Kenneth Frampton
was born in 1930 and trained as
an architect at the Architectural Association School of
Architecture, London. He has worked as both architect and
architectural historian, and is at present Professor at the
Graduate School of Architecture and Planning, Columbia
University, New York. He was a fellow of the Institute for
Architecture and Urban Studies, New York, from 1972 to
1982, and he has also served as Senior Tutor in the School
of Environmental Design, Royal College of Art, London.
He is the author of numerous articles on the
history of the Modern Movement.

# WORLD OF ART

This famous series
provides the widest available
range of illustrated books on art in all its aspects.
If you would like to receive a complete list
of titles in print please write to:
THAMES AND HUDSON
30 Bloomsbury Street, London WC1B 3QP
In the United States please write to:
THAMES AND HUDSON INC.
500 Fifth Avenue, New York, New York 10110

kenneth frampton

# modern architecture
a critical history

# architecture

with 336 illustrations

revised and enlarged edition

 thames and hudson

*To my parents*

First published 1980

Revised and enlarged edition 1985

Reprinted 1987

Printed and bound in the German Democratic Republic

# Contents

# Preface to the Second Edition

The success of the first edition of this book shows that it answered a need, particularly, I think, among students. I have taken advantage of a second edition to make a number of minor corrections, to enlarge the existing final chapter substantially, and to add a completely new chapter at the end.

During the last four or five years contemporary architecture has taken no radically new directions, but inevitably one's assessment of the recent past alters with a change of perspective. In particular I have now addressed, or given more space to, recent Japanese architecture, with the work of Arata Isozaki, Kazuo Shinohara and Toyo Ito; the phenomenon of Populism, promoted initially by Venturi, Scott-Brown and Izenour, explicated by Charles Jencks, expressed scenographically and often seemingly far from seriously by Venturi himself, Robert Stern, Helmut Jahn and Charles Moore, subverted by Frank Gehry, and absorbed into the European mainstream through the façades of Paolo Portoghesi's 'Strada Novissima' at the 1980 Venice Biennale; Neo-Rationalism and related modes of thought, in the Ticino, Spain, France and Germany (where O. M. Ungers has been a major theoretician and teacher), and in the United States as manifested in the work of the New York Five and carried through to Richard Meier's High Museum in Atlanta; I have looked more analytically at Productivism, acknowledging the designers who, taking Mies at his word in the cult of 'almost nothing', have concentrated on inflatable structures (Yukata Murata) or on cable-suspended tents (Frei Otto), and taking the story up to Foster Associates' building for the Hongkong and Shanghai Banking Corporation; and finally I have addressed Post-Avant-Gardism, that move away from Late Modernist positions that has characterized the more recent work of Michael Graves, Philip Johnson, James Stirling and Hans Hollein, and which ranges in its expression from the arbitrarily 'painted' scenography of Graves's Portland Building through the critical wit of Hollein's designs to the brutally kitsch classicism of Ricardo Bofill's housing in the region of Paris.

The new last chapter attempts to deal with the phenomenon of Critical Regionalism. Like other 'isms' that I have assumed in dealing with recent developments, Critical Regionalism is a critical category rather than an identifiable artistic movement in the avant-gardist sense. In writing about it I wish to draw attention to the fact that a regionally inflected but critical and 'revisionist' form of modern architecture has been in existence for the past forty years or more; certainly since Amancio Williams's famous house over a stream at Mar del Plata of 1945.

Finally, the Bibliography has been extensively revised and enlarged, reflecting the current state of research in the various sections into which I have divided the 'modern' period.

*New York 1984*                                                                    Kenneth Frampton

# Introduction

A Klee painting named 'Angelus Novus' shows an angel looking as though he is about to move away from something he is fixedly contemplating. His eyes are staring, his mouth is open, his wings are spread. This is how one pictures the angel of history. His face is turned towards the past. Where we perceive a chain of events, he sees one single catastrophe which keeps piling wreckage upon wreckage and hurls it in front of his feet. The angel would like to stay, awaken the dead, and make whole what has been smashed. But a storm is blowing from Paradise; it has got caught in his wings with such violence that the angel can no longer close them. This storm irresistibly propels him into the future to which his back is turned, while the pile of debris before him grows skyward. This storm is what we call progress.

Walter Benjamin
*Theses on the Philosophy of History*
1940

One of the first tasks to be faced in attempting to write a history of modern architecture is to establish the beginning of the period. The more rigorously one searches for the origin of modernity, however, the further back it seems to lie. One tends to project it back, if not to the Renaissance, then to that moment in the mid-18th century when a new view of history brought architects to question the Classical canons of Vitruvius and to document the remains of the antique world in order to establish a more objective basis on which to work. This, together with the extraordinary technical changes that followed throughout the century, suggests that the necessary conditions for modern architecture appeared some time between the physician–architect Claude Perrault's late 17th-century challenge to the universal validity of Vitruvian proportions and the definitive split between engineering and architecture which is sometimes dated to the foundation in Paris of the Ecole des Ponts et Chaussées, the first engineering school, in 1747.

Here it has been possible to give only the barest outline of this prehistory of the Modern Movement. The first three chapters, therefore, are to be read in a different light from the rest of the book. They treat of the cultural, territorial and technical transformations from which modern architecture emerged, offering short accounts of architecture, urban development and engineering as these fields evolved between 1750 and 1939.

The critical issues to be broached in writing a comprehensive but concise history are first, to decide what material should be included, and second, to maintain some kind of consistency in the interpretation of the facts. I have to admit that on both counts I have not been as consistent as I would have wished; partly because information often had to take priority over interpretation, partly because not all the material has been studied to the same degree of depth, and partly because my interpretative stance has varied according to the subject under consideration. In some instances I have tried to show how a particular approach derives from socio-economic or ideological circumstances, while in others I have restricted myself to formal analysis. This variation is reflected in the structure of the book itself, which is divided into a mosaic of fairly short chapters that deal either with the work of particularly significant architects or with major collective developments.

As far as possible I have tried to allow for the possibility of reading the text in more than one way. Thus it may be followed as a continuous account or dipped into at random. While the sequence has been organized with the lay reader or undergraduate in mind, I hope that a casual reading may serve to stimulate graduate work and prove useful to the specialist who wishes to develop a particular point.

Apart from this, the structure of the text is related to the general tone of the book, inasmuch as I have tried whenever possible to let the protagonists speak for themselves. Each chapter is introduced by a quotation, chosen either for its insight into a particular cultural situation or for its capacity to reveal the content of the work. I have endeavoured to use these 'voices' to illustrate the way in which modern architecture has evolved as a continuous cultural effort and to demonstrate how certain issues might lose their relevance at one moment in history only to return at a later date with increased vigour. Many unbuilt works feature in this account, since for me the history of modern architecture is as much about consciousness and polemical intent as it is about buildings themselves.

Like many others of my generation I have been influenced by a Marxist interpretation of history, although even the most cursory reading of this text will reveal that none of the established methods of Marxist analysis has been applied. On the other hand, my affinity for the critical theory of the Frankfurt School has no doubt coloured my view of the whole period and made me acutely aware of the dark side of the Enlightenment which, in the name of an unreasonable reason, has brought man to a situation where he begins to be as alienated from his own production as from the natural world.

The development of modern architecture after the Enlightenment seems to have been divided between the utopianism of the avant garde, first formulated at the beginning of the 19th century in the ideal physiocratic city of Ledoux, and that anti-Classical, anti-rational and anti-utilitarian attitude of Christian reform first declared in Pugin's *Contrasts* of 1836. Ever since, in its effort to transcend the division of labour and the harsh realities of industrial production and urbanization, bourgeois culture has oscillated between the extremes of totally planned and industrialized utopias on the one hand, and, on the other, a denial of the actual historical reality of machine production.

While all the arts are in some degree limited by the means of their production and reproduction, this is doubly so in the case of architecture, which is conditioned not only by its own technical methods but also by productive forces lying outside itself. Nowhere has this been more evident than in the case of the city, where the split between architecture and urban development has led to a situation in which the possibility of the former contributing to the latter and vice versa, over a long period of time, has suddenly become extremely limited. Increasingly subject to the imperatives of a continuously expanding consumer economy, the city has largely lost its capacity to maintain its significance as a whole. That it has been dissipated by forces lying beyond its control is demonstrated by the rapid erosion of the American provincial city after the end of the Second World War, as a consequence of the combined effect of the freeway, the suburb and the supermarket.

The success and failure of modern architecture to date, and its possible role in the future, must finally be assessed against this rather complex background. In its most abstract form, architecture has, of course, played a certain role in the impoverishment of the environment — particularly where it has been instrumental in the rationalisation of both building types and methods, and where both the material finish and the plan form have been reduced to their lowest common denominator, in order to make production cheaper and to optimize use. In its well-intentioned but sometimes misguided concern to assimilate the technical and processal realities of the 20th century, architecture has adopted a language in which expression resides almost entirely in processal, secondary components, such as ramps, walkways, lifts, staircases, escalators, chimneys, ducts and garbage chutes. Nothing could be further from the language of Classical architecture, where such features were invariably concealed behind the façade and where the main body of the building was free to express itself – a suppression of empirical fact that enabled architecture to symbolize the power of reason through the rationality of its own discourse. Functionalism has been based on the opposed principle, namely the reduction of all expression to utility or to the processes of fabrication.

Given the inroads of this modern reductionist tradition, we are now being urged once again to return to traditional forms and to render our new buildings – almost without regard for their status – in the iconography of a kitsch vernacular. We are told that popular will demands the reassuring image of homely, hand-crafted comfort and that 'Classical' references, however abstract, are as incomprehensible as they are patronizing. Only rarely does this critical opinion extend the scope of its advice beyond the surface issue of style to demand that architectural practice should re-address itself to the issue of *place* creation, to a critical yet creative redefinition of the concrete qualities of the built domain.

The vulgarization of architecture and its progressive isolation from society have of late driven the discipline in upon itself, so that we are now confronted with the paradoxical situation in which many of the more intelligent, younger members of the profession have already abandoned all ideas of realization. At its most intellectual this tendency reduces architectonic elements to pure syntactical signs that signify nothing outside their own 'structural' operation; at its most nostalgic it celebrates the loss of the city through metaphorical and ironic proposals that are either projected into 'astral wastes' or set in the metaphysical space of 19th-century urban splendour.

Of the courses of action which are still open to contemporary architecture – courses which in one way or another have already been entered upon – only two seem to offer the possibility of a significant outcome. While the first of these is totally coherent with the prevailing modes of production and consumption, the second establishes itself as a measured opposition to both. The former, following Mies van der Rohe's ideal of *beinahe nichts* or 'almost nothing', seeks to reduce the building task to the status of industrial design on an enormous scale. Since its concern is with optimizing production, it has little or no interest in the city. It projects a well-serviced, well-packaged, non-rhetorical functionalism whose glazed 'invisibility' reduces form to silence. The latter, on the other hand, is patently 'visible' and often takes the form of a masonry enclosure that establishes within its limited 'monastic' domain a reasonably open but nonetheless concrete set of relationships linking man to man and man to nature. The fact that this 'enclave' is often introverted and relatively indifferent to the physical and temporal continuum in which it is situated characterizes the general thrust of this approach as an attempt to escape, however partially, from the conditioning perspectives of the Enlightenment. The sole hope for a significant discourse in the immediate future lies, in my view, in a creative contact between these two extreme points of view.

1 *Opposite*, Soufflot, Ste-Geneviève (now the Panthéon), Paris, 1755–90; crossing piers strengthened by Rondelet in 1806.

# Part 1
## Cultural developments and predisposing techniques
## 1750–1939

# Chapter 1
# Cultural transformations: Neo-Classical architecture 1750-1900

The Baroque system had operated as a kind of double intersection. It had often contrasted with rationalized gardens, building façades decorated with plant motifs. The reign of man and the reign of nature had certainly remained distinct but they had exchanged their characteristics, merging into each other for the sake of ornamentation and prestige. On the other hand the 'English style' park, in which man's intervention was supposed to remain invisible, was intended to offer the *purposefulness* of nature; while within, but separate from the actual park, the houses constructed by Morris or Adam manifested the *will* of man, isolating clearly the presence of human reason in the midst of the irrational domains of freely growing vegetation. The Baroque interpenetration of man and nature was now replaced by a separation, thus establishing the distance between man and nature which was a prerequisite for nostalgic contemplation. Now . . . this contemplative separation arose as a compensatory or expiatory reaction against the growing attitude of practical men towards nature. While technical exploitation tended to wage war on nature, houses and parks attempted a reconciliation, a local armistice, introducing the dream of an impossible peace: and to this end man had continued to retain the image of untouched natural surroundings.

Jean Starobinski
*L'Invention de la liberté,* 1964

The architecture of Neo-Classicism seems to have emerged out of two different but related developments which radically transformed the relationship between man and nature. The first was a sudden increase in man's capacity to exercise control over nature, which by the mid-17th century had begun to advance beyond the technical frontiers of the Renaissance. The second was a fundamental shift in the nature of human consciousness, in response to major changes taking place in society, which gave birth to a new cultural formation that was equally appropriate to the life styles of the declining aristocracy and the rising bourgeoisie. Whereas technological changes led to a new infrastructure and to the exploitation of an increased productive capacity, the change in human consciousness yielded new categories of knowledge and a historicist mode of thought that was so reflexive as to question its own identity. Where the one, grounded in science, took immediate form in the extensive road and canal works of the 17th and 18th centuries and gave rise to new technical institutions, such as the Ecole des Ponts et Chaussées, founded in 1747, the other led to the emergence of the humanist disciplines of the Enlightenment, including the pioneer works of modern sociology, aesthetics, history and archaeology — Montesquieu's *De l'esprit des lois* (1748), Baumgarten's *Aesthetica* (1750), Voltaire's *Le Siècle de Louis XIV* (1751) and J. J. Winckelmann's *Geschichte der Kunst des Altertums* (History of Ancient Art) of 1764.

The over-elaboration of architectural language in the Rococo interiors of the Ancien Régime and the secularization of Enlightenment thought compelled the architects of the 18th century, by now aware of the emergent and unstable nature of their age, to search for a true style through a precise reappraisal of antiquity. Their motivation was not simply to copy the ancients but to obey the principles on which their work had been based. The archaeological research that arose from this impulse soon led to a major controversy: to which, of four Mediterranean cultures – the Egyptians, the Etruscans, the Greeks and the Romans – should they look for a true style?

One of the first consequences of reassessing the antique world was to extend the itinerary of the traditional Grand Tour beyond the frontiers of Rome, so as to study at its periphery those cultures on which, according to Vitruvius, Roman architecture had been based. The discovery and excavation of Roman cities at Herculaneum and Pompeii, during the first half of the 18th century, encouraged expeditions further afield and visits were soon being made to ancient Greek sites in both Sicily and Greece. The received Vitruvian dictum of the Renaissance – the catechism of Classicism – was now to be checked against the actual ruins. The measured drawings that were published in the 1750s and 1760s, J.-D. Le Roy's *Ruines des plus beaux monuments de la Grèce* (1758), James Stuart and Nicholas Revett's *Antiquities of Athens* (1762), and Robert Adam and C.-L. Clérisseau's documentation of Diocletian's palace at Split (1764), testify to the intensity with which these studies were pursued. It was Le Roy's promotion of Greek architecture as the origin of the 'true style' that raised the chauvinist ire of the Italian architect-engraver Giovanni Battista Piranesi.

Piranesi's *Della Magnificenza ed Architettura de' Romani* of 1761 was a direct attack on Le Roy's polemic: he asserted not only that the Etruscans had antedated the Greeks but that, together with their successors the Romans, they had raised architecture to a higher level of refinement. The only evidence that he could cite in support of his claim was the few Etruscan structures that had survived the ravages of Rome – tombs and engineering works – and these seem to have orientated the remainder of his career in a remarkable way. In one set of etchings after another he represented the dark side of that sensation already classified by Edmund Burke in 1757 as the Sublime, that tranquil terror induced by the contemplation of great size, extreme antiquity and decay. These qualities acquired their full force in Piranesi's work through the infinite grandeur of the images that he portrayed. Such nostalgic

Classical images were, however, as Manfredo Tafuri has observed, treated 'as a myth to be contested . . . as mere fragments, as deformed symbols, as hallucinating organisms of an "order" in a state of decay'.

Between his *Parere su l'Architettura* of 1765 and his Paestum etchings, published only after his death in 1778, Piranesi abandoned architectural verisimilitude and gave his imagination full rein. In one publication after another, culminating in his extravagantly eclectic work on interior ornamentation of 1769, he indulged in hallucinatory manipulations of historicist form. Indifferent to Winckelmann's pro-Hellenic distinction between innate beauty and gratuitous ornament, his delirious inventions exercised an irresistible attraction on his contemporaries, and the Adam brothers' Graeco-Roman interiors were greatly indebted to his flights of imagination.

In England, where the Rococo had never been fully accepted, the impulse to redeem the excess of the Baroque found its first expression in the Palladianism initiated by the Earl of Burlington, though something of a similar purgative spirit may be detected in the last works of Nicholas Hawksmoor at Castle Howard. By the end of the 1750s, however, the British were already assiduously pursuing instruction in Rome itself where, between 1750 and 1765, the major Neo-Classical proponents could be found in residence, from the pro-Roman and pro-Etruscan Piranesi to the pro-Greek Winckelmann and Le Roy, whose influence had yet to take effect. Among the British contingent were James Stuart, who was to employ the Greek Doric order as early as 1758, and the younger George Dance, who soon after his return to London in 1765 designed Newgate Gaol, a superficially Piranesian structure whose rigorous organization may well have owed something to the Neo-Palladian proportional theories of Robert Morris. The final development of British Neo-Classicism came first in the work of Dance's pupil John Soane, who synthesized to a remarkable degree various influences drawn from Piranesi, Adam, Dance and even from the English Baroque. The Greek Revival cause was then popularized by Thomas Hope, whose

*Household Furniture and Interior Decoration* (1807) made available a British version of the Napoleonic 'Style Empire', then in the process of being created by Percier and Fontaine.

Nothing could have been further from the British experience than the theoretical development that attended the emergence of Neo-Classicism in France. An early awareness of cultural relativity in the late 17th century prompted Claude Perrault to question the validity of the Vitruvian proportions as these had been received and refined through Classical theory. Instead, he elaborated his thesis of *positive* beauty and *arbitrary* beauty, giving to the former the normative role of standardization and perfection and to the latter such expressive function as may be required by a particular circumstance or character.

This challenge to Vitruvian orthodoxy was codified by the Abbé de Cordemoy in his *Nouveau Traité de toute l'architecture* (1706), where he replaced the Vitruvian attributes of architecture, namely *utilitas, firmitas* and *venustas* (utility, solidity and beauty) by his own trinity of *ordonnance, distribution* and *bienséance*. While the first two of his categories concerned the correct proportioning of the Classical orders and their appropriate disposition, the third introduced the notion of fitness, with which Cordemoy warned against the inappropriate application of Classical or honorific elements to utilitarian or commercial structures. Thus, in addition to being critical of the Baroque, which was the last rhetorical, public manner of the Ancien Régime, Cordemoy's *Traité* anticipated Jacques-François Blondel's preoccupation with appropriate formal expression and with a differentiated physiognomy to accord with the varying social *character* of different building *types*. The age was already having to confront the articulation of a much more complex society.

Apart from insisting on the judicious application of Classical elements, Cordemoy was concerned with their geometrical purity, in reaction against such Baroque devices as irregular columniation, broken pediments and twisted columns. Ornamentation too had to be subject to propriety, and Cordemoy, anticipating Adolf Loos's *Ornament und Verbrechen* (*Ornament and Crime*) by two hundred years, argued that many buildings required no ornament at all. His preference was for astylar masonry and orthogonal structures. For him, the free-standing column was the essence of a pure architecture such as had been made manifest in the Gothic cathedral and the Greek temple.

The Abbé Laugier in his *Essai sur l'architecture* (1753) reinterpreted Cordemoy, to posit a universal 'natural' architecture, the primordial 'primitive hut' consisting of four tree trunks supporting a rustic pitched roof. After Cordemoy, he asserted this primal form as the basis for a sort of classicized Gothic structure in which there would be neither arches nor pilasters nor pedestals nor any other kind of formal articulation, and where the interstices between the columns would be as fully glazed as possible.

Such a 'translucent' structure was realized in Jacques-German Soufflot's church of Ste-Geneviève in Paris, begun in 1755. Soufflot, who in 1750 had been one of the first architects to visit the Doric temples at Paestum, was determined to recreate the lightness, the spaciousness and the proportion of Gothic architecture in Classical (not to say Roman) terms. To this end he adopted a Greek cross plan, the nave and aisles being formed by a system of flat domes and semicircular arches supported on a continuous internal peristyle.

The task of integrating the theory of Cordemoy and the magnum opus of Soufflot into the French academic tradition fell to J.F. Blondel who, after opening his architectural school in Rue de la Harpe in 1743, became the master of that so-called 'visionary' generation of architects that included Etienne-Louis Boullée, Jacques Gondoin, Pierre Patte, Marie-Joseph Peyre, Jean-Baptiste Rondelet and, probably the most visionary of all, Claude-Nicolas Ledoux. Blondel set out his main precepts, concerning *composition, type* and *character*, in his *Cours d'architecture*, published from 1750 to 1770. His ideal church design, published in the second volume of his *Cours*, was related to Ste-Geneviève and prominently displayed a representational front, while articulating each internal element as part of a continuous spatial system whose infinite vistas evoked a sense of the Sublime. This church project hints at the simplicity and grandeur that were to inform the work of many of his pupils, most notably Boullée, who after 1772 devoted his life to the projection of buildings so vast as to preclude their realization.

In addition to representing the social character of his creations in accordance with the teachings of Blondel, Boullée evoked the sublime emotions of terror and tranquillity through the grandeur of his conceptions. Influenced by Le Camus de Mézières' *Génie de l'architecture, ou l'analogie de cet art avec nos sensations* (1780), he began to develop his *genre terrible*, in which the immensity of the vista and the unadorned geometrical purity of monumental form are combined in such a way as to promote exhilaration and anxiety. More than any other Enlightenment architect, Boullée was obsessed with the capacity of light to evoke the presence of the divine. This intention is evident in the sunlit diaphanous haze that illuminates the interior of his 'Métropole', modelled partly on Ste-Geneviève. A similar light is portrayed in the vast masonry sphere of his projected cenotaph for Isaac Newton, where by night a fire was suspended to represent the sun, while by day it was extinguished to reveal the illusion of the firmament produced by the daylight shining through the sphere's perforated walls.

While Boullée's political sentiments were solidly republican, he remained obsessed with imagining the monuments of some omnipotent state dedicated to the worship of the Supreme Being. Unlike Ledoux, he was unimpressed by the rural decentralized utopias of Morelly or Jean-Jacques Rousseau. Despite this, his influence in post-Revolutionary Europe was considerable, primarily through the activity of his pupil Jean-Nicolas-Louis Durand, who reduced his extravagant ideas to a normative and economic building typology, set out in the *Précis des leçons données à l'Ecole Polytechnique* (1802–09).

After fifteen years of millennial disarray the Napoleonic era required useful structures of appropriate grandeur and authority, on the condition that they be achieved as cheaply as

2   Boullée, project for a cenotaph for Isaac Newton, c.1785. Section by 'night'.

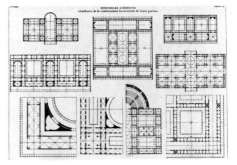

3   Durand, possible combinations and permutations of plan forms, from his *Précis*, 1802–09.

possible. Durand, the first tutor in architecture at the Ecole Polytechnique, sought to establish a universal building methodology, an architectural counterpart to the Napoleonic Code, by which economic and appropriate structures could be created through the modular permutation of fixed plan types and alternative elevations. Thus Boullée's obsession with vast Platonic volumes was exploited as a means to achieve an appropriate character at a reasonable cost. Durand's criticism of Ste-Geneviève, for example, with its 206 columns and 612 metres (2008 feet) of wall, involved him in making a counter-proposal for a circular temple of comparable area that would require only 112 columns and 248 metres (814 feet) of wall – a considerable economy, with which, according to him, one would have achieved a far more impressive aura.

Ledoux, after his career had been terminated by the Revolution, returned during his im-

4  Ledoux, ideal city of Chaux, 1804.

prisonment to develop the scheme of the salt works that he had built for Louis XVI at Arc-et-Senans in 1773–79. He expanded the semicircular form of this complex into the representational core of his ideal city of Chaux, published in 1804 under the title *L'Architecture considérée sous le rapport de l'art, des moeurs et de la législation*. The semicircular salt works itself (which he developed into the oval centre of his city) may be seen as one of the first essays in industrial architecture, inasmuch as it consciously integrated productive units with workers' housing. Each element in this physiocratic complex was rendered according to its character. Thus the salt evaporation sheds on the axis were high-roofed like agricultural buildings and finished in smooth ashlar, with rusticated dressings, while the director's house in the centre was low-roofed and pedimented, rusticated throughout and embellished with Classical porticos. Here and there the walls of the salt sheds and the workers' houses were relieved by grotesque 'spouts' of petrified water, which not only symbolized the saline solution on which the enterprise was based but also suggested that the productive system and the labour force had an equally processal status.

In fictitiously developing this limited typology to include all the institutions of his ideal city, Ledoux extended the idea of an architectural 'physiognomy' to symbolize the social intention of his otherwise abstract forms. The meanings are established either by conventional symbols, such as the fasces evoking justice and unity on the courthouse, the so-called *Pacifère*, or by isomorphism, as in the case of the *Oikema*, planned in the shape of a penis. This last structure was dedicated to libertinage, whose curious social purpose was to induce virtue through sexual satiety.

A whole world separates Durand's rational permutation of received Classical elements from Ledoux's arbitrary but purgative reconstitution of fragmented Classical parts demonstrated in the toll-gates that he designed for Paris between 1785 and 1789. These *barrières*

16

were just as disconnected from the culture of their time as the idealized institutions of Chaux. With their gradual demolition after 1789 they suffered the same fate as the abstract and unpopular customs boundary that they were intended to administer, the Enceinte des Fermiers Généraux, of which it was said, 'Le mur murant Paris rend Paris murmurant.'

After the Revolution, the evolution of Neo-Classicism was largely inseparable from the need to accommodate the new institutions of bourgeois society and to represent the emergence of the new republican state. That these forces were initially resolved in the compromise of constitutional monarchy hardly detracted from the role that Neo-Classicism played in the formation of the bourgeois imperialist style. The creation of Napoleon's 'Style Empire' in Paris and Frederick II's Francophile 'Kulturnation' in Berlin are but separate manifestations of the same cultural tendency. The former made an eclectic use of antique motifs, be they Roman, Greek or Egyptian, to create the instant heritage of a republican dynasty – a style that revealed itself significantly in the theatrical tented interiors of the Napoleonic campaigns and in the solid Roman embellishments of the capital city, such as Percier and Fontaine's Rue de Rivoli and Arc du Carrousel and Gondoin's Place Vendôme column dedicated to the Grande Armée. In Germany the tendency was first manifested in Carl Gotthard Langhans's Brandenburg Gate, built as the western entry to Berlin in 1793, and in Friedrich Gilly's design for a monument to Frederick the Great, of 1797. Ledoux's primary forms inspired Gilly to emulate the severity of the Doric, thereby echoing the 'archaic' power of the Sturm und Drang movement in German literature. Like his contemporary Friedrich Weinbrenner, he projected a spartan Ur-civilization of high moral value, with which to celebrate the myth of the ideal Prussian state. His remarkable monument would have taken the form of an artificial acropolis on the Leipzigerplatz. This temenos would have been entered from Potsdam through a squat triumphal arch capped by a quadriga.

Gilly's colleague and successor, the Prussian architect Karl Friedrich Schinkel, acquired his

5   Schinkel, Altes Museum, Berlin, 1828–30.

early enthusiasm for Gothic not from Berlin or Paris, but from his own first-hand experience of Italian cathedrals. Yet after the defeat of Napoleon in 1815, this Romantic taste was largely eclipsed by the need to find an appropriate expression for the triumph of Prussian nationalism. The combination of political idealism and military prowess seems to have demanded a return to the Classic. In any event this was the style that linked Schinkel not only to Gilly but also to Durand, in the creation of his masterpieces in Berlin: his Neue Wache of 1816, his Schauspielhaus of 1821 and his Altes Museum of 1830. While both the guardhouse and the theatre show characteristic features of Schinkel's mature style, the massive corners of the one and the mullioned wings of the other, the influence of Durand is most clearly revealed in the museum, which is a prototypical museum plan taken from the *Précis* and split in half – a transformation in which the central rotunda, peristyle and courtyards are retained and the side wings eliminated (see p. 236). While the wide entry steps, the peristyle and the eagles and Dioscuri on the roof symbolized the cultural aspirations of the Prussian state, Schinkel departed from the typological and representational methods of Durand to create a spatial articulation of extraordinary delicacy and power, as the wide peristyle gives way to a narrow portico containing a symmetrical entry stair and its mezzanine (an arrangement which would be remembered by Mies van der Rohe).

The main line of Blondel's Neo-Classicism was continued in the mid-19th century in the career of Henri Labrouste, who had studied at the Ecole des Beaux-Arts (the institution that

6  Labrouste, book stack of the Bibliothèque Nationale, Paris, 1860–68.

succeeded the Académie Royale d'Architecture after the Revolution) with A.-L.-T. Vaudoyer, who had been a pupil of Peyre. After winning the Prix de Rome in 1824 Labrouste spent the next five years at the French Academy, devoting much of his time in Italy to a study of the Greek temples at Paestum. Inspired by the work of Jakob-Ignaz Hittorff, Labrouste was among the first to argue that such structures had originally been brightly coloured. This, and his insistence on the primacy of structure and on the derivation of all ornament from construction, brought him into conflict with the authorities after the opening of his own atelier in 1830.

In 1840 Labrouste was named architect of the Bibliothèque Ste-Geneviève in Paris which had been created to house part of the library impounded by the French state in 1789. Based apparently on Boullée's project for a library in the Palais Mazarin, of 1785, Labrouste's design consists of a perimeter wall of books enclosing a rectilinear space and supporting an iron-framed, barrel-vaulted roof which is divided into two halves and further supported in the centre of the space by a line of iron columns.

Such Structural Rationalism was further refined in the main reading room and book stack that Labrouste built for the Bibliothèque

Nationale in 1860–68. This complex, inserted into the courtyard of the Palais Mazarin, consists of a reading room covered by an iron and glass roof carried on sixteen cast-iron columns and a multi-storey wrought- and cast-iron book stack. Dispensing with the last trace of historicism, Labrouste designed the latter as a top-lit cage, in which light filters down through iron landings from the roof to the lowest floor. Although this solution was derived from Sydney Smirke's cast-iron reading room and stack built in the courtyard of Robert Smirke's Neo-Classical British Museum in 1854, the precise form of its execution implied a new aesthetic whose potential was not to be realized until the Constructivist work of the 20th century.

The middle of the 19th century saw the Neo-Classical heritage divided between two closely related lines of development: the Structural Classicism of Labrouste and the Romantic Classicism of Schinkel. Both 'schools' were confronted by the same 19th-century proliferation of new institutions and had to respond equally to the task of creating new building types. They differed largely in the manner in which they achieved these representative qualities: the Structural Classicists tended to emphasize structure – the line of

Cordemoy, Laugier and Soufflot; while the Romantic Classicists tended to stress the physiognomic character of the form itself – the line of Ledoux, Boullée and Gilly. Where one 'school' seems to have concentrated on such types as prisons, hospitals and railway stations, in the work of men like E.-J. Gilbert and F.A. Duquesney (designer of the Gare de l'Est, Paris, in 1852), the other addressed itself more to representational structures, such as the university museum and library of C.R. Cockerell in England or the more grandiose monuments erected by Leo von Klenze in Germany – above all the latter's highly Romantic Walhalla, completed at Regensburg in 1842.

In terms of theory, Structural Classicism began with Rondelet's *Traité de l'art de bâtir* (1802) and culminated at the end of the century in the writing of the engineer Auguste Choisy, particularly his *Histoire de l'architecture* (1899). For Choisy the essence of architecture is construction, and all stylistic transformations are merely the logical consequence of technical development: 'To parade your Art Nouveau is to ignore the whole teaching of history. Not so did the great styles of the past come into being. It was in the suggestion of construction that the architect of the great artistic ages found his truest inspiration.' Choisy illustrated the structural determination of his *Histoire* with axonometric projections which revealed the essence of a type of form in a single graphic image, comprising plan, section and elevation. As Reyner Banham has observed, these objective illustrations reduce the architecture that they represent to pure abstraction, and it was this, plus the amount of the information they synthesized, that endeared them to the pioneers of the Modern Movement after the turn of the century.

The emphasis that Choisy's history placed on Greek and Gothic architecture was a late 19th-century rationalization of that Graeco-Gothic ideal which had first been formulated over a century before by Cordemoy. This 18th-century projection of Gothic structure into Classical syntax found its parallel in Choisy's characterization of the Doric as wooden structure transposed into masonry. Just such a transposition was to be practised by Choisy's

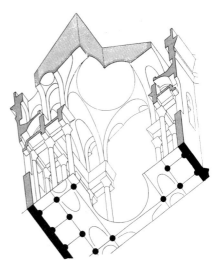

7  Choisy, axonometric projection of part of the Panthéon, Paris (see ill. 1), from his *Histoire de l'architecture*, 1899.

disciple, Auguste Perret, who insisted on detailing his reinforced-concrete structures after the manner of traditional wood framing.

A Structural Rationalist to the core, Choisy was nonetheless capable of responding to the Romantic sensibility when he wrote of the Acropolis: 'The Greeks never visualized a building without the site that framed it and the other buildings that surrounded it . . . each architectural motif, on its own, is symmetrical, but every group is treated like a landscape where the masses alone balance out.'

Such a Picturesque notion of partially symmetrical balance would have been as foreign to the teaching of the Beaux-Arts as it was to the polytechnical approach of Durand. Certainly it would have had a limited appeal for Julien Guadet, who sought, in his lecture course *Eléments et théorie de l'architecture* (1902), to establish a normative approach to the composition of structures from technically up-to-date elements, arranged as far as possible according to the tradition of axial composition. It was through Guadet's teaching at the Beaux-Arts, and his influence on his pupils Auguste Perret and Tony Garnier, that the principles of Classical 'Elementarist' composition were handed down to the pioneer architects of the 20th century.

## Chapter 2

# Territorial transformations: urban developments 1800-1909

[With] the development of increasingly abstract means of communication, the continuity of rooted communication is replaced by new systems which continue to perfect themselves throughout the 19th century, allowing the population greater mobility and providing information that is more precisely synchronized with the accelerating rhythm of history. Railway, daily press and telegraph will gradually supplant *space* in its previous informative role.

Françoise Choay
*The Modern City: Planning in the 19th Century*, 1969

The finite city, as it had come into being in Europe over the previous five hundred years, was totally transformed in the space of a century by the interaction of a number of unprecedented technical and socio-economic forces, many of which first emerged in England during the second half of the 18th century. Prominent among them from a technical point of view must be counted such innovations as Abraham Darby's mass-production of cast-iron rails, from 1767, and Jethro Tull's seed-drill cultivation of crops in rows, generally adopted after 1731. Where Darby's invention led to Henry Cort's development of the puddling process for the simplified conversion of cast- to wrought-iron in 1784, Tull's drill was essential to the perfection of Charles Townshend's four-crop rotational system – the principle of 'high farming' that became general towards the end of the century.

Such productive innovations had multiple repercussions. In the case of metallurgy, English iron production increased forty-fold between 1750 and 1850 (rising to two million tons a year by 1850); in the case of agriculture,

after the Enclosures Act of 1771 inefficient husbandry was replaced by the four-crop system. Where the one was boosted by the Napoleonic Wars, the other was motivated by the need to feed a rapidly growing industrial population.

At the same time the cottage-weaving industry, which had helped to sustain the agrarian economy of the first half of the 18th century, was rapidly changed, first by James Hargreaves's spinning jenny of 1764, which greatly increased the individual's spinning capacity, and then by Edmund Cartwright's steam-powered loom, first used for factory production in 1784. This last event not only established textile production as a large-scale industry, but also led immediately to the invention of the multi-storey fireproof mill. Thus traditional textile manufacturing was forced to abandon its predominantly rural base and to concentrate both labour and plant, first next to water courses and then, with the advent of steam power, close to coal deposits. With 24,000 power looms in production by 1820, the English mill town was already an established fact.

This process of uprooting – *enracinement*, as Simone Weil has called it – was further accelerated by the use of steam traction for transport. Richard Trevithick first demonstrated the locomotive on cast-iron rails in 1804. The opening of the first public rail service between Stockton and Darlington in 1825 was followed by the rapid development of a completely new infrastructure, Britain having some 10,000 miles of track in place by 1860. The advent of long-distance steam navigation after 1865 greatly increased European migration to the Americas, Africa and Australia. While this migration brought the populations needed to expand the economy of colonial terrirories and to fill the growing grid-plan cities of the New World, the military, political and economic obsolescence of the traditional European walled city led, after the liberal-national revolutions of 1848, to the wholesale demolition of ramparts and to the extension of the formerly finite city into its already burgeoning suburbs.

These general developments, accompanied by a sudden drop in mortality due to improved standards in nutrition and medical techniques, gave rise to unprecedented urban concentrations, first in England and then, at differing rates of growth, throughout the developing world. Manchester's population grew eight-fold in the course of the century, from 75,000 in 1801 to 600,000 by 1901, as compared to London's six-fold increase over the same period, from around 1 million in 1801 to $6\frac{1}{2}$ million by the turn of the century. Paris grew at a comparable rate but had a more modest beginning, expanding from 500,000 in 1801 to 3 million by 1901. Even these six- to eight-fold increases are modest compared with New York's growth over the same period. New York was first laid out as a gridded city in 1811, in accordance with the Commissioners' Plan of that year, and grew from its 1801 population of 33,000 to 500,000 by 1850 and $3\frac{1}{2}$ million by 1901. Chicago grew at an even more astronomical rate, rising from 300 people at the time of Thompson's grid of 1833 to around 30,000 (of whom something under half had been born in the States) by 1850, and going on to become a city of 2 million by the turn of the century.

The accommodation of such volatile growth led to the transformation of old neighbourhoods into slums, and also to jerry-built new houses and tenements whose main purpose, given the general lack of municipal transport, was to provide as cheaply as possible the maximum amount of rudimentary shelter within walking distance of the centres of production. Naturally such congested developments had inadequate standards of light, ventilation and open space and poor sanitary facilities, such as communal outside lavatories, wash-houses and refuse storage. With primitive drainage and inadequate maintenance, this pattern could lead to the piling up of excrement and garbage and to flooding, and these conditions naturally provoked a high incidence of disease – first tuberculosis and then, more alarmingly for the authorities, a number of outbreaks of cholera in both England and Continental Europe in the 1830s and 1840s.

These epidemics had the effect of precipitating health reform and of bringing about some of the earliest legislation governing the construction and maintenance of dense conurbations. In 1833 the London authorities instructed the Poor Law Commission, headed by Edwin Chadwick, to make enquiries about the origins of a cholera outbreak in Whitechapel. This led to Chadwick's report, *An Inquiry into the Sanitary Conditions of the Labouring Population in Great Britain* (1842), to the Royal Commission on the State of Large Towns and Populous Districts of 1844 and, eventually, to the Public Health Act of 1848. This Act, in addition to others, made local authorities legally responsible for sewerage, refuse collection, water supply, roads, the inspection of slaughter-houses and the burial of the dead. Similar provisions were to occupy Haussmann during the rebuilding of Paris between 1853 and 1870.

The result of this legislation in England was to make society vaguely aware of the need to upgrade working-class housing; but as to the models and means by which this should be achieved there was little initial agreement. Nonetheless, the Chadwick-inspired Society for Improving the Conditions of the Labouring Classes sponsored the erection of the first working-class flats in London in 1844 to the design of the architect Henry Roberts, and followed this resolute beginning with its Streatham Street flats of 1848–50 and a prototypical two-storey worker's cottage containing four flats, again to the design of Roberts, for the Great Exhibition of 1851. This generic model for the stacking of apartments in pairs around a common staircase was to influence the planning of working-class housing for the rest of the century.

The American-backed philanthropic Peabody Trust and various English benevolent societies and local authorities attempted, after

8  Godin, Familistère, Guise, 1859–70.

1864, to upgrade the quality of working-class housing, but little of significance was achieved until the slum clearance Acts of 1868 and 1875 and the Housing of the Working Classes Act of 1890, under which local authorities were required to provide public housing. In 1893, when the London County Council (established in 1890) began to build workers' flats under the auspices of this Act, its Architect's Department made a remarkable effort to deinstitutionalize the image of such housing by adapting the Arts and Crafts domestic style (see p.47) to the realization of six-storey blocks of flats. Typical of this development is the Millbank Estate, begun in 1897.

Throughout the 19th century the effort of industry to take care of its own assumed many forms, from the 'model' mill, railway and factory towns to projected utopian communities intended as prototypes for some future enlightened state. Among those who manifested an early concern for integrated industrial settlements one must acknowledge Robert Owen, whose New Lanark in Scotland (1815) was designed as a pioneering institution of the co-operative movement, and Sir Titus Salt, whose Saltaire, near Bradford in Yorkshire (founded in 1850), was a paternalistic mill town, complete with traditional urban institutions such as a church, an infirmary, a secondary school, public baths, almshouses and a park.

Neither of these realizations could match in scope and liberating potential the radical vision

of Charles Fourier's 'new industrial world', as formulated in his essay of that title (Le Nouveau Monde industriel) published in 1829. Fourier's non-repressive society was to depend on the establishment of ideal communities or 'phalanxes', housed in phalanstères, where men were to be related in accordance with Fourier's psychological principle of 'passional attraction'. Since the phalanstery was projected as being in open country, its economy was to be predominantly agricultural, supplemented by light manufacturing. In his earliest writings Fourier outlined the physical attributes of his communal settlement; it was modelled on the layout of Versailles, its central wing being given over to public functions (dining hall, library, wintergarden, etc.), while its side wings were devoted to the workshops and the caravanseray. In his Traité de l'association domestique agricole (1822) Fourier wrote of the phalanstery as being a miniature town whose streets would have the advantage of not being exposed to the weather. He saw it as a structure whose grandeur, if generally adopted, would replace the petit-bourgeois squalor of the small individual free-standing houses that were, by then, already filling the outer interstices of towns.

Fourier's disciple Victor Considérant, writing in 1838, mixed the metaphor of Versailles with that of the steamship and questioned whether it was 'easier to house 1800 men right in the middle of the ocean, six hundred leagues from every shore, . . . than to house in a unitary construction some 1800 good peasants in the heart of Champagne or firmly on the soil of Beauce?' This particular conflation of commune and ship was to be returned to by Le Corbusier, over a century later, in his self-contained commune or Unité d'Habitation, realized with Fourierist overtones at Marseilles in 1952 (see p.227).

The enduring importance of Fourier lies in his radical criticism of industrialized production and social organization, for, despite numerous attempts to create phalansteries in both Europe and America, his new industrial world was fated to remain a dream. Its closest realization was the Familistère, built by the industrialist J.-P. Godin next to his factory at Guise in 1859–70. This complex comprised three residential blocks, a crèche, a kindergarten, a theatre, schools, public baths and a laundry. Each residential block enclosed a top-lit central courtyard which took the place of the elevated corridor streets of the phalanstery. In his book *Solutions sociales* (1870) Godin absorbed the more radical aspects of Fourierism by showing how the system could be adapted to co-operative family living without resorting to the eccentric theories of 'passional attraction'.

Aside from accommodating the labouring masses, London's 18th-century matrix of streets and squares was extended throughout the 19th century to meet the residential requirements of a growing urban middle class. No longer satisfied, however, with the scale and texture of the occasional green square – delimited on all sides by streets and continuous terraces – the English Park Movement, founded by the gardener Humphrey Repton, attempted to project the 'landscaped country estate' into the city. Repton himself succeeded in demonstrating this, in collaboration with the architect John Nash, in their layout of Regent's Park in London (1812–27). After the victory over Napoleon in 1815, the proposed development enclosing the park was augmented, under royal patronage, by a continuous 'display' façade, penetrating into the existing urban fabric and extending as a more or less uninterrupted ribbon of terraced accommodation from the aristocratic vistas of Regent's Park in the north to the palatial urbanity of St James's Park and Carlton House Terrace in the south.

The squirearchical concept of the Neo-Classical country house set in an irregular landscape (an image derived from the Picturesque work of Capability Brown and Uvedale Price) was thus translated by Nash to the provision of terraced housing on the perimeter of an urban park. This model was first systematically adapted to general use by Sir Joseph Paxton, at Birkenhead Park, built outside Liverpool in 1844. Frederick Law Olmsted's Central Park in New York, inaugurated in 1857, was directly influenced by Paxton's example, even down to its separation of carriage traffic from pedestrians. The concept received its final elaboration in the Parisian parks created by J.C.A. Alphand, where the circulation system totally dictated the manner in which the park was to be used. With Alphand, the park becomes a civilizing influence for the newly urbanized masses.

The irregular lake that Nash created in St James's Park in 1828 out of the rectangular basin that the Mollet brothers had made in 1662 may be taken to symbolize the victory of the English Picturesque over the French Cartesian conception of landscape dating from the 17th century. The French, who had hitherto regarded greenery as another order of architecture and had rendered their avenues as colonnades of trees, were to find the romantic appeal of Repton's irregular landscape irresistible. After the Revolution they remodelled their aristocratic parks into Picturesque sequences.

Yet, for all the power of the Picturesque, the French impulse towards rationality remained, first in the *percements* (wholesale demolition in a straight line to create an entirely new street) of the Artists' Plan for Paris, drawn up in 1793 by a committee of revolutionary artists under the leadership of the painter Jacques-Louis David; and then in Napoleon's arcaded Rue de Rivoli, built after 1806 to the designs of Percier and Fontaine. Where the Rue de Rivoli was to serve as the architectural model not only for Nash's Regent Street but also for the scenographic 'façade' of Second Empire Paris, the Artists' Plan demonstrated the instrumental strategy of the *allée*, which was to become the prime tool for the rebuilding of Paris under Napoleon III.

Napoleon III and Baron Georges Haussmann left their indelible mark not only on Paris but also on a number of major cities in France and Central Europe which underwent Haussmann-like regularizations throughout the second half of the century. Their influence is even present in Daniel Burnham's 1909 plan for the gridded city of Chicago, of which Burnham wrote: 'The task which Haussmann accomplished for Paris corresponds with the work which must be done for Chicago in order to overcome the intolerable conditions which invariably arise from a rapid growth in population.'

In 1853 Haussmann, as the newly appointed Prefect for the Seine, saw these conditions in Paris as being polluted water supply, lack of an

9 The regularization of Paris: streets cut by Haussmann are shown in black.

adequate sewer system, insufficient open space for both cemeteries and parks, large areas of squalid housing and last, but by no means least, congested circulation. Of these, the first two were undoubtedly the most critical for the everyday welfare of the population. As a consequence of drawing the bulk of its water from the Seine, which also served as the main collector sewer, Paris had suffered two serious outbreaks of cholera in the first half of the century. At the same time, the existing street system was no longer adequate for the administrative centre of an expanding capitalist economy. Under the brief autocracy of Napoleon III, Haussmann's radical solution to the physical aspect of this complex problem was *percement*. His broad purpose was, as Choay has written, 'to give unity and transform into an operative whole the "huge consumer market, the immense workshop" of the Parisian agglomerate'. Although the Artists' Plan of 1793 and before that Pierre Patte's plan of 1765 had clearly anticipated the axial and focal structure of Haussmann's Paris, there is, as Choay points out, a discernible shift in the actual location of the axes, from a city organized around traditional *quartiers*, as in the plan made under David, to a metropolis united by the 'fever of capitalism'.

Saint-Simonian economists and technocrats, mostly from the Ecole Polytechnique, influenced Napoleon III's views as to the economic means and the systematic ends to be adopted in the rebuilding of Paris, emphasizing the importance of rapid and efficient systems of communication. Haussmann converted Paris into a regional metropolis, cutting through its existing fabric with streets whose purpose was to link opposing cardinal points and districts, across the traditional barrier of the Seine. He gave top priority to the creation of more substantial north-south and east-west axes, to the building of the Boulevard de Sébastopol and the easterly extension of the Rue de Rivoli. This basic cross, which served the main railway termini to the north and south, was encircled by a 'ring' boulevard which in turn was tied into Haussmann's major traffic distributor, his Etoile complex built around Chalgrin's Arc de Triomphe.

During Haussmann's tenure the city of Paris built some 137 kilometres (85 miles) of new boulevards, which were considerably wider, more thickly lined with trees and better lit than the 536 kilometres (333 miles) of old thoroughfare they replaced. With all this came standard residential plan types and regularized façades, and equally standard systems of street furniture – the *pissoirs*, benches, shelters, kiosks, clocks, lamp-posts, signs, etc., designed by Haussmann's engineers Eugène Belgrand and Alphand. This entire system was 'ventilated' whenever possible by large areas of public open space, such as the Bois de Boulogne and the Bois de Vincennes. In addition, new cemeteries and many small parks, such as the Parc des Buttes Chaumont and the Parc Monceau, were either created or upgraded within the extended boundaries of the city. Above all, there was an adequate sewer system and fresh water piped into the city from the Dhuis valley. In achieving such a comprehensive plan, Haussmann, the apolitical administrator par excellence, refused to accept the political logic of the régime he served. He was finally broken by an ambivalent bourgeoisie, who throughout his tenure supported his 'profitable improvements' while at the same time defending their proprietorial rights against his intervention.

Prior to the collapse of the Second Empire, the principle of 'regularization' was already

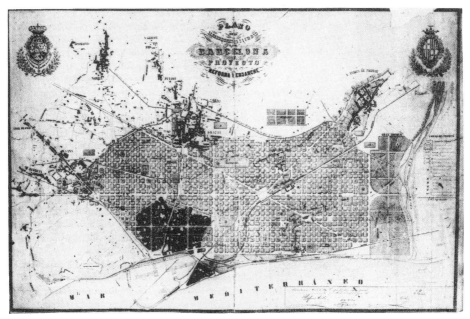

10 Cerdá, project for the expansion of Barcelona, 1858. The old city appears in black.

being practised outside Paris, particularly in Vienna, where the replacement of demolished fortifications by a display boulevard was taken to its logical extreme in the ostentatious Ringstrasse, built around the old centre between 1858 and 1914. The free-standing monuments of this 'open' city expansion, structured around a cranked thoroughfare of enormous width, provoked the critical reaction of the architect Camillo Sitte, who in his influential *Der Städtebau nach seinen künsterlerischen Grundsätzen* (*City Planning According to Artistic Principles*) of 1889 argued for the enclosure of the major Ringstrasse monuments by buildings and arcades. Sitte's remedial concern cannot be better characterized than in his critical comparison of the traffic-ridden 'open' city of the late 19th century with the tranquillity of the medieval or Renaissance urban core:

During the Middle Ages and Renaissance public squares were often used for practical purposes . . . they formed an entirety with the buildings which enclosed them. Today they serve at best as places for parking vehicles,

and they have no relation to the buildings which dominate them. . . . In brief, activity is lacking precisely in those places where, in ancient times, it was most intense, near public structures.

Meanwhile, in Barcelona, the regional implications of urban regularization were being developed by the Spanish engineer Ildefonso Cerdá, the inventor of the term *urbanización*. In 1859 Cerdá projected the expansion of Barcelona as a gridded city, some twenty-two blocks deep, bordered by the sea and intersected by two diagonal avenues. Driven by industry and overseas trade, Barcelona filled out this American-scale grid plan by the end of the century. In his *Teoriá general de la urbanización* ('General Theory of Urbanization') of 1867 Cerdá gave priority to a system of circulation and, in particular, to steam traction. For him transit was, in more ways than one, the point of departure for all scientifically-based urban structures. Léon Jaussely's plan for Barcelona of 1902, derived from Cerdá's, incorporated this emphasis on movement into the form of a

25

proto linear city where the separate zones of accommodation and transportation are organized into bands. His design anticipated in certain respects the Russian linear city proposals of the 1920s.

By 1891 intensive exploitation of the city centre was possible, due to two developments essential to the erection of high-rise buildings: the invention in 1853 of the passenger lift, and the perfection in 1890 of the steel frame. With the introduction of the underground railway (1863), the electric tram (1884) and commuter rail transit (1890), the garden suburb emerged as the 'natural' unit for future urban expansion. The complementary relationship of these two American forms of urban development − the high-rise downtown and the low-rise garden suburb − was demonstrated in the building boom that followed the great Chicago fire of 1871.

The process of suburbanization had already started around Chicago with the layout in 1869 of the suburb of Riverside, to the Picturesque designs of Olmsted. Based in part on the mid-19th-century garden cemetery and in part on the early East Coast suburb, it was linked to downtown Chicago by both a railway and a bridle path.

With the entry into Chicago in 1882 of the steam-powered cable car, the way became open to further expansion. The immediate beneficiary was Chicago's South Side. Yet suburban growth did not really prosper until the 1890s, when, with the introduction of the electric streetcar, suburban transit greatly extended its range, speed and frequency. This led at the turn of the century to the opening up of Chicago's Oak Park suburb, which was to be the proving ground for the early houses of Frank Lloyd Wright. Between 1893 and 1897 an extensive elevated railway was superimposed on the city, encircling its downtown area. All these forms of transit were essential to Chicago's growth. Most important of all for the city's prosperity was the railway, for it brought the first piece of modern agricultural equipment to the prairie − the essential McCormick mechanical reaper invented in 1831 − and collected in return both grain and cattle from the great plains, trans-shipping them to the lakeside silos and stockyards which had begun to be built on Chicago's South Side in 1865. It was the railway that redistributed this abundance from the 1880s on, in Gustavus Swift's refrigerated packing cars, and the corresponding growth in trade greatly augmented the extensive passenger traffic centring on Chicago. Thus the last decade of the century saw radical changes in both the methods of town building and the means of urban access − changes which, in conjunction with the grid plan, were soon to transform the traditional city into an

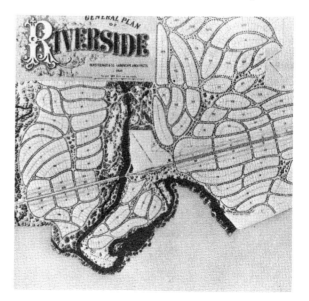

11   Olmsted, plan of Riverside, Chicago, 1869.

ever-expanding metropolitan region where dispersed homestead and concentrated core are linked by continual commuting.

The puritanical entrepreneur George Pullman, who helped to rebuild Chicago after the fire, had been one of the first to appreciate the expanding market in long-distance passenger travel, bringing out his first Pullman sleeping car in 1865. After the achievement of the transcontinental rail link in 1869, Pullman's Palace Car Company prospered, and in the early 1880s he established his ideal industrial town of Pullman, south of Chicago, a settlement that combined workers' residences with a full range of communal facilities, including a theatre and a library as well as schools, parks and playgrounds, all in close proximity to the Pullman factory. This well-ordered complex went far beyond the facilities provided by Godin at Guise some twenty years earlier. It also far exceeds, in its comprehensiveness and clarity, the Picturesque model towns founded in England by the confectioner, George Cadbury at Bournville, Birmingham, in 1879 and by the soap manufacturer W.H. Lever at Port Sunlight, near Liverpool, in 1888. The paternalistic, authoritarian precision of Pullman bears a closer resemblance to Saltaire or to the workers' settlements first established as company policy by Krupp at Essen in the late 1860s.

Rail transit on a much smaller scale, by tram or by train, was to be the main determinant of the two alternative models of the European garden city. One was the axial structure of the Spanish linear garden city, first described by its inventor Arturo Soria y Mata in the early 1880s, and the other was the English concentric garden city, shown as circumnavigated by rail in Ebenezer Howard's *Tomorrow: A Peaceful Path to Real Reform* of 1898. Where Soria y Mata's dynamic interdependent *ciudad lineal* comprised, in his own words of 1882, 'A single street of some 500 metres [1640 feet]

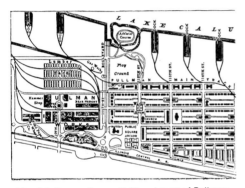

12   S.S. Beman, factory (left) and town of Pullman, Chicago, illustrated in 1885.

13   Howard, 'Rurisville', schematic garden city from his *Tomorrow*, 1898.

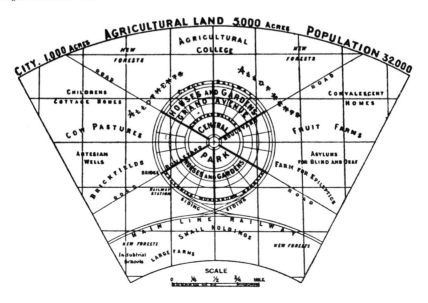

width and of the length that may be necessary ... [a city] whose extremities could be Cadiz or St Petersburg or Peking or Brussels', Howard's static yet supposedly independent 'Rurisville' was encircled by its rail transit and thereby fixed at an optimum size of between 32,000 and 58,000 people. Where the Spanish model was inherently regional, undetermined and Continental, the English version was self-contained, limited and provincial. Soria y Mata described his 'locomotion vertebrae' as incorporating, in addition to transit, the essential services of the 19th-century city — water, gas, electricity and sewerage — compatible with the distribution needs of 19th-century industrial production.

Apart from being an antithesis to the radially planned city, the linear city was a means for building along a triangulated network of pre-existing routes connecting a set of traditional regional centres. While the diagrammatic projection of Howard's city as a satellite town in open country was equally regional, the form of the city itself was less dynamic. On the model of Ruskin's ill-fated St George's Guild of 1871, Howard conceived of his city as an economically self-sufficient mutual aid community, producing little beyond its own needs. The difference between these city models lay finally in the fundamentally different attitudes they adopted to rail transit. Whereas Howard's Rurisville was intended to eliminate the journey to work — the railway being reserved for objects rather than men — the *ciudad lineal* was expressly designed to facilitate communication.

It was, however, the English garden city in its modified form that came to be widely adopted, rather than the linear model sponsored by Soria y Mata's Compañía Madrileña de Urbanización, which only built some 22 kilometres (14 miles) of the 55-kilometre (34-mile) long 'necklace' originally projected for the encirclement of Madrid. The failure of this sole example condemned the linear city to a theoretical rather than practical future, and at this level it persisted from the Russian linear cities of the late 1920s to Le Corbusier's ASCORAL planning thesis, first published as *Les Trois Etablissements humains* in 1945.

The radical reinterpretation of Howard's original diagrams, reflected in the layout of the first garden city, Letchworth in Hertfordshire (started in 1903), inaugurated the neo-Sittesque phase in the English garden city movement. That the engineer-planner Raymond Unwin was impressed by Sitte is evident from his highly influential book *Town Planning in Practice*, published in 1909. The preoccupation of Unwin and his colleague Barry Parker with 'imaginary irregular towns' — of a kind exemplified for them by such medieval German towns as Nuremberg and Rothenburg-ob-der-Tauber — clearly lies behind their picturesque layout for Hampstead Garden Suburb, designed in 1907. Yet for all his contempt for 'bye-law' architecture, Unwin remained as conditioned as any other planner by the constraints imposed by modern standards of hygiene and circulation. Thus, despite the renowned empirical' success of these pioneering garden cities, the debilitating environment produced subsequently by the English school of town planning stems, at least in part, from Unwin's failure to resolve this implacable dichotomy, that is to reconcile medieval nostalgia with bureaucratic control. The 'train-accident' block layouts of the 20th century are among the enduring formal legacies of this failure.

Chapter 3
# Technical transformations: structural engineering 1775–1939

With iron, an artificial building material appeared for the first time in the history of architecture. It went through a development whose tempo accelerated during the course of the century. This received its decisive impulse when it turned out that the locomotive, with which experiments had been made since the end of the 'twenties, could only be utilized on iron rails. The rail was the first unit of construction, the forerunner of the girder. Iron was avoided for dwelling-houses, and made use of for arcades, exhibition halls, railway stations, buildings which served transitory purposes. Simultaneously the architectonic areas in which glass was employed were extended. But the social conditions for its increased utilization as a building material only came into being a hundred years later. In Scheerbart's 'Glasarchitektur' (1914) it still appeared in the context of a Utopia.

Walter Benjamin
*Paris: Capital of the 19th Century*, 1930

Rotary steam power and the iron frame came into being at around the same time through the interdependent efforts of three men: James Watt, Abraham Darby and John Wilkinson. Of these, the last was the 'iron-master' of his day, whose invention of the cylinder boring machine in 1775 was essential to the perfection of Watt's steam engine of 1789. Wilkinson's experience in working iron was to prove equally indispensable to the first structural use of iron, since he assisted Darby and his architect, T.F. Pritchard, in designing and erecting the first cast-iron bridge, a 30.5-metre (100-foot) span built over the Severn near Coalbrookdale in 1779. The Coalbrookdale achievement aroused considerable interest, and in 1786 the Anglo-

American revolutionary, Tom Paine, designed a monument to the American Revolution in the form of a cast-iron bridge spanning the Schuylkill River. Paine had the parts for this bridge made in England, where they were exhibited in 1791, just a year before he was charged with treason and forced into exile in France. In 1796 a 71-metre (236-foot) cast-iron bridge was built across the Wear at Sunderland to the designs of Thomas Wilson, who adopted Paine's 'voussoir' method of assembly. About the same time Thomas Telford made his début as a bridge builder with his 39.5-metre (130-foot) Buildwas Bridge erected over the Severn, a design which employed only 176 tonnes (173 tons) of iron, as opposed to the 384 tonnes (378 tons) used at Coalbrookdale.

Over the next thirty years Telford went on to prove his unparalleled stature as a road and bridge builder and as the last great canal engineer of the waning waterway era. His pioneer career was brought to a close with his brick-encased, iron-framed warehouses at St Katharine Dock in London, designed with the architect Philip Hardwick and erected in 1829. They were based on the system of fireproof multi-storey mill construction developed in the Midlands during the last decade of the 18th century. The main structural antecedents for St Katharine's were William Strutt's six-storey calico mill, built at Derby in 1792, and Charles Bage's flax-spinning mill erected at Shrewsbury in 1796. While both of these structures employed cast-iron columns, the pressing need to perfect a fireproof system for mill buildings led, in the space of four years, to the replacement of the timber beams used at Derby by T-section iron beams. In each instance the

29

beams carried shallow brick vaults, the whole assembly being stiffened by an outer shell and by wrought-iron tie rods restraining the structure in a lateral direction. This use of vaulting seems to have derived directly from the 18th-century development of the Roussillon or Catalonian vault in France, which was first adopted there as a means of achieving a fire-proof structure in Château Bizy, built at Vernon by Constant d'Ivry in 1741.

Aside from its use in 13th-century cathedrals, wrought-iron masonry reinforcement in France had its origins in Paris, in Perrault's east façade of the Louvre (1667) and Soufflot's portico of Ste-Geneviève (1772). Both works anticipate the development of reinforced concrete. In 1776 Soufflot proposed a wrought-iron trussed roof for part of the Louvre that prepared the way for the pioneering work of Victor Louis, that is for Louis's wrought-iron roof for the Théâtre Français of 1786 and his theatre in the Palais-Royal of 1790. This last combined an iron roof with a hollow-pot, fire-proof floor structure, a system that once again was derived from the Roussillon vault. That fire was a growing urban hazard can be seen from the Halle au Blé, Paris, whose burnt-out roof was replaced in 1808 by an iron-ribbed cupola, designed by the architect F.J. Bélanger and the engineer F. Brunet — incidentally, one of the first instances of a clear division of labour between architect and constructor. In the meantime the earliest French application of iron to bridge construction had occurred with the building of the elegant Pont des Arts over the Seine, erected to the designs of L.A. de Cessart in 1803.

With the foundation of the Ecole Polytechnique in 1795, the French strove towards establishing a technocracy appropriate to the achievement of the Napoleonic Empire. While this emphasis on applied technique only served to reinforce the growing specialization of architecture and engineering (a division already institutionalized through Perronet's Ecole des Ponts et Chaussées), architects such as J.-B. Rondelet, who had supervised the completion of Ste-Geneviève after Soufflot's death, began to record the pioneering work of Soufflot, Louis, Brunet, de Cessart and others. And while

Rondelet documented the 'means' in his *Traité de l'art de bâtir* (1802), J.-N.-L. Durand, lecturer in architecture at the Ecole Polytechnique, catalogued the 'ends' in his *Précis des leçons données à l'Ecole Polytechnique* (1802–09). Durand's book disseminated a system whereby Classical forms, conceived as modular elements, could be arranged at will for the accommodation of unprecedented building programmes, i.e. the market halls, libraries and barracks of the Napoleonic Empire. First Rondelet and then Durand codified a technique and a design method whereby a rationalized Classicism could be brought to accommodate not only new social demands but also new techniques. This comprehensive programme influenced Schinkel who, at the beginning of his architectural career in 1816, began to incorporate elaborate iron elements into his Neo-Classical embellishments for the city of Berlin.

Around this time the technique of iron suspension construction underwent an independent evolution, beginning with the American James Finlay's invention of the stiffened, flat-deck suspension bridge in 1801, an achievement that was disseminated by Thomas Pope's *Treatise on Bridge Architecture* published in 1811. The climax of Finlay's brief but critical career was his 74.5-metre (244-foot) span iron-chain suspension bridge across the Merrimac River at Newport in 1810.

Finlay's work, as documented by Pope, had an immediate influence on the application of chain suspension technique in Britain, where Samuel Brown and Telford became involved in its development. Brown's wrought-iron flat bar links were patented in 1817 and applied with lasting success to his 115-metre (378-foot) span Union Bridge, built over the Tweed in 1820. Telford and Brown collaborated briefly on a chain bridge for Runcorn, and this collaboration no doubt informed Telford's design for his 177-metre (580-foot) span Menai Straits bridge, which after eight years of arduous work was finally opened in 1825. British wrought-iron suspension construction culminated in Isambard Kingdom Brunel's 214-metre (702-foot) span Clifton Bridge, Bristol, designed in 1829 but not completed until 1864, five years after Brunel's death.

14  J. A. and W.A. Roebling, Brooklyn Bridge, New York, under construction, c.1877. Initial cable-spinning in progress.

Since the manufacture of wrought-iron links capable of withstanding tension was always an expensive and hazardous affair, the idea of using cables of drawn wire instead of chains seems to have suggested itself, first in 1816 to White and Hazard, in their footbridge over the Schuylkill Falls in Pennsylvania, and then to the Séguin brothers, who constructed a wire bridge over the Rhône at Tain-Tournon in 1825. The Séguins' work formed the subject for an exhaustive analytical study carried out for the Ecole des Ponts et Chaussées by L.-J. Vicat, and the publication of this work in 1831 inaugurated the golden age of the suspension bridge in France, where some hundred such structures were built in the next decade. Vicat recommended that all future suspension members should be fabricated out of wire rather than bar iron, and to this end he invented a method for spinning wire cable in place.

A similar device was eventually used by the American engineer John Augustus Roebling, whose own patent for the manufacture of wire cable was taken out in 1842, just two years

before he used this material for the suspension of an aqueduct over the Allegheny River at Pittsburgh. Roebling's cables were spirally wrapped like those of Vicat, and he used this basic suspension material for the rest of his heroic career, from his 243.5-metre (800-foot) span Niagara Falls railway viaduct of 1855 to his 487-metre (1600-foot) span Brooklyn Bridge, New York, completed, after his death, by his son Washington Roebling in 1883.

With the virtual completion of the British railway infrastructure by 1860, British structural engineering entered a fallow period that lasted for the rest of the century. Few works of outstanding brilliance and ingenuity remained to be built after the middle of the century: these included the Stephenson and Fairbairn Britannia Tubular Bridge of 1852 over the Menai Straits and Brunel's Saltash Viaduct of 1859. Both made use of plated wrought iron, that is to say of riveted rolled sheet, a technique which had been greatly advanced by the studies of Eton Hodgkinson and the experimental work of William Fairbairn. Robert Stephenson had

31

15  Stephenson and Fairbairn, Britannia Tubular Bridge over the Menai Straits, 1852.

already utilized the findings of Hodgkinson and Fairbairn in his development of the plate girder in 1846, a system that was to be fully demonstrated in the Britannia Bridge. This structure comprised two independent, single-track, iron-plated box tunnels which bridged the straits in two spans of 70 metres (230 feet) each and one main span of 140 metres (460 feet). Stephenson's stone towers had been intended for the anchorage of supplementary suspension members, but the plated 'tubes' acting alone proved more than adequate for the span. Comparable spans were achieved in the Saltash Viaduct, where a single track is carried over the Tamar River on two bowstring trusses each spanning 138.5 metres (455 feet). Rolled, riveted plates were again used to form the hollow elliptical chords, measuring 4.9 by 3.7 metres (16 by 12 feet) across their respective axes. These chords interacted with underslung iron chain catenaries to carry vertical standards from which the roadbed was finally suspended. In its imaginative stature Brunel's last work equalled the great viaducts which Gustave Eiffel was to build in the Massif Central over the next thirty years, and its use of hollow plated sections anticipated the gigantic tubular steel framing to be employed by John Fowler and Benjamin Baker in the 213-metre (700-foot) cantilevers of their Forth Bridge, completed in 1890.

The railway development that had begun with George Stephenson's trial run from Stockton to Darlington in 1825 expanded over the second quarter of the century at a formidable rate. In England there were over 3,200 kilo-

metres (2,000 miles) of track after less than twenty years, while in North America 4,600 kilometres (3,000 miles) had been laid by 1842. In the interim, the materials of the railway, cast and wrought iron, gradually became integrated into the general building vocabulary, where they constituted the only available fireproof elements for the multi-storey warehouse space required by industrial production.

From the time of Boulton and Watt's 33-centimetre (13-inch) cast-iron beam, used in their Salford Mill, Manchester, of 1801, a continual effort was made to improve the spanning capacity of both cast- and wrought-iron beams and rails. The typical section of the 'railway' evolved during the first decades of the century, and from this section the standard structural I-beam eventually emerged. Jessop's cast-iron rail of 1789 gave way to Birkenshaw's wrought-iron T-rail of 1820, and this led in turn to the first American rail, rolled in Wales in 1831, with a section in the form of an I broader at the base than at the top. This form became gradually adopted for the permanent way, but did not come into general structural use until after 1854, when heavier versions with greater spanning capacity were successfully rolled. Meanwhile, engineers tried various ways to increase the spanning capacity of the material by building up deep members from the standard wrought-iron angles and plates that were then being used in ship building. Fairbairn reputedly made and tested such composite I-beams as early as 1839.

These ingenious attempts to produce wide-span elements through reinforcing or assembling iron components were more or less eclipsed at mid-century by the successful rolling of a wrought-iron beam 17.8 centimetres (7 inches) deep. Fairbairn's book *On the Application of Cast and Wrought Iron to Building Purposes* (1854) presented an improved system of mill construction, consisting of rolled iron beams 40.6 centimetres (16 inches) deep that supported shallow vaults made of sheet iron, the whole topped out with concrete. Since the wrought-iron tie rods, still used to stabilize the structure, were cast into the concrete floor, this proposal brought Fairbairn fortuitously close to the principles of reinforced concrete.

In a similar vein, a remarkable four-storey cast- and wrought-iron framed building was erected in the Naval Dockyard at Sheerness. This boat store, clad in corrugated iron, was designed by Colonel Greene and erected in 1860, some twelve years before the pioneering all-iron, skeleton-framed Menier chocolate factory was built by Jules Saulnier at Noisiel-sur-Marne. In its systematic use of iron I-sections throughout (cast in the case of the columns and wrought in the case of the beams) the Sheerness boat store anticipated both the standard section and the assembly method of modern steel-frame construction.

By mid-century, cast-iron columns and wrought-iron rails, used in conjunction with modular glazing, had become the standard technique for the rapid prefabrication and erection of urban distribution centres — market halls, exchanges and arcades. This last type was developed in Paris. Fontaine's Galerie d'Orléans, built in the Palais Royal in 1829, was the earliest arcade to have a glass barrel vault. The prefabricated nature of these cast-iron systems guaranteed not only a certain speed of assembly but also the possibility of transporting building 'kits' over large distances: from mid-century on the industrialized countries began to export prefabricated cast-iron structures all over the world.

The sudden expansion in urban growth and trade on the eastern American seaboard in the 1840s encouraged men such as James Bogardus and Daniel Badger to open casting shops in New York for the manufacture of multistorey architectural fronts in iron. Up to the late 1850s, however, their 'packaged' structures relied on the use of large timber beams to span the internal space, iron being reserved for the internal columns and the façades. One of the finest works of Bogardus's extensive career is his Haughwout Building, New York, of 1859, built to the designs of the architect John P. Gaynor. This was the first building to be served by a passenger elevator, just five years after Elisha Graves Otis had made his historic demonstration of the device in 1854.

The fully glazed structure, whose environmental attributes were exhaustively discussed by J.C. Loudon in his *Remarks on Hot Houses*

16    Fontaine, Galerie d'Orléans, Paris, 1829.

(1817), had little chance of having a more general application, at least in England, until the repeal of the excise duty on glass in 1845. Richard Turner and Decimus Burton's Palm House at Kew Gardens, built in 1845–48, was one of the first structures to take advantage of the sudden availability of sheet glass. The first large permanent enclosures to be significantly glazed thereafter were the railway termini that were built during the second half of the 19th century, a development that began with Turner and Joseph Locke's Lime Street Station, Liverpool, of 1849–50.

The railway terminus presented a peculiar challenge to the received canons of architecture, since there was no type available to express and articulate adequately the junction between the head building and the train shed. This problem, which saw its earliest architectural resolution in Duquesney's Gare de l'Est, Paris, of 1852, was of some concern since these termini were effectively the new gateways into the capital city. The engineer Léonce Reynaud, designer of the first Gare du Nord in Paris (1847), was aware of this issue of 'representation' when he wrote in his *Traité d'architecture* (1850):

Art does not have the rapid progress and sudden developments of industry, with the result that the majority of buildings today for the service of railroads leave more or less to be desired, be it in relation to form or arrangement. Some

33

stations appear to be appropriately arranged but having the character of industrial or temporary construction rather than that of a building for public use.

Nothing could be more exemplary of this predicament than St Pancras Station in London, where the vast shed, 74 metres (243 feet) in span, built in 1863–65 to the designs of W.H. Barlow and R.M. Ordish, was totally divorced from the Gothic Revival hotel-cum-head building completed in 1874 to the designs of George Gilbert Scott. And what was true for St Pancras also applied to Brunel's designs for Paddington in London (1852), where once again, despite the conscientious efforts of the architect Matthew Digby Wyatt, the rather rudimentary station building was left inadequately related to the vaulted profiles of the shed.

The free-standing exhibition structure presented none of the problems of the terminus, for where the issues of cultural context could scarcely arise the engineer reigned supreme. This was never more so than in the case of the Crystal Palace in London, built for the Great Exhibition of 1851, where the gardener Joseph Paxton was given a free hand to design in accordance with a method for the fabrication of glasshouses that he had developed through a rigorous application of Loudon's hothouse principles. Paxton had developed his method in a series of glasshouses built for the Duke of Devonshire at Chatsworth. When commissioned

17   Paxton, Crystal Palace, London, 1851, under construction, showing glaziers' cradles.

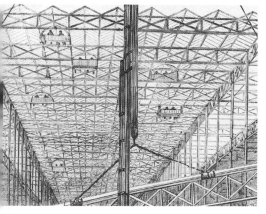

at the eleventh hour to design the Crystal Palace, Paxton was able to produce, in just eight days, an enormous orthogonal three-tiered glasshouse, whose components were virtually identical to those of the giant lily house that he had built at Chatsworth in the previous year. Except for three entrance porches, symmetrically disposed, its glazed perimeter was uninterrupted. During its development, however, a revised scheme had to be prepared in order to retain a group of mature trees. Since the remaining public opposition to the Great Exhibition of 1851 turned on this question of tree preservation, Paxton was quick to realize that these troublesome items could easily be accommodated by a central transept with a high curved roof, and thus the double symmetry of the final form emerged.

The Crystal Palace was not so much a particular form as it was a building process made manifest as a total system, from its initial conception, fabrication and trans-shipment, to its final erection and dismantling. Like the railway buildings, to which it was related, it was a highly flexible kit of parts. Its overall form was structured around a basic 2.44-metre (8-foot) cladding module, assembled into a hierarchy of structural spans varying from 7.31 to 21.95 metres (24 to 72 feet). Its realization, which took barely four months, was a simple matter of mass production and systematic assembly. As Konrad Wachsmann has remarked in his book *Wendepunkt im Bauen* (*The Turning Point of Building*) of 1961, 'Its production requirements included studies which indicated that for easy handling no part should weigh more than one ton and that the greatest economies could be obtained by using glass panels of the largest possible size.'

While the Crystal Palace engendered through its open lattice work spectacular parallel and oblique perspectives whose lines diminished into a diaphanous haze of light, its total envelope, comprising nearly 93,000 square metres (a million square feet) of glass, presented a climatic problem of unprecedented scale. The desirable environmental conditions, however, remained the same as they had been in Loudon's curvilinear hothouses – to maintain comfortable air movement and to moderate the heat of the sun. While the elevation of the building off the ground and the provision of a slatted floor, together with adjustable louvers in the walls, provided satisfactory ventilation, the accumulation of solar heat constituted a problem to which the railway engineer Charles Fox, who was responsible for the detailing of the structure, could find no adequate solution. The eventual ad hoc use of canvas awnings to shade the roof could hardly be regarded as an integral part of the system, and many of the international exhibitors chose to shield themselves from the 'greenhouse' effect by canopies of festooned draperies, which were no doubt hung as much against the unacceptable 'objectivity' of the structure as they were against the sun.

The British abandonment of the international exhibition field, after the triumph of 1851 and a further exhibition in 1862, was at once exploited by the French, who mounted five major international exhibitions between 1855 and 1900. The degree to which these displays were regarded as national platforms from which to challenge the British command over industrial production and trade may be judged from the emphasis placed each time on the structure and content of the 'Galerie des Machines'. The young Gustave Eiffel worked with the engineer J.-B. Krantz on the most significant exhibition building to be erected after 1851, that for the Paris World Exhibition of 1867. This collaboration revealed not only Eiffel's expressive sensibility but also his capacity as an engineer, since in detailing the Galerie des Machines, with its 35-metre (114-foot) span, he was able to verify the validity of Thomas Young's modulus of elasticity of 1807, a hitherto solely theoretical formula for determining the elastic behaviour of material under stress. The whole oval complex, of which the Galerie des Machines was merely the outer ring, was itself a testament to the conceptual genius of P.G.F. Le Play, who had suggested that the building be arranged as concentric galleries exhibiting machinery, clothing, furniture, liberal arts, fine arts and the history of labour.

After 1867 the sheer size and diversity of the objects produced, and the independence demanded by international competition, seem to have demanded multiple exhibition structures. By the time of the International Exhibition of 1889 no pretence was made of housing the exhibits in one self-contained building. This penultimate exhibition of the century was dominated by two of the most remarkable structures that French engineering was ever to achieve – Victor Contamin's vast Galerie des Machines, 107 metres (350 feet) in span, designed with the architect C.-L.-F. Dutert, and Eiffel's tower, 300 metres (984 feet) high, designed in collaboration with the engineers Nouguier and Koechlin and the architect Stephen Sauvestre. Contamin's structure, based on statical methods perfected by Eiffel in his hinged viaducts of the 1880s, was one of the first to use the three-hinged arch form in the achievement of a large span. Contamin's shed not only exhibited machines: it was itself an 'exhibiting machine', in which mobile viewing platforms, running on elevated tracks, passed over the exhibition space on either side of the central axis, affording the visitor a fast and comprehensive view of the entire show.

In the last half of the 19th century the Massif Central had been found to be sufficiently rich in minerals to justify the considerable expense of equipping it with a railway network. The railway viaducts that Eiffel designed there between 1869 and 1884 exemplify a method and an aesthetic that found their ultimate celebration in the design of the Eiffel Tower. The boat-shaped base and the parabolic vertical section

18 Dutert and Contamin, Galerie des Machines at the Paris Exhibition, 1889, showing the mobile viewing platform.

of the tubular iron pylon that Eiffel evolved for these viaducts is formally indicative of his constant attempt to resolve the dynamic interaction of water and wind.

The need to make wider river crossings led Eiffel and his associates to devise an ingenious system of viaduct support. The spur to such a solution came in 1875, with the commission to construct a railway viaduct over the river Douro in Portugal. The availability of cheap steel after 1870 afforded a material in which a wide-span solution might be readily achieved. A decision was therefore made to cross the ravine in five spans, two short spans supported on pylons on either side and a central longer span of 160 metres (524 feet) carried on a two-pinned arch. The procedure of erection, to be repeated a few years later at Garabit, was to construct the flanking spans with their supporting pylons and then to erect the central section from these continuous structures on either side. Truss extensions were cantilevered out at track level, and the hinged arch was simultaneously constructed, in two halves, from the water below. The initial hinged sections were floated and jacked into position and then maintained at a correct incline during their final assembly by cables suspended from the caps of the adjacent pylons. The outstanding success of the Douro Viaduct, completed in 1878, immediately brought Eiffel a commission to build the Garabit Viaduct over the River Truyère in the Massif Central.

Just as the Douro Viaduct provided the necessary experience to build Garabit, so the achievement of Garabit was essential to the design and conception of the Eiffel Tower. Like the Crystal Palace, but at a slower rate, the tower was designed and erected under considerable pressure. First exhibited as a design in the spring of 1885, it was in the ground by the summer of 1887 and well over 200 metres (654 feet) high by the winter of 1888. As in Contamin's Galerie des Machines, the structure had to be provided with an access system for the rapid movement of visitors. Speed was essential, since there was no way of gaining access to the tower except via elevators that ran on inclined tracks within its hyperbolic legs and rose vertically from first platform to

pinnacle. The guide rails for these elevators were exploited during erection as tracks for climbing cranes, an economy in working method reminiscent of the mounting technique used in the case of the hinged viaducts. As much a by-product of the railway as the Crystal Palace, the tower was, in effect, a 300-metre (974-foot) high viaduct pylon, whose type-form had originally been evolved out of the interaction of wind, gravity, water and material resistance. It was a hitherto unimaginable structure that could not be experienced except by traversing the aerial matrix of the space itself. Given the futuristic affinity of the tower to aviation – celebrated by the aviator Santos Dumont, when he circled the structure with his dirigible in 1901 – it is hardly surprising that thirty years after its erection it should have been appropriated and reinterpreted as the prime symbol of a new social and technical order, in Vladimir Tatlin's monument to the Third International, projected in 1919–20.

As iron technology developed through the exploitation of the earth's mineral wealth, so concrete technology, or at least the development of hydraulic cement, seems to have arisen out of traffic on sea. In 1774, John Smeaton established the base of his Eddystone Lighthouse using a 'concrete' compound of quicklime, clay, sand and crushed iron slag, and similar concrete mixes were used in England in bridge, canal and harbour works throughout the last quarter of the 18th century. Despite Joseph Aspdin's pioneering development of Portland Cement for use as imitation stone in 1824, and various other English proposals for metal-reinforced concrete construction, such as that made by the ever inventive Loudon in 1792, the initial English lead in the pioneering of concrete gradually passed to France.

In France the economic restrictions that followed the Revolution of 1789, the synthesis of hydraulic cement by Vicat around 1800 and the tradition of building in *pisé* (rammed earth), combined to create the optimum circumstances for the invention of reinforced concrete. The first consequential use of the new material was made by François Coignet, who was already familiar with the *pisé* building method of the Lyons district. In 1861 he developed a technique for strengthening concrete with metal mesh, and on the basis of this established the first limited company to specialize in ferroconcrete construction. Coignet worked in Paris under Haussmann's direction, building sewers and other public structures in ferro-concrete – including, in 1867, a remarkable series of six-storey apartment blocks. Despite these commissions, Coignet failed to uphold his patent and by the end of the Second Empire his company was dissolved.

Another French pioneer of concrete was the gardener Joseph Monier who, following his successful production of concrete flower pots in 1850, took out, after 1867, a series of patents for metal-reinforced applications, the partial rights of which he ill-advisedly sold in 1880 to the engineers Schuster and Wayss. Further rights were obtained from Monier in 1884 by the firm of Freytag, and soon afterwards the large German civil engineering concern of Wayss and Freytag came into being. Their monopoly over the Monier system was consolidated by G.A. Wayss's standard work on the Monier method (*Monierbau*), published in 1887. The publication of important theoretical studies on differential stress in reinforced concrete by the German theorists Neumann and Koenen served to consolidate the German lead in this type of construction.

The period of most intense development in reinforced concrete occurred between 1870 and 1900, with pioneering work being carried on simultaneously in Germany, America, England and France. In building his reinforced-concrete Hudson River home in 1873, the American William E. Ward became the first constructor to take full advantage of the tensile strength of steel by situating bars below the neutral axis of the beam. The inherent structural advantage of this was almost immediately confirmed by the concrete beam experiments conducted in England by Thaddeus Hyatt and Thomas Rickets, whose joint results were published in 1877.

Despite these ·international developments, the systematic exploitation of modern rein-forced-concrete technique was to wait upon the inventive genius of François Hennebique.

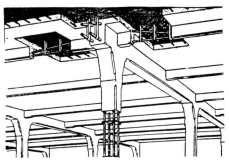

19 Hennebique, monolithic reinforced-concrete joint, patented in 1892.

Hennebique, a self-educated French builder, first used concrete in 1879. He then conducted an extensive programme of private research before patenting his own uniquely compre-hensive system in 1892. Before Hennebique the great problem in ferroconcrete had been the provision of a monolithic joint. The compound concrete and steel systems that had been patented by Fairbairn in 1845 were far from being monolithic, and the same restrictions applied to the work of Hyatt and Rickets. Hennebique overcame this difficulty through the use of bars of cylindrical section which could be bent round and hooked together. Integral to his system alone was the cranking up of reinforcement bars and the binding of joints with stirrup hoops in order to resist local stress. With the perfection of the monolithic joint, the monolithic frame could be realized, leading promptly to the first large-scale application of such a system to three spinning mills that Hennebique built in the region of Tourcoing and Lille in 1896. The results were at once acclaimed as a success, and Hennebique's firm immediately prospered. His partner, L.-G. Mouchel, took the system to England in 1897, building the first concrete road bridge there in 1901 and exhibiting a spectacular free-standing, helical, reinforced-concrete stair at the Franco-British exhibition of 1908.

The wide success of the Hennebique firm dates from around 1898, with the regular publication of its house magazine *Le Béton armé* ('Reinforced Concrete') and the extensive use of its system in the eclectic structures of the Paris Exhibition of 1900. Despite the false façades of the Château d'Eau, constructed out of ferroconcrete by François Coignet's son, the Paris Exhibition of 1900 gave an enormous boost to concrete construction, and by 1902, a decade after its foundation, the Hennebique firm had grown into a large international concern. By then innumerable works were being constructed in concrete throughout Europe, with Hennebique acting as the main contractor. In 1904 he built his own reinforced-concrete villa at Bourg-la-Reine, complete with roof garden and minaret. Its solid walls were formed out of ferroconcrete poured in place between permanent pre-cast concrete shuttering, and its almost totally glazed façade was dramatically cantilevered out from the main plane of the building. By the turn of the century, Hennebique's monopoly over his system began to wane, although his patents still had a number of years to run. In 1902 his chief assistant, Paul Christophe, popularized the system by publishing *Le Béton armé et ses applications*. Four years later Armand-Gabriel Considéré, who had already carried out concrete research for the department of Ponts et Chaussées, headed the national committee that established the French code for reinforced-concrete practice.

In 1890 the engineer Cottancin patented his own system of *ciment armé*, which depended on the combined reinforcement of concrete and brick, the bricks being bonded into the concrete with wire reinforcement. In this hybrid system the main function of the ferroconcrete element was to maintain structural continuity in areas of high tension. In areas of compression brick naturally predominated. The system had a

strong appeal for the rationalist architect Anatole de Baudot who, as a pupil of the great French 'structural' theorist Viollet-le-Duc, was preoccupied with revealed structure as the only valid basis for expression in architecture. On these grounds, de Baudot consigned monolithic *béton armé* to the field of engineering, while reserving for the architect the statically more explicit and articulate technique of *ciment armé*, a technology whose expressive qualities were most fully demonstrated in his church of St-Jean-de-Montmartre in Paris (begun in 1894).

The intricate vaulting there was closely related to a whole sequence of *grande salle* projects which de Baudot designed between 1910 and 1914. After Viollet-le-Duc, he was concerned with the problem of the great space as the necessary proving ground for any architectural culture. In this context his *grande salle* series, which commenced with a vast project for the 1900 Exhibition, may be seen as anticipating the reticulated flat slabs and prefabricated folded shells that were to be achieved half a century later by the Italian engineer Pier Luigi Nervi, most typically in the Turin Exhibition Hall of 1948 and the Gatti Wool Factory, built outside Rome in 1953.

In opposition to de Baudot's principle of reticulated form, the challenge of the great space was answered by Max Berg through the use of reinforced-concrete elements of enormous size, in his Jahrhunderthalle, built by Konwiarz and Trauer for the Breslau Exhibition of 1913. Inside this vast, centralized hall, 65 metres (213 feet) in diameter, the concrete ribs of the cupola sprang from a perimeter ring beam which was in its turn supported by massive pendentive arches. This awkward Herculean structure was concealed on the outside by concentric tiers of glazing, the organic plan and dynamic structure being suppressed by the superimposition of Neo-Classical elements.

Up to 1895, ferroconcrete work in North America was inhibited by its dependence on the importation of cement from Europe. Soon after, however, the epoch of the grain silo and the flatted factory commenced, first in Canada, with the reinforced-concrete silo structures of

20 Berg, Jahrhunderthalle, Breslau (Wroclaw), 1913.

Max Toltz, and then, from 1900 onwards, in the United States, in the work of Ernest L. Ransome, who was the inventor of twisted reinforcement. With the building in 1902 of his 91-metre (300-foot) machine shop at Greensburg, Pennsylvania, Ransome became the pioneer of the monolithic concrete frame in the United States. Here he applied for the first time the principle of spiral column reinforcement in accordance with the theories of Considéré. It says something for the technical precociousness of Frank Lloyd Wright that he began to design reinforced-concrete structures at around the same time: his unrealized Village Bank project of 1901, and the E-Z Polish factory and Unity Temple, completed in Chicago in 1905 and 1906 respectively.

Meanwhile, in Paris, Perret Frères had begun to design and build their first all-concrete structures, beginning with Auguste Perret's seminal Rue Franklin apartment block of 1903 and his Théâtre des Champs-Elysées of 1913. At about the same time, Henri Sauvage explored the expressive 'plastic' potential of this new monolithic material in his set-back apartments in the Rue Vavin, completed in 1912. By this date the reinforced-concrete frame had become a normative technique, and from now on most of the development was to lie in the scale of its application and in its assimilation as an expressive element. While its first use on a megastructural scale was in Matté Trucco's 40-hectare (100-acre) Fiat Works, begun in Turin in 1915, its appropriation as the primary expressive element of a architectural language came with Le Corbusier's 'Maison Dom-Ino' proposal of around the same date. Where the one clearly demonstrated that flat concrete roofs could sustain the vibration of dynamic moving loads – the Fiat factory has a test track on its roof – the other postulated the Hennebique system as a 'patent' primal structure to which, after the manner of Laugier's primitive hut, the development of the new architecture would have to refer.

From an engineering standpoint, this period was to reach its most sublime expression in the early work of the engineers Robert Maillart and Eugène Freyssinet. By 1905 in his Rhine Bridge at Tavanasa, the great Swiss engineer Maillart had already arrived at his characteristic bridge form – a three-hinged arch of hollow box section, with triangular openings cut into its sides to reduce unnecessary weight and to impart a light and expressive character to the overall form. By 1912, Maillart had achieved the first beamless floor slab in Europe, in a five-storey warehouse that he built in Altdorf. His beamless system seems to have been an advance over the mushroom slab construction developed slightly earlier by the American engineer C.A.P. Turner. In Turner's 'four-way' reinforcement, as opposed to Maillart's 'two-way' system, the bars were required to pass over all column heads, with the consequence that the steel could not be accommodated within an economic depth if the tendency of the column to punch through the slab was to be resisted. The floor structure in the Turner system was, in effect, a network of heavily reinforced flat beams with large column heads to resist the resulting shear. The beamless 'two-way' Maillart system was

21   Trucco, Fiat Works, Turin, 1915–21.

lighter and generated far less shear, with a corresponding reduction in the dimensions of both the slab and the column heads.

In his Aare Bridge at Aarburg (1911) Maillart succeeded in articulating the bridge platform from its supporting arch while stiffening the platform through transverse frames set into the haunch of the arch. He had still to articulate the abutments of the bridge in relation to its overall form. In almost all his bridges, even where supported by ribbed arches, Maillart designed the platform as a box section so that as far as possible the road bed was made to support itself. He reached the height of his powers as a bridge builder with his 90-metre (295-foot) span Salginatobel Bridge, erected in the Alps in 1930, but the formula that he had first worked out at Aarburg received its finest expression in the Arve Bridge, built at Vessey near Geneva in 1936.

The high twin airship hangars that the French engineer Freyssinet realized at Orly between 1916 and 1924, each 62.5 metres high and 300 metres long (205 by 984 feet), were one of first attempts, after the projects of de Baudot, to design monolithic structures whose assembled elements were capable of supporting themselves. These pioneer prefabricated folded slab constructions influenced a remarkable series of aircraft hangars designed by Nervi in the latter half of the 1930s. While still at work at Orly, Freyssinet designed for the concrete contractor Limousin a series of reinforced-concrete 'bow-string' warehouse structures, including a number of hangars and factory buildings lit through monitor lights in the shell roof. The culmination of all this work was two large bow-string bridges in reinforced concrete, at St-Pierre-du-Vauvray (1923) and at Plougastel (1926–29), the latter crossing the Elorn estuary in Brittany in three spans with a total length of 975 metres (3,200 feet).

The problem of the intense compressive and tensile stresses induced in the curing and loading of large parabolic arches led Freyssinet by the mid-1920s to experiment with the artificial inducement of stress in the reinforcement before casting. Within a few years pre-stressed concrete as we now know it had been invented. This extremely economical system for large spans – reducing the beam depth by about half for the same concrete section – was first patented by Freyssinet in 1939.

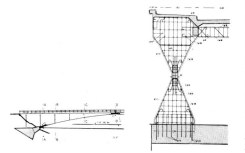

22  Maillart, Arve Bridge, Vessey, 1936. Half-section of bridge and section through transverse 'haunch', with reinforcement layout.

23  Freyssinet, Plougastel Bridge, Brittany, 1926–29. Half-section of one span, and transverse section at apex (b-b), showing the railway at lower level with roadway above. Where arch and railway diverge, in the half-section, a deflection joint is introduced (a).

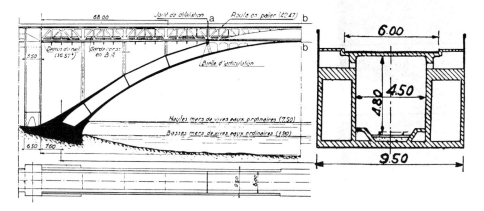

# Part 2
## A critical history
## 1836–1967

24  Terragni, Casa del Fascio, Como, 1932–36,
during a demonstration (see p. 205).

## Chapter 1

# News from Nowhere: England 1836-1924

The enthusiasm of the Gothic revivalists died out when they were confronted by the fact that they form part of a society which will not and cannot have a living style, because it is an economical necessity for its existence that the ordinary everyday work of its population shall be mechanical drudgery; and because it is the harmony of the ordinary everyday work of the population which produces Gothic, that is living architectural art, and mechanical drudgery cannot be harmonized into art. The hope of our ignorance has passed away, but it has given place to the hope of fresh knowledge. History taught us the evolution of architecture, it is now teaching us the evolution of society; and it is clear to us, and even to many who refuse to acknowledge it, that . . . the new society will not be hag-ridden as we are by the necessity for producing ever more and more market-wares for a profit, whether any one needs them or not; that it will produce to live and not live to produce, as we do.

William Morris
*The Revival of Architecture*, 1888

Prefigured in the Puritan and apocalyptic works of Milton and Blake, the Scottish *philosophe* Thomas Carlyle and the English architect A.W.N. Pugin separately called forth the spiritual and cultural discontents of the second half of the 19th century. The former was atheistic and consciously aligned to the radical Chartist movement of the late 1830s; the latter was a Catholic convert who advocated a direct return to the spiritual values and architectural forms of the Middle Ages. After the publication, in 1836, of his *Contrasts; or a parallel between the noble edifices of the 14th and 15th centuries and similar buildings of the present day*, Pugin's influence was immediate and extensive. To him we owe largely the homogeneity of the Gothic Revival, which profoundly affected English building in the 19th century. Carlyle, on the other hand, was in many respects in opposition to Pugin. His *Past and Present* of 1843 was an implicit critique of Catholicism in its decadence, presenting the case for a brand of paternalistic socialism on the model of Saint-Simon's New Christianity, of 1825. Whereas Carlyle's radicalism was politically and socially progressive, even if ultimately authoritarian, Pugin's reformism was essentially conservative and related to the right-wing, High Church Oxford Movement, whose foundation preceded by two years his conversion to Catholicism in 1835. What Carlyle and Pugin had in common was distaste for their materialistic age: through this shared antagonism they were to influence that mid-19th-century prophet of cultural doom and redemption, John Ruskin, who in his prime in 1868 became the first Slade Professor of Fine Art at the University of Oxford.

Ruskin, who acquired his intellectual following in 1846 with the appearance of the second volume of his *Modern Painters*, did not begin to declare himself unequivocally and extensively on socio-cultural and economic matters until 1853, when he published *The Stones of Venice*. There, in a whole chapter devoted to the place of the craftsman in relation to the work of art, Ruskin first spoke out against the industrialist 'division of labour' and the 'degradation of the operative into a machine' — a text that was to be reissued as a pamphlet by the first Working Men's College, at which Ruskin subsequently taught. In it, after Adam Smith, Ruskin compared traditional craftsmanship with the mechanical labour of mass production.

He wrote, 'It is not, truly speaking, the labour that is divided; but the men . . . so that all the little piece of intelligence that is left in a man is not enough to make a pin or a nail, but exhausts itself in making the point of a pin or the head of a nail.' This was an extension of his attitude to ornament, already outlined in *The Seven Lamps of Architecture* (1849), where he wrote that 'the right question to ask, respecting all ornament, is simply this: was it done with enjoyment?' With this brand of radicalism, Ruskin began to move away from his earlier High Anglican sympathies to a position much closer to that of Carlyle. On the publication in 1860 of his essays in political economy, *Unto this Last*, he finally revealed himself as an uncompromising socialist.

Through their influence on the English cultural climate via Pugin, Friedrich Overbeck — whom Pugin described as 'that prince of Christian painters' — and the German Nazarenes became the moral and artistic model for the short-lived, Chartist-inspired, Pre-Raphaelite brotherhood, formed at the instigation of the brothers Dante Gabriel and William Michael Rossetti, Holman Hunt and John Everett Millais in 1848.

In 1851 Ruskin became spiritually affiliated to this movement, which had as its aim the foundation of a school of painting which would be expressive of profound ideas and emotions. The ideal was to create an art form derived directly from nature and not from artistic conventions of Renaissance origin. This eminently anti-Classical, Romantic attitude was propagated in 1850 in the Pre-Raphaelite magazine, *The Germ*. Yet the brotherhood lacked the monastic strictness and conviction of the Nazarenes. Both it and its magazine were too individualistic to last for long, and by 1853 Pre-Raphaelitism as a collective movement was defunct.

The second, craft-oriented, phase of Pre-Raphaelite activity turns upon the meeting of William Morris and Edward Burne-Jones when undergraduates at Oxford, in 1853. Oxford exposed them to the lectures of Ruskin and to the all-pervasive influence of Pugin. After their graduation, in 1856, they became closely involved with the poet and painter Dante Gabriel Rossetti, eventually collaborating with him in 1857 on murals for the Union Society building at Oxford, an enterprise that deliberately echoed the Nazarene frescoes in Rome. Although Burne-Jones had already determined to become a painter, it was some months before Rossetti could lure Morris to London, away from his articled position in the Oxford office of the Gothic Revivalist architect G.E. Street. Somewhat paradoxically, Morris's career as a designer dates from his decision, late in 1856, to abandon architecture for painting: but that had to wait upon the furnishing of his rooms in London, for which he designed his first 'intensely medieval furniture . . . as firm and as heavy as a rock'. These unpretentious pieces, no doubt inspired by the craft ideals of Ruskin, were designed under the guidance of Philip Webb, with whom Morris had previously worked in Street's office. In 1858 Pre-Raphaelite domestic culture was crystallized, as it were, in Morris's only known easel work, a portrait of his wife, Jane Burden, as *Queen Guinevere* or *La Belle Iseult*, wearing ornate clothes in an ideal Pre-Raphaelite interior. Morris then gave up painting entirely and addressed himself to the task of furnishing his new home, the Red House, which Philip Webb built for him in 1859 at Bexley Heath, Kent, in a style which except for minor details was close to the work of Street and more particularly to William Butterfield's Gothic Revival vicarages dating from the 1840s and 1850s.

In the Red House (so called on account of its brickwork) Webb established the principles which were soon to inform the work of his brilliant contemporaries, William Eden Nesfield and Richard Norman Shaw, and for which he was to be known throughout his career — his concern for structural integrity and his desire to integrate buildings into their site and into the local culture. These aims he achieved through practical design, sensitive site layout and the use of local materials, coupled with a profound respect for traditional building methods. Like Morris, his first client and lifelong colleague, Webb had an almost mystical respect for the sacredness of craftsmanship and for the earth in which both life and architecture were ultimately founded. Even more than Morris,

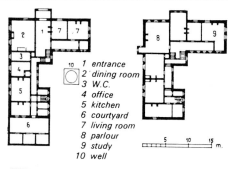

1 entrance
2 dining room
3 W.C.
4 office
5 kitchen
6 courtyard
7 living room
8 parlour
9 study
10 well

he was against any excessive use of ornament. According to his biographer, W.R. Lethaby, Webb once complained that an over-elegant grate was 'hardly fit for the holy fire'. Such a sentiment could hardly be further removed from the mannered interpretation that his approach was to be given at the hands of Nesfield and Shaw, for instance in the latter's picturesque 'Old English' country house, Leyswood, Sussex, designed in 1866.

The whole exuberant unfolding of the English Free Architecture movement, from the eccentricities of A.H. Mackmurdo and C.R. Ashbee to the refined professionalism of Shaw, Lethaby and C.F.A. Voysey, may be said to have had its origin in the creation of the Red House. At all events, this work was catalytic in launching Morris on his destined career, and two years later he organized an association of Pre-Raphaelite artists, including Webb, Rossetti, Burne-Jones and Ford Madox Brown, into an atelier which would design and execute on commission anything from murals to stained glass and furniture, from embroidery to metalwork and carved wood. The aim, as in Pugin's extensive furnishings designed for the Houses

25, 26   Webb, Red House, Bexley Heath, Kent, 1859. View, and plans of ground and first floors.

27   Shaw, Leyswood, Sussex, 1866–69.

of Parliament in the 1830s and 1840s, was the creation of a total work of art. This much, with all modesty, the prospectus of the firm made clear: 'It is anticipated that by such co-operation . . . the work must necessarily be of a much more complete order than if any single artist were incidentally employed in the usual manner.' Apart from the precedent established by Pugin, the foundation of this atelier may well have been influenced by the Art Manufactures organization, started by Henry Cole under the pseudonym of Felix Summerly in 1845. In any event, the Pre-Raphaelite craft work that had hitherto occurred spontaneously now took on a public character. It is fitting that the first work to be sold at the London premises of the firm was glass tableware designed by Webb.

With the prospering of the atelier, Morris was paradoxically compelled to leave the idyllic Red House in 1864 and to move permanently to London. A year later he gave over the management of the firm to Warrington Taylor, in order to devote himself exclusively to two-dimensional design and to literature, the two activities which were to consume the rest of his life. The first Morris wallpapers date from this period, as do the earliest works in stained glass by himself and Burne-Jones. Morris's models varied from Persian décor, illustrated in Owen Jones's *Grammar of Ornament* of 1856, to the medieval style which he naturally adopted for his stained-glass work — a product for which there was a steady, if limited, demand throughout his life. Morris, Marshall, Faulkner & Co. achieved public recognition in 1867 with the Green Dining Room or tea room that Webb designed for the South Kensington Museum (now Victoria and Albert) in London. The room was entirely furnished and decorated by Morris and the artist-craftsmen of his firm.

After this date, Webb started to design and execute large domestic commissions on his own, culminating in his last great house, Standen, built near East Grinstead, Sussex (1891–94), with furnishings provided — as was usually the case — by Morris's firm. Morris became increasingly involved with literature, from which he attempted fanatically to expunge all words of Latin origin, producing by the mid-1870s extensive translations of Icelandic sagas, in addition to numerous volumes of his own Romantic poetry. At that time it would seem as if medieval Iceland was the final 'Nowhere' that his idealistic spirit pined for, while it remained sequestered within the industrial reality of the 19th century.

The year 1875 was a watershed in Morris's life. The firm was dissolved and reorganized as Morris & Co. under his sole control, and he began to increase the number of crafts in which he and hence the firm could work. He taught himself dyeing and carpet weaving and, in 1877, established a London showroom as a prime commercial outlet. From then on, aside from the management of the firm and the design and production of a whole range of wallpapers, hangings and carpets, Morris's concerns gradually became increasingly public and less 'poetic' and craft-oriented. He seems to have felt it his duty to take up publicly the socialist and preservationist causes of Ruskin, who was by now mentally ill. Thus, in 1877 he wrote his first political pamphlet and founded the Society for the Protection of Ancient Buildings, in a successful attempt to foil Sir George Gilbert Scott's intentions to restore, or rather partly to rebuild, Tewkesbury Abbey.

In the decade following his reorganization of the firm, Morris divided his life equally between politics and design, producing during this period, according to his first biographer, Mackail, over six hundred designs for various fabrics. In 1883, however, Morris began to read the works of Karl Marx and joined the Social Democratic Federation, headed by Engels, in the company of such committed socialists as Eleanor Marx and Edward Aveling. Two years later he left the Federation and founded the Socialist League, shifting virtually all of his energies from design to politics. At frequent intervals, until his death in 1896, he wrote and published essays on the related themes of socialism, culture and society, beginning with his Fourierist essay of 1885 entitled *How We Live and How We Might Live*, and culminating in his famous utopian romance, *News from Nowhere*, of 1891.

To the coming generations, to Morris's associate Walter Crane, to Ruskin's protégé Mackmurdo and to the principal pupils of

Shaw, namely Lethaby, E.S. Prior and Ernest Newton, even to Shaw himself, and to relative outsiders such as Ashbee and Voysey, Morris's somewhat contradictory position was patently clear. Above all there was his utopian vision of 'Nowhere', a land where the state had withered away according to Marxist prophecy and where all distinction between town and country had disappeared. The city no longer existed as a dense physical entity and the great engineering achievements of the 19th century had been dismantled: wind and water were once more the sole sources of power, and the waterway and the road were the sole means of transport. A society without money or property, without crime or punishment, without prison or parliament, where social order depended solely upon the free association of family groups within the structure of the commune. Finally, a society where work was based on the banded workshop, the guild or *Werkbund*, and where education was free and like labour itself unforced.

This single-minded socialist vision stood out in strong contrast to the context of Morris's own life and to the latent inconsistency of his thought. There was his prosperous firm itself, a laissez-faire phenomenon par excellence, whose diverse luxury goods were consumed by the upper middle class; then there was his highly radical socialism, largely unintegrated with his innate anarchic leanings — a revolutionary socialism totally unacceptable to the more liberal of his followers, such as Ashbee; and finally, for Fabian Socialists and architects alike, there was within Morris's theory and practice the ameliorative suggestion of the garden city as a form of settlement to be based on the craft guild or co-operative, as a means for achieving not only work, but also evolutionary social reform and re-education, and so, by degrees, some public recognition for both. In contrast to this progressive (if somewhat disturbing) breadth of concern, there was the latent phobic quality of Morris's own design and — more critical still — there was his stubborn refusal to come to terms with industrial method and his ambiguous, not to say hostile, attitude to all architecture after the 15th century. Not only was the Classical past condemned but even sympathetic contemporary work was

indifferently received: Webb's fine designs singularly failed to draw from Morris any public recognition. Could it be that Webb's eclecticism was finally too much for Morris; that the Classical and Elizabethan elements incorporated into his houses between 1879 and 1891 were sufficient cause for disaffection?

In the event, the historicism of the period was hardly capable of sustaining Morris's anti-Classical line. By the early 1870s worldly architects like Shaw were already manipulating and classicizing, in an urban context, the Queen Anne style that he, Webb and Nesfield had developed out of the English and Dutch domestic traditions. Before his wholesale conversion to Neo-Georgian in the early 1890s, Shaw established a respectable precedent for adopting a classic, if mannered, format in town, such as the Old Swan House, Chelsea of 1875—77, and a free, Picturesque, convenient one in the country, such as Pierrepoint, at Frensham in Surrey, of 1876—78.

Despite his sophistry, Shaw was influenced by Ruskinian socio-cultural concerns. In 1877 he began to design, for the artistic property speculator Jonathan T. Carr, houses for the first garden suburb, located on the western outskirts of London. The red brick and tile-hung style of this upper-middle-class garden 'village', known as Bedford Park, was celebrated in the flippant 'Ballad of Bedford Park', published in the *St James's Gazette* in 1881:

Here trees are green and bricks are red
And clean the face of man.
We'll build our gardens here he said
In the style of good Queen Anne.
Tis here a village I'll erect
With Norman Shaw's assistance
Where man will lead a chaste
Correct, aesthetical existence.

This brick style extended even into the church, rendered significantly secular by the absence of any vertical feature; a structure which, although executed in a vague Gothic Revival manner, audaciously displayed a Wren-like lantern on its roof. The earliest houses of Bedford Park were built in 1876 to the designs of the *japoniste* architect E.W. Godwin. Shaw took over in 1877 and a number of different archi-

28 Bedford Park, London, showing Shaw's church of St Michael, 1879–82. The prototypical suburb.

tects worked there under his influence over the next decade, including at the tail-end Voysey, who built a remarkable house in The Parade in 1890.

In 1878, Shaw published his *Sketches for Cottages and Other Buildings*. This highly influential book illustrated numerous designs for workers' houses of various sizes. It also included the essential public building typology for a self-contained ideal village community, such as a school, a village hall, an almshouse and a cottage hospital. In the following year the first of the paternalistic garden cities appeared: Bournville, Birmingham, founded by George Cadbury and designed by Ralph Heaton and others. It was largely the Bedford Park model that W.H. Lever followed when, less than ten years later in 1888, he founded Port Sunlight.

The evolution of the garden city movement in the last decade of the century was intimately linked to the development of the Arts and Crafts movement. As presented by Ebenezer Howard in 1898, its social policy combined urban dispersal with rural colonization and decentralized government. As a complement to the co-operative movement, it advocated that such a city should derive its revenue from a balanced combination of industry and agriculture. Howard postulated trade union backing for the financing of housing, co-operative ownership of land, comprehensive planning and temperance reform. He fixed the optimum size of the garden city at 32,000, to be restricted from

further growth by an isolating green belt. Each city was to be regionally located as a satellite settlement and linked to a major centre by means of a railway. In this form the garden city complemented continuing attempts to improve, by social reform, the living and working conditions of the industrial proletariat. On his return from America in 1876, Howard had become involved in those socialist circles frequented by Bernard Shaw and Sidney and Beatrice Webb, a group which later, as Fabian Socialists, initially rejected the garden city idea. Howard's position, in accordance with the spirit if not with the letter of Fabianism, was at once practical and ameliorative. The very title of his book of 1898, *Tomorrow: a Peaceful Path to Real Reform*, announced his position as a man of compromise. Howard was committed to free enterprise within the limits of social control and favoured a piecemeal approach to reform rather than revolutionary action. Apart from Ruskin's St George's Guild of 1871, Howard was to depend for the socio-political model of his city on thinkers as diverse as the anarchist Peter Kropotkin and the American economist Henry George, who in his *Progress and Poverty* of 1879 had advocated a single tax on all ground rent. Howard was equally eclectic in deriving the diagrammatic form of his city from sources as varied as James Silk Buckingham's ideal town, Victoria, of 1849 and Paxton's Great Victorian Way proposal of 1855.

It is hard to imagine anything further removed from Howard's initial diagram than the realization of Letchworth Garden City, begun in 1904. The railway bisects the city, the shopping area is exposed to the weather, and industry is mixed with residential areas in a totally expedient way. Its architects, Raymond Unwin and Barry Parker, had, it seems, little to offer Howard save enfeebled essays in the style of Shaw and Webb. Hampstead Garden Suburb, designed by Unwin in 1907, would have been equally insipid had it not been for his collaboration with Lutyens.

Following in the Arts and Crafts tradition of Cole and Morris, Mackmurdo founded the Century Guild in 1882. Once again this comprised a group of artists who were to engage in the design and production of domestic objects. From the outset Mackmurdo worked with equal facility as a graphic artist and as a wallpaper and furniture designer. He publicized his views in collaboration with Selwyn Image, founding the Century Guild design group in 1882 and its magazine, *The Hobby Horse* in 1884. In his applied art of the early 1880s Mackmurdo developed a unique style, anticipatory of the Art Nouveau; a style which, deriving directly from William Blake, was spiritually at variance with the elegant but severe forms of his architecture. This found its most strict expression in the highly original flat-roofed house that he built at Enfield around 1883, and in his more gratifying Century Guild Exhibition Stand of 1886.

In 1887, Ashbee followed the well-established guild model with his foundation in the East End of London of the Guild of Handicraft, which incorporated into its programme the goal of direct social reform. His guild was established for the express purpose of usefully employing and training London journeymen and their apprentices, who would otherwise have remained unemployed. Ashbee, as we may judge from the house that he built for himself in Chelsea in 1904, was a more delicate and correct designer than Mackmurdo. With his post-graduate Toynbee Hall tutoring experience, he was also more committed to direct social action as a means of reform. However, although profoundly influenced by Morris and Ruskin, he took issue with both for their dogmatic antipathy to the machine and for their revolutionary socialism. In opposition to his more radical predecessors Ashbee styled himself a Constructive Socialist. After his meeting with Frank Lloyd Wright, around the turn of the century, he was confirmed in his belief that the resolution of the cultural dilemma posed by modern industry depended on a proper use of the machine. Like Howard, Ashbee was a man committed to compromise. He advocated the decentralization of existing urban concentrations and their institutions, thereby lending further support to a link between the Arts and Crafts movement and the garden city idea. Again following Howard, Ashbee remained opposed to the nationalization of land. Convinced that the cultural function of craftwork was to be that of human 'individuation',

Ashbee feared the reductionist aspects of radical socialism. Thus later in life he welcomed the foundering of the Socialist International on the 'rock of race'. In its place, he favoured a somewhat dated Disraeli style of social reform and in consequence was unduly sanguine about the virtues of British imperialism. A strong sense of economic reality was not part of Ashbee's make-up, and his precious Guild of Handicraft, established as a craft-based agrarian community at Chipping Campden in Gloucestershire in 1906, collapsed after only two years. A shareholder responded to Ashbee's appeal for further capital with the following words:

Cadbury's village at Birmingham is excellent as far as the cottages and all the life out of business hours goes, but modern conditions of cheap production and full use of machinery rule supreme in work hours, they have humanized leisure, you have tried to humanize work as well.

Such ambitious social ends were not the concern of Mackmurdo's individualistic disciple Voysey, who in 1885 arrived at a strength and simplicity of style that was to elude most of his contemporaries. Voysey derived his style from Webb's principles of respect for traditional methods and local materials, rather than from Shaw's inventiveness and spatial virtuosity. In an unrealized house project of 1885, intended for his own occupation, Voysey formulated (despite Shavian half-timbering) the essential components of his style: a slate roof with overhanging eaves, wrought-iron gutter brackets, and rendered rough-cast walls pierced by horizontal windows and marked at intervals by battered buttresses and chimneys. These features were to characterize his work for the next thirty years. Stylistically, Voysey's manner was a direct attempt to recover the basic merits of English yeoman building. However, his early association with Mackmurdo introduced a flowing and highly sophisticated element into his work which became manifest in his wallpaper and metalwork designs of around 1890. These details provided accents in Voysey's otherwise austere interiors. Unlike Morris, Voysey was possessed by a sense of restraint, almost to a fault. Thus he stipulated that either the fabrics or wallpapers should be patterned, but never both. His own house, The Orchard, built at Chorley Wood, Hertfordshire, in 1899, exemplifies the lively restraint of his interior style: gridded balusters flooded with light, low picture-rails, tiled fireplace surrounds, plain oak furniture and thick carpets. While these elements were repeated with little variation throughout his career, his designs became less figurative as the years advanced, and where his early furniture tended towards the organic, his later pieces are based on Classical themes.

Between 1889 and 1910 Voysey designed some forty houses, a number of which transcended the latent historicism of his style. Among these are the artist's residence for J.W. Forster built in Bedford Park in 1890, the Sturgis House in Guildford of 1896, and Broadleys on Lake Windermere, his finest house, realized in 1898. Nowhere else did he equal the clarity of its plan, the generosity of its layout and landscaping and the boldness of its massing and fenestration. In all this, Voysey's influence was as extensive as his career, C.R. Mackintosh, C.H. Townsend, and the Viennese architects J.M. Olbrich and Josef Hoffmann being among the architects influenced by his work.

During the first phase of Voysey's career the English Arts and Crafts movement became firmly institutionalized: initially with the foundation in 1884 of the Art Workers' Guild, at the instigation of Lethaby and other members of Shaw's office, then in 1887 with the establishment of the Arts and Crafts Exhibition Society, presided over by Morris's protégé, Walter Crane. The last twenty-five years of the movement prior to the outbreak of the First World War are inseparable from the career of Lethaby. After serving for twelve years as Shaw's chief assistant, he set up on his own in 1895 with the design of Avon Tyrrell, a large mansion in the New Forest. Five years later he was installed, jointly with George Frampton, as the first principal of the Central School of Arts and Crafts in London. Thus, apart from his very brief career as a designer, Lethaby's role within the Arts and Crafts movement turned upon his marked abilities as a teacher. In 1892 he published his first book, *Architecture, Mysticism and Myth*, in which he demonstrated how architecture in the past had always been universally informed by cosmic and religious paradigms. He attempted to incorporate such symbolism into his own work, while his general argument seems to have had an impact on the work of his close colleague, E.S. Prior, whose famous 'butterfly plan' house, The Barn, built at Exmouth in 1897, exhibited certain features that were decidedly symbolic. (Similar butterfly plan forms were proposed by M.H. Baillie-Scott, for Yellowsands in 1902 and for Hampstead Garden Suburb in 1908.)

29  Voysey, Broadleys, Cumbria, 1898.

With his entry into teaching, Lethaby shifted his attention from poetic content to the problem of developing the correct method for the evolution of form. Thus, by 1910, he was arguing against poetic self-consciousness:

Building has been and may be an art, imaginative, poetic, even mystic and magic. When poetry and magic are in the people and in the age they will appear in the arts . . . there is not the least good in saying let us build magic buildings.

For Lethaby, the tradition of which he had been a part appeared quite suddenly to be played out. The last in a long line of 'Gothic Revival' socialists, he was by the turn of the century arguing for pure functionalism. In 1915, while helping to organize the foundation of the Design and Industries Association, he was urging his colleagues to look to Germany and the Deutsche Werkbund for the way to the future.

As the first waves of the 1914 war broke across Europe, that golden age of dreamlike English country houses, ushered in by Webb, Shaw and Nesfield and rendered at its most exotic in the elaborate *Country Life* creations of Edwin Landseer Lutyens and Gertrude Jekyll, came definitely to a close. Yet this era had effectively ended even earlier, in a spate of large Neo-Georgian houses, built, as Robert Furneaux Jordan has remarked, for 'those aesthetic rich who after the Boer War had beaten their swords into gold shares'. Irrespective of this triumph of Neo-Palladianism in Edwardian

30   Lutyens, Thiepval Arch, Picardy, 1924.

taste — Lutyens's passion after the turn of the century for what he called the 'Wrenaissance' — it is unlikely that the forms and ideals of the English Arts and Crafts movement would have survived the socio-cultural trauma of the first large-scale industrialized war. Something of this can be sensed from the fate of Liberty & Co. after the war, for the holocaust of 1914–18 effectively divided the craft output of the firm like a guillotine. In the space of some five years, the inventive rigour and brilliance of its Art Nouveau silverware gave way to a décor of banal blue china, Tudor furniture and the pastiche production of pseudo-Pre-Raphaelite stained glass. Liberty & Co. were to opt for this degenerated style even in their new premises built in 1924 to the designs of E.T. Hall and E.S. Hall. This half-timbered department store epitomized the so-called 'Stockbroker's Tudor' that in various debased domestic versions was to line the newly built by-passes linking London to the suburban commuter regions that were to become its life's blood.

In the interim, Lutyens, now elevated to the position of being the unofficial 'architect laureate' to the state, found himself suspended in an aftermath that could not even afford the relatively modest luxury of his early country houses, with their small but complex gardens designed by Jekyll (e.g. his Prioresque Tigbourne Court of 1899). As the century advanced, Lutyens's taste for Palladianism, first wittily expressed in his house, Nashdom, of 1905, was to find its estranged fulfilment in the solemnity of his Somme memorial to the British dead, at Thiepval (1924), and in the superannuated monumentality of his masterly Viceroy's House, New Delhi, 1923–31 (ill. 200). In these two brilliant Neo-Classical monuments, Lutyens ruthlessly renounced his Arts and Crafts heritage. It would be hard to imagine anything more removed from Morris's utopian vision than these austere monuments isolated in the midst of flat and alien landscapes. 'Nowhere' was now to be embodied not in Morris's homely revival of the medieval guild, but rather in an arch raised to the memory of a martyred generation, and in a Baroque vista opening onto an empire that was already on the edge of being lost.

# Adler and Sullivan:
# the Auditorium and the high rise 1886-95

I should say that it would be greatly for our aesthetic good if we should refrain entirely from the use of ornament for a period of years, in order that our thought might concentrate acutely upon the production of buildings well formed and comely in the nude. We should thus perforce eschew many undesirable things, and learn by contrast how effective it is to think in a natural, favorous and wholesome way. . . . We shall have learned, however, that ornament is mentally a luxury, not a necessity, for we shall have discerned the limitations as well as the great value of unadorned masses. We have in us romanticism, and feel a craving to express it. We feel intuitively that our strong, athletic, and simple forms will carry with natural ease the raiment of which we dream, and that our buildings thus clad in a garment of poetic imagery, half hid as it were in choice products of loom and mine, will appeal with redoubled power, like a sonorous melody overlaid with harmonious voices.

Louis Sullivan
*Ornament in Architecture*, 1892

H.H. Richardson's Neo-Romanesque Marshall Field Wholesale Store, begun in 1885 and completed a year after his death in 1887, was the point of departure for the important achievements of the Chicago architectural partnership of Adler and Sullivan. Before joining Dankmar Adler as an assistant in 1879 (he was to become designing partner in 1881), Louis Sullivan had received a somewhat varied education; formally at two prestigious academies, where on each occasion he stayed for something under a year; at MIT in 1872 and then at J.-A.-E. Vaudremer's atelier in the

Ecole des Beaux-Arts, Paris, in 1874. Between these academic forays, Sullivan worked for a year in Frank Furness's office in Philadelphia, a year which was to prove critical to his career, not only because of his experience of Furness's 'Orientalized' Gothic manner — an episode which had an enduring effect on his own approach to ornament — but also because he met the young intellectual architect John Edelman, who introduced him, after 1875, to the Chicago architectural establishment — first to William Le Baron Jenney, later to become the pioneer of steel frame construction in his Fair Store of 1892, and then to Dankmar Adler. Edelman's unusual cultivation, including his anarcho-socialist views, derived from Morris and Kropotkin, exercised an influence over Sullivan's theoretical development, evidenced in the latter's *Kindergarten Chats* of 1901.

During the early years of their careers, Adler and Sullivan were preoccupied with meeting the urgent demands of a booming Chicago, then in the process of being rebuilt as the Midwestern capital after its destruction by fire in 1871. In the later 1870s, while Adler was still

31   Chicago, 1898: view from Michigan Boulevard westwards. In the centre (no. 2) is the Auditorium Building (see ill. 33).

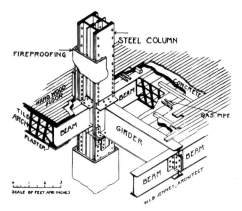

FIREPROOFING · STEEL COLUMN · CONCRETE · HARD WOOD FLOOR · BEAM · BEAM · GAS PIPE · TILE ARCH · BEAM · GINDER · BEAM · PLASTER · BEAM · W.L.B. JENNEY, ARCHITECT

SCALE OF FEET AND INCHES

32   Jenney, Fair Store, Chicago, 1890–91. Detail of fireproof steel-frame construction.

establishing his practice, Sullivan worked for Jenney, thereby becoming familiar with the technical aspects of Chicago construction. In his 1926 essay, *The Autobiography of an Idea*, Sullivan wrote of the powerful forces that led to this method of building.

The tall commercial building arose from the pressure of land prices, the land prices from pressure of population, the pressure of population from external pressure. . . . But an office building could not rise above stairway height without a means of vertical transportation. Thus pressure was brought on the brain of the mechanical engineer, whose creative imagination and industry brought forth the passenger elevator. . . . But it was inherent in the nature of masonry construction to fix a new limit of height; as its ever-thickening walls ate up ground and floor space of ever-increasing price, as the pressure of population rapidly increased./. . . [This] Chicago activity in erecting high buildings finally attracted the attention of the local sales managers of Eastern rolling mills; and their engineers were set to work. The mills for some time past had been rolling those structural shapes that had long been in use in bridge work. Their own ground work was thus prepared. It was a matter of vision in salesmanship based upon engineering imagination and technique. Thus, the idea of a steel frame which should carry all the load was

tentatively presented to Chicago architects . . . the trick was turned; and there swiftly came into being something new under the sun. . . . The architects of Chicago welcomed the steel frame and did something with it. The architects of the East were appalled by it and could make no contribution to it.

As Sullivan indicated, the Chicago architects of the 1880s had no choice but to master advanced modes of construction if they wanted to remain in practice; and while the great fire had demonstrated the vulnerability of cast-iron, the subsequent development of the fireproof steel frame — with its ability to provide multi-storey rentable space — enabled speculators to develop downtown sites to the absolute optimum. The contemporary critic Montgomery Schuyler remarked in 1899, 'the elevator doubled the height of the office building and the steel frame doubled it again'.

Before 1886, Adler and Sullivan were occupied primarily with small office structures, warehouses and department stores, a commercial practice that was varied from time to time by residential commissions. These early buildings, limited to about six floors, afforded little scope, except for the expression of the frame, be it in iron, masonry or a mixture of the two, and one could do little save manipulate the Classical division of the façade into base, middle and top.

All this was changed in 1886 by the commission to design the Auditorium Building, a structure whose overall contribution to Chicago culture was to be as much technological as conceptual. The basic arrangement of this multi-use complex was exemplary. The architects had been asked to install, within a half-block of the Chicago grid, a large modern opera house flanked on two sides by eleven storeys of accommodation, to be given over in part to offices and in part to a hotel. Their unique organization of this brief incorporated such innovations as locating the hotel kitchen and dining facilities on the roof so that the fumes would not disturb the residents. At the same time the auditorium itself offered plenty of scope for Adler's technological imagination. He met the demands for a variable capacity by using folding ceiling panels and vertical screens which could vary the auditorium from a concert size of 2,500 to a convention capacity of 7,000. The client's faith in Adler's technical ability finds some reflection in Adler's own description of the hall:

The architectural and decorative forms found in the auditorium are unconventional in the extreme and are determined to a great extent by the acoustic effects to be attained. . . . A series of concentric elliptical arches effect the lateral and vertical expansion of sound from the proscenium opening to the body of the house. The soffits and faces of these elliptical surfaces are ornamented in relief, the incandescent electric lamps and . . . inlet openings of the ventilating system forming an essential effective part of the decoration. . . . Much attention has been paid to the heating, cooling and ventilating apparatus. Fresh air, taken from the top of the building, is forced into the house by a fan . . . 10 feet [3 metres] in diameter. . . . This washes from the air much dust and soot. . . . A system of ducts carries the air into different parts of the auditorium, . . . stage, . . . corridor foyers and dressing-rooms. The general movement of air is from the stage outward and from the ceiling downward. . . . Ducts are carried to . . . exhaust fans from openings in the risers of all the steppings for the seats.

Adler was possibly one of the last architect-engineers to prove his competence over a wide technical range. He mastered a multitude of difficulties, from the air-conditioning of the auditorium to the trussed steel girder supporting its acoustical interior; from the accommodation of a complex revolving stage to the provision of extensive foyers to both the opera house and the hotel. The whole complex was housed in a massive masonry and iron structure, ingeniously

33   Adler and Sullivan, Auditorium Building, Chicago, 1887–89. Longitudinal section through the stage and auditorium.

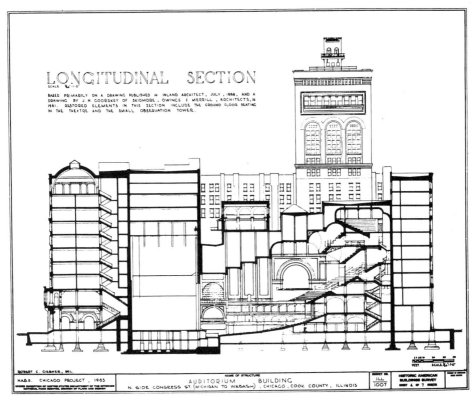

34  Sullivan, Getty tomb, Graceland cemetery, Chicago, 1890.

ballasted during construction so as to compensate for the differential loading of its foundations.

The aesthetic of this eleven-storey complex was based on an attenuation of the syntax of Richardson's Marshall Field Store. Where Richardson had used rusticated stone blocks throughout, Sullivan varied the facing material of the Auditorium Building to modulate its greater height and mass, changing from rusticated blocks to smooth ashlar above the third floor. However, the bleakness and austerity of the final result dismayed Adler, who wrote in 1892:

It is to be regretted that the severe simplicity . . . rendered necessary by the financial policy of the earlier days of the enterprise, the deep impression made by Richardson's 'Marshall Field Building' upon the Directors of the Auditorium Association, and a reaction from a course of indulgence in . . . highly decorative effects on the part of its architects, should have happened to coincide . . . and thereby deprive the exterior of the building of those graces . . . so characteristic of its internal treatment

Nevertheless, there is something forceful, taut and rhythmic about its overall character, while the colonnade of the hotel verandah on the lake front is echoed by similar delicate motifs in the tower. The slight hint of Orientalism in this verandah anticipates the decidedly Turkish feeling of the Charnley House in Chicago that Sullivan was to design in 1892, in close collaboration with his assistant Frank Lloyd Wright.

Richardson was to remain the ultimate determinant of Sullivan's early style. In Sullivan's hands Richardson's finely modulated use of the Romanesque became brutally simplified into an almost Neo-Classical manner, which was first developed in his Walker Warehouse of 1888 and in his Dooly Block of 1890. These were surely those buildings, 'well formed and comely in the nude', to which he referred in *Ornament in Architecture* of 1892. From now on Sullivan's delimitation of mass depended on pronounced string-courses and projecting cornices. Fenestration is grouped in elongated arcades, while smooth, flush façades are articulated by taut decorative episodes. The Getty and Wainwright tombs, designed in 1890 and 1892, epitomize the consolidation and refinement of this approach, which was rendered on a large scale in the Wainwright Building, completed in St Louis, Missouri, in 1891. As in the work of the Viennese architect Otto Wagner, the basic austerity of Sullivan's stereometric structures was in opposition to the ornamentation by which they were enriched and articulated. Yet, in contrast to Wagner's flowing ornament, there is always something decidedly Islamic about Sullivan's disposition of decoration. Even where his ornament is not intrinsically geometric it is almost always contained by geometric form. In this recourse to the aesthetic and even the symbolic content of the East, Sullivan sought to reconcile that schism in Western culture between the intellectual and the emotional, poles which he was to associate later with the Greek and the Gothic. Between the Auditorium and the Wainwright Building, the character of Sullivan's ornament alternates from being organically free to conforming to the outline of a precise geometry. In the Transportation Building for the Chicago World's Columbian Exposition of 1893, it becomes predominantly geometric, or, where free, strictly contained within a geometric grid. As Frank

Lloyd Wright wrote in his book, *Genius and the Mobocracy* (1949), this 'crystallization' finally arrived at its definitive form in Sullivan's Guaranty Building at Buffalo, New York, of 1895.

Neither Sullivan nor Jenney can be credited with the invention of the skyscraper, if by that term one simply means a multi-storey structure of great height, since such heights had already been achieved in load-bearing brick just prior to Sullivan's Wainwright structure, most notably in Burnham and Root's sixteen-storey Monadnock Block, Chicago (1889–92). Sullivan, however, may be credited with the evolution of an architectural language appropriate to the high-rise frame. The Wainwright Building is the first statement of this syntax, in which the suppression of the transom already evident in Richardson's Marshall Field Warehouse is taken to its logical conclusion. The façade, no longer arcaded, is articulated by gridded piers, clad in brick, while transoms are recessed and faced in terracotta so as to fuse with the fenestration. The piers rise out of a taut two-storey stone base and terminate abruptly at a massive and ornate terracotta cornice. Four years later Sullivan refined this expressive formula in his second masterwork, the Guaranty Building.

The Guaranty Building is Sullivan at the height of his powers: it is without doubt the fullest realization of the principles that he outlined in his essay of 1896, *The Tall Office Building Artistically Considered*. In this thirteen-

35 Adler and Sullivan, Guaranty Building, Buffalo, 1895.

storey office building Sullivan created a decorative structure in which, in his own words, 'The ornament is applied in the sense of being cut in or cut on . . . yet it should appear when completed, as though by the outworking of some beneficient agency, it had come forth from the very substance of the material.' Ornamental terracotta envelops the exterior in an opaque filigree, whose motifs penetrate even into the ornate metalwork of the lobby. Only the ground-floor plate-glass windows and marble walls were exempt from this intense, not to say delirious treatment.

Sullivan, like his pupil Frank Lloyd Wright, saw himself as the lone creator of the culture of the New World. Nurtured on Whitman, Darwin and Spencer and inspired by Nietzsche, he regarded his buildings as emanations of some eternal life force. For Sullivan nature manifested herself in art through structure and ornamentation. His famous slogan, 'form follows function', found its ultimate expression in the concave cornice of the Guaranty Building, where the ornamental 'life force' on the surface of the mullions expands in swirls around the circular attic windows, metaphorically reflecting the mechanical system of the building which, to quote Sullivan, 'completes itself and makes its grand turn, ascending and descending.' This organic metaphor was established in a more fundamental form in the significance which Sullivan attached to the winged seed of the sycamore, the 'germ' featured on the first page of his discourse on architectural ornament, *A System of Architectural Ornament According with a Philosophy of Man's Powers*, published in 1924, the year of his death. Under this image Sullivan placed a Nietzschean caption: 'The Germ is the real thing; the seat of identity. Within its delicate mechanism lies the will to power, the function of which is to seek and eventually to find its full expression in form.'

For Sullivan, as for Wright, this form could only evolve in a millennialistic, democratic America, where it would emerge as 'an art that will live because it will be of the people, for the people, and by the people'. As a self-appointed cultural prophet of democracy Sullivan was largely ignored. His over-idealized egalitarian culture was rejected by the people themselves. His morbid insistence on the creation of a new civilization comparable to that of the Assyrians, particularly as expressed in the coexistent delirium and restraint of his Orientalized architecture, left them both confused and alienated. Uprooted in their very essence and living through an economic depression on the edge of a frontier, they preferred the gratifying distractions of an imported Baroque, the 'White-City', East Coast emblems of imperialistic fulfilment that were so seductively presented to them in Daniel Burnham's Columbian Exhibition of 1893. This rejection destroyed Sullivan's morale, and despite a residual brilliance his powers began to decline. Separated from his urbane partner, Adler, he lost control over his professional destiny so that after the turn of the century he received few commissions. Among these must be acknowledged his inventive, eccentric and highly ornate Midwestern bank buildings of the period 1907–19, and last but not least the proportional magnificence and ornamental vitality of his prophetic Schlesinger and Mayer department store (now Carson, Pirie, Scott), built in Chicago between 1899 and 1904.

## Chapter 3

# Frank Lloyd Wright
# and the myth of the Prairie 1890-1916

When in early years I looked south from the massive stone tower of the Auditorium Building, a pencil in the hand of a master, the red glare of the Bessemer steel converters to the south of Chicago would thrill me as pages of the Arabian Nights used to with a sense of terror and romance.

Frank Lloyd Wright
'The Nature of Materials',
*Architectural Record*, Oct. 1928

These words written by Wright of the formative period that he spent with Adler and Sullivan in the early 1890s hint at the exotic vision that inspired his early career: the transformation of industrial technique through art. Yet what form this transformation should take was for Wright, at the turn of the century, far from clear. Like his masters, Sullivan and Richardson, he oscillated between the authority of Classical order and the vitality of asymmetrical form. Richardson, after the manorial and urban manner of Norman Shaw, had adopted an asymmetrical style for domestic settings while reserving the symmetrical mode for most of his public institutions. Yet Richardson's houses always display a unifying density, and wherever possible he tried to adapt the Romanesque gravity of Vaudremer's Second Empire manner and turn it into an appropriate style for the New World. Even in his early timber houses a certain feeling of weight pervades the shingled façades, while in his later domestic work, such as the Glessner House in Chicago of 1885, where shingle gave way to stone, the asymmetrical composition was imbued with an irrefutable monumentality.

This issue of monumentality seems to have been equally problematic for both Sullivan and Wright. Sullivan had already used monumental forms in his Getty and Wainwright tombs of the 1890s, but were they equally suitable to house the living? The initial solution seems to have turned on the doubly articulated formula of Classical and stone if urban, and Gothic and shingle if rural. Wright, who was virtually in charge of Sullivan's domestic work after 1890, demonstrated this dual principle first in his own house, erected in 1889 in what was still the prairie of American mythology – the nascent Chicago suburb of Oak Park – and then in the Orientalizing, Italianate Charnley House that he designed with Sullivan for downtown Chicago in 1892. Wright's own house was derived in both profile and plan, as Vincent Scully has shown, from the cruciform and T-plan Richardsonian pyramid-shaped houses that Bruce Price was then building in Tuxedo Park, New York.

For Sullivan and Wright, the young, egalitarian culture of the New World could not be based on something so ponderous and conventionally Catholic as Richardson's Romanesque. In consequence they turned to the work of a fellow Celt, Owen Jones, whose *Grammar of Ornament* had first been published in 1856. Over sixty per cent of Jones's ornamental examples were exotic, that is of Indian, Chinese, Egyptian, Assyrian or Celtic origin, and it was to such sources, all removed from the West, that Sullivan and Wright resorted in their search for an appropriate style in which to embody the New World. This not only accounts for the Islamic motifs to be found in Sullivan's work but also for the 'science-fiction' semicircular décor over the playroom in Wright's Oak Park studio of 1895, a mural featuring a recumbent Arab, transfixed before the celestial muse of an emergent civilization.

In Wright's Winslow House, built at River Forest, Illinois, in 1893, the problem of evolving

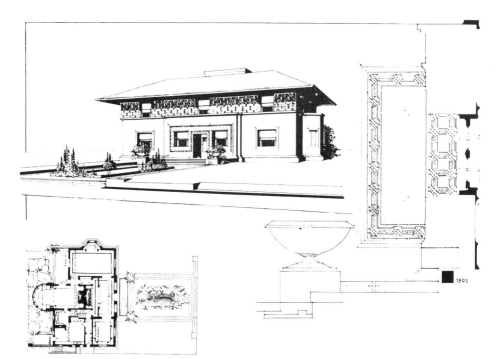

36   Wright, Winslow House, River Forest, Ill., 1893. View and site plan.

an egalitarian but appropriate format was provisionally resolved by providing two distinctly different aspects, the street or 'urban' façade being symmetrical and entered on axis and the garden or 'rural' façade being asymmetrical and entered to one side. This anticipates the planning strategy of Wright's Prairie Style, in which irregular distortions to the rear of a formal façade conveniently accommodate awkward ingredients such as service elements.

That the Winslow House was a transitional work is clearly confirmed by the mixed fenestration, part sash and part casement. Here, as Grant Carpenter Manson has written (in *Frank Lloyd Wright to 1910*, of 1958), Wright began 'to discard the sash window in favour of the casement, to prepare his work for the final change from fenestration in spots to fenestration in strips': While the characteristic Wrightian low-hipped Prairie roof appears here for the first time, the animation of surfaces with Sullivan-esque bands of ornament and string-courses

testifies to the continued influence of Wright's master. The ornamented entrance elevation clearly derives from Sullivan's tombs of the early 1890s, while the arcaded fireplace screen of the entry hall is an introverted version of the façade of Sullivan's Schiller Theatre.

This early emphasis on the fireplace testifies to another more critical influence, that of Japanese architecture, to which Wright on his own admission had been subject since 1890, and certainly since the Chicago World's Columbian Exposition of 1893, when the Japanese Government housed their national exhibit in a reconstruction of the Ho-o-den Temple. The role that this structure may have played in Wright's evolution has been best characterized by Manson:

If we assume that actual confrontation with Japanese concepts was the hint required at a certain juncture in his career to give his architecture its final and unequivocal direction,

58

many steps in its evolution become rational rather than metaphysical. As examples: the translation of the *tokonama*, the permanent element of a Japanese interior and the focus of domestic contemplation and ceremony, into its Western counterpart, the fireplace, and the expansion of the fireplace to an animistic importance; the frank revelation of the masonry of the fireplace and chimney as an expression of shelter and emphasized as the one desired solid substance in an interior of ever-increasing fluidity; the opening out of the interior away from the chimney towards shifting areas of glass at its outer limits; the extension of the great eaves over them to modify and control the intensity of the light which they admit and to protect them from the weather; the subdivision of the interior into its differing units by screens instead of partitions, thereby acknowledging and accommodating the fluctuating human uses to which it is put; the elimination of all sculptured and varnished trim in favour of flat surfaces and unpainted wood – all these and more could have been suggested by the lesson of the Ho-o-den as salutary improvements as yet missing or undeclared.

Irrespective of the final provenance of the *tokonama* motif, by the time of the Winslow House, the fireplace, despite the provision of central heating, had become even more of a ceremonial core to the home than it had been in Wright's own Oak Park house of four years before. Yet in 1893 Wright remained uncommitted, for he could still design a thoroughly Classical façade for the Milwaukee Library. Two years later he extended his own home with a studio in that quasi Pre-Columbian manner which we have come to regard, after Manson, as his Froebel style: a geometric proclivity supposedly influenced by the impact of Froebel toys on his education. Around 1895 he also produced two surprisingly radical designs, his Luxfer Prism offices, faced entirely in glass, and the McAfee House, which was an ingenious reinterpretation of Richardson's *parti* for the Winn Memorial Library of 1878.

Wright appears almost desperate at this point to break through to a new style: his public work is still part Italianate, part Richardsonian, while his domestic work is now consistently characterized by low-pitched roofs, poised at various heights over elongated asymmetrical plans. Typical of these two modes are his Francisco Terrace apartments and his Heller and Husser Houses, all built in Chicago between 1895 and 1899.

It was to take Wright two more years to resolve all these various influences into that integrated domestic style with which he was to express his myth of the Prairie, and of which he was to write in 1908: 'The Prairie has a beauty of its own and we should recognize and accentuate this natural beauty, its quiet level. Hence . . . sheltering overhangs, low terraces and out reaching walls, sequestering private gardens.'

The final emergence of the Prairie Style coincided with Wright's theoretical maturity, as manifest in his famous lecture of 1901, 'The Art and Craft of the Machine', which was first delivered, appropriately enough, at Jane Addams's Hull House Settlement in Chicago. Taking as his point of departure his youthful despair on reading Victor Hugo's *Notre Dame de Paris* (1832), in which the author had concluded that printing would eventually eliminate architecture, Wright countered that the machine could be intelligently used, in accordance with its own laws, as an agent for abstraction and purification – processes by which architecture may be redeemed from the ravages of industrialization. He led his audience to contemplate the awe-inspiring panorama of Chicago as a giant machine, and concluded with the exhortation that this was 'the thing into which the forces of Art are to breathe the thrill of ideality! A SOUL!'

From the early 1890s on, the sculptor Richard Bock served as the iconographer of this 'soul', that is to say as the image-maker of Wright's Prairie Style. Bock's early work, in its nature symbolism, was close to the European Secession Style and complemented the residual Sullivanesque aspects in Wright's work. After 1900, however, under Wright's influence, Bock's sculpture became increasingly abstract, as is evident from the 'Muse' that he created for Wright's Dana House of 1902. This figure, situated in the entrance hall, was depicted as

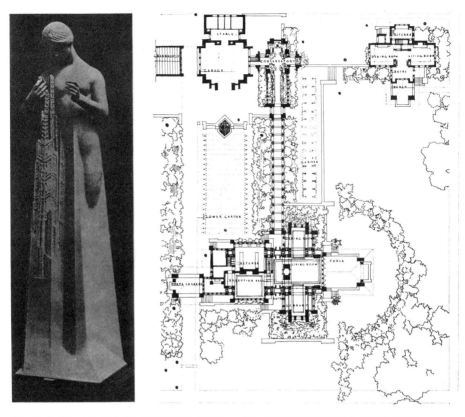

37  Bock, 'Muse' for Wright's Dana House, Spring-
field, Ill., 1902.

38  Wright, Martin House, Buffalo, 1904.

assembling the abstract elements of an exotic
machine culture, piece by piece.

Wright's Prairie Style crystallized finally in
the house plans designed for the *Ladies' Home
Journal* in 1900 and 1901. Its elements were
now established: an open ground-plan contained within a horizontal format comprising
low-pitched roofs and low bounding walls —
the low profile being integrated deliberately
into the site, in strong contrast to the vertical
chimneys and internal double-height volumes.
Yet Wright is still hesitant about the profile at
this point, oscillating between the Richardsonian
density of his Heurtley House of 1902 and
the light-weight Japanese framing of his
Hickox House, completed at Kankakee, Illinois,
two years before.

This split between a monolithic versus an
articulate expression resolved itself when
Wright started to work for the entrepreneurial
Martin family in Buffalo. The Larkin Building
and the Martin House, both built in 1904 for
Darwin D. Martin, owner of the Larkin Mail
Order Co., represent the emergence of Wright's
mature style. They were followed at once by
Wright's first visit to Japan in 1905 and by the
realization of his first concrete building, the
Unity Temple at Oak Park, Illinois, in 1906. By
now the Classical base, overlaid with the exotic,
had been transformed into a style that was
Wright's own, a unique manner soon to be
made available in Europe through the portfolios
of his work issued by Wasmuth in Berlin in 1910
and 1911.

The masterpieces of 1904–06, a house, a church and an office building, all display essentially the same architectural system. The Martin House is the first work by Wright to be consistently based on a modulated tartan plan form. Similar gridded articulations of support and void occur in the main volumes of the Unity Temple and the Larkin Building, although where the church is centralized about two axes the office building is structured around one. Both these public buildings comprise a single internal space, top-lit and surrounded by galleries on all four sides served by stairways at each of the four corners. The elevations of the church are effectively the same on all sides, symbolizing 'unity', whereas those of the Larkin Building differ on the longer and shorter sides. Apart from being monumental variations of the same architectural *parti*, both buildings pioneered ingenious systems of environmental control. The Unity Temple was equipped with built-in ducted hot air heating, while the Larkin Building was one of the first 'air-conditioned' office structures, inasmuch as its air was cooled as well as heated.

In these works Wright, the Unitarian, appeared to imbue his vision of a new life with a universal sense for the sacred, running from the sacrament of the family hearth through to the sacrament of work and to the house of religious assembly. His goal, like that of many of his European contemporaries, was the achievement

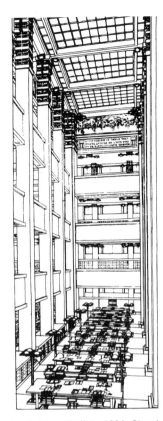

40  Wright, Larkin Building, Buffalo, 1904. Glazed central space.

of a total environment, embracing and affecting the whole of society. This would explain his obsessive exaltation of the hearth as the moral and spiritual centre to be projected, with the aid of well-placed inscriptions, into the more public realms of worship and work. It would also in part account for Wright's disappointment when, having designed the Larkin office furniture, he was not permitted to restyle the telephones. It is this same intent that embellished the main entrance to the building, where employees entered dutifully past a cascade of water falling from a symbolic relief by Bock bearing the paternalistic inscription: 'Honest labour needs no master, simple justice needs no slaves.' The same idealistic spirit is manifest in Wright's disgust at changes made to

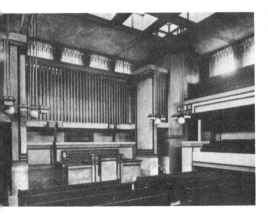

39  Wright, Unity Temple, Oak Park, Ill., 1904–06.

the Larkin structure during the course of its daily use. 'They', he wrote bitterly of the management, 'never hesitated to make senseless changes . . . it was just one of their factory buildings.' Despite his artistic patronage, Martin was obviously unable to place restrictions on the organization and management of his offices, and where the home could be preserved in all its purity, the workplace remained vulnerable to the dictates of production.

In these fertile years Wright carefully assembled an atelier of technicians and artist-craftsmen to design and realize his vision of a *Gesamtkunstwerk*, a 'total work of art'. This team included the engineer Paul Mueller, the landscape architect Wilhelm Miller, the cabinetmaker George Niedecken, the mosaic designer Catherine Ostertag, the sculptors Richard Bock and Alfonso Ianelli, and the talented Orlando Giannini, who served as Wright's fabricator of glass and textiles from 1892.

By 1905 the syntax of the Prairie Style was firmly established. Its expression, however, constantly oscillated between two poles, the one rambling, asymmetric and picturesque, as exemplified in the Avery Coonley House of 1908, and the other compact, gridded, symmetrical and architectonic, as displayed in the masterly Robie House of 1908–09. The Hardy House, built in 1905 in Racine, Wisconsin, is the purest formulation that Wright was ever to make of a symmetrical, frontalized house.

Midway Gardens, built in 1914, was the last concerted work of Wright's design team in Chicago. With the Imperial Hotel in Tokyo, it constituted the last attempt by the early Wright to establish his vision as a universal expression. Built in the short time of ninety days by the ever ingenious Mueller, Midway Gardens was, as Wright put it, 'a social response to the dance craze'. Based on the German beer garden, it was the embodiment of a new social institution, and took the form of a sequence of stepped terraces, focused axially on an orchestra shell at one end and linked by flanking arcades to a galleried restaurant and winter garden complex at the other. It was in many respects Wright's most cogent attempt at a popular culture. As such it afforded full scope to the rhetoric of his Prairie Style, with Bock and Ianelli designing figures, finials and reliefs and Giannini providing the glass. Inside there were large reliefs and abstract murals comprising concentric circular elements, which were reminiscent of Wright's fanciful idea of decorating the gardens with gas-filled coloured balloons moored to the roof.

Wright's Prairie sub-culture played itself out as a hermetic style in the building of the Imperial Hotel in Tokyo during the years 1916–22. This structure derived in both plan and section from Midway Gardens. The restaurant/ winter garden of the Chicago complex reappeared as the auditorium and lobby of the hotel, while the flanking arcades of the gardens themselves became transformed into its residential wings. The internal murals and reliefs also extended Midway themes, while the galleried accessways of the hotel recalled the café terraces of the Midway layout. Removed from an American context, Wright sought affinities with the local masonry tradition by

41  Wright, Robie House, Chicago, 1908–09.

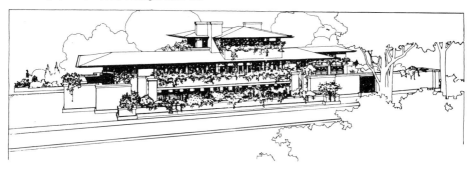

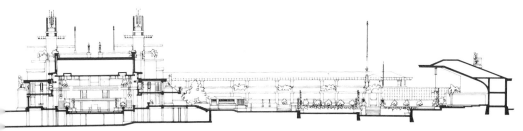

42, 43 Wright, Midway Gardens, Chicago, 1914. *Above*, longitudinal section, showing the restaurant (left) and bandshell (right); *below*, general view of the beer gardens in their heyday.

employing a battered and castellated profile, executed in brick and dressed in Oya stone. Internally this lava stone was modelled so as to allude to Pre-Columbian profiles, as had been done with the blockwork of Midway Gardens. Such exotic references were to become a theatrical formula in Wright's Hollywood houses of the 1920s. In the Imperial Hotel they amounted to a petrification of his New World culture.

As it happened, the Imperial Hotel was to be valued as much for its structural ingenuity as for its architecture, much of the credit for its miraculous survival amid the ruins of the 1922 Tokyo earthquake disaster going to the engineer, Mueller. Nevertheless, it was fitting that this final work in the first phase of Wright's brilliant career should be praised by Sullivan, who just before his death in 1924, wrote in mystical terms of its survival: 'it stands today, uninjured, because it was thought-built so to stand. It was not an imposition upon the Japanese, but a free will contribution to the finest elements in their culture.'

63

# Structural Rationalism and the influence of Viollet-le-Duc: Gaudí, Horta, Guimard and Berlage 1880–1910

In architecture, there are two necessary ways of being true. It must be true according to the *programme* and true according to the *methods of construction*. To be true according to the programme is to fulfil exactly and simply the conditions imposed by need; to be true according to the methods of construction, is to employ the materials according to their qualities and properties . . . purely artistic questions of symmetry and apparent form are only secondary conditions in the presence of our dominant principles.

Eugène Viollet-le-Duc
*Entretiens sur l'architecture*, 1863-72

For the great French architectural theorist Eugène Viollet-le-Duc these principles, first outlined in his lectures at the Ecole des Beaux-Arts in 1853, clearly precluded the architectural tradition of French Classical Rationalism. In place of an 'abstract' international style, Viollet-le-Duc advocated a return to regional building. His illustrations to the *Entretiens*, which in certain aspects anticipated Art Nouveau, ostensibly indicated the kind of architecture that would evolve from his principles of Structural Rationalism. To the envy of Ruskin, Viollet-le-Duc provided more than a moral argument. He proffered not only models but also a method which would theoretically free architecture from the eclectic irrelevancies of historicism. In this way, his *Entretiens* came to serve as an inspiration to the avant garde of the last quarter of the 19th century, his method penetrating to those European countries where French cultural influence was strong but the tradition of Classicism was weak. Eventually his ideas spread even to England, where they influenced men such as

Sir George Gilbert Scott, Alfred Waterhouse and even Norman Shaw. Outside France his thesis, in particular its implicit cultural nationalism, had its most pronounced impact on the works of the Catalan Antoni Gaudí, the Belgian Victor Horta and the Dutch architect Hendrik Petrus Berlage.

The writings of Viollet-le-Duc, Ruskin and Richard Wagner were all part of Gaudí's adopted cultural background. Aside from these extra-Mediterranean influences, his achievement seems to have sprung from two rather antithetical impulses, the desire to revive indigenous architecture and the compulsion to create totally new forms of expression. In this, of course, save for his unusual powers of fantasy, Gaudí was hardly unique. This antithesis, latent in the whole of the Arts and Crafts movement, was reflected in the Irish Celtic literary revival which exercised such a strong influence on the Glasgow School in the 1890s. A comparable Catalan revival had arisen in Barcelona as early as the 1860s, when Madrid asserted its sovereignty over Catalonia by prohibiting the use of the Catalan language. First confined to socio-political reform, the revival soon sued for Catalan independence and, although such a status was never granted, the claim to autonomy re-emerged as a powerful factor in the Spanish Civil War and is alive again today. In the second half of the 19th century the Church supported Catalan claims to sovereignty and social reform, so that Gaudí was free from any conflict between his faith and his political allegiances.

Both Gaudí and his patron, the textile manufacturer and shipping magnate Eusebio Güell Bacigalupi, grew to their maturity under the influence of the Catalan separatist movement. Although this movement had its conservative aspects, it nonetheless supported various programmes for social reform, which were largely the work of the Catalan intelligentsia. Gaudí had in fact been subject to socialist ideas before his meeting with Güell in 1882. Immediately after his graduation he had been involved with the Mataró Workers' Co-operative, who commissioned him to design a workers' settlement comprising houses, a community structure and a workshop, of which only the last was built, in 1878.

Soon after this, Gaudí began to work for the bourgeoisie, building the exotic Casa Vicens in a quasi-Moorish style in 1878. This house, like most of Gaudí's work, testified to the influence of Viollet-le-Duc, in particular the latter's L'Art russe (1870), where the constituent elements of a national style were seen as being contingent on the principles of Structural Rationalism. In the Casa Vicens Gaudí first formulated the essence of his style, which while Gothic in structural principle was Mediterranean, not to say Islamic, in much of its inspiration. As Ary Leblond wrote in 1910, Gaudí sought 'a Gothic which was full of sunlight, structurally related to the great Catalan cathedrals, employing colour as both the Greeks and the Moors did, logical for Spain; a Gothic, half maritime, half continental, enlivened by Pantheistic richness'. The result in the Casa Vicens was a Mudéjar pastiche planned around a conservatory, which in its banded brick, glazed tiles and decorative ironwork was more exuberant than any house of comparable date (cf. Shaw's Pierrepoint, at Frensham in Surrey, of 1876). Yet the structure transcended its exotic expression; for this was the first occasion on which Gaudí used the traditional Catalan or Roussillon vault, in which arch-like forms are achieved through corbelling out laminated layers of tiles. This vault became a key feature of his style, appearing in its most delicate form in the thin shell structure of his Sagrada Familia School, Barcelona, of 1909.

The initial achievements of Gaudí's career are inseparable from the various works that he and his colleague, Francesc Berenguer, designed for Eusebio Güell. Count Güell was a progressive, and his house in Barcelona, the Palau Güell, which Gaudí designed for him in 1888, became a Mecca for the intelligentsia of

44   Gaudí, three progressive stages of the Sagrada Familia Church, Barcelona (left to right, 1898, 1915, 1918) and (far right) Viollet-le-Duc, plan for a cathedral, from his L'Art russe, 1870.

the 1890s. As the Casa Vicens had been built around a conservatory, so the Palau Güell was built around a music room, an organ loft and chapel. This composite space echoed the form of the typical Islamic court and ran through the entire upper section of the house.

Prominent among Güell's enthusiasms were Ruskin and Wagner, and Gaudí seems to have been as much affected by the theories of the one as by the music-dramas of the other. At any event Ruskin's reputation was at its height at the turn of the century, and his dictum, so compatible with Wagner, that the architect who was not a sculptor or a painter was 'nothing but a framemaker on a large scale' would clearly have appealed to Gaudí.

For Güell the transformation of society at large was to be effected through the garden city. To this end in 1891 he commissioned Gaudí and Berenguer to design a workers' community for his textile plant at Santa Coloma de Cervelló, later known as the Colonia Güell. This was to be followed by a commission in 1900 for a middle-class suburb, the Park Güell, situated on the Montaña Pelada over-looking Barcelona, a project eventually realized without its perimeter of houses between 1903 and 1914. In the meantime Berenguer continued with the sporadic development of the Colonia Güell, until Gaudí succeeded him there in 1908, to complete the work on the chapel. By then Gaudí's career as an ecclesiastical archi-tect had already begun, since he had taken over the building of the Sagrada Familia Church in Barcelona from Juan Martorell in 1906.

Gaudí's Park Güell emerged as the unin-hibited crystallization of his ecstatic vision. For all that the park commanded a spectacular view, the only buildings to be completed there were the gatehouse, the grand stairway leading to the covered market above and Gaudí's own house. The irregularly shaped undulating vault of the market was carried on sixty-nine grotesque Doric columns, while its roof, bounded by a continuous serpentine bench, was intended to function as an arena or open-air stage. This exotic, mosaic-faced perimeter terminated in an esplanade, which in turn merged into the naturalistic random rubble construction of the rest of the park. The park itself was structured by serpentine pathways which where necessary were supported on vaulted buttresses, shaped so as to suggest petrified tree trunks.

The Park Güell is the first of Gaudí's works to evoke directly, through the undulating profile of its arena, the obsessive image of his life — the famous mountain near Barcelona known as Montserrat. According to the medieval legend, celebrated by Wagner in *Parsifal*, the Holy Grail was concealed in the castle of Montsalvat, a site later identified with Montserrat and its monastery, housing the patron saint of Cata-lonia. Gaudí, who first worked for the monas-tery in 1866, remained haunted by the serrated profile of the mountain for the whole of his life.

The peaks and chimneys of the Casa Milà rise out of the rational grid of Barcelona as the crown of an undulating cliff face, a cyclopean gesture whose overwhelming sense of weight seems to contradict its free and delicate organization about three irregularly shaped courts. This contradiction finds its parallel in the perverse suppression of the building's steel structure behind massive stone facing. As in the Park Güell, the articulation of the structure has been sacrificed to the evocation of some primal force. Nothing could have been further from Viollet-le-Duc, for neither the fabric nor its mode of assembly was explicitly rendered. Instead, huge blocks were laboriously worked so as to suggest a rock face eroded by time. A similar cosmic reference seems to be intended in the iron balconies, wrought by the Gaudí atelier in such a way as to suggest petrified strands of storm-tossed seaweed. Departing from the principles of Viollet-le-Duc, Gaudí finally transformed his raw material into an assembly of powerful images, whose emotive force recalls the operatic genre of Wagner. Seen in retrospect, the Casa Milà seems to anticipate something of the ethos of the Expressionism that was soon to emerge in Central Europe. In 1910, its symbolic solemnity served to isolate Gaudí, not only from the tradition of Structural Rationalism, but also from the lighter aspects of Symbolism, those flutters of 'farewells in space' that constitute the general tenor of Catalan 'Modernismo'.

The situation in Brussels at the end of the century was similar in many respects to that in Barcelona. In the Flemish capital a comparable accumulation of industrial wealth was paralleled by an equally obsessive preoccupation with national identity, although in Belgium the wealth was more evenly distributed and the nationalism mitigated by actual independence. All the same, Belgian architects were quite as anxious as the Catalans for the evolution of a truly modern but nonetheless national style. The architectural avant garde of the 1870s accused the Beaux-Arts architect Joseph Poelaert of cultural mendacity for his Neo-Classical Palais de Justice, completed in 1883: not only was it Piranesian and megalomaniacal, but it evoked a past which was international and hence by definition un-Flemish. As far as they were concerned, the model for a new 'native' architecture could be found in the local 16th-century brick traditions, in which the principles of Viollet-le-Duc could flourish.

One year after the publication of *Entretiens*, the newly formed Société Centrale d'Architecture de Belgique started to campaign vigorously in their magazine *L'Emulation* for a new national style. The issue of 1872 declared: 'We are called to create something which is our own, something to which we can give a new name. We are called upon to invent a style.' E. Allard,

45    Gaudí, Palau Güell, Barcelona, 1888.

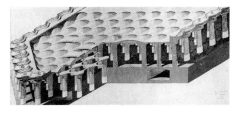

46    Gaudí, Park Güell, 1903–14. Cut-away diagram showing the structure of the covered market. The vaulted Doric colonnade supports the esplanade.

47    Gaudí, Casa Milà, Barcelona, 1906–10.

the major theorist of *L'Emulation*, later wrote: 'We must try first and foremost to create Belgian artists — we must free ourselves from foreign influences.' Throughout the 1870s *L'Emulation* continued to propagate the principles of a hypothetical style that was more constrained in its Structural Rationalism than that adopted by Gaudí. 'Nothing is beautiful in architecture unless true.' 'Shun painted plaster and stucco.' 'Architecture is drifting towards decadence; towards a veritable cacophony.'

Despite these exhortations, a convincing style took its time to materialize, and nothing of consequence was achieved in Belgium until 1892, when Victor Horta began his mature career with the realization of the Hôtel Tassel in Brussels. In this narrow-fronted, three-storey town house of traditional terrace format, Horta went beyond the achievement of his early career to become one of the first architects to make an extensive use of iron in domestic architecture. He treated iron as though it were an organic filament insinuated into the fabric to subvert the inertia of stone. Other than the

48    Horta, Hôtel Tassel, Brussels, 1892.

works of Eiffel and Contamin, which he would have seen at the Paris Exhibition of 1889, the most influential image behind Horta's peculiar 'strapwork' style was the contemporary graphic work of the Dutch-Indonesian artist Jan Toorop. This connection underlines the importance of painting in the Belgian Art Nouveau. Toorop was a member of that influential Post-Impressionist group, Les XX, whose later re-formation as La Libre Esthétique was to play a key role in disseminating the aims and principles of the English Arts and Crafts movement.

In the open planning of the Hôtel Tassel Horta exploded the 18th-century Parisian *hôtel* formula. As the octagonal vestibule on the ground floor rose upwards through a half-level towards the garden, it expanded laterally into an adjacent foyer space covered by an iron superstructure. The free-standing columns of this space, embellished with iron tendrils, echo similar serpentine forms throughout the rest of the metalwork. From the balustrades to the light-fittings the same aesthetic is dominant, a linear exuberance that is delicately echoed in the mosaic floor and wall finishes and in the coloured glass panels of the door to the salon. Yet for all this florid profusion the main volumes are still tempered by the use of Rococo mouldings, which serve to relate the more exotic elements to the received tradition of Louis Quinze. A similar balance is achieved on the exterior, where the ductile elements of the inner armature find their discreet expression. In an otherwise Classical façade, the stone quoins of an iron bay window are wrought in such a way as to imply the thrust of the inner metallic structure.

Over the next decade Horta continued this dialogue between the tensility of iron and the massiveness of stone in a number of other town houses in Brussels, including residences for the chemist Solvay and the industrialist Van Eet-velde and his own house and studio in the Rue Américaine, all built before 1900. All were partial elaborations of the Hôtel Tassel syntax, yet none, save the Hôtel Solvay, equalled its simplicity and impressiveness.

The Maison du Peuple, built for the Belgian Workers' Socialist Party in 1897–1900, is the most original work of Horta's career and the only one in which he seems to have felt free to pursue the principles of Viollet-le-Duc to their logical conclusion. Here a native brick and stone vernacular was brilliantly exploited to create an architecture of revealed construction – brickwork being consistently modulated and moulded to receive stone, and stone being dressed to receive iron and glass. While externally this tectonic was comprised by the elevational expression of a complex programme and by the displacement of a concave plan-form over a sloping site, internally it achieved a dramatic and highly fluid expression through the exposed steel framework of all the major volumes, the offices, meeting rooms, lecture theatre and cafeteria. This consistent but strangely unresolved 'Neo-Gothic' assembly of masonry, iron and glass was Horta's most influential achievement and one which he was not to surpass in his more resolved and last essay in this idiom, his Innovation department store, built in Brussels in 1901.

In France, the line of succession linking Viollet-le-Duc to Hector Guimard passes through Guimard's master Anatole de Baudot, who had been a pupil of both Viollet-le-Duc and Labrouste. In 1894 de Baudot had designed, in association with the engineer Paul Cottancin, the church of St-Jean-de-Montmartre in Paris, a structure of reinforced brickwork and *ciment armé* that was surely the most profound essay in Structural Rationalism to date. Thus Guimard, in his early Parisian works, reveals his debt to both de Baudot and Viollet-le-Duc, particularly in his Ecole du Sacré Coeur and his Maison Carpeaux in the Boulevard Exelmans, both completed by 1895. While the former, a small school building with V-supports to the upper floor, was almost a direct realization of the famous illustration to *Entretiens*, the latter, a bourgeois town house, displayed the same tendencies towards a vestigial Classicism that we find in the works of Horta.

In a letter to L.-C. Boileau in 1898, Guimard openly acknowledged his debt to Viollet-le-Duc: 'Decoratively, my principles are perhaps new but they derive from those already in use with the Greeks. . . . I have only applied the

49 Horta, Maison du Peuple, Brussels, 1897–1900. Detail of façade.

theories of Viollet-le-Duc without being fascinated by the Middle Ages.' Yet Guimard was concerned to achieve that native style prescribed by the French theorist as conforming to usage, climate and national spirit and 'to the progress which has been made in science and practical knowledge'. Thus we find him writing in 1903:

A style of architecture, in order to be true, must be the product of the soil where it exists and of the period which needs it. The principles of the Middle Ages and those of the 19th century, added to my doctrine, should supply us with a foundation for a French Renaissance and an entirely new style. Let the Belgians, the Germans and the English evolve for themselves a national art and assuredly in so doing they will perform a true, sound and useful work.

We may assume that what Guimard, like Gaudi and Horta, had in mind was the evolution of the 'constituent elements' of a national style as advocated by Viollet-le-Duc. Yet by the turn of the century there were at least three versions of Guimard's own style: a loose, rustic, mixed-media expression, as found in the country

69

chalets that he built between 1899 and 1908, of which his Castel Henriette of 1900 is typical; an urban style of precisely assembled brick and

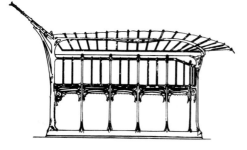

dramatically sculptured stonework such as we find in his own house in the Avenue Mozart, Paris, of 1910; and finally a spidery ferrovitreous manner which was mass-produced soon after 1899, when he was awarded the commission for the Paris Métro stations. The entrances were made up of interchangeable standard iron pieces, cast in the form of naturalistic elements and framing enamelled steel and glass. Paradoxically, they were closer to the linear expressiveness of Horta than to the moral rigour of de Baudot; and Guimard even treated the typography and illumination of these structures as the sinuous continuation of their form. Thereafter, over the next four years, these apparently natural emanations from a wondrous subterranean world erupted over the streets of Paris, to make Guimard notorious as the creator of the 'Style Métro'.

This well-earned notoriety has unfortunately helped to eclipse the one short-lived master-piece of Guimard's whole career, his Humbert de Romans concert hall, completed in Paris in 1901 and demolished in 1905. Like Horta's Maison du Peuple, this surely has to be regarded as one of the major achievements of Structural Rationalism. Fernand Mazade's text of 1902 is still capable of evoking the power of an interior that, save for a few faded photographs, is entirely lost:

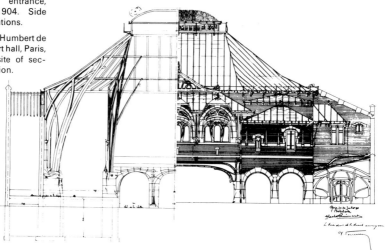

[its] main branches, eight in number, support a rather high cupola, pierced, like the sides, with bays filled with pale yellow stained glass, through which an abundance of light finds its way into the hall. The framework is of steel, but the metal is covered with mahogany . . . the result is the most elaborate roof ever conceived by a French architect.

Throughout the two decades that spanned the turn of the century, there remained quietly in the background the Dutch architect Hendrik Petrus Berlage, who contrived to practise in a consistent manner until his death in 1934. Unlike Horta, Berlage did not allow his principles to become compromised by the acquired, 'alien' tastes of an arriviste middle class. In Holland, in any case, the middle class was fully integrated into the general society, social co-operation being second nature in a country that was constantly threatened with inundation. In such a stable context Berlage enjoyed almost fifty years of uninterrupted practice, over a period that due to Dutch neutrality was not even disturbed by the hostilities of the First World War.

Berlage received his professional education at the Eidgenössische Technische Hochschule, Zürich, in the late 1870s. There he studied under the immediate followers of Gottfried Semper, from whom he would have received an extremely rational and typological education. On his return to Amsterdam in 1881 he began to associate with P.J.H. Cuijpers, nearly thirty years his senior, who was already a disciple and correspondent of Viollet-le-Duc. In accordance with the principles of Structural Rationalism, Cuijpers sought to rationalize his own eclecticism in an effort to evolve a new national style, an attempt which culminated in his Neo-Flemish Rijksmuseum, Amsterdam, of 1885. This work strongly influenced Berlage's entry for the Amsterdam Exchange competition of 1883, which he designed in association with Theodorus Sanders in a similar turreted and gabled manner.

Twelve years later Berlage received the commission for the Exchange, despite the fact that he had only been awarded fourth place in the competition. At once he began to rework the design after an arched brick syntax that he had developed in the interim, first in a villa built at Groningen in 1894, and then in an office building erected in The Hague in the following year. These crenellated, Neo-Romanesque brick structures, influenced without doubt by Richardson's work in the United States, were vehicles for an architecture of explicit construction, a fact that was most evident in the brick-vaulted stair complex of the office building. Yet for all the profundity of these early essays (reminiscent in their structural probity of the rigour of de Baudot) the final formulation of the Berlage idiom was to depend on the realization of the Exchange.

The four versions of the Exchange that followed the initial project represent different stages in an arduous process of simplification. In this development Berlage seems to have been guided by a complex of theoretical ideas, some drawn from Viollet-le-Duc, some from Semper and some from his colleague Jan Hessel de Groot, who was the originator of the Amsterdam school of mathematical aesthetics. After the Exchange was opened in 1903, Berlage began to publish his own synthesis of these ideas in a series of theoretical studies, first in his *Gedanken über den Stil in der Baukunst* ('Thoughts on Style in Architecture') of 1905 and then in his *Grundlagen und Entwicklung der Architektur* ('Principles and Evolution of Architecture') of 1908. As Reyner Banham has observed, the salient principles stressed in these writings were 'the primacy of space, the importance of walls as creators of form and the need for systematic proportion'. The distillation of the Exchange into its final form takes on a richer significance once we become aware of Berlage's views on the essential role of masonry, as first set forth in these texts. 'Before all else the wall must be shown naked in all its sleek beauty and anything fixed on it must be shunned as an embarrassment.' Or again, 'The art of the master builder lies in this, in the creation of space, not the sketching of façades. A spatial envelope is established by means of walls, whereby a space . . . is manifested according to the complexity of the walling.'

In his gradual refinement of the Exchange Berlage largely retained the original plan of

52, 53 Berlage, Exchange, Amsterdam. *Above,* second design, 1896–97; *below,* as built, 1897–1903.

end he gradually reduced the number of gables and turrets and slowly eliminated all lanterns and every trace of banded stonework. At one stage the scheme vaguely resembled Gull's Landesmuseum, then nearing completion in Zürich, while at the penultimate stage the reduced forms attained their final definition through the superimposition of a diagonal lattice derived from De Groot. After this all subsequent changes were largely confined to the design of the main entrance and its adjacent tower, which were conceived by Berlage as the prime representative elements of both the institution and the city.

The load-bearing brick structure of Berlage's Exchange was precisely articulated in accordance with the principles of Structural Rationalism. Inside, a mosaic frieze or a filigreed lamp are but inflections within large brick volumes where granite abutments, quoins, corbels and cappings consistently mark the points of structural transference and bearing. The same dressed stones which in one instance are corbelled out to receive a steel truss in another articulate the keying of an arch. In this way the ethos and the logic of Viollet-le-Duc pervade the entire fabric as in no other structure of the 19th century.

To this achievement the philosophical tenor of Berlage's thought added dimensions which went beyond any single structure, first into the immediate urban context and then, by extension, into the body politic at large. His model for an ideal urban society was first outlined in a set of essays published in 1910, of which one in particular, *Kunst en Maatschappij* ('Art and Society'), most clearly reveals the depth of his socio-political commitment. While socialism for Berlage was a prime article of faith, he nonetheless subscribed to Hermann Muthesius's view that the general level of a culture could only be raised through the production of high quality, well designed objects. On the other hand, he remained convinced as to the supreme cultural importance of the city, and deplored the disurbanizing tendency of the English garden city.

In 1901 Berlage was given an opportunity to put his urban theory into practice, when the city of Amsterdam commissioned him to pre-

three top-lit rectangular volumes, one for each exchange, housed in an orthogonal matrix of four-storey perimeter walls. The progressive aim was to simplify this *parti* and its structure into an extremely astringent form, and to this pare a plan for Amsterdam South. For Berlage the street was essentially an outdoor room, the necessary consequence of the housing lining its length. This insistence on enclosure, prefigured in the medieval city, had already been postulated by Berlage in his design for the Exchange. After Alphand and the theories of the German planner Stübben, the qualities of the street spaces in Amsterdam South vary according to their width and furnishing. The wider streets were furnished with *parterres* and flanking avenues of trees; the narrower ones were simply lined with trees and paving. At the major intersections centralized spaces were created somewhat after the principles of Stübben and Camillo Sitte (see above, p. 25). The whole was fed by a modern system of mass transit in the form of the electric tram.

In 1915 Berlage totally revised his plan to incorporate avenues of Haussmann-like scale, two of which, converging at a sector known as Amstellaan, were completed with their environs in the early 1920s. Their realization, which unequivocally demonstrated Berlage's concern for the physical continuity of the urban environment, eventually brought him into conflict with the anti-street polemic of the Congrès Internationaux d'Architecture Moderne (CIAM), founded in 1928. Yet today the value of his urban achievement seems to be more pertinent than ever, for as Giorgio Grassi has written of Amstellaan:

it is still the key point on the outskirts of Amsterdam, the point where one finds expressed most clearly the concept of collective living, where the civic value of single parts blends into a unified vision that – being less concerned with the optimum dwellings of certain rationalist experiments – has, in its nuclear concept of housing, expressed well the values of the city. And it has recognized not only the physical need of the dwellers for recreation and rest. but their impulse to form communities and to assume in this act a symbol of life.

54  Berlage, Exchange, Amsterdam, 1897–1903. Main hall.

55  Berlage, revised development plan for Amsterdam South, 1917.

73

# Chapter 5
# Charles Rennie Mackintosh and the Glasgow School 1896-1916

On the second floor of a modest building in the great industrial smoky town of Glasgow there is a drawing room amazingly white and clean looking. Walls, ceiling and furniture have all the virginal beauty of white satin. The note throughout is white – white and violet. From the upper part of two large violet plaques, which form centre pieces, there hang long tendrils threaded with little globes of old silver. . . . The carpet and the leaded glass window are violet, and one can trace the same colour note on the narrow frames of two choice drawings. . . . In the stillness of the studio, among a bevy of plants and strewn with the novels of Maeterlinck, two visionary souls, in ecstatic communion from the heights of loving mateship, are wafted still further aloft to the heavenly regions of creation.

E. B. Kalas
*De la Tamise à la Sprée*
*l'essor des industries d'art*, 1905

By 1905, Charles Rennie Mackintosh and his wife, Margaret Macdonald, had already acquired an international reputation. In England they had achieved notoriety in 1896, when with Herbert McNair and Margaret's sister Frances Macdonald, as the 'Glasgow Four', they had exhibited their early works at the London Arts and Crafts Exhibition Society show. Such was the impact of their work on this occasion that, despite official disapproval stemming from Walter Crane, they were appreciatively acclaimed as the 'Spook School' by Gleeson White, editor of *The Studio*. This sudden success, which had been preceded by an exhibition of their student work at Liège in 1895, was further confirmed by the acceptance in 1896 of Mackintosh's design for the new

Glasgow School of Art, on which work commenced in the following year.

The Four had been making furnishings since 1894, so Gleeson White's article in *The Studio* of 1897 could illustrate, in addition to their graphic work, repoussé metal plaques, mirrors, sconces and clocks designed by the Macdonald sisters and cupboards and cabinets designed by McNair and Mackintosh. In all this, the Four had evolved a sensibility which for White was the expression of a 'quasi-malignant paganism', a style which took its linear manner from the graphic work of William Blake, Aubrey Beardsley and Jan Toorop and its sentiment, part nationalist and part Symbolist, from old cymric motifs of Celtic origin and from names drawn from the mystical works of Maurice Maeterlinck and Dante Gabriel Rossetti.

Mackintosh's architecture also had other, somewhat less exotic, origins. Through his education within the mainstream of the Gothic Revival he had naturally acquired an affinity for a solid craft approach to buildings. Like Philip Webb, his architectural precursors were the Gothic Revivalists of the mid-century, men such as Butterfield and Street. This much is evident in his own early ecclesiastical work, such as his Queens Cross Church of Scotland, Glasgow, of 1897. In his secular work, however, he managed to temper the revivalist impulse with a more direct approach, deriving partly from Voysey and partly from the Scottish Baronial tradition (cf. James MacLaren's Fortingall cottages of 1892). His first and last statements in this manner are incorporated in the gradual realization of the Glasgow School of Art.

Throughout Mackintosh's unique and highly influential development, Lethaby's *Architec-*

*ture, Mysticism and Myth* of 1892 was to serve as an important catechism — not only because it revealed the universal metaphysical basis of all architectural symbolism but also because, coming from Lethaby's hand, it formed a bridge between the other-worldliness of Celtic mysticism and the more pragmatic Arts and Crafts approach to the creation of form. With regard to this last, Mackintosh took the traditionalist Ruskinian line and argued that modern materials, such as iron and glass, 'will never worthily take the place of stone because of this defect, the want of mass'.

There was to be no want of mass in the Glasgow School of Art, which was built from a local grey granite on three of its sides and from roughcast brickwork on the fourth. Yet, despite Mackintosh's avowed respect for masonry, glass and iron were present in abundance in the extensive studio northlights, which occupy the full length of the main façade. At the same time, from a technical standpoint,

Mackintosh — like his American contemporary Frank Lloyd Wright — made every effort to incorporate ingenious and up-to-date systems for environmental control, such as the still effective system of ducted heating and ventilation, built into the school from the beginning.

Following the Gothic Revival tradition, Mackintosh designed the main body of the school as a loose-fitting envelope, with the bulk of the studio space being stacked on four floors. This mass, which effectively reads as two storeys throughout the length of the main façade, was complemented by ancillary elements (such as the library and museum) located to the sides, the centre and the rear. The result was an E plan-form, with an eccentrically counterbalanced main elevation, in which subtle displacements in both the main entrance and the forecourt railings simultaneously engender symmetrical and asymmetrical readings. The return east and west façades, steeply sloping down towards the rear of the

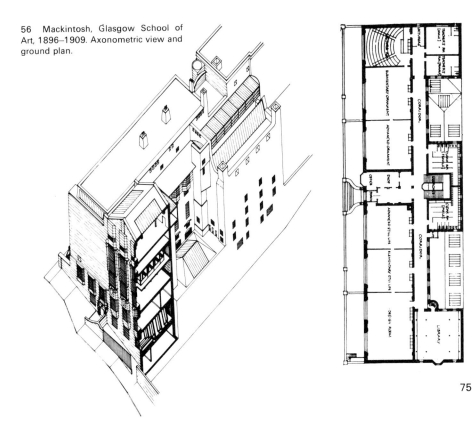

56  Mackintosh, Glasgow School of Art, 1896–1909. Axonometric view and ground plan.

site, were left partly blank so as to express the depth of the studio space. With the aid of finials, gables, projecting turrets and incised windows, this inherent asymmetry imparts to the east façade an overtly Gothic Revival character, which would have been repeated on the west had it not been for Mackintosh's radical redesign of the second stage in 1906. This west façade as finally completed represents Mackintosh at the height of his power. In no other work was he able to reach such authority and grandeur. Its three vertical oriels with their gridded fenestration serve dramatically to light and express the rich volume of the library and its adjacent upper floor.

Built in two stages, the art school is a record of Mackintosh's stylistic development from 1896 to 1909. The difference between the Voyseyesque entry hall and stair of the first stage and the double-height library of the final stage, patently influenced by Norman Shaw, reflects the full range of his development by

that date. In a matter of a few years he had fully crystallized that sinuous architectural syntax which he had first used on a grand scale in the design of the Willow Tea Rooms, Glasgow, in 1904. In contrast to those 'white and willowy' interiors, the art school library is austere and geometrical, and executed in dark wood throughout. There is almost a Japanese quality about its structural articulation. It must be seen as a transitional work, lying somewhere between Mackintosh's Art Nouveau period and the later, modern, almost Art Deco manner that characterizes his final work for Bassett-Lowke.

The brief and brilliant, violet and silver period of organic ornamentation set against plain white surfaces, commonly regarded as the touchstone of the Mackintosh style and eulogized as such by Kalas in 1905, came to its maturity at the turn of the century. It was already developed in full in the furniture and décor of Mackintosh's Glasgow apartment,

57  Mackintosh, Glasgow School of Art. Library, 1905–09.

designed in 1900. It was further elaborated in the Scottish section of the Viennese Secession Exhibition of the same year and in the music salon built for Fritz Wärndorfer in Vienna in 1902. As a fully integrated aesthetic, both internally and externally, it reached its apotheosis in the Willow Tea Rooms, completed two years after the Wärndorfer salon.

Externally, the restrained yet moulded white façade of the Willow Tea Rooms was of the same genre as Mackintosh's Voysey-like house projects of the turn of the century or the two quasi-Baronial roughcast houses that he realized at Kilmacolm and Helensburgh between 1899 and 1903. As Robert Macleod has written, 'these houses were an expression of conscious gaucheness, and an anti-pretty attitude that had as its chief historical exponents William Butterfield and Philip Webb'. Mackintosh's perverse attempt to fuse the ornamental with the gauche was often far from successful, and the houses appear somewhat chaotic and unresolved when compared to the magnificent and highly influential 'Haus eines Kunstfreundes', which Mackintosh designed as his entry to the limited competition organized in Darmstadt by Alexander Koch in 1901.

The unrealized 'House for an Art-lover' and the Glasgow School of Art represent Mackintosh's essential contribution to the mainstream of 20th-century architecture. In the house he created a work which passed well beyond the constraints of the traditional Voysey model to display a formal plasticity of almost Cubist affinity. The organization of the house around a number of countervailing axes and its division into two major longitudinal masses that appear to be on the point of sliding past each other resulted in a tense but consolidated composition, and the enrichment of its otherwise plain surface with precisely proportioned windows and occasional accents of embossed ornament suggests at once the strong influence it must have exercised over Josef Hoffmann, in particular on his design for the Palais Stoclet, Brussels, of 1905. Nothing in any event could have been further from the yeoman rusticity of the winning design by Baillie Scott.

It is ironic that Mackintosh should have begun and ended his career as an independent

58   Mackintosh, Hill House, Helensburgh, 1902–03.

architect with the Glasgow School of Art, the effective years of his practice being from 1897 to 1909. In 1914 the Mackintoshes moved from Scotland to England, where Mackintosh, suddenly and somewhat inexplicably discouraged as an architect, turned to painting. In 1916, however, he made a brief comeback with the brilliant remodelling of a small terrace house for W.J. Bassett-Lowke, No. 78 Derngate in Northampton. The rich, abstract interiors are equal to any Continental work of comparable date. The plain geometrical bedroom furniture and the striped graphic décor bonding the twin beds together were well in advance of their time, inasmuch as they anticipated the spatial and plastic devices to be employed by the Continental avant garde after the First World War (De Stijl, Art Deco, etc.). During the war Mackintosh designed clocks, furniture and posters for Bassett-Lowke, but even this patronage was withdrawn after 1918.

Rejected in Scotland and isolated in England, Mackintosh could sustain neither the values of his earlier life nor the creative impulse of his pre-war career. The last decade of his life was one of progressive decline, in which the commissioning in 1925 of the German architect Peter Behrens to design a new house for Bassett-Lowke was but a final blow. It was a tragic fate for one who, as P. Morton Shand has written, 'was the first British architect since Adam to be a name abroad and the only one that has ever become the rallying point for a Continental school of design'.

## Chapter 6

# The Sacred Spring:
# Wagner, Olbrich and Hoffmann 1886-1912

A series of edifices expressed the Bildungsideal of Liberal Austria: university, museum, theatre and – grandest of all – the opera. The culture once confined to the palace had poured into the market place, accessible to all. Art ceased to serve only as an expression of aristocratic grandeur or ecclesiastical pomp; it became the ornament, the communal property, of an enlightened citizenry. The splendiferous structures of the Ringstrasse bore massive witness to the fact that Austria had replaced despotism and religion with constitutional politics and secular culture . . . the economic growth of Austria created the basis for an increasing number of families to pursue an aristocratic style of life. Wealthy burghers or successful bureaucrats, many of whom acquired patents of nobility like Stifter's Freiherr von Risach [in the novel Der Nachsommer, 1857], established urban or suburban variants of the Rosenhaus, museum-like villas which became centres of a lively social life. Not only gracious manners, but also intellectual substance were cultivated in the salons and soirées of the new élite . . . the English Pre-Raphaelites inspired the Art-Nouveau movement (under the name of 'Secession') in fin de siècle Austria, but neither their pseudo-medieval spirituality nor their strong social-reformist impulse penetrated to their Austrian disciples. In brief, the Austrian aesthetes were neither as alienated from their society as their French soul-mates nor as engaged in it as their English ones. They lacked the bitter anti-bourgeois spirit of the first and the warm melioristic thrust of the second. Neither degagé nor engagé, the Austrian aesthetes were alienated not from their class, but with it from a society that defeated its expectations and rejected its values. Accordingly, Young Austria's Garden of Beauty was a retreat of the beati possidentes, a garden strangely suspended between reality and utopia. It expressed both the self-delight of the aesthetically cultivated and the self-doubt of the socially functionless.

Carl Schorske
The Transformation of the Garden: Ideal and Society in Austrian Literature, 1970

As Carl Schorske informs us, that which realized itself in 1898 as the 'sacred spring', through the appearance of the Secessionist magazine Ver Sacrum, had some of its origins at mid-century in Der Nachsommer, the Indian Summer of Adalbert Stifter's idealistic novel of 1857. Otto Wagner's first suburban villa of 1886 may be seen as a realization of the Rosenhaus which Stifter had invented as the ideal location for the cultivation of a private aesthetic life. While Wagner had been born into the same class as Stifter's Freiherr von Risach, he did not attain immediate success. After a distinguished academic career, first at the Vienna Polytechnic and then at the prestigious Bauakademie in Berlin, purveyor of the Schinkel tradition, he practised independently for some fifteen years before receiving his first state commission, the décor for the Emperor's silver wedding celebrations in 1879. Even this royal recognition did not bring him wide acclaim, so that when in 1886 he built his own Italianate version of the Rosenhaus at Hütteldorf he was still far from being professionally established. Four years later, however, he had not only arrived artistically but had achieved some worldly success with the building of a small but lavish town house in Vienna for his own use.

Wagner's influence as a teacher dates from his succession in 1894 to Karl von Hasenauer as professor at the school of architecture in the Academy of Fine Arts in Vienna. In 1896, at the age of fifty-four, he published his first theoretical work, *Moderne Architektur*. This was followed in 1898 by the first publication of the work of his students, given under the title *Aus der Wagnerschule*. Having been formed in Berlin by one of Schinkel's prime pupils, Wagner's architectural affinities at this time seem to have lain somewhere between the rationalism of the *Schinkelschüler* and the more rhetorical manner of those last great architects of the Ringstrasse, Gottfried Semper and Karl von Hasenauer, whose State Museums, Burgtheater and Neue Hofburg were under construction in the Ring throughout the last quarter of the century.

Wagner's polytechnical education had left him acutely aware of the technical and social realities of his epoch. At the same time, his romantic imagination was drawn towards the radical stirrings of his more talented pupils – to the anti-academic art movement co-founded by his assistant Joseph Maria Olbrich and by his most brilliant pupil Josef Hoffmann, who had graduated with a Prix de Rome in 1895. These men were not only influenced by the work of the Glasgow Four, then being illustrated in *The Studio*, but were also under the spell of the exotic vision of two young Viennese painters, Gustav Klimt and Koloman Moser. Under the leadership of Klimt, Olbrich, Hoffmann and Moser banded together in their revolt against the Academy and in 1897, with Wagner's blessing, they founded the Vienna Secession. In the following year Wagner declared his own sympathies for the Secession through the creation of a florid abstraction in faience for the façade of his pseudo-Italianate Majolica House in Linke Wienzeile, and in 1899 he scandalized the establishment by becoming a full member of the Secession.

In 1898 Olbrich built the Secession building, apparently after a sketch by Klimt, who was to remain the prime mover of the revolt. From Klimt came the battered walls, the axiality and especially the laurel motif – with its dedication to Apollo – the latter being rendered by Olbrich as a perforated metal dome, suspended between four short pylons and set above planar masses

59    Olbrich, Secession building, Vienna, 1898.

whose severe modelling recalls the work of such British architects as Voysey and Charles Harrison Townsend. A comparable symbol of organic vitality occurred on the cover of the first issue of *Ver Sacrum* – an ornamental shrub whose vital roots were depicted bursting through its tub into the earth beneath. Such was Olbrich's symbolic point of departure, a conscious return to the fertility of the unconscious, from which, ever subject to the influence of Voysey and Mackintosh and the claims of Klimt's pan-eroticism, he began to evolve a style of his own.

This evolution took place largely in Darmstadt, where Olbrich had been invited by the Grand Duke Ernst Ludwig in 1899. Later in that year he was joined by six other artists, the sculptors Ludwig Habich and Rudolf Bosselt, the painters Peter Behrens, Paul Bürck and Hans Christiansen, and the architect Patriz Huber. Two years later, this artists' colony exhibited its life style and 'habitat' as a total work of art, under the title 'Ein Dokument deutscher Kunst'. The exhibition was opened in May 1901 by a mystical ceremony called 'Das Zeichen' (The Sign), which took place on the steps of Olbrich's Ernst Ludwig House. In this ceremony an 'unknown' prophet descended from the golden portal of the building to receive a crystalline form, as a symbol of base material transformed into art, just as carbon

initial focus, around which a number of individual artists' houses were eventually built. With its high, blank, horizontally fenestrated façade, shielding north lights to the rear, and its ornate, recessed circular entrance flanked by giant statues carved by Habich, it was the ultimate monumentalization of themes that Olbrich had broached in the Secession building.

Between this early masterpiece and the final 'classicization' of his style in 1908 – the year of his premature death – Olbrich continued his search for a uniquely expressive mode. Throughout the last decade of his life he created works of exceptional originality, culminating in his cryptic and brooding Hochzeitsturm or Wedding Tower, which, with the adjacent exhibition buildings, was completed on the Mathildenhöhe in Darmstadt for the Hessische Landesausstellung of 1908. With its pyramidal composition the Mathildenhöhe complex, built on top of a reservoir, was in effect a 'city crown' whose form anticipated the symbolic centre of Bruno Taut's 'Stadtkrone' of 1919. Girded by a series of tiered concrete pergolas, it was drawn by Olbrich as a mountainous labyrinth of dense foliage, whose colour would change with the seasons from green to russet brown. Rising from the high ground like a mystical mountain, it consciously opposed the Edenic serenity of the formal plane-tree garden, or Platanenhain, on which it fronted.

60   Olbrich, Ernst Ludwig House, Darmstadt. 'Das Zeichen', May 1901.

61   Olbrich, Hochzeitsturm and exhibition buildings, Darmstadt, 1908.

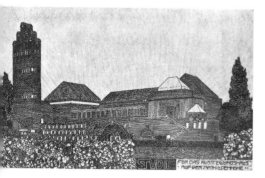

may be changed into the brilliance of a diamond.

The Ernst Ludwig House, built in 1901, was undoubtedly the most progressive work that Olbrich designed during his nine-year residence in Darmstadt. Consisting of eight studio living spaces, four on each side of a common meeting hall, it was in effect the colony's

Over the whole of Olbrich's career there stood the challenging figure of Peter Behrens, initially a graphist and painter, who had come to Darmstadt from the Munich Secession in 1899. He emerged as an architect and a designer with the building and furnishing of his own house at Darmstadt in 1901. In their rivalry as *Gesamtkünstler* to the house of Hesse-Darmstadt it was Olbrich rather than Behrens who was to be the brilliant designer of objects, while in their careers outside Darmstadt, as architects, it was Behrens who became the more powerful creator of form. Above all it was he who anticipated their common return to the kind of crypto-Classicism that characterizes the work of Olbrich's final years, his Tietz department store in Düsseldorf and the mansion that he built for the cigar manufacturer Feinhals in Cologne, both completed in 1908.

In 1899 Josef Hoffmann began to teach at the applied art school attached to the Austrian Museum for Art and Industry in Vienna (which had been founded, in accordance with Semper's educational programme, some thirty-five years before). A year later, he replaced Olbrich as the designer of the élite Hohe Warte suburb on the outskirts of Vienna, building four villas there between 1901 and 1905. He had succeeded Olbrich as the leading architect to the Secession, and his first work on this site, designed in the manner of English Free Architecture, was for Koloman Moser. By 1902, however, Hoffmann was already beginning to move towards a more planar and Classical mode of expression, based largely on the post-1898 work of Otto Wagner, that is towards a handling of mass and surface which was far removed from the British preoccupation with medieval, yeoman form.

By the time of the Vienna Secession Exhibition of 1900, at which Mackintosh's actual work was shown in Austria for the first time, Hoffmann had already arrived at a furnishing style of refined rectilinear form. This was his initial move away from the obsessive curvilinearity of his 'Apollo' shop in Vienna of the previous year. By 1901 he was preoccupied with the possibilities for abstract form in design. 'I am particularly interested in the square as such,' he wrote, 'and in the use of black and white as dominant colours, because these clear elements have never appeared in earlier styles.' Together with Moser and other Secessionists, he became interested in the craft production of decorative and applied art objects, along the lines of Ashbee's Guild of Handicraft. By 1902, with his setting for Klinger's Beethoven statue, exhibited in the Secession Building, he had arrived at his own abstract style, in which certain contours or proportions are emphasized through the use of projecting beads and clusters of small squares. A year later, in 1903, with the backing of Fritz Wärndorfer, the Hoffmann/Moser Wiener Werkstätte was started for the design, production and marketing of high-quality domestic objects. This organization and its output had achieved world fame by the time of its precipitate and inexplicable closure by Hoffmann in 1933.

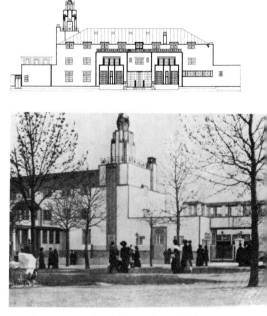

62, 63    Hoffmann, Palais Stoclet, Brussels, 1905–10

The last issue of *Ver Sacrum* was published in 1903: with its demise the high period of the Secession was over. In 1904, Hoffmann and Josef August Lux started to edit a new periodical, entitled *Hohe Warte*, named after the garden suburb. From the outset it was dedicated to the propagation of 'back to nature' garden city values, and later, in less liberal times, it became the garden city platform of the Austrian National Socialist movement. Unlike Hoffmann, Lux was quick to react against its chauvinistic exaggeration of folklorish values, resigning his editorship in protest against its *Heimatstil* policy as early as 1908.

By 1903 Hoffmann had moved closer to the style of his master Wagner, particularly in the design of the Classical and austere Purkersdorf Sanatorium, which was to have such an influence on Le Corbusier's early development. In 1905 Hoffmann began to work on his masterpiece, the Palais Stoclet, built in Brussels between 1905 and 1910. As in Perret's Théâtre des Champs-Elysées, its reduced Classical decoration paid veiled homage to the

Symbolist aesthetic of the Belle Epoque. But, unlike Perret's theatre, the Palais Stoclet is (as Eduard Sekler has observed) essentially atectonic: its thin white marble facing with its metal seams has all the mannered and hand-crafted elegance of a Wiener Werkstätte object on a large scale. Of its conscious denial of structure and mass Sekler wrote:

A strongly linear element is introduced by these articulated metal bands but it has nothing to do with 'lines of force', the way linear elements did in the architecture of Victor Horta. At the Stoclet house, we have lines which occur equally along horizontal and vertical edges – they are tectonically neutral. At the corners . . . where two or more of these parallel mouldings come together, the effect tends towards a negation of the solidity of the built volume. A feeling persists as if the walls had not been built in a heavy construction, but consisted of large sheets of thin material, joined at the corners with metal bands to protect the edges.

These bands, which issue from the apex of the stair tower, where four male figures support a Secessionist dome of laurels, are vaguely reminiscent of Wagner's stylized cable mouldings, and serve as they cascade down over the corners to unite the whole building through the continuity of the seam.

Wagner's mature style dates from his sixtieth year, with the completion of his Vienna Stadtbahn network in 1901. Not a trace of his Italianate manner remains in his *Die Zeit* telegraph office of 1902, or in his Kaiserbad Dam Works of 1906, both of which seem to relate in their engineered elegance and punctilious revetment to the atectonic style of Hoffmann. Yet the dematerialization of the Palais Stoclet seems to have been anticipated by Wagner's own masterwork, his Imperial Post Office Savings Bank built in Vienna in 1904. Wagner, unlike his Secessionist pupils, always built for the reality of the present rather than for some remote Symbolist utopia that looked towards the aesthetic redemption of man. Thus his 'Grosstadt' plan of 1910, with its hierarchy

64  Wagner, Post Office Savings Bank, Vienna, 1904. Detail of façade.

65   Wagner, Post Office Savings Bank, Vienna, 1904. Banking hall.

of neighbourhood units, was projected as a rationally planned and realizable metropolitan future. In all his public work Wagner built with great technical precision for a bureaucratic state which he could only regard as lasting indefinitely. Crowned by an honorific pergola hung with laurel wreaths and flanked by winged Victories whose arms are raised skyward, the Post Office Savings Bank represented the republican benevolence of the Austro-Hungarian Empire at the height of its power.

Like the Palais Stoclet, the Post Office Savings Bank resembles a gargantuan metal box, an effect due in no small measure to the thin polished sheets of white Sterzing marble that are anchored to its façade with aluminium rivets. Its glazed canopy frame, entrance doors, balustrade and parapet rail are also of aluminium, as are the metal furnishings of the banking hall itself. Faced in ceramic, lit from above and resting in its turn on a suspended concrete floor, studded with glass lenses for the illumination of the basement, this hall existed until recently in its original form. Its unadorned, riveted steel-work was formally related to the industrial lighting standards and the aluminium heating cowls which flanked its perimeter. As Stanford Anderson has observed,

The details of an engineered building are not placed before us in the *sachlich* manner of nineteenth-century exhibition halls or railway sheds; the concept of an engineered building is revealed to us instead through the building's own modernist symbols of exposed industrial materials, structure and equipment.

By 1911 the 'classicization' of the Secession was complete, and for all his continuing interest in the evolution of an appropriate *Heimatstil*, Hoffmann represented Austria at the Rome International Art Exhibition of that year with a pavilion design whose atectonic Classicism anticipated the rhetorical monumentality of Mussolini's New Rome. Equally prophetic was Behrens's representation of Prussia in St Petersburg with an embassy whose solemnity would point towards the official rhetoric of the Third Reich. In such a climate it fell to Wagner to close the Secession as it had begun, with the vigour of his extremely austere yet elegantly proportioned second villa, built in Hütteldorf in 1912. In this lucidly planned house, lyrically decorated by Moser and influenced to an equal degree by the work of Wagner's own pupils and the recently published works of Wright, Wagner was to spend his last six years.

## Chapter 7

# Antonio Sant'Elia and Futurist architecture 1909-14

We had been awake all night my friends and I, under the mosque shaped chandeliers which starry like our souls were lit by the inner radiance of an electric heart. For hours we had trampled opulent oriental carpets; soiled quantities of paper with frantic thought. . . . We were alone before the hostile stars, alone with the stokers who sweat before the satanic furnaces of great ships, alone with those black phantoms who ferret in the bellies of red hot locomotives as they hurtle forward at insensate speeds. . . . We all started up, at the sound of a tram rumbling past, ablaze with multicoloured lights, like a village in festival dress that the flooded Po tears from its banks and sweeps through the gorges and rapids, down to the sea. Afterwards the silence grew deeper and we heard only the muttered devotions of the old canal and the creaking of the arthritic, ivy-bearded palaces. . . . Suddenly we heard the roar of starving cars. . . . Let us go, I cried, let us depart. Mythology and Mystic Idealism are defeated at last. We are in at the birth of the centaurs, we shall see the first angels fly. We must rattle the doors of life, test the hinges and the bolts. Let us go. There on earth is the first dawn of history and there is nothing to match the red sword of the sun, slashing for the first time through the shadows of a thousand years.

Filippo Tomaso Marinetti
'Le Futurisme', *Le Figaro*, Paris,
20 February, 1909

With bombastic rhetoric, Italian Futurism announced its iconoclastic principles to the complacent bourgeoisie of the Belle Epoque. This millennialistic introduction was followed by an account of an impromptu automobile race on the outskirts of Milan ending in an accident which, as Reyner Banham has observed, had all the overtones of being 'the mimic baptism of a new faith'. In a text that pretended to be part autobiographical, Marinetti told of the overturning of his car into a factory ditch:

Oh beautiful, maternal factory ditch, how greedily I tasted your fortifying mire, that reminded me of the dark breasts of my Sudanese nurse. Yet when I emerged, ragged and sodden from the overturned vehicle, I felt the hot iron of a delicious joy pierce my heart. And so, our faces covered in good factory mud, plastered in slag, sweat and soot, bruised and in splints, but undaunted yet, we pronounced our fundamental will to live to all the live spirits of the world.

Then followed the eleven points of the Futurist Manifesto, the first four of which extolled the virtues of temerity, energy and audacity, while asserting the supreme magnificence of mechanical speed in the now famous passage that declared a racing car to be more beautiful than the Winged Victory of Samothrace. Points five to nine went on to idealize the driver of such a vehicle as being integral with the trajectories of the universe and to celebrate other diverse virtues, such as patriotism and the glorification of war; point ten called for the destruction of academic institutions of every kind; and point eleven itemized the ideal context of a Futurist architecture:

We will sing of the stirring of great crowds – workers, pleasure seekers, rioters and the confused sea of colour and sound as revolution sweeps through a modern metropolis. We will sing of the midnight fervour of arsenals and shipyards blazing with electric moons; insatiable stations swallowing the smoking serpents of their trains; factories hung from the clouds by the twisted threads of their smoke; bridges flashing like knives in the sun, giant gymnasts that leap over rivers; adventurous steamers that scent the horizon, deep chested locomotives that paw the ground with their wheels, like stallions harnessed with steel tubing; the easy flight of aircraft, their propellers beating the wind like banners with a sound like the applause of a mighty crowd.

Apart from its debt to the *aeropoesia* of the nationalist poet Gabriele D'Annunzio and a feeling for the 'simultaneity' of Cubist vision, this evocative passage was a straightforward homage to the triumph of industrialization – to the technical and social phenomena of the 19th century as they were then being extended through aviation and electrical power. In the face of Italian Classical, passéist values, it proclaimed the cultural primacy of a mechanized environment that later informed to an equal degree the architectural aesthetic of Italian Futurism and Russian Constructivism. In 1909, as Joshua Taylor has remarked, Futurism was an impulse rather than a style, so that for all its explicit opposition to both the Secession and to the classicizing Post-Secession, the form that a Futurist architecture might take was not immediately clear. After all, Futurism had proclaimed itself as being fundamentally opposed to culture, and this polemically negative stance could hardly have excluded architecture.

In 1910, with the crucial contribution of the artist Umberto Boccioni, Futurism began to extend its 'anti-cultural' polemic to the domain of plastic art. Boccioni produced two Futurist manifestos on painting in that year, and they were followed in April 1912 by his *Manifesto tecnico della scultura futurista* (*Technical Manifesto of Futurist Sculpture*). This later text, like most of the pre-war Futurist writings, gave evidence of a developed architectural sensibility. Thus Boccioni's opening critique, while ostensibly addressing itself to the *pompier* dead-end that he wished to confront in contemporary sculpture, could have applied, with just as much pertinence, to the post-1904 work of

Secessionist architects such as Joseph Olbrich and Alfred Messel – the former for his Tietz department store in Düsseldorf and the latter for his Wertheim store in Berlin. Boccioni wrote: 'We find in Germanic countries a ridiculous obsession with a Hellenized Gothic style that is industrialized in Berlin and enervated in Munich.' By the same token Boccioni's positive concern to extend the field of the sculptural object to incorporate its immediate milieu had connotations which were intrinsically architectural. This he made explicit as a converse principle in his preface to the catalogue of the first exhibition of Futurist sculpture in 1913: 'The search for naturalistic form removes sculpture (and painting also) from both its origins and its ultimate end: architecture.

In his concern for a non-naturalistic expression, Boccioni developed a plastic aesthetic that was entirely removed from the concerns of the 1896 Secession. Again in his catalogue preface of 1913 he wrote:

All these convictions compel me to search in sculpture not for pure form but *pure plastic rhythm*; not the construction of bodies, but the *construction of the action of bodies*. Thus I have as my ideal not a pyramidal architecture (static state), but a spiral architecture (dynamism). . . . My inspiration moreover seeks through assiduous research a complete fusion of environment and object by the means of the interpenetration of planes.

To achieve this sculptural simultaneity, Boccioni had already recommended, in his sculpture manifesto of 1912, that sculptors henceforth exclude the nude and exalted subject matter and the use of honorific materials such as marble or bronze in favour of heterogeneous media: 'Transparent planes of glass or celluloid, strips of metal, wire, interior or exterior electric lights can indicate the planes, the tendencies, the tones and half tones of a new reality.' Paradoxically, this concept of a spirally structured, non-monumental, mixed-media object to be extended into the immediate environment was to have more influence on Russian Post-Revolutionary 'Cubo-Futurist' Constructivism than on the evolution of Futurist architecture.

66 Sommaruga, Faccanoni Mausoleum, Sarnico, 1907.

Nevertheless, Boccioni's sculpture manifesto of 1912 and Marinetti's *La Splendeur Géomé-trique et Mécanique* (*Geometric and Mechanical Splendour and the Numerical Sensibility*) of 1914 jointly gave the intellectual and aesthetic frame of reference within which a Futurist architecture could be postulated. Marinetti wrote: 'Nothing in the world is more beautiful than a great humming power-station, holding back the hydraulic pressures of a whole mountain range, and the electric power for a whole landscape, synthesized in control panels bristling with levers and gleaming commutators.' This pristine vision of mechanical splendour was fittingly paralleled by the young Italian archi-tect Antonio Sant'Elia's power-station designs of the same date.

Prior to 1912 Sant'Elia was still relatively isolated from the Futurists, and involved with the Italian Secessionist movement. This so-called 'Stile Floreale' was to enjoy an extensive, if brief, national popularity after the resounding success of Raimondo D'Aronco's flamboyant pavilion for the Exhibition of Decorative Arts held in Turin in 1902. Thereafter, in Udine, D'Aronco continued to follow the lead of Olbrich, while the Milanese architects of the 'Stile Floreale' attempted to integrate their taste for the Neo-Baroque with motifs drawn

from the *Wagnerschule*. In Milan this impulse found its most powerful synthesis in the works of Giuseppe Sommaruga, who seems to have exercised a particular influence over Sant'Elia's early development. Many of the characteristic elements of Sant'Elia's *dinamismo architetto-nico* were surely anticipated in Sommaruga's hotel at Campo de' Fiori, while Sommaruga's Faccanoni Mausoleum, built at Sarnico in 1907, seems to have served as the point of departure for Sant'Elia's design of 1912 for a cemetery at Monza.

In 1905, at the age of seventeen, Sant'Elia obtained his diploma as a master builder from a technical school in Como. He then moved to Milan and started to work, first for the Villoresi Canal Company and later for the city of Milan. In 1911 he took architectural courses at the Brera Academy, and in the same year he designed a small villa above Como for the industrialist Romeo Longatti. By 1912 he was back in Milan, working on a competition entry for the central station. In the same year he collaborated with his friends Ugo Nebbia, Mario Chiattone and others to form the group Nuove Tendenze. At the first exhibition of this group, in 1914, Sant'Elia showed his drawings for the Futurist 'Città Nuova'. At what date he had first made contact with Marinetti and the

Futurist circle remains unclear, but he was fully under their influence by the time of writing, with the help of Nebbia, his *Messaggio*, as a preface to the 1914 exhibition.

The *Messaggio*, signed only by Sant'Elia, finally specifies — without once using the word 'Futurist' — the rigorous form that architecture should adopt in the future. The most specific parts of this text, now categorically anti-Secessionist, read:

The problem of modern architecture is not a problem of rearranging its lines; not a question of finding new mouldings, new architraves for doors and windows; nor of replacing columns, pilasters and corbels with caryatids, hornets and frogs, etc. . . . but to raise the new built structure on a sane plane, gleaning every benefit of science and technology . . . establishing new forms, new lines, new reasons for existence solely out of the special conditions of modern living and its projection as aesthetic value in our sensibilities.

The text then turns to contemplate the invigorating large-scale landscape of a new industrial world, paraphrasing the spirit if not the letter of Marinetti's diatribe against Ruskin and the whole of the English Arts and Crafts movement, delivered at the Lyceum Club in London in 1912. Against the passéism of Morris's 'Nowhere', Marinetti asserted that

cosmopolitan travel, the spirit of democracy and the decay of religions had made completely useless the vast permanent and ornate buildings that once used to express royal authority, theocracy and mysticism . . . the right to strike, equality before the law, the authority of numbers, the usurping power of the mob, the speed of international communications and the habits of hygiene and comfort demand instead large well-ventilated apartment houses, railways of absolute reliability, tunnels, iron bridges, vast high speed liners, immense meeting halls and bathrooms designed for the rapid daily care of the body.

In short, he correctly recognized the implacable advent of a new cultural milieu dedicated to a large-scale and highly mobile society; a

67    Sant'Elia, design for Monza Cemetery, 1912.

society to be equipped in detail according to Sant'Elia's *Messaggio* in which he wrote:

Calculations of the resistance of materials, the use of reinforced concrete and iron exclude 'Architecture' as understood in the Classical or traditional sense. Modern structural materials and our scientific concepts absolutely do not lend themselves to the disciplines of historical styles. . . . We no longer feel ourselves to be the men of the cathedrals and ancient moot halls, but men of the Grand Hotels, railway stations, giant roads, colossal harbours, covered markets, glittering arcades, reconstruction areas and salutary slum clearances. We must invent and rebuild *ex novo* our modern city like an immense and tumultuous shipyard, active, mobile and everywhere dynamic, and the modern building like a gigantic machine. Lifts must no longer hide away like solitary worms in the stairwells, but the stairs — now useless — must be abolished, and the lifts must swarm up the façades like serpents of glass and iron. The house of cement, iron and glass, without carved or painted ornament, rich only in the inherent beauty of its lines and modelling, extraordinarily brutish in its mechanical simplicity, as big as need dictates, and not merely as zoning rules permit, must rise from the brink of a tumultuous abyss; the street which, itself, will no longer lie like a doormat at the level of the thresholds but plunge storeys deep into the earth, gathering up the traffic of the metropolis connected for necessary transfers to metal catwalks and high-speed conveyor belts.

This prescription, specifying the form of Sant' Elia's *casa a gradinata* designs of 1914, is of such a dynamic nature as to suggest precedents other than Henri Sauvage's set-back apartment block completed in Rue Vavin, Paris, in 1912. The subtitle of the Nuove Tendenze exhibition, 'Milano l'anno due mille', suggests the precedent of Antoine Moilin's book *Paris, l'an 2000* (1896), a work which Marinetti would have known through his contact with the Parisian poet Gustave Kahn.

Sant'Elia's sketches for the Città Nuova are not entirely consistent with his precepts. Where the *Messaggio* took a stand against all commemorative architecture and, in consequence, against all static and pyramidal forms, Sant'Elia's drawings are replete with such monumental images. In retrospect it seems but a step from Sommaruga's Faccanoni Mausoleum to the soaring, massive and often symmetrical power-houses and tall blocks that rise like mirages out of the scenographic landscape of the Città Nuova. In this context, it is fitting and ironic that Sant'Elia's memory should have been honoured in a monument to the dead of the First World War, that was erected on the shores of Lake Como in 1933 — to a design by Giuseppe Terragni based on one of Sant'Elia's sketches.

The official *Manifesto dell' architettura futurista* (*Manifesto of Futurist Architecture*), published in July 1914, seems to have had as its prime goal the public recognition of Sant' Elia as a Futurist. It amounted to a new version of the *Messaggio*, edited, to all appearances, by Marinetti and signed by Sant'Elia alone. Apart from the interjection of the word 'Futurist' on every possible occasion, this text added little to the original save a number of militant propositions at the end, including the contradictory opposition to any kind of permanence, the assertion that 'our houses will last less time than we do and that every generation will have to make its own'.

By now Sant'Elia was fully involved in Futurism and in 1915 he signed, with Boccioni, Marinetti, Piatti and Russolo, the Futurist proto-Fascist political manifesto, *Italian Pride*. In July of that year he enlisted with other Futurists in the Lombardy Volunteer Cyclist Battalion and entered on a military career that ended with his front-line death in 1916. With the loss of Boccioni two months before (in a riding accident) the generative period of Futurism was brought to an abrupt end, ironically divested of its major talent in part by the first industrialized war. Out of this Futurist holocaust, Marinetti survived to remind his fellow Futurists, such as Balla, Carrà, Severini and Russolo, of their duty to lead the post-war generation towards the final fulfilment of Italian nationalism in the triumph of a Fascist state.

Typical of the confusion of Futurism in its decline, which undoubtedly paralleled Mussolini's rapprochement with the Vatican, was Marinetti's 1931 *Manifesto of Sacred Futurist Art*, where he urged that church candlelight 'must be replaced by powerful electric bulbs of brilliant white and blue light', that 'for the representations of Hell, Futurist painters must depend on their memories of shell-scarred battlefields', and that 'only Futurist artists . . . can give form to interpenetrated space-time, to the super-rational mysteries of the Catholic dogmas'.

That this absurd bravado had been anticipated in the initial manifesto (with its violence reminiscent of Georges Sorel) does not entirely account for the state of decadence to which Futurist 'culture' had descended by 1931. After 1919 it was the revolutionary Russian Constructivists, and not the Italians, who took up the early militant modernism of Marinetti, Boccioni and Sant'Elia. Some time was to elapse before the Italian Rationalist movement would begin to respond to the images of the Città Nuova, and even then it would do so only in a climate that was concerned for the integration of modern values into the Classical traditions of Italian architecture.

68   Sant'Elia, *casa a gradinata* for the Città Nuova, 1914.

# Chapter 8
# Adolf Loos and the crisis of culture 1896-1931

May I lead you to the shores of a mountain lake? The sky is blue, the water green and everything is profoundly peaceful. Mountains and clouds are reflected in the lake, and so are houses, farmyards, courtyards and chapels. They do not seem man-made, but more like the product of God's workshop, like the mountains and trees, the clouds and the blue sky. And everything breathes beauty and tranquillity.

Ah, what is that? A false note in this harmony. Like an unwelcome scream. In the centre, beneath the peasants' homes which were created not by them, but by God, stands a villa. Is it the product of a good or a bad architect? I do not know. I only know that peace, tranquillity and beauty are no more. . . .

And I ask yet again: Why does the architect both good and bad violate the lake? Like almost every town dweller, the architect possesses no culture. He does not have the security of the peasant to whom this culture is innate. The town dweller is an upstart.

I call culture, that balance of inner and outer man, which alone can guarantee reasonable thought and action.

Adolf Loos
*Architektur*, 1910

Adolf Loos, the son of a stonemason, was born in Brno, Moravia, in 1870. Following a technical education at the Royal and Imperial State Technical College and further studies at the Dresden College of Technology, he left for the United States in 1893 – apparently to visit the World's Columbian Exposition in Chicago. Although he seems not to have found work as an architect during his three-year stay in the States, he nonetheless became familiar with the pioneer achievements of the Chicago School

and with the theoretical writings of Louis Sullivan, in particular with Sullivan's essay *Ornament in Architecture* (1892), which patently influenced his own essay *Ornament und Verbrechen* (*Ornament and Crime*), published sixteen years later.

After his return to Vienna in 1896, Loos began his career by designing interiors and writing articles for the liberal *Neue Freie Presse*, on a wide variety of topics ranging from clothes to architecture and from manners to music. In 1908 he published *Ornament and Crime*, in which he elaborated the nature of his quarrel with the artists of the Viennese Secession, an argument that he had already enjoined by 1900 in the form of an anti-*Gesamtkunstwerk* fable, 'The Story of a Poor Rich Man'. There Loos portrayed the fate of a wealthy businessman who had commissioned a Secessionist architect to design a 'total' house for him, including not only the furnishings but also the clothes of the occupants.

Once it happened that he was celebrating his birthday. His wife and children had given him many presents. He liked their choice immensely and enjoyed it all thoroughly. But soon the architect arrived to set things right, and to take all the decisions in difficult questions. He entered the room. The master greeted him with pleasure, for he had much on his mind. But the architect did not see the man's joy. He had discovered something quite different and grew pale. 'What kind of slippers are these you've got on?' he ejaculated painfully. The master of the house looked at his embroidered slippers. Then he breathed in relief. This time he felt quite guiltless. The slippers had been made to the architect's original designs. So he answered

69  A 1911 cartoonist's comment on Loos's Goldman and Salatsch façade (1910–11). The original caption read: 'Brooding about art, the most modern man walks through the streets. Suddenly he stops transfixed. He has found that for which he has searched so long.'

in a superior way, 'But Mr Architect! Have you already forgotten? You yourself designed them!' 'Of course,' thundered the architect, 'but for the bedroom! They completely disrupt the mood here with these two impossible spots of colour. Can't you see that?'

The Belgian artist Henry van de Velde is as much the unidentified cultural martinet of this sardonic piece as Joseph Maria Olbrich. For it was he and not Olbrich who designed special clothes for his wife to harmonize with the lines of their house, built at Uccle in 1895. Nonetheless, Olbrich remained the essential focus of Loos's anti-Secessionist attacks throughout the next decade: he was even cited by name in *Ornament and Crime* as the progenitor of illegitimate ornament. 'Where will Olbrich's work be in ten years' time?' wrote Loos. 'Modern ornament has no forebears and no descendants, no past and no future. It is joyfully welcomed by uncultivated people to whom the true greatness of our time is a closed book, and after a short time is rejected.'

Loos's ultimate argument against ornament was not only that it was wasteful in labour and material, but that it invariably entailed a punitive form of craft slavery that could only be justified for those to whom the highest achievements of bourgeois culture were inaccessible –

for those craftsmen who could only find their aesthetic fulfilment in the spontaneous creation of ornament. Loos justified the ornamentation of his bespoke footwear – which he would have preferred to be plain – in the following terms: 'We go to Beethoven or *Tristan* after the cares of the day. My shoemaker can't. I must not take away his joy as I have nothing to replace it with. But whoever goes to the Ninth Symphony and then sits down to design a wallpaper is either a rogue or a degenerate.'

Such challenging ethical and aesthetic pronouncements isolated Loos not only from the Secession and his conservative contemporaries, but also from his true successors, those latter-day 'purists' who even now have yet to comprehend fully the profundity of his insights. By the time of his critical essay *Architektur* of 1910, Loos had already begun to sense the full force of a modern predicament, which persists to this day. Given, as Loos argued, that the architect from the city was uprooted by definition and hence categorically alienated from the innate agrarian (or alpine) vernacular of his distant forebears, then it followed that he could not compensate for this loss by pretending to inherit the aristocratic culture of Western Classicism. For the urban bourgeoisie – whence he invariably came and whom he naturally served – were, whatever else they might be,

70  Cover of *Das Andere*, edited by Loos, Vienna, 1903.

patently *not* aristocrats. That much was already clear to Loos in 1898 when he wrote in *Die potemkinsche Stadt*, his satire on the Ringstrasse:

Whenever I stroll along the Ring, I always feel as if a modern Potemkin had wanted to make somebody believe he had been transported into a city of aristocrats. All that the Italian Renaissance could produce in noble mansions had been plundered in order to conjure up for Her Highness the common people a New Vienna, which only people in a position to own an entire palace from the cellars to the chimney-pots could inhabit. . . . Viennese landlords were delighted with the idea of owning a mansion and the tenants were equally pleased to be able to live in one.

Loos's solution to this dilemma, as posited in *Architektur*, was to argue that most modern building tasks were appropriate vehicles for *building* rather than architecture: 'Only a very small part of architecture belongs to art: the tomb and the monument. Everything else, everything that serves a purpose, should be excluded from the realms of art.'

At the same time Loos considered that all culture depended on a certain continuity with the past; above all, on a consensus as to a typification. He could not accept the romantic notion of the highly gifted individual transcending the historical limits of his own epoch. Instead of self-conscious ornamental design, Loos favoured understated dress, anonymous furniture and efficient plumbing of the Anglo-Saxon middle class. Naturally in this respect he had America in mind rather than England. In this he anticipated Le Corbusier's notion of the *objet-type*, the refined, normative object, spontaneously produced by the craft-based industries of the society. To this end, objects of Anglo-Saxon affinity, such as clothing, sportswear and personal accessories, appeared as advertisements in Loos's short-lived periodical *Das Andere* ('The Other') of 1903, significantly subtitled 'A Journal for the Introduction of Western Civilization into Austria'.

Despite all his Anglophilia, the 'vernacular' of the English Arts and Crafts movement (as documented in Hermann Muthesius's book *Das Englische Haus* of 1904) presented Loos with a problem: where was one to draw a line between such architecture, however sensible and convenient, and the self-conscious, craft-based, hermetic fantasies of the Secession? Since for Loos the last Western architect of stature had been Schinkel, his self-imposed predicament seems to have been how to combine the informal comfort of the Anglo-Saxon interior with the asperities of Classical form.

Until 1910, Loos's practice was largely confined to the conversion of existing interiors. His best works of this period were the luxury shops that he designed in Vienna around the turn of the century, and his famous Kärntner or American Bar of 1907. Externally these works, designed for the purveyors of Anglocentric civilization, were finished in elegant, unobtrusive materials, while internally the style varied from the Japanese ambience of his first interior for Goldman & Salatsch in the Graben (1898) to the classicized club-room elegance of the Kärntner Bar.

In Loos's domestic interiors the expression was even more eclectic, reflecting the fundamental split in his work between a comfortable rusticity on the one hand and a severe monumentality on the other. He invariably panelled his walls up to dado or picture-rail level in polished stone or wood; above this they were either left blank or topped with an ornamental pattern or Classical frieze in plaster. (In *Ornament and Crime*, Loos had admitted the eclectic appropriation of archaeological ornament, while categorically excluding the invention of modern decoration.) Ceilings, where public, were often blank; where private, they were coffered in wood or metal. On other occasions, particularly in dining spaces, they might be relieved by Richardsonian timber beams, which were often of grotesque proportions, as in the Steiner House of 1910. Floors were generally of stone or parquet and always covered with oriental carpets, while fireplace surrounds, frequently of brick, stood out in textured contrast to the highlights invariably provided by vitrines, mirrors, lamps and sundry metalware. As far as possible furniture was always built in. Otherwise it was selected by the client, although where it was movable and the building public, Loos restricted himself to standard Thonet bentwood furniture, as in his somewhat Wagner-like Café Museum of 1899. In his essay on the abolition of furniture he wrote: 'The walls of a building belong to the architect. There he rules at will. And as with walls so with any furniture that is not movable.' Of movable pieces he wrote: 'The wrought-iron bedstead, table and chairs, hassocks and occasional chairs, desks and smoking stands — all items made by our craftsmen in the modern idiom (never by architects); everyone may buy these for himself according to his own taste and inclination.' This categorical anti-*Gesamtkunstwerk* attitude was complemented by Loos's passion for rich materials of which he wrote in the vein of Semper: 'Rich material and good workmanship should not only be considered as making up for lack of decoration, but as far surpassing it in sumptuousness.'

The Steiner House, built in Vienna in 1910, initiated a series of houses in which Loos gradually evolved his conception of the *Raumplan* or 'plan of volumes', a complex system of internal organization that culminated in the split-level houses realized towards the end of

71, 72 Loos, Steiner House, Vienna, 1910. *Below*, dining room.

his life: the Moller House in Vienna and the Müller House near Prague. By the time of the Steiner House, Loos had already arrived at a highly abstract external idiom — his white unadorned prism, which anticipated by at least eight years the so-called 'International Style'. He began to elaborate his *Raumplan* concept in his Rufer House, Vienna (1912), where, in contrast to his later houses, the openings are quite freely disposed, following the free disposition of the internal volumes — an elevational counterpoint that anticipated the canonical works of De Stijl.

93

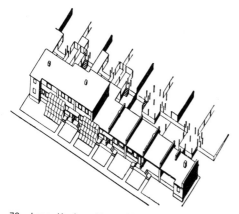

73 Loos, Heuberg Estate, Vienna, 1920, showing conservatories and allotments.

Loos's *Raumplan* reached its apotheosis in his last domestic works, the Moller and Müller houses of 1928 and 1930. As anticipated in the open stair hall of the Rufer House, both these works are organized about displacements in the respective levels of their principal floors, elisions that serve not only to create spatial movement but also to differentiate one living area from the next. The typically irregular Gothic Revival plan, documented in Muthesius's *Das Englische Haus*, clearly inspired Loos's wholly unprecedented development of the *Raumplan*, yet with his Classical predilection for cubic form he could not accept the picturesque massing that was its natural consequence. From this, no doubt, came the tortuous manipulation of the available volume of the prism as though it were just so much raw material from which to create a dynamic composition in section.

Such plastic intentions were basically incompatible with an architecture of consistent distinction between structural and non-structural elements, and while Loos strove to maintain such distinctions in his public work, at a domestic level he gave primacy to the sensation of space, rather than to the revelation of architectonic structure. The principles of Viollet-le-Duc were in any event alien to him, since he deliberately contorted plans for the sake of providing an architectural promenade of sensual significance as Le Corbusier was to do. In almost all his domestic work structural

junctions are invariably masked by revetment, either with the aim of hiding unresolved conditions or out of a desire to provide an appropriate level of decorum.

During his tenure as chief architect to the Housing Department of Vienna, from 1920 to 1922, in the austere aftermath of the war, Loos applied his as yet undeveloped *Raumplan* to the problem of mass housing. The result was a number of remarkable housing studies, in which his preferred form, the cube, became transformed into a stepped terrace section. In 1920 he designed a brilliant and economical housing scheme, known as the Heuberg Estate. Terrace houses were integrated with greenhouses and allotments, in which the occupants were expected to grow their own food — a typical urban survival strategy of the inflationary post-war period, which became adopted as general policy in many German housing settlements during the 1920s.

It is one of the paradoxes of Loos's career that he, the bourgeois architect and man of taste, should create his most sensitive larger projects in the service of the underprivileged. His disillusioned resignation as housing architect in 1922 and his subsequent migration to Paris, at the invitation of the Dadaist poet Tristan Tzara — for whom he was to design a house in 1926 — restored him to the cosmopolitan circles of the high bourgeoisie. There he became part of the fashionable world that surrounded the dancer Josephine Baker, for whom he designed a rather ostentatious villa in 1928. Save for Tzara and his old Viennese client, the internationally famous tailor Kniže, for whom he had first designed a store in Vienna in 1909, none of his Parisian patrons had either the resources or the faith to realize any of the large-scale projects that he designed during his expatriate years. In 1928 he returned to Vienna, five years before his death, his career virtually at an end.

In the final analysis Loos's significance as a pioneer depended not only on his extraordinary insights as a critic of modern culture, but also on his formulation of the *Raumplan* as an architectural strategy for transcending the contradictory cultural legacy of bourgeois society which, having deprived itself of the

94

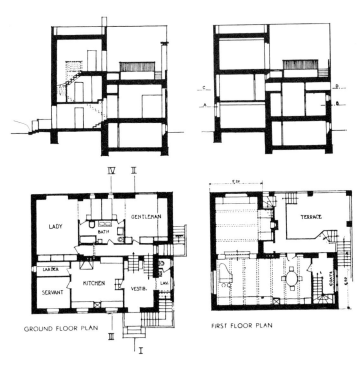

74, 75  Loos, villa project for the Venice Lido, 1923. *Left*, transverse sections (through I–II and III–IV), and plans of ground and first floor: *below*, model.

vernacular, could not claim in exchange the culture of Classicism. No one was better prepared to receive this hyperconscious sensibility than the post-war Parisian avant garde, in particular the circle editing *L'Esprit Nouveau*, namely the proto-Dadaist poet Paul Dermée and the Purist painters Amédée Ozenfant and Charles-Edouard Jeanneret (Le Corbusier), who in 1920 reprinted the 1913 French translation of *Ornament and Crime*. And while (as Reyner Banham has observed) the roots of Purism lay in the abstract classicizing tendencies of Parisian culture, notwithstanding the 'ready-made' sensibility of Marcel Duchamp, there is little reason to doubt that the influence of Loos was decisive in refining the typological programme of Purism; that impulse to synthesize, at every conceivable scale, the 'type-objects' of the modern world.

Above all, Loos must now be seen as the first to postulate the problem that Le Corbusier was eventually to resolve with his full development of the free plan. The typological issue posited by Loos was how to combine the propriety of Platonic mass with the convenience of irregular volume. This proposition was never more lyrically stated than in his 1923 project for a villa on the Lido in Venice; and this house was destined to become the type-form for Le Corbusier's canonical Purist villa, his villa at Garches of 1927.

95

## Chapter 9
# Henry van de Velde
# and the abstraction of empathy 1895-1914

I tell you that the time will come when the furnishing of a prison cell by Professor Van de Velde will be considered an aggravation of the sentence.

Adolf Loos
*Trotzdem*, 1931

The Belgian designer and theorist Henry van de Velde set out on what he called the *voie sacrée* of architecture in 1894, at the age of thirty-one, when after ten years as a Neo-Impressionist painter he published his famous essay, 'Déblaiement d'art', in the Belgian Nietzschean journal *La Société nouvelle*. This essay, which called for the redeployment of art in the service of the society, was clearly influenced by those Pre-Raphaelite precepts which Van de Velde would have learned through his association with the avant-garde group, Les XX. Since its inception in 1889, this Belgian group of artists had had strong ties with England and in particular with William Morris's protégé Walter Crane. Under Crane's influence, the group turned from its fine art preoccupations to a concern for the design of the environment as a whole. Reorganized under the leadership of Octave Maus, Les XX became the Salon de la Libre Esthétique, whose first exhibition in 1894 featured the work of the Belgian cabinet-maker Gustave Serrurier-Bovy. Serrurier-Bovy brought back to Belgium an Arts and Crafts sensibility that he had acquired in England during the second half of the 1880s. In 1894 he displayed the exceptional qualities of his unpainted furniture in a suite of strikingly sculptural pieces that recalled that Anglo-Japanese style, developed some twenty years before by Edward Godwin and Christopher Dresser.

Van de Velde made his début as an architect and as a designer in 1895, when he designed and built a house for himself at Uccle near Brussels. This without question was intended to demonstrate the ultimate synthesis of all the arts, for apart from integrating the house with all its furnishings, including the cutlery, Van de Velde attempted to consummate the whole *Gesamtkunstwerk* through the flowing forms of the dresses that he designed for his wife. The fall, cut and decoration of these clothes already exhibited that energetic serpentine line that

76 Van de Velde's wife, Maria Sèthe, wearing a dress to his design, *c.*1898.

77 Van de Velde's furniture atelier, Brussels, c.1897. He is bending over a drawing on the right.

78 Van de Velde, desk for Meier-Graefe, 1896, and Ferdinand Hodler's Symbolist painting *Day*, c.1896.

was to be Van de Velde's prime contribution to the vocabulary that he inherited from Serrurier-Bovy. Derived from Gauguin, it was used as an expressive device for imparting a more vigorous profile to the formal legacy of the Arts and Crafts.

For Van de Velde the ameliorative thrust of the English Arts and Crafts movement was complemented by the more anarchic but equally reformist visions of Tolstoy and Kropotkin. While he could share with the Pre-Raphaelites their intense antipathy to all architecture after the Gothic, he could not accept their conscious drive towards the medievalization of the present. As a socialist, he was more influenced by the young militants of the Belgian Socialist Party, with whom he had been in contact since the mid-1880s: Emile Vandervelde, the socialist client of Horta's Maison du Peuple, and the poet-critic Emile Verhaeren, whose critical study of urbanization, *Les Villes tentaculaires*, had been published in 1895. Yet in spite of these radical affiliations, Van de Velde still believed in the reform of society through the design of the environment; that is, he still adhered to a sensationalist faith in the primacy of physical form over programmatic content. For him, as for the whole of the Arts and Crafts tradition, the single family house was the prime social vehicle through which the values of the society

could be gradually transformed. 'Ugliness', he held, 'corrupts not only the eyes but also the heart and mind.' In his fight against ugliness, Van de Velde concentrated on the design of every aspect of the domestic environment. He was ill-equipped, either by temperament or training, to think at an urban scale: in his layout for the Hohenhagen garden colony, built at Hagen in Germany for Karl Ernst Osthaus in 1906, he singularly failed to demonstrate how the individual house might be aggregated into larger and more significant social units. And he was no more successful than William Morris in reconciling the contradictions between his socialist commitments and his patronage by the upper middle class.

From the mid-1890s on, Van de Velde was profoundly influenced by the aesthetic theories of the Viennese art-historian Alois Riegl and the Munich psychologist Theodor Lipps. Where the one stressed the creative primacy of the individual *Kunstwollen* or 'will to form', the other postulated *Einfühlung* or 'empathy' as the quasi-mystical projection of the creative ego into the art object. These complementary ideas had already been given a more specific context in Nietzsche's essay of 1871, *Die Geburt der Tragödie aus dem Geiste der Musik*, wherein the Apollonian and the Dionysian were seen as the irreducible duality of Hellenic culture, the former aspiring to the typical and freedom within the law and the latter to superabundance and pantheistic expression. These loosely related ideas, which vaguely informed Van de Velde's work after 1896, found a certain synthesis in Wilhelm Worringer's *Abstraktion und Einfühlung* (*Abstraction and Empathy*), published in 1908. Van de Velde studied Worringer's text assiduously and found that his own work seemed to combine in a single entity the two antagonistic aspects of Worringer's cultural model – on the one hand the impulse towards the *empathetic* expression of vital psychic states, and on the other the tendency towards achieving transcendence through *abstraction*.

While Van de Velde strove for an empathetic and vital culture of form, he was nonetheless aware of the innate tendency of all architecture towards abstraction. In this context, his lifelong respect for the Gothic may be regarded as a nostalgia for an architecture in which the immediate vitality of the form-force would come to be transcended by the sublime structural abstraction of the whole. The embodiment of such a force was the mainspring of his own aesthetic, from its initial appearance in the so-called 'Yachting Style' suite of furniture that he designed in 1895 for Samuel Bing's Maison de l'Art Nouveau in Paris to his theoretical formulation in 1902, in Weimar, of the principles of what he called 'structurally linear ornament'.

Van de Velde maintained a subtle distinction between *ornamentation* and *ornament*, arguing that the former, by virtue of being applied, was unrelated to its object, while the latter, by virtue of being functionally (i.e. structurally) determined, was integrated into it. This definition of functional ornament was inseparable from the importance that Van de Velde attached to the gestural 'crafted' line, as the necessary anthropomorphic trace of human creation. 'The line', he wrote in 1902, 'carries the force and the energy of that which has traced it.' For him the 'quasi-erotic' impulses governing the course of a line were to be regarded as a literature without an alphabet.

The powerful anti-decorative tendency of this purist view of culture was reinforced in 1903 when Van de Velde returned from a tour of Greece and the Middle East, overwhelmed by the power and the purity of Mycenaean and Assyrian form. From this point on he tried to avoid both the gestural fantasy of the Secession and the rationality of Classicism. He attempted to create 'pure' organic form, such form as could only be found, in his opinion, in the cradle of civilization or in the monumental cryptic gestures of Neolithic man. This no doubt accounts for the telluric forms of the houses that he built in Chemnitz and in Hagen between 1903 and 1906. Yet despite the curious megalithic quality of these works, there remained in all of Van de Velde's work after 1903 a trace of Classicism that was not entirely mediated by his feeling for the archaic. This is most evident in the domestic objects that he designed between 1903 and 1915, pieces that seem to reflect his passionate reaction to the classic, not to say ineffable, qualities that he found in the Parthenon:

On the Acropolis the living standing columns teach us that they do not exist, that they do not carry load, or rather that they are interspaced according to an end very different from that for which they were apparently erected. Even where they are still joined by an entablature, they proclaim in evidence that the columns around the Parthenon do not exist, but that between them gigantic perfect vases are poised, containing life, space and sun, sea and mountains, night and the stars. The entasis of the columns is transformed until the resultant space between one and the other has attained a perfect, eternal form.

Van de Velde's Apollonian conversion, so to speak, coincided with the climax of his career at Weimar. After having been consultant to the craft industries of the Grand Duchy of Saxe-Weimar since 1901, he was nominated in 1904 to serve as the professor to the newly created Grand Ducal School of Arts and Crafts. This appointment gave him the commission to design new premises for both the school and the existing Academy of Fine Art – the nucleus that fourteen years later would become the Weimar Bauhaus. Prior to the opening of these buildings in 1908, Van de Velde continued to lecture in Weimar and to give his *Kunstseminar* for the cultural instruction of trained artisans.

79   Van de Velde, Werkbund Exhibition Theatre, Cologne, 1914.

Yet this most triumphant moment of his entire career was overshadowed by profound inner doubts, in which he began to question the artist's prerogative to determine the form of objects. In 1905 he wrote: 'At what point do I have this right to impose on the world a taste and a wish which is so personal. Suddenly I no longer see the ties between my ideal and the world.'

After Gottfried Semper and Peter Behrens, Van de Velde had always sought to strengthen such socio-cultural ties through the agency of the theatre, conceiving its union of actors and spectators as the highest form of social and spiritual life. Directly influenced by scenographers such as Max Reinhardt and Gordon Craig, he devoted himself to the development of the tripartite stage, first formulated in a project for the Dumont Theatre in Weimar in 1904. He returned to this theme in 1911 in his compromise design for the Théâtre des Champs-Elysées, Paris (realized by Auguste Perret in a modified form in 1913), and again in his Cologne Werkbund Exhibition Theatre of 1914. The highly expressive but short-lived Werkbund Theatre was the apotheosis of all his pre-war work. Erich Mendelsohn wrote of it: 'Only Van de Velde, with his theatre, is really searching for new form. Concrete used in the Art Nouveau style, but strong in conception and expression.' Its surging masses demonstrated Van de Velde's masterly control over form in a manner that later served as a model for the profiling of Mendelsohn's Einstein Tower, built at Potsdam in 1919.

The much admired Werkbund Theatre was to be the last formulation of Van de Velde's 'form-force' aesthetic. Fusing actor with audience and auditorium with landscape, as in the open-air arenas of Neolithic man, it appeared as a unique empathetic expression. Such expression could of course find no place in the modest modular prefabricated house that Van de Velde built for himself after the First World War. The Werkbund dream of a world transformed by *gute Form* and industrial monopoly had proven just as vain as the reformist hopes of the socially conscious bourgeoisie whose fifty-year-old patronage of the Arts and Crafts and Art Nouveau had been brought to an abrupt end by the first industrialized war. One could no longer fantasize about a society transformed through art, industrial design, and the theatre, at a time when the provision of minimum shelter was a matter of the greatest urgency.

## Chapter 10

# Tony Garnier
# and the Industrial City 1899-1918

The city is imaginary: let us assume that the towns of Rive-de-Gier, St-Etienne, St-Chaumond, Chasse and Givors have conditions similar to those of this town. The site of this study is located in a region of south-east France, and regional materials have been used in its construction.

Determining factors in the establishment of a similar city should be the proximity of raw materials, or the existence of a natural force capable of being used for energy, or the convenience of methods of transportation. In our case the determining factor in the location of the city is the force of the tributary that is the power source; there are also mines in the region, but they could be located further away. The tributary is dammed; a hydroelectric plant distributes power, light, and heat to the factories and to the entire city. The principal factories are situated in the plain at the confluence of the river and its tributary. A mainline railroad passes between the factories and the town, which is located above the factories on a plateau. Higher still are placed the hospitals; they, as well as the city, are sheltered from cold winds, and have their terraces oriented to the south. Each of these main elements (factories, town, hospitals) is isolated so that it can expand. . . . Investigation of the most satisfactory programme for the material and moral needs of the individual has resulted in the creation of rules concerning road use, hygiene, and so on; the assumption is that a certain progress of social order resulting in an automatic adoption of these rules already has been realized, so that it will not be necessary to enact the actual laws. Distribution of land, everything related to the distribution of water, bread, meat, milk, and medical supplies, as well as the re-utilization of refuse, will be given over to the public domain.

Tony Garnier
Preface to *Une Cité industrielle*, 1917

It would be hard to imagine a more concise statement of the basic economic and technical precepts for the foundation and organization of a modern city. The very lucidity of this outline — the sole theoretical statement of Garnier's career — reflects in its tone and content the fundamentally radical nature of his life and work. Born in Lyons in 1869 and raised in a radical workers' quarter, he remained consistently committed to the socialist cause up to his death in 1948.

Garnier's education and the commitment of his professional career are both inseparable from the city of Lyons. The radical syndicalism and socialism that Lyons nurtured stemmed from the fact that it was one of the most progressive industrial centres in 19th-century France, with its silk and metallurgical industries well established by the time of Garnier's birth. In addition to its favourable location in the Rhône-Saône corridor, the growth of Lyons had been stimulated soon after mid-century by one of the first main railway links in France. By the 1880s, with the electrification of its trams and local railway systems, it was well placed to become a main centre for technical and industrial innovation. Photography, cinematography, hydro-electric generation, automobile production and aviation all saw their first beginnings there between 1882 and the turn of the century. The influence of this technical milieu certainly found its reflection in Garnier's project for a 'Cité Industrielle', first exhibited in 1904; a project which demonstrated his belief that the cities of the future would have to be based on industry.

Other aspects of Lyons culture were also featured in the plans of Garnier's Cité, most notably the French regionalist movement in favour of reviving local culture, which was as a result committed to the broader political policies of federalism and decentralization. Thus Garnier included an old medieval town within the confines of his industrial city. The importance that he attached to such foundations is reflected in his location of the main railway station in close proximity to this regional centre.

The municipality of Lyons was also important, even in Garnier's youth, for its progressive approach to urbanization. Its streets had been regularized between 1853 and 1864; after 1880 – as part of a slum clearance programme – the city began to improve its water and sanitation systems; and around 1883 it began to provide a whole range of welfare facilities, including schools, workers' housing, baths, hospitals and abattoirs.

Entering the Ecole des Beaux-Arts, first at Lyons in 1886 and then at Paris in 1889, Garnier came under the influence of Julien Guadet who, as Professor of Theory after 1894, taught not only the precepts of Rational Classicism but also programmatic analysis and the classification of building types. Guadet's *Eléments et théories de l'architecture* of 1902 was a programmatic updating of Durand's methods of 1805 for the rational combination of typified architectural forms, and it was this common elemental approach to design that was to inform the careers of Guadet's foremost pupils, Garnier and Auguste Perret. These two men, however, were to have very different careers, for while Garnier, after ten years in Paris, won the Prix de Rome in 1899 and spent another four years at the French Academy in the Villa Medici, Perret left the Beaux-Arts in 1897 after only three years of formal education to work for his father. Thus when the Cité Industrielle was first exhibited, in 1904, Perret had already made his mark as an architect and a builder with his pioneer reinforced-concrete-frame apartment building in the Rue Franklin.

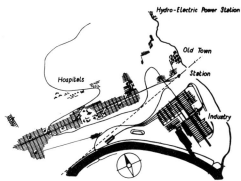

80  Garnier, Cité Industrielle: schematic plan, 1904–17. Below the hospitals is the administrative/cultural centre, flanked by housing.

From the time when Garnier was first a *logiste* for the Prix de Rome in 1892, he had been immersed in the increasingly radical climate of Paris, presided over by the figure of Jean Jaurès, who became a socialist deputy in 1893. The Parisian political scene was galvanized after 1897 by the Dreyfus affair, an event which converted Emile Zola into a passionate advocate of radical reform. Out of this came Zola's first utopian socialist novel, *Fécondite*, which was serialized in 1899 in the socialist journal *L'Aurore*. Given Garnier's long-standing affiliation with the Société des Amis d'Emile Zola, it is certain that he would have read these excerpts. In any event, the early sketches for the industrial city that he made in the same year seem to reflect Zola's vision of a new socio-economic order, which the writer was to elaborate in his second utopian socialist novel, *Travail* (1901).

Against great opposition at the Villa Medici, Garnier continued to work on his city project throughout his stay. For the required 'testimony of academic study' he prepared an imaginative and equally unprecedented reconstruction of the Roman hill city of Tusculum. Tusculum and the first version of the Cité Industrielle were jointly exhibited in Paris in 1904, the year when Garnier returned in triumph to Lyons. Over the next thirty-five years he was to work exclusively in and for this city, largely at the command of the progressive mayor, Edouard Herriot, and it was in Lyons, at the beginning of his public career, that Le Corbusier first met him in 1908.

Set on a river escarpment, in a mountainous landscape that corresponded generally to that of the Lyons region, Garnier's industrial city of 35,000 inhabitants was not only a regional centre of medium size, sensitively related to its environment, but also an urban organization that anticipated in its separate zoning the principles of the CIAM Athens Charter of 1933. It was above all a socialist city, without walls or private property, without church or barracks, without police station or law courts; a city where all the unbuilt surface was public parkland. Within the built area Garnier eventually established a varied and comprehensive housing typology, in accordance with strict standards for the provision of light, ventilation and green space. These codes and the combinational patterns they generated were inflected by a hierarchy of tree-lined streets of varying widths. At an average height of only two storeys, such an open layout yielded a low density, and Garnier supplemented a 1932 edition of his scheme with residential sectors at a higher density. Integral to the residential quarters were different categories of schools, sited to serve specific districts, while facilities for technical and professional education were located between the residential and industrial sectors.

It has recently been shown that Garnier did not arrive at the concept of his city in isolation, and that among the remarkable young *pensionnaires* who were his colleagues at the French Academy in Rome must be counted Léon Jaussely, whose Prix de Rome entry of 1903, 'A Metropolitan Square in a Large Democratic State', resembled in many respects the layout, content and ethos of the cultural and administrative centre of Garnier's Cité, which was rendered as a 'space of public appearance' where a museum, a library, a theatre, a stadium and a vast public indoor swimming pool or *hydrothérapie* building are grouped around the axis of an assembly complex. The prime organizing principle of this last-lozenge-shaped structure is a peristyle of reinforced-concrete columns which enclose a cluster of union meeting rooms and a central circular 3000-seat assembly hall, flanked on one side by an auditorium seating 1,000 and on the other by two 500-seat amphitheatres set side by side. Ostensibly dedicated to different democratic purposes, from parliamentary debate to conferences, committee work and cinematic display, the various kinds of assembly would have taken place here beneath the rationalistic image of a 24-hour clock and an entablature which bore Courbet-like reliefs and was inscribed with two quotations from Zola's *Travail*. The first of these texts alluded to the Saint-Simonian programme for achieving international harmony through industrial production and communication, and the second to the ritualistic celebration of a utopian socialist harvest:

This was the incessant production suitable for epochs of peace, rails and yet more rails, so that all frontiers might be passed over, and so

81    Garnier, Cité Industrielle: the centre (with lozenge-shaped assembly building) and housing, 1917.

that all peoples, reunited, might form a single people, on an earth entirely furrowed by routes. These were the great steel ships, no longer the abominable ships of war carrying devastation and death, but ships of solidarity and fraternity, exchanging the products of continents, increasing the domestic riches of humanity tenfold, to that point when tremendous abundance reigned throughout.

It was resolved that the feast would take place in the open air, near to the town, in a vast field, where the high corn sheaves stood, like the symmetrical columns of a giant temple, the colour of gold under the clear sun. The colonnade stretched to infinity, to the far horizon, sheaves and yet more sheaves, telling of the inexhaustible fertility of the earth. And there it was that they sang and danced, with the good smell of the ripe corn, in the middle of the immense fertile plain, from which the labour of men, reconciled at last, obtained enough bread for the happiness of all.

This last passage directly evoked that Classical arcadian life and landscape that Garnier had first fully understood after his visit to Greece in 1903. Like the agora, of which it was intended to be the modern counterpart, Garnier's assembly building was depicted as being populated by shadowy figures whose latter-day Biedermeier clothing evoked an appropriately Classical atmosphere. Their houses were to be equally plain, without cornices and mouldings and in many instances planned around courtyards and drained by *impluvia*. In

short, despite its use of advanced constructional methods, its adoption of reinforced-concrete construction throughout (Hennebique) and its use of large steel spans in the industrial sector, after Contamin's Galerie des Machines of 1889, the Cité Industrielle remained above all else the vision of a Mediterranean socialist arcadia.

For all that Garnier in Rome had been influenced by other important French urbanists, such as Léon Jaussely and Eugène Hénard, whose first articles on urban transformation appeared in 1903, the unique contribution of his city lay as much in the extraordinary level of detail to which it was developed as in the 'modernity' of its vision. Garnier's project not only stipulated the principles and the layout for a hypothetical industrial city; it also delineated, at many different scales, the specific substance of its urban typology, while giving at the same time precise indications as to the mode of its construction in concrete and steel. Nothing as comprehensive as this had been attempted since Ledoux's ideal city of Chaux of 1804. While *Une Cité industrielle* was not published until 1917, its author's contribution to contemporary urbanism was already being acknowledged by 1920, when Le Corbusier published material from the Cité folio in the Purist review *L'Esprit Nouveau*.

Despite the obvious impact of the Cité on urbanistic thought of Le Corbusier, its overall influence was limited since, aside from Garnier's isolated works in Lyons, its basic propositions were never tested nor extensively published.

82   Garnier, Cité Industrielle: detail of assembly building, 1904–17.

Unlike Ebenezer Howard's garden city model of 1898, which was realized as a developmental strategy at Letchworth Garden City in 1903, it could hardly be referred to as a proven model. These two alternatives could not in fact have been more opposed, for where Garnier's Cité was inherently expandable and graced with a certain autonomy due to its base in heavy industry, Howard's Rurisville was limited in size and economically dependent, with its base in light industry and small-scale agriculture. And where Garnier's Cité, in conjunction with Jaussely's Barcelona project of 1904, was to influence the theoretical planning models developed during the first decade of the Soviet Union, Howard's schema was to lead to the reformist proliferation of 'garden city' communities and eventually to the equally pragmatic New Town programme that emerged in England after the Second World War.

Garnier's urbanistic thought was expressed in his *Grands travaux de la ville de Lyons* of 1920, his abattoirs of 1906–32, his Grande Blanche hospital of 1909–30 and his Etats-Unis quarter, designed in 1924 and built by 1935. Each of these complexes amounted to a city in miniature that reasserted through its amenities the sovereignty of the city as a civilizing force – a mission for which the Anglo-Saxon garden city had little capacity.

83  Garnier, abattoir, La Mouche, Lyons, 1917.

## Chapter 11

# Auguste Perret: the evolution of Classical Rationalism 1899-1925

In the beginning architecture is only wooden framework. In order to overcome fire one builds in hard material. And the prestige of the wooden frame is such that one reproduces all the traits, including the heads of the nails.

Auguste Perret
*Contribution à une théorie de l'architecture*
Paris, 1952

In 1897, after abruptly terminating a brilliant career at the Ecole des Beaux-Arts, Auguste Perret left the academic guidance of his master Julien Guadet to work for his father. This move consolidated his previous part-time involvement in the family contracting firm. Of his works from this period, starting as early as 1890, those designed after Perret left the Beaux-Arts are the most interesting, since they set the stage for the rest of his career. Of these, two are of considerable significance: a casino at St Malo, of 1899, and an apartment building in the Avenue Wagram, Paris, of 1902. Where the one was a Structural Rationalist essay in the 'national-romantic' style then being popularized in the rustic villas of Hector Guimard, the other was an eight-storey Louis-Quinze-cum-Art-Nouveau essay in dressed stone. Of the two, the latter has to be regarded as Perret's essential point of departure, since it demonstrated his conscious return to the Classical tradition, a return that even anticipated, by a few years, the 1907 'crystallization' of the Secession Style in the work of such men as Behrens, Hoffmann and Olbrich.

The Avenue Wagram building projected by a bay-window depth over the pavement as it ascended to its colonnaded sixth floor. This swelling stone profile was subtly complemented by a carved vine ornament which rose sinuously from the threshold to blossom forth in petrified abundance under the plinth of the sixth-floor colonnade. Attached to Symbolism, Perret had designed the masonry of this structure so as to evoke the floral imagery of the Belle Epoque. At the same time, not wishing to violate the *ordonnance* of a Parisian street, he took care to align its moulded openings with those of the Classical façades on either side. All this, however, contradicted the Structural Rationalist canon, for it was patently not the architecture of articulate structure such as had been advocated by Viollet-le-Duc. Nor was it the naturally expressive and vernacular use of structure which Perret had displayed in the Casino at St Malo.

Two books seem to have been influential in bringing Perret to adopt a trabeated concrete structure for his apartment block in the Rue Franklin of 1903: Auguste Choisy's monumental *Histoire de l'architecture* (1899) and Paul Christophe's text on the Hennebique system, *Le Béton armé et ses applications* (1902). Where the first cited Greek trabeation as the Classical precedent for such structures, the second provided a definitive technique for the fabrication and design of a reinforced-concrete frame.

84  Perret, Casino, St Malo, 1899.

85　Perret, 25 bis Rue Franklin, Paris, 1903.

Choisy, Professor of Architecture at the Ecole des Ponts et Chaussées, cultivated a deterministic view of history in which he argued that the various styles had arisen not as the sports of fashion but as the logical consequence of developments in building technique. His preferred examples of such technically determined styles were (after Viollet-le-Duc) the Greek and the Gothic, although it was, of course, his reference to the former that made him the last influential theorist of Classical Rationalism. Choisy succeeded a long line of such Rationalists, dating back like Guadet and Labrouste to the 18th-century theorists Cordemoy and Laugier. Like most proponents of this school, Choisy saw nothing irrational in the Greek transposition of timber forms into the masonry components of the Doric order.

Perret's initial use of ferroconcrete accorded more closely with Choisy's characterization of the Gothic as an architecture of rib-work and infill. In compositional terms, the Rue Franklin block compressed the format adopted one year earlier in the Avenue Wagram. In each case street façades, divided into five bays, with end bays corbelling out over the pavement, rise five or six storeys in height and terminate in an additional 'capping' floor, before setting back. This floor in the Avenue Wagram is emphasized through an attached colonnade, while in the Rue Franklin its elemental character is stressed by the frame of two open loggias. There, however, all correspondence ends, for whereas the Wagram building is monolithic and horizontally expansive, the Rue Franklin block is articulated and vertically attenuated. The articulation of its columns and the rise of its high pitched set-back roof give something of a Gothic feeling to this otherwise orthogonal structure, recalling the 17th-century work of Mansart. This was the closest that Perret was to come to the detailed prescription of Viollet-le-Duc. The reason for its hollow U-form front, so suggestive of the attentuations of the Gothic, was in fact eminently pragmatic: Perret could get more floor area by providing the regulation court at the front, rather than the rear. With equal ingenuity, he clad the rear wall of the building with glass lenses in order not to infringe an easement.

After 1903 Perret, like Choisy, regarded the *charpente* or structural frame as the quintessential expression of built form. The ferroconcrete frame of the Rue Franklin block was tiled in such a way as to suggest post and lintel construction in wood – the remainder being either windows or solid panels faced in ceramic mosaic. While the tessellated sunflowers of the latter gave the building that quality of fossilized Art Nouveau so peculiar to the end of the Belle Epoque, the frame itself, and the open planning it permitted, pointed towards Le Corbusier's later development of the free plan.

The firm of Perret Frères, consisting of Auguste and his brother Gustave, played an essential role in the development of Perret's style. In 1905 they erected a remarkable four-storey mechanical stacking garage in the Rue de Ponthieu. This was followed in 1912 by a house designed by Paul Guadet, Julien Guadet's son. Executed in reinforced concrete and rising in each instance to an attic floor or frieze capped by a projecting cornice, these works show the progressive refinement of a rational, trabeated Perret 'house-style'. Where the former may be regarded as having anticipated the format of Perret's later ecclesiastical style, the latter must be seen as the prototypical Perret façade, a modulated format that was given its ultimate expression in his reconstruction of Le Havre after the end of the Second World War.

In 1911–13 came the tour de force of the Théâtre des Champs-Elysées, following the unhappy confrontation between Auguste Perret and Henry van de Velde. Commissioned by the theatrical director G. Astruc in 1910, Van de Velde soon realized that on such a restricted site it was necessary to work in reinforced concrete, and he therefore hired Perret Frères as contractors. The decision was unfortunate, for Perret challenged the structural feasibility of his design, and proposed a similar scheme of his own. Within six months Perret's views had prevailed and Van de Velde had been reduced in status from collaborating architect to *architecte-consultant*.

While the plan and elevation of the Théâtre des Champs-Elysées were essentially Van de Velde's, its realization proved both Perret's mastery of detail and the technical prowess of the firm of Perret Frères. The programme required three auditoria, seating 1,250, 500 and 150 people respectively, with full ancillary space comprising stage, backstage, foyers, cloakrooms, etc., all on a site some 37 metres wide and 95 metres deep (120 by 310 feet). Perret suspended his main circular auditorium within a perimeter of eight columns and four bowspring arches, both elements being integral with a continuous monolithic frame that rose from a raft foundation. The basic matrix of the skeleton was augmented by the intelligent application of cantilevers and trussed girders, so that the required volumes could be accom-

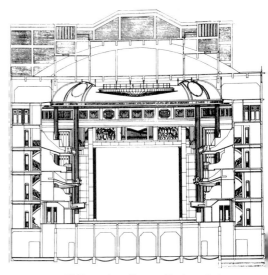

86  Perret, Théâtre des Champs-Elysées, Paris, 1911–13. Section of the large auditorium, with reliefs by Bourdelle.

modated exactly within the confines of the site. Little of this dynamic structure is expressed on the exterior, which at the back and sides is generally rendered as a trabeated frame filled with brick. The main façade, however, is Classically treated, being faced with stone in a regular manner which is only tenuously related to the rich columnar subdivision of the foyer within. At the same time, the Symbolist culture of Paris, inherited from the Belle Epoque, still found a certain expression – both internally and externally – in the low reliefs and friezes of Antoine Bourdelle, and in the mural paintings of Maurice Denis. This nostalgia for a mythological antiquity found further reflection in the handrails, light fittings and furnishings designed by Perret himself.

In the decade following the inauguration of this theatre in 1913, Perret Frères were occupied with a remarkable series of utilitarian ferroconcrete structures, including dock buildings in Casablanca and various workshops in the vicinity of Paris. Then suddenly, in 1922, came Auguste Perret's first church commission, Notre-Dame du Raincy, completed in 1924. Here Perret arrived at the most pure formulation of his ferroconcrete style, almost twenty years after it first appeared in the Rue Franklin. The church was important not only for its elegant proportions and syntactic refinement but also for its formulation of the cylindrical column articulated within a non-load-bearing envelope. The precepts of Choisy were respected throughout, from the perforated, prefabricated wall screens to the fluted, tapered columns — each component reduced to its most explicit structural essence.

Immediately after Le Raincy there came two temporary structures which were the climax of Perret's early career: his art gallery, the Palais de Bois, built in 1924 of standard timber scantlings which were reused after dismantling, and his small arena theatre in the Exposition des Arts Décoratifs of 1925. Whereas the art gallery, like the Le Raincy church, was one of Perret's most articulate structures, the temporary theatre of light-weight construction was designed to simulate a heavy monolithic frame. The actual structure consisted of circular timber columns carrying a grid of steel-reinforced light-weight clinker beams. The whole was finished internally in lathe and plaster and clad externally in synthetic stone. As such it was certainly removed from the structural purity that had always been essential to the Rationalist thesis. This 'deception' was excused by the designer on the grounds that had it been permanent he would have built it in reinforced concrete.

For all its impurity, the Arts Décoratifs theatre was the most lucid and lyrical statement that Perret ever made. Eight internal free-standing columns supported a ceiling 'ring' beam which through ingenious transformations across its four diagonal corners supported a gridded and coffered skylight over the cruciform arena. The transverse loads of this inner structure were to be transferred to a perimeter beam, supported by a system of free-standing columns regularly spaced around the outside of the auditorium. Externally, however, the expression remained awkward and these apparently 'redundant' columns that articulated the blank exterior reflected Perret's preoccupation with the creation of a new 'national-classical' style, an obsession that was severely to limit the development of his later work.

Apart from the lucidity of his architecture, and the extraordinary refinement attained in his built work, Perret's significance as a theoretician lay in his aphoristic, dialectical turn of mind — in the importance that he attached to such polarities as order versus disorder, frame versus infill, permanent versus impermanent, mobile versus immobile, reason versus imagination, and so on. Comparable oppositions may be found throughout the entire corpus of Le Corbusier's work. In the Exposition des Arts Décoratifs of 1925, however, the ways of these two figures had already begun to diverge, and not only in their respective exhibition structures, but also at the level of theory, for nothing could have been more removed from Perret's precepts than *Les 5 points d'une architecture nouvelle* that Le Corbusier published a year later in 1926.

87    Perret, theatre, Exposition des Arts Décoratifs, Paris, 1925.

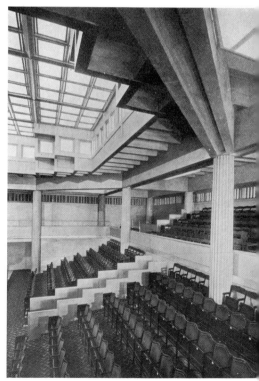

## Chapter 12

# The Deutsche Werkbund 1898-1927

Britain, the pioneer, found it more profitable to invest her surpluses abroad than to modernise her home environment and production. This meant that the élan of 20th-century industrialism did not emerge in Britain. It emerged in a newer industrial nation like Germany, which, wishing to penetrate into new overseas markets traditionally preserved by the older maritime powers, systematically studied the products of her competitors, and by typological selection and re-design helped to forge the machine aesthetic of the 20th century.

C.M. Chipkin
'Lutyens and Imperialism',
*RIBA Journal,* 1969

With the Prussian suppression of the Saxon Revolt in 1849 — a revolt in which both Mikhail Bakunin and Richard Wagner played prominent roles — Gottfried Semper, architect and liberal revolutionary, fled from Dresden, first to Paris, and then two years later, as the result of a special commission, to London. There, on the occasion of the 1851 Exhibition, he wrote his famous essay *Wissenschaft, Industrie und Kunst (Science, Industry and Art),* published in German in 1852, where he examined the impact of industrialization and mass consumption on the entire field of applied art and architecture. A decade before William Morris and his associates produced their first domestic objects, Semper crystallized his critique of industrial civilization: 'We have artists but no actual art.' In tough-minded opposition to the Pre-Raphaelite dream of returning to a pre-industrial era, Semper took the view that

Unremittingly science enriches itself and life with newly discovered useful materials and natural powers that work miracles, with new methods and techniques, with new tools and machines. It is already evident that inventions no longer are, as they had been in earlier times, means for warding off want and for helping consumption; instead, want and consumption are the means to market the inventions. The order of things has been reversed.

Later in the same text, he analyzed the impact on design of new methods and materials:

the hardest porphyry and granite are cut like butter and polished like wax, ivory is softened and pressed into shapes, caoutchouc and gutta percha are vulcanized and used to produce deceptive imitations of carvings in wood, metal, or stone, whereby the natural aspects of the simulated materials are greatly surpassed. . . . The abundance of means is the first serious danger with which art has to struggle. This term is in fact a paradox (there is no abundance of means, but rather a lack of ability to master them), yet it is justified in so far as it correctly describes the absurdities of our situation.

He then went on to ask:

Where will the depreciation of material that results from its treatment by machines, from substitutes for it from so many new inventions, lead? And where the depreciation of labour, of paintings, of fine art and furnishings, which originates from the same causes. . . . How will time or science bring law and order into this until now thoroughly confused state of affairs? How will it prevent the general devaluation from expanding into the area of work which is executed by hand in the true old fashion, so that one may find in it more than affection, antiquarianism, superficial appearance and obstinacy?

In this militant and incisive manner Semper raised the prime issues of the century, and touched on a range of cultural problems which even today are far from resolved. His ideas gradually became integrated into 19th-century German cultural theory, largely through the publication of his major theoretical text, *Der Stil in den technischen und tektonischen Künsten oder praktische Ästhetik* ('Style in industrial and structural arts or practical aesthetics') of 1860–63.

His general thesis of the socio-political influence on style was misunderstood until after the intense industrial expansion that occurred in Germany during the last quarter of the century. At the Philadelphia Centennial Exhibition of 1876 German industrial and applied art products were regarded as inferior to those from England and America. Franz Reuleaux, a mechanical engineer, who by then had been Semper's colleague for ten years at the Eidgenössische Technische Hochschule in Zürich, wrote from Philadelphia in 1877 that German products were 'cheap and nasty'. 'German industry must relinquish the principles of competition in price alone' and instead use 'the intellectual power and the skill of the worker to refine the product and this to a greater degree the more it approaches art'.

For twenty years after the unification of Germany in 1870, German industry had neither the time nor the cause to heed such criticism. Under Bismarck's stable leadership it was concerned solely with the task of development and expansion. A crucial factor in this development was the founding by Emil Rathenau in 1883 of the Allgemeine Elektricitäts Gesellschaft (AEG) in Berlin. This electrical company grew, in the space of seven years, into a vast industrial combine, with a wide range of products and interests extending all over the world.

After the resignation of Bismarck in 1890, a great change occurred in the cultural climate of Germany. Numerous critics held that improved design in both craft and industry was essential to future prosperity, and that Germany, without a cheap source of materials or a ready outlet for inexpensive goods, could only begin to compete for a share of the world market with products of exceptionally high quality. This argument was enlarged upon by the nationalist and Christian-Social Democrat Friedrich Naumann in his 1904 essay *Die Kunst im Maschinenzeitalter* ('Art in the Epoch of the Machine'). There he argued, in opposition to William Morris's Luddism, that such quality could only be economically achieved by an artistically cultivated people, oriented towards machine production.

This spur of industrialism and Pan-German nationalism made the Prussian bureaucracy react against the philistinism of Wilhelmine Germany and encourage the incipient Arts and Crafts revival of an 'intrinsic' Germanic culture. To this end, in 1896, Hermann Muthesius was sent to London as an attaché to the German Embassy, with a charge to study English architecture and design. He returned to Germany in 1904 and took up the post of privy councillor to the Prussian Board of Trade, with a special assignment to reform the national programme of education in applied art. This official *Kunstgewerbeschule* (school of arts and crafts) reform movement had been anticipated by Karl Schmidt's foundation in 1898 of the Dresdner Werkstätten für Handwerkskunst (Dresden Workshop for Manual Art) at Dresden. In 1903 the whole movement had gained considerable impetus from the appointment of Peter Behrens as principal of the Düsseldorf Kunstgewerbeschule. In 1904 Muthesius propagated his ideal model of a native craft culture in his book *Das Englische Haus*. For him the importance of British Arts and Crafts architecture and furniture lay in its demonstration of craftsmanship and economy as the basis of good design.

Two years later, in 1906, as *Arbeitskommissar* to the third German Exhibition of Arts and Crafts in Dresden, Muthesius aligned himself with Naumann and Schmidt against the conservative and protectionist group of artists and craftsmen known as the Alliance for German Applied Arts by severely criticizing the state of applied art in Germany, while at the same time advocating the adoption of mass production. In the following year the three men founded the Deutsche Werkbund, whose initial membership comprised twelve independent artists and twelve craft firms. The individuals were Peter

Behrens, Theodor Fischer, Josef Hoffmann, Wilhelm Kreis, Max Laeuger, Adelbert Niemeyer, J. M. Olbrich, Bruno Paul, Richard Riemerschmid, J. J. Scharvolgel, Paul Schultze-Naumburg and Fritz Schumacher. The firms were Peter Bruckmann & Söhne, Deutsche Werkstätten für Handwerkskunst Dresden-Hellerau und München, Eugen Diederichs, Gebrüder Klingspor, Kunstdruckerei Kunstlerbund Karlsruhe, Poeschel & Trepte, Saalecker Werkstätten, Vereinigte Werkstätten für Kunst und Handwerk München, Werkstätten für deutschen Hausrat Theophil Müller Dresden, Wiener Werkstätten, Wilhelm & Co. and Gottlob Wunderlich.

The Werkbund members dedicated themselves to the betterment of craft education and to the establishment of a centre for advancing the aims of their institution. As one might suspect from the heterogeneous nature of the founding group, the Werkbund was by no means totally committed to Muthesius's ideal of normative design for industrial production. It is significant that the site first proposed for the founding ceremony of the Werkbund was in Nuremburg — the setting of Wagner's guild opera *Die Meistersinger*.

The subsequent development of the Werkbund, particularly in its relationship to industry, is inseparable from that phase of Behrens's career which started in 1907 with his appointment as architect and designer to the AEG, for whom he was to evolve a house style ranging from graphics to product design and industrial plant. He brought to this challenging task his innate graphic ability and his experience as a precocious Jugendstil designer during his period at the Darmstadt colony in 1899–1903. His Darmstadt style was to be transformed under the influence of the Beuronic monastic school of geometrical proportion, as then practised by the Dutch architect J.L.M. Lauweriks, who joined Behrens in Düsseldorf when the latter became principal of the applied arts school there in 1903.

Behrens's 'empathetic' manner, his so-called 'Zarathustrastil', was epitomized in his Vorhalle for the Turin International Exhibition of 1902. Here energetic sinuous line and expressive arcuated form were combined in an attempt to evoke the Nietzschean 'will to form'.

88   Behrens, poster for AEG bulbs, before 1910

This rhetoric gave way, under the influence of Lauweriks, to an airless atectonic style, first manifest in the pavilions that Behrens built at Oldenburg in 1905. This Neo-Quattrocento-Beuronic manner was elaborated by Behrens in his design for a crematorium built at Hagen in 1906 and adapted, with Neo-Classical overtones, to the pavilion he designed for the AEG at the Berlin ship-building exhibition of 1908.

On joining AEG, Behrens was confronted with the brute fact of industrial power. In exchange for his youthful visions of revitalizing German cultural life through an elaborately staged mystic ritual, he had to accept industrialization as the manifest destiny of the German nation; or, as he conceived of it, as the composite issue of *Zeitgeist* and *Volksgeist*, to which it was his duty as an artist to give form. Thus the Turbine Factory that he built for AEG in 1909 was a deliberate reification of industry as the one vital rhythm of modern life. Far from being a straightforward design in iron and glass (such as the 19th-century railway shed), Behrens's Turbine Factory was a conscious work of art, a temple to industrial power. While accepting the ascendancy of science and industry with pessimistic resignation, Behrens sought to bring the factory under the rubric of the farm – to restore to factory production that sense of common purpose innate in agriculture, a feeling for which the newly urbanized semi-skilled labour of Berlin would supposedly still have a certain nostalgia. How else should one account for the faceted gable roof of the Turbine Hall or for the Sittesque farmyard layout of the AEG Brunnenstrasse complex of 1910? On joining AEG, Behrens had modified his Oldenburg manner, retaining its formal strength but dispensing with its rigid geometry. Thus the light steel frame of the street façade of the Turbine Factory is terminated at the ends by solid battered corner elements whose surfaces are rendered in such a way as to deny any capacity for sustaining load. This atectonic formula of flanking light trabeated frames with massive corners characterizes virtually all the industrial structures that Behrens designed for AEG. Where the skeletal frame was not a functional prerequisite, as in his Neo-Classical German Embassy in St Petersburg of 1912, this Schinkelesque corner emphasis is evident but less pronounced.

In 1908 Behrens revealed his essentially conservative nature in an essay entitled *Was ist monumentale Kunst?* ('What is Monumental Art?'), where he defined such art as an expression of the dominant power group in any given epoch. In this same text he took issue with Semper's theoretical derivation of environmental form from technical and material exigencies. He rejected the importance which Semper attached to the typical tectonic element – to the expressive load-bearing column as it appears in Classical architecture. Instead Behrens was profoundly influenced by Alois Riegl's élitist theory of the *Kunstwollen* or 'will to form' which acts through the agency of talented individuals as an ordained 'atectonic' principle. For Riegl this force was destined to oppose the specific technical propensities of an epoch. Consistent with this thesis, Behrens's contribution to AEG product design was to be in the realm of style rather than technique.

This split between *Norm* and *Form*, between *type* and *individuality*, was soon to preoccupy the members of the Deutsche Werkbund. The issue came to a head with Hermann Muthesius's address to the Werkbund assembly on the occasion of the Deutsche Werkbund Exhibition, held in Cologne in 1914. Muthesius's ten-point programme, highly influenced by the writings of Naumann, concentrated on the need for refining typical objects (cf. Le Corbusier's *objet-type*). In points 1 and 2 he argued that architecture and industrial design can attain significance only through the development and refinement of types (*Typisierung*), and in points 3–10 he dealt with the national need for products of high standard, so that these could be readily sold on the world market. Point 9 dealt with mass production and read: 'A precondition for export is the existence of efficient big firms, whose taste is impeccable. Particular single objects designed by artists would not even cover the demand in Germany'.

This opportunistic emphasis on designing cultural objects for an international middle class was immediately challenged by Henry van de Velde who, in presenting his counter-thesis, at once rejected 'export' art and proclaimed the essential creative sovereignty of the individual artist. For him, as for Behrens, only the natural process of Riegl's *Kunstwollen* could gradually bring about the evolution of a civilized *Norm*. Despite much controversy over this issue, there was enough support for Van de Velde's position, from figures as diverse as Walter Gropius and Karl Ernst Osthaus, for Muthesius to be forced to withdraw his programme. In his ten-point presentation Muthesius had elaborated his idea of type as follows: 'The way from individualism to the creation of types is

89 Behrens, German Embassy, St Petersburg, (Leningrad), 1912.

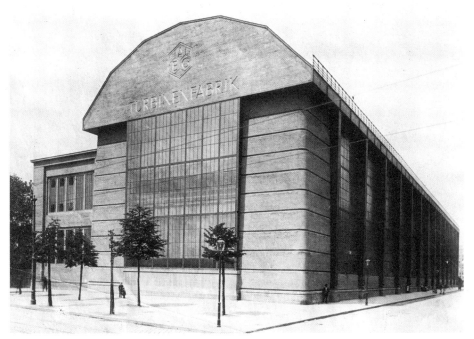

90  Behrens, AEG Turbine Factory, Berlin, 1908–09.

91  Behrens, AEG Factory complex, Berlin, in 1912. Left, the high-voltage works; right, the assembly plant.

the organic way of development', he argued. 'This is, today, the way in manufacture, where the product . . . is steadily being improved.' Again, he declared: 'Essentially, architecture tends towards the typical. The type discards the extraordinary and establishes order.' Thus for Muthesius, as for Semper before him, 'type' had two connotations: the 'product object' gradually refined through use and production, and the 'tectonic object', which was an irreducible building element functioning as a basic unit of architectural language.

The need for such a syntax, in the face of the sudden collapse of the Jugendstil, brought most of the architects at the 1914 Deutsche Werkbund Exhibition, including Muthesius, Behrens and Hoffmann, to express themselves in the language of a reinterpreted Neo-Classicism. The only two exceptions to this were Van de Velde's Werkbund Theatre, endowed by his form-force aesthetic with a quasi-theosophical aura, and its close rival, Bruno Taut's Glass Pavilion, which evoked the ritualistic mysticism of Behrens's Turin Vorhalle of 1902.

The 1914 Exhibition introduced to a wide public a new generation of Werkbund artists,

including in particular Gropius and Adolf Meyer, who up to 1910 had worked together in the office of Behrens. Gropius's activity between 1910 and 1914 followed along the lines of Behrens's Berlin career. In March 1910 he submitted to Emil Rathenau of AEG a memorandum on rationalized house production, as exemplified by workers' houses that he had projected for Janikow in 1906. This text, written by Gropius at the age of twenty-six, remains even today one of the most exhaustive and lucid expositions ever made of the essential preconditions for the successful prefabrication, assembly and distribution of standardized housing units. In 1911 the new partnership of Gropius and Meyer was commissioned by Karl Benscheidt to design the Fagus shoe-last factory, at Alfeld-an-der-Leine. In 1913 the Deutsche Werkbund *Jahrbuch* carried an article by Gropius on industrial building, illustrated by grain silos and multi-storey factories taken from the industrial vernacular of the New World. In the same year he started to work as an industrial designer, designing the body-work and layout of a diesel locomotive and then the interior of a railway sleeping car. Finally, he and Meyer designed a model factory for the Werkbund Exhibition of 1914.

In the Faguswerk, Gropius and Meyer adapted the syntax of Behrens's Turbine Factory to a more open architectural aesthetic. The corners still serve to contain the composition, as in all of Behrens's large AEG structures, but where Behrens's corners are invariably of masonry here they are of glass. The vertical panels of glazing, set forward from the battered brick facing, give the illusion of being miraculously suspended from the upstand at roof level. This 'pendant' effect, plus the translucent corner, inverts the composition of the Turbine Factory, the sheer planar quality of the vertical glass façade being accentuated by the 'Classical' entasis of the brick-faced frame. Despite such transpositions, the Faguswerk, with its atectonic glazing and its nostalgia for the Classical, remained subject to the influence of Behrens.

This particular disposition, which manifested itself compositionally in emphatic corners and string-courses, was to characterize all the

92 Gropius and A. Meyer, detail of the Fagus Factory, Alfeld-an-der-Leine, 1911.

public work of Gropius and Meyer up to Gropius's design for the Dessau Bauhaus in 1924. Certainly it was the stratagem adopted in their model factory complex designed for the Werkbund Exhibition of 1914. Here the corporeality of the glass skin was developed as a continuous membrane to embrace spiral staircases at either end of the building. Within this sheer glass envelope stood a brick armature, its separateness being accentuated by two end pavilions, each capped by a flat roof overhang after the style of Frank Lloyd Wright. In spite of this dramatic reversal of the roles of glass and masonry, the factory layout was highly conventional, not only in its axiality but also in its hierarchic and syntactical separation into 'administrative' and 'productive' elements. The public, 'Classical', 'white-collar' façade was placed to the fore, thus screening the private, utilitarian, 'blue-collar' steel-frame structure to the rear. Such a dualistic solution, however well articulated, would never have been acceptable to Behrens.

The split between Muthesius and Van de Velde effectively exposed the reactionary spirit that was already evident in much of the Werkbund work by the time of the 1914 Exhibition. Whereas the yearbooks of 1913 and 1914 were respectively devoted to 'Art in Industry and Trade', and 'Transport' recording the design of the furnishing of industrial structures, rolling stock, shipping and aircraft, the 1915 yearbook bore the ominous title 'German Form in the War Year', and nostalgically devoted its pages to the predominantly neo-Biedermeier work of the 1914 Exhibition. That the promise and triumph of a progressive industrial state would soon be consumed by an industrialized war seems hardly to have been foreseen. This tragedy was not to be transcended by the quality of the war graves that the Werkbund artists were commissioned to design, which formed the exclusive subject of the Werkbund yearbook issued in 1916/17.

After the war Behrens was a changed man, for the *Volksgeist* was patently no longer the same. Accordingly he gave up his frigid Classicism and his preoccupation with symbolizing the authority of industrial power. His renewed search for an art of building which

93 Gropius and A. Meyer, part of model factory complex, Werkbund Exhibition, Cologne, 1914, with office block on the left.

would express the true spirit of the German people led back, via the pages of Bruno Taut's magazine *Frühlicht*, beyond Behrens's own Neo-Romantic Nietzschean past to forms of medieval origin and association. However, his faith in the redeeming power of Riegl's 'will to form' remained unshaken. When I.G. Farben commissioned him to design their new premises at Frankfurt-Höchst in 1920 he attempted in a brick and stone structure to reinterpret the lost syntax of medieval civic architecture. The building has at its core a mystic space of public ritual and renewal (going back to Behrens's Turin Vorhalle of 1902) in the form of a faceted five-storey hall of corbelled brickwork, capped by a crystalline rooflight. This was an allusion to that theatrical space of public appearance which had inspired his youth, to the *Kultursymbol* that obsessed, with equal intensity, the members of Bruno Taut's Glass Chain (see the next chapter). A similar impulse informed his small exhibition structures of the 1920s — his steeply pitched Dombauhütte (cathedral masons' lodge) with its diagonal banded brickwork, designed for the Munich Kunstgewerbeschau of 1922, and his Wrightian glass conservatory built for the Paris Exposition des Arts Décoratifs in 1925. From then on Behrens's work was to remain close to the Art Deco style, while the future of the Deutsche Werkbund was to be inseparable from the Neue Sachlichkeit movement, which saw its apotheosis, under Werkbund auspices, in the international housing exhibition (including the famous Weissenhofsiedlung) that opened at Stuttgart in 1927.

## Chapter 13

# The Glass Chain: European architectural Expressionism 1910-25

In order to raise our culture to a higher level, we are forced, whether we like it or not, to change our architecture. And this will be possible only if we free the rooms in which we live of their enclosed character. This, however, we can only do by introducing a glass architecture, which admits the light of the sun, of the moon, and of the stars into the rooms, not only through a few windows, but through as many walls as feasible, these to consist entirely of glass – of coloured glass.

Paul Scheerbart
*Glasarchitektur*, 1914

The poet Paul Scheerbart's vision of a culture elevated through the use of glass served to consolidate those aspirations towards a non-repressive sensibility that had first emerged in Munich in 1909 with the foundation of the Neue Künstler Vereinigung. This proto-Expressionist art movement, led by the painter Wassily Kandinsky, gained immediate support in the following year from two anarchist publications, Herwarth Walden's journal *Der Sturm* and Franz Pfemfert's paper *Die Aktion*. These Berlin journals promoted a counter-culture, in opposition to the state culture that had been initiated with the foundation of the Deutsche Werkbund. In 1907 Scheerbart had independently proffered a 'science-fiction' image of a utopian future that was equally inimical to both bourgeois reformism and the culture of the industrial state.

The Cologne Werkbund Exhibition in 1914 gave expression to an ideological split within the Werkbund between the collective acceptance of normative form (*Typisierung*), on the one hand, and the individually asserted, expressive 'will to form' (*Kunstwollen*) on the

other. This opposition, reflected in the contrast between Behrens's Neo-Classical Festhalle and the organic form of Van de Velde's theatre, was comparable in many respects to the difference between the Gropius and Meyer model factory and Bruno Taut's fantasmagoric pavilion for the glass industry; a parallelism which confirms that the split affected more than one generation of Werkbund designers. Where Behrens and Gropius tended towards the normative mode, that is the Classical, Van de Velde and Taut in their buildings manifested a freely expressed *Kunstwollen*.

The aphoristic text of Scheerbart's *Glasarchitektur* was dedicated to Taut, whose Glass Pavilion was inscribed with Scheerbart's aphorisms: 'Light wants crystal'; 'Glass brings a new era'; 'We feel sorry for the brick culture'; 'Without a glass palace, life becomes a burden'; 'Building in brick only does us harm'; 'Coloured glass destroys hatred'. These words dedicated Taut's pavilion to the light that filtered through its faceted cupola and glass block walls to illuminate an axial seven-tiered chamber, lined with glass mosaic. According to Taut this crystalline structure, modelled after his Leipzig Steel Pavilion of 1913, had been designed in the spirit of a Gothic cathedral. It was in effect a *Stadtkrone* or 'city crown', that pyramidal form postulated by Taut as the universal paradigm of all religious building, which together with the faith it would inspire was an essential urban element for the restructuring of society.

The socio-cultural implications of Scheerbart's vision were enlarged on in 1918 by the architect Adolf Behne:

It is not the crazy caprice of a poet that glass architecture will bring a new culture. *It is a fact.*

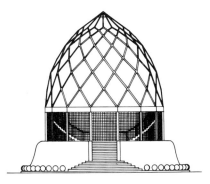

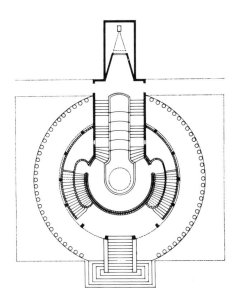

94, 95   Taut, Glass Pavilion, Werkbund Exhibition, Cologne, 1914. *Above*, elevation and plan; *right*, stepped interior with waterfall.

New social welfare organizations, hospitals, inventions, or technical innovations and improvements – these will not *bring a new culture* – but glass architecture will. . . . Therefore the European is right when he fears that glass architecture might become uncomfortable. Certainly it will be so. And that is not its least advantage. For first of all the European must be wrenched out of his cosiness.

With the armistice of November 1918, Taut and Behne began to organize the Arbeitsrat für Kunst, which eventually merged with the somewhat larger Novembergruppe formed at the same time. This Workers' Council for Art declared its basic aims in Taut's *Architekturprogramm* of December 1918, which argued for a new total work of art, to be created with the active participation of the people. In the spring of 1919 the manifesto of the Arbeitsrat für Kunst reasserted this general principle: 'Art and people must form an entity. Art shall no longer be a luxury of the few, but should be enjoyed and experienced by the broad masses.

The aim is the alliance of the arts under the wing of a great architecture.' Led by Behne, Gropius and Taut, and affiliated to the painters of Die Brücke, the Arbeitsrat für Kunst comprised some fifty artists, architects, and patrons living in and around Berlin, including the artists Georg Kolbe, Gerhard Marcks, Lyonel Feininger, Emil Nolde, Hermann Finsterlin, Max Pechstein and Karl Schmidt-Rottluff, and the architects Otto Bartning, Max Taut, Bernhard Hoetger, Adolf Meyer, and Erich Mendelsohn. In April 1919, these last five staged an exhibition of visionary works under the title

'An Exhibition of Unknown Architects'. The introduction that Gropius wrote for this exhibition was, in effect, the first draft of his Weimar Bauhaus programme, published in the same month:

We must want, imagine, and create the new architectural concept co-operatively. Painters, sculptors, break down the barriers around architecture and become co-builders and comrades-in-arms towards art's ultimate goal: the creative idea of the Cathedral of the Future [*Zukunftskathedrale*], which will once more encompass everything in one form – architecture and sculpture and painting.

This call for a new religious building, capable of unifying the creative energy of the society as in the Middle Ages, was echoed by Behne in 1919, in his reply to a group opinion poll, published under the title *Ja! Stimmen des Arbeitsrates für Kunst in Berlin* ('Yes! Voices from the Art Soviet in Berlin'):

The most important thing seems to me to be to construct an ideal House of God, not a denominational one, but a religious one. . . . We must not wait until a new religiosity is upon us, for it may be waiting for us while we are waiting for it.

The suppression of the Spartacist Revolt in 1919 put an end to the overt activities of the Arbeitsrat für Kunst, and the energies of the group were channelled into a series of letters, known as 'Die Gläserne Kette' or the Glass Chain. This was Bruno Taut's 'Utopian Correspondence,' which began in November 1919 after Taut's suggestion that 'everyone of us will draw or write down at brief intervals of time, informally and as the spirit moves him . . . those ideas which he would like to share with our circle.' The correspondence involved fourteen people, of whom only about half created works of enduring importance. Apart from Taut, who called himself *Glas*, there was Gropius (*Mass*), Finsterlin (*Prometh*), and Bruno Taut's brother Max, who wrote under his own name. This inner circle was complemented by architects who had previously only had a peripheral involvement with the Arbeitsrat, notably the brothers Hans and Wassili Luckhardt and Hans

Scharoun. Apart from providing material for Taut's magazine *Frühlicht* ('early light'), the Utopian Correspondence served to expose and develop the various attitudes represented by the circle. Taut and Scharoun especially stressed the important creative role of the unconscious, Scharoun writing in 1919:

We must create just as the blood of our ancestors brought on waves of creativity; and we shall be content if we are ourselves thereafter able to reveal a complete comprehension of the character and the causality of our creations.

By 1920, however, the solidarity of the Glass Chain began to break, with Hans Luckhardt's recognition that free unconscious form and rational prefabricated production were in certain respects incompatible. In that year he wrote:

Opposite to this profoundly spiritual striving is the trend toward automatic processes. The invention of the *Taylor System* is a typical characteristic of this. It would be completely erroneous to refuse to recognize this tendency of the time, as it is a historic fact. Moreover, it can in no way be proven to be hostile toward art.

While Luckhardt's rationalism had the effect of returning the debate to the issues that had divided the Werkbund in 1914, Taut maintained the Scheerbartian views first expressed in books such as *Alpine Architektur* and *Die Stadtkrone* of 1919, publishing his famous *Die Auflösung der Städte* ('The dissolution of cities') in 1920. In common with the socialist planners of the Russian Revolution, he recommended the break-up of cities and the return of the urbanized population to the land. At his most practical, he attempted to formulate models for agrarian and handicraft-based communities; at his most fantastic, he projected the building of glass temples in the Alps. Typical of Taut's Kropotkinian propositions was his model of a circular, radially subdivided, agricultural settlement. In its core were three separate residential sections, one for each class of citizen – *Künder, Künstler und Kinder* (the 'enlightened', artists and children) – each grouped around lozenge-shaped courts.

This tripartite organization led axially to the central crystalline 'Haus des Himmels' or 'House of Heaven', where the governors of the community convened. It is one of the paradoxes of Taut's anarchic socialism that the hierarchic, not to say authoritarian, social institutions imagined for these communities contained the seeds of a fascism that was soon to find its vulgarization in the 'blood and soil' culture of the National Socialist movement.

After becoming city architect to Magdeburg in 1921, Taut attempted to realize his Stadtkrone in the form of a municipal exhibition hall, designed in the following year. By that date, however, the movement propagated by *Frühlicht* was losing its impetus. Taut, like Hans Luckhardt before him, was beginning to come to terms with the harsh reality of the Weimar Republic, where pragmatic social need gave little scope for the achievement of Scheerbart's glass paradise. This much became explicit in 1923, when he started to work with his brother on the design of the first low-cost housing schemes to be commissioned by the government.

Paradoxically, it was not Taut but Hans Poelzig who was to realize the quintessential image of the crystalline 'city crown'. The 5,000-seat theatre that he designed for Max Reinhardt in Berlin in 1919 came closer to Scheerbart in its scintillating luminous·dissolution of form and space than any post-war achievement by Taut. Of its fantastic stalactite interior, Wassili Luckhardt wrote:

The interior of the large dome is hung with an infinite variety of pendants which are given a softly curving movement by the hollow of the cupola on to which they are fastened, so that especially when light is thrown against the tiny reflectors on each tip, the impression of a certain dissolution and infinity results.

After establishing himself as an architect in Breslau in 1911, Poelzig had realized two seminal works which anticipated the later formal language of both Taut and Mendelsohn: a water tower for Posen (a Stadtkrone image if ever there was) and an office building for Breslau, which led to the architectural format of Mendelsohn's *Berliner-Tageblatt* building of

96  Poelzig, Grosse Schauspielhaus, Berlin, 1919.

97  Poelzig, chemical plant, Luban, 1912.

1921. In addition, Poelzig's highly articulated brick chemical plant built at Luban in 1912 came close to rivalling the industrial style that Behrens had just invented for AEG.

After the war, in his address as chairman of the Werkbund in 1919, Poelzig returned to the controversy over *Typisierung* and effectively argued yet again for the principle of the *Kunstwollen*. A year later, he announced his affinity with the artists of the Glass Chain, in his Salzburg Festspielhaus project where his newly invented pendentive motif was piled up into a Stadtkrone image of heroic proportions. As in his Istanbul 'Freundschaftshaus' (House of Friendship) project of 1917, these arched forms were assembled in such a way as to create a ziggurat whose interior was a prismatic cavern made up entirely of pendentive elements. Apart from his sets for Paul Wegener's film *The Golem* (1920), the Schauspielhaus for Reinhardt was Poelzig's last fully Expressionist work. By 1925, with his Capitol Cinema for Berlin, he had already returned to the crypto-Classical fold.

Mendelsohn realized his own version of the Stadtkrone in the observatory that he built for Albert Einstein at Potsdam in 1917–21. Combining as it did the sculptural forms of Van de Velde's Werkbund Theatre and the overall profile of Bruno Taut's Glass Pavilion, the design's point of departure lay in the 1914 Werkbund Exhibition. In its final silhouette, however, the Einstein Tower displayed a certain formal affinity to the thatched-roof vernacular of the Dutch architects Eijbink and Snellbrand, who, with Theo van Wijdeveld, represented the extreme organic wing of Dutch Expressionism, centred around Wijdeveld's magazine *Wendingen* ('Turnings'). It is hardly surprising, therefore, that soon after the completion of the observatory Mendelsohn visited Holland, at Wijdeveld's invitation, to see the work of the *Wendingen* circle for himself. In Amsterdam he visited a number of Expressionist housing schemes which were then under construction, as part of Berlage's plan for Amsterdam South, including Michel de Klerk's Eigen Haard (1913–19) and Piet Kramer's De Dageraad (1918–23). Executed in moulded brickwork and tile-

98  Mendelsohn, Einstein Tower, Potsdam, 1917–21. Front and side elevations and half-plan.

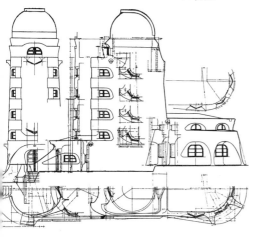

hanging, they exemplified a much more structural approach than the highly plastic and folkish preoccupations of Wijdeveld's 'vernacular' architects. Outside the Amsterdam School of Wijdeveld, De Klerk and Kramer, Mendelsohn met and was influenced by a number of Dutch architects of quite different persuasion, such as the rationalist Rotterdam architect J.J.P. Oud and the Wrightian architect W.M. Dudok, practising in Hilversum. In a letter to his wife, Mendelsohn explained how neither the Amsterdam nor the Rotterdam school met with his full approval:

Analytic Rotterdam refuses vision; visionary Amsterdam does not understand objectivity. Certainly the primary element is function but function without sensibility remains mere construction. More than ever, I stand by my reconciliatory programme. . . . Otherwise, Rotterdam will pursue the way of mere construction, with deathly chill in its veins, and Amsterdam will be destroyed by the fire of its own dynamism. Function plus dynamics is the challenge.

As this letter suggests, the more structural of the Dutch Expressionists had an immediate impact on Mendelsohn's own development: after his visit to Holland he turned from the plasticity of his Potsdam observatory towards a concern for the intrinsic structural expressiveness of materials. The hat factory that he built at Luckenwalde in 1921–23 reflects this influence. Its ridged and pitched-roofed dye shop and production sheds, modelled in the manner of De Klerk, stood in strong contrast to the smooth flat-roofed power house whose layered 'cubist' expression in brick and concrete recalls the early work of Dudok. The principle established here, of setting dramatic tall pitched industrial forms against horizontal administrative elements, was repeated by Mendelsohn in his Leningrad textile mill project of 1925. In this instance, however, a further step was taken, for the banded modelling of the administration block anticipated the profiling of his metropolitan department stores, built in Breslau, Stuttgart, Chemnitz and Berlin between 1927 and 1931. From now on, as Reyner Banham has observed, he thought 'in

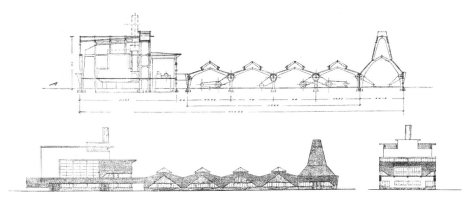

99  Mendelsohn, hat fac-
tory, Luckenwalde, 1921–
23. *Above*, section; *below*,
elevation from front to
back, and rear elevation of
building at front.

100  Mendelsohn, Peters-
dorff Store, Breslau (Wroclaw), 1927.

121

GUT GARKAU

101   Häring, farm at Garkau, 1924. Buildings for
animals (upper left) and barns.

terms of structural assemblies of geometrical,
simple units which presented themselves to the
eye as tidily profiled edges.'

In the masterwork of Hugo Häring, the farm
complex at Garkau near Lübeck built in 1924,
we find a somewhat similar expressive use of
pitched-roof forms contrasted with bulky
tectonic elements and rounded corners. A few
years earlier, Häring had shared an office in Berlin with Mies van der Rohe, four years his
junior, and there is evidence that for a brief
while the two men exercised a certain influence
on each other. This is particularly noticeable in
their entries to the famous Friedrichstrasse
office building competition of 1921, where they
adopted a similar organic approach to the
genesis of form. As one might expect, however,
it was Mies rather than Häring who put forward
a structure made entirely of glass. Mies's
Scheerbartian obsession with the reflectivity of
this material also manifested itself in an extraordinary project for a glass skyscraper which was
published in 1922 in the last issue of Taut's
magazine Frühlicht.

Although Häring, like Mendelsohn, believed
in the ultimate primacy of function, he sought
to transcend the primitive nature of mere utility
by evolving his forms from a more profound
understanding of the programme. Like Scharoun, however, his attitude to massing was
often naïvely imitative of biological form.
In this respect, one may see Scharoun's Home
and Work Exhibition building at Breslau of
1928 as influenced by Häring's Prinz Albrecht
Garten residential project of 1924. Despite an
overtly Expressionist tendency, Häring re-

mained preoccupied with the inner source of
form, with that which he termed the Organwerk
or the programmatic essence of the 'organism',
as opposed to its surface expression or Gestalt-
werk. Of this duality he wrote:

We want to examine things and allow them to
discover their own images. It goes against the
grain to bestow a form on them from the outside. . . . In nature, the 'image' is the result of
a co-ordination of many parts in such a way
as to allow the whole as well as each of its
parts to live most fully and most effectively. . . .
If we try to discover the 'true' organic form,
rather than to impose an extraneous form, we
act in accord with nature.

At the Berlin Secession Exhibition in 1923
Hans and Wassili Luckhardt, together with
Mies and some of his contemporaries, had
begun to show a more functional and objective
mode of building, a development which led in
the following year to their formation of the
Zehnering. By 1925, when the Zehnering
became Der Ring, with Häring as its secretary,
no divisions between the various positions had
appeared, as their collective energy was
devoted to overcoming the reactionary policies
of the Berlin city architect, Ludwig Hoffmann.

In 1928, however, when this battle had been
won, Häring's concern for the 'organic' naturally led him into conflict with Le Corbusier
when, as secretary of Der Ring, he participated
in the foundation of the Congrès Internationaux
d'Architecture Moderne, at La Sarraz, Switzerland. While Le Corbusier here proclaimed an
architecture of functionalism and pure geometrical form, Häring tried in vain to win the
Congress over to his own conception of
'organic' building. His failure to do so not only
emphasized the non-normative, 'place'-orien-
tated nature of his approach but also denoted
the final eclipse of the Scheerbartian dream.
For all that Scharoun extended this vision into
the post-war period, in his Romeo and Juliet
apartments, built in Stuttgart in 1954–59, and
his last masterwork, the Philharmonie, built in
Berlin in 1956–63, the idiosyncratic nature of
the 'organic' approach has since been given
little chance to prevail.

## Chapter 14

# The Bauhaus:
# the evolution of an idea 1919-32

Let us create a new guild of craftsmen, without the class distinctions which raise an arrogant barrier between craftsman and artist. Together let us conceive and create the new building of the future, which will embrace architecture and sculpture and painting in one unity and which will rise one day toward heaven from the hands of a million workers like the crystal symbol of a new faith.

Proclamation of the Weimar Bauhaus, 1919

The Bauhaus was the outcome of a continuous effort to reform applied art education in Germany around the turn of the century, first with the establishment in 1898 of Karl Schmidt's Dresdner Werkstätten (which became the Deutsche Werkstätten, and moved to the garden city of Hellerau in 1908), then with the appointment in 1903 of Hans Poelzig and Peter Behrens to the directorships of applied art schools in Breslau and Düsseldorf, and finally, in 1906, with the founding of the Grand Ducal School of Arts and Crafts in Weimar under the direction of the Belgian architect Henry van de Velde.

Despite the ambitious structures that he designed for both the Fine Arts Building and the School of Arts and Crafts, Van de Velde did little more in his tenure than establish a relatively modest *Kunstseminar* for craftsmen. After his enforced resignation as an alien in 1915, he advised the Saxon State Ministry that Walter Gropius, Hermann Obrist or August Endell would make a suitable successor. Protracted discussions took place throughout the war between the Ministry and Fritz Mackensen, head of the Grand Ducal Academy of Fine Art, as to the relative pedagogical status of fine and applied art, with Gropius arguing for the relative autonomy of the latter. Gropius advocated a workshop-based design education for both designers and craftsmen, while Mackensen stuck to the Prussian idealist line, insisting that artist-craftsmen should be trained in a fine art academy. This ideological conflict was resolved in 1919 in compromise: Gropius became director of a composite institution, consisting of the Academy of Art and the School of Arts and Crafts, an arrangement that was to divide the Bauhaus, conceptually, throughout its existence.

The principles of the Bauhaus Proclamation of 1919 had been anticipated in Bruno Taut's architectural programme for the Arbeitsrat für Kunst, published late in 1918. Taut argued that a new cultural unity could be attained only through a new art of building, wherein each separate discipline would contribute to the final form. 'At this point,' he wrote, 'there will be no boundaries between the crafts, sculpture and painting; all will be one: Architecture.'

This anarchic reworking of the *Gesamtkunstwerk* ideal was elaborated by Gropius first in the pamphlet written in April 1919 for the 'Exhibition of Unknown Architects', organized by the Arbeitsrat für Kunst, and then in his Bauhaus Proclamation of about the same date. Where the one called on all fine artists to reject salon art and to return to the crafts in the service of a metaphorical cathedral of the future – 'to go into buildings, endow them with fairy tales . . . and *build in fantasy* without regard for technical difficulty' – the other exhorted the members of the Bauhaus 'to create a new guild of craftsmen, without the class distinctions which raise an arrogant barrier between craftsman and artist'.

Even the word *Bauhaus*, which Gropius persuaded the reluctant state government to adopt as the official title of the new institution, intentionally recalled the medieval *Bauhütte* or masons' lodge. That such connotations were deliberate is confirmed by a letter written by Oskar Schlemmer in 1922:

Originally the Bauhaus was founded with visions of erecting the cathedral of socialism and the workshops were established in the manner of the cathedral building lodges [*Dombauhütten*]. The idea of the cathedral has for the time being receded into the background and with it certain definite ideas of an artistic nature. Today we must think at best in terms of the house, perhaps even only *think* so. . . . In the face of the economic plight, it is our task to become pioneers of simplicity, that is, to find a simple form for all life's necessities, which is at the same time respectable and genuine.

For the first three years of its existence the Bauhaus was dominated by the charismatic

102  Feininger, woodcut for the Bauhaus Proclamation, 1919. *Zukunftskathedrale*, the cathedral of the future as the cathedral of socialism.

presence of the Swiss painter and teacher, Johannes Itten, who arrived in the autumn of 1919. Three years earlier he had started his own art school in Vienna, under the influence of Franz Cizek. In a highly charged milieu, coloured by the anarchic anti-Seccessionist activities of the painter Oskar Kokoschka and the architect Adolf Loos, Cizek had developed a unique system of instruction based on stimulating individual creativity through the making of collages of different materials and textures. His methods had matured in a cultural climate impregnated with progressive educational theory, from the systems of Froebel and Montessori to the 'learning-through-doing' movement, initiated by the American John Dewey and vigorously propagated in Germany after 1908 by the educational reformer Georg Kirschensteiner. The teaching in Itten's Viennese school and in the *Vorkurs*, or preliminary course, that he initiated in the Bauhaus was derived from Cizek, although Itten enriched the method with the form and colour theory of his own master Adolf Hölzel. The aims of Itten's foundation course, mandatory for all first-year students, were to release individual creativity and to enable each student to assess his own particular ability.

Up to 1920, when, at Itten's request, the artists Schlemmer, Paul Klee and Georg Muche joined the Bauhaus, he taught, single-handed, four separate craft courses in addition to the *Vorkurs*, while Gerhard Marcks and Lyonel Feininger gave marginal courses in ceramics and printing respectively. Itten's anarchic position at the time may be gleaned from his 1922 response to a referendum on the provision of state welfare for artists:

The mind stands outside any organization. Where it has nevertheless been organized (religion, church) it has become estranged from its innate nature. . . . The state *should* take care that none of its citizens starve, but it *should not support art.*

Itten's anti-authoritarian, even mystical, position was substantially reinforced in 1921 by his extended stay in the Mazdaznan centre at Herrliberg near Zürich. He returned in the middle of the year to convert his pupils and his

103 Itten, in the Mazdaznan work costume that he designed, 1921.

The growing division between Gropius and Itten was exacerbated by the appearance in Weimar of two equally powerful personalities: the Dutch De Stijl artist Theo van Doesburg, who took up residence in the winter of 1921, and the Russian painter Wassily Kandinsky, who joined the Bauhaus, at Itten's instigation, in the summer of 1922. Where the former postulated a rational, anti-individualist aesthetic, the latter taught an emotive and ultimately mystical approach to art. Although the two men did not come into direct conflict, Van Doesburg's extramural De Stijl polemic instantly appealed to many Bauhaus students. His teaching not only had an immediate impact on the production of the workshops, but also directly challenged the open-ended precepts of the original Bauhaus programme. His influence was even reflected in the furnishing of Gropius's own office, and in the asymmetrical composition of Gropius's entry for the

colleague Muche to the rigours of this updated version of an archaic Persian religion. The cult demanded an austere life style, periodic fasting and a vegetarian diet flavoured with cheese and garlic. The physical and spiritual well-being deemed to be essential to creativity was further assured by breathing and relaxation exercises. Of this inner-directed orientation Itten later wrote:

The terrible losses and horrible events of World War I and a close study of Spengler's *Decline of the West* made me realize that we had reached a crucial point in our scientific-technological civilization. For me, it was not enough to embrace the slogans 'return to craft' or 'art and technology, hand in hand'. I studied Eastern philosophy, delved into Persian Mazdaism and Indian yoga teachings, and compared them with early Christianity. I reached the conclusion that we must counterbalance our externally-orientated scientific research and technological speculation with inner-directed thought and practice. I searched for something, for myself and my work, on which to base a new way of life.

104 Gropius and A. Meyer, project for the *Chicago Tribune* Building, 1922.

1922 *Chicago Tribune* competition, designed with Adolf Meyer.

In 1922, after Van Doesburg had been proselytizing for nine months, the generally critical socio-economic situation brought Gropius to modify the craft orientation of the original programme. His initial attack on Itten appeared in his circular to the Bauhaus masters, where he indirectly criticized Itten's monastic rejection of the world. This text was in effect a draft for his essay *Idee und Aufbau des Staatlichen Bauhauses Weimar* ('The Theory and Organization of the Bauhaus'), published on the occasion of the first Bauhaus exhibition held in Weimar in 1923. He wrote:

The teaching of craft is meant to prepare for designing for mass production. Starting with the simplest tools and least complicated jobs, he [the Bauhaus apprentice] gradually acquires ability to master more intricate problems and to work with machines, while at the same time he keeps in touch with the entire process of production from start to finish, whereas the factory worker never gets beyond the knowledge of one phase of the process. Therefore the Bauhaus is consciously seeking contacts with existing industrial enterprises, for the sake of mutual stimulation.

This carefully worded argument for the reconciliation of craft design and industrial production brought about Itten's immediate resignation.

His position on the faculty was immediately filled by the Hungarian artist and social radical László Moholy-Nagy. On his arrival in Berlin in 1921 (as a refugee from the short-lived Hungarian revolution), Moholy-Nagy had come into contact with the Russian designer El Lissitzky, who was then in Germany for the preparations of the Russian Exhibition of 1922. This encounter encouraged him to pursue his own Constructivist leanings, and from this date forward his paintings featured Suprematist elements, those modular crosses and rectangles soon to become the substance of his famous 'telephone' pictures, executed in enamelled steel. Of these he wrote:

In 1922 I ordered by telephone from a sign factory five paintings in porcelain enamel. I had the factory's colour chart before me and I sketched my paintings on graph paper. At the other end of the telephone the factory supervisor had the same kind of paper, divided into squares. He took down the dictated shapes in the correct position.

This spectacular demonstration of programmed art production seems to have impressed Gropius, for in the following year he invited Moholy-Nagy to take over both the preliminary course and the metal workshop. Under Moholy-Nagy's leadership the products of the latter were at once orientated towards a 'Constructivist Elementarism', which was tempered over the years by a mature concern for the convenience of the objects produced. In the meantime he introduced into the preliminary course, which he shared with Josef Albers, exercises in equilibrium structures in a variety of materials, including wood, metal, wire and glass. The aim was no longer to demonstrate a feeling for contrasting materials and forms, usually assembled as reliefs, but rather to reveal the statical and aesthetic properties of free-standing asymmetrical structures. The epitome of such 'exercises' was the building of his own Light-Space Modulator, on which he was to be occupied from 1922 to 1930.

The 'Constructivist Elementarist' style, which Moholy-Nagy had partly derived from the Vkhutemas (Higher Technical and Artistic Studios) of the Soviet Union, was complemented elsewhere in the Bauhaus by the De Stijl influence of Van Doesburg and by a post-Cubist approach to form, as evidenced in the sculpture workshops under Schlemmer's direction from 1922. An early manifestation of this 'Elementarist' aesthetic, instantly adopted as a house style after Itten's resignation, was the sans serif typography used by Herbert Bayer and Joost Schmidt for the Bauhaus Exhibition of 1923.

Two model houses, largely built and furnished by the Bauhaus workshops, characterize this period of transition, revealing common elements and striking dissimilarities. They are the Sommerfeld House, designed by Gropius and Meyer and completed in Berlin-Dahlem in 1922, and the Bauhaus 'Versuchshaus' or

Experimental House, designed by Muche and Meyer for the Bauhaus Exhibition of 1923. Where the first was designed as a traditional *Heimatstil* log house, with an interior enriched with carved wood and stained glass so as to create a *Gesamtkunstwerk*, the second was conceived as a *sachlich*, smoothly rendered object, furnished with the latest labour-saving devices so as to be a *Wohnmaschine* or living machine. This minimum-circulation house was organized around an 'atrium' — not an open court but a clerestory-lit living-room surrounded on all sides by bedrooms and other ancillary spaces. Each of these perimeter rooms was equipped in an austere manner, with exposed metal radiators, steel windows and door frames, elemental furniture and unshaded tubular light fittings. While most of these pieces were hand-made in the Bauhaus workshops, Adolf Meyer, in his report on the house in *Bauhausbücher 3* (1923), emphasized its furnishing with standard bathroom and kitchen equipment and its construction with entirely new materials and methods.

The changing ideology of the Bauhaus was further demonstrated in an article by Gropius in the same issue of *Bauhausbücher*; entitled 'Wohnhaus-Industrie', it illustrated a remarkable round house projected by Karl Fieger, the centralized, light-weight conception of which anticipated Buckminster Fuller's Dymaxion House of 1927. In addition, Gropius published his own 'Serienhäuser', or extending house units, intended as prototypes for the Bauhaussiedlung, a housing estate which he hoped to build on the outskirts of Weimar. These serial houses were finally realized as masters' residences built at the Dessau Bauhaus in 1926.

After 1923 the Bauhaus approach became extremely 'objective', in the sense of being closely affiliated to the Neue Sachlichkeit movement. This affiliation, which was reflected, despite their rather formalistic massing, in the buildings for the Dessau Bauhaus itself, was to become more pronounced after Gropius's resignation in 1928. The last two years of Gropius's tenure were distinguished by three major developments: the politically enforced and well-orchestrated move from Weimar to Dessau, the completion of the Dessau Bauhaus, and finally the gradual emergence of a recognizable Bauhaus approach, in which a greater

105   Muche and A. Meyer, Experimental House, Bauhaus Exhibition, Weimar, 1923.

106, 107   Gropius, Bauhaus, Dessau, 1925–26. Exterior showing the pinwheel composition (see p. 138); *below*, bridge linking administration and workshop blocks, on inauguration day, 1926.

108 Jucker, adjustable piano lamp, 1923.

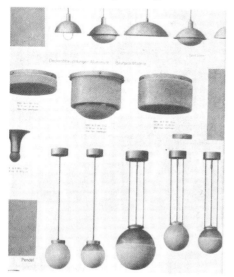

109 Bauhaus light fittings, of pressed metal and opalescent glass, mass-produced under the direction of H. Meyer.

Bauhaus typography finally matured with Bayer's austere layout and sans serif type, about to become world famous for its exclusion of upper-case letters. The year 1927 also saw the formation of the architectural department, under the leadership of the Swiss architect Hannes Meyer. A number of Breuer's prefabricated house designs of around this time reflect the immediate impact of Meyer's influence. Meyer brought with him his talented colleague Hans Wittwer who, like him, had been a member of the left-wing ABC group in Basle (see below, p. 132).

Early in 1928 Gropius tendered his resignation to the mayor of Dessau and appointed Meyer as his successor. The relative maturity of the institution, the unremitting attacks on himself and the growth of his practice all convinced him that it was time for a change. This move radically transformed the Bauhaus and, paradoxically enough, given the growing reactionary climate of Dessau, shifted its orientation still further left and even closer to the Neue Sachlichkeit position. For a variety of reasons Moholy-Nagy, Breuer and Bayer fol-

110 Gropius, Bauhaus, Dessau, 1925–26. Main hall with Breuer furniture.

emphasis was placed on deriving form from productive method, material constraint and programmatic necessity.

The furniture workshops, under Marcel Breuer's brilliant direction, started in 1926 to produce tubular steel light-weight chairs and tables which were convenient, easy to clean and economical. These pieces, together with the light fittings from the metal workshop, were used to furnish the interior of the new Bauhaus buildings. By 1927 the 'licensed' industrial production of such Bauhaus designs was in full swing, including the Breuer furniture, the textured fabrics of Gunta Stadler-Stölzl and her colleagues, and the elegant lamps and metalware of Marianne Brandt. In that year too,

lowed Gropius's lead and resigned. As Moholy-Nagy indicated in his letter of resignation, he disliked Meyer's immediate insistence on the adoption of a rigorous design method:

I can't afford a continuation on this specialized purely objective and efficient basis – either productively or humanly.... Under a programme of increased technology I can only continue if I have a technical expert as my aide. For economic reasons this will never be possible.

Largely liberated from the inhibiting influence of Gropius's star faculty, Meyer was able to steer the work of the Bauhaus towards a more 'socially responsible' design programme. Simple, demountable, inexpensive, plywood furniture came to the fore and a range of wallpaper was produced. More Bauhaus designs were being manufactured than ever before, although the emphasis was now placed on social rather than aesthetic considerations. Meyer organized the Bauhaus into four major departments: architecture (now called 'building' for polemical reasons), advertising, wood and metal production, and textiles. Supplementary scientific courses, such as industrial organization and psychology, were introduced into all departments, while the building section shifted its emphasis to the economic optimization of plan arrangements and to methods for the precise calculation of light, sunlight, heat loss/gain, and acoustics. This ambitious programme required an increase in faculty, so that Wittwer's appointment as a technician was soon complemented by that of the architect/planner Ludwig Hilberseimer, the engineer Alcar Rudelt and a studio staff comprising Alfred Arndt, Karl Fieger, Edvard Heiberg and Mart Stam.

Despite Meyer's concern to prevent the Bauhaus from becoming a tool of left-wing party politics (he resisted an attempt to form a student Communist cell), a remorseless campaign against him finally forced the mayor to demand his resignation. Meyer revealed his understanding of the situation in an open letter to the mayor, Fritz Hesse:

It was no use explaining [to you] that a 'Bauhaus Dessau' group of the German Com-

munist Party was an impossibility from the party organization point of view, no use my assuring you that my political activities were of a cultural and never a party character.... Municipal politics require you to provide resounding Bauhaus successes, a brilliant Bauhaus façade and a prestigious Bauhaus director.

Municipal politics and German right-wing reaction in the event required considerably more. They required the Bauhaus closed and its *sachlich* façade capped by an 'Aryan' pitched roof. They required the Marxists impeached and the liberal émigrés banished along with their obscure art works – later to be designated as decadent. The desperate attempt of the mayor of Dessau to shore up the Bauhaus, in the name of liberal democracy, through the patriarchal directorship of Mies van der Rohe, was doomed to failure. The Bauhaus remained in Dessau for but two more years. In October 1932 what was left of it moved into an old warehouse on the outskirts of Berlin, but by now the floodgates of reaction were open, and nine months later the Bauhaus was finally closed.

111 Yamawaki, 'The End of the Dessau Bauhaus', collage, 1932.

## Chapter 15

# The New Objectivity:
# Germany, Holland and Switzerland 1923-33

The expression *Neue Sachlichkeit* was in fact coined by me in the year 1924. A year later came the Mannheim exhibition which bore the same name. The expression ought really to apply as a label to the new realism bearing a socialist flavour. It was related to the general contemporary feeling in Germany of resignation and cynicism after a period of exuberant hopes (which had found an outlet in expressionism). Cynicism and resignation are the negative side of the *Neue Sachlichkeit*; the positive side expresses itself in the enthusiasm for the immediate reality as a result of a desire to take things entirely objectively on a material basis without immediately investing them with ideal implications. This healthy disillusionment finds its clearest expression in Germany in architecture.

G.F. Hartlaub
Letter to Alfred H. Barr, Jr, July 1929

The term *Sachlichkeit* had been current in German cultural circles long before 1924, when the art critic G.F. Hartlaub hit upon the phrase 'die neue Sachlichkeit' ('the new objectivity') to identify a post-war school of anti-Expressionist painting. *Sachlichkeit* seems to have been first used in an architectural context in a series of articles written by Hermann Muthesius for the journal *Dekorative Kunst* between 1897 and 1903. These articles attributed the quality of *Sachlichkeit* to the English Arts and Crafts movement, particularly as manifest in the handicraft guilds (such as that of Ashbee) and the early garden suburbs. *Sachlichkeit* for Muthesius seems to have meant an 'objective', functionalist and eminently yeoman attitude to the design of objects, tending towards the reform of industrial society itself. The term

was given somewhat different connotations by Heinrich Wölfflin, in his book, *Kunstgeschichtliche Grundbegriffe* (*The Principles of Art History*) of 1915, when he wrote of the 'linear' vision of 1800: 'The new line comes to serve a new objectivity.' *Sachlichkeit* had thus been qualified by the objective 'new' well before Hartlaub gave the title 'Die Neue Sachlichkeit' to his 1925 exhibition in Mannheim of 'Magical Realist' painters, artists who since the First World War had depicted both the appearance and the essence of an austere social reality. Yet, as Fritz Schmalenbach has observed,

In reality, it was not the 'objectivity' of the new painting which the term was intended in the first place and above all to formulate, but something more universal underlying this objectivity and of which it was the expression, a revolution in the general mental attitude of the times, a general new *Sachlichkeit* of thought and feeling.

By the early 1930s, the expression had achieved wide circulation and had come to connote, as Hartlaub had intended, an unsentimental approach to the nature of society. In 1926 the phrase was first used to designate a 'new-objective' and explicitly socialist attitude to architecture, although, as Schmalenbach has noted, this transference did not derive from a community of style between Magical Realism and the new architecture. The first polemical post-1918 use of the word 'object' (*Gegenstand*) in Germany came directly from a Russian source, and this interjected into the development of Neue Sachlichkeit architecture a specific set of socio-political connotations.

With the advent of the Russian Revolution in 1917 and the military collapse of Germany in the following year, Russia and Germany both found themselves confronted by hostile Western powers. While the Soviet Union had to contend with foreign intervention in the midst of a civil war and with the deprivations of an economic blockade, Germany was crippled by the punitive reparation agreements of Versailles. The end of the Russian Civil War in 1921 and the easing of foreign pressure induced Lenin to proclaim his new Economic Policy, designed to attract foreign capital into corporate partnership with the Soviet Union. Soon afterwards Germany ratified a series of earlier negotiations with the Soviets, signing in 1922 the Treaty of Rapallo, which re-established diplomatic relations and pledged both countries to economic co-operation. With the opening up of Russo-German relations at the end of 1921, El Lissitzky and Ilya Ehrenburg came to Berlin as unofficial cultural ambassadors of the Soviet Union, their immediate task being to organize an official exhibition of Russian avant-garde art. In May 1922 they published the first number of a trilingual art review, *Veshch/Gegenstand/Objet*, which featured on its cover two significant images: a photograph of a snow plough locomotive, and the basic icons of Suprematism, a black square and a black circle. *Veshch* thus invoked the *sachlich* engineered object and the Suprematist 'non-objective' world.

In 1923 Lissitzky became further involved with such cultural propaganda, editing, with Hans Richter and Werner Graeff, the first issue of the Berlin magazine *G* (for *Gestaltung*, 'Form') and demonstrating his architectural ideas in the Prounenraum built for the Grosse Berliner Kunstausstellung of that year. By his invented term 'Proun' (from *Pro-Unovis*, 'for the school of the new art'), Lissitzky evoked a new realm of art somewhere between painting and architecture. Of the Proun room, comprising a small rectilinear cell, articulated and animated by a continuous relief extending over the floor and ceiling, Lissitzky wrote:

The room . . . is designed with elementary forms and materials . . . and with surfaces which are spread flat on to the wall (colour) and surfaces which are perpendicular to the wall

112 Lissitzky, cover of *Veshch/Gegenstand/Objet*, 1922.

(wood) . . . the equilibrium which I seek to attain in the room must be elementary and capable of change so that *it cannot be disturbed by a telephone or a piece of standard furniture.* The room is there for the human being – not the human being for the room.

Here, as on the cover of *Veshch*, Suprematist abstraction is seen as being compatible with standard objects. Unlike Frank Lloyd Wright in the Larkin Building, Lissitzky did not feel any need to restyle such manufactured objects as telephones, although as early as 1920 he had rejected the 'anti-art' utilitarianism proclaimed by Tatlin's Productivist Group. While he recognized that empirically engineered (*sachlich*) structures could possess both spatial beauty and symbolic significance, his Lenin Tribune of 1920 exemplified his own subtle combination of engineering and Suprematism: the basic structure consisted of an inclined lattice girder, with Lenin photomontaged into position at its crown, while the rostrum and the base were treated as Elementarist forms, miraculously suspended in space. This incongruous juxtaposition of abstract, non-objective elements with empirically engineered form was to characterize Lissitzky's work until the early 1930s. Although this synthesis was not strictly compatible with the notion of *Sachlichkeit*, Lissitzky's approach came to be a point of departure for an international and 'objective' style of building.

In 1922 the Dutch architect Mart Stam, then twenty-three years old, went to work for Max Taut in Berlin. There, while working independently on a competition for an office block in Königsberg, he met Lissitzky and for the rest of their stay in Berlin the two men remained in close contact. In 1923 Lissitzky projected his 'suspended' office block for Moscow, the 'Wolkenbügel', of which two separate versions were eventually produced, one by Lissitzky alone and the other in conjunction with Stam. When, late in 1923, Lissitzky contracted tuberculosis and was forced to move to Zürich, Stam went with him. During the next year they acquired a Swiss following and in 1925, largely at Lissitzky's instigation, they formed the left-wing ABC group, centred on Basle. The Swiss members of the group included Emil Roth of Zürich and Hans Schmidt, Hannes Meyer and Hans Wittwer of Basle. These men dedicated themselves to the design of socially relevant buildings in accordance with scientific principles.

In 1924 the ABC group began to propagate their views in the magazine *ABC: Beiträge zum Bauen*, edited by Stam, Schmidt and Lissitzky in collaboration with Roth. Although they did not adopt the phrase 'Neue Sachlichkeit', they nonetheless made their *sachlich* orientation explicit. The first number contained Stam's essay 'Kollektive Gestaltung' ('Collective Design') and Lissitzky's seminal text, 'Element und Erfindung' ('Element and Invention'), in which he outlined the duality of his approach, his synthesis of functional structure with abstract elements. The second issue introduced the group's characteristic preoccupation with normative standards, particularly in Paul Artaria's essay on the standardization of paper sizes, while Nos 2 and 3, a double issue, included an essay on reinforced-concrete construction, as exemplified in Le Corbusier's 'Dom-Ino' system of 1914–15, as well as in Mies van der Rohe's glass skyscraper projects of 1922 and Stam's Königsberg block and extendable house proposals of the same date. By dramatically comparing the relative weights and thicknesses of metal and wooden window frames the magazine stressed the intrinsic economy of modern building technology. Soon afterwards the ABC group summed up its distaste for massive architecture in the equation: 'building × weight = monumentality'.

With the publication of Meyer and Wittwer's Petersschule project for Basle of 1926, the ABC group crystallized its Functionalist and anti-monumental programme. Meyer's description reveals the ABC preoccupation with precise calculation and social relevance, both to be made manifest through light-weight technique:

The ideal would be to skylight all the rooms . . . and to set aside a new site as part of the town. At present there appears to be no prospect of such demands being realized and the following is a compromise solution on the basis of the old building. . . . The School itself is raised as far as possible above the ground to a level where there is sunlight and fresh air. On the ground floor there is only the swimming bath and the gymnasium in an enclosed space. The remaining area of the playground is released for public traffic and parking. Instead of a playground, two open spaces (suspended platforms) and all the flat roofs of the building are assigned to the children for recreation. . . . The dead weight of the building is used to carry on four cables the unsupported steel structure of the two suspended platforms.

113 The ABC group's published disapproval of Östberg's Stockholm Town Hall, Bonatz's Stuttgart Railway Station and a house by Van Doesburg and Van Eesteren (1923: see ill. 128), from *ABC*, 1926.

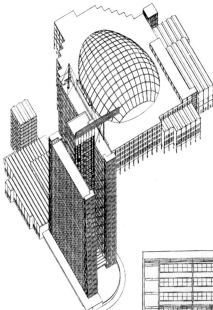

This steel-frame 'Constructivist' work recalls a Soviet Vkhutemas project for a suspended restaurant, published by Stam in the ABC magazine in 1924. The machine-like furnishing of the Petersschule proposal, its steel windows, aluminium doors, rubber floors and asbestos-cement cladding, anticipated the finishes proposed in the Meyer/Wittwer entry for the League of Nations competition of 1927.

The claim by Meyer and Wittwer that their League of Nations design was a scientific solution merits examination. Structurally the assertion appears tenable, inasmuch as their use of a standard module throughout would have been highly suitable for prefabrication. As in Paxton's Crystal Palace, the modular extension or contraction of any section would have been possible without altering the basic

114   H. Meyer and Wittwer, project for the League of Nations Building, Geneva, 1926–27. (Compare Le Corbusier's entry, ill. 144.)

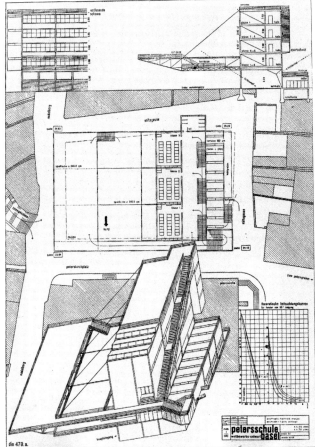

115   H. Meyer and Wittwer, project for the Petersschule, Basel, 1926.

order of the building. The raising of the assembly building on columns was more than adequately justified by the provision of parking beneath. Meyer's much-proclaimed 'objectivity' also found reflection in the determination of the auditorium profile through elaborate acoustical calculation. But one may question the designer's 'objectivity' when elevator shafts are glazed (after Russian Constructivist models) so as to reveal the 'machine aesthetic' in action. Further doubts arise when one considers the undeniably picturesque qualities of the composition. And although Meyer claimed in his report that 'our building symbolizes nothing', and that its objective indifference to the site lay beyond aesthetic evaluation, he disclosed a certain symbolizing intent when he wrote:

If the intentions of the League of Nations are sincere, then it cannot possibly cram such a novel social organization into the straitjacket of traditional architecture. No pillared reception rooms for weary monarchs but hygienic workrooms for the busy representatives of their people. No back corridors for backstairs diplomacy but open glazed rooms for public negotiation of honest men.

The latent symbolism of Meyer's functional approach also finds expression in his proposal to classify the users of the assembly building by their parking position and to conduct them inconspicuously from this point to their assigned places in the auditorium above.

The ABC commitment to an objective approach to both building and life arose out of a determination to serve only collective necessity of which Stam wrote in 'Kollektive Gestaltung':

The dualistic view of life — heaven and earth, good and evil — the idea that there is an eternal inner conflict, has thrown the emphasis on the individual and drawn him away from society. . . . The individual's isolation has led him to be dominated by his emotions. But the modern outlook . . . sees life as the single reaching out of a *single* force This means that what is special and individual must yield to what is common to all.

Meyer expressed a similar view in his essay 'Die neue Welt' ('The New World') published in *Das Werk* (1926):

The standardization of our requirements is shown by: the bowler hat, bobbed hair, the tango, jazz, the co-op product, the DIN standard size, etc. . . . Trade union, co-operative, Ltd, Inc., cartel, trust, and the League of Nations are the forms in which today's social conglomerations find expression, and the radio and the rotary press are their media of communication. Co-operation rules the world. The community rules the individual.

In 1925, Stam returned to Holland to work under L.C. van der Vlugt, as job captain on the reinforced-concrete mushroom-columned Van Nelle Factory, completed in 1929. If the Meyer/Wittwer project for the League of Nations can be regarded as the canonical work of the ABC group, then the Van Nelle tobacco, tea and coffee packing plant may be considered as the realization of similar technical and aesthetic premises. As in the Meyer/Wittwer design, the structure and the movement systems were explicitly revealed, although naturally in a packing process the prime movers were not elevators but glazed conveyors, running diagonally between the curtain-walled packing block and the canal warehouse. The significance of such an open and dynamic expression was not lost on an observer as sensitive as Le Corbusier, who saw it as a confirmation of his own utopian socialist convictions, and wrote in 1931:

The road that runs into the factory is smooth, flat, bordered with brown tiled sidewalks; it is as clean and bright as a dance floor. The sheer façades of the building, bright glass and grey metal, rise up . . . against the sky. . . . The serenity of the place is total: *Everything is open to the outside.* And this is of enormous significance to all those who are working, on all eight floors *inside*. . . . The Van Nelle tobacco factory in Rotterdam, a creation of the modern age, has removed all the former connotations of despair from that word 'proletarian'. And this deflection of the egoistic property instinct towards a feeling for collective action leads to

116, 117 Brinkman and Van der Vlugt (architect in charge: Stam), Van Nelle Factory, Rotterdam, 1927–29. Transverse section showing concrete mushroom column construction, and exterior.

a most happy result: the phenomenon of *personal participation* in every stage of the human enterprise.

Despite Stam's major participation in this design, the role of Van der Vlugt cannot be discounted, particularly as he later designed a work of comparable 'objectivity' without the aid of Stam – his *Existenzminimum* Bergpolder flats, built in Rotterdam in 1933. Nonetheless Stam must be credited for introducing the polemic of objectivity into Dutch architecture, for all that J.J.P. Oud had by this date already built extensive amounts of flat-roofed Functionalist workers' housing, most particularly his Kiefhoek Estate in Rotterdam, under construction by 1925. In all this work Oud, as Rotterdam City Architect, remained committed to Berlage's traditional urban precept of the street, regarded as an enclosed, external room.

The full measure of Stam's revolt against this tradition may be judged from his 1926 project for the Rokin district of Amsterdam, where the continuity of the existing street is vitiated by a continuously elevated office block, served by escalator access and an aerial railway, the ground being reserved for traffic parking, display and pedestrian movement. This provocative yet economically questionable project was typical of Stam's preoccupation with the subversion of the traditional urban pattern. It epitomized his concept of the 'open city', of which he wrote in the late 1920s:

The ever increasing volume of traffic due to the growing economic struggle makes traffic organization the determining factor in architectural town planning. Architectural thinking must break free from aesthetic attitudes left over from earlier generations. The conception of a town as an enclosed space is one of these and must give way to the open town.

Stam's extreme materialism served to isolate him from the Functionalist Opbouw group, already established in Rotterdam by 1920. Despite their commitment to the 'Nieuwe Zakelijkheid', Opbouw members such as Brinkman and Van der Vlugt and their industrialist client Kees van der Leeuw sought to transcend 'objectivity' through a concern for universal 'spiritual' values. This they expressed through their participation in the Dutch theosophical movement and through their building, in 1930, of a small retreat at Ommen for Krishnamurti and his followers.

Similar spiritual aspirations were inherent in the work of Johannes Duiker and Bernard Bijvoet, who departed from their initial Wrightian manner in the boarded house that they built at Aalsmeer in 1924. This asymmetrical, monopitched house initiated the Zakelijkheid period of Duiker's career, a period that culmin-

135

118 Duiker and Bijvoet, house, Aalsmeer, 1924.

119 Duiker, Zonnestraal Sanatorium, Hilversum, 1928. Administration and medical complex with radiating ward blocks.

120 Duiker, Open Air School, Amsterdam, 1930.

ated in two reinforced-concrete and glass structures of a decidedly Constructivist character — his Zonnestraal Sanatorium at Hilversum of 1928 and his Open Air School in Amsterdam of 1930. Despite his receptivity to the necessity for programmatic distortion, as in the asymmetrical gymnasium wing of the Open Air School, Duiker's latent idealism found expression in his preference for symmetrical organization. Only at the end of his life did he begin to abandon his characteristic 'butterfly' *parti*, in favour of the more serial, aformal approach of Stam. This came with his Cineac Cinema, Amsterdam, of 1934 and with the Gooiland Hotel, Hilversum, completed in 1936 by Bijvoet after Duiker's death.

In 1928, having designed housing for the 1927 Weissenhofsiedlung at Stuttgart, Stam once again left Holland for Germany, this time for Frankfurt, where he was to work under the City Architect Ernst May on the Hellerhof housing scheme — a residential sector within May's large 'Neue Frankfurt' development. Later that year, in the curious company of Rietveld and Berlage, Stam represented Holland at the foundation meeting of the Congrès Internationaux d'Architecture Moderne (CIAM) at La Sarraz in Switzerland. Soon after this meeting the Dutch Nieuwe Zakelijkheid movement became consolidated through the fusion of the Amsterdam Functionalist circle known as De 8 with the Opbouw group. This formation, called De 8 in Opbouw, remained active as the Dutch wing of CIAM until 1943.

The emergence of the Neue Sachlichkeit in Germany was inseparable from the Weimar Republic's crash housing programme, initiated by the stabilization of the Rentenmark in November 1923. In that year, Otto Haesler, the pioneer of *Zeilenbau* (row) housing, completed the Siedlung Italienischer Garten at Celle, near Hanover. Flat-roofed, with polychromatic rendered façades, its modernistic formula was to be adopted by Ernst May as a model for the first units to be built in Frankfurt, in 1925. In 1924, in the Siedlung Georgsgarten, his second work at Celle, Haesler developed Theodor Fischer's Alte Heide row housing model of 1919 into a general system, the housing being laid out in rows an optimum distance apart for sun penetration and ventilation. This pattern, based on Heiligenthal's rule (ill. 125) that the rows should be spaced no less than twice their block height apart, became the normative Neue Sachlichkeit formula, to be repeated in any number of housing schemes realized in Germany between 1925 and 1933. In such layouts, following Haesler's example, south- or west-facing living-rooms open onto communal green space. In Georgsgarten, Haesler added short south-facing blocks to the terraces, which ran north-south, thereby creating a series of L-shaped green courts, extending out into adjacent allotments. These allotments were subdivided into family plots for the cultivation of food (cf. Adolf Loos's Heuberg Estate, Vienna, of 1926). At Georgsgarten, Haesler also evolved the basic apartment type, of which he was to design many variations throughout his career. His typical apartment, stacked on three floors, with staircase access in pairs, consisted of a living/dining room, a small kitchen, a w.c., and three to six bedrooms. The replacement of the traditional *Wohnküche* by a separate kitchen was a radical departure in mass housing, and had the critical social impact of shifting the household focus towards an austerity version of the bourgeois 'salon'. Haesler was to upgrade his typical apartment in the Siedlung Friedrich Ebert-Ring at Rathenow, built in 1929, where a separate bathroom was introduced into the standard walk-up unit.

Both these early settlements were equipped with communal facilities such as laundries, meeting rooms, libraries, sports fields, etc., while Georgsgarten was further provided with a kindergarten, a café and a hairdresser. The sparse furnishing of these spaces, with their standard Thonet furniture and bare light bulbs, relieved by carefully detailed pipework and electrical conduit, synthesized the typical Neue Sachlichkeit interior: cold and austere and yet at the same time scintillating. Such qualities were echoed on the exterior, where plain rendered surfaces, steel windows, patent glazing and metal railing were combined to create the universal *sachlich* syntax.

Despite the national and ideological divergence of the seventeen architects involved — including, from Germany alone, figures as diverse as Behrens, Döcker, Gropius, Hilberseimer, Rading, Scharoun, Schneck, Mies van der Rohe and the brothers Taut — this objective mode of expression was more or less universally adopted in the Deutsche Werkbund Weissenhofsiedlung, erected outside Stuttgart in 1927.

In the subsequent development of his own work, Haesler began to move away from the expression of the *Siedlung* as a corporate entity to the assertion of the terraced block as a free-standing, infinitely repeatable unit. His initial plan of 1929 for the Siedlung Rothenberg at Kassel is typical in this respect, not only of his own work, but of most other Neue Sachlichkeit housing of comparable date.

With May's appointment as City Architect of Frankfurt in 1925, the building of workers' settlements began there on an unprecedented scale. Yet, owing to his early training with both Theodor Fischer in Munich and Raymond Unwin in England, May's rationalism was tempered by a feeling for tradition. Whereas Haesler had created an indented but continuous form at Georgsgarten and a serried open-ended layout at Rothenburg, May (like Bruno Taut and Martin Wagner in their contemporary Berlin-Britz housing) was more concerned with the creation of self-contained urban space, after the model of the traditional Prussian *Anger* village. Thus May's first work for Frankfurt, his Bruchfeldstrasse development of 1925, designed with C.H. Rudloff, consisted of a large courtyard of 'zigzag' housing, enclosing an elaborately landscaped communal garden. This unique layout, formally reminiscent of the Cité Moderne designed by Victor Bourgeois for Brussels in 1922, gave way to a more generalized approach in May's master-plan for Neue Frankfurt of 1926 and in his Römerstadt, Praunheim, Westhausen and Hohenblick settlements built as parts of the Nidda Valley complex between 1925 and 1930.

The 15,000 units completed under May's direction account for more than ninety per cent of the housing built in Frankfurt over the entire period. This impressive figure could hardly have been achieved without May's insistence on efficiency and economy in both design and construction. Such an objective approach, re-

121　May and Rudloff, Bruchfeldstrasse Estate, Frankfurt, 1925.

122　Schütte-Lihotzky, *Frankfurter Küche*, 1926.

inforced by the realities of building costs, led inevitably to the formulation of 'existence-minimum' space standards, which became the contentious theme of CIAM Frankfurt Congress of 1929. In contrast to Le Corbusier's 'idealistic' appeal for an 'existence-maximum', May's minimum standards were dependent on the extensive use of ingenious built-in storage, fold-away beds and above all on the development of the ultra-efficient, laboratory-like kitchen, the *Frankfurter Küche*, designed by the architect G. Schütte-Lihotzky. Escalating costs finally led May to pioneer prefabricated concrete slab construction, the so-called 'May System' being used for the Praunheim and Höhenblick housing sectors started in 1927.

Walter Gropius's Bauhaus complex of 1926 and his Törten housing of 1928 represent two stages in his gradual conversion to the principles of the Neue Sachlichkeit. While the 'railroad' layout of Törten reflected not only the standardization of its units but also the linear process of their prefabricated assembly by travelling crane, the Dessau Bauhaus still amounted to a formalist composition of asymmetrical elements. Its centrifugal, pinwheeling form, reminiscent of De Stijl planning, had first been attempted by Gropius and Meyer in their *Chicago Tribune* project of 1922 (ill. 104) and reformulated by them as an asymmetrical, horizontal distribution of masses in their Erlangen Academy design of 1924. While the expression of a comparable aesthetic in the Dessau Bauhaus necessitated the wilful suppression of its structural frame, this was compensated for by the *sachlich* detailing of its secondary components, such as the radiators, the fenestration, the balustrading and the light fittings. All the same, the ultimate articulation of these large intersecting masses could not be achieved without recourse to changes in colour or to a shallow modelling of the façade that effectively recalled the Neo-Classical *modenature* of the Gropius and Meyer Werkbund Building of 1914.

Gropius's most unequivocal Neue Sachlichkeit work was his 1927 Total Theatre project, designed for Erwin Piscator's Volksbühne in Berlin. Piscator had founded his Proletarian Theatre in 1924 after the model of the Russian revolutionary producer Meyerhold, whose October Theatre had been proclaimed in Moscow in 1920. Thus Gropius's 'Piscator-bühne' was largely designed to satisfy the requirements of a bio-mechanical stage, to provide the space for a 'theatre of action' as outlined by Meyerhold and his Proletkult colleagues. The actor-acrobat was the ideal type for such a theatre, in which a circus-like mechanized performance was presented on an apron stage. Meyerhold's prescriptions for a bio-mechanical production made a certain political content more or less mandatory:

The auditorium is to be kept permanently illuminated, a permanent visual link being thus maintained between actor and audience. . . . The 'soul junk' of the bourgeois stage is to be avoided. The theatre must not be considered as *culturally independent*. The stage is to be used as a political forum or as the simulator of profound social experience.

In his remarkably elegant and flexible solution, Gropius provided Piscator with an auditorium which could be rapidly transformed into any one of the three 'classic' stage forms, the proscenium, the apron, or the arena. How this provision was to be made, and to what theatrical ends, has been best described in Gropius's own words. In 1934, at a conference in Rome, he stated:

A complete transformation of the building occurs by turning the stage platform and part of the orchestra through 180°. Then the former proscenium stage becomes a central arena entirely surrounded by rows of spectators! This can even be done during the play. . . .

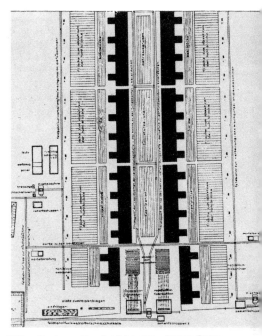

123   Gropius, rationalized housing, Dessau-Törten, 1928. The site layout is apparently organized around tower crane tracks.

124   Gropius, Total Theatre project, 1927. View from above, and alternative plans showing proscenium, apron and arena stages.

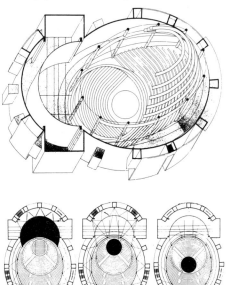

**8**

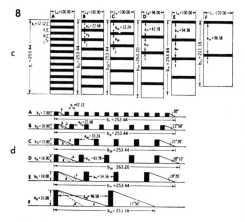

125  Gropius, diagram presented at CIAM in 1930 demonstrating the increased density and open space to be obtained by using high-rise slabs.

This attack on the spectator, moving him during the play and unexpectedly shifting the stage area, alters the existing scale of values, presenting to the spectator a new consciousness of space and making him participate in the action.

The convertible auditorium was also equipped with a peripheral stage, on which the action could encircle the audience. Alternatively this *Spielring* could be sealed off by a segmented back-projection screen, for the display of cinematic images complementary to the action on the stage. A similar demountable cyclorama was also available for the stage itself. The adaptability of this auditorium was to be further augmented by the provision for acrobatic display, just above the central arena. This aerial stage would have had the effect of transforming Gropius's egg-like void into a truly three-dimensional 'play' space, with the audience either surrounding or surrounded by the action on every side. Finally, the auditorium itself was a transparent box, through which its basic structure could be easily perceived, the open lattice of the ovoid roof being ingeniously reconciled with the column nodes of its elliptical 'ring' support (cf. the Meyer/Wittwer League of Nations auditorium).

Of approximately the same date as the Total Theatre were the Haselhorst housing and Elberfield Hospital projects, designed by Marcel Breuer and Gustav Hassenpflug in 1928, and Hannes Meyer's Trades Union School, completed at Bernau in 1930. Breuer's unrealized Elberfield project and Meyer's Bernau school were comparable *sachlich* works, inasmuch as they each comprised asymmetrical sequences of repeated elements, arranged in stepped formation, responding 'simultaneously' to the respective demands of the programme, orientation and topography. Where the ward units of the sanatorium, supported on a concrete superstructure, were set back to provide a stepped sequence of sun decks, one for each ward, the bulk of Meyer's school was made up of three-storey residential blocks, set back at their corners in such a way as to break up the overall length. Both these buildings were stepped in relation to gently sloping sites, and yet both were freely and functionally related to their major atypical elements, such as operating suites and x-ray units in the sanatorium or lecture halls and common facilities in the case of the school.

After his resignation from the Bauhaus at the end of 1927, Gropius became increasingly involved with the problem of housing, so that apart from the extensive low-cost schemes that he designed and saw built in the late 1920s, in Dessau, Karlsruhe and Berlin, he became theoretically concerned with the improvement of housing standards and the development of the housing block into a classless system for community settlement. His unrealized housing projects for Berlin of 1929 were a significant advance over his previous work, offering higher living standards and more comprehensive social services, while his 1931 proposal for high-rise middle-class housing, on the Wannsee near Berlin, constituted his first attempt at a self-contained commune block equipped with a restaurant and a gymnasium-solarium on the roof. Gropius's views in the late 1920s lay to the left of the Social Democratic position, as his essay, *Die Soziologischen Grundlagen der Minimalwohnung* (*The Sociological Bases of Minimum Housing*), of 1929 makes clear. There he put forward the familiar socialist argument in favour of state involvement in the provision of housing:

Since technology operates within the framework of industry and finance and since any cost reduction achieved must first of all be exploited for the benefit of private industry, it will only be able to provide cheaper and more varied dwellings if the government increases private industry's interest in dwelling construction by increased welfare measures. If the minimum dwelling is to be realized at rent levels which the population can afford, the government must be requested to: (1) prevent waste of public funds for apartments of excessive size . . . for which an upper limit of apartment size must be established; (2) reduce the initial cost of roads and utilities; (3) provide the building sites and remove them from the hands of speculators; (4) liberalize as far as possible the zoning regulations and building codes.

These prescriptions were only barely in advance of the official housing policy of the Weimar Republic, which, between 1927 and 1931, was to subsidize publicly through social insurance and property tax the design and erection of around one million dwellings – about seventy per cent of the new housing starts made over the entire period.

Such an extensive Welfare State system could not, however, be maintained in the face of the stock market collapse, which accompanied the world economic depression of 1929. Foreign trade slumped, loans were called in, and Germany was once more plunged into economic and political chaos. This had the effect of swinging the opinion of the country to the right, and with this political shift the fate of the German Neue Sachlichkeit architects was more or less sealed. Nothing remained for them but to emigrate, and this they did, each

126   An architect leaves Germany for the Soviet Union: cover of *Das Neue Frankfurt*, Sept. 1930, devoted to 'Germans building in the USSR'.

according to the colour of his political conviction. May left for the Soviet Union early in 1930, with a team of architects and planners, to work on a master plan for a steel smelting plant and town at Magnitogorsk in the Urals. His team included Fred Forbat, Gustav Hassenpflug, Hans Schmidt, Walter Schwagenscheidt and Mart Stam. At the same time Meyer left to take up a teaching post in Moscow. Others, such as Arthur Korn and Bruno Taut, followed suit in the early 1930s. On the National Socialist seizure of power in 1933, the remaining Neue Sachlichkeit architects of more moderate persuasion were either forced to retire or compelled to leave the country, Gropius and Breuer hurriedly migrating to England in 1934, en route to America.

## Chapter 16

# De Stijl: the evolution and dissolution of Neo-Plasticism 1917–31

1   There is an old and a new consciousness of the age. The old one is directed towards the individual. The new one is directed towards the universal. The conflict of the individual and the universal is reflected in the World War as well as in art today.

2   The war is destroying the old world with all that it contains: the pre-eminence of the individual in every field.

3   The new art has revealed the substance of the new consciousness of the age: an equal balance between the universal and the individual.

4   The new consciousness is ready to be realized in everything, including the every-day things of life.

5   Traditions, dogmas and the pre-eminence of the individual (the natural) stand in the way of this realization.

6   Therefore the founders of Neo-Plasticism call on all those who believe in the reform of art and culture to destroy those things which prevent further development, just as in the new plastic art, by removing the restriction of natural forms, they have eliminated what stands in the way of the expression of pure art, the extreme conse-quence of every concept of art.

From the first manifesto of De Stijl, 1918

The Dutch De Stijl movement, which lasted for barely fourteen years, was centred about the work of three men: the painters Piet Mondrian and Theo van Doesburg and the cabinet-maker and architect Gerrit Rietveld. The other artists who constituted the original formation, in 1917, under Van Doesburg's leadership — the painters Bart van der Leck, Georges Vantongerloo, and Vilmos Huszar, the architects J.J.P. Oud,

Robert van 't Hoff and Jan Wils and the poet Anthony Kok — soon departed in their various ways from the main line of the movement. All, however, with the exception of Van der Leck and Oud, were signatories of the eight-point manifesto published in 1918 in the second issue of the magazine De Stijl. This, the first manifesto of De Stijl, called for a new balance between the individual and the universal and for the liberation of art from both the constraints of tradition and the cult of individuality. Influenced as much by the philosophical thought of Spinoza as by the Dutch Calvinistic background from which they all came, they sought a culture that would transcend the tragedy of the individual by its emphasis on immutable laws. This universal and utopian aspiration was succinctly summed up by their aphorism: 'The object of nature is man, the object of man is style.'

By 1918 the movement had already been influenced by the Neo-Platonic, not to say Theosophical, philosophy of the mathematician M.H. Schoenmaekers, whose major works, Het nieuwe Wereldbeeld ('The New Image of the World') and Beeldende Wiskunde ('The Principles of Plastic Mathematics'), had been published in 1915 and 1916 respectively. Schoenmaeker's metaphysical world-view was complemented by more concrete attitudes and concepts drawn directly from Berlage and Wright, the latter having become known in Europe through the publication in 1910 and 1911 of the two famous Wasmuth volumes dedicated to his work. Berlage, on the other hand, was more influential for his socio-cultural criticism, and it was from him that the De Stijl artists had appropriated the title 'The Style' which he in turn had probably taken from Gottfried Semper's critical study, *Der Stil in den technischen und tektonischen Künsten oder praktische Ästhetik*, of 1860.

The appearance of Mondrian's first post-Cubist compositions, consisting largely of broken horizontal and vertical lines, coincided with his return to Holland from Paris in July 1914 and with the period that he and Van der Leck spent in Laren in almost daily contact with Schoenmaekers. From Schoenmaekers came the term 'Neo-Plasticism' – from his coinage of *nieuwe beelding* – and from him too came the restriction of the palette to the primary colours of whose cosmic significance he wrote in *Het nieuwe Wereldbeeld:* 'The three principal colours are essentially yellow, blue and red. They are the only colours existing . . . yellow is the movement of the ray (vertical) . . . blue is the contrasting colour to yellow (horizontal firmament) . . . red is the mating of yellow and blue.' Elsewhere in the same text he provided a comparable justification for limiting Neo-Plastic expression to orthogonal elements: 'The two fundamental, complete contraries which shape our earth and all that is of the earth are: the horizontal line of power, that is the course of the earth around the sun, and the vertical, profoundly spatial movement of rays that originate in the centre of the sun'.

For all his formative influence Schoenmaekers played no direct role in the aesthetic evolution of De Stijl. This was left to Van der Leck and Vantongerloo, whose very independence as artists caused them to split from Van Doesburg at an early date. Yet without their contributions it is doubtful if the characteristic De Stijl aesthetic could have been formulated with such clarity in so short a time. It is obvious, for example, that Van Doesburg's famous abstraction *The Cow*, of 1916, owes much to Van der Leck, while Vantongerloo's sculpture *Interrelation of Masses*, of 1919, clearly anticipates the general massing of the Van Doesburg and Cor van Eesteren house projects of 1923. And even the aloof Mondrian, in the last number of *De Stijl* (1932) – dedicated to the memory of Van Doesburg – brought himself to acknowledge his debt to Van der Leck, for the latter's use, as early as 1917, of saturated primary colours.

The years 1914–16 had seen Mondrian in Laren, in frequent contact with Schoenmaekers. During this period he wrote his basic theoretical text, 'De Nieuwe Beelding in de Schilderkunst' ('Neo-Plasticism in Painting'), which appeared in 1917 in the first issue of *De Stijl*. The enforced seclusion and meditation of the war years brought Mondrian to a new point of departure. His work now comprised a series of compositions consisting of floating, rectangular, coloured planes. Both he and Van der Leck had now arrived at what they each considered to be a totally new and pure plastic order, with the much younger Van Doesburg closely following their lead. Yet while Mondrian remained involved in planar compositions set within the 'shallow space' of the picture plane, as represented in his *Composition with Coloured Planes on a White Ground* of 1917, Van der Leck and Van Doesburg were to arrive at a linear structuring of the picture plane itself, through the use of narrow bars of colour, etched in a white field. Van Doesburg's *The Cow* dates from this period, as does his *Rhythm of a Russian Dance* of 1918, both works being influenced by Van der Leck.

The first architectural work associated with De Stijl was created by Robert van 't Hoff, who had seen Wright's work on a visit to America before the war, and in 1916 built a remarkably convincing Wrightian villa on the outskirts of Utrecht. Aside from this pioneering reinforced-concrete house at Huis ter Heide and a number of less elegant Wrightian works by Wils, there was comparatively little architectural activity in the early phases of De Stijl. Oud, who became City Architect to Rotterdam in 1918, at the age of twenty-eight, was never wholeheartedly affiliated with the movement. After abstaining from the 1918 manifesto he took pains to establish his artistic independence. He seems to have found in the compositions of the Austrian architect Josef Hoffmann a means for detaching himself from the more 'structural' interests of De Stijl. The single exception to this was his Purmerend factory project of 1919, wherein Neo-Plastic elements were rather diffidently applied to an otherwise bland assembly of masses. There was, in effect, very little Neo-Plastic architecture before 1920, when it made its first appearance in the work of Rietveld. Prior to 1915 Rietveld had taken courses with the architect P.J. Klaarhamer, who, while never associated with De Stijl, was collaborating at the time with Van der Leck.

The year 1917 saw the creation of the famous Red/Blue chair designed by Rietveld. This simple piece of furniture, based on a traditional folding bed-chair, provided the first occasion for a projection of the Neo-Plastic aesthetic into three dimensions. In its form, the bars and planes of Van der Leck's compositions were now realized as articulated and displaced elements in space. Aside from its articulation, the chair was distinguished by its exclusive use of primary colours in conjunction with a black frame – a combination which, with grey and white added, was to become the standard colour scheme of the De Stijl movement. Its structure enabled Rietveld to demonstrate an open architectonic organization that was manifestly free from the influence of Wright. It still predicated a *Gesamtkunstwerk*, but one that was free from the biological analogies of 19th-century synthetic Symbolism, that is to say from Art Nouveau.

Few, if any, of Rietveld's colleagues could have foreseen the full potential of the modest pieces of furniture that he went on to design between 1918 and 1920 – the buffet, baby cart and wheelbarrow which, as direct developments of the Red/Blue chair, were assembled from rectilinear wooden spars and planes, simply dowelled together. None of these pieces, however, fully anticipated the architectural environment attempted by Rietveld in his design for Dr Hartog's study, built at Maarssen in 1920. In this work each piece of furniture,

including the suspended light fitting, appeared to be 'elementarized', and the effect was to imply, like Mondrian's later paintings, an infinite series of co-ordinates in space.

In many respects Van Doesburg embodied the movement in himself, for by 1921 the composition of the group had radically altered. Van der Leck, Vantongerloo, Van 't Hoff, Oud, Wils and Kok had all by then disassociated themselves from De Stijl, while Mondrian had re-established himself as an independent artist in Paris. This Dutch defection convinced Van Doesburg that it was necessary to proselytize for De Stijl abroad. The fresh blood brought into the movement in 1922 reflected his international orientation. Of the new members of that year only one was Dutch, the architect Van Eesteren; the others were Russian and German – the architect, painter and graphic designer El Lissitzky and the film-maker Hans Richter. It was at Richter's invitation that Van Doesburg first visited Germany in 1920, and from this visit followed an invitation from Gropius to come to the Bauhaus in the following year. Van Doesburg's brief stay in Weimar in 1921 engendered a crisis within the Bauhaus, the repercussions of which have since become legendary, for the impact of his ideas on the students and faculty was both immediate and marked. Even Gropius who, under the circumstances, had reason to be apprehensive, designed in 1923 a suspended light for his own study which displayed an undeniable affinity to the Rietveld fitting designed for Hartog.

Of greater importance for the second phase of the De Stijl movement, lasting until 1925, was Van Doesburg's meeting with Lissitzky. Just two years before this meeting Lissitzky

127 Rietveld, buffet, 1919.

had developed his own form of Elementarist expression, evolved in collaboration with Kasimir Malevich at the Suprematist school in Vitebsk. Although Russian and Dutch Elementarism had quite independent origins – the one Suprematist, the other Neo-Plastic – Van Doesburg's work was transformed. After 1921, under the impact of Lissitzky's Proun compositions, both he and Van Eesteren began to project, as axonometric drawings, a series of hypothetical architectural constructs, each comprising an asymmetrical cluster of articulated planar elements suspended in space about a volumetric centre. Van Doesburg invited Lissitzky to become a member of De Stijl and in 1922 Lissitzky's abstract-typographic children's fable of 1920, 'The Story of Two Squares', appeared in the pages of the magazine. It is significant that the magazine itself changed its format at this juncture, Van Doesburg replacing the frontal composition and woodcut logotype designed by Huszar with an asymmetrical, Elementarist layout and a 'Constructivist' logo.

In 1923 Van Doesburg and Van Eesteren managed to crystallize the architectural style of Neo-Plasticism in an exhibition of their work, at Léonce Rosenberg's Paris gallery, 'L'Effort moderne'. This show was an immediate success and in consequence was restaged elsewhere in Paris and later in Nancy. Apart from the axonometric studies previously mentioned it included their project for a house for Rosenberg and two other seminal works, their study for the interior of a university hall and their project for an artist's house.

Meanwhile in Holland Huszar and Rietveld collaborated on the design for a small room to be built as part of the Grosse Berliner Kunstausstellung of 1923. Huszar designing the environment and Rietveld the furniture, including the important Berlin chair. Simultaneously, Rietveld began to work on the design and detailing of the Schröder-Schräder House in Utrecht. This house, built at the end of a late 19th-century terrace, was in many respects a realization of Van Doesburg's *Tot een beeldende architectuur* ('16 points of a Plastic Architecture'), published at the time of its completion. It fulfilled his prescription, being *elementary, economic and functional; un-*

128  Van Eesteren (left) and Van Doesburg, preparing for the Rosenberg exhibition in Paris, 1923, with a model of their 'artist's house'.

*monumental and dynamic; anti-cubic* in its form and *anti-decorative* in its colour. Its main living level on the top floor, with its open 'transformable plan', exemplified, despite its traditional brick and timber construction, his postulation of a dynamic architecture liberated from the encumbrance of load-bearing walls and the restrictions imposed by pierced openings. Van Doesburg's eleventh point reads like an idealized description of the house:

The new architecture is *anti-cubic*, that is to say, it does not try to freeze the different functional space cells in one closed cube. Rather, it throws the functional space cells (as well as the overhanging planes, balcony volumes, etc.) centrifugally from the core of the cube. And through this means, *height, width, depth, and time* (i.e. an imaginary four-dimensional entity) approaches a totally 'new plastic expression in open spaces. In this way architecture acquires a more or less floating aspect that, so to speak, works against the gravitational forces of nature.

The third and last phase of De Stijl activity, lasting from 1925 to 1931, was announced by

145

129, 130   Rietveld, Schröder-Schräder House, Utrecht, 1924. *Right*, plans of the upper floor, 'closed' (above) and 'open'.

52. Schröder House, plan, upper floor, closed

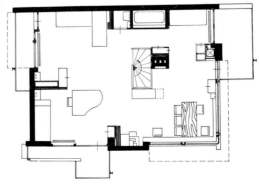

53. Schröder House, plan, upper floor, open

a dramatic rift between Mondrian and Van Doesburg over the latter's introduction of the diagonal into his paintings, in a series of 'counter-compositions' that he had completed in 1924. By now the initial unity had been lost, as much by Van Doesburg's incessant polemical activity as by his arbitrary modification of the Neo-Plastic canon. From his association with Lissitzky he had come to regard social structure and technology as among the prime determinants of form, irrespective of any concerns he might still entertain for the De Stijl ideal of universal harmony. By the mid-1920s he realized that universality could, by itself, only produce an artificially delimited culture, which by virtue of its antipathy to everyday objects could only be against the initial De Stijl concern — subscribed to even by Mondrian — for the unification of art and life. Van Doesburg seems to have opted for a Lissitzkian solution to this dilemma, whereby both the environmental scale and status of the object should determine the degree to which it may be manipulated in accordance with an abstract conception. Thus, while furniture and equipment as produced by the society at large ought to be accepted as the ready-made objects of the culture, the built environment itself could and indeed should still be made to conform to a higher order.

Van Doesburg and Van Eesteren gave an idealized version of this position in their essay *Vers une construction collective* ('Towards a Collective Construction'), published in 1924, in which they tended towards a more objective and technical solution to the problem of architectural synthesis:

We must realize that life and art are no longer separate domains. That is why the 'idea' of 'art' as an illusion separate from real life must disappear. The word 'Art' no longer means anything to us. In its place we demand the construction of our environment in accordance with creative laws based upon a fixed principle. These laws, following those of economics, mathematics, technique, sanitation, etc., are leading to a new plastic unity.

Later one reads, under the seventh point of the manifesto, the essence of the spirit that was to inform Van Doesburg's last major work, the Café L'Aubette of 1928:

We have established the true place of colour in architecture and we declare that painting, without architectural construction (that is, easel painting), has no further reason for existence.

Rietveld had little association with Van Doesburg after 1925. Nonetheless, his work developed in a similar direction, away from the Elementarism of the Schröder House and his early orthogonal furniture, towards more 'objective' solutions arising out of the application of technique. Rietveld started in this direction by redesigning the seats and backs of his chairs as curved planes, not only because such shapes were more comfortable, but also because they possessed greater structural strength. This led naturally to the technique of wood lamination and from there it was but a step, once the inhibiting Neo-Plastic aesthetic had been relinquished, to moulding a chair out of a single sheet of plywood. Rietveld's two-story chauffeur's house, built in Utrecht in 1927, was largely the product of a similar approach, where despite — or rather because of — its use of advanced technique, little of the original De Stijl aesthetic was left. Instead of primary colours, the exposed steel frame and concrete panels were painted black, and the surface of the panels themselves overpainted with a grid of white squares. Removed from Van Doesburg's conception of anti-cubic space as set out in his '16 Points of a Plastic Architecture', it was more determined by technique than by any drive towards universal form.

The Café L'Aubette in Strasbourg, designed in 1928, comprised a sequence of two large public rooms and ancillary spaces set within an 18th-century shell. These rooms were designed and realized by Van Doesburg in association with Hans Arp and Sophie Tauber Arp. While Van Doesburg controlled the general theme each artist was free to design his own room. With the single exception of Arp's mural, all the rooms were modulated by shallow abstract wall reliefs, colour, lighting and equipment being integrated into each composition. Van Doesburg's own scheme was, in effect, a

131  Van Doesburg, Café L'Aubette, Strasbourg, 1928–29.

reworking of his 1923 project for a university hall, in which a diagonal Elementarist composition had been deliberately imposed on all the surfaces of a partially orthogonal space. Van Doesburg's interior in L'Aubette was similarly dominated and distorted by the lines of a huge diagonal relief or counter-composition, passing obliquely over all the internal surfaces. This fragmentation through relief – an extension of Lissitzky's Proun room approach of 1923 – was complemented by the fact that the furnishing was free of any Elementarist pieces. In their place Van Doesburg designed 'standard' bentwood chairs and elsewhere employed extremely objective detailing. The tubular railing throughout was simply welded, while the main lighting consisted of bare light bulbs bracketed off two metal tubes suspended from the ceiling. Of this design he wrote:

The track of man in space (from left to right, from front to back, from above to below) has become of fundamental importance for painting in architecture. . . . In this painting the idea is not to lead man along a painted surface of a wall, in order to let him observe the pictorial development of the space from one wall to the other; the problem is to evoke the simultaneous effect of painting and architecture.

L'Aubette, finished in 1929, is the last Neo-Plastic architectural work of any significance.

Thereafter those artists who were still affiliated with De Stijl, including Van Doesburg and Rietveld, came increasingly under the influence of the Neue Sachlichkeit and thereby subject to the cultural values of international socialism. Van Doesburg's own house, built in Meudon around 1929, barely fulfils any of the sixteen points of his. 1924 manifesto. It is simply a utilitarian studio, of rendered reinforced-concrete frame and block construction, superficially resembling the type of artisan dwelling that had already been projected by Le Corbusier in the early 1920s. For fenestration Van Doesburg chose to use the standard French industrial sash, and for furniture he designed his own version of a *sachlich* chair in tubular steel. By 1930 the Neo-Plastic ideal of uniting the arts and transcending the division of art and life had been relinquished and returned to its origins in abstract painting, to the *art concert* of Van Doesburg's counter-compositions hung on the walls of his studio in Meudon. Yet Van Doesburg's conscious concern for a universal order remained alive, for in his last polemic, *Manifeste sur l'art concret* (1930), he wrote: 'If the means of expression are liberated from all particularity, they are in harmony with the ultimate end of art, which is to realize a universal language.' How these means were to become liberated in the case of applied art, such as furniture and equipment, was not made clear. A year later, at the age of forty-eight, Van Doesburg died in a sanatorium in Davos, Switzerland, and with him died the moving force of Neo-Plasticism. Of the original De Stijl artists only Mondrian seems to have remained committed to the strict principles of the movement, to the orthogonal and the primary colours which were the constituent elements of his mature work. With these he continued to represent the harmony of an unrealizable utopia. As he wrote in his *Plastic and Pure Plastic Art* (1937): 'Art is only a substitute while the beauty of life is still deficient. It will disappear in proportion, as life gains in equilibrium.'

## Chapter 17

# Le Corbusier
# and the Esprit Nouveau 1907-31

You employ stone, wood and concrete, and with these materials you build houses and palaces; that is construction. Ingenuity is at work. But suddenly you touch my heart, you do me good, I am happy and I say: 'This is beautiful.' That is Architecture. Art enters in. My house is practical. I thank you, as I might thank railway engineers or the telephone service. You have not touched my heart. But suppose that walls rise towards heaven in such a way that I am moved. I perceive your intentions. Your mood has been gentle, brutal, charming or noble. The stones you have erected tell me so. You fix me to the place and my eyes regard it. They behold something which expresses a thought. A thought which reveals itself without word or sound, but solely by means of shapes which stand in a certain relationship to one another. These shapes are such that they are clearly revealed in light. The relationships between them have not necessarily any reference to what is practical or descriptive. They are a mathematical creation of your mind. They are the language of Architecture. By the use of inert materials and starting from conditions more or less utilitarian, you have established certain relationships which have aroused my emotions. This is Architecture.

Le Corbusier
*Vers une architecture*, 1923

The absolutely central and seminal role played by Le Corbusier in the development of 20th-century architecture is sufficient cause for us to examine his early development in detail; and the fundamental significance of his achievement only becomes apparent when it is seen against the extremely varied and intense in-fluences to which he was subject in the decade between his first house, built in La Chaux-de-Fonds in 1905, when he was eighteen, and his last works realized there in 1916, one year before moving to Paris. Above all it seems necessary to remark on the distant Albigensian background of his otherwise Calvinist family, on that half forgotten but latent Manichean view of the world which may well have been the origin of his 'dialectical' habit of mind. I am referring to that ever-present play with opposites — with the contrast between solid and void, between light and dark, between Apollo and Medusa — that permeates his architecture and is evident as a habit of mind in most of his theoretical texts.

Le Corbusier was born in 1887 in the Swiss watch-making town of La Chaux-de-Fonds, which is situated in the Jura, close to the French frontier. One of the prime images of his adolescence must have been this highly rational gridded industrial town that had been rebuilt after its destruction by fire some twenty years before his birth. During his training as a designer-engraver at the local school of arts and crafts, Charles Edouard Jeanneret (as he then was) became involved in his late teens in the last phases of the Arts and Crafts movement. The Jugendstil manner of his first house, the Villa Fallet of 1905, was a crystallization of all that he had been taught by his master, Charles L'Eplattenier, director of the *cours supérieur* at the applied art school in La Chaux-de-Fonds. L'Eplattenier's own point of departure had been Owen Jones, whose book *The Grammar of Ornament* (1856) was a definitive compendium of decorative art. L'Eplattenier aimed to create a native school of applied art and building for the Jura region and, after Jones, he taught his students to derive all ornament from their immediate natural environment. The vernacular type and décor of the Villa Fallet were exemplary in this respect: its overall form was essentially a variation on the wood and stone farmhouses of the Jura, while its decorative elements were derived from the flora and fauna of the region.

Despite his admiration for Owen Jones, for the Budapest-trained L'Eplattenier the cultural centre of Europe remained Vienna, and his one ambition was that his prime pupil should be apprenticed there to Josef Hoffmann. Accordingly, in the autumn of 1907 Le Corbusier was dispatched to Vienna. He was cordially received, but he seems to have rejected Hoffmann's offer of work and with it the sophistries of the now classicized Jugendstil. Certainly the designs that he made in Vienna for further houses, to be completed in La Chaux-de-Fonds in 1909, show little trace of Hoffmann's influence. This apparent disaffection with the Jugendstil in its decline was encouraged by a meeting with Tony Garnier in Lyons, in the winter of 1907, just as Garnier was beginning to amplify his 1904 project for a Cité Industrielle. Le Corbusier's utopian socialist sympathies and his susceptibility to a typological — not to say Classical — approach to architecture certainly date from this meeting, about which he wrote: 'This man knew that the imminent birth of a new architecture depended on social phenomena. His plans displayed a great facility. They were the consequence of one hundred years of architectural evolution in France.'

The year 1907 may be regarded as the turning point of Le Corbusier's life, for in that year he not only met Garnier, but he also made a crucial visit to the Charterhouse of Ema, in Tuscany. There he experienced for the first time the living 'commune' which was to become the socio-physical model for his own reinterpretation of the utopian socialist ideas that he had inherited in part from L'Eplattenier and in part from Garnier. Later he was to describe the Charterhouse as an institution in which 'an authentic human aspiration was fulfilled: silence, solitude, but also daily contact with men.'

In 1908, Le Corbusier obtained part-time employment with Auguste Perret in Paris, whose reputation had already been made through his 'domestication' of the reinforced-concrete frame in his apartment block built in the Rue Franklin in 1904. The fourteen months that Le Corbusier spent in Paris afforded him a totally new outlook on both life and work. Aside from receiving a basic training in reinforced-concrete technique the capital gave him the chance to broaden his knowledge of French Classical culture, by visiting the museums, libraries and lecture halls of the city. At the same time, much to the disapproval of L'Eplattenier, he became convinced through his contact with Perret, that béton armé was the material of the future. Aside from its malleable monolithic nature, its durability and inherent economy, Perret valued the concrete frame as an agent for resolving the age-old conflict between the structural authenticity of the Gothic and the Humanist values of Classical form.

The impact of all these diverse experiences may be gauged from the project that he made for his alma mater, on his return to La Chaux-de-Fonds in 1909. This building, evidently conceived in reinforced concrete, consisted of three stepped tiers of artists' studios, each with its own enclosed garden, arranged around a central communal space covered by a pyramidal glass roof. This free adaptation of the Carthusian cell form, with its connotations of communality, was the first instance on which Le Corbusier reinterpreted a received type in order to accommodate the programme of an entirely new type. Such typological transformations, with their spatial and ideological references, were to become an intrinsic part of his working method. Since this synthetic procedure was impure by definition, it was inevitable that his works should become charged with references to a number of different antecedents at once. For all that this process may at times have been partly unconscious, the art school must be seen as being as much an heir to Godin's Familistère of 1856 as it was a reinterpretation of Ema. Nevertheless Ema was to remain embedded in Le Corbusier's imagination as an image of harmony to be reinterpreted innumerable times, first on a large scale in his 'Immeuble-Villa' project of 1922 and then, less directly, in the residential block types that he designed, throughout the next decade, for his hypothetical city plans.

Le Corbusier went to Germany in 1910 ostensibly to further his knowledge of reinforced-concrete technique, but while he was there he was commissioned by the art school of La Chaux-de-Fonds to study the state of decorative art. This undertaking, which resulted in a book, brought him into contact with all the major figures of the Deutsche Werkbund, above all with Peter Behrens and Heinrich Tessenow, the two artists who were to exercise a strong influence on two of his later works in La Chaux-de-Fonds — the Villa Jeanneret Père of 1912 and the Scala Cinema of 1916. Aside from this, the Werkbund contact made him conscious of the achievements of modern production engineering, the ships, automobiles and aircraft that were to form the substance of his polemical essay 'Des Yeux qui ne voient pas.' At the end of the year, after five months in the office of Behrens, where he would certainly have met Mies van der Rohe, he left Germany to take up a teaching post at La Chaux-de-Fonds, offered him by L'Eplattenier. Before returning to Switzerland, however, he made an extensive tour of the Balkans and Asia Minor, and henceforth Ottoman architecture was to be a muted but decided influence on his work. This much is evident from his lyrical record of the trip, his *Voyage d'Orient* of 1913.

The five years prior to 1916 shaped the orientation of his future career in Paris. His final break with L'Eplattenier and his simultaneous rejection of Frank Lloyd Wright, whose work he would have known from the Wasmuth volumes of 1910-11, enabled him to remain open to the possibilities for rationalized production in reinforced concrete. In 1913 he established his own office in La Chaux-de-Fonds, ostensibly to specialize in *béton armé*.

In 1915, in conjunction with his boyhood friend, the Swiss engineer Max du Bois, he evolved two ideas that were to inform his development throughout the 1920s — his reinterpretation of the Hennebique frame as the Maison Dom-Ino, which was to be the structural basis of most of his houses up to 1935, and the 'Villes Pilotis', a city projected as being

built on piles; the concept of the elevated street evidently deriving from Eugène Hénard's 'Rue Future' of 1910.

The year 1916 saw the culmination of his early career in La Chaux-de-Fonds with the building of the Villa Schwob, which was an extraordinary synthesis of all that he had experienced so far. It was, above all else, an elaborate assimilation of the spatial potential of the Hennebique system, permitting its author to impose on a skeleton structure stylistic elements drawn from Hoffmann, Perret and Tessenow. There was even an erotic evocation of a seraglio, from which the building took its nickname of 'Villa Turque'. At the same time, it was the first occasion on which Le Corbusier conceived a house in honorific terms, that is, as a palace. The alternately wide and narrow bay system and the symmetrical organization of the plan bestowed on the Villa Schwob a structure that was undeniably Palladian. Similar Classical connotations were indicated in the text that accompanied its publication in *L'Esprit Nouveau* in 1921, wherein Julien Caron wrote:

Le Corbusier had to resolve a delicate problem which was contingent upon making a pure work of architecture, as postulated by a design in which the masses were of a primary geometry, the square and the circle. Such speculation in building a house has rarely been attempted except during the Renaissance.

For the first time Le Corbusier employed 'regulating lines', that Classical device used to maintain proportional control over the façade, manifest for instance in the disposition of the fenestration in accordance with the golden section. In the years that followed, this 'house-palace' theme saw its fulfilment in Le Corbusier's work on two different scales, with related but separate socio-cultural connotations. The first was the free-standing individual bourgeois villa of Palladian precedent, as exemplified in the masterly houses of the late 1920s; the second was the collective dwelling, conceived as a Baroque palace that could evoke through its 'set-back' plan the ideological connotations of a phalanstery.

Soon after he moved to Paris in October 1916 to establish a practice, Le Corbusier had the good fortune to be introduced by Auguste Perret to the painter Amédée Ozenfant, with whom he was to evolve the all-embracing machine asthetic of Purism. Grounded in Neo-Platonic philosophy, Purism extended its discourse to cover all forms of plastic expression from salon painting to product design and architecture. It was nothing less than a comprehensive theory of civilization which strenuously advocated the conscious refinement of all existing types. Hence it was as much against what Le Corbusier and Ozenfant regarded as the unwarranted distortions of Cubism in painting (see their first joint polemic entitled *Après le Cubisme* of 1918) as it was in favour of the 'evolutionary' perfection of, say, Thonet bentwood furniture or standard café tableware. Their first full formulation of this aesthetic came with their essay entitled 'Le Purisme', which appeared in 1920, in the fourth number of the magazine *L'Esprit Nouveau*, a literary and artistic journal which they were to continue to edit with the poet Paul Dermée until 1925. Without doubt the most fertile period of their collaboration came with the gestation of *Vers une architecture* which, prior to its publication as a book in 1923, was published in part in *L'Esprit Nouveau* under the double pseudonym of Le Corbusier-Saugnier.

This text – the credit for which in book form was appropriated by Le Corbusier – articulated the conceptual duality around which the rest of his work was to revolve: on the one hand the imperative need to satisfy functional requirements through empirical form, and on the other the impulse to use abstract elements to affect the senses and nourish the intellect. This dialectical view of form, introduced under the heading 'Esthétique et architecture de l'ingenieur', was exemplified by the most advanced engineering structures of the epoch, by Eiffel's Garabit Viaduct of 1884 and by Giacomo Matté Trucco's Fiat Works of 1915 to 1921

The other aspect of the Engineer's Aesthetic – product design – was represented by the ships, automobiles and aircraft which were featured as separate sub-sections under the general heading 'Des Yeux qui ne voient pas'. The third section returned the reader to the antithesis of Classical architecture, to the lucid poetry of the Athenian Acropolis, which was appraised in the penultimate chapter under the title 'Architecture, pure creation de l'esprit'. Such was Le Corbusier's admiration of engineering exactitude that the profiles of the Parthenon were presented as being analogous to those now wrought by machine tools. He wrote: 'All this plastic machinery is realized in marble with the rigour that we have learnt to apply in the machine. The impression is of naked, polished steel.'

Over the first five years of his intense activity in Paris, during which he painted and wrote in all his spare time, Le Corbusier earned his living during the day as the manager of a brickworks and building materials plant at Alfortville. In 1922 he relinquished this position to enter into practice with his cousin Pierre Jeanneret, a contract which lasted until the outbreak of the Second World War. One of the earliest undertakings of the office was to advance the 'constructional' idea first touched on with du Bois during the early years of the First World War, namely the Maison Dom-Ino and the Villes Pilotis.

The Dom-Ino prototype was evidently open to different levels of interpretation. While on the one hand it was simply a technical device for production, on the other it was a play on the word 'Dom-Ino' as a patent industrial name, denoting a house as standardized as a domino. This play acquired the force of a literal pun where the free-standing columns could be regarded in plan as domino dots and where the zigzag pattern of an aggregation of these houses resembled the formations of dominoes in play. With their symmetrical arrangement, however, such patterns could also acquire specific connotations by either resembling the typical Baroque palace plan of Fourier's phalanstery or alternatively by recalling Eugène Hénard's 'Boulevard à Redans' of 1903. With his own 'rue à redents' of 1920, Le Corbusier managed to combine the image of the phalanstery with his own 'anti-corridor street' polemic. At the same time he wished to

132, 133  Le Corbusier, Maison Dom-Ino, 1915.
*Below,* structure of 'Dom-Ino' unit; *above,* perspective and plan showing possible grouping.

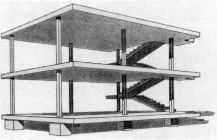

see the Dom-Ino as a piece of equipment, analogous in its form and mode of assembly to a typical piece of product design. Such elements were seen by Le Corbusier as *objets-types*, whose forms had already become refined in response to typical needs. In *Vers une architecture* he wrote:

If we eliminate from our hearts and minds all dead concepts in regard to houses and look at the question from a critical and objective point of view, we shall arrive at the 'House Machine', the mass production house, healthy (and morally so too) and beautiful in the same way that the working tools and instruments which accompany our existence are beautiful.

The post-war attempt by the Voisin aeroplane company to break into the French housing market with an assembly-line production of timber houses was enthusiastically acclaimed by Le Corbusier in the second issue of *L'Esprit Nouveau*. Yet at the same time he realized that such production could only be obtained through the exercise of high-grade skills under factory conditions, a combination of circumstances rare in the building industry. He acknowledged these limitations in his Maison Dom-Ino proposal which aside from the formwork and the steel reinforcement was designed to be built by unskilled labour. As early as 1919 he had adopted a comparable

'collagist' approach to construction, when he proposed to use corrugated asbestos sheets as permanent shuttering for the concrete vaulted roof of his Maison Monol.

In 1922 both the Maison Dom-Ino and the Villes Pilotis were further developed as the 'Maison Citrohan' and the 'Ville Contemporaine', both projects being exhibited in the Salon d'Automne of that year. Where the latter was directly evolved, at least in section, out of Hénard's Rue Future of 1910, the former utilized the Hennebique frame to project a long rectilinear volume, open at one end, which approximated to the traditional megaron form of the Mediterranean. Within this basic type — designed in two successive versions — Le Corbusier projected for the first time his characteristic double-height living space, complete with a sleeping mezzanine and children's bedrooms on the roof. Aside from its roots in the Greek vernacular, this type, which he first produced in 1920, seems to have been derived from a workers' café in Paris, in the Rue de

153

134 Le Corbusier, Maison Citrohan, 1920. Perspective, ground and floor plans.

135 Le Corbusier, Pessac housing estate, near Bordeaux, 1926, on opening day.

136 Gropius (left), Frau Gropius and Le Corbusier in a Paris café.

Babylone where he lunched each day with his cousin. From this small restaurant they took the section and the basic arrangement of the Maison Citrohan: 'Simplification of the light source; one single bay at each end; two lateral bearing walls; a flat roof over; a veritable box which could be used as a house.'

While the Maison Citrohan, elevated on *pilotis*, came close to anticipating *Les 5 Points d'une architecture nouvelle*, which Le Corbusier finally formulated in 1926, it was hardly applicable to anything other than 'suburban' development. He was soon to use a version of it to this end in the garden city estates he built at Liège and Pessac in 1926. Among the 130 reinforced-concrete frame houses built at Pessac for the industrialist Henri Frugès, there was one prevalent type known as the 'sky-scraper' unit which was in effect a combination of the Maison Citrohan and the back-to-back units that he had designed for the 'city' of Audincourt in the same year. A true version of the Citrohan type was not realized, however, until his work at the Stuttgart Weissenhofsied-lung of 1927. Pessac, as its mixture of unit types would indicate, was a culmination of his incessant attempts in the early 1920s to put his various designs for the standardized dwelling into production. The name 'Citrohan' was a play on the patent name of the famous auto-mobile company, indicating that a house should be as standardized as a car. Pessac showed the first conscious integration of Purist colour displacements into architecture. The architect observed at the time:

The site at Pessac is very dry. The grey con-crete houses produce an insupportable com-pressed mass, lacking in air. Colour is able to bring us space. Here's how we have established certain invariable points. Some façades are painted in burnt sienna. We have made the lines of other houses recede, through clear ultramarine blue. Again we have confused certain sections with the foliage of gardens and trees, through pale green façades.

Unlike his European contemporaries, Grop-ius and Mies van der Rohe, Le Corbusier was anxious to develop the urban connotations of his architecture. The Ville Contemporaine for three million was the ultimate demonstration of this aspect in his work up to 1922. Influenced equally by the gridded skyscraper cities of the United States and the image of the 'city-crown' as put forward by Bruno Taut in his book *Die Stadtkrone* (1919), Le Corbusier projected the Ville Contemporaine as an élite capitalist city of administration and control, with garden cities for the workers being sited, along with industry, beyond the 'security zone' of the green belt encompassing the city.

The city itself, textured like an oriental carpet and some four times the surface area of Manhattan, consisted of residential blocks some ten to twelve storeys in height plus twenty-four 60-storey office towers in the centre, the whole surrounded by a Picturesque park which, like the traditional *glacis*, maintained the class separation of the urban élite from the suburban proletariat. The cruciform office towers themselves — the so-called Cartesian skyscrapers — were reminiscent in their serrated plan profile of stepped Khmer or Indian temple forms and as such they were evidently intended to replace as secular centres of power the religious structures of the traditional city. That such an authority was attributed to these forms is suggested by their proportional relation to the grid of the city, where they take up a golden section of the surface area in plan, within the double square occupied by the city as a whole.

None of this was lost on the Communist newspaper *L'Humanité*, which regarded the entire project as reactionary. Their sense of Le Corbusier's commitment to Saint-Simonian methods of management and control was entirely confirmed by the publication of his book *Urbanisme* (*The City of Tomorrow*) in 1925, its last plate depicting Louis XIV supervising the building of the Invalides. Even Le Corbusier was sufficiently embarrassed by this image to place underneath its caption the rider that it was not to be understood as support for the French Fascist party Action Française.

The Ville Contemporaine was no less ideological in the detailed organization of its residential districts, which were made up of two different block prototypes — the perimeter block and

137 Le Corbusier and Jeanneret, Plan Voisin proposal for Paris, 1925. The hand points towards the new business centre of the city.

the 'set-back' or *redent* formation — each postulating a different conception of the city. The former was still committed to the idea of a 'walled' city made up of streets, while the latter presupposed a wall-less 'open city', that vision finally to be achieved in the Ville Radieuse, of a dense city elevated above the surface of a continuous park. The implicity anti-street polemic of this vision was finally made explicit in an essay on the street that Le Corbusier wrote in 1929 for the Syndicalist newspaper *L'Intransigeant*.

Apart from providing the 'essential joys' of sunlight and green, the open city was supposed to facilitate locomotion, in accordance with Le Corbusier's entrepreneurial aphorism that 'A city made for speed is a city made for success.' This was part of the rhetoric that accompanied his 'Plan Voisin' proposal for Paris of 1925 — the paradoxical notion that the automobile having effectively destroyed the great city could now be exploited as an instrument for its salvation. Notwithstanding their financial support, the car/aircraft cartel, Voisin was no doubt only too aware of the economic and political impossibility of raising vast cruciform towers next to the Ile de la Cité.

The most important and enduring contribution of the Ville Contemporaine was its Immeuble-Villa unit, an adaptation of the Maison Citrohan as a general type for high-rise high-density living. These units, stacked up on six double floors, included garden terraces, one for each duplex, an arrangement

155

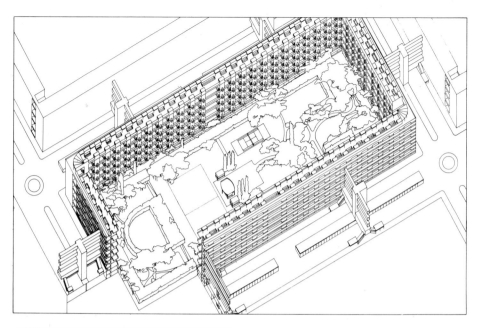

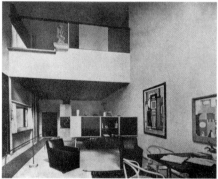

which today seems to be one of the few acceptable solutions for high-rise *family* living. In the so-called 'cellular' perimeter blocks of the Ville Contemporaine, these terraced duplexes opened at ground level to bounded rectangular green space, equipped with recreational facilities for communal use. The marginal provision of additional communal space within the block and around the periphery of this area and the intended provision of hotel service throughout situates this proposal some-where between the bourgeois apartment block and the socialist collective dwelling (cf. the phalanstery and Borie's Aérodromes). The Immeuble-Villa living unit was finally worked out in detail and exhibited as a prototype in the form of the Pavillon de L'Esprit Nouveau, built for the Exposition des Arts Décoratifs held in Paris in 1925. Unfortunately, subsequent attempts to market this unit, both as a freehold maisonette in the city and as a free-standing villa in the suburbs, did not meet with success. The Pavillon de L'Esprit Nouveau was a condensation of the Purist sensibility: while machinist in promise and urban by implication, since it was designed ostensibly for mass production and aggregation at high density, it was furnished in accordance with the Purist canon of *objets-types*, that is with English club armchairs, Thonet bentwood furniture and standard Parisian cast-iron park pieces, with *objets-tableaux* of Purist origin, with oriental rugs and South American pottery. This finely balanced assembly of folk, craft and machine-made objects, borrowed in spirit from Adolf Loos, was posited here under the patronage of the Minister for the Arts as a polemical gesture against the Art Deco movement.

In 1925 Le Corbusier also returned to the theme of the bourgeois villa, first in his Maison Cook, completed in the following year as a demonstration of *Les 5 points d'une architecture nouvelle*, which were published in 1926, and then in the project for the Villa Meyer, which anticipated the villa at Garches and the Villa Savoie at Poissy, completed in 1927 and 1929 respectively.

All these houses depended for their expression on the syntax of the 'five points': (1) the *pilotis* elevating the mass off the ground, (2) the free plan, achieved through the separation of the load-bearing columns from the walls subdividing the space, (3) the free façade, the corollary of the free plan in the vertical plane, (4) the long horizontal sliding window or *fenêtre en longueur*, and finally (5) the roof garden, restoring, supposedly, the area of ground covered by the house.

The latent potential of the Hennebique frame in the Maison Dom-Ino and the solid lateral walls of the Maison Citrohan determined to an equal degree the basic *parti* of all these houses, with the liberal use of free-standing columns, strip-windowed façades and cantilevered floor slabs. The structural subdivision of the Maison Dom-Ino (the rhythmic formula AAB comprising two wide bays plus a narrow one containing a stair) links the overt Palladianism of the Villa Schwob to the suppressed Palladianism of the villa at Garches, both houses seemingly organized about the classic Palladian ABABA rhythm, remarked on by Colin Rowe. Palladio's Villa Malcontenta of 1560 and Le Corbusier's villa at Garches of some 350 years later are equally predicated in the longitudinal direction on alternating double and single bays producing a rhythm of 2:1:2:1:2. As Rowe has pointed out, a similar syncopation obtains in the other dimension:

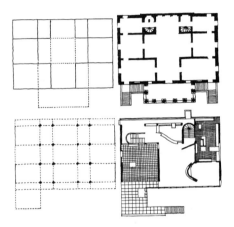

140  Le Corbusier and Jeanneret, Villa de Monzie, Garches, 1927.

141  Palladio's Villa Malcontenta, 1560 (top), and Le Corbusier's Villa de Monzie, Garches, 1927, with analyses of their proportional rhythm.

In both cases, six 'transverse' lines of support, rhythmically alternating single and double bays, are established; but the rhythm of the parallel lines of support, as a result of Le Corbusier's use of the cantilever, differs slightly. At the villa at Garches, it is $\frac{1}{2}:1\frac{1}{2}:1\frac{1}{2}:1\frac{1}{2}:\frac{1}{2}$ and at the Malcontenta $1\frac{1}{2}:2:2:1\frac{1}{2}$. In plan, Corbusier thus obtains a sort of compression for his central bay and interest seems transferred to his outer bays, which are augmented by the extra half unit of the cantilever; while Palladio secures a dominance for his central division, and a progression towards his portico, which

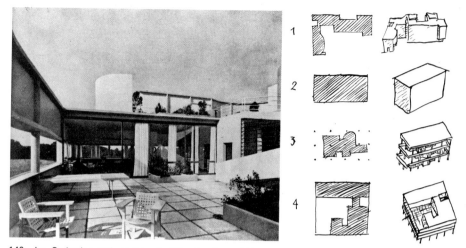

142 Le Corbusier and Jeanneret, Villa Savoie, Poissy, 1929–31. The first-floor 'jardin suspendu'.

143 Le Corbusier, the Four Compositions of 1929: (1) Maison La Roche, (2) villa at Garches, (3) Weissenhofsiedlung in Stuttgart, (4) Villa Savoie.

focuses interest there. In both cases the projecting element, terrace or portico, occupies $1\frac{1}{2}$ units in depth.

Rowe goes on to contrast the centralization of the Villa Malcontenta with the centrifugality of the villa at Garches:

At Garches the central focus has been consistently broken up, concentration at one point is disintegrated, and replaced by a peripheral dispersion of incident. The dismembered fragments of the central focus become, in fact, a sort of serial installation of interest round the extremities of the plan.

Aside from its Purist layering of frontalized planes in space and its play with literal and phenomenal transparency, remarked on by Rowe and Robert Slutzky, Garches was significant for its resolution of a problem that had first been posed by Loos: how to combine the comfort and informality of the Arts and Crafts plan with the asperities of geometrical, if not Neo-Classical, form — how to reconcile the private realm of modern convenience with the public façade of architectural order. As Le Corbusier's Four Compositions of 1929 would indicate, Garches was able to achieve this, with an

elegance denied to Loos, through the displacements afforded by the invention of the free plan. The disjunction, so to speak, of the complex interior was held away from the public front, by the elision of the free façade.

If Garches is to be associated with the Villa Malcontenta, the Villa Savoie, as Rowe again points out, may be compared to Palladio's Villa Rotonda. The almost square plan of the Villa Savoie, with its elliptical ground floor and centralized ramp, may be read as a complex metaphor for the centralized and biaxial plan of the Rotonda. There, however, all similarity ends, Palladio insisting on centrality and Le Corbusier asserting, within his self-imposed square, the spiralling qualities of asymmetry, rotation and peripheral dispersal. Nevertheless, in his book *Précisions sur un état présent de l'architecture et de l'urbanisme* (1930) Le Corbusier made the imminent Classicism of the Villa Savoie abundantly clear:

The inhabitants come here because this rustic landscape goes well with country life. They survey their whole domain from the height of their *jardin suspendu* or from the four aspects of their *fenêtres en longueur*. Their domestic life is inserted into a Virgilian dream.

158

With the Villa Savoie, one arrives at the last of Le Corbusier's Four Compositions of 1929. The first was his Maison La Roche of 1923, which he presented in 1929 as a Purist version of the Gothic Revival L-plan — a 'genre plutôt facile, pittoresque, mouvementé'; the second was shown as an ideal prism, and the third and fourth (the villa at Garches and the Villa Savoie) as alternative strategies for reconciling the first two, the former depending on a subtle integration of the first and second and the latter on the encompassing of the first by a prism.

With their 1927 entry to the international competition for the League of Nations (Société des Nations or SdN) headquarters in Geneva, Le Corbusier and Pierre Jeanneret produced their first design for a large public structure. Their attention had hitherto been focused on the house and on the concomitant simplicity of a basic prism. Now they addressed themselves to the necessary complexity of the 'palace' as a type. The competition's conditions stipulated two buildings, one for the secretariat and one for the assembly, and this programmatic duality led the architects to take an Elementarist approach to the design: the constituent 'elements' being first established and then manipulated in order to generate a number of alternative arrangements. This extension of the Elementarism professed at the turn of the century by the Beaux-Arts master Julien Guadet, would have come to Le Corbusier via Guadet's pupils, Garnier and Perret. That he was to adopt this approach generally when dealing with large complexes is shown by his preliminary studies for the Palace of the Soviets project, 1931. There under eight alternative arrangements we read the caption: 'the various stages of the project, wherein one sees the organs, already independently established, the one from the other, take up little by little their reciprocal places to culminate in a synthetic solution.' We find a comparable remark appended to an alternative scheme for the SdN project published in Le Corbusier's *Une Maison, Un Palais* (1928). Under a symmetrical layout (evidently more rational, from an operational point of view), we read: 'alternative proposition employing the same elements of composition'. The asymmetrical organization finally adopted suggests a conflict between the circulatory logic of the symmetrical layout and a Classical preference for an axial approach to the representative façade of the principal building.

The SdN project is both the climax and the crisis point of Le Corbusier's early career: a moment of acclaim, denied (if we are to believe him) by his disqualification on the grounds that he had not submitted his entry in the appropriate graphic medium. It represents the culmination of his Purist period, since it virtually coincides with the introduction into his painting of figurative elements and of what he later called *objets à réaction poétique*, loosely translatable as 'objects evocative of poetic emotion'. From now on, while his painting became organic and figurative, his architecture, at a public level at least, became increasingly symmetrical. In retrospect the League of

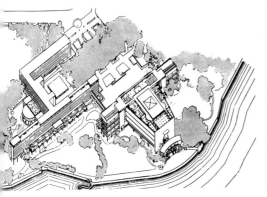

144   Le Corbusier and Jeanneret, project for the League of Nations Building, Geneva, 1927. (Compare H. Meyer and Wittwer's entry, ill. 114.)

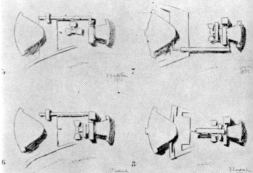

145   Le Corbusier and Jeanneret, project for the Palace of the Soviets, Moscow, 1931. Four alternative layouts using the same elements.

Nations entry must be considered as a watershed; as a point of division, not only within his own work, but also between himself and his following within the international Modern Movement, particularly where this concerned the support of those whose political convictions lay to the left. In 1927 the Constructivist affinities of the League of Nations entry, its commitment to free-floating asymmetry and technical innovation, its secretariat *à pilotis* (reminiscent, in plan, of Lissitzky's *Wolkenbügel*), its mechanized cleaning system, its air-conditioned assembly hall (acoustically profiled, tuned and flooded with light), could do nothing but command the enthusiastic support of the young, irrespective of their political allegiance. But the undeniable monumentality – expressed in its stone facing and in the hierarchical, seven-door, entry system proposed to conduct the various classes of user to their appointed place within the auditorium – seems to have had the effect of eventually arousing a certain ideological mistrust.

Le Corbusier's drive to resolve the dichotomy between the Engineer's Aesthetic and Architecture, to inform utility with the hierarchy of myth, was bound to bring him into conflict with the functionalist-socialist designers of the late 1920s. His 'Mundaneum' or 'Cité Mondiale', designed in 1929 for Geneva as a centre of world thought, provoked a sharp reaction from his Czech admirer, the left-wing artist and critic Karel Teige. It was not the content but the *form* of the Cité that provoked Teige's objections, particularly the helicoidal ziggurat of the 'Musée Mondial'. In 1927 Teige had publicly supported Le Corbusier in the international dispute over his League of Nations entry and had called on all other Czech artists to do the same. Now, barely two years later, he attacked him with such vehemence that Le Corbusier was prompted to reply, in the essay entitled 'The Defence of Architecture,' written for Teige's journal, *Stavba*. In his attack Teige had quoted from Hannes Meyer's essay of 1928, *Bauen* ('Building').

All things in the world are a product of the formula, function times economics, so none of these things are works of art; all art is composition and hence unsuited to a particular end. All life is function and therefore not artistic, the idea of the composition of a dock is enough to make a cat laugh. But how is a town plan designed or the plan of a dwelling? Competition or Function? Art or Life?

Le Corbusier placed this quotation at the head of his essay, making it clear that his riposte was directed as much to Meyer as to Teige. He then argued:

Today amongst the avant garde of the Neue Sachlichkeit, one has killed two words: *Baukunst* (Architecture) and *Kunst* (Art). One has replaced them by *Bauen* (To Build) and *Leben* (To Live). . . . Today, where mechanization brings us a gigantic production, architecture is above all in the battleship, Monsieur Hannes Meyer; as in the conduct of war or in the shape of a pen, or in a telephone. Architecture is a phenomenon of creation, according to an arrangement. Whoever determines the arrangement, determines the composition.

In the same year as the Teige attack he acknowledged in his book *Précisions* that the Mundaneum had been badly received by the German architectural Left, but he saw no reason to modify his ultimate position and hence maintained that

The buildings projected are strictly utilitarian – particularly this helicoidal Musée Mondial so violently incriminated. . . . The plans of the Cité Mondiale bring to buildings which are true machines a certain magnificence wherein some wish to discover at any cost an archaeological inspiration. But from my point of view, this harmonious quality arises from another thing, from a simple response to a problem well stated.

Nonetheless he could not, and indeed did not, deny that the site layout of the Cité Mondiale had been determined by a network of *tracés régulateurs*, comparable to those used to control the façade of the villa at Garches – a façade which, however much it subscribed to the canons of the Purist machine aesthetic, remained as Classical in its affinities as the Palladian plan type from which its structure had been derived.

## Chapter 18

# Mies van der Rohe
# and the significance of fact 1921-33

It then became clear to me that it was not the task of architecture to invent form. I tried to understand what that task was. I asked Peter Behrens, but he could not give me an answer. He did not ask that question. The others said, 'What we build is architecture', but we weren't satisfied with this answer . . . since we knew that it was a question of truth, we tried to find out what truth really was. We were very delighted to find a definition of truth by St Thomas Aquinas: 'Adequatio intellectus et rei', or as a modern philosopher expresses it in the language of today: 'Truth is the significance of fact'.

Berlage was a man of great seriousness who would not accept anything that was fake and it was he who had said that nothing should be built that is not clearly constructed. And Berlage did exactly that. And he did it to such an extent that his famous building in Amsterdam, The Beurs, has a medieval character without being medieval. He used brick in the way the medieval people did. The idea of a clear construction came to me there, as one of the fundamentals we should accept. We can talk about that easily but to do it is not easy. It is very difficult to stick to this fundamental construction, and then to elevate it to a structure. I must make it clear that in the English language you call everything structure. In Europe we don't. We call a shack a shack and not a structure. By structure we have a philosophical idea. The structure is the whole from top to bottom, to the last detail – with the same ideas. That is what we call structure.

Mies van der Rohe
(quoted by Peter Carter in *Architectural Design*, March 1961)

As the above quotation makes clear, Ludwig Mies – he later added his mother's name, Van der Rohe – was as much inspired by the work of the Dutch architect Berlage as by that Prussian school of Neo-Classicism to which he became the direct heir. Unlike his contemporary, Le Corbusier, he was not educated within the Arts and Crafts ethos of the Jugendstil. At the age of fourteen he entered his father's stone-mason's business and after two years at a trade school and a subsequent period as a stucco designer for a local builder, in 1905 he left his native town of Aachen for Berlin where he worked for a minor architect specializing in timber construction. There followed a further period of apprenticeship with the furniture designer Bruno Paul before he ventured briefly on his own in 1907, to build his first house in a restrained *englische* manner, reminiscent of the work of the Werkbund architect Hermann Muthesius. In the following year he joined Peter Behrens, whose newly established Berlin office was beginning to develop an overall house style for the electrical combine AEG.

During his three years in Behrens's office, Mies became aware of the *Schinkelschüler* tradition, which, apart from its Neo-Classical affiliation, was committed to the idea of *Baukunst*, not only as an ideal of technical elegance but also as a philosophical concept. Schinkel's brick-faced Bauakademie in Berlin, with its warehouse-like detailing, was later compared by Mies to the articulate construction of Berlage's Amsterdam Beurs or Exchange, which he had first seen when he visited Holland in 1912. On leaving Behrens's employ in 1911, after a brief stint as site architect on Behrens's German Embassy in St Petersburg, Mies opened his own office with the Perls

House, completed in Berlin-Zehlendorf in that year. This was the first of a series of five neo-Schinkelesque houses to be designed by Mies before the outbreak of the First World War. In 1912 he succeeded Behrens as architect to Mrs H.E.L.J. Kröller, who wanted a gallery and residence in The Hague to house the famous Kröller-Müller collection: the project was mocked up in canvas and wood at full size before being inexplicably abandoned. This year also saw his Boullée-like monument to Bismarck, which was to be the last significant project of his pre-war career.

The defeat and collapse of the German military-industrial imperium at the end of the First World War reduced the country to a state of economic and political turmoil and Mies, like every other architect who had fought in the war, sought to create an architecture that was more organic than that permitted by the autocratic canons of the Schinkel tradition. In 1919 he began to direct the architectural section of the radical Novembergruppe, named after the month of the Republican revolution and dedicated to the revitalization of the arts throughout Germany. This association brought him into contact with the Arbeitsrat für Kunst and with the ideas of Taut's Glass Chain (see Chapter

146 Mies van der Rohe, project for an office building in Friedrichstrasse, Berlin, 1921. First scheme.

13), and there can be little doubt that his first skyscraper project of 1920 was made in response to Paul Scheerbart's *Glasarchitektur* of 1914. The same faceted, crystal skyscraper theme occurred in his Friedrichstrasse competition entry of 1921, and the publication of both of these projects in the last issue of Taut's magazine *Frühlicht* confirmed his post-war Expressionist affiliation. Mies's intent at this time was to render glass as a complex reflective surface which would be constantly subject to transformation under the impact of light. This much is clear from the description that accompanied the first publication of his Friedrichstrasse proposal:

In my project for a skyscraper at the Friedrichstrasse Station in Berlin I used a prismatic form which seemed to me to fit best the triangular site of the building. I placed the glass walls at slight angles to each other to avoid the monotony of over-large glass surfaces. I discovered by working with actual glass models that the important thing is the play of reflections and not the effect of light and shadow as in ordinary buildings.

The results of these experiments can be seen in the second scheme published here. At first glance, the curved outline of the plan seems arbitrary. These curves, however, were determined by three factors: sufficient illumination of the interior, the massing of the building from the street, and lastly the play of reflections. I proved in the glass model that calculations of light and shadow do not help in designing an all glass building.

It is instructive in this context to compare Mies's entry with that of Hugo Häring. Where one is triangular, undulating, and convex, the other is triangular, faceted, and concave. Otherwise the two solutions are · similarly expressive, a coincidence that may be partly explained by the fact that Häring shared an atelier with Mies throughout the early 1920s.

Mies van der Rohe's so-called 'G' period began in 1923 with his participation in the first issue of the magazine *G*, subtitled *Material zur elementaren Gestaltung* and edited by Hans Richter, Werner Gräff and Lissitzky. His glass skyscrapers of the previous year, with their kinetic reflections on the surfaces of trans-lucent forms, had already anticipated some-thing of the peculiar G sensibility which seems to have combined a Constructivist objectivity with a Dadaist feeling for chance. Yet the seven-storey office building that Mies presented in the first issue of G broke different ground, for now the primary expressive mater-ial was not glass but concrete, projected in the form of concrete 'trays' cantilevered off a re-inforced-concrete frame. As in Frank Lloyd Wright's Larkin Building of 1904, the upstands of these 'trays' were high enough to accom-modate standard built-in filing cabinets, set below a band of recessed clerestory glazing. With this project Mies declared himself against formalism and aesthetic speculation and wrote with decidedly Hegelian overtones that 'Archi-tecture is the will of the age conceived in spatial terms. Living, changing, new.' At the same time he went on to declare: 'The office building is a house of work . . . of organization, of clarity, of economy. Bright, wide, workrooms, easy to oversee, undivided except as the undertaking is divided. The maximum effect with the mini-mum expenditure of means. The materials are concrete, iron, glass.'

Despite this objective advocacy of a 'skin-and-bones' architecture reminiscent of Le Corbusier's Dom-Ino proposal, a vestige of academic tradition was visible in the project in the widening of the end bays in order to 'strengthen' the corners of the building. This, however, was Mies's last overt reference to the Neo-Classical principles of Schinkel until his first gesture at a 'new monumentality' a decade later, with his Reichsbank project of 1933.

Apart from the ever-present undertones of Neo-Classicism, Mies's work after 1923 dis-plays, to a varying degree, three main influences: (1) the Berlage brick tradition and the dictum that 'nothing should be built that is not clearly constructed'; (2) the pre-1910 work of Frank Lloyd Wright, as filtered through the De Stijl group — an influence acknowledged in the horizontal profiles extending into the land-scape of Mies's brick country house of 1923; and (3) Kasimir Malevich's Suprematism, as interpreted through the work of Lissitzky. While the Wrightian aesthetic could be readily absorbed within the *Schinkelschüler* tradition of *Baukunst* — that is according to the highest standards of European masonry practice — Suprematism had the effect of encouraging Mies to develop the free plan. Where Mies's *Baukunst* ideal was fulfilled in the Karl Lieb-knecht and Rosa Luxemburg Monument and in the Wolf House, both built of brick and com-pleted in 1926, the free plan was to emerge fully armed, so to speak, in the Barcelona Pavilion of 1929.

Despite these diverse and compelling in-fluences, Mies still seems to have experienced difficulty in relinquishing the Expressionist aesthetic of his Novembergruppe period. A comparable sensibility, touched by a some-what Russian sense of colour, is still evident in the 1927 Berlin Silk Industry Exhibition, designed in collaboration with Lily Reich, who had initially trained as a fashion designer. The black, orange and red velvets and the gold, silver, black and lemon-yellow silks no doubt reflected her taste, as did the acid-green, cowhide upholstery used for the sitting-room furniture of the Tugendhat House. A latent feeling for Expressionism may still be detected, too, in the Deutsche Werkbund Weissenhof-siedlung Exhibition which opened in Stuttgart in the same year. Despite a tendency to regard every commission as a free-standing object, Mies initially planned this exhibition as a con-tinuous urban form, like a medieval town. It even had a vestigial *Stadtkrone*, a pseudo-Tautian gesture towards unity that had to be abandoned. In the final version of the layout Mies divided the site into rectilinear plots, on which free-standing 'display' houses were erected to the designs of various Werkbund architects, among them Walter Gropius and Hans Scharoun. A number of foreign archi-tects also participated, including Le Corbusier, Victor Bourgeois, J.J.P. Oud and Mart Stam.

Initially conceived in the spirit of the original Darmstadt exhibition of 1901, 'Ein Dokument Deutscher Kunst', the Weissenhofsiedlung be-came the first international manifestation of that white, prismatic, flat-roofed mode of building which was to be identified in 1932 as the International Style. Mies's contribution to both the style and the content of the exhibition

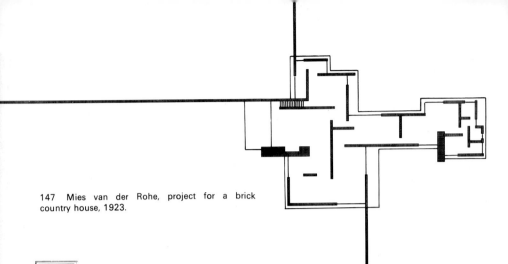

147  Mies van der Rohe, project for a brick country house, 1923.

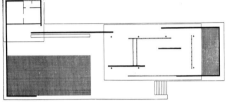

148  Mies van der Rohe, German Pavilion, World Exhibition, Barcelona, 1929.

was an apartment house that he designed as the central armature of the scheme. This five-storey structure was generally similar to the standard *Zeilenbau* block being developed at the time, but it differed from the typical row-house slab in the ease with which it could be brought to accommodate a variety of different apartment shapes and sizes. Of his solution Mies wrote in 1927:

Today the factor of economy makes rationaliza-tion and standardization imperative in rental housing. On the other hand, the increased complexity of our requirements demands flexi-bility. The future will have to reckon with both. For this purpose skeleton construction is the most suitable system. It makes possible rational-ized building methods and allows the interior to be freely divided. If we regard kitchens and bathrooms, because of their plumbing, as a fixed core, then all other space may be partitioned by means of movable walls. This should, I believe, satisfy all normal requirements.

The climax of Mies's early career came with the three masterworks that he designed in sequence after finishing the Weissenhofsied-lung: the German State Pavilion at the Barcel-ona World Exhibition of 1929, the Tugendhat House at Brno, Czechoslovakia, of 1930, and the model house erected for the Berlin Building Exhibition of 1931. In all these works a hori-zontal centrifugal spatial arrangement was subdivided and articulated by free-standing planes and columns. While this aesthetic (already anticipated in Mies's country house projects of 1922 and 1923) was basically Wrightian, it was Wright as reinterpreted through the sensibility of the G group and the metaphysical space conceptions of De Stijl. As Alfred Barr observed, the load-bearing walls of Mies's brick country house were disposed in a pinwheel fashion like the clustering elements of Van Doesburg's painting of 1917, *Rhythms of a Russian Dance*.

Despite the Classical associations of its regular eight-column grid and its liberal use of traditional materials, the Barcelona Pavilion was undeniably a Suprematist-Elementarist composition (cf. Malevich's *Future Planets for Earth Dwellers* of 1924 and the work of his indirect pupil Ivan Leonidov). Contemporary photographs reveal the ambivalent and in-effable quality of its spatial and material form. From these records we may see that certain displacements in its volume were brought about by illusory surface readings such as that effected by the use of green tinted glass screens, to emerge as the mirror equivalents of the main bounding planes. These planes, faced in polished green Tinian marble, in their turn reflected the highlights of the chromium vertical glazing bars holding the glass in place. A comparable play in terms of texture and colour was effected by the contrast between the internal core plane of polished onyx (the equivalent of Wright's centrally placed chimney core) and the long travertine wall that flanked the main terrace with its large reflecting pool. Here, bounded by travertine and agitated by the wind, the broken surface of the water distorted the mirror image of the building. In contrast to this, the internal space of the pavilion, modulated by columns and mullions, terminated in an enclosed court, containing a reflecting pool lined with black glass. Above and in this implacable, perfect mirror, there stood the frozen form and image of Georg Kolbe's *Dancer*. Yet despite all these delicate aesthetic contrasts the building was simply structured about eight free-standing crucifrom columns that supported its flat roof. The regularity of the structure and the solidity of its matt travertine base evoked the *Schinkelschüler* tradition to which Mies was to return.

Like the De Stijl room of 1923, the Barcelona Pavilion was the occasion for a classic piece of furniture, namely the Barcelona chair, which was one of five neo-Schinkelesque pieces that the architect designed in the years 1929–30 — the other four being the Barcelona stool and table, the Tugendhat armchair and a buttoned-down leather couch. The Barcelona chair, framed in welded and chromium-plated bar steel and upholstered in buttoned-down calfskin, was as integrated into the design of the pavilion as Rietveld's Red/Blue chair in the room designed for the Berlin Exhibition.

The Tugendhat House, built in 1930 on a steeply sloping site overlooking the city of Brno in Czechoslovakia, adapted the spatial conception of the Barcelona Pavilion to a domestic programme. One may also see it as an attempt to combine the layered, compartmentalized planning of Wright's Robie House — where the service block slides behind the main living volume — with the typical loggia form

149   Mies van der Rohe, German Pavilion, World Exhibition, Barcelona, 1929.

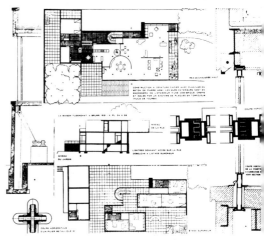

150   Mies van der Rohe, Tugendhat House, Brno, 1930.

of the Schinkel Italianate Villa. In any event, the free plan was reserved here solely for the horizontal living volume, which, modulated once again by chromium cruciform columns, opened on its long side to a panorama of the city and on its short side to a conservatory faced in large sheets of plate glass. While the mechanical lowering of the long glass wall converted the whole of the living area into a belvedere, the conservatory acted as a natural foil in a

165

151 Mies van der Rohe, Tugendhat House, Brno, 1930. Dining alcove.

symbolic scheme — as a mediation between natural vegetation and the fossilized onyx of the interior. In a comparable manner, the plywood dining alcove, faced in ebony veneer, evoked the sustenance of life to which its space was dedicated. Similarly, the rectilinear onyx plane dividing the living volume of the house signified through its surface the 'worldliness' of the spaces to be found on either side of it — the sitting-room and the study. Such rhetoric obtained only on the lower ground floor, the bedrooms on the entrance level being treated simply as hermetic volumes.

With the Berlin Building Exhibition house of 1931, on the other hand, Mies demonstrated the possibility of extending the free plan to the bedrooms, and for the next four years he elaborated this approach in a series of extremely elegant courtyard-houses that regrettably were never built.

Mies van der Rohe's idealism and his natural affinity for German Romantic-Classicism clearly served to remove him from the mass-production approach of the Neue Sachlichkeit. The sense of objectivity in each case was patently different. As far as the Neue Sachlichkeit was concerned, Mies declared the apolitical, not to say reactionary, nature of his position when, in 1930, he accepted the directorship of the Bauhaus, as Hannes Meyer's successor. In his essay *The New Era*, written on the occasion of his appointment, he attempted to formulate his own somewhat ambivalent position. In res-ponse to Hannes Meyer's 'materialist' essay, *Bauen*, he wrote:

The new era is a fact: it exists, irrespective of our 'yes' or 'no'. Yet it is neither better nor worse than any other era. It is pure datum, in itself without value content. Therefore I will not try to define it or clarify its basic structure.

Let us not give undue importance to mechanization and standardization.

Let us accept changed economic and social conditions as a fact.

All these take their blind and fateful course.

One thing will be decisive: the way we assert ourselves in the face of circumstance.

Here the problems of the spirit begin. The important question to ask is not 'what' but 'how'. What goods we produce or what tools we use are not questions of spiritual value.

How the question of skyscrapers versus low buildings is settled, whether we build of glass or steel, are unimportant questions from the point of view of spirit.

Whether we tend to centralization or decentralization in city planning is a practical question, not a question of value.

Yet it is just the question of value that is decisive.

We must set up new values, fix our ultimate goals so that we may establish standards.

For what is right and significant for any era — including the new era — is this: to give the spirit the opportunity for existence.

This Neo-Classical concern for spiritual value seems to have led directly to the idealized monumentality of Mies's Reichsbank proposal of 1933, submitted as a competition entry in the year when the National Socialists came to power. The non-Classical impulse that had sustained him up to this time — the Suprematist-Elementarism that had inspired his version of the free plan — now gave way to an impassive monumentality which, aside from the neutrality of its skin, intended nothing save the idealization of bureaucratic authority. This Suprematist sensibility was to remain suppressed in Mies's work until 1939, when, on his migration to the United States, it momentarily re-emerged in the first sketches for the IIT campus in Chicago.

Chapter 19
# The New Collectivity: art and architecture in the Soviet Union 1918-32

The simple, classical concept of internationalism underwent a considerable change towards the end of the 1920s, when hopes of immediate world revolution receded and the more autarchic stage of 'the building of Socialism in one country' was initiated. Simultaneously, the exuberant romantic conception of technique gave way to a sober realization that technique, in Russia, meant a hard uphill struggle to transform a peasant economy into a modern industrial organism, starting with the most primitive means.

Their failure to understand the significance of these changes, and to adjust themselves, led the profession, as happened earlier in the case of the formalists, to the brink of complete impotence.

Disarming itself by rejecting the whole of past architectural tradition, the profession gradually lost all confidence in itself and in its social purpose. Those architects who were most honest with themselves drew their own conclusion from the worship of the engineer and the denial of all architectural tradition, and actually abandoned their profession to become building technicians, administrators and planners.

The disparity between the vision of a supercharged technique and the reality of a primitive and backward building industry, in which, more and more, idealized technology had to give way to ordinary ingenuity on a low level, led others to a hollow and insincere aestheticism, indistinguishable from that of the formalists they had set out to replace, inasmuch as they were forced to reproduce the adulterated forms of an advanced technique in the absence of its real media.

All the aggressive self-assertion with which the Functionalists enunciated their creed could

mask neither the barrenness of their doctrine nor the sterility of their practice. The few remaining buildings of the period bear witness to it.

Berthold Lubetkin
'Soviet Architecture: Notes on Development from 1917 to 1932',
*AAJ*, 1956

The Russian Pan-Slavic cultural movement that came into being after the liberation of the serfs in 1861 manifested itself in a widespread Slavophile arts and crafts revival. This movement first appeared in the early 1870s on the Abramtsevo Estate outside Moscow, where the railway tycoon Savva Mamontov had established a retreat for the Populist or Narodniki painters, who, calling themselves 'The Wanderers', had seceded from the Petersburg Academy in 1863 in order to become itinerant artists carrying their 'art' to the people.

This movement took on a more applied form in the cottage-industry colony founded at Smolensk in 1890 by the Princess Tenisheva, for the purpose of reviving traditional Slavic crafts. Where the achievements of the Mamontov intelligentsia ranged from the medieval revivalism (Old Russian style) exemplified in V.M. Vasnetsov's Abramtsevo Chapel (1882) to Leonid Pasternak's designs for the first production of Rimsky-Korsakov's opera *The Snow Maiden* (1883), the works of the Tenisheva colony were more modest in scale, consisting of simple, light, fretted houses, furniture and domestic utensils which took much of their basic form from traditional timber construction and most of their decorative elements from peasant crafts, such as the traditional woodcut narrative art form known as *lubok*. The Populist-cum-Expressionist paintings of the Abramtsevo

167

circle were among the first tentative steps towards the radical Russian art of the early 20th century, presaging both the Dadaistic *zaum* poetry of Alexei Kruchonykh and the atonal music of Matyushin, while Tenisheva craftwork anticipated the Constructivist woodblock and stencil typography of the Post Revolutionary Proletkult movement.

In contrast to the exuberant vitality of the Pan-Slavic movement in the arts, Russian architecture, for all its prodigious output after 1870, remained stylistically divided (particularly in Moscow) between the Classical standards of the St Petersburg establishment and the slowly unfolding National Romantic movement. This last, initiated in 1838 by K.A. Thon's Neo-Byzantine Kremlin Palace, gave birth in the last decade of the century to the so-called Neo-Russian designers, such as Vasnetsov, A.V. Shchusev: V.F. Walcot and above all F.O. Shekhtel, whose Rayabushinsky Mansion of 1900 was quite comparable to August Endell at his best. Closely affiliated to Art Nouveau and referring to such figures as Voysey, Townsend and Richardson, the quality of expression varied from Shchusev's highly eclectic but ultimately retardataire Kazan Station (started in 1913) to Vasnetsov's brilliant Tretyakov Gallery (1900–05), which, despite its eclecticism, is still comparable to Olbrich's Ernst Ludwig House of 1901. All of this was largely independent of developments in the engineering field, particularly the work of the engineer V.A. Zhukov, designer of the glazed roof for A.N. Pomerantsev's New Trading Lines in Moscow (1889–93) and later designer of a light-weight radio tower in the form of a frustrum built in Moscow in 1926.

Of greater consequence for Post-Revolutionary architecture was the transformation of the Slavophile movement into a grass-roots cultural force largely inspired by the 'scientific' cultural theories of the economist Alexander Malinovsky, who, in 1895, styled himself 'Bogdanov' (the 'God-gifted'). Having abandoned the Social Democrats for the Bolsheviks in the revolutionary crisis of 1903, Bogdanov founded, in 1906, the Organization for Proletarian Culture, otherwise known as the Proletkult. This movement dedicated itself to the regeneration of culture through a new unity of science, industry and art. For Bogdanov, a super-science of 'tectology' would afford the new collectivity the natural means for raising both traditional culture and its own material product to a higher order of unity. As James Billington has written,

In the manner of Saint-Simon, rather than Marx, Bogdanov argued that the destructive conflicts of the past would never be resolved without a positive new religion; that the unifying role once played in society by a central temple of worship and religious faith must now be played by the living temple of the proletariat and a pragmatic, socially oriented philosophy of 'Empirio-monism'.

Bogdanov published the first instalment of his treatise on tectology, 'The Universal Organizational Science', in 1913, the very year in which Kruchonykh's Futurist play, 'Victory Over the Sun,' was first performed in St Petersburg with music by Matyushin and costumes and sets by Kasimir Malevich. Malevich's curtain for this apocalyptic play exhibited for the first time the black square motif that was to become the quintessential icon of Suprematism.

By the eve of the First World War, avant-garde Russian culture had already developed into two distinct but related impulses. The first of these was represented by a non-utilitarian synthetic art form that promised to transform everyday life into that millennial future evoked by the poetry of Kruchonykh and Malevich. The second, as proposed by Bogdanov, was a post-Narodnik hypothesis that sought to forge a new cultural unity from the material and cultural exigencies of communal life and production. After October 1917, the revolutionary reality of the newly formed Soviet state tended to bring these two positions – the 'apocalyptic' and the 'synthetic' – into conflict, leading to hybrid forms of socialist culture, such as Lissitzky's adaptation of Malevich's 'apocalyptic' and highly abstract art to the utilitarian ends of his self-styled Suprematist-Elementarism.

In 1920 Inkhuk (the Institute for Artistic Culture) and Vkhutemas (Higher Artistic and Technical Studios) were founded in Moscow as institutes for comprehensive education in art, architecture and design. Both these institutions were to serve as arenas for public debate, wherein mystical idealists such as Malevich and Wassily Kandinsky and objective artists such as the brothers Pevsner found themselves equally opposed by the so-called Productivists, Vladimir Tatlin, Alexander Rodchenko and Alexei Gan. In 1920 the challenge of the pure art position was most eloquently formulated by Naum Gabo (Pevsner), who later wrote of his critical reaction to the Tatlin Tower:

I showed them a photograph of the Eiffel Tower and said: 'That which you think is new has been done already. Either build functional houses and bridges or create pure art or both. Don't confuse one with the other. Such art is not pure constructive art, but merely an imitation of the machine.'

Despite the persuasive logic of such rhetoric, idealists such as Gabo and Kandinsky felt themselves constrained to leave the Soviet Union even though Malevich had succeeded in entrenching himself in Vitebsk, where shortly after 1919 he had founded his Suprematist school, Unovis (the School of the New Art). This institution was to exercise a definitive influence on Lissitzky's development, putting an end to his expressionistic graphics and starting him on his career as a Suprematist designer.

In the meantime, a specifically proletarian culture had spontaneously emerged from the communicational needs of the Revolution, imparting vitality to cultural forms which might otherwise have remained remote from the actual conditions of the period and from the real needs of a population which was still basically ill-housed, ill-fed, and above all illiterate. Graphic art came to play a salient role in spreading the message of the Revolution. It took the form of large-scale street art, displayed in the Agit-Prop propaganda trains and boats designed by Proletkult artists and in the 'monumental propaganda plan' launched by the authorities shortly after the Revolution with the express purpose of covering every available surface with inflammatory slogans and evocative iconography. The central task of Proletkult at this time was the propagation of official

152   Agit-Prop train, 1919.

information through theatrical production, film and exhortatory graphics, and its form was invariably nomadic and demountable. Everything had to be easily transportable and made at the simplest level of production. Apart from the dissemination of propaganda, Productivist artists such as Tatlin and Rodchenko addressed themselves to the design of light collapsable furniture and to the fabrication of durable clothing for workers. Tatlin designed a stove that was supposed to give off maximum heat while consuming the minimum of fuel. The universality of this 'nomadic' impulse is reflected in the light-weight furniture designed by European architects in the late 1920s – the conceptually 'knock-down', if not actually demountable, chairs produced by Mies van der Rohe, Le Corbusier, Mart Stam, Hannes Meyer and Marcel Breuer. Breuer was particularly susceptible to this influence: his famous Wassily chair of 1926 coincided with an almost identical canvas and tube chair of about the same date designed in Vkhutemas. It is now clear, from recently discovered correspondence between Moholy-Nagy and Rodchenko, that after 1923 the Bauhaus was subject to direct influence from Vkhutemas.

In the early 1920s, Proletkult attained its most synthetic expression through the theatre, most notably in Nikolai Evreinov's 'theatricalization of everyday life', which used the format of the tattoo to stage the annual re-enactment of the storming of the Winter Palace. On less momentous occasions, street parades were organized in which Constructivist lay figures, invariably representing either the Revolution or its capitalist enemies, served as the focusing icons for mass demonstrations. An equally polemical intention prompted V. Meyerhold's proclamation of 'The October Theatre', which attempted to translate such Agit-Prop street activity into the principles of the agitatory stage. Meyerhold's 'Octobrist' proclamation of 1920 prescribed a theatre comprised of the following elements and principles: (1) the use of a permanently illuminated arena stage so as to unite the audience with the actors; (2) an anti-naturalistic mode of mechanized production, featuring the actor-acrobat as the ideal type for Meyerhold's 'bio-mechanical' stage — a stage form that had obvious affinities with the circus; and finally, (3) the exclusion of illusion and the elimination of any of the Symbolism that was then still endemic to the bourgeois

153 Tatlin, model of monument to the Third International, 1919–20. Tatlin stands in the foreground, pipe in hand.

theatre, exemplified by Stanislavsky's Moscow Arts Theatre. Similar prescriptions were to inform Erwin Piscator's foundation of the Berlin Proletarian Theatre in 1924.

Lenin came to distrust, if not to fear, Bogdanov's radical assertion that there were three independent roads to socialism — the economic, the political and the cultural. Yet despite the official repudiation of Bogdanov in 1920 and the subsequent subjugation of the Proletkult movement to the authority of Narkompros (People's Commissariat for Education), the ethos of Agit-Prop culture persisted, particularly in Meyerhold's theatre. It also continued to find expression in the numerous projects for kiosks, tribunes and other didactic information-structures designed by Productivist artists such as G. Klutsis and Rodchenko. These projects constituted the first attempts to formulate a non-professional socialist style of architecture. Although intentionally 'unrealizable', Lissitzky's 1920 design for a Lenin Tribune (see p. 131), projected as a Proun, was an alternative for such an architecture. Lissitzky had coined the term *Proun* — from *Pro-Unovis*, 'For the School of the New Art' — to indicate an unprecedented creative realm, situated somewhere between painting and architecture.

Paramount among such pioneer works was Tatlin's 1919–20 design for a 400-metre (1,310-foot) high monument to the Third International, projected as two intertwining lattice spirals within which were to be suspended four large transparent volumes each rotating at progressively faster speeds, once a year, once a month, once a day, and presumably, once an hour. They were respectively dedicated to the purposes of legislation, administration, information, and cinematic projection. On one level Tatlin's Tower was a monument to the constitution and function of the Soviet state; on another it was intended to exemplify the Productivist/Constructivist programme of considering 'intellectual materials', such as colour, line, point, and plane, and 'physical materials', such as iron, glass and wood, as thematically equal elements. In this respect, one can hardly regard the tower as a purely utilitarian object. In spite of the anti-art and anti-religious slogans of the 1920 'Programme of the Productivist Group', the tower remained as a monumental metaphor for the harmony of a new social order. It was first exhibited under a banner which bore the slogan, 'Engineers Create New Forms'. The millennialistic symbolism of both its form and its material are clearly manifest in a contemporary description which presumably paraphrased Tatlin's own words:

Just as the product of the number of oscillations and the wavelength is the spatial measure of sound, so the proportion between glass and iron is the measure of the material rhythm. By the union of these fundamentally important materials, a compact and imposing simplicity and, at the same time, relation, is expressed, since these materials, for both of which fire is the creator of life, form the elements of modern art.

In its use of the spiral theme, in its enclosure of a series of progressively diminishing Platonic solids and in its rhetorical exhibition of iron and glass and mechanized movement, as the very stuff of the millennium, Tatlin's Tower anticipated the work of two distinct tendencies in Russian avant-garde architecture. One of these was the school which established itself within Vkhutemas, as part of the first- and second-year course given by Nikolai A. Ladovsky. This structuralist, or rather formalist, school attempted to evolve a totally new syntax of plastic form, based ostensibly on the laws of human perception. The other was a much more materialist and programmatic approach which clearly emerged in 1925 under the leadership of the architect Moisei Ginzburg.

In 1921 Ladovsky urged that a research institute be established at Vkhutemas for the systematic study of the perception of form. Vkhutemas basic designs, carried out under his supervision, always featured some rhythmic delineation of the surfaces of pure forms or, alternatively, studies into the growth and diminution of dynamic form according to the laws of mathematical progression. These Vkhutemas exercises often featured geometrically progressing volumes, rising or falling in both size and location. On occasions these studies were proposed as designs for actual buildings,

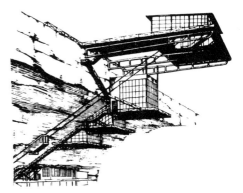

154  Simbirchev in the Vkhutemas atelier of Ladovsky, project for a suspended restaurant, c.1922–23.

as in the suspended restaurant designed by Simbirchev around 1923, a project whose total transparency and extravagant access system echoed the expressive utilitarianism of the Productivists. Such a fantastic structure was patently beyond the capacity of Soviet engineering at the time, while its numerous changes in level would surely have limited its use as a restaurant.

Ladovsky's so-called 'rationalism' was anything but programmatic, for he ultimately sought, as Lubetkin has observed, a universalism of the Larousse type. Like the Neo-Classical artists of the late 18th century, he preferred to use geometrical entities such as spheres and cubes, forms that could be hypothetically associated with specific psychological states. In 1923 Ladovsky tried to propagate his views through the foundation of Asnova (Association of New Architects), a professional group centred on Vkhutemas. This organization attained its greatest influence around 1925, when both Lissitzky and the architect Konstantin Melnikov were associated with it. Like the wooden demountable market stalls that he designed in 1924, Melnikov's USSR Pavilion for the Paris Exposition des Arts Décoratifs of 1925 was a synthesis of the more progressive aspects of Soviet architecture to date. In its imaginative use of lap-jointed timber struts and planks, it recalled not only the traditional vernacular of the Steppes, but also those exhibition pavilions which had been

155    Melnikov, Sucharev Market, Moscow, 1924–25.

designed for the All-Russian Agricultural and Craft Exhibition of 1923, including the Izvestia kiosk by the artists A.A. Exter, Gladkov and Stenberg, and Melnikov's own Makhorka Pavilion. In its basic conception, Melnikov's Pavilion reflected the rhythmic formalism of the Ladovsky school. Its rectangular plot was animated by a staircase traversing the diagonal which divided the ground floor into two identical triangles. This staircase, rising and falling through an open timber construction forming criss-crossing planes, gave access only to the upper levels of the structure. Such an intersecting roof form was soon to become as prevalent a 'geometrically progressive' device among the Russian avant garde as the logarithmic spiral of the Tatlin Tower. Melnikov's dynamic timber structure was complemented by Rodchenko's interior for an ideal workers' club featuring typical light-weight Productivist furniture, including a dialectically red and black chess-playing suite consisting of a table and two chairs.

The Asnova group sought not only to achieve a more scientific aesthetic, but also to devise new building forms which would satisfy and express the conditions of the new socialist state. Hence the preoccupation with workers' clubs and recreational facilities designed to function as new 'social condensers'. This drive to invent new forms also accounts for Lissitzky's attempt to reconstitute the American skyscraper in a socialist form, in his Wolkenbügel ('cloud-hanger') project of 1924, conceived as an elevated propylaeum opening onto the peripheral boulevard surrounding the centre of Moscow. This work, however bizarre,

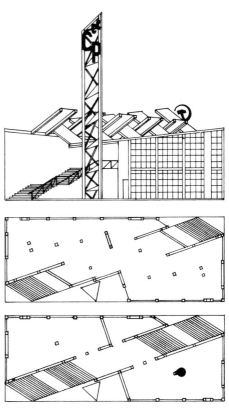

156    Melnikov, USSR Pavilion, Exposition des Arts Décoratifs, Paris, 1925. Ground plan (bottom), first-floor plan and elevation.

was intended as a critical antithesis to both the capitalist skyscraper and the Classical gate.

Melnikov's early Productivist works were all built in the period of relative economic stability that resulted from Lenin's New Economic Policy (NEP), introduced after the Civil War in March 1921 as a way of attracting foreign capital into partnership with the Soviet Union. Lenin's death in January 1924 not only brought the period of NEP culture to an end, but also presented the Party with the ironic problem of finding an appropriate style for his tomb. While the Productivist manner could be considered adequate for the representation of the Soviet Union at an international exhibition of decorative art, it was much too insubstantial to enshrine the founder of the first socialist state.

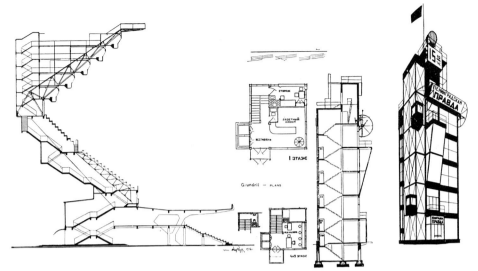

157 Typical Constructivist works of the 1920s: Korschev, Spartakiada Stadium, Moscow, 1926 (left: section of stand), and Vesnin, Pravda Building, Moscow, 1923 (right: plans, section and view).

Neo-Classicism, with its idealistic connotations, was equally inappropriate. Something of this uncertainty is reflected in the designs that the Academician Shchusev produced for Lenin's mausoleum. The first was a temporary wooden structure, which despite its symmetry displayed affinities with the Productivist aesthetic. The second, permanent version in stone was an attempt at recreating the form of a Central Asian Tartar tomb.

158 Shchusev, temporary wooden mausoleum for Lenin, Moscow, 1924.

With Lenin's death the heroic period of the Revolution came to a close. By now the Revolution had acquired a definitive history, from the hard-won victory over the Whites in the Civil War to the tragic suppression of the Kronstadt revolt against the Party and the NEP establishment of state capitalism within the proletarian state. Deprived of Lenin's charisma, the immediate prospect was one of conflict rather than resolution — the fight for succession within the Party, the modernization of industry and agriculture, the campaign against illiteracy, the daily struggle to provide shelter and food, the drive to electrify the country and the ever-present need to forge a real link between the industrial, urban proletariat and a dispersed and vestigially feudal peasant society. Above all, there arose the annual battle to extract sufficient food for the urban populace from a recalcitrant and alienated countryside, which had stubbornly resisted the inducements it had received under the provisions of the New Economic Policy.

The most chronic problem from an architectural standpoint was clearly housing. Nothing had been built since the beginning of the First World War, and the degree to which the pre-war stock had deteriorated was reflected in the proceedings of the 13th Party Congress of 1924, where housing was recognized as 'the most important question in the material life of the workers'. Faced with the task of meeting this deficiency, certain members of the younger generation of architects felt that they could no longer indulge in the formalist preoccupations of the Vkhutemas, still under the influence of Ladovsky.

This reaction precipitated the formation of a new group, the Association of Contemporary Architects (OSA), whose initial membership, under the leadership of Ginzburg, comprised M. Barshch, A. Burov, L. Komarova, Y. Kornfeld, M. Okhitovich, A. Pasternak, G. Vegman, V. Vladimirov and the brothers A. and V. Vesnin. Soon after its foundation OSA began to admit members from related fields, such as sociology and engineering. OSA's essentially programmatic orientation was as antipathetic to the Productivist culture of the Proletkult as it was to the perceptual aestheticism of Ladovsky. From the outset it attempted to change the modus operandi of the architect, from one who traditionally had a craftsmanlike relation to his client to a new type of professional who was first a sociologist, second a politician, and third a technician.

In 1926 OSA began to propagate these views in its magazine, *Sovremennaya Arkhitektura* ('Contemporary Architecture'), dedicated to the incorporation of scientific methods into architectural practice. In the fourth issue OSA conducted an international inquiry into flat-roofed construction, wherein Taut, Behrens, Oud and Le Corbusier were asked to comment on the technical viability and advantages of flat roofs. OSA also set itself the task of formulating the necessary programmes and type forms for an emerging Socialist society, concerning itself as well with the broader issues of energy distribution and population dispersal. Thus its prime concerns were: first the issue of communal housing and the creation of appropriate social units, and sec-

ond, the process of distribution, namely transit in all its forms.

In pursuit of the former, it launched a second inquiry in *SA* in 1927, as to the appropriate form of the new communal dwelling or *dom-kommuna*. The replies received were used as the basis for a fraternal competition that attempted to develop and refine a new residential prototype, something along the lines of Fourier's phalanstery. Most of the entries gave symbolic and operational importance to an internal double-loaded corridor, a volume formed by the interlocking of up- and down-going duplex apartments. A version of this section came to be adopted by Le Corbusier after 1932 as the 'cross-over' section of the typical block of his Ville Radieuse.

All this activity prompted the government to set up a research group for the standardization of housing, under the leadership of Ginzburg. The work of this group led to the development of a series of *Stroikem* units, one of which was adopted by Ginzburg for his Narkomfin apartment block built in Moscow in 1929. While its internal street or deck system gave direct access to an adjunct block containing a canteen, a gymnasium, a library, a day nursery and a roof garden, Ginzburg remained acutely aware that this implied collectivity could not be imposed on the residents through the built form alone. He wrote at the time:

We can no longer compel the occupants of a particular building to live collectively, as we have attempted to do in the past, generally with negative results. We must provide for the possibility of a gradual, natural transition to communal utilization in a number of different areas. That is why we have tried to keep each unit isolated from the next, that is why we

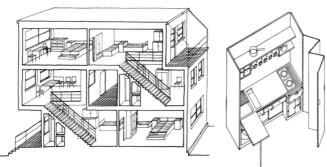

159  Ol, Ivanov and Lavinsky, interlocking duplex flats with central corridor, OSA competition, 1927.

160  Design for a compact kitchen module with concealing screens, by the Building Committee of the Economic Council of the USSR, 1928.

found it necessary to design the kitchen alcove as a standard element of minimum size that could be removed bodily from the apartment to permit the introduction of canteen catering at any given moment. We considered it absolutely necessary to incorporate certain features that would stimulate the transition to a socially superior mode of life, *stimulate but not dictate*.

In the previous year, OSA had turned its attention to the design of another type of 'social condenser', the workers' club. Anatole Kopp has observed:

The year 1928 witnessed a mutation in club architecture. In spite of all their innovations, the existing clubs, even the most modern, such as those designed by Melnikov and Golosov, were sharply criticized for being centred on the stage and tied to the professional theatre.

The reaction of Ginzburg's protégé, Ivan Leonidov, was to project a totally different type of club, one which focused more on educational institutions and athletic facilities. In 1928 he began to produce a series of designs that were all, in effect, versions of his remarkable Lenin Institute projected a year earlier for a site in the Lenin Hills outside Moscow. His design for this institute of advanced studies consisted of two primary glazed forms: a rectilinear library tower and a spherical auditorium resting on a single point. The whole suspended, floating complex, stabilized by guying cables, was to have been linked to the city by an elevated monorail. Leonidov's science-fiction concept of the club as a Suprematist megastructure – a vision clearly influenced by the work of Malevich – reached its climax in 1930 in his Palace of Culture project, whose glazed auditoriums, planetariums, laboratories and winter gardens were laid out on a gridded rectilinear matrix that made few concessions to traditional landscaping. Its inscribed, almost metaphysical surface was relieved by clumps of luxuriant vegetation and by prisms whose transparent forms, while revelatory of their interiors, were not functionally determined. The dirigible and mooring mast included in the composition were clearly intended to exemplify the same light-weight technology as would be used for the earthbound structures – buildings whose integrated space-frame construction anticipated the mid-century work of designers such as Konrad Wachsmann and Buckminster Fuller.

In such complexes, Leonidov envisaged the enactment of a continual process of education and recreation: athletics, scientific demonstrations, political meetings, films, botanical displays, manifestations, flying, gliding, car racing and military exercises. The very utopianism of this vision brought him under attack from the pro-Stalin group known as Vopra (an acronym standing for the 'All-Russian Association of Proletarian Architects'), who condemned such schemes for their vain idealism.

Before the consolidation of the Party line in architecture, instituted by the Ukase of April 1932, finally suppressed the extraordinary diversity of the Soviet architectural avant garde, OSA became involved in the question of 'social condensation' on a much larger scale, at the level of regional planning, which was then still in its infancy as an applied science. For the main OSA planning theorist, Okhitovich, the projected electrification of the Soviet Union offered itself as an infrastructural model

161  Leonidov, project for a Palace of Culture, from the cover of *SA*, 1930, showing (left to right) the 'physical culture sector', 'field for demonstrations' and 'popular activities sector'.

for all forms of regional planning. His strategy for the disurbanization of the country, to be carried out literally along the lines of the power grid and the road system, implied a critical attitude towards the *dom-kommuna* and the super-communes or *kombinats* then being proposed by the main theorist of urbanization, L. Sabsovich. Okhitovich wrote in 1930:

We have now arrived at a moment of disenchantment with the so-called 'commune' that deprives the worker of living space in favour of corridors and heated passages. The pseudo-commune that allows the worker to do no more than sleep at home, the pseudo-commune that deprives him of both living space and personal convenience (the lines that form outside bathrooms and cloakrooms and in the canteen) is beginning to provoke mass unrest.

In the event, the super-collective communes came to be discredited, not only for their social unacceptability but also because their massive scale would have entailed the use of sophisticated technology and scarce material resources. For a while the disurbanization proposals of Okhitovich and N.A. Milyutin found a favourable hearing in official circles. It proved easier, however, to gain acceptance for a theoretical policy than to devise an economical land settlement pattern that could be generally applied throughout the country, and for the remainder of its existence the OSA group was somewhat divided as to how this could be best achieved. After the linear city schemes of Soria y Mata, they finally proposed ribbon-like settlements which, however imaginative, were often quite arbitrary in their specific configuration. Typical of such proposals was Barshch and Ginzburg's Green City scheme for the extension of Moscow, published in 1930. This rather eccentric project comprised a cranked continuous spine of 'bachelor' units raised on stilts, which, aside from providing residential accommodation, was apparently conceived as signifying the presence of the city. On both sides of this spine communal facilities were provided at 500-metre (1,640-foot) intervals. These buildings were flanked with the usual complement of sports fields and swimming pools and sited within continuous park strips lying on either side of the central spine, green 'bands' of varying width which were delimited on their outer edges by the flow and return of one-way roads giving access to the entire system. Ginzburg's overall strategy was to use such arteries for the progressive decantation of the existing population of Moscow, thereby allowing the old capital to deteriorate and to revert gradually to semi-rustic parkland within which significant monuments would remain as reminders of past culture.

By far the most abstract and theoretically consistent proposition was the linear-city principle advanced by Milyutin, who argued in 1930 for a continuous city comprising six parallel strips or zones. These zones were to be arranged in the following sequence: (1) a railway zone; (2) an industrial zone containing within itself, in addition to production, centres for education and research; (3) a green zone accommodating the highway; (4) a residential zone subdivided into communal institutions, dwellings and a juvenile area containing schools and kindergartens; (5) a park zone with sports facilities; and finally (6) an agricultural zone.

A specific political and economic intent informed this arrangement. Both industrial and agricultural workers were to be unified in the same residential zone, while any surplus production from either industry or agriculture would flow directly into the warehouses situated in the railway or green zones, to be temporarily stored there and later redistributed throughout the country. In accordance with the same 'biological' model, solid waste from the residential zone would be channelled directly to the agricultural zone for recycling into food. After the principles laid down in the *Communist Manifesto* of 1848, all secondary and technical education was to be carried out in the place of work, thus assuring the unity of theory and practice. Of this biological schema Milyutin wrote:

There must be no departure from the sequence of these six zones as this would not only upset the whole plan but would make the development and extension of each individual unit impossible, create unhealthy living conditions, and completely nullify the important advantages in respect of production that the linear system embodies.

In January 1929 the Soviet Government declared its intention to found the city of Magnitogorsk in the eastern Urals for the exploitation of iron deposits, and Milyutin and other OSA architects such as Ginzburg and Leonidov submitted schematic proposals for the new city. These variously abstract schemes were rejected by the authorities, who chose instead to commission the German architect Ernst May and his Frankfurt team to design the official plan for the town. The endless theoretical disputes of the Russian architectural avant garde – the complex arguments and counter-arguments of the 'urbanists' and the 'disurbanists' finally brought the Soviet authorities to circumvent such factional issues and to invite the more pragmatic and experienced left-wing architects of the Weimar Republic to apply their normative methods of planning and production (their *Zeilenbau* layout and their rationalized building methods) to the task of realizing the building of the first Five Year Plan.

The failure of OSA to develop sufficiently concrete proposals for planning on a large scale or to evolve residential building types which were appropriate to the needs and resources of a beleaguered socialist state, in conjunction with the paranoid tendency that emerged under Stalin for state censorship and control, had the effect of bringing about the eclipse of 'modern' architecture in the Soviet Union. For all his justifications of the need for proletarian culture to be based on the 'organic development of those stores of knowledge which humanity has accumulated under the yoke of capitalism', there is little doubt that Lenin's repression of the Proletkult in October 1920 was something of an initial step in the other direction. It was certainly the first attempt to control the remarkable creative forces that had been released by the Revolution. Lenin's NEP programme was clearly a second step, inasmuch as it set limits on the scope of participatory Communism. Above all, the econ-

162  Leonidov, project for Magnitogorsk, 1930. A 20-mile (32-km) road links the industrial plant to an agricultural commune in the interior.

omic compromise of NEP seems to have entailed the recall and employment of 'politically unreliable' experts from the bourgeois era, men such as Shchusev, ironically commissioned to design Lenin's mausoleum. For all its effectiveness, this co-option of bourgeois professionals under state supervision involved a deep compromise that not only prejudiced the principles of the Revolution but also inhibited the development of a collective culture. On the other hand, the historical circumstances were such that the people were largely incapable of adopting the way of life posited by the socialist intelligentsia. Furthermore, the failure of the architectural avant garde to match their visionary proposals for such a life with adequate levels of technical performance led to their loss of credibility with the authorities. Finally, their appeal to an international socialist culture was clearly anti-thetical to Soviet policy after 1925, when Stalin announced the decision to 'build socialism in one country'. That Stalin had no use whatsoever for élitist internationalism was officially confirmed by Anatole Lunacharsky's nationalist and populist cultural slogan of 1932, his famous 'pillars for the people,' which effectively committed Soviet architecture to a regressive form of historicism from which it has yet to emerge.

## Chapter 20

# Le Corbusier
# and the Ville Radieuse 1928-46

The machinery of society, profoundly out of gear, oscillates between an amelioration, of historical importance, and a catastrophe. The primordial instinct of every human being is to assure himself of a shelter. The various classes of workers in society today no longer have dwellings adapted to their needs; neither the artisan nor the intellectual. It is a question of building which is at the root of the social unrest of today; architecture or revolution.

Le Corbusier
*Vers une architecture,* 1923

After the League of Nations competition of 1927 the Engineer's Aesthetic and Architecture seemed to refer increasingly to a schism within Le Corbusier's own ideology, rather than to an opposition that was capable of synthesis. By 1928, this split was most evident in the contrast between the undeniable monumentality of the Cité Mondiale and those delicate pieces of light-weight tubular steel furniture that he designed at the same time with Charlotte Perriand — *le fauteuil à dossier basculant, le grand confort, la chaise longue, la table 'tube d'avion'* and *le siège tournant* — all of which were exhibited at the Salon d'Automne of 1929. A certain rationalization of this difference in approach had been anticipated already in Purist aesthetic theory which had argued that the more intimate the relation between the man and the object, the more the latter must reflect the contours of his form, that is, the more it must approximate to being the ergonomic equivalent of the Engineer's Aesthetic — and that conversely the more distant the relation, the more the object will tend towards abstraction — that is towards Architecture.

As far as building was concerned this determination of form through proximity and use was complicated by the demands of large-scale production and by the consequent necessity to distinguish between the creation of the one-off monument and the potential advantage of using rationalized production methods for the general provision of shelter. Such a distinction seems to have been the motive for Le Corbusier abandoning his perimeter block, otherwise known as the Immeuble-Villa, in favour of a building form more suited to mass production, namely his *à redent* Ville Radieuse block projected as a continuous band of 'on-line' housing. Based on Eugène Hénard's Boulevard à Redans of 1903 ( the term *redan* being borrowed like the term *boulevard* from the vocabulary of fortification) Le Corbusier's *redent* form consisted of a continuous terrace whose frontage was alternately and regularly set back from or aligned with the outer limits of the street.

The difference in the organization of the dwelling units in these two types was as significant as the difference between their exterior form. Where the Immeuble-Villa was predicated (as its name suggests) on the *qualitative* provision of the house with its 'hanging garden' as an autonomous unit, the Ville Radieuse type seems to have been orientated towards more economic criteria; that is, towards the *quantitative* standards of serial production. Where the Immeuble-Villa incorporated an ample garden terrace and a double-height living space, of fixed dimensions irrespective of family size, the Ville Radieuse (VR) unit was a flexible single-storey apartment of varying extent, more economical in terms of space than the double-height duplex section. The VR unit optimized every available square centimetre of space, its partitions being reduced in thickness to the point of becoming inadequate as acoustical barriers. To similar ends, the service cores, namely the kitchens and bathrooms, were reduced to a minimum. Moreover, each apartment was made capable of a certain transformation from night to day use, through the withdrawal of sliding partitions. When closed these elements subdivided the sleeping spaces and when open they yielded a children's play area that could be made continuous with the living-room. Through such devices the typical VR apartment was designed to be as ergonomically efficient as the sleeping cabins of a *wagon-lit*, and indeed Le Corbusier used many of the same space standards. With air-conditioning and sealed façades, this was clearly an attempt to provide the normative equipment of a machine-age civilization. Close to product design and remote from architecture in the traditional sense, the VR block could hardly have been further from the ethos of the Cité Mondiale.

This shift from the self-contained perimeter block to the continuous housing terrace and from the bourgeois standard of the 'villa' to an industrialized norm, may well have been a response to the technocratic challenge of the left-wing of CIAM — those German and Czech Neue Sachlichkeit architects whom Le Corbusier would have first encountered at the founding CIAM congress of 1928 (see p. 136). These 'materialist' designers challenged Le Corbusier again, at Frankfurt in 1929, on the occasion of the first working session of CIAM, dedicated under the title 'Existenzminimum' to determining optimum criteria for the minimum standard dwelling. In repudiating the reductivist approach of architects such as Ernst May and Hannes Meyer, Le Corbusier rhetorically proclaimed the space standards of his *maison maximum*, which happened to be an ironic play with the name of the economy car, *voiture maximum*, that he had designed with Jeanneret in the previous year. In this last respect they were to be proven right, since their *voiture maximum* became the prototype for the austerity vehicles that were to be produced on a large scale in Europe after the Second World War.

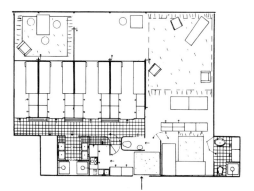

163   Le Corbusier and Jeanneret, Ville Radieuse, 1931. Plan of a five-bedroom unit.

164   Le Corbusier and Jeanneret, *voiture maximum*, 1928.

This Neue Sachlichkeit encounter and the three visits that Le Corbusier made to Russia between 1928 and 1930, brought him into close contact with the international Left; so much so that a Western reactionary critic, Alexandre de Senger, could denounce him soon after as being the Trojan Horse of Bolshevism. Of greater consequence for his later development however, was his exposure to the Russian OSA housing prototypes of 1927, with their interlocking duplex units; and his further encounter with the linear-city concepts of N.A. Milyutin. Both of these ideas soon emerged in his own work, the 'cross-over' duplex section in 1932 and the 'linear-industrial' city in 1935. Once assimilated, they were reformulated by him in the mid-1940s: the former as the prototypical section of his Unité d'Habitation and the latter as the Cité Industrielle that was central to his regional planning thesis entitled *Les Trois Etablissements humains*. By way of return, so to speak, he attempted to introduce the glass curtain wall into the Soviet Union, as part of his technically 'progressive' but ultimately troublesome Tsentrosoyuz building erected in Moscow in 1929. This double-layered glass wall (a standard technique of the Swiss Jura and used by him in the Villa Schwob) could not in the event withstand the rigours of a Russian winter. All the same, it was still included as a technical element in his 1930 reply to a Moscow questionnaire, entitled *Réponse à Moscou*, a document for which it seems the plates of the Ville Radieuse were specially prepared.

Transformations in his urban prototypes in the 1920s, in which the 'hierarchic' Ville Contemporaine of 1922 became the 'classless' Ville Radieuse of 1930, involved significant

165 Le Corbusier and Jeanneret, Ville Radieuse, 1931. Plan showing zoning in parallel bands: from offices (top) via housing (middle) to industry.

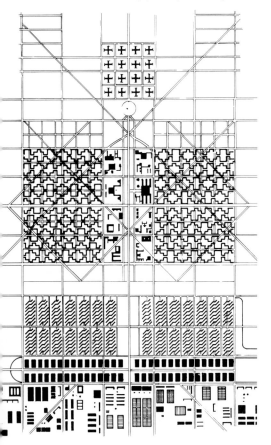

changes in Le Corbusier's way of conceiving the machine-age city; amongst which the most important was the move away from a centralized city model to a theoretically limitless concept, whose principle of order stemmed from it being zoned, like the Milyutin linear city, into parallel bands. In the Ville Radieuse these bands were assigned to the following uses: (1) satellite cities dedicated to education, (2) business zone, (3) transportation zone including passenger rail and air transport, (4) hotel and embassy zone, (5) residential zone, (6) green zone, (7) light industrial zone, (8) warehouses plus freight rail and (9) heavy industry. It was paradoxical, to say the least, that something of a Humanist, anthropomorphic metaphor was still inserted into this model. This much is evident from his explicatory sketches of the period which show the isolated 'head' of the sixteen cruciform skyscrapers above the 'heart' of the cultural centre, located between the two halves or 'lungs' of the residential zone. Aside from the distortions induced by such biological metaphors the linear model was strictly adhered to, thereby allowing less hierarchic zones to expand independently of each other.

The Ville Radieuse took the open-city concept of the Ville Contemporaine to its logical conclusion, and a typical section through the entire city showed all the structures raised clear of the ground, including the garages and the access roads. By virtue of elevating everything on *pilotis* the ground surface would have become a continuous park in which the pedestrian would have been free to wander at will. The typical transverse section of the VR block and the glass curtain wall or *pan-verre* in which it was enveloped were equally crucial to the provision of the 'essential joys' of 'sun', 'space' and 'green'; this last being guaranteed not only by the park, but also by the roof garden, running along the top of the continuous *redent* block.

In 1929, before finalizing his plans for the 'radiant city', Le Corbusier visited South America where, piloted by the pioneer aviators Mermoz and Saint-Exupéry, he had the stimulating experience of surveying a tropical landscape from the air. From such a vantage point,

Rio de Janeiro impressed him as a natural linear city, laid out like a narrow ribbon along its *corniche*, with the sea on one side and steep, volcanic rocks on the other. The form of this urban terrain seems to have spontaneously suggested the idea of the viaduct city, and Le Corbusier immediately sketched an extension of Rio in the form of a coastal highway, some 6 kilometres (3¾ miles) in length, elevated 100 metres (305 feet) above the ground and comprising fifteen floors of 'artificial sites' for residential use stacked beneath its road surface. The resultant megastructure was shown in section as elevated above the average roof height of the city.

This inspired proposal led directly to the plans for Algiers developed during the years 1930 to 1933. The first of these projected a motorway megastructure for the entire length of an equally spectacular *corniche*, given the code name 'Obus' because its concave enclosure of the bay resembled the trajectory of a shell. (Note once again the appropriation of a military term.) With six floors beneath its road

surface and twelve above the idea of the 'viaduct city' came into its own. Set some 5 metres (6 feet) apart, each of these floors constituted an artificial site, on which individual owners were envisaged as erecting two-storey units 'in any style they saw fit'. This provision of a public but pluralistic infrastructure, designed for individual appropriation, was destined to find considerable currency among the anarchistic architectural avant garde of the post Second World War period (for instance, in urban infrastructures proposed by Yona Friedman and Nicolaas Habraken).

The 'erotic' plan configurations created for the cities of Rio de Janeiro and Algiers seem to have been related to certain transformations in the expressive structure of Le Corbusier's painting, which after 1926 began to move from Purist abstraction towards sensuously figurative compositions, featuring his so-called *objets à réaction poétique*. Female figures first appeared in his painting at this time and the sensuous, heavy manner in which these were rendered lent a certain substance to his claim that, like Delacroix, he had rediscovered the essence of female beauty in the casbah of Algiers.

Le Corbusier's 1930 Algiers plan was his last urban proposal of overwhelming grandeur. Reminiscent of the sensuous spirit of Gaudí's Park Güell, his ecstatic enthusiasm seems to have spent itself here in a passionate poem to the natural beauty of the Mediterranean. From now on his approach to city planning was to be more pragmatic, while his urban building types gradually assumed less idealized forms.

166 Le Corbusier, *corniche* extensions for Rio de Janiero, 1930.

167 Le Corbusier and Jeanneret, 'Plan Obus' for Algiers, 1930.

168   Le Corbusier and Jeanneret, plan for Zlín, Czechoslovakia, 1935, showing it organized as a linear city in parallel bands.

The cruciform Cartesian skyscraper was abandoned in favour of the Y-shaped office block, with which it was possible to achieve a more favourable distribution of sun over the entire surface of the building. Similarly, his typical VR *redent* block was distorted into an Arabesque form in the Obus plan and then phased out entirely. This last modification which led to his adoption of the free-standing slab as his basic residential type (cf. the *Unité* slab of 1952) came with his 1935 proposals for the towns of Nemours in North Africa and Zlín in Czechoslovakia. While both of these plans were projected for steeply sloping sites — for which the free-standing slab was eminently suitable — their chequer-board layout, set appropriately against the fall of the land, became a formula which was soon to be applied everywhere irrespective of the topography. As the typical Corbusian solution to high-density housing it was to be copied with disastrous consequences in a great deal of subsequent urban development, and the alienating environment created in many of the post-war *grands ensembles* clearly owes much to the influence of this model.

Aside from the context it afforded for the evolution of the *Unité* slab form, the significance of Zlín, designed for the shoe manufacturer Bata, lies in its ingenious adaptation of the Milyutin linear-city proposal to a specific site. In linking the old town and manufacturing centre of Zlín at the bottom of the valley to the executive airport situated on the plateau, the road and railway paralleled the length of the valley, with the new industry on one side and the company housing on the other. Zlín thus became Le Corbusier's first formulation of the linear city after the Soviet model, a type to be designated by him later as one of the three productive units (i.e. *Etablissements humains*), the other two being the traditional radially planned city and the 'agricultural co-operative'.

The argument put forward in *Les Trois Etablissements humains* of 1944 was largely a reinterpretation of the regional planning theses that had already been advanced by the German geographer Walter Kristaller and the Spanish linear-city theorist Soria y Mata. Le Corbusier derived his own regional model from Kristaller's law of urban development which held that, other factors being equal, urban settlements in Germany had always occurred at the intersections of triangular or hexagonal grids. Using Soria y Mata's idea of the linear suburb Le Corbusier merely complemented the Kristaller analysis by proposing that all links between existing radio-concentric cities should be developed as linear-industrial settlements. He went on to show that the interstices within the grid could then be developed as agricultural co-operatives. For this comprehensive-regional approach it was necessary to develop a new typology on an increased scale. Zlín was to serve as the generic 'linear-industrial city', and the 'radiant farm' and the 'radiant village' designed in 1933 for the Syndicalist agricultural worker Norbert Bezard were to be posited as the constituent elements of the new agricultural co-operative.

*Les Trois Etablissements humains*, with which, according to Le Corbusier, one could both urbanize the town and urbanize the country, was an attempt to resolve the conflict that had bitterly divided the Russian urban planners of the late 1920s, between the de-urbanists who had wanted to redistribute the existing population throughout the Soviet Union and the urbanists who had advocated the maintenance of existing towns and the creation of additional urban centres.

While the radiant city was never realized, its influence as an evolving model on post-war urban development in Europe and elsewhere was extensive. In addition to innumerable housing schemes, the specific organization of two new capital cities was clearly indebted to ideas embodied in the Ville Radieuse: namely Le Corbusier's master plan for Chandigarh of 1950 and Lúcio Costa's plan for Brasilia of 1957. Le Corbusier's basic acceptance of the existing garden-city layout for Chandigarh, as produced by the American planner Albert Mayer in the very same year, made it sufficiently clear that he had effectively abandoned any notion of creating a finite city of significant form and that he had shifted his general approach to promoting models of dynamic growth on a regional scale. For all his modification of the Mayer plan, his 'ideal city' came to be reduced at this juncture to the government centre alone, the Chandigarh Capitol of 1950. This realist strategy had already been anticipated in his plan for St-Dié of 1946. From now on, like the masters of the Renaissance, he seems to have been prepared to make up for the unrealizable whole through the projection of a representational element on a monumental scale.

Throughout the first half of the 1930s this latent monumentalizing tendency in no way diminished Le Corbusier's interest in equipping the 'machine-age' civilization. He continued to address himself to industrialists and called attention wherever possible to his capacity for designing the large-scale *objets-types*, regarded by him as being essential to the equipment of a new age. Such indeed were the four major buildings that he realized between 1932 and 1933: the Maison Clarté apartments in Geneva, the Pavillon Suisse in the Cité Universitaire, the Salvation Army Building and his own

169   Le Corbusier, Porte Molitor apartments, Paris, 1933.

Porte Molitor apartments, these last three all being built in Paris. The modular, glass and steel, *pan-verre* façade employed in each case was intended to demonstrate the 'machine-age' aesthetic. As such it represented a break with the concrete frame and rendered blockwork used in the villas of the 1920s. This apotheosis of the Engineer's Aesthetic paradoxically occurred at just that moment when Le Corbusier was beginning to lose his faith in the inevitable triumph of the machine age. Soon after 1933 he began to react against the rationalized production of the *machine à habiter,* although whether from disillusion with modern technique as such or from despair in the face of a world torn apart by economic depression and political reaction it is hard to know. As Robert Fishman has recently pointed out, he had always maintained a certain ambivalence with regard to the promise of Taylorized mass-production:

Le Corbusier's quest for Authority in the Thirties reflects finally his deeply ambivalent attitude towards industrialization. His social thought and his architecture rested on the faith that industrial society had the inherent capacity for a genuine and joyous order. But behind that faith, there was the fear that a perverted, uncontrolled industrialization could destroy civilization. As a young man at La Chaux-de-Fonds he had seen ugly, mass-produced time-pieces from Germany virtually wipe out the watchmaker's crafts. The lesson was not forgotten.

Whatever the ultimate cause, primitive technical elements began to appear in his work with increasing frequency and freedom of expression from 1930 onwards. First in the pitched-roofed, timber and stone Errazuriz House projected in 1930 for Chile, then in the rubble-walled villa built for Madame Mandrot near Toulon in 1931, and finally in two remarkable works of 1935 and 1937 respectively: a concrete, vaulted weekend house built in the suburbs of Paris and his light-weight, canvas Pavillon des Temps Nouveaux, erected for the Paris International Exhibition of 1937. While the roof of the former recalled not only his Maison Monol of 1919, but more profoundly the traditional barrel-vaulted construction of the Mediterranean, the latter evoked not only the nomadic tent but also that reconstruction of the Hebraic temple in the wilderness which he had chosen to illustrate in *Vers une architecture* as an example of regulating lines. With this series of works the burden of expression now shifted from abstract form to the means of construction itself. As Le Corbusier was to

remark of his weekend house: 'The planning of such a house demanded extreme care, the elements of construction were the sole architectural means'. Despite the archaic and vernacular references, both works still exploited aspects of advanced technology, the weekend house making telling use of reinforced concrete, plywood and glass lenses and the pavilion making a spectacular demonstration of steel cable suspension in such a way as to recall the jointing techniques which were then the province of aeronautical construction. Finally both works seemed to be sophisticated metaphors for a less doctrinaire future when men would freely mix primitive and advanced techniques according to their needs and resources (see Chapter 25).

How resources in general might best be allocated in socio-political terms was first explicitly formulated by Le Corbusier in the contributions that he made from January 1931 to the monthly Syndicalist journal, *Plan*, edited by Philippe Lamour, Hubert Lagardelle, François Pierrefeu and Pierre Winter. In December 1931, in an essay entitled 'Décisions', he established the political preconditions under which his urban ideas might be fulfilled. His recommendation that urban land should be requisitioned by the state gave adequate ammunition to the forces of reaction, who had already chosen to see him as a Bolshevik in disguise; while his demand that the state should forbid by edict the

170   Le Corbusier and Jeanneret, Errazuriz House, Chile, 1930.

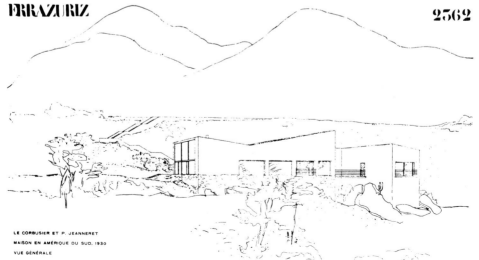

LE CORBUSIER ET P. JEANNERET
MAISON EN AMÉRIQUE DU SUD, 1930
VUE GÉNÉRALE

production of useless consumer goods must have disturbed those on the technocratic right, who might otherwise have taken him as an unequivocal representative of their interests.

In 1932 Le Corbusier broke with Lamour and became a member of the Committee for Regionalist and Syndicalist Action and a contributory editor of its journal *Prélude*, edited by Hubert Lagardelle. As a protégé of Sorel, Lagardelle had close ties with the left wing of the Italian Fascist movement and as such was cautiously pro-Fascist. The text of *La Ville Radieuse*, issued as a book in 1933, had previously appeared in instalments under the sign of an authoritarian brand of Syndicalism, first in *Plan* and then, after 1932, in *Prélude*. Le Corbusier, influenced no doubt by the strong Syndicalist traditions of the Jura region, vacillated, like his fellow Syndicalists, between the authoritarian utopian socialism of Saint-Simon and the anarchic-socialist tendencies latent in the writings of Fourier. In *La Ville Radieuse*, Le Corbusier advocated, along Syndicalist lines, a direct system of government through the *métiers* (trade guilds or unions), yet like his editorial colleagues he seems to have had only the vaguest idea as to how this reign of the *métiers* could be established.

Tacitly accepting yet forever postponing the eventuality of a general strike as the only access to power, the French Syndicalists of the 1930s were for reform rather than revolution and for the rationalization of the state rather than its abolition. While pro-industrialist and progressive, they remained nostalgic for a pre-industrial harmony; while anti-capitalist, they were nonetheless promoters of a technocratic élite; for while opposed to the oligarchy of the Bolshevik state, they simultaneously advocated technocratic authority. With greater consistency they were fervently internationalist and pacifist and against the waste of armament production and laissez-faire consumption. To this end, in 1938 Le Corbusier was to write his most polemical book, bearing the prophetic – if ironic – title *Des canons, des munitions? Merci! Des logis . . . S.V.P.* Yet for all this, the Syndicalists were unable to establish a popular base. The gap between the provisions of a welfare state and the possibility of a mass culture of high quality did not escape Le Corbusier who with characteristic aloofness deprecated the proto-populist housing to be provided by the Lois Loucheur of 1929, under whose auspices his minimum dwellings for workers had been designed. He concluded his initial description of the project with the resigned statement:

We shall not make a single one. . . . Because your law has no real basis. There is no point of contact between the two sides involved: my plan (which is a way of life) and those for whom the law is made, the potential clients who have not been educated.

171 Le Corbusier, cover of *Des canons, des munitions? Merci! Des logis . . . S.V.P.*, 1938.

185

# Chapter 21
## Frank Lloyd Wright
## and the Disappearing City 1929-63

According to reports in the press Henry Ford has issued an order whereby all married workers and employees in their spare time are to cultivate vegetables in their own gardens to detailed instructions given by experts employed by him for this purpose, the idea being that by this means they will be able to supply the greater part of their own requirements. The necessary garden land is to be placed at their disposal. Henry Ford has said, 'Self help is the only means of combatting the economic depression. Anyone refusing to cultivate his garden will be dismissed.'

*Die Heimstätte*, No. 10, 1931

172   Wright, project for the National Life Insurance Building, Chicago, 1924.

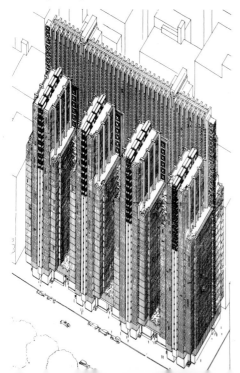

The second significant phase of Wright's career was initiated by the completion of the last of his concrete-block houses, in Tulsa, Oklahoma, in 1929, and by the first of his projects to exploit to the limit the cantilevering capacity of reinforced concrete, his Elizabeth Noble Apartments projected for Los Angeles. The crystalline aesthetic of these apartments had already been anticipated in his National Life Insurance Building project for Chicago of 1924, whose scintillating copper and glass façade was a direct translation of his 'textured concrete block' aesthetic into glass.

The economic mass production of the automobile by Henry Ford and the impact of the Depression seem to have had the effect of rousing Wright from his Eldorado dreams, from the 'instant' culture of his Mayan houses, built for rich, displaced aesthetes in the lush hills of southern California. Influenced by the role then being played by the Neue Sachlichkeit in Europe, Wright was induced to formulate a new role for architecture in restructuring the social order of the United States.

Ever since his address, 'The Art and Craft of the Machine' (1901), Wright had recognized that it was the destiny of the machine to bring about a profound change in the nature of civilization. His initial reaction, lasting until 1916, had been to adapt the machine to the creation of a high-level craft culture; that is, to apply it to the direct formation of his Prairie Style. Despite the fact that, for Wright, 'machine' expression always seemed to involve a certain rhetorical use of the cantilever (the Robie House of 1909 is a typical example), he still insisted on the ultimate authority of traditional materials and methods. Although anticipated in the Coonley House (1908) and in Midway

Gardens (1914) it was the mid-1920s before Wright considered the assembly of entire structures from mass-produced synthetic elements, such as the concrete-block mosaic of his Californian houses or the modular curtain wall system that he devised for the enclosure of monolithic concrete structures.

In being forced by the economy to recognize the limits of traditional materials and construction, Wright was caused to abandon the earthbound syntax of his Prairie Style, and through a singular combination of reinforced concrete and glass he created a prismatic, faceted architecture whose glass exterior, borne on an armature of floating planes, conveyed an illusion of total weightlessness. It was as though, like Scheerbart before him, he had suddenly been possessed by the expressive qualities of glass, whose crystalline translucence could be best complemented by the liberating attributes of the column-free plan. The first occasion on which Wright, the master of masonry, acclaimed glass as the modern material par excellence was in his famous Kahn Lectures, given at Princeton University in 1930. In 'Style in Industry' he stated:

Glass has now a perfect visibility, thin sheets of air crystallized to keep air currents outside or inside. Glass surfaces, too, may be modified to let the vision sweep through to any extent up to perfection. Tradition left no orders concerning this material as a means of perfect visibility;

173  Wright, plan for the subdivision of a typical section of land, Chicago, 1913.

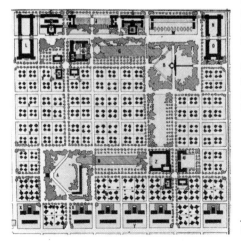

hence the sense of glass as crystal has not, as poetry, entered yet into architecture. All the dignity of colour and material available in any other material may be discounted with permanence. Shadows were the 'brush work' of the ancient Architect. Let the Modern now work with light, light diffused, light reflected – light for its own sake, shadows gratuitous. It is the Machine that makes *modern* these rare new opportunities in Glass.

In 1928 Wright coined the term 'Usonia' to denote an egalitarian culture that would spontaneously emerge in the United States. By this he seems to have intended not only a grassroots individualism but also the realization of a new, dispersed form of civilization such as had recently been made possible by mass ownership of the automobile. The car as *the* 'democratic' mode of locomotion was to be the *deus ex machina* of Wright's anti-urban model, his Broadacre City concept, in which the concentration of the 19th-century city was to be redistributed over the network of a regional agrarian grid (already anticipated in his entry for the City Club, Chicago, competition of 1913 for a subdivision on the outskirts of Chicago). He had first spoken out against the traditional city in the last of his Kahn Lectures, which began: 'Is the city a persistent form of social disease, eventuating in the fate all cities have met?' It is one of the ironies of our century that Broadacre City corresponded more closely than any other form of radical urbanism to the central precepts of the *Communist Manifesto* of 1848, advocating 'the gradual abolition of the distinction between town and country by a more equable distribution of the population over the land.'

Nevertheless, Wright's first building projects for this new Usonian culture, the St Mark's apartment tower and the *Capital Journal* newspaper building, both of 1931, were urban rather than agrarian in tone. Eventually realized

174  Wright, project for the *Capital Journal* Building, Salem, Oregon, 1931. Section.

175, 176   Wright, S. C. Johnson & Son Administration Building, Racine, Wis., 1936–39. General view by night and interior.

as the Price Tower in Bartlesville, Oklahoma (1952–55), and as the Johnson Wax Administration Building in, Racine, Wisconsin (1936–39), both of these projects consisted of reinforced-concrete cantilevered systems covered in a crystalline membrane. At a symbolic level they embodied the essential polarity that had been evident in Wright's work ever since his Martin House and Larkin Building of 1904 – the fundamentalist assimilation of the building of the home to the processes of nature and of the work place to the idea of sacrament. This polarization was to be brilliantly reformulated in Wright's Usonian period in two masterworks of unsurpassed richness and generosity, the Kaufmann weekend house at Bear Run, Pennsylvania, of 1936, better known as Falling Water, and the Johnson Wax Administration Building begun in the same year.

For Wright, the word 'organic' (which he first applied to architecture in 1908) came to mean the use of the concrete cantilever as though it were a natural, tree-like form. He seems to have conceived of such a form as a direct extension of Sullivan's vitalist metaphor

of the 'seed germ', extended now to include the whole structure rather than the ornament alone. Just before his death, Wright wrote of the vulva-shaped pool in the foyer of the Guggenheim Museum: 'Typical of the details of this edifice, the symbolic figure is the oval seed pod containing globular units.'

In the Johnson Wax Administration Building this organic metaphor revealed itself in tall, slender mushroom columns tapering towards their bases, which form the prime support within a 9-metre (30-foot) high open-planned air-conditioned office space. These columns resolve themselves at roof level into broad circular lily pads of concrete, between which is 'interwoven' a membrane of pyrex glass tubing. These horizontal roof lights delicately supported by columns, and the columns themselves (whose hollow cores serve as storm water drains and whose hinged bases are pin-jointed into bronze shoes), jointly represent the apotheosis of Wright's technical imagination. This was the expressive destiny of Usonia, a poetry of miraculous technique arising out of a daring inversion of the traditional elements. Thus where one would have expected solid (the roof) one found light; and where one would have expected light (the walls) one found solid. Of this inversion Wright wrote:

Glass tubing laid up like bricks in a wall composes all the lighting surfaces. Light enters the building where the cornice used to be. In the interior the box-like structure vanishes completely. The walls carrying the glass ribbing are of hard red brick and red Kasota sandstone. The entire fabric is reinforced concrete, cold-drawn mesh being used for the reinforcement.

This concrete mushroom construction brought Wright to develop, for the first time, a curved corner profile and a predominantly circular vocabulary, which, executed in hard, precise materials and lit throughout by translucent glass tubing, imparted to the structure a Moderne streamlined aura which time has done little to dispel. At the same time this science-fiction atmosphere rendered the Johnson Wax Building as a self-contained, monastic place of work. As Henry-Russell Hitchcock wrote: 'There is a certain illusion of sky seen from the bottom of an aquarium'. Here again, as in his Larkin Building, Wright had created an hermetic environment whose physical exclusion of the outside world was reinforced by the form and colour of the special office equipment designed for its furnishing.

While Johnson Wax reinterpreted the sacramental place of work, Falling Water embodied Wright's ideal of the place of living fused into nature. Once again, reinforced concrete afforded the point of departure; only this time the cantilevering gesture was extravagant to the point of folly, in contrast to the implacable calm of the mushroom structure of Johnson Wax. Falling Water projected itself out from the natural rock in which it was anchored, as a free floating platform poised over a small waterfall. Designed in a single day, this dramatic structural gesture was Wright's ultimate romantic statement. No longer restricted by the extended earth line of his Prairie Style, the terraces of this house appeared as an agglomeration of planes miraculously suspended in space, poised at varying heights above the trees of a densely wooded valley. Tied back into the escarpment by the reinforced-concrete upstand beams of its terraces, Falling Water defies photographic record. Its fusion with the landscape is total, for, despite the extensive use of horizontal glazing, nature permeates the structure at every turn. Its interior evokes the atmosphere of a furnished cave rather than that of a house in the traditional sense. That the rough stone walls and flagged floors intend some primitive homage to the site is borne out by the living-room stairs which, descending through the floor to the waterfall below, have no function other than to bring man into more intimate communion with the surface of the stream. Wright's perennial ambivalence towards technique was never more singularly expressed than in this house, for although concrete had made the design feasible he still regarded it as an illegitimate material – as a 'conglomera' that had 'little quality in itself'. His initial intent had been to cover the concrete of Falling Water in gold leaf, a kitsch gesture from which he was dissuaded by the discretion of the client. He finally settled for finishing its surface in apricot paint!

From now on, aside from his remarkably practical Usonian houses, Wright continued to develop a curious kind of science-fiction architecture which, judging from the exotic style of his late renderings, seemed intended for occupation by some extraterrestial species. This selfconscious exoticism fell to the level of ultra-kitsch in his Marin County Courthouse, California, commissioned in 1957 and finished in 1963, four years after his death. Wright had already acknowledged this compulsion towards the fantastic when he wrote in 1928: 'The fact remains Usonia wanted romance and sentiment. The failure to get it is less significant than the fact that it was sought.'

Wright's Usonian vision, first crystallized in his masterworks of the mid-1930s, attained its fulfilment in his Guggenheim Museum, New York, of 1943. The structural idea and *parti* for

177   Wright, Falling Water, Bear Run, Pa., 1936.

178   Wright, preliminary project for the Solomon R. Guggenheim Museum, New York, 1943.

the museum dates back to his sketch for the Gordon Strong Planetarium of 1925 — a science-fiction proposal par excellence, a 'ziggurat' destined for the semi-religious gratification of 'nature-worshipping' pilgrims. At the Guggenheim, he simply turned the diminishing helix of the planetarium inside out, inverting and thereby converting what had previously been a car ramp into an internal, spiralling gallery, an extended spatial helix which Wright later referred to as an 'unbroken wave'. The Guggenheim Museum must be regarded as the climax of Wright's later career, since it combines the structural and spatial principles of Falling Water with the top-lit containment of Johnson Wax. His declaration that the museum was more like a temple in a park than a mundane business building or residential structure may be seen as an ironic reference to its origin in these projects.

In his first book on city planning, *The Disappearing City* (entitled in the first draft *The Industrial Revolution Runs Away*), published in 1932 on the completion of his Broadacre City study, Wright declared that the future city will be everywhere and nowhere, and that 'it will be a city so greatly different from the ancient city or from any city of today that we will probably fail to recognize its coming as the city at all'. Elsewhere he stated: 'America needs no help to build Broadacre City. It will build itself, haphazard.' Wright neither sought nor found any satisfactory resolution to the inherent contradiction of this polemic. On the one hand, he argued that men should con-sciously establish a new system of dispersed land settlement, anti-urban by definition; on the other, he stated that there was little need to do so since this would happen spontaneously!

In his historical determinism, Wright looked to the machine as the one agent with which the architect has no choice but to come to terms. But the old dilemma remained: how to do this without being brutalized? For Wright, this was the constant cultural quest of his long career. Thus, in *The Living City* (1958), we find him writing: 'Miracles of technical invention with which our "hit and run" culture has nothing to do are — despite misuse — new forces with which any indigenous culture must reckon.' While he consigned steam power and the railway to instant oblivion, he welcomed (like the Soviet de-urbanists of his day) electricity as a source of silent power and the automobile as the provider of limitless movement. He identified the new forces which would transform the entire basis of Western civilization as follows: (1) Electrification, the communicational annihilation of distance and the constant illumination of human occupation; (2) Mechanical Mobilization, the immeasurable widening of human contact due to the invention of the airplane and the automobile, and finally (3) Organic Architecture which, although it always escaped any precise definition, seems to have eventually meant for Wright the economic creation of built form and space in accordance with the latent principles of nature as these may be revealed through the application of the reinforced-concrete construction. On another

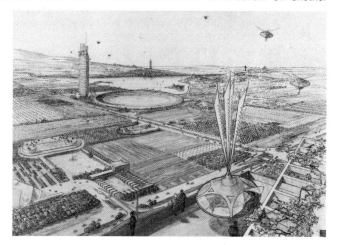

179  Wright, Broadacre City project, 1934–58.

occasion, Wright characterized the resources that would implacably shape Broadacre City as the car, the radio, the telephone, the telegraph, and, above all, standardized machine shop production.

For Wright, Usonian culture and Broadacre City were inseparable concepts, the former providing the prime intention behind a whole range of buildings which were the architectural substance of the latter. Falling Water and the Johnson Wax Building would no doubt have found their appointed places in Broadacre City. Yet, by Usonia Wright generally intended something altogether more modest: warm, open-planned, small houses designed for convenience, economy and comfort. The heart of the Usonian house was the 'time-and-motion' kitchen, an alcove work space freely planned off the living volume, which, as Henry-Russell Hitchcock observed, was an important contribution to American domestic planning. Of almost equal import to the modern interior was Wright's introduction at this time of continuous wall-seating to maximize space in small houses. While single-family Usonian homes were projected as the housing stock of Broadacre City, they were also actually realized in the numerous suburban houses that Wright designed and built between 1932 and 1960, including the famous four-family Suntop Homes, arranged in a pinwheel formation, that were erected on the outskirts of Philadelphia in 1939.

By far the most important building type designed for Wright's ideal city was not a house at all but the Walter Davidson Model Farm projected in 1932. This unit, designed to facilitate the economic management of both home and land, was critical to the overall economy of Broadacre City, where every man was to grow his own food on an acre of land which, reserved at his birth, would be placed at his disposal as soon as he was of age.

Apart from a number of contingent social ideas such as the single tax system or social credit — both popular remedial notions in the Depression — Broadacre City was above all an updating of that smallholding cottage-industry economy first advocated by Peter Kropotkin in his *Factories, Fields and Workshops* of 1898.

In reviving such a propositon there was at least one awkward contradiction which Wright, like Henry Ford, stubbornly refused to recognize: namely, that an individualistic quasi-agrarian economy would not necessarily be able to guarantee to an industrialized society either its subsistence or the benefits of mass production, since the latter, despite automation, still demanded some concentration in both labour and resources. Even Kropotkin acknowledged the need to concentrate labour and resources for the processes of heavy industry. Wright's vision of a city in which part-time smallholders would drive to work, to rural factories, in secondhand Model T Fords, suggests that a migrant, 'sweat equity' labour force would have been essential for the success of the Broadacre economy.

As Meyer Schapiro pointed out at the time, Wright, despite his unremitting attack on rent and profit and his prescience in foreseeing the dissolution of the city, failed to confront the urgent issue of power that was fundamental to the Broadacre concept. Like Buckminster Fuller, who was already active by this date, he could not bring himself to acknowledge that architecture and planning must, of necessity, address themselves to the class struggle. Schapiro summed up Wright's utopianism correctly in 1938, when he wrote:

The economic conditions that determine freedom and a decent living are largely ignored by Wright. He foresees, in fact, the poverty of these new feudal settlements when he provides that the worker set up his own factory-made house, part by part, according to his means, beginning with a toilet and kitchen, and adding other rooms as he earns the means by his labor in the factory. His indifference to property relations and the state, his admission of private industry and second-hand Fords in this idyllic world of amphibian labor, betray its reactionary character. Already under the dictatorship of Napoleon III, the state farms, partly inspired by the old Utopias, were the official solution of unemployment. The democratic Wright may attack rent and profit interest, but apart from some passing reference to the single tax, he avoids the question of class and power.

# Alvar Aalto and the Nordic tradition: National Romanticism and the Doricist sensibility 1895-1957

The first essential feature of interest is Karelian architecture's uniformity. There are few comparable examples in Europe. It is a pure forest-settlement architecture in which wood dominates almost one hundred percent both as material and as jointing method. From the roof, with its massive system of joists, to the movable building parts, wood dominates, in most cases naked, without the dematerializing effect that a layer of paint gives. In addition, wood is often used in as natural proportions as possible, on the scale typical of the material. A dilapidated Karelian village is somehow similar in appearance to a Greek ruin, where, also, the material's uniformity is a dominant feature, though marble replaces wood. . . . Another significant special feature is the manner in which the Karelian house has come about, both its historical development and its building methods. Without going further into ethnographic details, we can conclude that the inner system of construction results from a methodical accommodation to circumstance. The Karelian house

is in a way a building that begins with a single modest cell or with an imperfect embryo building, shelter for a man and animals, and which then figuratively speaking grows year by year. 'The expanded Karelian house' can in a way be compared with a biological cell formation. The possibility of a larger and more complete building is always open.

This remarkable ability to grow and adapt is best reflected in the Karelian building's main architectural principle, the fact that the roof angle isn't constant.

Alvar Aalto
*Architecture in Karelia*, 1941

In this perceptive essay on the farmhouse vernacular of eastern Finland, Aalto evoked, almost by chance, the two prominent architectural modes of the second half of the 19th century, Romantic Classicism and the Gothic Revival. Where Aalto's account of native agrarian form with its stress on the variation in roof pitches comes close to Pugin's original prescription for a revived medieval domestic style, his characterization of a decayed Karelian village as a Greek ruin rendered in wood rather than stone is a sort of mirror-image of Auguste Choisy's thesis that the metopes of the Parthenon are nothing but vestigial forms of timber construction. Aside from making us aware of his own Classical consciousness and of his interest in an all but primeval vernacular, this passage also serves to introduce the two stylistic themes of the Nordic tradition: the National Romantic manner dating from 1895 and the Doricist sensibility which emerged in Scandinavia around 1910. Aalto's long and brilliant career can scarcely be appreciated without making explicit reference to these

180 Sonck, Tampere Cathedral, 1902. Ground plan showing 'log-cabin' corners.

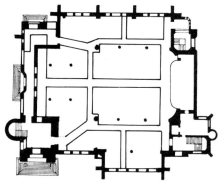

themes, for, while he was never a committed participant in either, his life's work reflected a constant debt to either National Romantic tactility or the astringencies of Doricist form.

The origin of these modes is significant, the one patently stemming from the Gothic Revival, via the American Shingle style of H.H. Richardson, and the other arising out of the Romantic Classicism of Schinkel. Helsinki, founded as the Finnish capital in 1817 on the basis of J.A. Ehrenström's orthogonal grid, was to be particularly prone to the influence of the Romantic Classical style, since it was laid out around an armature of representative Classical buildings – the Senate House, the University and the Cathedral, all built after 1818 on the designs of Schinkel's fellow pupil, Carl Ludwig Engel. As for National Romanticism, such is Aalto's debt to this movement that it is hardly possible to appreciate his later career without first examining its origins and aims.

Initially, National Romanticism was as prevalent in Sweden as in Finland, particularly in the work of the architect Gustaf Ferdinand Boberg who was responsible in his Gävle Fire Station of 1890 for introducing the work of Richardson into Scandinavia. However, in general, Swedish architects were incapable of transforming this Neo-Romanesque manner into a convincing national style. What was true of Sweden was even more true of Denmark, where Martin Nyrop's popularly acclaimed neo-medieval Copenhagen Town Hall of 1892 remained complacently rooted in a highly eclectic, if successful form of historicism, totally unmoved by the conviction and integrity of Richardson's heroic example. Indeed the Swedes and the Danes were only able to achieve an authentic national revivalist manner after the main impulse of the nationalist cultural movement was already over, most notably in Ragnar Östberg's castle-like Stockholm City Hall (1909–23), and in P.V. Jensen-Klint's proto-Expressionist Grundtvig Church, Copenhagen, designed in 1913 but not realized until 1921–26.

National Romanticism in Finland had already become a significant force by 1895, when a group of artists came to their ideological and artistic maturity at the same time – the composer Jean Sibelius, the painter Akseli Gallén-Kallela and the architects Eliel Saarinen, Herman Gesellius, Armas Lindgren and, at some distance, Lars Sonck. The basic inspiration behind all their work was the Finnish folk epic, the *Kalevala*, which had been collected and transcribed by Elias Lönnroth at the beginning of the 19th century.

The compelling force behind National Romanticism in Finland derived, in part at least, from the need to find a national style other than Romantic Classicism, which was the imperialist manner of Helsinki, built under Russian auspices. A further cause for the particular form taken by Finland's rather ready acceptance of the Richardsonian syntax, derived from the need to exploit the abundance of local granite, reflected in the dispatch of a mission to Aberdeen in the early 1890s to study the Scottish technique of building in this material. The first National Romantic architect to use granite was Sonck, whose Neo-Gothic church of St Michael, built in Turku in 1895, was enriched by columns and furnishings in finely carved granite, in contrast to its otherwise stark and sparsely decorated interior. That this interior with its etched precision shows something of the same surface articulation as is found, say, in Otto Wagner's Steinhof Church in Vienna built a decade later, is perhaps partly explained by the fact that Sonck's generation had been trained in the Finnish Polytechnic under the tutorship of the technocratic but Classically-educated Carl Gustav Nyström. Nyström, aside from pioneering granite construction, had established himself as a Wagnerian 'technocrat' in his National Archives Building of 1890. He was later to distinguish himself as a Structural Rationalist, when in 1906 he added an exemplary steel and concrete bookstack to the rear of C.L. Engel's University Library.

Sonck's major buildings, Tampere Cathedral (1902) and the Telephone Building in Helsinki (1905), were patently influenced by the work of Richardson, whose masonry syntax, as Asko Salokorpi has remarked, resembled the Finnish medieval tradition. This Richardsonian manner was soon to be adapted by Eliel Saarinen and Armas Lindgren, in their Orientalizing Neo-

Romanesque Finnish Pavilion for the Paris Exposition of 1900, and a domestic version of this manner was used in their highly romantic Villa Hvitträsk, designed in 1902 in collaboration with Gesellius. Inside, however, Hvitträsk was less Richardsonian, and in many respects a reworking of Gallén-Kallela's log cabin studio built at Ruovesi, in 1893. Aside from its spirited interpretation of Finnish timber vernacular, the

181   Gallén-Kallela, the artist's studio at Ruovesi, 1893. Ground plan and elevation.

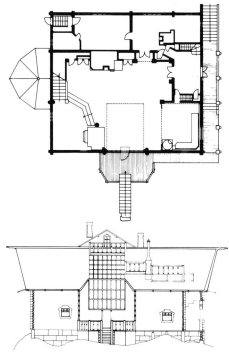

interior décor of Hvitträsk reiterated Gallén-Kallela's attempt to evoke the lost forms and images of Finno-Ugric culture. Two years later, in 1904, the 'guild' idyll of Saarinen, Gesellius and Lindgren – who, in anticipation of Wright, not only worked but also lived together at Hvitträsk – came to an abrupt end. This happened when Saarinen, acting independently, entered and won the competition for the Helsinki Railway Terminus with a design whose architectonic invention reflected the 'crystallized' Jugendstil of such buildings as Hoffmann's Palais Stoclet, Brussels, of 1905 and Olbrich's Hochzeitsturm, Darmstadt, of 1908. Saarinen was not the only Finn to entertain the late Jugendstil manner: Onni Tarjanne's *Wagnerschule* style matched and in many ways surpassed that of Saarinen, particularly in his Takaharju Sanatorium of 1903. (It is measure of Tarjanne's brilliance that he had designed the Finnish National Theatre at Helsinki in a National Romantic, Richardsonian manner only five years earlier.) The swan song of the Finnish Jugendstil came with the extremely delicate Hoffmannesque work of Selim A. Lindquist, as exemplified in Helsinki in the Suvilhati Power Station of 1908 and the Villa Ensi of 1910.

Naturally enough, given Finland's long history as an imperial colony, first of Sweden and then of Russia, the revival of Romantic Classicism in Scandinavia – the so-called Doricist sensibility – began in Denmark. It came into being there under the influence of writers such as Vilhelm Wansher, whose first articles on Neo-Classicism appeared in 1907, and the German Paul Mebes, whose book *Um 1800* was published in 1908. The interest of these men (and others including H. Kampmann and

182   Saarinen, Lindgren and Gesellius, Villa Hvitträsk, near Helsinki, 1902.

E. Thompsen) in a non-historicist, primordial Doric simplicity, based on primal architectonic elements which were neither Classic nor vernacular, drew attention to the Danish school of Romantic Classicism, to the work of Gottlieb Bindesbøll (1800–56) and Christian Frederick Hansen (1756–1845). This whole sensibility crystallized in 1910, after the Carlsberg Brewery had publicly demanded that a spire be added to Hansen's Fruekirche. The architect Carl Petersen responded to their arrogant gesture by organizing an exhibition of Hansen's drawings. In the following year a group of painters responded by commissioning Petersen to design the Faaborg Museum, generally regarded as the first building of the Romantic Classical Revival.

It was to take some time for this movement to enter Sweden. The impulse is just discernible in Carl Westman's Stockholm Law Courts of 1915, a part National Romantic, part Classical work, which was followed by Ivar Tengbom's Neo-Classical Stockholm Concert Hall (1920–26) and Gunnar Asplund's Stockholm Public Library (1920–28), the movement culminating in Finland at the point of its exhaustion, with J.S. Sirén's Finnish Parliament Building (1926–31). In Sweden the Romantic Classical Revival, far from being *sachlich* and normative, was distorted by a tendency towards the inflection of the plan and by an obsession with local allusion, such as had been established in the skewed planning and iconography of Östberg's National Romantic manner. This was a restrained and synthetic form of expression that invariably alluded to the topography and the genius loci. This drive towards distortion was deeply engrained in Asplund who, having been influenced by both Östberg and Tengbom at the Klara School, sought sporadically throughout his career to transcend the 'battle of styles' by fusing the vernacular and the Classical into a primitive and more authentic form of expression. The first opportunity to do this came with his Woodland Chapel (1918–20) in the Stockholm South Cemetery, which he had planned as a competition design with Sigurd Lewerentz in 1915. Basically Classical in design, this small single-cell structure, with its crisply profiled shingle roof set on a Tuscan peristyle, was in fact derived from a 'primitive hut' that Asplund had happened to see in a garden at Liselund. Up to the time of his brief 'Functionalist' period, lasting from 1928 to 1933, his work seems to have been subject to influences as diverse and as separate in time as the French Neo-Classicists, Josef Hoffmann and above all Bindesbøll, whose Thorwaldsen Museum, Copenhagen, of 1848 furnished Asplund with the Egyptoid and Neo-Classical motifs that recur in his work throughout the 1920s, first in the Carl Johan School at Göteborg of 1915, then in the Skandia Cinema at Stockholm of 1921, and finally in the Stockholm Public Library, completed in 1928.

In Alvar Aalto's early career it was Asplund who was the catalyst, despite the *Wagnerschule* influence of Aalto's teacher, Usko Nyström. By 1922, when he started on his own, Aalto, like Asplund before him, appeared to be moving in several directions. The four buildings that he designed for the Industrial Exhibition held at Tampere in that year obviously allude to quite different levels of cultural development. In all the rhetorical diversity of his later career, no contrast is so expressive as that to be found in his work there, between, say, his 'Classical' industrial pavilion, built of modular panels, along the lines of Otto Wagner's Karlsplatz Station of 1899, and his 'vernacular' thatched-roofed kiosk designed for the display of Finnish handicrafts.

Aalto's early practice in Jyväskylä between 1923 and 1927 was remarkably varied, includ-

183  Asplund, Stockholm Public Library, 1920–28.

184 Aalto, project for Viipuri Library, 1927.

ing workers' apartments and a workers' club (both built in 1924), a surprising number of churches and church renovations, and two civilian guard houses, built at Seinäjoki and Jyväskylä in 1927. All these works were carried out under Asplund's influence in a vaguely Doricist style, which, while compounded in part of the local timber vernacular, was at the same time indebted to Hoffmann's austerity of line and to Schinkel's Italianate mode. In 1927 Aalto moved decisively towards Romantic Classicism in his Viinika Church and his Viipuri Library competition entry. The latter (realized in a modified form in 1935) was unequivocally influenced by Asplund, its form including features taken directly from the Stockholm Public Library. Of these, the Neo-Classical plan with its axial *scala regia*, the atectonic façade and its frieze, and the giant Egyptoid door were patently items which Asplund in his turn had drawn from Bindesbøll. It was Aalto's prize-winning entry for the Paimio Sanatorium of 1928 that firmly established the fundamental Functionalist style of his first mature period (1927–34).

Aside from Asplund, the other catalytic figure in Aalto's early development was clearly the slightly older Finnish architect Erik Bryggman, with whom Alvar and his wife Aino briefly collaborated after their move to the booming city of Turku in southern Finland at the end of 1927. Alvar Aalto was soon to outdo the stripped Classicism of Bryggman's Atrium Apartments of 1925 in his own Asplundian South-Western Agricultural Co-operative Building, realized in Turku in 1928. The colour scheme of the theatre in this building – a dark blue auditorium offset by grey and pink plush upholstery – is obviously taken from Asplund's Skandia Cinema, as is the frieze running below the exterior cornice. The fruit of Aalto's collaboration with Bryggman was first an office building project for the town of Vaasa and

then, in 1929, an exhibition celebrating the 700th anniversary of Turku. As in Asplund's 1928 sketch proposals for the Stockholm Exhibition, with their exposed, light-weight, cantilevered trusses, suspended sky signs and 'agitatory' graphics, this commission led Bryggman and Aalto to follow the Soviet Agit-Prop lead in architectural rhetoric.

After the realization of his Constructivist-influenced *Turun-Sanomat* newspaper building at Turku in 1928 (reminiscent of the Vesnins' *Pravda* project of 1923), Aalto was able to take advantage of his growing reputation by participating in international conferences on modern architecture and construction. At a conference on reinforced concrete in Paris in 1928 he became acquainted with the work of Duiker (pp. 135–6), whose reinforced-concrete Zonnestraal Sanatorium was the point of departure for Aalto's own competition design for the Paimio Sanatorium, submitted in January 1929. From this date on Aalto was decidedly under the influence of both Dutch and Russian Constructivism, particularly as it was manifest in the work of Duiker and in the urban projects of N.A. Ladovsky's Asnova and ARU groups. The serial, geometrical schemes proposed at different times by ARU (Association of Urban Architects), such as Ladovsky's Kostino Quarter for Moscow of 1926, are obviously the source for the entry trajectory and the serial landscape formations that appear in Paimio. As well as reflecting the urban approach of ARU, Paimio also marked a turning point in the matter of detail, for it abounded in Constructivist quotation.

Although he kept his distance from international polemics, in this period Aalto drew surprisingly close to the exclusively economic position adopted by the German Neue Sachlichkeit architects at the 1929 Frankfurt CIAM Congress on 'Existenzminimum', such concerns being reflected in his 1930 apartment designs for the Finnish Arts and Crafts Society, and in his prototypical minimum house for the Nordic Building Conference of 1932.

At around the same time, Aalto met Harry and Maire Gullichsen, an event which opened up his practice to industrial production. Mrs Gullichsen, heiress of the large Ahlström timber, paper and cellulose concern, had seen Aalto's earliest furniture in a Helsinki store, and invited him to design a range of furniture for serial production. The eventual consequences were the foundation in 1935 of the Artek Furniture Company (to distribute Aalto's furniture) and the Sunila Pulp Mill and workers' housing designed and realized at Kotka between 1935 and 1939. Fortunately Aalto's pieces readily lent themselves to mass production. He had already started to design plywood furniture as early as 1926 when he produced a stacking chair for the Jyväskylä guard house, and he followed this success with a laminated armchair for Paimio, a prototype which was finally put into production in 1933. It is interesting to note that Aalto took the technique of this design from the standard bent plywood seating that Otto Korhonen produced in the late 1920s.

Aalto's patronage by the Finnish timber industry — the large industrial concerns of Ahlström and Enso-Gutzeit were to be his patrons for the rest of his life — led him to reappraise the value of timber over concrete as a primary expressive material. With this he seems to have gradually returned to the highly textured architectural manner of the Finnish National Romantic movement, to the work of Saarinen, Gallén-Kallela and Sonck. The first indication of this move away from international Constructivism came with his own house built in Munkkiniemi, Helsinki, in 1936. This somewhat irregular L-shaped building, executed as a collage in rendered masonry, grooved planking and exposed brickwork, was followed by his prizewinning entry design for the Finnish Pavilion for the Paris World Exhibition of 1937, a timber structure significantly entitled 'Le Bois est en marche'. It was a rhetorical display of wooden construction, its various bearing elements expressing the specific characteristics of wood. The battened timber siding of the main hall and the skeleton timber structure of the perimeter exhibition space made up a virtuoso display of different techniques for jointing in wood. Yet for all its constructional ingenuity, the Finnish Pavilion was chiefly important for its formulation of the site-planning principle of Aalto's later career, wherein a given building is invariably separated

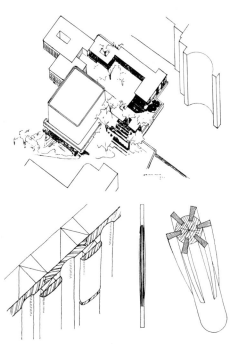

185 Aalto, Finnish Pavilion, World Exhibition, Paris, 1937. Details show (left to right) boarded siding, a reinforced wooden column of the loggia and part of a column with projecting reinforcement fins.

into two distinct elements and the space between is articulated as a space of human appearance (see the Villa Mairea, Säynätsalo Town Hall, etc.: below, p. 201). He wrote of the pavilion in his collected works:

One of the most difficult architectural problems is the shaping of the building's surroundings to the human scale. In modern architecture where the rationality of the structural frame and the building masses threaten to dominate, there is often an architectural vacuum in the left-over portions of the site. It would be good if, instead of filling up this vacuum with decorative gardens, the organic movement of people could be incorporated in the shaping of the site in order to create an intimate relationship between Man and Architecture. In the case of the Paris Pavilion, this problem fortunately could be solved.

186  Aalto, Viipuri Library, 1927–35. Lending department, and reading room at higher level.

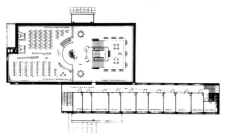

187  Aalto, Viipuri Library, 1927–35. First-floor plan.

In his later career, Aalto was to regard the shift from reinforced-concrete expression to wood and natural materials as being of the utmost importance for the development of his architecture. He saw his laminated furniture as exemplifying an intuitive, indirect and more critical approach to design, which was capable of achieving a more responsive and inflected environment than that usually achieved by linear logic. Thus in 1946, on the occasion of an exhibition of his furniture in Zürich, he wrote:

In order to achieve practical goals and valid aesthetic forms in connection with architecture, one cannot always start from a rational and technical standpoint – perhaps even never. Human imagination must have free room in which to unfold. This was usually the case with my experiments in wood. Pure playful forms, with no practical function whatsoever,

have, in some cases, led to a practical form after ten years have elapsed. . . . The first attempt to construct organic form from volumes of wood without the use of cutting techniques led later, after nearly ten years, to triangular solutions, considering the orientation of wood fibres. The vertical bearing portion of furniture forms is truly the smaller sister of the architectural column.

This organic approach to design already lies behind the detailing of the Viipuri Library and the Paimio Sanatorium, those masterworks of the late 1920s, which, although they were built of reinforced concrete, still afforded Aalto an occasion for extending the precepts of Functionalism to include the satisfaction of a full range of physical and psychological needs (cf. Neutra's 'biological' approach). Aalto's life-long concern for the overall ambience of a space and for the way it may be modified through the responsive filtration of heat, light and sound, was first fully formulated in these works. In Paimio the two-person wards were carefully arranged to meet the patient's needs not only at the level of environmental control but also in terms of identity and privacy, direct light and heat being kept away from the patient's head, while ceilings were coloured to reduce glare, and wash-hand basins were designed to function noiselessly. Similarly, the main reading rooms of the Viipuri Library were indirectly lit at all times – by day through the funnel-shaped roof lights, and at night through retractable spot lights which bounced their light off the walls opposite. Aalto gave equally careful consideration to the library's acoustical properties, isolating reading rooms from traffic noise and equipping the rectangular lecture hall with an undulating ceiling reflector for the whole of its length. In general the 'free planning' principles adopted in the library and sanatorium established Aalto's organic approach to architecture, an approach which for all its inherent freedom rarely suffered, in formal terms, from a loss of control. His concern for the natural modification of the environment and for the intrinsic nature of the site gave his work a unique continuity from his Functionalist period in the late 1920s to the more expressive phase of his work that started in the early 1950s. Of his anti-mechanistic attitude he wrote in 1960:

To make architecture more human means better architecture, and it means a functionalism much larger than the merely technical one. This goal can be accomplished only by architectural methods – by the creation and combination of different technical things in such a way that they will provide for the human being the most harmonious life.

In 1938, Aalto achieved the masterwork of his pre-war career, the Villa Mairea, a summer home built for Maire Gullichsen at Noormarkku. The initial sketch for this L-shaped building makes explicit reference to National Romanticism: the plan of the main living hall refers directly to the plan of Gallén-Kallela's Ruovesi studio of 1893. Both works also feature a prominent, rendered, sculptural fireplace and a stepped living level which eventually leads to a mezzanine stair. Like his Munkkiniemi House, the Villa Mairea is compounded out of a mixture of brickwork, rendered masonry and timber siding.

More than any other pre-war work of Aino and Alvar Aalto, the villa represents a conceptual link between the rational-constructivist tradition of the 20th century and the evocative heritage of the National Romantic movement. Its primary spaces, the dining and living rooms, border a sheltered garden court, set within a roughly circular forest clearing. The 'geologically striated' mass of the house and the irregularly contoured perimeter of the sauna plunge pool suggest a metaphorical opposition between artificial and natural form, and this principle of duality obtains throughout the work. Thus the 'head' of Mrs Gullichsen's prow-like studio opposes the 'tail' of the sauna, and the wooden siding of the public rooms stands in strong contrast to the white rendering of the private areas. Similarly complex formal operations abound throughout the house: an example is the 'metonymy' of the entrance canopy, the irregular rhythm of its timber screen echoing the irregular spacing of the pine trees in the forest – a device that is repeated in the railing of the interior stair. This is followed, in terms of sequence, by the repetition of the same plan form in the studio,

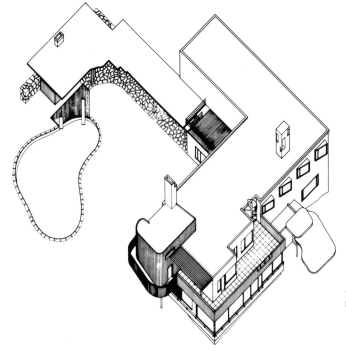

188  Aalto, Villa Mairea, Noormarkku, 1938–39.

189, 190  Aalto, Villa Mairea, Noormarkku, 1938–39. View towards the living hall, and exterior.

191  Aalto, Säynätsalo Town Hall, 1949–52.

the entry canopy and the plunge pool, all recalling the sinuous perimeter of a typical Finnish lake. The finishes of the ground floor are also coded as an internal landscape in which changes from tiles to boarding or to rough paving stones denote subtle transformations in mood and status, as one moves from, say, the family hearth to the sitting room and conservatory. Finally, structure itself is used symbolically to refer to origins: as in the Villa Hvitträsk, the sauna represents the native culture — linked by an outriding rubble wall to the main house, it is a traditional timber-sided structure roofed with sod, and built according to the canons of Finnish timber vernacular, in opposition to the sophisticated tectonic of the house itself.

After the rhetorical exuberance of his pavilion for the New York World's Fair in 1939 and the somewhat unresolved design of the Baker Dormitory, built for MIT at Cambridge, Massachusetts, in 1947, there was an expressive uncertainty in Aalto's work, until 1949, when the second phase of his career took decisive shape with his Säynätsalo Town Hall. Where the Villa Mairea had depended for its articulation on wooden revetment, at Säynätsalo the syncopation of the form depended on the rhythmic spacing of the fenestration and on the subtle modelling of brickwork. For all their differences, however, the works had the same conceptual basis in their division into two parts, grouped around an atrium. These elements, which took the form of an L-shaped house and a plunge pool in the Villa Mairea, are at Säynätsalo a U-shaped administration building and a free-standing library block, the two forms enclosing a court raised above the street level. This *parti*, which Aalto used again in his National Pensions Institute at Helsinki, seems to have been derived from the traditional Karelian farm and village complexes that he had first written about in 1941. Another source for the duality of these compositions may be Aalto's idiosyncratic view of the process of architectural creation, of which he wrote in 'The Trout and the Mountain Stream' (1947):

I would like to add that architecture and its details are connected in a way with biology.

They are perhaps like large salmon or trout. They are not born mature, they are not even born in the sea or body of water where they will normally live. They are born many hundreds of miles from their proper living environment. Where the rivers are but streams, small shining bodies of water between mountains . . . as far from their normal environment as man's spiritual life and instincts are from his daily work. And as the fish egg's development to a mature organism requires time, so it also requires time for all that develops and crystallizes in our world of thoughts. Architecture needs this time to an even greater degree than any other creative work.

All these buildings seem to symbolize this duality of architectural creation, wherein the enclosing L or U form of the main mass, the 'fish' element, is contrasted with the independent form of the adjacent 'egg'. In the Villa Mairea and Säynätsalo Town Hall the head of the fish form appears to accommodate the most honorific public element – the studio in the house, and the council chamber in the town hall.

Such hierarchical differentiation is complemented by changes in material and structure. At Säynätsalo the brick paving of the 'secular' access corridor and stair gives way to the suspended wooden floor of the 'sacred' council chamber above. This change in status is confirmed by the elaborate detailing of the roof trusses over the council room, an obvious reference to medieval practice. Similar shifts in symbolic content occur in the 'egg' element: in the Villa Mairea the 'egg' is the swimming pool – the agent of physical regeneration – while in Säynätsalo Town Hall it is the library, the repository of intellectual nourishment. Furthermore the detailing of the atrium itself, particularly at Säynätsalo and in the Pensions Institute, reflects a comparable mythic intent. In both instances the path through the 'acropolis' is treated like a 'rite of passage', between over-civilized urbanity on one side of the complex and native rusticity on the other. In each instance, the space is enriched by the presence of water, hinting again at the process of birth and regeneration.

The Pensions Institute in Helsinki, designed for a competition of 1948 and built in 1952–56, established Aalto as one of the master architects of the post-war period. As much as any work from the last twenty-five years of his career, this large bureaucratic complex demonstrated an architecture that would, in his own words, add 'a more sensitive structure to living'. This intent, evident in the warmth and convenience of the smallest details, from the foyer seats to the visitors' coat-racks and from the light-fittings to the built-in heating, was manifest above all in the delicately scaled interviewing booths ranged in rows under the skylit hall. This hall, paved in black and white marble, established the honorific 'key' for the rest of the building. Thereafter each space is colour-coded in order to suggest a change in status – the main entry in white and dark blue wall tiles, the staff refectory in brown, white and beige, and so on.

Aalto's resolve to serve the common man reappeared in his adaptation of the 'atrium' concept to the design of a multi-storey apartment block, built for the Berlin 'Hansaviertel Interbau' exhibition in 1955. This ingenious design comprised one of the most significant apartment types to have been invented since the end of the Second World War. Le Corbusier's famous Unité maisonette (so extensively copied in low-cost housing throughout the world) compares with it rather unfavourably as a family dwelling. The primary virtue of Aalto's apartment type is that it provides the attributes of the single-family home within the confines of a small flat. Within its U organizat-

192  Aalto, National Pensions Institute, Helsinki, 1952–56. Centre of south front.

ion a generous atrium terrace is flanked by the living and dining rooms, while the whole is surrounded on two sides by private spaces, such as bedrooms and bathrooms. The disposition of these apartment units within the block is equally good, their 'clustering' about naturally lit stair-halls enabling Aalto to avoid that sense of an infinite number of 'monotype' apartments stacked in a single high-rise structure.

Aalto's lifelong attempt to satisfy social and psychological criteria effectively set him apart from the more dogmatic Functionalists of the 1920s, whose careers were already established when he designed his first significant works. Despite his initial response to the dynamic forms of Soviet Constructivism, Aalto always focused his attention on the creation of environments which would be conducive to human well-being. Even his most Functionalist works, such as his *Turun-Sanomat* Building of 1928, reflect his perennial sensitivity to light, constantly enriching a structure that would otherwise be extremely dogmatic and austere.

Such a consistently organic approach brought Aalto conceptually close to the ethos of Bruno Taut's Glass Chain, above all to the work of Hans Scharoun and to Hugo Häring. So he may be seen as belonging to that 'group' of Northern European Expressionist architects who were concerned that building should be life-giving rather than repressive. This meant that the latent tyranny of the normative orthogonal grid should always be fractured and inflected where the idiosyncrasies of the site or the programme demanded it. In 1960 Leonardo Benevolo effectively summed up Aalto's achievement from this standpoint in the following terms:

In the first modern buildings the constancy of the right angle served mainly to generalize the compositional process of instituting *a priori* geometrical relationships between all the elements, which meant that all conflicts could be resolved geometrically with the balancing of lines, surfaces, and volumes. The use of the oblique (as at Paimio) pointed the way towards the contrary process, that of making the forms more individual and precise, allowing imbalance and tension to exist and to be balanced by the physical consistency of the elements and surroundings. Such architecture lost in didactic rigours but gained in warmth, richness, and feeling, and ultimately extended its field of action because the process of individuation was based on the already recognized generalizing method and indeed presupposed it.

At its best this was a discreet yet highly responsive mode of building, one which continued the essential Nordic tradition of fusing the vernacular with the Classical — the idiosyncratic with the normative — through fifty years of unbroken development, from Östberg's Bonnier Villa of 1909 to Aalto's Finlandia Concert Hall, completed in Helsinki some four years before his death in 1976.

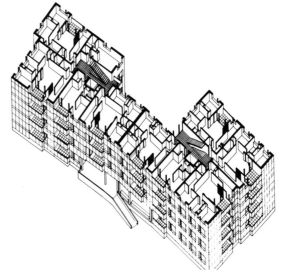

193   Aalto, Hansaviertel apartment block, Berlin, 1955.

## Chapter 23

# Giuseppe Terragni and the architecture of Italian Rationalism 1926–43

We no longer feel ourselves to be the men of the cathedrals and the ancient moot halls, but men of the Grand Hotels, railway stations, giant roads, colossal harbours, covered markets, glittering arcades, reconstructed areas and salutary slum clearances.

Antonio Sant'Elia
*Messaggio* (text for the *Città Nuova*, 1914)

Our past and present are not incompatible. We do not wish to ignore our traditional heritage. It is the tradition which transforms itself and assumes new aspects recognizable only to a few.

gruppo 7
'Note', in *Rassegna Italiana*, December 1926

The Classical and oneric expression that emerged in Italy after the end of the First World War — first in painting, in the highly metaphysical Valori Plastici movement led by Giorgio de Chirico, and then in architecture, with the Classical Novecento movement started by the architect Giovanni Muzio — was as much the complex point of departure for the development of Italian Rationalism as was the heritage of pre-war Futurist polemic.

The Rationalist 'gruppo 7' who first declared themselves, after graduating from the Milan Polytechnic, in the *Rassegna Italiana*, comprised the architects Sebastiano Larco, Guido Frette, Carlo Enrico Rava, Adalberto Libera, Luigi Figini, Gino Pollini and Guiseppe Terragni. All sought to achieve a new and more rational synthesis between the nationalistic values of Italian Classicism and the structural logic of the machine age. In their 'Note' of 1926 they committed themselves to exploring a middle ground between the arcane language of the Novecento — of which Muzio's Ca' Brutta apartment block built in Milan in 1923 was an influential example — and the dynamic vocabulary of industrial form bequeathed to them by the Futurists. The group also showed a certain sympathy for the Deutsche Werkbund and for the works of the Russian Constructivists. Yet for all their enthusiasm for the machine age, the gruppo 7 gave more weight to a reinterpretation of tradition than to modernity *per se*. Thus, in 1926, they wrote critically of the Futurists:

The hallmark of the earlier avant garde was a contrived impetus and a vain, destructive fury, mingling good and bad elements; the hallmark of today's youth is a desire for lucidity and wisdom. . . . This must be clear . . . we do not intend to break with tradition. . . . The new architecture, the true architecture should be the result of a close association between logic and rationality.

Despite this declaration of faith in tradition, the early works of the Rationalists, particularly those projected by Giuseppe Terragni, displayed a preference for compositions based on industrial themes. Terragni's projects for a gasworks and a steel tube factory exhibited at the IIIrd Monza Biennale of 1927 seem to have more to do with the Engineer's Aesthetic than with Architecture, to use the polarities of Le Corbusier's *Vers une architecture*, a book which exercised considerable influence on the Rationalisti after its publication in 1923. An early and naïve response to this influence was indubitably Pietro Lingeri's boat house, built at Como in 1926, which, with its allusion to marine engineering, paid somewhat simplistic homage to the work of Le Corbusier.

194 Piacentini and team, University of Rome, 1932. Senate building on inauguration day.

More susceptible to the influence of Muzio, Terragni established himself in 1928 with the completion of his Novocomun apartments in Como. This symmetrical five-storey composition, popularly known as the Transatlantico, manifested that characteristic Rationalist concern for the rhetorical displacement of mass. Where the corners of the building should have been reinforced in accordance with Classical canon, they were dramatically cut away so as to expose glass cylinders, which were capped by the massive weight of the oversailing top floor and bound into the composition by the overruns of the third-floor balcony and the mass of the second floor. This solution obviously owed more to Russian Constructivism than to Purism, Golossov's initial project for his Zuyev Workers' Club, completed in Moscow in 1928, being the most obvious precedent.

The Italian Rationalist movement briefly constituted itself as an official body in the Movimento Italiano per l'Architettura Razionale (MIAR), founded in 1930 just one year before the third exhibition of the gruppo 7 staged in Bardi's Galleria d'Arte in Rome. Its influence was short-lived since it was soon to be undermined by the forces of cultural reaction. Where earlier manifestations of Rationalist work had left the more conservative professionals relatively undisturbed, this show was accompanied by a provocative pamphlet entitled 'Report to Mussolini on Architecture', written by the art critic Pietro Maria Bardi. He claimed that Rationalist architecture was the only true expression of Fascist revolutionary principles. A MIAR declaration of the period put forward an equally opportunistic assertion: 'Our movement has no other moral aim than that of serving the [Fascist] Revolution in the prevailing harsh climate. We call upon Mussolini's good faith to enable us to achieve this.'

Mussolini opened the exhibition, but his faith was little proof against the hostile reaction of the National Union of Architects, subject to the influence of the classicist Marcello Piacentini. Three weeks after the opening of the exhibition, the National Union of Architects repudiated the very work that it had previously sponsored, publicly declaring that Rationalist architecture was incompatible with the rhetorical demands of Fascism. It was left for Piacentini to mediate between the metaphysical traditionalism of the Novecento and the avant gardism of the Rationalists and to propose his highly eclectic Stile Littorio (Lictorial Style) as the 'official' party manner. First formulated in the Revolutionary Tower, completed in Brescia to his designs in 1932, this manner was finally consolidated in Piacentini's Palace of Justice started in Milan in 1932.

Piacentini's position was reinforced by the founding of the Fascist Raggruppamento Architetti Moderni, which avoided any categorical condemnation of either the Novecentisti or the Rationalists and gave its support to the vestigial Classicism of the Stile Littorio. The guidelines that Piacentini imposed on the nine architects who collaborated with him in 1932 on the new University in Rome established, through the repetition of simple elements, the rudiments of the official Fascist manner. This remarkably consistent style was expressed almost always in four-storey brick or stone masses, capped by rudimentary cornices and articulated solely through a modulation of rectangular openings. Since a certain irregularity and asymmetry was permitted in the detailed planning, representative expression was largely restricted to the entrances where, with colonnades, bas reliefs and lettered friezes, it took a Classical form. Although none of gruppo 7 worked on the University, three buildings by the Piacentini team betrayed a certain Rationalist affinity: Gio Ponti's School of Mathematics,

Giovanni Michelucci's Mineralogy Building and, above all, Giuseppe Pagano's elegantly brick-faced Institute of Physics.

By 1932 Pagano had already made his contribution to the polemic surrounding the evolution of an appropriate national style, for in 1930 he had started to edit the magazine *Casabella* in collaboration with the Turinese art critic and designer Edoardo Persico. These men endeavoured through their editorials to persuade the undecided members of the Novecento to abandon the Stile Littorio of Piacentini in favour of the Rationalism of Terragni. In 1934 Persico wrote of the Rationalist predicament: 'Today, artists must tackle the thorniest problem of Italian life: the capacity to believe in specific ideologies and the will to pursue the struggle against the claims of an "anti-modernist" majority.'

In 1932 Terragni produced the canonical work of the Italian Rationalist movement, the Casa del Fascio (now the Casa del Popolo) in Como. Planned within a perfect square and half as high as its width of 33 metres (110 feet), the half cube of the Casa del Fascio established the basis of strictly rational geometry. Within this volume, it not only revealed the logic of its trabeated frame but also the 'rational' code underlying the modelling of its layered façade. On every side (except the south-east elevation which stresses the main stair) the fenestration and the external layers of the building are manipulated in such a way as to express the presence of the internal atrium. Earlier studies for the building reveal that like other works by Terragni (such as his Saint'Elia School of 1936) it was originally planned around an open courtyard, on the model of the traditional palazzo. In subsequent stages of the design this *cortile* became a central double-height meeting hall, top-lit through a glazed concrete roof and surrounded on four sides by galleries, offices and meeting rooms. As in Mies van der Rohe's Barcelona Pavilion of 1929, the monumental status of the entire structure is established by its slight elevation on a masonry base, described by Terragni as a *piano rialzato*. The original political purpose of the structure is expressed in almost literal terms through the battery of glass doors which separates the entrance foyer from the piazza. These, when simultaneously opened by an electrical device, would have united the inner agora of the *cortile* to the piazza, thereby permitting the uninterrupted flow of mass demonstrations from street to interior (ill. 24). Comparable political connotations are evident in the treatment of the main meeting room with its photomontage relief by Mario Radice and in the shrine commemorating the fallen of the Fascist movement. There is, needless to say, an aspect of this work which transcends these ideological considerations to concern itself with the creation of metaphysical spatial effects — the building is treated as though it were a continuous spatial matrix, without any particular orientation such as up or down, left or right, etc. Thus the mirror effects of glass are used in the lining of the foyer ceiling to create the illusion of an infinite

195 Terragni, Casa del Fascio, Como, 1932–36. Proportional system of façade, and ground plan.

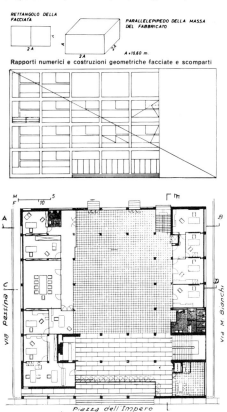

trabeated construction existing in volumes which are in fact quite differently occupied. At the same time the subtle implantation of the work in an historic urban core, its facing throughout in Bolticino marble and its use of glass block to designate its honorific space, combine to create a work which is at once tectonic, meticulous and monumental.

This ideal symbolization of Fascism was by no means unique. Other rhetorical overtures to the movement were made by the Rationalists before their final disillusionment in the mid-1940s. Amongst these, mention must be made of the building for the 'Mostra della Rivoluzione Fascista', staged in Rome in 1932, on the occasion of the tenth anniversary of the March on Rome. This temporary structure, strongly reminiscent of the work of Leonidov and built to the designs of Libera and De Renzi, contained along with other set pieces the commemorative 1922 Room designed by Terragni as a dynamic wall relief, combining plastic, graphic and photographic elements in a manner which recalled Lissitzky's Soviet International Hygiene Exhibit, staged in Dresden in 1930.

By the mid-1930s actual Rationalist architecture varied widely from the highly intellectual work of Terragni to the bland International Style of the short-lived Comasco group, whose artist's house was exhibited at the Vth Milan Triennale of 1933. The participation of Terragni as a member of this eight-man design team seems to have had little effect on the quality of

the outcome, and a comparable loss of intensity can be detected when one compares the very first work of Figini and Pollini, namely their Casa Elettrica built for the Milan Triennale of 1930, to their artist's house built for the next Triennale in 1933. And indeed the facts indicate that by the time of the Vth Triennale, Italian Rationalism was already becoming compromised, either by a banal modernism on the one hand or by a reactionary historicism on the other.

In 1934 Persico and Marcello Nizzoli designed their famous Medaglia d'Oro room for the Italian Aeronautical Show in Milan. An elegant labyrinth of white wooden lattices, raised well above the floor, supported a field of graphic and photographic images that appeared to float in space and to advance and recede throughout the depth of the hall. This suspended construction established a new standard for exhibition design that was to exercise a strong influence until well after the Second World War. By this date, with the exception of such occasional masterpieces as this extraordinary work by Persico and Nizzoli, Italian Rationalism had entered its decline. This much is evident from the subsequent work of Persico himself, who moved in the space of two years from designs of great vivacity and sophistication to the cold, atectonic monumentality of his Salone d'Onore for the 1936 Triennale, designed in collaboration with Nizzoli, Palanti and Fontana. Only Terragni, working with

196 Terragni, Casa del Fascio, Como, 1932–36. Main meeting room. The panel on the end wall, by Radice, includes a portrait of Mussolini.

Pietro Lingeri and Cesare Cattaneo, was able to maintain the intellectual intensity of the Rationalist approach, with its concern for the total integration of conceptual, structural and symbolic form.

After Persico's untimely death in 1936, the political and cultural difficulties of the Rationalists increased. Pagano, always close to official circles, compromised himself further through collaborating with Piacentini on the plan for the 'Esposizione Universale Roma '42', to be held outside Rome in 1942. Like the new Fascist towns of Littoria, Sabaudia, Carbonia and Pontinia (this last being built in the Pontine marshes), the permanent structures of the EUR '42, the museums, memorials and palaces, were designated by Mussolini to form the core of the Third Rome. Not even Pagano's intelligence could prevent this extravagant ideological gesture from degenerating into the most banal assembly of Neo-Classical forms. Its major set-piece, the Palazzo della Civiltà Italiana by Guerrini, La Padula and Romano, was nothing if not the ultimate vulgarization of the Valori Plastici movement. One imagines that its empty, cubic, arcuated forms could have hardly delighted any sensibility more than that of De Chirico himself. Of the same spirit as Mussolini's 1931 plan for the Haussmannization of Rome (a proposal for the wholesale removal of the medieval urban tissue from the antique ruins) Piacentini's EUR '42 plan was caught, like the various architectural factions including the Rationalists, between a post-Futurist drive to create a modern civilization and the need to legitimize this same civilization through an appeal to the glories of the Roman imperium. Thus the EUR complex turned its principal axis towards the Tyrhenian coast and inscribed one of its monuments with the prophecy: 'The Third Rome will spread over the other hills along the sacred river [Tiber] to the beaches of the sea.' As for the involvement of the Rationalists in this Faustian enterprise, Leonardo Benevolo has written:

The compromise attempted by Pagano was thus untenable: by following 'ideal links' back to Roman times, architects would arrive at one result only, Neo-Classical conformism; the difference of tone between Brasini's applied archaeology and Foschini's measured simplification, between the sophisticated elegance of the young Romans and the calculated rhythms of the young Milanese, which seemed important in the plans, disappeared entirely in the execution. What had happened in Germany, Russia, and France was repeated here too: this was the *internationale des pompiers*.

The reactionary architectural and political climate prevailing in Italy in the mid-1930s was partly offset by the Saint-Simonian aspirations of one man, Adriano Olivetti, who had succeeded his father as director of the famous business-machines concern in 1932. In 1934

197 Persico and Nizzoli, Medaglia d'Oro room, the first Italian Aeronautical Show, Milan, 1934.

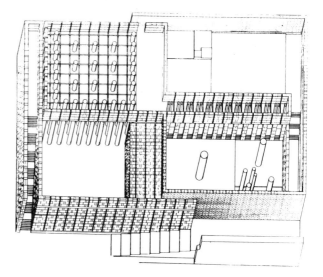

198 Terragni, Danteum project, Rome, 1938.

Adriano began to reveal his concern for the contribution to be made by modern design to industrial welfare by successively commissioning Figini and Pollini to design a whole sequence of buildings for the Olivetti enterprise in Ivrea; first a new administrative centre in 1935 and then workers' housing and community facilities between 1939 and 1942. In 1937 he extended his partronage to regional planning, calling upon Figini and Pollini and BBPR (Banfi, Belgiojoso, Peressutti and Rogers) to prepare a plan for the Aosta valley.

In the meantime, a set of closely related designs continued to pour forth from Terragni's studio, including his competition entries for the Casa Littoria of 1937 and the EUR Congress Building of 1938, both projects designed in collaboration with Cattaneo and Lingeri. Around the same time Terragni produced the most metaphysical work of his entire career, his Danteum, projected in 1938 as a monumental embellishment to the Via Del Impero cut by Mussolini through the ancient city. This project, comprising progressively less dense blocks of rectangular space arranged as a labyrinth and symbolizing the stages of Inferno, Purgatory and Paradise, was in many respects an abstraction of the *parti* used for the EUR building.

Terragni's obsession with a 'transparent' architecture – a sublimation of the Futurist programme of projecting the street into the house – was first advanced in his Casa del Fascio. Thereafter it reappeared as a constant drive throughout all his public work, from the Sarfatti Monument, built at Col d'Echele in 1934 to the final design for the EUR Congress Building. Aside from the ultimate state of 'lucidity' attained in the Paradise volume of the Danteum, with its thirty-three glass columns and its glass ceiling, Terragni achieved a sense of conceptual transparency through two basic devices which were ingeniously fused together in his seven-storey apartment block, the Casa Rustici, Milan (1936–37). These devices were (1) the use of a duality which, following the form of his 1931 War Memorial in Como, generally comprised two parallel rectilinear masses with a slot of space in between, and (2) frontalized parallel rectilinear voids or masses, receding like successive picture planes from a given vantage point, as in the flying balconies and bridges, etc., of the Casa Rustici or the glazed office slabs of the Casa Littoria, whose receding spatial layers established the domain of the ancillary ground level accommodation, the auditoria, etc.

This frontalized formula of alternately built and non-built parallel volumes came to be asymmetrically rotated in the EUR proposal and in a condensed form in Terragni's last building, his four-storey Giuliani Frigerio Apartments completed in Como in 1940. As in the Casa del Fascio the intention seems to have been one of inflecting the orientation of the prism by arranging for a primary and secondary façade to be placed at right angles to one another. A similar rotatory 'cubist' composition had already appeared in Terragni's early villas and the same 'format' was adopted by Cattaneo in his apartment house built in Cernobbio in 1938.

The final work of the series, in which Terragni did not participate, is the Fascist Trades Union Building at Como, under construction on a site next to the Casa del Fascio from 1938 to 1943 and built to the designs of Terragni's prime pupil Cattaneo, in collaboration with Lingeri, Augusto Magnagni, L. Origoni and Mario Terragni. This orthogonal, trabeated structure, organized about a Palladian ABABABABA grid in one direction and a regular but partially syncopated modular grid in the other, is in many respects the most sublime resolution of compositional and typological themes initiated by the Como Rationalists, so much so that one may even claim that this building is one of the major inspirations behind the so-called 'autonomous architecture' of the Italian Tendenza produced over the past decade (cf. Giorgio Grassi's design for a Students' Hostel at Chieti of 1974 with Monestiroli, Conti and Guazzoni). The Trades Union Building consists of two five-storey slabs separated by a courtyard in which a two-storey ancillary block is suspended, comprising an entry podium, a secretariat and a 500-seat auditorium.

The completion of this building in 1943 coincided with the premature and still somewhat mysterious deaths of both Terragni and Cattaneo. Although their deaths brought the movement to an abrupt close, their works still

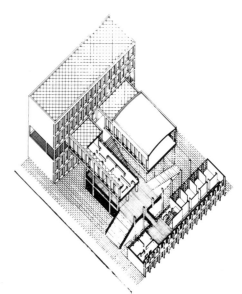

199 Cattaneo, Lingeri, Magnagni, Origoni and M. Terragni, Trades Union Building, Como, 1938–43. Cut-away axonometric view.

testify to their efforts to realize an ideal setting for a society which would be at one and the same time both rationally organized and culturally classless. The fact that this ideal attained its fulfilment in the transparent logic of their architecture rather than in the society at large was touched on by Sylvia Danesi when she wrote of the two men in 1977:

In both there is a complete trust in the guiding role of the middle class and of its organizing capacity in its administrative function as a pivot of the social contract. They did not sense the crisis that was about to involve their generation. They felt that the class to which they too belonged would be perfectly capable of carrying out the task delegated to them by the rest of the country. They did not realize that the local industrial middle class was gradually losing ground to the new State bourgeoisie that was being formed on the strength of the 1929 crisis (nationalization of banks, foundation of the IRI, etc.) and which still governs us to this day; a class who got on fine with big capital interests and felt at ease with the totalitarian regime.

# Chapter 24
# Architecture and the State: ideology and representation 1914-43

The road describes a curve and embarks imperceptibly on a gradient. Suddenly, on the right a scape of towers and domes is lifted from the horizon, sunlit pink and cream dancing against the blue sky, fresh as a cup of milk, grand as Rome. Close at hand the foreground discloses a white arch.

The motor turns off the arterial avenue, and skirting the low red base of the gigantic monument, comes to a stop. The traveller heaves a breath. Before his eyes, sloping gently upward, runs a gravel way of such infinite perspective as to suggest the intervention of a diminishing glass; at whose end, reared above the green tree tops, glitters the seat of government, the eighth Delhi, four square upon an eminence – dome, tower, dome, tower, dome, tower, red, pink, cream and white-washed gold and flashing in the morning sun.

Robert Byron
'New Delhi', in *The Architectural Review*, 1931

The modernist tendency to reduce all form to abstraction made it an unsatisfactory manner in which to represent the power and ideology of the state. This iconographic inadequacy largely accounts for the survival of an historicist approach to building in the second half of the 20th century. It is to Henry-Russell Hitchcock's credit as a historian that long ago he felt it necessary to acknowledge the persistence of this vestigial tradition. However, his term 'The New Tradition', coined in 1929 in an effort to distinguish a certain conservative trend from the works of the pioneers, has hardly stood the test of time. The attributes and the chronology that he attached to this tradition were too vague to gain general acceptance. Nevertheless, the need to treat the problems posed by representation or the lack of it has increased rather than diminished over the years, and the cultural predicament of Social Realism in its broadest sense can now no longer be excluded from our critical scrutiny. In a general sense, the term may be taken as evidence of the failure of abstract form to communicate. In the face of this, as Hitchcock wrote in 1958: 'The historian *must* attempt to give some sort of account of things like the Stockholm City Hall or the Woolworth Building.'

The origin of the New Tradition, outside the main line of the Modern Movement, can be seen to lie in the emergence between 1900 and 1914 of a consciously 'modernized' historicist style. In the first place, the generic style of the establishment, the late 19th-century public mode which oscillated constantly between Neo-Gothic and Neo-Baroque, began to lose its definition. In England and Germany, in particular, it degenerated into an eclectic elaboration which in the event demonstrated little capacity for achieving a convincing architectural expression. At the same time the main line of European Classicism, the Beaux-Arts, reached its *pompier* dead end in the Paris Exhibition of 1900. The scintillating yet overblown rhetoric of the Grand Palais, for example, was patently ill-equipped to represent the progressive ideology of an advanced industrialized society. What could after all be more symbolic of repression than the ferrovitreous interior of the Grand Palais incarcerated in an elaborate scenography of stone? The subsequent attempt to revivify this perennial preference for lithic form with sinuous floral motives drawn from Art Nouveau led to equally lugubrious examples of petrified Classicism with heavy Symbolist overtones, such as Boileau's Hôtel Lutetia, Paris (1911), much despised by Le Corbusier.

On the other hand, the essentially anti-establishment Anglo-Saxon Free Style or its even more liberated successor on the Continent, generally known as Art Nouveau, had by this time degenerated into a very rigid, crystallized form of expression. In addition, as Henry van de Velde realized in 1908, the very idea of a *Gesamtkunstwerk* had the unfortunate consequence of privatizing the socio-cultural significance of the work in question. Neither the protracted Pre-Raphaelite myth of a return to an agrarian craft economy nor the urbane exoticism of Art Nouveau could be exploited to represent either parliamentary democracy or the ideological aspirations of a liberal and progressive society. Even Peter Behrens who, around 1910, stood on the threshold of a new normative style expressly conceived for the representation of the cartel, if not of the modern industrial state (Max Weber's *Machtstaat*), was to lose his creative nerve by the time of the Werkbund Exhibition of 1914 and to retreat into the security of the all but Neo-Classical formula of his Werkbund Festhalle.

Ragnar Östberg's unique adaptation of the principles of the English Free Style to the purpose of representing a public institution came with his Stockholm City Hall of 1909–23, an iconographic triumph that seems to have owed its singular success to the fact that it represented a traditional Burgher port rather than an industrial state. In this respect it hinted at the architectural policies of the Third Reich, which reserved certain styles for particular ideological ends.

The eve of the First World War saw the creation of a number of works representative of the New Tradition, 'historicist' buildings which were far from being historically determined in their overall conception. Thus the Gothic detailing of Cass Gilbert's Woolworth Building in New York (1913) was incidental compared to the way in which its uncompromising organization and exotic profile were to anticipate the post-war skyscraper developments of Frank Lloyd Wright and Raymond Hood.

In Europe the inauguration of the New Tradition was more selfconscious, marked by works which independently broke with the received public style of the Neo-Baroque to return, in spirit if not in form, to the gravity and clarity of ancient Rome – typical examples include Paul Bonatz's Stuttgart Railway Station, built in 1913–27, and Edwin Lutyens's New Delhi, commissioned in 1912 but not realized in its final form until 1931.

George V's proclamation, founding the capital of New Delhi at a durbar or mass pageant held there in his honour, was nothing if not an elaborate ideological gesture, designed to mask the sheer expediency that lay behind the British removal of their Indian capital from Calcutta to Delhi in 1911. Evidently the British hoped that by reviving the pageantry of the Moghul Court – in the name of the Raj and in the heart of the Empire – they might still pursue their contradictory policy of welcoming home-rule while maintaining their colonial economy. The fact that much of the imperial kudos was lost because the King entered the city on a horse rather than an elephant is not without a certain significance. The diplomatic effort at a liberal compromise had altered the traditional code beyond recognition and the King passed through the gates of Delhi largely unobserved. That the building of New Delhi was a reification of this fragile ideological gesture is evident from the protracted efforts made between 1913 and 1918 to arrive at a convincing Anglo-Indian style which would satisfy all concerned. Above all, it had to convince Lutyens himself, who finally decided that the Moghul city of Fatehpur Sikri presented the only native architecture that could be effectively incorporated into the humanist tradition. Humanism, that is to say Classicism, had been hastily revalidated in English architectural culture after the turn of the century, first in the architecture of Shaw and Lutyens and then with great sophistication, at a theoretical level, in Geoffrey Scott's *The Architecture of Humanism* published in 1914.

The need to assimilate a powerful exotic culture while asserting the standards of humanism brought Lutyens to a level of abstract precision and balance which he had never attained before and which he was only to equal again in his memorials to the fallen of the First World War – the Cenotaph in London, unveiled

200 Lutyens, Viceroy's House, New Delhi, 1923–31.

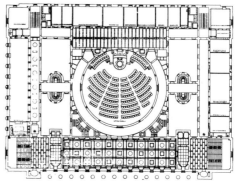

201 Sirén, Finnish Parliament Building, Helsinki, 1926–31. Plan of main level.

in 1920, and the Thiepval Memorial Arch to the dead and missing of the Somme, of 1924 (ill. 30). In the Viceroy's House at New Delhi, under construction from 1923 to 1931, Lutyens transcended the ultimately effete historicism of his country houses to postulate, like Wright, the possibility of a 'frontier' culture, a synthetic imperium on which the sun would never set. It is ironic that history would permit only another fifteen years of British rule, given that New Delhi was the most monumental complex they had ever built. The Viceroy's House alone, despite its almost domestic interiors, covers an area equal to that of Versailles.

As with Versailles, the commissioning of New Delhi in 1912 inaugurated a period of building in which architecture would once again be exploited in the cause of the state — first, to represent new nations which had emerged as independent democracies from the cataclysm of the First World War, and then to celebrate the revolutionary 'millennium' as it became manifest in its various guises between 1917 and 1933 — first in the Soviet Union, then in 1922 in Fascist Italy, and finally in the Third Reich. In more general terms, it was called upon to represent the revival and manifest destiny of monopoly capital both before and after the stock market disaster of 1929.

The ideological charge laid on official architecture during this period, and the Classical, not to say Beaux-Arts, background of most of the architects involved, served to isolate the whole

development from the progressive aspirations of the Modern Movement, and in most instances this isolation seems to have been consciously desired. Sirén's Finnish Parliament Building, erected in Helsinki for the newly independent state in 1926–31, established the neo-Neo-Classical norm of the New Tradition. His brilliantly planned Riksolagshus came directly out of the Scandinavian Neo-Classical revival, and as such was closely related to Asplund's Stockholm Public Library of 1920–28. Sirén's work, however, appears almost theatrical when compared to Asplund's, his shallow peristyle being nothing more than a scenographic relief on a tightly organized building whose strictly stereometric volume would have otherwise remained uninflected.

The explicit confrontation between the Modern Movement and the New Tradition came with the League of Nations competition of 1927, when a jury consisting of Beaux-Arts academicians and Art Nouveau veterans — men like John Burnet, Charles Lemaresquier and Carlos Gato from the one camp and Hoffmann, Victor Horta and Hendrik Berlage from the other — chose twenty-seven designs representing the three basic approaches of the period. Nine of the premiated places were given to the Beaux-Arts; the Modern Movement was recognized by eight, including the famous projects by Le Corbusier and Hannes Meyer (ills. 144, 114); and the New Tradition by ten, including entries by L.-C. Boileau, Paul Bonatz and Marcello Piacentini. Three of the premiated Beaux-

Arts competitors and Giuseppe Vago, whose work represented the New Tradition, were commissioned to prepare a final design, which came surprisingly close to the stripped Classicism of Russian Social Realism.

## THE SOVIET UNION 1931–38

The struggle between the Modern Movement and the New Tradition had to be fought all over again in the Palace of the Soviets competition, staged in 1931 as a deliberate Russian response to the building of the League of Nations. The impact of this competition on Soviet architecture was decisive, for it not only drew entries from all over the world, including projects by Le Corbusier, Perret, Gropius, Poelzig and Lubetkin, but it also stimulated an equal amount of activity inside the Soviet Union, involving a large number of individual designers as well as entries from the major architectural factions, including Asnova, OSA and Vopra.

That Le Corbusier's project (see p. 159) was the most Constructivist of his entire career is evident from the exposed roof structure of its auditoria and from the total transparency of its external skin. Yet, despite the reductive nature of these elements, the symbolism of the project was quite explicit in the speaker's tribune situated at the end of the library block, overlooking the *res publica* podium, to the rear of the larger auditorium. Few entries were so literal in according symbolic value to the functionality of their various components, and one recognizes here a work as didactic in its organization and form as Gropius's theatre for Piscator, designed some four years earlier. However, the jury found that Le Corbusier's entry 'indulged in a too pronounced cult of machinism and aestheticization'.

This could also have been said of many of the Russian projects, which were often little more than elaborate exercises in technological rhetoric projected as metaphors for the newly industrialized socialist state. It is one of the ironies of this competition that the monumental Socialist Realist line, which was to be officially adopted by the Central Committee of the Party in April 1932, was not represented by the entry

of the most left-wing faction, the Proletkult group or All Russian Association of Proletarian Architects. Instead the SR style was first tentatively advanced in the winning entry of B.M. Iofan, whose Constructivist auditoria were shown as semicircular terminal buildings delimiting the confines of a rectangular, Classical court. From the centre of this enclosure rose an equally Classical pylon surmounted by the statue of a worker. This figure seems to have been a conscious reference to the Statue of Liberty, its raised arm projecting the light of revolt, if not of freedom. In the subsequent

202 Nénot, Broggi, Vago and Lefebvre, League of Nations, Geneva. Council chamber with murals by J. M. Sert.

203 Iofan, project for the Palace of the Soviets, Moscow, 1934.

development of the design after 1933, by Iofan in collaboration with the Academicians Gel'-freikh and V. Shchuko, it became increasingly rhetorical. By 1934, the two auditoria of the original version had been absorbed into a 'wedding cake' of colonnaded tiers and pinnacled statuary, culminating in a gargantuan figure of Lenin offering his hand to the universe, at a height of 450 metres (1,500 feet). Three years later, although the general form remained the same, the total mass was smaller and the colonnades had been regrouped as Art Deco pilasters.

After 1932 those Academicians such as A.V. Shchusev (whose eclectic National Romantic Kazan Station in Moscow was under construction by 1913), who had established themselves before the Revolution and had laid low since, began to build one pseudo-Neo-Classical monument after another. Shchuko's Lenin State Library of 1938 typifies this bastard style of asymmetrical volumes, stripped pilasters and inconsequential Classical episodes enriched by sculpure. The emergence of the New Tradition in the Soviet Union was due to several contributory factors. First there was the doctrinal and unanswerable challenge made by Vopra against the Constructivist intellectuals to the effect that only the proletariat could create a proletarian culture; then there were the rehabilitated pre-war Academicians who, while technically indispensable to the building programme, were to remain unsympathetic to Constructivism; finally there was the Party itself which sensed that the people were incapable of responding to the abstract aesthetics of modern architecture. The absolute ideological expediency of the Party Social Realist line instigated in 1932 accounts for Anatole Lunacharsky's sophistries of the following year, his over-elaborate apologia for Social Realism in which, while acknowledging the remoteness of Hellenic culture, he insisted that 'this cradle of civilization and art' could still serve as a model for architecture in the Soviet Union. The success of this state culture, which has been maintained as a consistent policy for more than forty years, has perhaps never been more justly assessed than by Berthold Lubetkin, who wrote in 1956:

Festooned as they are with haberdashery, draped in theatrical marginalia, and wrapped in irrelevant pages from a monumental mason's catalogue, some of the Soviet buildings (if by no means all) are yet able to form, by virtue of vigorously conceived layouts, of prodigious use of open spaces and of breathtaking scale, grand, orderly ensembles whose impact is not easily forgotten by a Western architect of the epoch of picturesque fragmentation and 'mixed development'.

## FASCIST ITALY 1931-42

A similar conflict between modernity and tradition coloured the architectural ideology of the Italian Fascist movement, between Mussolini's March on Rome in October 1922, and 1931 when the government-backed Union of Architects withdrew its support from the newly founded Movimento Italiano per l'Architettura Razionale (MIAR) and rallied under the leadership of Marcello Piacentini to support the cause of reconciling the rival factions into a single ideological formation, the Raggruppamento Architetti Moderni Italiani.

The development of Fascist ideology after the war had stemmed from two distinct aspects of the pre-war Futurist movement: from its revolutionary concern for the restructuring the society, and from its cult of war and its worship of the machine. Both aspects provided elements that could be effectively incorporated into Fascist rhetoric, but the war and its aftermath had been a disaster – destructive even of Futurism itself – and the idea of a 'machine-culture' was suddenly regarded with a good deal of scepticism, and not only at a popular level but also by the intelligentsia.

Indeed, the cultural reaction against Futurism had been formulated before Futurism had fully emerged, first with Benedetto Croce's *Filosofia come scienza dello spirito* (*The Philosophy of the Spirit*) of 1908–17, which insisted on the exclusively formal domain of art, and then with Giorgio de Chirico's painting *The Enigma of the Hour* (1912) which depicted an arcuated peristyle in failing light – a haunting metaphysical image which immediately seemed

205   De Chirico, *The Enigma of the Hour*, 1912.

204   Poster for the Universal Exhibition, Rome (EUR), 1942, exhibiting Libera's project for an arch leading to the site and the future.

to prefigure the form and the mood of the Italian New Tradition.

Influenced by De Chirico and by the metaphysical painters of the Novecento movement, by men who were cognizant of modernity but not seduced by it, the Milanese architectural avant garde headed by Giovanni Muzio began to reinterpret the Classical forms of the Mediterranean as a conscious antithesis to the machine cult of Futurism. The inaugural work of this movement, Muzio's Ca' Brutta apartments built in the Via Moscova, Milan, in 1923, was as much a point of departure for the work of the Italian Rationalists as it was an influence on Piacentini's Stile Littorio, which emerged with the University of Rome begun under his direction in 1932. Muzio's defence of the Classical tradition, written in 1931, displayed

an awareness of the universality of the New Tradition that transcended the Piranesian conceits of his own style. He wrote of the Novecento movement as being of an anti-Futurist conviction. He argued that the Classical schemas of the past would always be applicable, and went on to ask: 'Are we not perhaps anticipating a movement whose imminent birth is announced throughout Europe by hesitant but widespread symptoms?'

The conflict between modernity and tradition took a peculiarly subtle form in Italy, since the young Rationalists were just as committed as Muzio and Piacentini to a reinterpretation of the Classical tradition. But the MIAR approach was extremely intellectual and their austere works lacked an iconography which could be readily understood. Aware that Futurism could not represent a nationalistic ideology, Fascist power opted, in 1931, for a simplified and easily reproducible Classical style whose apotheosis came with the ill-fated EUR of 1942. This wishful implantation of a new capital, outside the limits of the Eternal City, was as utopian and reactionary in its aspirations as New Delhi. It posited a monumentality that was totally divorced from social reality, De Chirico's *The Enigma of the Hour* being almost literally realized in the Palazzo della Civiltà Italiana, the six-storey prism, filled with arches, that terminated the main axis of site.

215

206 Guerrini, La Padula and Romano, Palazzo della Civiltà Italiana, EUR, 1942.

## THE THIRD REICH 1929–41

The Italian struggle between two alternative interpretations of the Classical tradition – the rationalist versus the historicist – was absent in Germany, where the rational line of the Modern Movement suffered instant eclipse after the National Socialist seizure of power in January 1933. Modern architecture was dismissed as cosmopolitan and degenerate save for those occasions when efficient industrial production and factory welfare demanded a Functionalist approach; but the question as to the appropriate style for Hitler's 'social revolution' could not be resolved, as in Italy or Russia, by an open conflict ending in the adoption of a single style to be used on almost all occasions. The subtle ideological policies of the Third Reich were inimical to such a blanket solution.

While striving at a public level to represent National Socialism as the heroic fulfilment of of German destiny, the Nazis also wished to gratify the popular desire for an architecture of psychological security and to compensate for a world where industrialized warfare, inflation and political upheaval had already undermined traditional society. This initial stylistic dichotomy reflected, in a perverse form, the ideological division that had permeated the history of the Modern Movement – the split first identified by Pugin in the 1830s as the opposition between the utilitarian, universal standards of industrial production (reified in Neo-Classical form) and a basic Christian desire to return to the *rooted* values of an agrarian craft economy. For the former the Nazis had only to look to the enlightened Prussian culture of the authoritarian state, expressed in the philosophy of Hegel and the architecture of Schinkel; for the latter they could return to the Germanic myth of the *Volk*, to that anti-Western cult first advanced by the Prussian patriot F.L. Jahn in 1806.

The National Socialist updating of Jahn's philosophy came with the publication in 1929 of Richard Walter Darré's book *Das Bauerntum als Lebensquell der nordischen Rassen* ('The Peasantry as the Life Source of the Nordic Race'), which first advanced the idea of a 'blood and soil' culture, advocating a return to the land. Darré, who had started his career as an agronomist, was to play a salient role in developing the anti-urban racial ideology of National Socialism, and although his view was never fully embraced by the Nazi élite, it remained the rationale behind the *Heimatstil* or vernacular housing built under party auspices after 1933.

Given that the conflicting ideologies within the Third Reich could not be adequately expressed in two polarized styles, other modes had to be adduced. The remote party political schools, the Ordensburgen, were built in a pseudo-medieval castellated manner, and the various leisure facilities of Robert Ley's Kraft durch Freude (Strength Through Joy) movement demanded an escapist environment of their own. A popular pseudo-Rococo décor was applied indiscriminately to the interiors of theatres, ships and other buildings dedicated to light recreation. This stylistic schizophrenia frequently led to different parts of the same

207　Kraft durch Freude poster, 1936. The Volkswagen was an integral part of Ley's movement.

Scharoun. For Schultze-Naumburg, however, the issue of form had political connotations, and in opposing the Neue Sachlichkeit architecture of the Weimar Republic he soon adopted right-wing, not to say racist, attitudes that were readily assimilable to the reactionary ideology of the Party. By 1930, when Schultze-Naumburg finally joined Alfred Rosenberg's cultural front, the Kampfbund für deutsche Kultur, Darré had already cleared the field for an attack on modern culture in general, with his diatribe against industrial urbanization and the destruction of the peasantry. For him the agrarian settlement was not only the stronghold of patriotism but also the hypothetical habitat of a pure Nordic race.

Schultze-Naumburg took up a parallel position in his 1932 Kampfbund book, *Kampf um die Kunst* ('The Struggle over Art'), where he castigated those nomads of the metropolis who had lost any concept of the homeland. Elsewhere, almost paraphrasing Darré, he praised the pitched-roofed German house with its roots sunk deep into the soil, contrasting it to the flat-roofed architecture of an uprooted

208　Rimpl, Heinkel workers' housing (above) and factory, Oranienburg, 1936.

development being treated in a totally different manner, as in Herbert Rimpl's Heinkel factory at Oranienburg of 1936, which ranged in its expression from the Neo-Classical portico of the administration building to the *Heimatstil* of the workers' housing and the functionalism of the plant itself.

The sudden shift in the style of state-sponsored housing, from the cubic flat-roofed forms of the Weimar Republic to the pitched-roofed forms of the Third Reich, was enthusiastically supported by the architect Paul Schultze-Naumburg who, despite his own austere manner, had long ago reacted against Functionalist architecture. An associate of Heinrich Tessenow in the creation of a whitewashed, pitched-roofed *Heimatstil* manner, Schultze-Naumburg sought as early as the mid-1920s to resist the internationalist and mechanistic tendencies of modern life. His anti-rationalist rhetoric grew out of a late Arts and Crafts concern for simple, earthbound organic forms subscribed to equally by Tessenow, Häring and

people. He had announced these views as early as 1926, when he wrote that the flat roof 'is immediately recognizable as the child of other skies and other blood' – a comment which seems to have inspired that sardonic photomontage of the Stuttgart Weissenhof-siedlung in the guise of an Arab village, complete with Bedouin and camels. Schultze-Naumburg's racial prejudice was made explicit in his book *Kunst und Rasse* ('Art and Race') (1928), where he attempted to prove that Germany's cultural 'decadence' had a biological origin. In his second theoretical work, *Das Gesicht des deutschen Hauses* ('The Face of the German House') of 1929, he wrote that the German dwelling

gives one the feeling that it grows out of the soil, like one of its natural products, like a tree that sinks its roots deep in the interior of the soil and forms a union with it. It is this that gives our understanding of home [*Heimat*], of a bond with blood and earth [*Erden*], for one kind of men this is the condition of their life and the meaning of their existence.

However appropriate for mass housing, a 'blood and soil' *Heimatstil* could hardly represent the myth of the thousand-year Reich, and for this purpose the party exploited the Classical heritage of Gilly, Langhans and Schinkel. Paul Ludwig Troost and Albert Speer (successively Hitler's personal architects from 1933 to the mid-1940s) effectively established a reduced version of the Schinkelschüler tradition as the representative style of the state. From Troost's embellishments of Munich as the 'capital of the party' to Speer's colossal set-pieces for the Nazi state in its heyday, his Zeppelinfeld stadium for the Nuremburg rally of 1937 and his new Chancellery in Berlin, completed in the following year, the same spartan Classicism prevails.

The conscious elimination of Schinkel's proportional delicacy in the name of the millennium evolved only slightly as it passed from Troost's frigid version of the Tuscan order to Speer's preference for plain or fluted rectangular columns. This sterilization of Romantic Classicism – built with fanatical precision – only came

to life when these vast set-pieces were used for mass assembly, for a style of pageantry which Speer himself had first formulated in his so-called 'cathedral of ice', a virtual column of flag standards and searchlights created for the Tempelhof rally at Berlin in 1935. Under Goebbels's direction, such arenas became the setting for the inculcation of Nazi ideology, not only on the spot but throughout the Reich: for the first time the 'state as a work of art' could be channelled into the mass media of radio and film. Leni Riefenstahl's documentary film of the Nuremberg rally of 1934, *Triumph des Willens* (*The Triumph of the Will*), was the first occasion on which architecture, in the form of Speer's temporary setting, was pressed into the service of cinematic propaganda. Henceforth Speer's designs for stadia at Nuremberg were determined as much by camera angles as by architectural criteria. This cinematic exploitation of architecture was totally at variance with Speer's insistence on the use of load-bearing masonry to insure the future of the Zeppelinfeld as a sublime ruin. This idiosyncratic 'law of the ruins', forbidding the use of metal reinforcement, was a nostalgic reference to the Enlightenment (he was thinking of Piranesi's Paestum engravings, for instance); so was Wilhelm Kreis's insistence that Neo-Classicism expressed the spirit of the German earth, the people's cult of the *Heimat*.

The National Socialist version of the New Tradition could not transcend this reduction of the 'space of public appearance' to mass hysteria, this subordination of all real relationships to the illusion of film or to the histrionic rituals of the *Thingplätze* – open-air arenas built after 1934 for nature worship and the celebration of Teutonic rites. The language of Romantic Classicism stripped of its Enlightenment imagery and faith was now reduced to scenography. With the notable exceptions of Werner March's Olympic Stadium of 1936 and Bonatz's *Autobahn* bridges of the same date, the New Tradition degenerated into meaningless megalomania, terminating after 1941 in Kreis's 'Totenburgen', brilliantly conceived, Boullée-like 'castles of the dead' built throughout Eastern Europe, whenever there was time, to immortalize the remains of the fallen.

## THE MODERNISTIC STYLE IN AMERICA
## 1923–32

That aspect of the New Tradition which took the form of a stripped Classical style emerged

209  Kreis, project for a war memorial, Kutno, 1942.

210  World Exhibition, Paris, 1937. Speer's representation of the Third Reich (far left) confronts Iofan's USSR Pavilion (far right).

as the ruling taste in the 1930s, wherever power wished to represent itself in a positive and progressive light. As Speer observed, the Soviet Pavilion for the Paris World Exhibition of of 1937 employed a pseudo-Classical syntax almost identical to that of the German Pavilion which Speer had designed for the same occasion. This taste for Neo-Classical monumentality was not restricted, as Speer noted, to totalitarian states, but could be seen in Paris, where it was displayed in such works as J.C. Dondel's Musée d'Art Moderne and Auguste Perret's Musée des Travaux Publics, both works completed in 1937. It also made itself manifest in the United States, where it gradually emerged out of Beaux-Arts Neo-Classicism — the 'official' style in the States from the World's Columbian Exposition of 1893 to the First World War. As one may judge from the Neo-Classical embellishments of Washington, such as Henry Bacon's Lincoln Memorial of 1917, the Federal Government was too conservative to become a patron of the New Tradition. With the universities more or less committed after the turn of the century to copybook Gothic, the one patron capable of sponsoring a more adventurous eclecticism seems to have been the railroads, from the eclectic Romanism of the New York termini built in the decade prior to the First World War — Warren and Wetmore's Grand Central Station (1903–13) and McKim, Mead and White's Pennsylvania Station (1906–

10) — to such Moderne pieces as the Cincinnati Union Station designed by Feilheimer & Wagner in 1929.

The other source of patronage for a Moderne expression was, of course, high-rise office development, and from the time of Cass Gilbert's Woolworth Building of 1913 the New Tradition, as far as the skyscraper was concerned, displayed a preference for the Gothic. This tendency was reinforced by the results of the *Chicago Tribune* competition of 1922. Once again the premiated designs of an international competition seem to have been decisive in the formation of a ruling style, Eliel Saarinen's second-prize entry being as important an influence on Raymond Hood's subsequent career as Hood and Howell's own winning design. This can be seen in the development of Hood's 'skyscraper style' from his black-and-gold American Radiator Building, New York, of 1924, to his earliest sketches, made in 1930, for Rockefeller Center, New York. As Jacques Greber was to remark in 1920, a 'stripped Gothic' enabled the architect to overcome the problem of a large number of windows 'by means of strongly marked ribs which accentuated the verticalism and therefore the impressive appearance of towers'.

The synthesis of the Art Deco or the Modernistic Style in the States had just as many roots in the mainstream of the Modern Movement as it did in the historicism of the turn of the century. Above all its affinities lay with German Expressionism (Poelzig, Höger, etc.) as we may judge from the evolution of the New York work of McKenzie, Voorhees, Gmelin and Walker, from their inaugural Barclay-Vesey Building of 1923 to their Western Union Building of 1928. However, no one source can ever be credited for this highly synthetic style, the need for which seems to have arisen out of a spontaneous desire to celebrate the triumph of democracy and capitalism in the New World. From the American point of view the First World War had been favourably concluded; America had emerged a creditor nation and the boom of the 1920s was about to start. In what style could such an enthusiasm for 'progress' be expressed? Certainly not in the historicist styles of waning European power —

nor for that matter could it adopt the avant-garde mode of the new Europe. Its sources, as Forrest F. Lisle has remarked of Chicago's Century of Progress Exposition of 1933, had to be more open and eclectic:

the Paris 1925 Fair, Frank Lloyd Wright, cubism, machine ethics, Mayan forms, Pueblo patterns, Dudok, the Viennese Secession, modern interiors, the zoning-law set back. This large number of weakly related sources, readily identified as underlying the Moderne in America, begins to suggest the loose, broad, inclusive, less intense, rather indiscriminate, thus democratic, perimeters of the modern movement *here* as opposed to the impersonal, reductive, exclusive, more idealistic, more moralistic thrust of avant-garde Europe at this time.

Something of the intent behind the Modernistic Style may be adduced from the way in which it was used. Aside from domestic interiors, etc., it was reserved for the worldy realm of offices, in-town apartment blocks hotels, banks, department stores and buildings dedicated to modern media, newspapers, publishing ventures, tele-communications, etc. It was an exclusively urban style: the suburban work of Moderne architects such as Ely-Jacques Kahn and Raymond Hood — their private houses and country clubs — were usually carried out in variations of the English Free Style, tempered by the occasional Colonial portico. There was in fact a sense of stylistic propriety comparable to that which obtained according to 'party line' in totalitarian countries: one style for the office, another for the suburban retreat, and still another for the idyll of the university — this last being more often than not from the medieval hand of Ralph Adams Cram.

However, the precise manner in which the Modernistic Style was woven into the ideological and historical fabric of its time is perhaps best revealed by the case history of the Rockefeller Center, New York, which started off as a large piece of real estate development predicated on the Metropolitan Opera Company's desire for a new auditorium in a new location. It was completed as a precarious speculation, in the midst of the Depression, significantly enough without the opera, but *with* the aid of the newly fledged and flourishing communications industry, the Radio Corporation of America and its subsidiaries NBC and RKO, as the primary client. Thus, instead of being focused about a 'city beautiful' plaza before an Art Deco opera house façade as in the 1928 design by B.W. Morris, it was soon to be reinterpreted both ideologically and architecturally as a Radio City – 'within a city'. The Rockefeller Center management were only too aware that the economic threat of such a huge development in the midst of a depression would have to be presented as an unequivocal contribution to the public weal. To this end they abetted their major client in commissioning the vaudeville and radio personality and impressario Roxy (S.L. Rothafel) to work in collaboration with the architects on the creation of the 6,200-seat Radio City Music Hall for the presentation of a hybrid entertainment comprising vaudeville and film, and the 3,500-seat luxury cinema known as the Center Theater. The generally popular flavour of Radio City – the city of illusion and distraction in the midst of crisis (Roxy's slogan was 'a visit to Radio City is as good as a month in the country') – was reinforced in 1936 when the failure of the shops in the sunken plaza led to the substitution of an open-air skating rink with restaurants situated to either side.

It is to the lasting credit of Hood, as the prime designer of the architectural troika of Reinhard & Hofmeister, Corbett Harrison & Macmurray, and Hood & Fouilhoux, that he was able to control not only the overall composition and the detail but also a good deal of the programme; it was he, for instance, who first suggested the idea of roof gardens. Under his supervision, the Center, eventually amounting to eight blocks and fourteen buildings, had its representative core – the seventy-storey

211 Van Alen, Chrysler Building, New York, 1928–30, between the RCA Victor (now G.E.) Building, by Cross & Cross, and Schultze and Weaver's Waldorf Astoria, both of 1930–31.

212 Reinhard & Hofmeister, Corbett Harrison & Macmurray, and Hood & Fouilhoux, Rockefeller Center, New York, chiefly 1932–39. The tallest structure, in the centre, is the RCA Building. Below it on the right is Radio City Music Hall. Between the RCA Building and 5th Avenue (bottom) are the sunken garden with Prometheus statue and two low buildings with roof gardens flanking a fountain walk.

RCA slab and plaza and the Radio City Music Hall — all completed in eighteen months, in time for the gala opening at the end of 1932.

Roxy's formula of the Rockettes floor show plus a movie was as extemporary and transitional in its cultural nature as the artistic programme of the entire Center, where one artistic work after another, be it sculpture or mural, took as its subject matter such themes as light, sound, radio, television, aviation and progress in general, culminating in two major set-pieces on the central axis of the entire composition. These were Paul Manship's gilded Prometheus, surrounded by the Zodiac and overlooking the sunken plaza, and Diego Rivera's ill-fated mural to the entrance hall of the RCA Building, *Man at the Crossroads*, which, with its unequivocal revolutionary iconography including even an image of Lenin, had the effect of placing his patrons in an impossible public position, in which politically they had no choice but to insist on its removal. This contradictory New Deal gesture of monopoly capital consciously commissioning an emblematic work from a communist artist seems now, almost half a century later, to be as remote and fictitious as Hugh Ferriss's vision of Manhattan transformed into an endless repetition of skyscraper ziggurats, in his book *The Metropolis of Tomorrow* of 1929. Recording Art Deco skyscrapers that were then either

213  Ferriss, 'The Business Centre', 1927, from *The Metropolis of Tomorrow*, 1929.

completed or already under way and anticipating the apotheosis of the Rockefeller Center, this was a science-fiction vision of a city of towers as scenographic and theatrical as the style itself — a New Babylon born of euphoria, land values and the set-back profiles imposed by the 1916 New York City zoning code.

## THE NEW MONUMENTALITY 1943

With the exception of the Soviet Union, Roosevelt's New Deal and the Second World War had the effect of bringing the New Tradition to an abrupt end, but not before architects like J.J.P. Oud had been touched by its influence (see for instance his Shell Building, built at The Hague in 1938). After the war the general ideological climate of the West was hostile to any kind of monumentality. The League of Nations had been discredited, the British had granted India her independence and the régimes that had made the New Tradition into an instrument of national policy were regarded as anathema. Moreover, the manipulative advantages of less permanent but cheaper, more flexible and more penetrating modes of ideological representation were soon seen as far surpassing the effectiveness of architecture. As anticipated by the intense and brilliant use of radio and film in the propaganda of the Third Reich and in the popular mass productions of RCA and Hollywood during the Depression, governments after the Second World War came to give increasing attention to the content and impact of media rather than to built form. And where the former became increasingly rhetorical and intense, the latter became more and more abstract and devoid of iconographical content. The highly abstract quality of the post-1956 extension of Rockefeller Center west of 6th Avenue for Time Inc., Exxon and McGraw-Hill already testifies to this reductive process.

The reasons for the eclipse of the Modernistic New Tradition in 1939 were not, however, entirely ideological; for one thing the high quality craftsmanship readily available for the realization of such remarkable structures as William van Alen's Chrysler Building, New York (1930), was largely absorbed and dispersed by the war effort. In addition, the enthusiasm with which the American establishment embraced the Modern Movement increased each successive year, after the Hitchcock and Johnson exhibition 'Modern Architecture' of 1932, and by 1945, when the New Deal was at its height, the Functionalist line in architecture was virtually the ruling style (cf. the work of Lescaze, Neutra, the Bowman brothers, etc.)

It is ironic that the demise of the New Tradition and the triumph of the Modern Movement should coincide with a reaction in favour of monumentality coming from the heart of the movement itself. Only five years separate Giedion's Charles Eliot Norton Lectures, given at Harvard University in 1938–39 (published as *Space, Time and Architecture* in 1941), from his polemical *Nine Points on Monumentality* of 1943, written in collaboration with Fernand Léger and José Luis Sert. The most important articles of this document read:

(1)　Monuments are human landmarks which men have created as symbols for their ideals, for their aims, and for their actions. They are intended to outlive the period which originated them, and constitute a heritage for future generations. As such, they form a link between the past and the future.

(2)　Monuments are the expression of man's highest cultural needs. They have to satisfy the eternal demand of the people for translation of their collective force into symbols. The most vital monuments are those which express the feeling and thinking of this collective force – the people.

(4)　The last hundred years have witnessed the devaluation of monumentality. This does not mean that there is any lack of formal monuments or architectural examples pretending to serve this purpose; but the so-called monuments of recent date have, with rare exceptions, become empty shells. They in no way represent the spirit and the collective feeling of modern times.

(6)　A new step lies ahead. Post-war changes in the whole economic structure of nations may bring with them the organization of community life in the city which has been practically neglected up to date.

(7)　The people want the buildings that represent their social and community life to give more than functional fulfilment.

This position paper – destined to become the brief for CIAM VIII of 1952 – formulated a sharply discriminative approach to the problem of representation, which seems to be as valid today as when it was first written. In the first instance, there is its recognition of the fact that neither the monumentality of the New Tradition nor the functionalism of the Modern Movement was capable of representing the collective aspirations of the people. In the second, there is the implication, never explicitly stated, that a genuine collectivity can only realize an appropriate expression of its values and historical continuity at a 'cantonal' or municipal level, and that large centralized or authoritarian states are incapable, by definition, of authentically representing the hopes and desires of the people. In the years since 1943 the issue of representation – the fundamental problem of meaning in architecture – has recurred again and again, only to be met by repression and denial, or by escapist withdrawal into the supposedly spontaneous and hence popular significance of advertising and media in the consumer economy. The practice of architecture now lapses into 'silence' – see Manfredo Tafuri's *Progetto e Utopia (Architecture and Utopia, Design and Capitalist Development)* of 1973 – and even into disrepute solely because one of the primary subjects of which it should speak, namely the destiny of the society, is constantly denied it. Unfortunately, the political institutions that would be capable of rearticulating this particular form of significance are today as fragile as the culture of architecture itself.

## Chapter 25

# Le Corbusier and the monumentalization of the vernacular 1930-60

This construction, built by local contractors, consists of reinforced-concrete floors carried on exposed masonry walls made of the local stone. Despite the use of ordinary masonry, the usual conceptions employed in our houses reappear here. That is to say, a complete distinction is maintained between the bearing walls which are considered as supports for the floors and the glazed partitions which fill the empty spaces.

The composition is structured by the landscape. The house occupies a small promontory dominating the plain behind Toulon, backed by a magnificent silhouette of mountains. The site offers the striking spectacle of a vast unfolding landscape, and the unexpected nature of this has been kept by walling in the principal rooms on the side to the view and by having only a door that opens onto a veranda from which the sudden vista is like an explosion. On descending the small staircase that leads down to the ground one sees a large stele by Lipschitz rising up, its terminal *palmette* outlined against the sky above the mountains.

Le Corbusier,
*Oeuvre complète, 1929–34,* 1935

Le Corbusier and Pierre Jeanneret had already thought of their domestic architecture of the late 1920s as having a strong link with the natural environment, but they had never previously conceived of this connection as taking place on such a monumental scale. Now, with this holiday house designed for Hélène de Mandrot and built outside Toulon in 1931, and their Errazuriz House projected for a remote site in Chile (1930), they began to envisage their works as reaching out across landscapes of titanic proportions. This subtle shift towards a topographic sensibility contrasted with their apparently spontaneous acceptance of 'vernacular' construction as a mode of expression. Although they had used load-bearing crosswalls before they had never exploited the expressive qualities of rough-hewn stonework.

This break with the dogmatic aesthetic of Purism (already anticipated in Le Corbusier's painting of 1926) coincides with the conceptual point in his career when he began to abandon his faith in the *inevitably* beneficient workings of a machine-age civilization. From now on, disillusioned by industrial reality and increasingly under the 'Brutalist' influence of the painter Fernand Léger, his style began to move in two opposite directions at once. On the one hand he returned, at least in his domestic work, to the language of the vernacular; on the other, as in his project for Paul Otlet's Cité Mondiale of 1929, he embraced a monumentality of Classical, not to say Beaux-Arts, grandeur.

However, to think of this schism as a simple differentiation in the expressive mode between 'building' and 'architecture' is to give an oversimplified account of the practice at this time. For, despite the 'inner doubt', not only had the machine aesthetic not been totally abandoned (as we may judge from 'curtain-walled' structures built by the practice between 1930 and 1933), but also works such as the de Beistegui Penthouse unexpectedly revealed a Surrealist side to Le Corbusier's imagination. This dreamlike exercise – reminiscent of Adolf Loos's interiors for the Tristan Tzara house of 1926 – manifested its 'aesthetic' disjunctions on more than one level. While it emphasized the strangeness of objects at a domestic scale (the lawn of the solarium appeared like a living carpet!) it also evoked unlikely urban (topographic) associations such as the isomorphic similarity between the solarium's false fireplace and the Arc de Triomphe, poised on the artificial horizon of the bounding wall. This Surrealist sensibility (cf. Magritte and Piranesi) is latent throughout the whole of Le Corbusier's return to the vernacular, from the de Mandrot House of 1931 to the Ronchamp pilgrimage chapel built in the mid-1950s.

In many of the 'vernacular' essays prior to Ronchamp the remoteness of the site itself became the rationale for the mode of building. The extreme example of this is the very cheap house at Mathes, near Bordeaux (1935), which was built from drawings without the architect visiting the site. Le Corbusier wrote:

The impossibility of supervising the construction and the necessity of employing a small contractor from the village led even to the conception of the plan itself. The house had three successive and absolutely separate stages of work:

(a) the masonry built at one time,

(b) the carpentry built at one time,

(c) the joinery, comprising windows, doors, shutters and cupboards, all to a standard and to a unitary principle of construction; assembled independently and variously panelled in glass, plywood and asbestos cement.

The same justification of limited resources could be put forward in the case of the Errazuriz and de Mandrot houses, but it could hardly apply to the weekend house built in the Parisian suburbs in 1935. Here the vernacular was being consciously embraced for its material articulation, for its capacity to enrich the abstract and reductive nature of the Purist style. Le Corbusier wrote:

The designing of such a house demanded extreme care since the elements of construction were the only architectonic means. The architectural theme was established about a typical bay whose influence extended as far as the little pavilion in the garden. Here one was confronted by exposed stonework, natural on the outside, white on the interior; wood on the walls and ceilings; and a chimney out of rough brickwork, with white ceramic tiles on the floor,

Nevada glass block walls and a table of Cippolino marble.

In short, one experienced, as at Toulon and Mathes, an expressive *bricolage*. From now on the juxtaposition of contrasting materials became an essential aspect of Le Corbusier's style, not only as an expressive 'palette' but also as a means of building.

This shift to natural materials and primitive methods had consequences that went beyond a mere change in technique or surface style. Above all it meant abandoning the Classical envelope that had been used in the villas of the late 1920s in favour of an architecture predicated on the expressive force of a single architectonic element, be this a monopitched roof supported by cross-walls or a barrel-vaulted megaron. While the former mode (anticipated at Mathes) appeared in the rammed-earth walls and lean-to thatched roofs of the 'Maisons Murondins' proposed in 1940 for the accommodation of refugees, the latter was the basic structural module of both the weekend house and the farm complex projected for Cherchell, North Africa, in 1942. That Le Corbusier's preoccupation with the Mediterranean after the Second World War took a vernacular rather than a Classical form is demonstrated by a sequence of works stemming from the Cherchell project, and leading via the Roq et Rob stepped-terrace housing designed for Cap Martin in 1949 to the Sarabhai House in Ahmedabad and the Maisons Jaoul in Paris, these last two works being completed in 1955.

As James Stirling was to make clear, the Maisons Jaoul design was an affront to those

214 Le Corbusier and Jeanneret, weekend house, Paris, 1935.

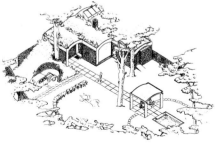

sensibilities which had been nurtured on the myth that modern architecture should manifest itself as smooth, machine-wrought, planar surfaces set within an articulated structural frame. It was disturbing to find that this complex was 'being built by Algerian labourers equipped with ladders, hammers and nails', and that with the exception of glass no synthetic materials were being used. For Stirling, the almost medieval level of the technology was enough to relegate the work to the realm of art for art's sake, and he saw it, justifiably, as being in direct opposition to the Rationalist tradition of the Modern Movement. However, Le Corbusier's 'arationality' went beyond the anachronistic, if expedient, application of Catalan vaulting or exposed brickwork and concrete struck directly from timber shuttering. The concrete waterheads, the narrow openings in the cross-walls, and the transverse bays (these last being largely filled with plywood panelling), combined to create the impression of a consciously hostile attitude to the outside world. The archetypal window was now no longer the *fenêtre en longueur* to be looked through, but rather a framed and panelled insert to be looked at. 'The eye finding interest in every part of a surface impasto', wrote Stirling, 'does not, as at Garches, seek relief from the hard textureless finish by examining the contours and the form of the plane.' Instead of Purist form, the Maisons Jaoul offered a tactile reality far removed from the utopian visions of the late 1920s; a pragmatism which was ready to embrace, as Reyner Banham has observed, the contradictions and confusions of suburbia.

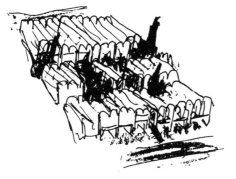

215   Le Corbusier, Roq et Rob project, Cap Martin, 1949. A reinterpretation of the weekend house as a housing prototype.

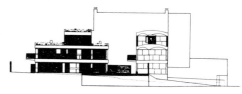

216   Le Corbusier, Maisons Jaoul, Paris, 1955. North-east elevation.

The Maisons Jaoul design was a monumental reinterpretation of a Mediterranean vernacular, whose effect stemmed as much from its introspective solemnity as from its scale. This Surrealistic syntax could hardly be used for the eighteen-storey Unité d'Habitation, built at Marseilles in 1947–52. And yet in abandoning the light-weight machine technology of the pre-war era the Unité showed itself equally committed to 'brutalist' methods of construction. This is especially evident in the casting of its basic concrete superstructure from rough timber formwork, a deliberate revelation of built process which Le Corbusier was to justify on grounds which were almost existential.

Aside from this *béton brut* appearance, the Unité was far more complex in its organization than the typical pre-war Ville Radieuse block. Where the VR slab was a continuous horizontal volume, hermetically contained behind glass, the Unité revealed its cellular structure through the use of concrete sun-baffle balconies and canopies projecting from the main body of the building. These *brise-soleil* with their side walls stressed the volume of the two-storey units extending through the width of the block — megaron forms constructed as independent elements and suspended within the concrete frame in much the same manner as bottles are set into a rack. Interior 'streets' on every other floor provided the horizontal access to these interlocking cross-over units.

This cellular morphology automatically expressed an agglomeration of private dwellings (cf. Roq et Rob), while the shopping arcade and the rooftop communal facilities served to establish and represent the public realm. The honorific status of this larger whole was expressed at ground level in the carefully profiled columns supporting the underbelly

of the building. These *pilotis*, precisely proportioned in accordance with Le Corbusier's
*Modulor*, suggested the invention of a new
'Classical' order. Uniting its 337 dwellings with
a shopping arcade, a hotel and a roofdeck, a
running track, a paddling pool, a kindergarten
and a gymnasium, the Unité was just as much
of a 'social condenser' as the Soviet commune blocks of the 1920s. This total integration of community services recalled the 19th-
century model of Fourier's phalanstery, not
only through its size but also in its isolation
from the immediate environment. And just
as the phalanstery was intended to house the
ordinary man in a princely domain (Fourier
detesting the meanness of the individual
house), so the Unité was seen by its author
as restoring the dignity of architecture to the
simplest private dwelling.

The pilgrimage chapel at Ronchamp, first
projected in 1950, and the Dominican monastery of La Tourette, built at Eveux outside
Lyons in 1960, represent the two principal
building types – the sacred building and
the retreat – that preoccupied Le Corbusier
throughout the 1950s. The monastery, effectively combining both types, served to remind

217  Le Corbusier, Unité d'Habitation, Marseilles,
1947–52.

218  Le Corbusier, Unité d'Habitation, Marseilles,
1947–52. Children's pool on the roof.

219  Le Corbusier, monastery of La Tourette, near
Lyons, 1957–60. Section and second-floor plan.

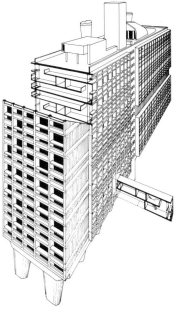

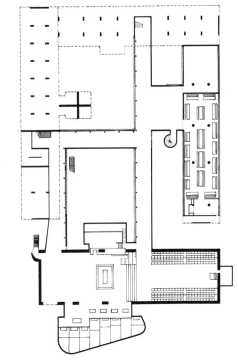

220  Le Corbusier and Jeanneret, Pavillon des Temps Nouveaux, World Exhibition, Paris, 1937.

221  Le Corbusier, Ronchamp Chapel, near Belfort, 1950–55.

him of that paradigm of 'solitude and communion' which had so deeply moved him when he first visited the Charterhouse of Ema in 1907. La Tourette simply reinterpreted this ideal model as a bipartite scheme comprising 'public' church and 'private' cloister. Elevated off the ground rather than terraced into its site, this opposition between the vertical volume of the chapel and the horizontal layer of the ambulatory was dramatically exposed by the fall of the land. Colin Rowe has written:

At La Tourette the site is everything and nothing. It is equipped with an abrupt slope and a lavishly accidental cross-fall. It is by no means a local condition which would really justify the quintessential Dominican establishment which seems to have been preconceived. Rather it is the reverse; architecture and landscape, lucid and separate experiences, are like rival protagonists of a debate who progressively contradict and clarify each other's meaning.

Nothing could have been further from this than the rapport established between building and site at Ronchamp, where the crustacean forms which make up the whole — the shell roof with its giant gargoyle, the side chapels and the altar — were all precisely tuned to respond to the 'visual acoustics' of an undulating landscape. Ronchamp brought Le Corbusier

back to the 1930s, not only to the de Mandrot House for its integration into the site but also to the basic form of the Pavilion des Temps Nouveaux built for the Paris Exhibition of 1937. Unlikely as it may seem, this wire-cable suspension structure was the fundamental prototype for Ronchamp, inasmuch as it was inspired by the reconstruction of the Hebrew temple in the wilderness, previously reproduced in *Vers une architecture*. As a further transposition of the same metaphor, the dominant concrete shell roof of Ronchamp echoed the profile of the canvas-and-cable catenary roof to the 1937 pavilion. The recurrence of this profile in the Chandigarh Capitol and elsewhere in his later work makes it seem that Le Corbusier was trying to establish this form as the 20th-century equivalent of the Renaissance dome, i.e. as a sign for the sacred.

Beyond this, Ronchamp resists analysis — in part Maltese tomb, in part Ischian vernacular, its half-cylindrical side chapels, toplit through spherical cowls and orientated towards the trajectory of the sun, serve to remind one that this Christian site was once the location of a sun temple. Built as it is around a hidden reinforced-concrete frame, the vernacular in this instance is simulated rather than reinterpreted in monumental terms. As in the villa at Garches, the rough masonry infill is rendered

228

over with 'gunite', but the desired finish is no longer the machine precision of Purism but the stippled, whitewashed texture of Mediterranean folk building.

Le Corbusier's concern for the sculptural resonance of a building in relation to its site was first formulated in 1923, when he characterized the Acropolis and its Propylea as that point 'when nothing more might be taken away, when nothing would be left but these closely knit and violent elements, sounding clear and tragic like brazen trumpets'. This passionate image of the Acropolis, conveying a feeling for unity just prior to breaking up, reappears as a constant theme throughout his life and with heightened pathos towards the end of his career. This was as much the principle underlying Ronchamp's 'visual acoustics' as it was the reason for the diminutive volcanic, mountainous forms that erupt on the roofdeck of the Unité.

A more Cartesian approach informed the design of Chandigarh, the new administrative capital of the Punjab, founded in 1951. Since the terrain here was flat, the siting of the monuments was determined by the imposition of a proportional grid. Le Corbusier had already used such 'regulating lines' on an urban scale in his Cité Mondiale of 1929 and in his centre

222  Le Corbusier, Ronchamp Chapel, near Belfort, 1950–55.

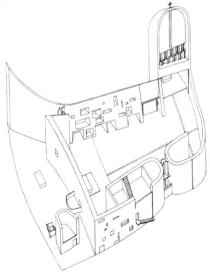

for St-Dié of 1945. His description of the Capitol makes it clear he was convinced that such delicate refinements were perceptible, irrespective of the distances involved. 'The composition of the Park of the Capitol, vast as it is, is today regulated to the centimetre in nearly all of its dimensions both overall and in detail. Such are the means, the powers, and the objectives of "proportioning".' That similar modular devices had been used by Sir Edwin Lutyens when designing New Delhi was not lost on Le Corbusier, who wrote appreciatively of that new capital that it was 'built by Lutyens over thirty years ago with extreme care, great talent, and with true success. The critics may rant as they will, but the accomplishment of such an undertaking earns respect.'

Unlike New Delhi or the Cité Mondiale, Chandigarh achieved monumentality without referring directly to the traditional vocabulary of Western Classicism. The striking profiles of its three monuments were derived, in the first instance, from a direct response to the severity of the climate. Unlike Lutyens, who had exploited only the secondary elements of Moghul architecture, Le Corbusier appropriated the traditional 'parasol' concept of Fatehpur Sikri as a monumental coding device to be varied from one structure to the next. By using this shell form either as a prelude (the Assembly entrance canopy), or as a constant (the vaulted roof of the High Court), or as a dominant (the crowning parasol of the Governor's Palace), he was able to suggest the character and status of each institution. The subtle

223  Le Corbusier, with Jeanneret, Drew and Fry, Chandigarh, 1951–65. The Capitol (top of plan) is represented as a wooden model in the foreground, showing (left to right) the Secretariat, Assembly, Governor's Palace and High Court.

profiles of these shell forms were derived in part from the livestock and landscape of the region. The evident intent was to represent a modern Indian identity that would be free from any association with its colonial past.

At the same time, the enormous scale of the Capitol deprived it of those public attributes of the 'heart of the city' which, at CIAM VIII, held at Hoddesdon in 1952, Sert had seen as being dependent on 'walking distances and man's angle of vision'. Within the temenos of the Capitol, where it takes over twenty minutes to walk from the Secretariat to the High Court, the presence of man is more metaphysical than real (once again recalling De Chirico). Le

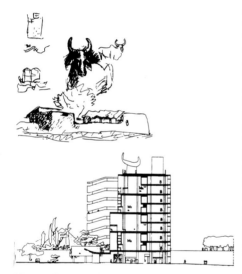

224   Le Corbusier, Chandigarh, c.1951. Sketches of cattle and vernacular building forms, and section through the Secretariat.

Corbusier's Neo-Classical heritage had emerged to evoke the landscape of the *genre terrible*: the representative buildings of the 'three powers' — the High Court, the Assembly and the Secretariat — were related not, as on the Acropolis, by the configuration of the site, but rather by abstract sight lines, receding across vast distances, a progressive foreshortening whose only limits seemed to lie with the mountains on the horizon.

The realization of Chandigarh proper, as an abstract and ill-advised plan, can (as Stanislaus von Moos has argued) hardly be separated from the political aspirations of India at the time of its independence. For Chandigarh was more than the capital of the Punjab: it was the symbol of the New India. It epitomized the idea of a modern industrial state, the utopian destiny which Nehru had envisaged for India in total opposition to Gandhi's will. Thus Chandigarh had already been laid out as a picturesque 'motopian' suburbia by the American planner Albert Mayer before its hasty rationalization into a more or less orthogonal road network at the hands of Le Corbusier, in association with Pierre Jeanneret, Jane Drew and Maxwell Fry. The emerging crisis of Western Enlightenment, its inability to nurture an existing culture or even to sustain the significance of its own Classical forms, its lack of any goal beyond constant technical innovation and optimum economic growth, all seem to be summed up in the tragedy of Chandigarh — a city designed for automobiles in a country where many, as yet, still lack a bicycle.

225   Le Corbusier with Jeanneret, Drew and Fry, Chandigarh Capitol, 1957–65. Secretariat (left) and Assembly Buildings.

## Chapter 26

# Mies van der Rohe and the monumentalization of technique 1933-67

In architecture there is only one man whom even the young men can defend and that is Mies van der Rohe. Mies has always kept out of politics and has always taken his stand against functionalism. No one can accuse Mies's houses of looking like factories. Two factors especially make Mies's acceptance as the new architect possible. First, Mies is respected by the conservatives. Even the *Kampfbund für Deutsche Kultur* has nothing against him. Secondly, Mies has just won . . . a competition for the new building of the Reichsbank. The jury were older architects and representatives of the bank.

If (and it may be a long if) Mies should build this building it would clinch his position. A good modern Reichsbank would satisfy the new craving for monumentality, but above it all it would prove to the German intellectuals and to foreign countries that the new Germany is not bent on destroying all the splendid modern arts which have been built up in recent years.

Philip Johnson
'Architecture in the Third Reich',
*Horn and Hound*, 1933

Mies van der Rohe's entry for the Reichsbank competition of 1933 was the beginning of a transformation in his work, from informal asymmetry to symmetrical monumentality. This move towards the monumental eventually culminated in the development of a highly rationalized building method that was widely adopted in the 1950s by the American building industry and its corporate clientele. The Reichsbank design hinted at this future development in more ways than one, for it established a preference not only for symmetry but also for a certain tectonic which tended to move away from the dynamic spatial effects of his earlier

career. At the same time the client was the institutional establishment, a patron that Mies was to serve throughout his practice in the United States.

The Reichsbank design was not simply a return to Schinkel, who, except in Mies's work of the early 1920s, had always been a latent influence. It was more a return to the tectonics of Mies's concrete office building, first published in the magazine *G* in 1923, the emphasis in both projects being on the expressive qualities of an objective building technique, logically conceived and rigorously executed. In 1926 Mies had spoken of architecture as being 'the will of the epoch translated into space'. In Hegelian terms, he saw this will as historically determined technique, as a self-evident fact, only to be refined by the spirit. The intrinsic monumentality of his later work was predicated on such a refinement. For Mies, technology was the cultural manifestation of modern man, and in this respect

226   Mies van der Rohe, project for the Reichsbank, Berlin, 1933.

the Reichsbank must be regarded as his first essay in the monumentalization of technique. This accounts for its warehouse-like appearance, for the neutral, scarcely modulated treatment of its curtain wall.

Between 1933 and the early 1950s, Mies's work was to oscillate between asymmetry and symmetry, between technique as found and the monumentalization of technique as form. This variation in expression occurred not only from one building to the next but also within a single structure. He summed up the overriding cultural import that he attached to technique in his address to the Illinois Institute of Technology in 1950:

Technology is rooted in the past. It dominates the present and tends into the future. It is a real historical movement – one of the great movements which shape and represent their epoch.

It can be compared only with the classic discovery of man as a person, the Roman will to power, and the religious movement of the Middle Ages.

Technology is far more than a method, it is a world in itself. As a method it is superior in almost every respect. But only where it is left to itself, as in gigantic structures of engineering, there technology reveals its true nature. . . . Whenever technology reaches its real fulfilment, it transcends into architecture. It is true

that architecture depends on facts, but its real field of activity is in the realm of significance.

Mies van der Rohe's development after the mid-1930s concerned itself with the conciliation of two opposed systems. One was the heritage of Romantic Classicism which, when translated into the skeleton steel frame, pointed towards the dematerialization of architecture, to the mutation of built form into shifting planes suspended in diaphanous space – the image of Suprematism. The other was the authority of trabeated architecture as it had been inherited from the ancient world, the implacable elements of roof, beam, column and wall. Caught, as it were, between 'space' and 'structure', Mies constantly sought to express simultaneously both transparency and corporeality. The dichotomy revealed itself most sublimely in his attitude to glass, which he used in such a way as to allow it to change under light from the appearance of a reflective surface to the disappearance of the surface into pure transparency: on the one hand, the apparition of nothing, on the other, an evident need for support.

In this respect, the preliminary scheme for the Illinois Institute of Technology (IIT) campus in Chicago, prepared in 1939, two years after his arrival in the United States, is clearly as Suprematist in feeling as parts of the Barcelona Pavilion. As in the Reichsbank project, the

227    Mies van der Rohe, preliminary scheme for the Illinois Institute of Technology, Chicago, 1939.

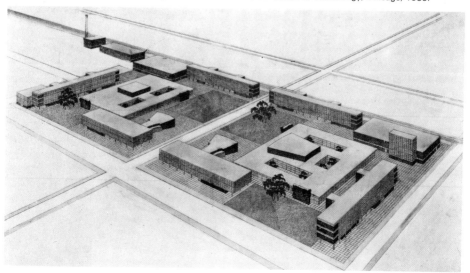

plan is disposed about a single axis of symmetry. All the structures are four storeys high and rendered as pure prisms, faced in graph-paper curtain walls, their surfaces animated by skyscape reflections. These walls are shown sliding behind occasional clumps of trees, eliding into projecting ivy-clad brick planes, poised on the edge of their stereometric masses. Apart from a Neo-Classical insistence on the visual reinforcement of corners with panels of brickwork, the effect is close to the Suprematist aesthetic of Ivan Leonidov, in particular to his Culture Park project of 1930.

At this point, Mies appears to be struggling with the generic relation of column to wall, particularly where the wall in question is largely of glass. The implicit solution in the first IIT proposal (as in the Reichsbank project) is to set the columns back from the glass face, but in the final 1940 version the columns are integrated into the wall. This development becomes explicit in the first building for the campus. The articulation of the column system in conjunction with the glazed plane becomes increasingly idealized and monumental with each successive structure.

This progressive idealization depended on the replacement of Mies's generic cruciform column section of the early 1930s by the standard American I-beam. The asymmetrical pin-wheeling plans of the Barcelona Pavilion and the Tugendhat House at Brno demanded a non-directional column form, similar to the point supports that Mies used in his Berlin Building Exhibition house of 1931. By contrast, his preference from the Reichsbank onwards for a single axis of symmetry favoured the articulation of façades in terms of the directional axis of the I-beam. The development of his work at IIT, from the Minerals and Metals Research Building and the Library of 1942 to the Alumni Memorial Hall of 1945, is towards the idealization of the I-beam column, culminating in the square, concrete-clad steel columns of the Alumni Memorial Hall.

With the Library and the Alumni Memorial Hall, Mies was on the threshold of the building typology and structural syntax of his late career. At the same time, in the IIT Library he first projected a work whose monumentality

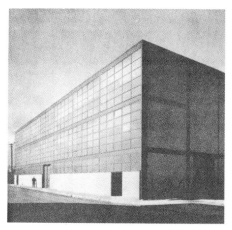

228   Mies van der Rohe, Minerals and Metals Research Building, IIT, Chicago, 1942.

depended on its great size — a gargantuanism that has obsessed Chicago architectural practice ever since (see the recent work by the leading designers of Skidmore, Owings and Merrill, and C.F. Murphy). Here Mies audaciously proposed a clear structural span of 20 metres (66 feet) wide, with glass panels measuring 5.5 x 3.7 metres (18 x 12 feet) and a single triple-height volume 91 x 61 metres (300 x 200 feet) in plan, broken only by a floor-to-floor book stack, an enclosed court and a suspended mezzanine. Where the Library anticipated Mies's later single-storey clear-span type (first clearly formulated in his drive-in restaurant project of 1946), the Alumni Memorial Hall anticipated his typical multi-storey slab, in which the glazing, the mullions and the structure of the external wall combine to form an articulated façade. Where the IIT Library led, by way of the drive-in restaurant, to Mies's project for the Mannheim Theatre of 1953 — a technological monument par excellence consisting of a large flat roof measuring 162 x 81 metres (530 x 266 feet) suspended from seven steel trusses — the detailing of the Alumni Hall was the formulation of the language that Mies would soon use for the realization of 860 Lake Shore Drive.

The Lake Shore Drive apartments, under construction between 1948 and 1951, took the kitchen, bathrooms and access cores of Mies's

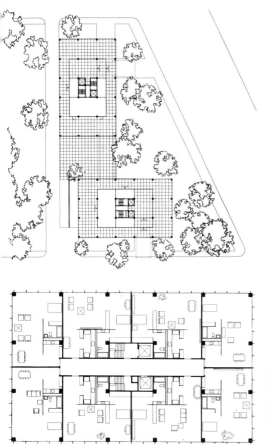

The structural frame and its glass infill become architecturally fused, each losing a part of its particular identity in establishing the new architectural reality. The mullion has acted as a kind of catalyst for this change. The columns and mullion dimensions determine window widths. The two central windows (in each structural bay) are, therefore, wider than those adjacent to the column. These variants produce visual cadences of expanding and contracting intervals; column – narrow window – wide window, then reversing – wide window, narrow window – column, and so on, of an extraordinarily subtle richness. And to this is added the alternating opacity of the steel and reflectivity of the glass caused by the blinker quality of the mullions *en masse*.

In short, more than in any other work by Mies, the wall is rendered here – after Semper's prescription – as a woven fabric; a subtle integration of structure with fenestration that displays the same capacity as load-bearing masonry for limiting any extension of the space.

230 Mies van der Rohe, 860 Lake Shore Drive, Chicago, 1948–51.

229 Mies van der Rohe, 860 Lake Shore Drive, Chicago, 1948–51. Ground plan of towers and typical floor plan.

1927 Weissenhofsiedlung apartments and compacted them about two elevators in the middle of a thick slab. In this arrangement one gained access, through a service zone comprising kitchens and bathrooms, to a continuous living space running around the perimeter that could be subdivided according to variations in unit size and type. The initial wall/column articulations of the Alumni Hall were here elaborated into a modulated façade which was subtly related to the Suprematist, pinwheeling juxtaposition of the two blocks. Of this relationship Peter Carter has written:

234

This restriction may well have contributed, as Colin Rowe has suggested, to Mies's preoccupation with the creation of an unobstructed clear-span single-storey, unitary volume. This, Mies's other generic type, was to absorb him from the IIT Library onwards. As an archetypal form it was inherently public, yet it did not always accommodate a public programme. In domestic terms the type was first crystallized in the house designed in 1946 for Dr Edith Farnsworth, realized four years later at Plano, Illinois. Here a 23 x 9-metre (77 x 29-foot) single-volume house was sandwiched, as it were, between floor and roof slabs and raised some 1.5 metres (5 feet) above the ground on exterior I-columns set 6.7 metres (22 feet) apart. The resultant box was enclosed by a plate-glass skin, the apotheosis of Mies's phrase *beinahe nichts*, 'almost nothing'.

An evident asymmetry deriving in part from Suprematism was here beautifully balanced by the symmetry of the *Schinkelschüler* tradition. Thus the entry platform slid past the base of the house as a flat plane carried on six columns in opposition to a prismatic volume carried on eight — the asymmetry being evident in the overlapping of two symmetrical elements. For all its limited size, this was the elevation of a house to the status of a monument. The podium, the steps, the terrace and the floor itself were all face in travertine. The exposed steel work was sprayed white after having been ground down to remove all the welds. The windows were curtained in natural off-white shantung silk. One is hardly surprised to learn that the inordinate cost of the house led to a rupture between Mies and Dr Farnsworth. Now the weekend residence of a distant millionaire, it stands appropriately furnished but nonetheless largely unoccupied; like some well maintained but otherwise forgotten Shinto shrine.

At a public level Mies's single-span volume found its most 'Classical' realization in IIT's Crown Hall, built in 1952–56, and its most monumental expression in the convention hall for Chicago, projected in 1953. Where the former took Mies away from the Suprematism of his early American career (his designs of

231   Mies van der Rohe, Farnsworth House, Fox River, Plano, Ill., 1946–50.

232 Mies van der Rohe, Crown Hall, IIT, Chicago, 1952–56.

1939–50), the latter must still be regarded as his final Suprematist statement. Unbuilt, this 18-metre (60-foot) high, marble-panelled, lattice-braced, steel frame structure, elevated 6 metres (20 feet) above the ground, would have enclosed an assembly hall roofed by a space-frame with the colossal clear span of 220 metres (720 feet).

Crown Hall, designed at about the same time as the Mannheim Theatre, was a decisive return to the tradition of Schinkel and in particular to Schinkel's Altes Museum in Berlin, always admired by Mies. This *Schinkelschüler* type-form is generally evident as an organizing paradigm throughout Mies's work of the late 1960s, from the Bacardi Building in Mexico City (1963) to the School of Social Service Administration at the University of Chicago (1965). Needless to say, the programme could not always be appropriately accommodated within such a simple paradigm. Thus, where the School of Social Services with its centralized library to the rear permitted a more or less direct transposition of the portico entry and rotunda of the Altes Museum, Crown Hall could but barely reflect these constituent elements and then only at the expense of the programme.

Colin Rowe has argued that the whole evolution of the International Style in architecture was profoundly affected by a conceptual schism between centripetal and centrifugal space, the one stemming from Palladianism and the other ultimately deriving from the anti-monumentality of Wright's extension of the English Free Style plan. This schism, Rowe claims, is demonstrated in Crown Hall (significantly enough, the IIT school of architecture), where the 67 x 37-metre (220 x 120-foot) span glazed box does not afford an unequivocal reading of its centralized composition. As Rowe has written:

Like the characteristic Palladian composition, Crown Hall is a symmetrical and, probably, a mathematically regulated volume. But, unlike the characteristic Palladian composition, it is not a hierarchically ordered organization which projects its centralized theme vertically in the form of a pyramidal roof or dome. Unlike the Villa Rotonda, but like so many of the compositions of the Twenties, Crown Hall is provided with no effective central area within which the observer can stand and comprehend the whole . . . once inside, rather than any spatial climax, the building offers a central solid, not energetically stated, it is true, but still an isolated core around which the space travels laterally with the enclosing windows.

233 Schinkel's Altes Museum, Berlin, 1823–30 (above), and Mies van der Rohe's Crown Hall, Chicago, 1952–56.

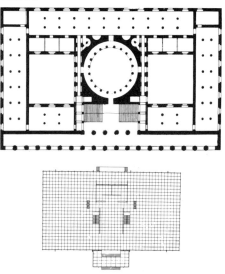

Also, the flat slab of the roof induces a certain outward pull and, for this reason, in spite of the centralizing activity of the entrance vestibule, the space still remains, though in very much simplified form, the rotary, peripheric organization of the Twenties, rather than the predominantly centralized composition of the true Palladian or Classical plan.

Mies's typical suppression of all that was programmatically incompatible with the monumental manifested itself most strikingly at Crown Hall, where the department of industrial design was banished to the basement to rest, literally and symbolically, beneath the grandeur of the department of architecture. Yet, despite the impositions of an *a priori* idealism, Mies was never grandiose and his structures were relatively inexpensive, particularly when they entailed repetitious cellular elements as found in multiple residential or office accommodation.

Mies's approach offered the publicity-conscious client an impeccable image of power and prestige. After the completion of 860 Lake Shore Drive (built for the developer Herbert Greenwald) in 1951, he began to work increasingly for the real-estate and institutional establishment, the final 'breakthrough' coming in 1958 when he was commissioned through the agency of Phyllis Lambert to design the 39-storey Seagram Building in New York. In this bronze and brown glass office tower, Mies once again achieved that Semperian interweaving of fenestration with structure. This time, however, unlike Lake Shore Drive, he created a frontalized axial composition facing a granite piazza, the slab itself being set back some 27 metres (90 feet) from the building line, as a compliment to the 1917 Racquet Club by McKim, Mead and White on the other side of Park Avenue. This concession on the part of the client enabled Mies to achieve his one and only monument in Manhattan, and to rival, in grandeur, the one New York structure that he had long since admired, the George Washington Bridge.

As director of the department of architecture at the Illinois Insitute of Technology from 1939 to 1959, Mies had ample opportunity to develop a 'school' of architecture in the broadest possible sense and to generate a culture of simple, logical building, amenable to refinement (*Baukunst*) and open in principle to the optimum utilization of industrial technique. Unfortunately, he could not transmit with equal force that *Schinkelschüler* sensibility which was second nature to him. And while the great strength of the school lay in the clarity of its principles, the followers of Mies, as recent events suggest, were by and large unable to grasp the delicacy of his sensibility, that feeling for the precise proportioning of profiles that alone guaranteed his mastery over form.

234 Mies van der Rohe and Johnson, Seagram Building, New York, 1958.

237

# The Eclipse of the New Deal: Buckminster Fuller, Philip Johnson and Louis Kahn 1934–64

Those, like Kahn, who show a marked individualism in a world in which team work is becoming widely accepted, who aim to build for eternity in a world of economy of consumption, find themselves in a certain sense beyond the contingencies of time; and it is from this position that their personalities are consolidated. Kahn's personality evokes a picture of the masterly welding together of coexistent elements in antithesis. While Kahn is classical in fact, in the stability and symmetry of his forms, he is romantic in his nostalgia for the Middle Ages. He earnestly applies the most advanced technological means, but this does not prevent him from using stone supporting pillars for the Adler House. He has gone beyond the schemes of functionalism in his distribution, but in many instances he utilizes functionalist aesthetics. He has a rationalist's cult of stereometry, which the thin casings and total transparency of his blocks tends to refute. He has mastered the vital concepts of the organic, but he does not share in its disturbing morphology.

Enzo Fratelli
*Zodiac* 8, 1960

The European economic and political crises of the 1930s and the social provisions of Roosevelt's New Deal brought to the United States both a refugee intelligentsia and extensive programmes for social welfare and reform. While the Museum of Modern Art and Harvard University were to play major roles in the cultural assimilation of this migration, the Federal Government provided the infrastructural basis for the numerous welfare works that were to be executed between Roosevelt's Housing Act of 1934 and the end of the Second World War. The most famous planning and settlement projects of the New Deal were the Tennessee Valley Authority and Clarence Stein's Greenbelt New Towns, the latter realized after 1936 under the auspices of the Federal Resettlement Administration. Unlike the remarkable dams, gantries and slipways built in the Tennessee Valley, Stein's Greenbelt settlements were not graced by works of architectural distinction. From this point of view finer results were obtained in the workers' villages financed over the same period by the Farm Security Administration, a typical example being the adobe farm community at Chandler, Arizona, built in 1937 to the designs of Vernon de Mars. An equally efficient and elegant housing standard was reached in other settlements financed by similar government agencies, including New Kensington village, Pennsylvania, built in 1940 to the designs of Walter Gropius and Marcel Breuer, and Channel Heights, San Pedro, Los Angeles, designed in 1943 by Richard Neutra. An inexplicably ungainly work built under similar auspices was

235  Tennessee Valley Authority architects and engineers, Norris Dam, 1933–37.

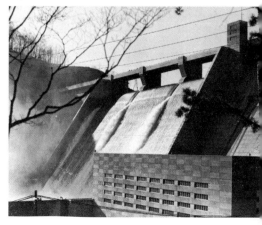

Carver Court Housing at Coatesville, Pennsylvania, designed in 1944 by George Howe, Oscar Stonorov and Louis Kahn. This work seems all the more surprising when one realizes that Kahn had already proven his ability while working for Alfred Kastner on the Jersey Homesteads at Hightstown, New Jersey, between 1935 and 1937.

Irrespective of their architectural merit, all of these works evinced the presence of a 'New Objectivity' in the United States. That this movement was hardly as self-conscious or as polemical as its European counterpart was due to the fact that a comparable ideological basis did not exist. The 'movement' had, in any event, to be more sensitive to the issue of popular acceptance and to this end its anti-monumentality stemmed directly from its use of native materials and from its response to the vagaries of topography and climate.

A unique and contentious figure within the American architectural avant garde during the New Deal, Richard Buckminster Fuller had adopted a recognizably 'objective' – not to say Constructivist – attitude as early as 1927, when he designed the first version of his free-standing Dymaxion House; the name being a neologism, signifying *dynamism plus efficiency*. Fuller, like the more extreme members of the Swiss ABC group, had no concern whatsoever for the idiosyncrasies of any given context and projected his house as though it were a prototype for serial production. Hexagonal in plan and sandwiched between two hollow decks, it was suspended and triangulated (on the wire wheel principle) from a central mast. In this form, it was advanced, like Fuller's even more eccentric Dymaxion automobile of 1933, as the one and only inevitable solution. Fuller, never at a loss for rhetoric, described this light-weight metal house in his *Shelter* magazine of May 1932 as a synthesis between the American skyscraper and the oriental pagoda. Ingeniously equipped with a hollow hexagonal mast containing all the necessary services, it was the first in a series of centralized structures which culminated in Fuller's much simpler geodesic dome, first adapted for domestic use on his own account at Carbondale, Illinois, in 1959. The rugged reductive ethic of the pioneering individualist is evident from the doggerel chorus to be sung to the tune of 'Home on the Range' that Fuller composed while teaching as a visitor at Yale University in the mid-1950s:

Roam home to a dome
Where Georgian and Gothic once stood
Now chemical bonds alone guard our blondes
And even the plumbing looks good.

Such a utilitarian and yet complacent attitude seems a far cry from the proposals that Fuller seriously made in 1932 for the conversion of empty skyscraper office structures (vacant as a result of the Depression) into emergency residential accommodation. Fuller claimed that by the end of the year ninety per cent of the people then still living in the city would be unable to pay taxes or to buy food. This, more than anything else, tends to confirm the affinity that then coincidentally existed between the concerns of the European Neue Sachlichkeit and the Structural Study Associates group – Simon Breines, Henry Churchill, Theodore Larsen and Knud Lönberg-Holm – Fuller's associates during his brief editorship of *Shelter* in 1932.

236 Fuller, prefabricated bathroom, patented 1938–40.

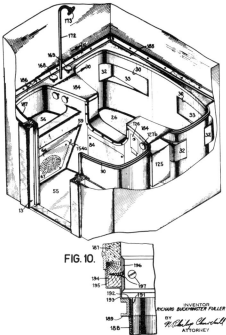

The year 1945 appears as the watershed between the socially committed ethos of the New Deal and an incipient impulse towards monumentality. This last seems to have emerged partly out of the demands of America's status as a world power and partly out of the cultural anxiety that attended the end of the Second World War. Two texts published in 1945 establish the climate of the period with some precision: they are *Built in U.S.A. 1932–1944*, edited by Elizabeth Mock, which accompanied an exhibition at the Museum of Modern Art, New York — in which over half the illustrations were devoted to the works of the New Deal — and *New Architecture and City Planning*, edited by Paul Zucker, which recorded the proceedings of a symposium conducted in the same year. This symposium was devoted to the growing need for monumental expression, a theme most elaborately formulated by Sigfried Giedion in his paper of 1944, *The Need for a New Monumentality*. Kahn himself had argued on the same occasion that

Monumentality is enigmatic. It cannot be intentionally created. Neither the finest material nor the most advanced technology need enter a work of monumental character for the same reason that the finest ink was not required to draw up the Magna Carta.

The issue emerged again in 1950 in the first number of *Perspecta – The Yale Architectural Journal*, founded by George Howe, wherein Henry Hope Reed argued that the New Deal had dealt a severe blow to the culture of affluence, and that the provisions arising out of the Depression had effectively inhibited any capacity for the monumental:

To be sure, the New Deal proved to be the greatest patron of the arts in that decade, but never on the basis of pomp and ceremony, or for reasons of national prestige or democratic grandeur. The government instead reached a charitable and philanthropic hand to the starving artist, not that of a magnificent and 'wasteful' patron. It is hardly surprising that architects and city planners were ripe for a message from across the waters about a new

style which banished 'waste', tolerated only the functional, and declared the house to be a machine for living, a fitting phrase for a technocratic era.

Although Reed concluded that the tools to create the monument had been lost, he was soon to be proven wrong, for America was about to enter on a spate of all but unprecedented monument-building. Intimations of this in the 1944 Zucker symposium were vindicated a few years later, in 1949, when Philip Johnson built his small but monumental Glass House at New Canaan, Connecticut. Although inspired by Mies van der Rohe's 1945 sketches for the Farnsworth House, this work wilfully departed from Mies's preoccupation with the expression of structural logic. That the Glass House already anticipated Johnson's later adaptation of the Miesian syntax to decorative ends is hinted at in his description of it written in 1950:

Many details of the house are adapted from Mies's work, especially the corner treatment and the relation of the column to the window frames. The use of standard steel sections to make a strong and at the same time decorative finish to the façade is typical of Mies's Chicago work. Perhaps if there is ever to be 'decoration' in our architecture it may come from the manipulation of stock structural elements such as these (may not Mannerism be next?).

Johnson's determination to obscure structure through surface manipulation was to characterize his work throughout the next decade. This approach, first fully broached in monumental terms in his Port Chester Synagogue, New York, of 1954, attained its fullest development in his New York State Theater in Lincoln Center, New York, and in his Klein Laboratory Tower built for Yale University at New Haven, both of which were complete for occupation by 1963.

While the Graduate School of Design at Harvard (under the direction of Gropius after 1963) helped to consolidate the anti-historicist and 'objective', Functionalist approach of the New Deal, the School of Architecture at Yale,

237, 238   Johnson, Glass House, New Canaan, Conn., 1949.

239   Kahn, Yale University Art Gallery, New Haven, Conn., 1950–54.

alistic' monument of the period was surely Edward Durrell Stone's U.S. Embassy built at New Delhi in 1957, a work whose level of decorative, not to say laboured, monumentality was only to be surpassed in respect of its authoritarian overtones by Eero Saarinen's far superior U.S. Embassy in London, completed in 1960.

The Yale Art Gallery, like Johnson's Glass House, was based on a subtle transposition of the late Miesian aesthetic. Yet where Mies had always given priority to the direct expression of structural frame, both Kahn and Johnson concealed the frame, at least externally, placing their particular emphasis on the monumentalization of what might be considered 'secondary' components, such as walls, floors and ceilings. By a similar token, where Mies always chose to emphasize the axiality of his composition, Kahn and Johnson masked the inherent symmetrical order of their work by suppressing the frame. Where Kahn used the palpable opacity of brick for this purpose, Johnson relied on the reflectivity of glass. He exploited its innate capacity, when set flush with the surface, to appear as a continuous membrane: to seem to be of the same metalled substance and formal order as the supporting metal frame. However, these two seminal works had more in common than their 'hermetic' attitude to surface. In both instances the main orthogonal volume was animated by a cylindrical form housing primary service elements: the major access stair in the case of the gallery, and the fireplace and bathroom in the case of the house. And while the schema of the Glass House — namely a circle in a rectangle — also served as the essential *parti* of Kahn's gallery, it was Kahn and not Johnson who was to go on to elaborate the notion of the cylinder as the *servant* and the rectangle as the *served* into the dialectic of a general architectural theory.

These early works of Johnson and Kahn created a kind of post-Miesian space: an asymmetrical architecture of 'almost nothing', which depended no longer on the manifestation of structure as frame, but rather on the manipulation of surface as the ultimate agent for the revelation of light, space and support.

under George Howe's leadership after 1950, played a formative role in the development of American post-war monumentality. Howe's own professional career had certainly been as varied as Gropius's, ranging from the arch conservatism of his country house practice in Philadelphia to the avant-garde Functionalism of his brief partnership in 1929 with William Lescaze. Howe championed the cause of monumentality not only through his founding of *Perspecta*, but also through his influence on the selection of architects for Yale's expansion programme which began in the early 1950s. Indeed, when Reed's article appeared in *Perspecta* in 1950, Louis Kahn had already been selected to design the Yale Art Gallery.

With the completion of the art gallery in 1954, Kahn established American post-war monumentality as a cultural force in its own right. He did so with a building that was hardly to be compared to the vulgar rhetoric generally attained by American official architecture throughout the 1950s. A typical 'imperi-

Thus the space of Kahn's art gallery was as much determined by the concrete tetrahedral space-frame that constituted its floors as it was by the regular grid of rectangular columns that divided its internal volume into four basic sections. As Reyner Banham remarked:

> The exact equipartition of the plan contributes little to its functional organization or the visual experience of the visitor. In other words, no significant architectural promenade arose out of the rhythm of the structural grid or at least not one that in any way transcended the sporadic and ever-changing disposition of the gallery partitions.

From the early 1950s on, first Johnson and then Kahn came to be increasingly concerned with reactivating the formal systems of the past. Johnson's own 'historicism' — evident in the Neo-Classical qualities of the Glass House — came directly from his understanding of late Mies and, again after Mies, something of Schinkel's Romantic Classicism. The beginning of Kahn's concern with the past is more difficult to establish. Beaux-Arts trained in Philadelphia under Paul Cret but close in the late 1930s and 1940s to the radicalism of men like Buckminster Fuller and Frederick Kiesler, Kahn was to return after the New Deal to a remote historical tradition, through his preoccupation with the creation of hierarchic order out of heavy structural form. Certainly Kahn's whole approach changed with his project for the Trenton Jewish Community Centre of 1954, made some two years after he had returned from his sabbatical at the American Academy in Rome.

By the mid-1950s the points of reference were becoming more complex, for while Johnson had shifted his attention from Schinkel to Soane, simultaneously keeping his eye fixed on the totally independent Baroque forays then being made in Brasilia by Oscar Niemeyer, Kahn had begun to be preoccupied with the concept of an architectural totality, whose ultimate historical reference would prove Islamic rather than Western.

At this juncture in Kahn's career one encounters one of the central paradoxes in the work and influence of Buckminster Fuller. For

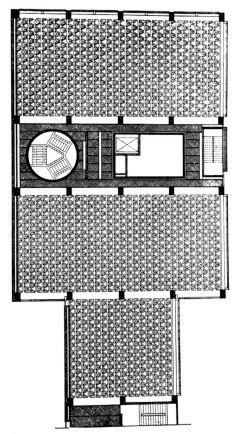

240   Kahn, Yale University Art Gallery, New Haven, Conn., 1950–54. Floor plan with diagrid ceiling reflected.

whereas Fuller's contribution was posited by both himself and his followers as the only truly functionalist approach of the age, it has since become evident that his geodesic structural systems should be regarded as evoking through their universal geometry an attitude to both form and life that is fundamentally mystical. It is clear from Kahn's subsequent career that this side of Fuller's thought exercised a strong hold over his development, and never more so than during the period of his association with Ann Tyng, who was an ardent follower of the Fuller line. The various versions of Kahn's multi-storey triangulated city hall for

Philadelphia, designed in association with Tyng between 1952 and 1957, bracket the period during which he was most directly under Fuller's influence. The basic concept of a geodesic skyscraper, stabilized by tetrahedronal concrete floors — ' a vertical truss against the wind' — enabled Kahn to return to an architectural intention that would have been appreciated by Viollet-le-Duc. This much is evident from one of the clearest statements of intent that he ever produced:

In Gothic times, architects built in solid stones. Now we can build with hollow stones. The spaces defined by the members of a structure are as important as the members. These spaces range in scale from the voids of an insulating panel, voids for air, lighting and heat to circulate, to spaces big enough to walk through and live in. The desire to express voids positively in the design of a structure is evidenced by the growing interest and work in the development of space-frames. The forms being experimented with come from a closer knowledge of nature and the outgrowth of the constant search for order. Design habits leading to the concealment of structure have no place in this implied order. Such habits retard the development of an art. I believe that in architecture, as in all art, the artist instinctively keeps the marks which

reveal how a thing was done. The feeling that our present-day architecture needs embellishment stems in part from our tendency to fair joints out of sight, to conceal how parts are put together. Structures should be devised which can harbour the mechanical needs of rooms and spaces. . . . If we were to train ourselves to draw as we build, from the bottom up, when we do, stopping our pencil to make a mark at the joints of pouring or erecting, ornament would grow out of our love for the expression of method. It would follow that pasting over the construction of light and acoustical material, the burying of tortured unwanted ducts, conduits and pipe lines would become intolerable. The desire to express how it is done would filter through the entire society of building, to architect, engineer, builder and draftsman.

The fundamental themes of Kahn's subsequent career are all basically outlined in this remarkable passage, from the notion of conceptually transposing solid and void — see the reference to hollow stones — to the idea of explicitly integrating mechanical systems with the structure and the important corollary that the universal ordering principle (namely 'what the building wants to be') could only make itself manifest through the revelation of the constructional process.

The integrated development of these principles, from the Yale Art Gallery to the Richards Laboratories built for the University of Pennsylvania between 1957 and 1964, led to the first phase of Kahn's postponed maturity. In both works Kahn used a method and mode of expression where the empirical details of the programme have little or no impact on the overall form. It was in fact a case of discrete function having to accommodate itself — as in the past — to the form, but only insofar as the form itself had been invented from a profound understanding of the overall task in the first place. In the case of the Richards Laboratories, the problematic aspect of Kahn's method lay exactly in this issue, as to whether or not the overall form was typologically justified. The subsequent difficulties encountered in using the building would suggest that it was not. We

241   Kahn and Tyng, project for Philadelphia City Hall, 1952–57. Model.

seem to be confronted here with the traditional American impulse to idealize the work place — to monumentalize the space of process — an intention which is as evident in the Richards Laboratories as it is in Johnson's Klein Tower. The precedent for all this would seem, not surprisingly, to be Wright, first in his Larkin Building at Buffalo of 1904 and then in his complex for Johnson Wax, built at Racine in Wisconsin, 1936–39. It is an appropriate irony, to say the least, that both Kahn and Johnson should come to debate in *Perspecta 2* (1953) the validity of Wright's later addition to his Racine complex, namely the laboratory tower built there in 1946. With marked indifference to the status of the tower as it might be determined by the programme in relation to the society, Kahn remarked:

It has to do with the full complexity of making architecture work in the psychological sense. It works because it is so motivated. It fills the desires and the needs. And so the tower should work, as psychological satisfaction.

Along more aesthetic lines and with greater flamboyance, Johnson declared his own indifference to the issue of function:

It was the terrific problem of a man who wants a beautiful building but the only thing he has to build is a laboratory. Wright puts it into a tower. It doesn't work; it doesn't have to work. Wright had that shape conceived long before he knew what was going into it. I claim that is where architecture starts, with the concept.

It is a measure of Kahn's achievement and of his continuing influence today that the 'concept' was exactly where architecture always started for him, even if he was sufficiently flexible to allow the initial 'Form' (Kahn's term for 'type') to be modified by the exigencies of the programme. For him, building remained a spiritual act, and it is hardly an accident that his best work was reserved for religious or extremely honorific structures. In many subsequent commissions he ascribed a highly spiritual connotation to the programme and never more so than in the case of the research centre that he designed for Dr Jonas Salk, at La Jolla, California, between 1959 and 1965. In this instance, the separation of the whole complex into *working*, *meeting* and *living* sectors seems to have released Kahn from the compulsive need to reduce the laboratory space to an ideal form. The final version of the Salk Laboratories brought him to accept a solution in which the services were as 'repressed' or concealed as in any office building by Mies van der Rohe. Kahn's provision of a whole full-height service floor under each laboratory — a provision which today is fully utilized — yielded a much more flexible space than that generally achieved at Philadelphia. The unbuilt Salk meeting complex was also the first occasion on which Kahn had a chance to develop his anti-glare concept of setting a 'building within a building', a notion which he had first broached at a conceptual level in his 1959 sketches for the American Consulate at Luanda, Angola. This idea, destined to remain

242   Kahn, A.N. Richards Laboratories, University of Pennsylvania, Philadelphia, 1957–61. Third-floor plan.

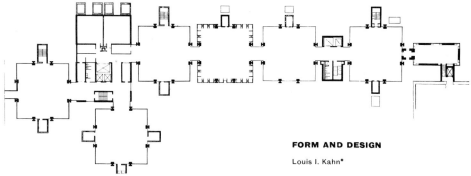

**FORM AND DESIGN**

Louis I. Kahn*

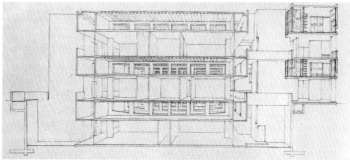

243 Kahn, Salk Institute of Biological Studies, La Jolla, Calif., 1959–65. Section through laboratory wing.

244 Kahn, 'dock, complex projected for Philadelphia, 1956, comprising a multi-storey car park surrounded by apartment and office buildings.

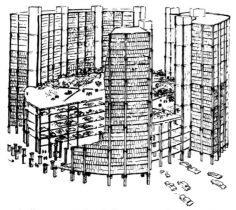

unbuilt even at La Jolla, was to become the main theme of his magnificent National Assembly Building, under construction at Dacca in East Pakistan (now Bangladesh) from 1965 to 1974.

Kahn's rejection of a simple-minded if socially committed functionalism in favour of an architecture capable of transcending utility led him to postulate a parallel approach to urban form. Once again this shift reflected his own development, in which he progressed from projecting the Ville Radieuse onto the centre of Philadelphia — in his so-called Rational City studies of 1939–48 — to postulating, in his maturity, the need to make an explicit distinction between the architecture of the 'viaduct' and building at a human scale. This was perhaps never more dramatically expressed than in his plan for midtown Philadelphia of 1956, where he attempted to press

the forms of Piranesi's Rome of 1762 into the service of the modern city. Yet for all the rational poetry of this proposition, and the ingenuity of his subtly rearranged traffic patterns (his distinction for instance between the expressways as 'rivers' and the 'stop-go' traffic-light-controlled streets as 'canals'), Kahn's midtown planning proposals remained paradoxically unspecific when it came to imagining the precise relations that should obtain between the pedestrian and the automobile. Kahn, conscious of the profound antipathy between the automobile and the city and of the fatal link between consumerism, the suburban shopping centre and the decline of the urban core (a link that stemmed incidentally from the combined effects of the post-war federal highway subsidy and the mortgage provisions of the G.I. Bill), was no more capable than any other architect of conceiving a satisfactory interchange between the human scale and the scale of the car. His Piranesian 'dock' proposal of 1956, comprising a six-storey cylindrical silo housing 1,500 cars and surrounded on its perimeter by eighteen-storey blocks, was as deprived as any other megastructure of the period of the necessary elements with which to establish a human scale at its base. The limits of Kahn's profound historicism were never more poignant than in his likening of his Philadelphia midtown plan to Carcassonne. It was surely a vain utopian hope to argue, as he did, that the ordering of movement within a city would of necessity assure its defence against destruction by the automobile.

# Part 3
## Critical assessment and extension into the present 1925–84

245  Foster Associates, Willis-Faber & Dumas Building, Ipswich, 1974 (see pp. 301–3).

# Chapter 1
# The International Style:
# theme and variations 1925-65

The effect of mass, of static solidity, hitherto the prime quality of architecture, has all but disappeared; in its place there is an effect of volume, or more accurately, of plane surfaces bounding a volume. The prime architectural symbol is no longer the dense brick, but the open box. Indeed, the great majority of buildings are in reality, as well as in effect, mere planes surrounding a volume. With skeleton construction enveloped only by a protective screen, the architect can hardly avoid achieving this effect of surface, of volume, unless in deference to traditional design in terms of mass he goes out of his way to obtain the contrary effect.

Henry-Russell Hitchcock and Philip Johnson
*The International Style*, 1932 (exhibition
catalogue, Museum of Modern Art,
New York)

In many respects, the International Style was little more than a convenient phrase denoting a cubistic mode of architecture which had spread throughout the developed world by the time of the Second World War. Its apparent homogeneity was deceptive, since its stripped planar form was subtly inflected so as to respond to different climatic and cultural conditions. Unlike the Neo-Classical manner of the Western world in the late 18th century, the International Style never became truly universal. Nonetheless, it implied a universality of approach which generally favoured light-weight technique, synthetic modern materials and standard modular parts so as to facilitate fabrication and erection. It tended as a general rule towards the hypothetical flexibility of the free plan, and to this end it preferred skeleton frame construction to masonry. This predisposition became formalistic where specified conditions, be they climatic, cultural or economic, could not support the application of advanced light-weight technology. Le Corbusier's ideal villas of the late 1920s anticipated such formalism inasmuch as they masqueraded as white, homogeneous, machine-made forms, whereas they were in fact built of rendered concrete block-work held in place by a reinforced-concrete frame.

Dr Philip Lovell's Health House, built in Los Angeles in 1927 to the designs of the Austrian émigré architect Richard Neutra, may be regarded as the apotheosis of the International Style, its architectural expression deriving directly from a skeleton steel frame, clad in a light-weight synthetic skin. Set on a bluff overlooking a romantic, half-wild parkscape, its asymmetrical composition of dramatically suspended floors was reminiscent of Wright's West Coast block-house style of the 1920s, and this formal similarity already suggests the catholic sources from which the supposed

246  Neutra, Lovell Health House, Griffith Park, Los Angeles, 1927.

homogeneity of the International Style initially derived.

Almost incidentally, the open-plan form of the house was an appropriate reflection of Lovell's expansive personality and served to represent his callisthenic lifestyle. As David Gebhard suggests in his study of Neutra's compatriot and early partner Rudolph Schindler (who had realized a house at Newport Beach

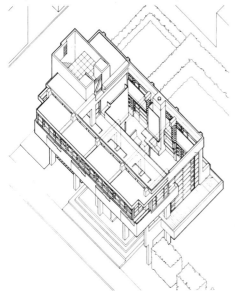

247 Schindler, Lovell Beach House, Newport Beach, Calif., 1925–26.

248 Rudolf Schindler (right) with Richard and Dione Neutra and their son, at Schindler's Kings Rd house (1921–22), Los Angeles, 1928.

for Lovell just one year before), Lovell could have been regarded as embodying the athletic and progressive attributes of the International Style in his own persona:

Dr Lovell was a characteristic southern California product. It is doubtful whether his career could have been repeated anywhere else. Through his *Los Angeles Times* column, 'Care of the Body', and through 'Dr Lovell's Physical Culture Center', he had an influence which extended far beyond the physical care of the body. He was, and he wished to be considered, progressive, whether in physical culture, permissive education, or architecture.

The ideology of Lovell and its direct expression in the Health House exercised a decisive influence over the rest of Neutra's career. From now on his work was at its best where the building programme could be interpreted as making a direct contribution to the psycho-physiological wellbeing of its occupants. The central theme of both Neutra's work and his writings was the beneficial impact of a well-designed environment upon the general health of the human nervous system. And while his so-called 'bio-realism' rested largely on unproven arguments linking architectural form to overall health, it is difficult to discredit the extraordinary sensitivity and supra-functional attitude that coloured his whole approach. Nothing could be further removed from the exclusively formal motivations attributed to the International Style by Hitchcock and Johnson than the overall biological concerns addressed by Neutra in his book *Survival Through Design* (1954), where he wrote:

It has become imperative that in designing our physical environment we should consciously raise the fundamental question of survival in the broadest sense of the term. Any design that impairs or imposes excessive strain on the natural human equipment should be eliminated or modified in accordance with the requirements of our nervous, and more gradually, our total physiological functioning.

Thus, the primary concern for Schindler and Neutra alike — both of whom had served their American apprenticeships with Wright — was

249

not abstract form as such, but rather the modulation of sun and light and the sensitive articulation of the screens of plants between the building and its general context. This ambient hedonism was never more subtly expressed than in the Sachs Apartments, Los Angeles, built to Schindler's design in 1929, or in Neutra's second masterwork, his Kaufmann Desert House, built at Palm Springs, California, in 1946–47.

For Alfred Roth, practising in Zürich throughout the 1930s, the essential touchstone of the International Style was a sensitive and strictly doctrinaire approach to the creation of built form. In his remarkable anthology of 1940, *The New Architecture*, he attempted to show that the Neue Sachlichkeit was at its best where neither advanced technique nor the free-plan was allowed to become an end in itself. A well-formulated programme and a concern for the environmental impact of detailing seem to have been more highly valued by Roth than the achievement of spectacular solutions in either spatial or technical terms. Roth thus gave as much space to traditional techniques, such as load-bearing masonry, as to advanced systems of frame construction in timber and steel. And while the latter included Neutra's completely straightforward but beautifully detailed open-air school in Los Angeles of 1934, the former ranged from Vernon de Mars's two-storey adobe terrace housing built in New Mexico in 1939 to the 1932 Neubühl Siedlung built in Zürich to the designs of Roth's compatriots Max Haefeli, Carl Hubacher, Rudolf Steiger, Werner Moser, Paul Artaria and Hans Schmidt. While meeting the non-rhetorical (anti-monumental), social and technical criteria of the ABC group, by whose members ir was largely designed, the Neubühl Estate was able to humanize the rigorous *Zeilenbau* approach of the Neue Sachlichkeit, not only through the stepped inflection of the row house unit over a sloping site, but also through the delicacy of its landscaping.

In featuring other equally restrained but elegant works, such as the Bad-Allenmoos swimming facility in Zürich by Werner Moser of 1935 or Roth's own Doldertal apartments, built for Sigfried Giedion in Zürich in 1936 to designs made with Marcel Breuer and his cousin Emil Roth, *The New Architecture* proclaimed the maturity of the Swiss Modern Movement. But despite its decided bias in favour of the work of CIAM members, Roth's anthology was just as cosmopolitan as *The International Style*, featuring works from Czechoslovakia, England, Finland, France, Holland, Italy and Sweden and thereby acknowl-

249  Neutra, Kaufmann Desert House, Palm Springs, Calif., 1946–47.

250  Haefeli, Hubacher, Steiger, Moser, Artaria and Schmidt, Neubühl Siedlung, Zürich, 1932. Site plan (sloping down from bottom to top) and stepped elevations.

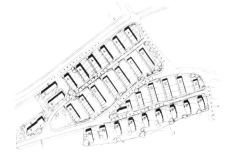

edging the establishment of the New Architecture (Roth's own term) in all these countries by the late 1930s. France was represented by two works: by the Perretesque open-air school built at Suresnes outside Paris to the design of Beaudouin and Lods, and by Le Corbusier's proto-Brutalist rubble-walled and timber-roofed house built at Mathes in 1935. Holland was represented by the work of the Opbouw group (the Dutch wing of CIAM), most notably by the practices of Brinkman and Van der Vlugt, and Van Tijen and Maaskant. Britain was accounted for in the singular masterwork of the engineer Owen Williams, the famous Boots Pharmaceutical Plant, built at Beeston in 1932. Williams was an outsider in the whole anthology since he was neither an architect nor a member of CIAM. Nonetheless, his reinforced-concrete and glass factory rivalled the brilliance of Brinkman and Van der Vlugt's Van Nelle packing plant, built outside Rotterdam in 1929. Williams's audacious use of giant mushroom columns, supporting bays up to $9.75 \times 11$ metres ($31 \times 36$ feet) in plan, together with the ingenious use of $45\degree$ clipped set-backs in the containing curtain wall, gave to this four-storey industrial shed a sculptural form of remarkable precision and energy.

The one country which has always been inadequately represented in any account of the International Style is Czechoslovakia, and an adequate history of the Czechoslovakian Functionalist movement has yet to be written. Roth's anthology did include the insurance offices built in Prague in 1934 to the designs of J. Havlíček and K. Honzík, and *The International Style* featured Otto Eisler's 'double-house' of 1926 and Bohuslav Fuchs's 'formalist' exhibition pavilion of 1929, both built in Brno. Above all they showed Ludvik Kysela's eight-storey Bata shoe store in Prague, built in 1929 and faced entirely in plate glass. Hitchcock and Johnson failed, however, to include such brilliant figures as Jaromir Krejcar, although admittedly his most spectacular work, his Czechoslovakian pavilion for the 1937 Paris World Exhibition, had yet to come. Perhaps most serious of all, they failed to mention the catalytic role played by the critic Karel Teige, whose Devenstil group was the driving

251   Williams, Boots Pharmaceutical Plant, Beeston, Notts., 1932.

252   Kysela, Bata Shoe Store, Prague, 1929.

253 Lubetkin and Tecton, Highpoint 1, Highgate, London, 1935.

force behind the Czechoslovakian left-wing Functionalist movement.

As in the United States, where the International Style was first practised by Viennese and Swiss émigrés, in England it had its origin in the work of outsiders. First and foremost was Peter Behrens's house for W.J. Bassett-Lowke, New Ways, built at Northampton in 1926. Then came Amyas Connell's house, High and Over, built at Amersham in 1930 for the archaeologist Bernard Ashmole, Connell coming from New Zealand in the late 1920s and soon after founding the London firm of Connell, Ward and Lucas. By far the most influential émigré to enter England at this moment was the Russian architect Berthold Lubetkin, whose impact on the development of modern architecture in England has never been adequately appreciated. Lubetkin, who came from a modest but brilliant career in Paris, brought to Tecton, the firm that he founded in 1932, a capacity for logical organization which has rarely graced English architecture. His 1935 block of flats in Highgate, London, Highpoint 1, remains a masterpiece even by the standards of today, its internal layout and disposition on an awkward site being a model of both formal and functional order. Despite the success of their subsequent work for the London and Whipsnade Zoos, Lubetkin and his Tecton team — Chitty, Drake, Dugdale, Harding and Lasdun — never attained this level again. Their Highpoint

2 block, built in 1938, already shows a decided mannerist reaction. One is left to speculate on the extent to which Lubetkin, as an architect of anarcho-socialist persuasion, had become sensitive to Soviet Social Realism, for certainly his essays on Soviet architecture written in the 1950s reveal a sympathy in this direction. The shift in expression between Highpoint 1 and Highpoint 2 was noted at the time, and the ensuing discussion established the ground rules for the ideological struggles of the 1950s. Their central issue, that of the primacy of the formal concept in architecture and the ultimate significance of built form, was touched on by Anthony Cox in 1938 when he wrote of Highpoint 2:

Highpoint 1 stands on tiptoe and spreads its wings; Highpoint 2 sits back on its haunches like Buddha. That this effect is deliberate, Tecton themselves would probably be the first to admit; one has the feeling that a *form* has been imposed on the rooms (which is an altogether different thing from giving the *rooms* form). It is as if, during the three years that separate the buildings, rigid conclusions had been reached as to what is formally necessary in architecture. The important point isn't whether or not one personally likes these formal conclusions, but whether one thinks that any such rigid conclusions are expedient. . . . The intellectual approach which has produced what we know as modern architecture is fundamentally a functionalist approach. I take it that most of us do not need to argue about that. Functionalism is a rotten name for the antithesis of formalism, because it carries with it dehumanized ideas which nobody wishes to defend — but interpreted in a wide sense, I think the word conveys the method of work underlying this movement. . . . My contention is that the recent work of Tecton shows a deviation from this approach. It is more than a deviation of appearance; it implies a deviation of aim. It is more than an adjustment within legitimate limits; it is prepared to set certain formal values above the use values, and marks the re-emergence of the *idea* as a motive force.

Preoccupied with the need to create a generally accessible modern architecture, Tecton's work after 1938 seems to have been determined by a conscious attempt to assimilate the rhetorical tradition of the Baroque to the rigours of a cubist syntax. The critical acceptance of Tecton's manneristic neo-Corbusian style, as exemplified by their Finsbury Health Centre, London, of 1938, gave Lubetkin a position of ascendance in the British scene immediately after the war, and the ten-year period following 1945 was effectively dominated by the language invented by Lubetkin and his colleagues in the previous decade. The Royal Festival Hall, to take one of the most prominent examples, designed in 1950 by a team including Leslie Martin, Robert Matthew and Peter Moro, was obviously indebted to Lubetkin throughout, as was the work of the young ex-Tecton partnership of Lindsay Drake and Denys Lasdun, whose Bishop's Bridge housing, built in Paddington, London, in 1953, extended Lubetkin's façadism to indulge in a crude masking of reality, with syncopated fretwork façades and appliqué columns.

MARS (Modern Architectural Research Group), the English wing of CIAM, was founded in 1932, on the initiative of the Canadian émigré Wells Coates, who represented MARS at the 1933 Congress dedicated to the theme of 'The Functional City'. While the MARS group possessed, at least initially, the necessary élan to attract the more avant-garde members of the British profession — including Connell, Ward and Lucas, Lubetkin, E. Maxwell Fry and the historian/critic P. Morton Shand — its sole achievement aside from its 'New Architecture' Exhibition staged in the Burlington Galleries in 1938 was its brilliant, if highly utopian, plan for London, drawn up in the early 1940s under the direction of the German architect Arthur Korn and the Viennese engineer Felix Samuely. The MARS group naively hoped for a future which, in the words of Coates, 'must be planned, rather than a past which must be patched up'; yet, unlike Tecton, it was incapable of formulating a truly progressive methodology for the organization of this future. Lubetkin seems to have been the first to sense this lack of orientation, and he abandoned MARS at the end of 1936 to become affiliated with the left-wing ATO (Archi-

tects' and Technicians' Organization), which up to the early 1950s was to concern itself exclusively with the problem of working-class housing.

A parallel polemical movement developed in Spain after 1930 under the leadership of the socialist architects José Luis Sert and Garcia Mercadal. Initiated in 1929 as a Catalan cultural movement, it was organized on a national basis, as the Spanish wing of CIAM, under the abbreviation GATEPAC (Grupo de Arquitectos y Técnicos Españoles para el Progreso de la Arquitectura Contemporánea). Its membership included important figures such as Sixte Yllescas, Germa Rodríguez Arias and Torres Clave. Before the Spanish Civil War, in the space of some eight years, these men produced three major theoretical studies, including the Maciá Plan for Barcelona, designed in collaboration with Le Corbusier in 1933. This remarkable low-rise residential project achieved the exceedingly high density of 1,000 persons per hectare (400 per acre), without exceeding two storeys. The most significant realization of GATEPAC was the seven-storey Casa-Bloc communal dwelling, including duplexes, a library, a crèche, a kindergarten and a swimming pool — a type-form that was clearly derived from the *redent* prototype of Le Corbusier's Ville Contemporaine.

The last significant gesture of the Spanish Modern Movement was made under the aegis of the doomed Second Republic, in the form of Sert's Spanish Pavilion designed for the Paris Exhibition of 1937. This pavilion was the occasion for the first showing of Picasso's *Guernica* which commemorated the aerial bombardment of this Basque town earlier in the same year. Commissioned by the Republican government, as a monument to the dead of Guernica, this work was intended as a solemn rebuke to the international betrayal of the Republican cause.

After the Hitchcock and Johnson exhibition of 1932 the International Style expanded outside Europe and North America and began to emerge in areas as far flung as South Africa, South America and Japan. The pioneering South African movement, lasting from 1929 to 1942, was a special case since Le Corbusier

254 Sert, Spanish Pavilion, World Exhibition, Paris, 1937, showing Picasso's *Guernica*.

associated himself with it directly by dedicating the second edition of his first *Oeuvre complète* to Rex Martienssen and his Transvaal Group. He opened his dedicatory letter of 1936 with the words:

It is a very moving experience to turn over the pages of your *South African Architectural Record*. Firstly, because one is amazed to find something so vital emanating from a distant point in Africa which lies far beyond the equatorial forests, but yet more because one can discover so much of youth's faith in it, such solicitude for architecture, and so fervent a desire to attain a cosmic philosophy.

By this date a close rapport had already been established between Le Corbusier and the Transvaal Group, with Le Corbusier contributing a special article to the *South African Architectural Record* and men like Martienssen and Norman Hanson building houses in Johannesburg in an extremely sophisticated post-Corbusian style. By 1942, however, before the group could become the South African wing of CIAM, Martienssen had died and Hanson had begun to challenge the socio-economic validity of Le Corbusier's planning, arguing against the in-vacuo abstraction of his simplified urbanism.

In Brazil modern architecture had its origins in the mid-1920s partnership of Lúcio Costa and Gregori Warchavchik, an émigré Russian architect who had been influenced by Futurism during his studies in Rome and who was responsible for the first cubistic houses in Brazil. With the revolution headed by Getúlio Vargas in 1930 and the appointment of Costa as head of the School of Fine Arts, modern architecture came to be welcomed in Brazil as a matter of national policy. In 1936 Le Corbusier had a direct impact on South America when he was invited to Brazil to act as adviser for the design of a new building for the Ministry of Education in Rio de Janeiro. After working with Costa and his design team, Le Corbusier seems to have endorsed the sixteen-storey slab solution which departed dramatically from his initial sketches. Yet the final version, raised on a peristyle of *pilotis*, was an occasion for the first monumental application of many of the characteristic Corbusian elements, including the *toit-jardin*, the *brise-soleil*, and the *pan-verre*. The young Brazilian followers of Le Corbusier immediately transformed these Purist components into a highly sensuous native expression which echoed in its plastic exuberance the 18th-century Brazilian Baroque. The most brilliant exponent of this rhetorical manner was Oscar Niemeyer, who had worked with Costa, Affonso Reidy, Jorge Moreira and others on the design for the Ministry of Education. Niemeyer's freely planned Brazilian Pavilion for the 1939 New York World's Fair, designed with Costa and Paul Lester Wiener, gained world recognition for the Brazilian movement and confirmed his own exceptional ability. Niemeyer brought Le Corbusier's concept of the free plan to a new level of fluidity and interpenetration. Initially planned around an exotic garden court of Brazilian flora and fauna – a micro-Amazonian landscape complete with orchids and snakes – this plastic concept evoked the tropical corniche of Rio itself. The garden layout was the work

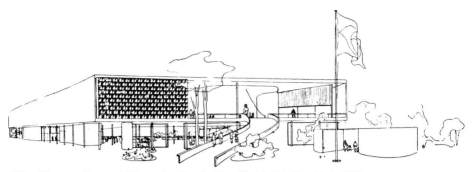

255　Niemeyer, Costa and Wiener, Brazilian Pavilion, World's Fair, New York, 1939.

of the painter Roberto Burle Marx, whose landscapes after 1936 became a seminal force in the Brazilian movement. Burle Marx exploited the Purist concept of the *mariage de contour* in order to organize 'paradise gardens', artciulated and textured in many instances with newly domesticated plants which he himself had taken from the jungle. With Burle Marx's landscape a new national style came into being, based to a large extent on indigenous Brazilian vegetation.

Niemeyer's genius reached its height in 1942 when, at the age of thirty-five, he achieved his first masterwork, the Casino at Pampulha. Here Niemeyer reinterpreted the Corbusian notion of a *promenade architecturale* in a spatial composition of remarkable balance and vivacity. This was a narrative building in every respect, from the welcoming double-height foyer to the gleaming ramps rising to the gaming floor; from the elliptical corridors leading towards the restaurant to the ingenious backstage access to the dance area; in short, an explicit *promenade* which articulated the space of the building as the structure of an elaborate game, a game as intricate as the habits of the society it was intended to serve. The restaurant with its complex accessways, interlocking like the turns of a labyrinth, established not only the routes but also the class roles of the various 'actors' divided between clients, entertainers, and serving staff. Strong and hedonistic in its general treatment, the building had a severe yet theatrical atmosphere, a contrast in mood established by the propriety of the façades faced in travertine and

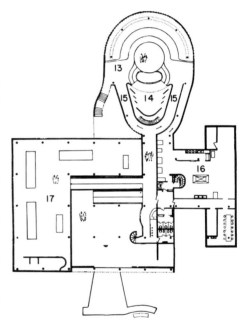

256　Niemeyer, Casino, Pampulha, Minas Gerais, Brazil, 1942. Second-floor plan.

juparana stone and the exoticism of an interior lined with pink glass, satin and brilliantly coloured panels of traditional Portuguese tiles. Rendered obsolete as a casino through a subsequent interdiction on gambling, the building now serves as an art museum. Niemeyer was well aware of the limitations of working for such an under-developed society when he wrote in 1950:

Architecture must express the spirit of the technical and social forces that are predominant in a given epoch; but when such forces are not balanced, the resulting conflict is prejudicial to the content of the work and to the work as a whole. Only with this in mind may we understand the nature of the plans and drawings which appear in this volume. I should very much have liked to be in a position to present a more realistic achievement: a kind of work which reflects not only refinements and comfort but also a positive collaboration between the architect and the whole society.

For all that this collaboration was earnestly sought by the reformist president Juscelino Kubitschek, for whom Niemeyer had worked since 1942, such a balance remained elusive. A singular achievement was Reidy's Pedregulho complex, built outside Rio between 1948 and 1954, comprising apartments, a primary school, a gymnasium and a swimming pool; the whole constituting a prototypical neighbourhood unit. Throughout Kubitschek's presidency, from 1955 on, surprisingly little architecture was realized in the name of the whole society.

Brasilia, planned by Costa in the mid-1950s, brought the progressive development of Brazilian architecture to a point of crisis. This crisis, destined eventually to provoke a global reaction against the precepts of the Modern Movement, permeated the entire project, not only at the level of the individual building but also at the scale of the plan itself. The conceptual schism that had already occurred at Chandigarh in 1951, between the isolated monumentality of the government centre as designed by Le Corbusier and the rest of the city, was to be repeated at Brasilia where the overall plan was somewhat less systematic in its basic conception. Where Chandigarh, in the last analysis, at least paid lip service to the time-honoured logic of the colonial grid, Brasilia, despite its orthogonal pattern of *supercuadras*, was fundamentally based on a cross form. It would seem as if the mythic principles of European humanism, as reinterpreted through the late work of Le Corbusier, determined the structure of Brasilia with unfortunate con-

sequences, at least from the point of view of accessibility. Moreover, soon after its foundation, Brasilia emerged as *two* cities: the monumental city of government and big business to which the bureaucrats commuted by air from Rio, and the 'shanty town' or *favela*, whose inhabitants served the 'radiance' of the high city. Even within its own confines, Brasilia, like Le Corbusier's Ville Radieuse of 1933, was a divided city, zoned into separate sections to accord with its class structure. Yet, aside from the manifest social inequality enforced by such an arrangement, Brasilia also produced formalistic and repressive results at the level of its own representation. In this connection it may be argued that Le Corbusier's development at Chandigarh foreshadowed a critical point in Niemeyer's own career, for clearly Niemeyer's work became increasingly simplistic and monumental after the publication of the first sketches for Chandigarh.

Although Niemeyer could not return to the formal delicacy of his Pampulha Casino, his command of free form, deriving in part from his continual association with Burle Marx, grew in its lyrical authority from the time of his Pampulha restaurant of 1942 to the extraordinary 'organic' house that he built for himself in 1953–54 at Gavea, overlooking Rio. At this juncture, however, Niemeyer broke with the informal functionality on which his fluid plan forms had been based, to concentrate on the creation of pure form: to move closer, that is, to the Neo-Classical tradition. One may date this break with his 1955 project for a Museum of Modern Art in Caracas, where he proposed the dramatic use of an inverted pyramid, to be poised on the edge of a precipitous terrain. Inverted or not, this use of the pyramid seems to have signalled a return to Classical absolutes, and the same may be said of his work at Brasilia which, together with Costa's grid, evoked the aura of the *genre terrible*, the assertion of implacable form against remorseless nature; for beyond the order of Brasilia's Capitol, edged by an artificial lake, there lay the infinite extent of the jungle. In a direct paraphrase of Chandigarh, Brasilia's Three Powers Square, at the head of the north/south axis, was assigned to accommodate the execu-

257  Niemeyer and Costa, Brasilia, 1956–63. View up the north/south axis between ministry buildings, towards Three Powers Square. On the right, the cathedral.

tive, legislative, and judicial powers, paralleling in content, if not in form, the Secretariat, High Court, and Assembly Building at Chandigarh. In both instances, the Capitol was located exactly in the conceptual 'head' position that had been zoned for administrative purposes in the initial projection of the Ville Radieuse. The 'head' at Brasilia, represented by Niemeyer's twin-slab Secretariat block, acted like a 'gun sight' marker for an axis dividing the convex dome of the Senate from the concave bowl of the House of Representatives.

In contrast to the adjustable *brise-soleil* judiciously applied, some twenty years before, to the north façade of the Ministry of Education, the curtain walls at Brasilia were left unshielded from the sun, although faced with heat-absorbent glass. This indifference to climate seems to have arisen out of a desire to represent the institutions of government by Platonic forms whose purity would stand in strong contrast to the glazed and repetitive slabs housing the ministries. That the initial exuberance of modern Brazilian architecture contained within itself the seeds of such decadent formalism seems to have been most clearly appreciated by Max Bill, who condemned Niemeyer's 1954 Palace of Industry for São Paulo in the following decisive terms:

In a street here in São Paulo I have seen under construction a building in which *pilotis* construction is carried to extremes one would have supposed impossible. There I saw some shocking things, modern architecture sunk to the depths, a riot of anti-social waste, lacking any sense of responsibility toward either the business occupant or his customers. . . . Thick *pilotis*, thin *pilotis*, *pilotis* of whimsical shapes lacking any structural rhyme or reason, disposed all over the place. . . . One is baffled to account for such barbarism as this in a country where there is a CIAM group, a country in which international congresses on modern architecture are held, where a journal like *Habitat* is published and where there is a biennial exhibition of architecture. For such works are born of a spirit devoid of all decency and of all responsibility to human needs. It is the spirit of decorativeness, something diametrically opposed to the spirit which animates architecture, which is the art of building, the social art above all others.

Japan, susceptible to Western influence for over fifty years, was well prepared for the assimilation of the International Style, whose arrival may be dated to 1923, with the realization of Antonin Raymond's first reinforced-concrete house, built in Tokyo for his own occupation. Once again, it was a question of the style being introduced, in its most accomplished form, by an émigré. Raymond was a much-travelled Czech-American who had come to Tokyo at the end of 1919 to work as the supervising architect on Frank Lloyd Wright's Imperial Hotel. As in the case of the careers of Neutra and Schindler in the States, the style emerged from the hands of a Central European who had been formally educated in

258 Raymond, the architect's house, Reinanzaka, Tokyo, 1923.

Europe and afterwards trained by Wright. It is interesting to note that Neutra, Schindler and Raymond freed themselves from the constraints of Wright's stylistic influence within a few years of leaving his employ.

Raymond's own house was remarkable in a number of ways. It was one of the first occasions on which a concrete frame was detailed so as to recall traditional Japanese wooden construction, a mannerism which was to become the architectonic touchstone of Japanese architecture after the Second World War. Its interior was equally in advance of its time by the standards of the International Style, since Raymond made one of the earliest uses of cantilevered tubular steel furniture, antedating the pioneering chairs of Mart Stam and Marcel Breuer. The house itself was detailed with metal fenestration and tubular steel trellises. At the same time, Raymond attempted to integrate into its form elements taken straight from the local vernacular, such as the use of rope rain leaders instead of traditional Western downpipes. Otherwise, in the profiling of its window canopies, the house still recalled something of Wright's Unity Temple style of 1905.

Despite the previous brilliance of Wright's 'reworking' of Japanese culture in America

and Paul Mueller's ingenious use of reinforced-concrete technique, the Imperial Hotel in Tokyo gave no indication as to how its ponderous architectural style could ever contribute to an intelligent reinterpretation of Japanese light-weight construction. Its stylistic affinities were closer to the isolated castles of the 16th and 17th centuries than to aristocratic Shinto building of the Heian era; contrary to Louis Sullivan's opinion of 1924 it remained firmly removed from the architectural mainstream of the indigenous culture. Nonetheless, its spectacular survival of the 1923 Tokyo earthquake disaster provided a *post facto* justification for the expense of anti-seismic structure, particularly in the case of public buildings. This 'proof' of reinforced monolithic construction enabled Raymond to take full advantage of the latest concrete technology in his major works of the late 1920s, including his Rising Sun Petroleum Company offices of 1926 and his elaborate and highly mannered Tokyo Golf Club, built outside the capital in 1930. At this juncture Raymond seems to have shifted his stylistic allegiance to Auguste Perret, apparently sensing that an appropriate syntax for exposed reinforced concrete was hardly to be found in Wright.

With the Akaboshi and Fukui houses of 1933–35, Raymond and his wife Noemi Pernessin reached the high point of their early career in the service of an arriviste industrialist class. Together they determined the design of everything from the building itself to its furnishings and fabrics. In these years, they produced a whole series of houses for different members of the Akaboshi family, loosely attempting to integrate their own rather tasteful furniture with the severity of the traditional *tatami* floor and the implacable surface of the *shoji* screen. Their unique Eurasian style seems to have reached its apotheosis in a house and bathing facility that the Raymonds designed for the Fukui family at Atami Bay in 1935, where they reinterpreted traditional forms in such a way as to liberate themselves finally from the influence of both Wright and Perret.

In 1926, a relatively independent Japanese movement began to develop around the Japanese Secession Group, which included

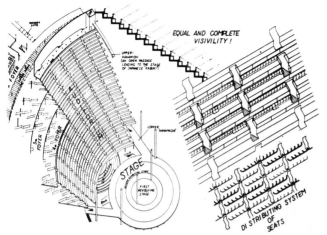

EQUAL AND COMPLETE VISIVILITY!

259   Kavakita, project for Kharkov Theatre, 1931.

260   Tange, National Olympic Gymnasium, Tokyo, 1964. Air view showing small basketball stadium and large pools stadium, and interior of pools stadium.

among its early members Mamoru Yamada, who designed the Central Telephone Office in Tokyo in 1926, and Tetsuro Yoshida, who designed the Tokyo General Post Office in 1931. At the same time, those of an even younger generation, such as Kunio Mayekawa and Junzo Yoshimura, began either to work for Raymond or to study abroad. A number of Japanese even ended up by studying at the Bauhaus in the late 1920s, while others such as Mayekawa and Junzo Sakakura worked for Le Corbusier. Sakakura even managed to complete his European experience with a work of international importance, the Japanese Pavilion at the Paris Exhibition of 1937, in which the architectonic order of the traditional tea house was reinterpreted in modern, not to say Corbusian, terms. Sakakura's open-space planning, together with the clear articulation of his structure and its ramped interconnection of exterior and interior space, bore but a distant resemblance to the spatial order of traditional Japanese architecture.

A more restrained interpretation of tradition informed the domestic practice of Isoya Yoshida, while against such conservatism stood the conceptual boldness of men such as Rentchitchiro Kavakita whose entry for the Soviet Kharkov Theatre competition of 1931 was far removed from the received modernism of the

period; that is to say, it was as distant from conventional Constructivist motifs as it was from the Japanese tradition. It was primarily concerned with the excitement of mechanical movement and the rhetoric of structural invention on an enormous scale. This work surely anticipated the quite extraordinary audacity of Kenzo Tange's post-war development, culminating in the twin Olympic stadia that he designed for the Tokyo games in 1964. While Tange was not concerned with movement, the elliptical and circular volumes of these stadia were covered by catenary steel roofs hung from the prow-like 'horns' of elliptical concrete

259

ring beams which also supported the upper tiers of the raked seating.

Just prior to his now famous Hiroshima Peace Memorial of 1955 — marking the epicentre of the first nuclear bomb — Tange, a former assistant of Mayekawa, began his career with a whole series of governmental commissions, starting with his rather schematic city halls for Shimizu and Tokyo (1952–54) and culminating in the Kagawa Prefectural Office (1955–58) and the city hall for Kurashiki (1957–60). Where Tokyo City Hall was a meticulous but nonetheless contrived parody in concrete of Jomon timber technique, the Kagawa Prefecture attained a state of almost classic balance which, through its remarkably lucid spatial organization, fused concepts drawn from the Heian era with elements discreetly abstracted from the received vocabulary of the International Style. This work, for all its historicism and its mixed reference to both Buddhist and Shinto prototypes, established Tange as one of the major figures to emerge in Japan after the Second World War. Despite common roots in the work of Le Corbusier, no two designs of the late 1950s could be farther apart than Niemeyer's Three Powers Square in Brasilia, with its simplistic Classicism, and Tange's Kagawa Prefecture, with its extraordinarily articulate detailing. That he was acutely aware of the energy released by the intense industrial development of Japan and of the ambivalent role to be played by tradition in relation to this socially 'liberating' force is born out by Tange's incisive and optimistic analysis made at the time of the Prefecture's completion:

Until only very recently, Japan was constantly under the control of an absolute state, and the cultural energy of the people as a whole – the energy with which they might have created new forms – was confined and suppressed. This was especially true in the Tokugawa period, when the government strove relentlessly to prevent social change. Only in our own times has the energy of which I speak begun to be released. It is still working in a confused medium, and much remains to be done before real order is achieved, but it is certain that this energy will do much to convert Japanese tradition into something new and creative.

The older generation, the men born at the turn of the century, such as Mayekawa and Sakakura, continued to make significant, if less dramatic, contributions: Mayekawa's theoretical work effectively challenging the whole orientation of 20th-century architecture and its fatal link to the instrumentality of the West. Both the Kamakura Museum of Modern Art

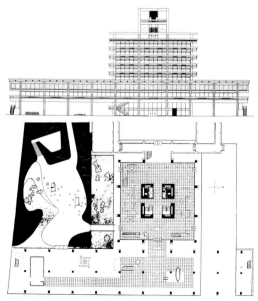

261   Tange, Kagawa Prefectural Office, Takamatsu, 1955–58. Elevation and site plan.

by Sakakura (1951) and the Harumi Apartments, Tokyo, by Mayekawa (1957), were hybrid works revealing a certain cultural dependency: the one being truly Neo-Classical in a cross-cultural sense, the other being derived from Le Corbusier's Unité d'Habitation at Marseilles. Where Tange was ultimately to lose any sense of human scale or place in the enormous residential megastructures that he began to propose in the late 1950s, specifically his Boston Bay project of 1959 and his Tokyo Bay proposal of 1961, Mayekawa was to make a bold attempt to accommodate a part-Western, part-Japanese life style within the multi-storey layers of a giant anti-seismic structure. That the Harumi apartment block, like the synthetic life style it was intended to house, could be, at best, only a qualified success, seems to have been acknowledged by Mayekawa himself when in 1965, in an essay entitled *Thoughts on Civilization in Architecture*, he came to the sobering conclusion that:

Modern architecture is and must be squarely based on the solid achievements of modern science, technology, and engineering. Why then does it so often tend to become something inhuman? I believe that one of the main reasons is that it is not always created merely to satisfy human requirements, but rather for some other reason, such as the profit motive. Or an attempt is made to cramp the architecture into the framework of some budget formulated by the mechanical operations of a powerful bureaucratic system of the modern state, this budget having nothing to do with human considerations. Another possibility is that inhuman elements may be contained within science, technology, and engineering themselves. When man attempts to understand a certain phenomenon, science analyses it, breaking it down into the simplest possible elements. Thus, in structural engineering when one attempts to understand a certain phenomenon, the methods adopted are those of simplification and abstraction. The question arises of whether the use of such methods may not cause a departure from human realities. . . . Modern architecture must recall its rudiments, its initial principles as a human architecture. Whereas science and engineering are the products of human brains, the modern architecture and the modern cities which are built by them tend to become inhuman. That which has beclouded the rudimentary principles of modern architecture, that which is distorting its sense of mission is today's ethical system regulating human action, and the system of value judgments concealed behind this ethical system. These ethical and value criteria are the forces which are moving modern civilization but are also obliterating human dignity and making a mockery of the Declaration of Human Rights. The conclusion of the tragedy is by no means simple. We must go back to the beginnings of Western civilization and discover whether the power to bring about such an ethical revolution can really be found in the inventory of Western civilization itself. If not, then we must seek it, together with Toynbee, in the Orient, or perhaps in Japan.

With this paradoxical proposition, that traditional Japanese culture may yet in its essence survive as the one force capable of redeeming the technocratic excesses of the West, the era of the International Style was brought to its definitive close, not only in Japan but throughout the rest of the world.

262    Mayekawa, Harumi Apartments, Tokyo, 1957.

## Chapter 2
# New Brutalism
# and the architecture of the Welfare State:
# England 1949-59

In January 1950 I shared offices with my esteemed colleagues Bengt Edman and Lennart Holm. These architects were at the time designing a house at Uppsala. Judging from their drawings I called them in a mildly sarcastic way 'Neo-Brutalists'. (The Swedish word for 'New Brutalists'!) The following summer, at jollification with some English friends, among whom were Michael Ventris, Oliver Cox and Graeme Shankland, the term was mentioned again in a jocular fashion. When I visited the same friends in London last year, they told me that they had brought the word back with them to England, and that it had spread like wildfire, and that it had, somewhat astoundingly, been adopted by a certain faction of younger English architects.

Hans Asplund,
Letter to Eric de Maré, *Architectural Review*,
Aug. 1956

After the Second World War Britain possessed neither the material resources nor the necessary cultural assurance to justify any form of monumental expression. If anything the post-war tendency lay in the opposite direction, since in architecture, as in other matters, Britain was in the final stages of relinquishing its imperial identity. While Indian independence initiated the disintegration of the Empire in 1945, the class conflict that had so bitterly divided the country during the Depression came to be partially alleviated by the welfare provisions of the Attlee Labour Government. Post-war social reconstruction gained its first impetus from two important Parliamentary Acts: the Education Act of 1944, raising the school leaving age to fifteen, and the New Towns Act

of 1946. This legislation was the effective instrument of an extensive government building programme, resulting in the construction of some 2,500 schools within a decade and in the designation of ten new towns, to be built on the model of Letchworth Garden City, with populations ranging from 20,000 to 69,000.

A great deal of this work — outside such precocious authorities as the Hertfordshire County Council which, under the leadership of C.H. Aslin, was to pioneer the wholesale prefabrication of schools — came to be carried out either in the 'reduced' Neo-Georgian manner of the average municipal architect, or in the so-called Contemporary Style, which was largely modelled on the official architecture of Sweden's long-established Welfare State. The syntax of this style — which was presumably considered to be sufficiently 'popular' for the realization of English social reform — comprised an architecture of shallow-pitched roofs, brick walls, vertically boarded spandrels and squarish wood-framed picture windows, the latter either left bare or painted white. This so-called 'people's detailing' became, with local additions, the received vocabulary of the left-wing architects of the London County Council, and it acquired a wider acceptance through the influence of the more active editors of *The Architectural Review*, J.M. Richards and Nikolaus Pevsner, who, from having first argued for a stringent modernism, began in the early 1950s to opt for a less rigorous approach to the creation of built form. Pevsner's Reith Lectures of 1955, 'The Englishness of English Art', publicly asserted picturesque informality as the very essence of British culture. This humanized version of the Modern Movement even came to be propagated under the title of 'The

263   Alison and Peter Smithson, Secondary School, Hunstanton, Norf., 1949–54.

New Humanism' by the editorial of *The Architectural Review*.

The Festival of Britain in 1951 served to give this undemanding cultural policy a progressive and modern dimension by parodying the heroic iconography of the Soviet Constructivists. Its two most potent symbols, the Skylon by Philip Powell and John Hidalgo Moya, and the Dome of Discovery by Ralph Tubbs, represented nothing more consequential through their structural rhetoric than the 'circus' of life for which presumably the 'bread' was soon to be provided. It was not that the exhibition was not without content, but that its content was presented in a gratuitious manner.

While the work of Edman and Holm may have sparked the invention of the term 'New Brutalism', it was in England rather than Sweden that the radical reaction that it denotes first arose. The gratifying populism of the Festival of Britain was rejected outright by Alison and Peter Smithson, the initial proponents of the Brutalist ethos, who counted among their sympathizers and colleagues many of the immediate post-war generation, including Alan Colquhoun, William Howell, Colin St John Wilson and Peter Carter, all of whom were working in the early 1950s for the LCC Architect's Department without subscribing to the 'Swedish line'. Of this situation Reyner Banham observed:

The negative aspect of the younger generation's attitude may be best summed up in the exasperated statement by James Stirling: 'Let's face it, William Morris was a Swede!' The factual accuracy of this statement need not detain us here; it is its emotional truth as a total rejection of the style of all forms of Welfare architecture

that is of consequence. The William Morris revival or People's Detailing or whatever term was commonly employed to satirize attempts to revive 19th-century brick-building techniques, complete with small shoulder-arched windows, etc., was occasionally dignified by the grandiose title of 'The New Humanism', which was in itself a reworking of a title invented (by *The Architectural Review*) for the Swedish retreat from Modern Architecture: The New Empiricism.

Inasmuch as Brutalism embraced an identifiable Palladian tendency, the Brutalist response to the New Humanism of *The Architectural Review* was to assert the old Humanism, that had in any event always been latent in the pre-war Modern Movement. The 1949 publication of Rudolf Wittkower's *Architectural Principles in the Age of Humanism* had the unexpected effect of engaging the interest of the rising generation in the methodology and aims of Palladio. On another level the Brutalists responded to the challenge of 'people's detailing' by making a direct reference to the socio-anthropological roots of popular culture, while rejecting outright the petit-bourgeois respectability of Swedish empiricism. This anthropological aestheticism (closely related as an impulse to the painter Jean Dubuffet's anti-art cult of *art brut*) brought the Smithsons into contact in the early 1950s with the remarkable personalities of the photographer Nigel Henderson and the sculptor Eduardo Paolozzi, from both of whom Brutalism derived much of its existential character.

The years 1951–54 were crucial to the architectural formation of this sensibility. Already heavily involved with the realization of their Palladian-cum-Miesian school designed for

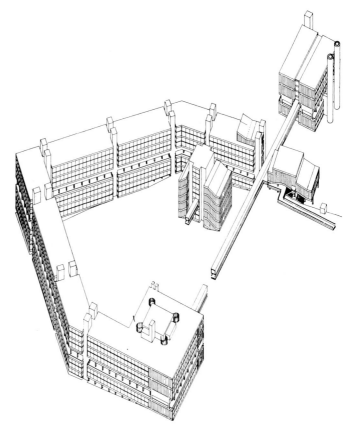

264 Alison and Peter Smithson, Sheffield University extension, 1953.

Hunstanton in Norfolk in 1949 and completed some five years later, the Smithsons followed their early success with a sequence of highly original competition entries — projects which, as Banham has remarked, can only be seen as attempts to invent a totally 'other' kind of architecture. Indeed, what little Palladianism there is left in their projects of this period is heavily mediated, from their Coventry Cathedral of 1951 to their Golden Lane housing, London of 1952, or their equally remarkable Sheffield University extension of the following year. If anything, these projects are 'Constructivist' in their affinities, although their restrained structural rhetoric seems in retrospect to have been of Japanese rather than Russian persuasion. That the failure to premiate any of these designs

was a loss to English architectural culture may be judged from the absolute banality of the structures that were eventually erected in their place.

The underlying ethos of the original Brutalist sensibility — the cryptic element that transcended its Palladianism — first came to public notice with the 'Parallel of Life and Art' exhibition, staged at the Institute of Contemporary Arts, London, in 1953. This show comprised a didactic collection of photographs assembled and annotated by Henderson, Paolozzi and the Smithsons. Drawn from news photos and arcane archaeological, anthropological and zoological sources, many of these images 'offered scenes of violence and distorted or anti-aesthetic views of the human figure, and all had a coarse grainy texture which was clearly regarded by the collaborators as one of their main virtues'. There was something decidedly existential about an exhibition that insisted on viewing the world as a landscape laid waste by war, decay and disease – beneath whose ashen layers one could still find traces of life, albeit microscopic, pulsating within the ruins. Henderson, writing of his work in this period, stated: 'I feel happiest among discarded things, vituperative fragments, cast casually from life, with the fizz of vitality still about them. There is an irony in this and it forms at least a partial symbol for an artist's activity.'

That this was the underlying motivation of Brutalism in the 1950s was not lost on the visitors to 'This Is Tomorrow', a show staged in 1956 by the ICA Independent Group at the Whitechapel Art Gallery, under the leadership of Lawrence Alloway. For this exhibition, the Smithsons, once again in collaboration with Henderson and Paolozzi, designed a symbolic temenos – a metaphorical shed in an equally metaphorical backyard, an ironic reinterpretation of Laugier's primitive hut of 1753 in terms of the back-yard reality of Bethnal Green, about which Banham remarked:

One could not help feeling that this particular garden shed with its rusted bicycle wheels, a battered trumpet and other homely junk, had been excavated after an atomic holocaust, and discovered to be part of a European tradition of site planning that went back to archaic Greece and beyond.

But this gesture was by no means entirely retrospective, for within this cryptic and almost casual metaphor of the shed the distant past and the immediate future fused into one. Thus the pavilion patio was furnished not only with an old wheel and a toy aeroplane but also with a television set. In brief, within a decayed and ravaged (i.e. bombed out) urban fabric, the 'affluence' of a mobile consumerism was already being envisaged, and moreover welcomed, as the life substance of a new industrial vernacular. Richard Hamilton's ironic collage for this exhibition, entitled *Just what is it that makes today's homes so different, so appeal-*

*ing*, not only inaugurated Pop culture but also crystallized the domestic image of the Brutalist sensibility. The Smithsons' 'House of the Future', exhibited at the Daily Mail Ideal Home Exhibition in 1956, was evidently intended as the ideal home for Hamilton's muscle-bound 'punch-bag' natural man and his curvaceous companion.

Split between a sympathy for old-fashioned working-class solidarity and the promise of consumerism, the Smithsons were ensnared in the intrinsic ambivalence of an assumed populism. Throughout the second half of the 1950s they moved away from their initial sympathy for the life style of the proletariat towards more middle-class ideals that depended for their appeal on both conspicuous consumption and mass ownership of the automobile. At the same time, they remained far from sanguine about the evident potential for such new-found 'mobility' to destroy both the structure and the density of the traditional city. In their London Roads Study of 1956 they attempted to resolve this dilemma by projecting the elevated freeway as the new urban fix. Meanwhile at a domestic scale they continued to regard the chromium consumer product in the crumbling tenement or the plastic interior as the ultimate liberating icon of their conciliatory style.

Up to the mid-1950s truth to materials remained an essential precept of Brutalist architecture, manifesting itself initially in an obsessive concern for the expressive articulation of mechanical and structural elements, as in the Smithsons' Hunstanton school, and reasserting itself in a more normative but nonetheless anti-aesthetic manner in the small Soho house projected by the Smithsons in 1952. Designed to be built in brick, with exposed concrete lintels and an unplastered interior, this four-storey box made numerous references to the British warehouse vernacular of the late 19th century, antedating by a year the publication of the equally brutal *avant project* for Le Corbusier's Maisons Jaoul, Paris, and anticipating the various projects for village infill housing designed by James Stirling, William Howell and the Smithsons themselves, and exhibited at the CIAM Aix-en-Provence Congress of 1953.

The mid-1950s clearly saw an extension of the Brutalist base beyond the hermetic pre-occupations of the Smithsons, Henderson and Paolozzi. By 1955 both Howell and Stirling were part of a Brutalist formation, although Stirling has since denied that he ever thought of himself as such. While his Sheffield University entry of 1953 was indeed Tectonesque his house project of the same year returned Stirling to the utilitarian brick aesthetic of the 19th century, though this work remained removed, in its Neo-Plastic composition of interlocking squares, from the brutal anti-art aura of the Smithsons' Soho house. Meanwhile, within the LCC, architects such as Colquhoun, Carter, Howell and John Killick had begun to realize a number of Corbusian housing schemes culminating in that parody of the 'radiant city', the Alton East Estate built at Roehampton in 1958.

Despite the fact that Mies's IIT campus had been the initial influence in shaping the Smithsons' first building, the subsequent development of the Brutalist style found much of its vocabulary in the late work of Le Corbusier. His revitalization of the Mediterranean vernacular, manifest in his 1948 Roq et Rob project, proved seminal to the formation of the

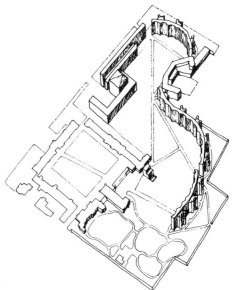

266    Stirling and Gowan, project for Selwyn College, Cambridge, 1959.

Brutalist sensibility, and the Smithsons followed their enthusiasm for Mies with a subtle reworking of Le Corbusier's *béton brut* manner: as they put it in 1959, 'Mies is great but Corb communicates.' Similarly, the shock first experienced by Stirling on visiting the Maisons Jaoul in 1955 was soon outweighed by the enthusiasm with which he followed its example. The close correspondence between the syntax of the Maisons Jaoul and the style of Stirling's Ham Common housing of 1955 can hardly be disputed, although load-bearing cross walls were used in the two cases to entirely different architectural ends.

The ultimate integration of the British Brutalist aesthetic — the fusion of its contradictory 'formalist' and 'populist' aspects into a glass and brick 'vernacular' drawn from the industrial structures of the 19th century — came with the works of Stirling and his partner James Gowan in 1959, their dormitory project for Selwyn College, Cambridge, and their Engineering Building for Leicester University. Some acknowledgment must be made here of the work of the late Edward Reynolds, whose structurally expressive (not to say expression-

265    Stirling and Gowan, flats, Ham Common, Richmond, Surrey, 1955–58.

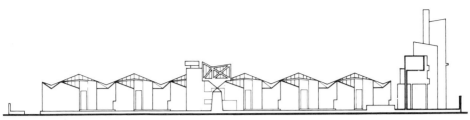

267  Reynolds, project for a delivery warehouse, Bristol, 1958.

ist) designs, which he made while still a student, exerted a decisive influence on the development of Brutalism, most notably in the Howell and Killick entry for Churchill College, Cambridge, of 1958, and then in Stirling's Leicester project of the following year.

The Stirling and Gowan Selwyn College proposal not only introduced the crystalline plasticity of their initial style but also presented for the first time the 'front' versus 'back' theme that was to be typical of their characteristic organization; a theme derived from the solid-versus-glazed expression of the Ville Radieuse slab. Once again it was Reynolds's warehouse project of 1958 that seems to have been the key influence on the form of the Leicester Engineering Building, a work in which Stirling and Gowan finally arrived at their unique expression. What had previously been the slab element in Le Corbusier's Pavillon Suisse was here transformed (via the Reynolds warehouse scheme), into the horizontal form of a crystalline-roofed laboratory block, while Le Corbusier's free-standing access tower reappeared as a vertical cluster, comprising flatted laboratories, lecture halls and offices. Leicester absorbed the fundamental contradictions of the initial Brutalist position by recombining the canonical forms of the Modern Movement with elements drawn from the industrial and commercial vernacular of Stirling's native Liverpool (see, for instance, the pioneering work of Peter Ellis). All that now remained of the Purist paradigm of the late 1920s was the marine detailing – the deck rails, companion ladders and cowls that had been polemically illustrated in *Vers une architecture*. For the rest, Leicester was an eclectic tour de force that recalled, in its remarkable juxtaposition of

diverse elements, not only the work of Telford and Brunel but also the work of William Butterfield as manifest in his All Saints' Church, Margaret Street, London, of 1849. What other strategy, one may argue, than the Gothic Revival could have succeeded in combining Purist formal elements with the Romantic imagery of Wright's Johnson Wax complex of 1936–39, while at the same time integrating such Brutal structural components as the exposed diagrid floors drawn from Kahn's Richards Laboratories of 1958?

268  Stirling and Gowan, Engineering Building, Leicester University, 1959.

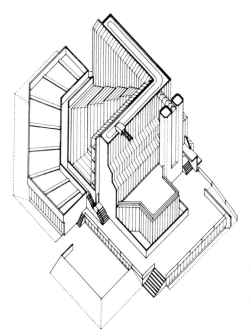

269 Stirling, History Faculty Building, Cambridge University, 1964.

While Leicester imposed, as it were, a 45° grid over an otherwise orthogonal geometry, Stirling's History Faculty Building at Cambridge of 1964 rendered the diagonal as the major organizing axis of the plan. At the same time, the History Building stretched the brick and glass syntax of Selwyn and Leicester until the crystalline form of the glass began to overwhelm the controlling armature of the brick. Despite this, it still displayed the coupled elevator stair tower, not only as an articulation of access reminiscent of Kahn's 'servant' element (cf. the Richards Laboratories) but also as a typological device that denoted the Stirling house style. This device was to be repeated in the last and least successful of the brick and glass series, namely the Florey Residential Building, designed by Stirling for Queen's College, Oxford, in 1966. The major

works of this series – Selwyn, Leicester, the History Faculty and the Florey Building – follow each other as a catalogue of types for the modern university. This typological orientation, with its tendency to dismember and recombine discrete architectural elements, partly in response to empirical demands and partly out of a determination to 'deconstruct' the received forms of the Modern Movement, shaped these late 'monuments' of Brutalism to a far greater degree than any concern for the attributes of place.

For all that programmatic demands have been invariably met, Stirling's significance to date has lain in the compelling quality of his style; in the brilliant architectonic of his form rather than in the consistent refinement of those 'place' attributes which do of necessity determine the quality of life. Despite his reverence for Aalto, Stirling's achievement has been largely removed from the receptive ambience and self-effacing sensibility of, say, Aalto's Säynatsalö City Hall. It is as though the formal mastery of his syntactical imagination came to disown the critical 'place-creating' potential that he himself had once posited in his village infill housing of the mid-1950s. As Manfredo Tafuri has written of Stirling's later work:

Suspending the public destined to use his buildings in a limbo of a space that ambiguously oscillates between the emptiness of form and a 'discourse on function' – that is architecture as an autonomous machine, as it is spelled out in the History Building at Cambridge and made explicit in the project for Siemens AG – Stirling carries out the most cruel of acts by abandoning the sacred precinct in which the semantic universe of the modern tradition has been enclosed. Neither attracted nor repulsed by the independent articulation of Stirling's formal machines, the observer is forced into a swinging course, itself just as oscillating as the perverse play of the architect with the elements of his own language.

*Chapter 3*

# The vicissitudes of ideology: CIAM and Team X, critique and counter-critique 1928-68

1. The idea of modern architecture includes the link between the phenomenon of architecture and that of the general economic system.

2. The idea of 'economic efficiency' does not imply production furnishing maximum commercial profit, but production demanding a minimum working effort.

3. The need for maximum economic efficiency is the inevitable result of the impoverished state of the general economy.

4. The most efficient method of production is that which arises from rationalization and standardization. Rationalization and standardization act directly on working methods both in modern architecture (conception) and in the building industry (realization).

5. Rationalization and standardization react in a threefold manner:
(a) they demand of architecture conceptions leading to simplification of working methods on the site and in the factory;
(b) they mean for building firms a reduction in the skilled labour force; they lead to the employment of less specialized labour working under the direction of highly skilled technicians;
(c) they expect from the consumer (that is to say, the customer who orders the house in which he will live) a revision of his demands in the direction of a readjustment to the new conditions of social life. Such a revision will be manifested in the reduction of certain individual needs henceforth devoid of real justification; the benefits of this reduction will foster the maximum satisfaction of the needs of the greatest number, which are at present restricted.

La Sarraz Declaration,
*Congrès Internationaux d'Architecture Moderne*, 1928

The 1928 CIAM declaration, signed by twenty-four architects, representing France (6), Switzerland (6), Germany (3), Holland (3), Italy (2), Spain (2), Austria (1), and Belgium (1), emphasized *building* rather than architecture as 'the elementary activity of man intimately linked with evolution and the development of human life'. CIAM openly asserted that architecture was unavoidably contingent on the broader issues of politics and economics and that, far from being removed from the realities of the industrialized world, it would have to depend for its general level of quality not on craftsmen but on the universal adoption of rationalized production methods. Where four years later Hitchcock and Johnson were to argue for the pre-eminence of style as determined by technique, CIAM emphasized the need for planned economy and industrialization, denouncing as it did so efficiency as a means for maximizing profit. Instead it advocated the introduction of normative dimensions and efficient production methods as a preliminary step towards a rationalization of the building industry. Thus, that which aesthetes would regard as a formal preference for regularity was for CIAM the initial prerequisite for increasing housing production and for superseding the methods of a craft era. The La Sarraz document took an equally radical attitude to town planning, when it declared:

Urbanization cannot be conditioned by the claims of a pre-existent aestheticism; its essence is of a functional order . . . the chaotic division of land, resulting from sales, speculations, inheritances, must be abolished by a collective and methodical land policy. This redistribution of the land, the indispensable preliminary basis for any town planning, must include the just division between the owners

269

and the community of the *unearned increment* from works of joint interest.

Between the La Sarraz declaration of 1928 and the last CIAM conference held in Dubrovnik in 1956, CIAM passed through three stages of development. The first, lasting from 1928 to 1933 and comprising the CIAM congresses held in Frankfurt in 1929 and Brussels in 1930, was in many respects the most doctrinaire. Dominated by the German-speaking Neue Sachlichkeit architects, who were mostly of socialist persuasion, these congresses addressed themselves first, at Frankfurt, under the title 'Die Wohnung für das Existenzminimum', to the problems of minimum living standards, and then, at Brussels (CIAM III), under the title 'Rationelle Bebauungsweisen', to the issues of optimum height and block spacing for the most efficient use of both land and material. CIAM II, initiated by the Frankfurt city architect, Ernst May, also established a working party, known as CIRPAC (Comité International pour la Résolution du Problème de l'Architecture Contemporaine), whose primary task was to prepare themes for future congresses.

The second stage of CIAM, lasting from 1933 to 1947, was dominated by the personality of Le Corbusier, who consciously shifted the emphasis to town planning. CIAM IV in 1933 was without doubt the most comprehensive congress from an urbanistic standpoint, by virtue of its comparative analysis of thirty-four European towns. Out of it came the articles of the Athens Charter, which for inexplicable reasons were not published until a decade later. Reyner Banham characterized the achievements of this congress in 1963 in the following rather critical terms:

CIAM IV – theme 'The Functional City' – took place in July and August 1933 aboard the S.S. *Patris*, in Athens, and in Marseilles at the end of the voyage. It was the first of the 'romantic' congresses, set against a background of scenic splendour, not the reality of industrial Europe, and it was the first *Congrès* to be dominated by Le Corbusier and the French, rather than the tough German realists. The

Mediterranean cruise was clearly a welcome relief from the worsening situation of Europe and in this brief respite from reality the delegates produced the most Olympian, rhetorical, and ultimately destructive document to come out of CIAM: the Athens Charter. The hundred and eleven propositions that comprise the Charter consist in part of statements about the conditions of towns, and in part of proposals for the rectification of those conditions, grouped under five main headings: Dwellings, Recreation, Work, Transportation, and Historic Buildings.

The tone remains dogmatic, but is also generalized and less specifically related to immediate practical problems than were the Frankfurt and Brussels reports. The generalization had its virtues, where it brought with it a greater breadth of vision and insisted that cities could be considered only in relation to their surrounding regions, but this persuasive generality which gives the Athens Charter its air of universal applicability conceals a very narrow conception of both architecture and town planning and committed CIAM unequivocally to: (a) rigid functional zoning of city plans, with green belts between the areas reserved to the different functions, and (b) a single type of urban housing, expressed in the words of the Charter as 'high, widely-spaced apartment blocks wherever the necessity of housing high density of population exists'. At a distance of thirty years we recognize this as merely the expression of an aesthetic preference, but at the time it had the power of a Mosaic commandment and effectively paralyzed research into other forms of housing.

While the summary consensus of the Athens Charter may well have served to inhibit any further examination of alternative housing models, the fact remains that there was a noticeable shift in tone. The radical political demands of the early movement had been dropped and while Functionalism remained the general credo, the articles of the Charter read like a neo-capitalist catechism, whose edicts were as idealistically 'rationalistic' as they were largely unrealizable. This idealistic approach acquired its pre-war formulation in the fifth congress, dedicated to the theme of dwelling and leisure and held in Paris in 1937. On this occasion CIAM was prepared to acknowledge not only the impact of historical structures but also the influence of the region in which the city happened to be situated.

With the third and final stage of CIAM, liberal idealism triumphed completely over the materialism of the early period. In 1947, at CIAM VI, held at Bridgwater in England, CIAM attempted to transcend the abstract sterility of the 'functional city' by affirming that 'the aim of CIAM is to work for the creation of a physical environment that will satisfy man's emotional and material needs.' This theme was developed further under the auspices of the English MARS group which prepared the topic, 'The Core', for CIAM VIII, held at Hoddesdon, England, in 1951. In choosing the theme 'The Heart of the City', MARS caused the congress to address itself to a topic that had already been broached by Sigfried Giedion, José Luis Sert and Fernand Léger in their manifesto of 1943, where they wrote: 'The people want buildings that represent their social and community life to give more functional fulfilment. They want their aspiration for monumentality, joy, pride and excitement to be satisfied.'

For Giedion, as for Camillo Sitte, the 'space of public appearance' was necessarily contingent on the monumental counterform of the public institutions enclosing it and vice versa. Yet, despite their now manifest concern for the concrete qualities of place, the old guard of CIAM gave no indication that they were capable of realistically appraising the complexities of the post-war urban predicament; with the result that new affiliates, drawn from the younger generation, became increasingly disillusioned and restless.

The decisive split came with CIAM IX held at Aix-en-Provence in 1953, when this generation, led by Alison and Peter Smithson and Aldo van Eyck, challenged the four Functionalist categories of the Athens Charter: Dwelling, Work, Recreation and Transportation. Instead of proffering an alternative set of abstractions, the Smithsons, Van Eyck, Jacob Bakema, Georges Candilis, Shadrach Woods, John Voelcker and William and Jill Howell searched for the structural principles of urban growth and for the next significant unit above the family cell. Their dissatisfaction with the modified Functionalism of the old guard – with the 'idealism' of Le Corbusier, Van Eesteren, Sert, Ernesto Rogers, Alfred Roth, Kunio Mayekawa and Gropius – is reflected in their critical reaction to the CIAM VIII report. They responded to the simplistic model of the urban core by positing a more complex pattern that would be, in their view, more responsive to the need for identity. They wrote:

Man may readily identify himself with his own hearth, but not easily with the town within which it is placed. 'Belonging' is a basic emotional need – its associations are of the simplest order. From 'belonging' – identity – comes the enriching sense of neighbourliness. The short narrow street of the slum succeeds where spacious redevelopment frequently fails.

In this singularly sharp paragraph they not only dismissed the Sittesque sentimentality of the old guard, but also the rationalism of the 'functional city'. Their critical drive to find a more precise relation between physical form and socio-psychological need became the subject matter for CIAM X, held at Dubrovnik in 1956 – the last CIAM meeting – for which this group, thereafter known as Team X, was basically responsible. The official demise of CIAM and the succession of Team X were confirmed in a further meeting that took place in 1959 in the elegiac setting of Van de Velde's Museum at Otterloo with the old master in attendance. But the essential epitaph of CIAM had already been written, in Le Corbusier's letter to the Dubrovnik congress, when he stated:

It is those who are now forty years old, born around 1916 during wars and revolutions, and those then unborn, now twenty-five years old, born around 1930 during the preparation for a new war and amidst a profound economic, social, and political crisis, who thus find themselves in the heart of the present period the only ones capable of feeling actual problems, personally, profoundly, the goals to follow, the means to reach them, the pathetic urgency of the present situation. They are in the know. Their predecessors no longer are, they are out, they are no longer subject to the direct impact of the situation.

The peculiar London cultural climate of the mid-1950s, subject as it was to the influence of Parisian Existentialism, not only decisively shaped the ethos of the British Brutalist movement but also contributed to the Team X polemic with which it was closely associated. In this respect credit must be given to the photographer Nigel Henderson, whose photographs of London street life were exhibited by the Smithsons at Aix-en-Provence and whose perception and way of life played such a crucial role in shaping the Smithsons' sensibility. That this sensibility was ultimately at odds with the tabula rasa implications of Le Corbusier's CIAM Grid, which was still being propagated as late as 1952, must in no small part be attributed to Henderson's record of the social and physical reality of London's East End – his photographs of community life in Bethnal Green. The Smithsons regularly visited Henderson's home in Bethnal Green from 1950 onwards and it was from their first-hand experience of the street life in the area (now obliterated by the high-rise housing blocks of the Welfare State) that they drew their first notions of *identity* and *association*. Thus the Bye-Law Street, albeit distorted by their own rationalization, became the conceptual 'armature' for their Golden Lane housing proposal of 1952.

For all its resemblance to Le Corbusier's 'Ilot Insalubre' project of 1937, Golden Lane was clearly intended as a critique of the Ville Radieuse and of the zoning of the four functions of the city into Dwelling, Work, Recreation and Transportation. The Smithsons opposed these functions with the more phenomenological categories of House, Street, District and City, although what they meant by these terms grew vaguer as the scale increased. The house in their Golden Lane project was clearly the family unit; the street was evidently a system of one-sided gallery access of generous width, elevated into the air. The district and the city

were understandably and realistically regarded as variable domains that lay outside the bounds of physical definition.

Yet, while remaining opposed to the pre-war determinism of the 'functional city', the Smithsons in their Golden Lane proposal became caught in a rationalization process comparable to that of CIAM. For all that the 'yards' in their Golden Lane scheme were indicated as adjunct areas to the streets, it was clear that the 'house in the air' did not have a yard that was in any way akin to the back-yard of the Bye-Law Street and that the street itself, now divorced from the ground, could no longer accommodate community life. Above all, its one-sided nature had only the capacity to stress the linearity of the route rather than engender a sense of place. The presence of life on both sides of the Bye-Law Street had clearly been responsible for its social vitality (as an early sketch by the Smithsons would indicate), but the nature of Golden Lane – high density on a small site – and the Smithsons' own acceptance of Functionalist norms precluded a solution that could have sustained such a life.

From their postulation of this housing pattern as a prototypical solution, one must conclude that the Smithsons were largely unaware of these contradictions: they proceeded to show their Golden Lane scheme, repeated ad infinitum over the metropolitan area, as though it were the manifest critical alternative to Le Corbusier's Ville Radieuse. And while its random, 'twig-like' distribution could no doubt be taken as a polemic against wholesale demolition and as an argument in favour of piecemeal development, their collage of the Golden Lane prototype as a phantom axonometric, apparently erecting itself amid the ruins of Coventry, returned its authors to the central dilemma of CIAM. As imposed on blitzed Coventry, Golden Lane appeared to be as much against the continuity of the existing city as the Haussmann-like projections of Le Corbusier's Plan Voisin of 1925. The axonometric depicted the 'edge conditions' between the old street pattern and the new work as a series of inevitable collisions. After the building-out of the Golden Lane concept in

1961 at Park Hill in Sheffield, to the design of Jack Lynn and Ivor Smith, it became obvious that aside from the perimeter block form, such as had been realized by Brinkman at Spangen, Rotterdam, in 1919 (a scheme well known to the Smithsons), there was little possibility of achieving any continuity between decks in the air and streets on the ground.

For all that Team X were committed to the multi-level city — an idea stemming via Le Corbusier from Hénard's visions of 1910 — it was to the Smithson's credit that they remained conscious of its limitations and in consequence produced one of the most critical sketches of their early career, namely a drawing which demonstrated that above the sixth floor one lost all contact with the ground. While the Smithsons were to use this sketch as a way of justifying a megastructural approach, their recognition of tree height as an experiential limit may well have exerted an influence in the 1960s on the general adoption of 'low rise, high density' as the preferred policy for family residential development. This critical awareness was amplified at the time by the Smithsons' own village-infill projects of the mid-1950s — their 'close' and 'fold' houses — and by their insistence, following the 'ecological' argument of their Doorn Manifesto of 1954, that 'habitat should be integrated into the landscape rather than isolated as an object within it.'

The socio-cultural challenge of Bethnal Green was largely lost on Bakema, despite the anti-Functionalism of his pronouncements in the early 1940s. He was the one member of Team X whose practice was hardly to deviate from the site planning principles of the Neue Sachlichkeit — the row-house principle of open-ended blocks of identical height an optimum distance apart. Bakema's constant point of reference was clearly the Amsterdam South Plan of 1934 and the pre-war work of Dutch Functionalists such as Merkelbach, Karsten and Stam. All the same, in the Opbouw studies for Pendrecht (1949–51) and for Alexander Polder (1953–56), in all of which Bakema participated, there was a move away from the rigid principle of blocks of uniform height and orientation to a more modulated layout, com-

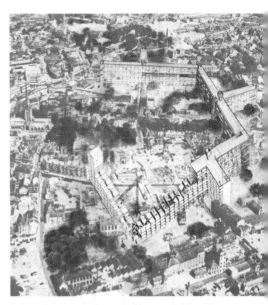

270 Alison and Peter Smithson, Golden Lane Housing system applied to central Coventry. (The parish church and ruined cathedral are on the left.)

271 Lynn and Smith, Park Hill, Sheffield, 1961.

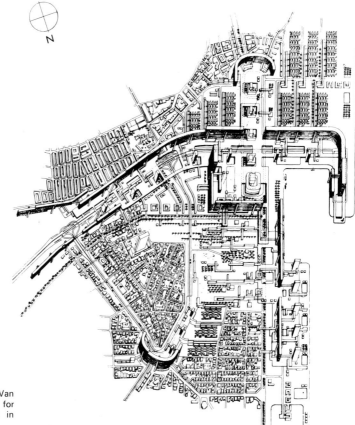

272 Bakema and Van den Broek, project for megastructural blocks in Tel Aviv, 1963.

prising 'swastika' formations, grouped into 'neighbourhoods' about clusters of public facilities, swimming pools, schools, etc.

The Kennermerland project, designed by Bakema in collaboration with J.M. Stokla and submitted to the Otterlo Congress of 1959, was a culmination of this research work, as Bakema admitted when challenged by Kenzo Tange as to the origin of the proposal. Yet it says something for the confusion of the time that both Tange and Bakema should insist on Corbusian rationalism as its point of departure, for clearly Kennermerland stemmed from the abstract 'neighbourhood' concept first developed by German planners such as Ernst May and Arthur Korn. Even as late as the early 1960s, Bakema was still proposing an extremely hierarchized form of neighbourhood planning as had first appeared in Korn's MARS plan for London of 1942.

Bakema did not truly come under Le Corbusier's influence until his Tel Aviv proposal of 1963, when he used the megastructural Obus block projected for Algiers in 1931 (ill. 167) as a means for giving order to the dispersed form of the city. Paradoxically, this continuous superblock in no way served to liberate Bakema from his deterministic tendencies, for while the fiction of the neighbourhood unit was given less importance, its structuring function was replaced by megaforms that either cut across topography, as in the case of his 1962 entry for Bochum University, or alternatively, as in Tel Aviv, paralleled the trajectory of a freeway spine running through the city.

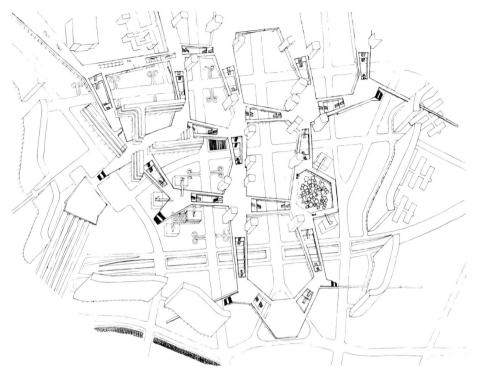

273, 274 Alison and Peter Smithson and Sigmond, project for Berlin-Haupstadt, 1958. *Above*, southern portion of pedestrian net, showing the growth of causeways above the old street grid; *below*, escalator access to shopping level and roof.

It is one of the paradoxes of Team X that Bakema proposed the megabuilding as the psychological 'fix' for the Megalopolitan land-scape just when the Smithsons had begun to entertain doubts as to the viability of such structures. The Smithsons' 'open city' thesis, influenced by the urbanistic concepts of Louis Kahn, was first broached after their initial visit to the States in 1958. In that year they also designed (with Peter Sigmond) their competition entry for the Hauptstadt district of Berlin. In this scheme (strangely similar to that of Scharoun) they posited the notion of the permanently 'ruined' city – ruined in the sense

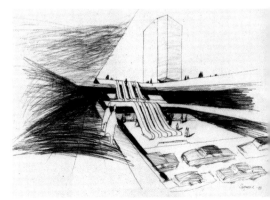

that accelerated movement and change in the 20th century were incapable of relating to the pattern of any pre-existing fabric.

While both Bakema and the Smithsons were preoccupied with the notion of 'urban fix' — with the sense of place to be established by architecture within the 'space endlessness' of Motopia — the Smithsons, rather than continuing to advocate the megastructure, opted for localized traffic-free enclaves, be they the elevated podiums of their Hauptstadt scheme or the Schinkelesque *Paradeplatzen* of their Mehringplatz proposal of 1962. Either way round, both Bakema and the Smithsons were, by this date, obsessed with the liberating promise of mass mobility, whose achievement they wanted to celebrate with an appropriate architectural counterform.

Of the various strategies proffered for dealing with this phenomenon, those of the Smithsons seem to have been the more feasible, and this is reflected in the partial realization of both their Hauptstadt and Mehringplatz prototypes — the one in their *Economist* office complex, London, of 1965, and the other in their Robin Hood Gardens housing, London, of 1969. Yet the sterile conditions imposed by these developments, particularly in the case of Robin Hood Gardens which was as isolated from its urban context as the towers of any 'functional city', would suggest that the Smithsons had yet to come to terms with the urban consequences of their 'landcastle' approach.

The essential pluralism of Team X found a direct reflection in the very different approach of Aldo van Eyck whose entire career has been devoted to evolving a 'place form' which would be appropriate to the second half of the 20th century. From the very outset Van Eyck addressed himself to issues which the majority of Team X would have preferred to have left unformulated, and where Team X kept its initial buoyancy through a naïve optimism Van Eyck was motivated by a critical impulse which verged on the pessimistic. No other Team X member seems to have been prepared to attack the alienating abstraction of modern architecture at its roots, possibly because no one else had had the benefit of Van Eyck's 'anthropological' experience. His personal pre-

occupation with 'primitive' cultures, and with the timeless aspects of built form that such cultures invariably reveal, dated from the early 1940s, so that by the time he joined Team X he had already developed a unique position. His statement at the Otterlo Congress of 1959, in which he declared his concern for the timelessness of man, was almost as foreign to the mainstream of Team X thought as it was to the ideology of CIAM:

Man is always and everywhere essentially the same. He has the same mental equipment though he uses it differently according to his cultural or social background, according to the particular life pattern of which he happens to be a part. Modern architects have been harping continually on what is different in our time to such an extent that even they have lost touch with what is not different, with what is always essentially the same.

Van Eyck's concern for transition, for the amplification of the 'threshold' so as to mediate symbolically between such universal twin phenomena as 'inside versus outside' and 'house versus city', was to make itself manifest in his own work of the late 1950s, most particularly in his children's home in Amsterdam which was then nearing completion. In this school Van Eyck demonstrated his notion of 'labyrinthine clarity' (see below, p. 293) through an interconnected sequence of domed 'family' units, all united under a continuous roof.

By 1966, however, that which had been the cause for enthusiasm became the occasion for despair. Five years of intense urban development had been enough to convince Van Eyck that the architectural profession, if not Western man as a whole, had so far proved incapable of developing either an aesthetic or a strategy for dealing with the urban realities of mass society. Van Eyck stated: 'We know nothing of vast multiplicity — we cannot come to grips with it — not as architects, planners or anybody else.' Elsewhere Van Eyck characterized this predicament in terms of the cultural void left by the loss of the vernacular. In his various writings of the period, he pointed to the role played by modern architecture in the eradication of both *style* and *place*. He argued that post-war Dutch planning had produced nothing save the organized uninhabitable nowhere of the 'functional city'. His doubts as to the ability of the profession to meet the pluralistic demands of society, without the mediation of a vernacular, led him to question the authenticity of the society itself. In 1966 he asked: 'If society has no form — how can architects build its counterform?'

By 1963, Team X had already passed beyond the stage of fertile exchange and collaboration, a transformation that was intuitively acknowledged by the Smithsons in their 1962 publication of the *Team X Primer*. From now on, Team X would continue as a movement only in name, since what there had been to achieve through a creative critique of CIAM had already been attained. Little more, in fact, was now to be accomplished in the way of critical reinterpretation, save possibly for the work of two men who had hitherto remained somewhat to one side — an American, Shadrach Woods, and an Italian, Giancarlo de Carlo.

The new departure made by Woods in his Frankfurt-Römerberg competition entry of 1963 was a direct response to Van Eyck's appeal for 'labyrinthine clarity': for what was being proffered in the Frankfurt proposal was a 'city in miniature'. In the place of the medieval centre destroyed in the Second World War, Woods, in collaboration with Manfred Schiedhelm, proposed an equally labyrinthine configuration of shops, public spaces, offices and dwellings, the whole being served by a double-decked basement containing service and parking. If Frankfurt was an urban 'event', it was certainly conceived in different terms from those of the Smithsons or Bakema, for while presenting an orthogonal *counterform* in opposition to the medieval *form* of the city, it also embodied a three-dimensional 'loft' system, served by escalators, whose interstices could be occupied according to demand. That this concept had been anticipated by the infrastructures of Yona Friedman's *L'Architecture mobile* of 1958 in no way detracted from the magnitude of Wood's achievement.

Frankfurt-Römerberg, although it remained a project, was without doubt the greatest

275   Candilis, Josic and Woods, project for Frankfurt-Romerberg, 1963. Model. (Designers: Woods and Schiedhelm.)

accomplishment of Woods's career and is probably one of the most important prototypes developed by Team X. In relating to the context of an existing city and refusing the escapism of both 'functional' and 'open' city models, it endeavoured to put the automobile in its place and to continue the tradition of urban culture.

That this Frankfurt scheme as built out in the Free University of Berlin in 1973 lost much of its conviction stems largely from the absence of an urban context. In Berlin-Dahlem it was deprived of that urban culture for which it had been conceived and to which it would have responded had it been built in Frankfurt. However much a university may function like a city in microcosm, it cannot generate the animated diversity of the city proper. Aside from this, Frankfurt's flexibility in terms of space was replaced in Berlin by an idealization of flexibility in terms of technique — by the 'poetic' but somewhat unserviceable detailing of Jean Prouvé's modular clip-on façade of Core 10 steel.

In 1964, the implicit ideology of Woods's Frankfurt scheme found its complement in De Carlo's plan for Urbino. This plan, proceeded by an exhaustive topographical study, devotes more space to the tactics of preservation and rehabilitation than to the accommodation of

TYPICAL TRANSVERSE SECTION

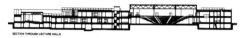

SECTION THROUGH LECTURE HALLS

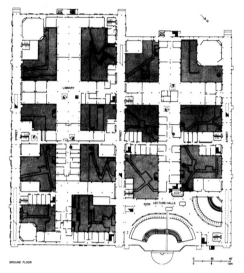

GROUND FLOOR

276 Woods and Schiedhelm, Free University, Berlin-Dahlem, 1963–73. Sections and ground plan of first phase.

new development. With De Carlo's Urbino, Team X finally arrived at the complete antithesis to the Cartesian projections of the Ville Radieuse. De Carlo's concern for the reuse of existing stock wherever possible has been confirmed as a policy by recent housing studies, which have shown conclusively that, despite the higher densities usually attained, it may take as long as fifty years for new housing to compensate for the statistical 'housing loss' incurred through the time spent in demolition and construction.

Considerations such as these finally had the effect of precipitating Team X into a realm that it had always strenuously avoided, namely politics. Never was this shift in consciousness more manifest than at the Milan Triennale

of 1968 when Woods, in sympathy with student radicals, assisted in the removal of his own work. Only one year before, he had written:

What are we waiting for? To read the news about a new armed attack with even more esoteric weapons, news which comes to us through the air captured by our marvellous transistorized instruments somewhere deep in our more and more savaged dwellings? Our weapons become more sophisticated; our houses more and more brutish. Is that the balance sheet for the richest civilization since time began?

This same theme was taken up by De Carlo in 1968 when he wrote his synoptic analysis of the ideological development of modern architecture, under the title *Legitimizing Architecture*, wherein he reviewed the consequences of the CIAM Declaration of 1928:

Today, forty years after the Congress, we find that those proposals have become houses and neighbourhoods and suburbs and then entire cities, palpable manifestations of an abuse perpetrated first on the poor and then even on the not-so-poor: cultural alibis for the most ferocious economic speculation and the most obtuse political inefficiency. And yet those 'whys' so nonchalantly forgotten in Frankfurt still have trouble coming openly to the surface. At the same time, we have a right to ask 'why' housing should be as cheap as possible and not, for example, rather expensive; 'why' instead of making every effort to reduce it to minimum levels of surface, of thickness, of materials, we should not try to make it spacious, protected, isolated, comfortable, well equipped, rich in opportunities for privacy, communication, exchange, personal creativity. No one, in fact, can be satisfied by an answer which appeals to the scarcity of available resources, when we all know how much is spent on wars, on the construction of missiles and anti-ballistic systems, on moon projects, on research for the defoliation of forests inhabited by partisans and for the paralyzation of the demonstrators emerging from the ghettos, on hidden persuasion, on the invention of artificial needs, etc.

277 Woods and Schiedhelm, Free University, Berlin-Dahlem, 1963–73. Core 10 steel cladding system, detailed by Prouvé.

For De Carlo, the students' revolt of 1968 was not only a necessary culmination of the crisis in architectural education, but also a reflection of the deeper and more significant dysfunctions of architectural practice and theory — the latter often serving to mystify the true network of power and exploitation permeating the entire society. As an example of this, De Carlo cited the proceedings of CIAM VIII, whose sentimental deliberations on 'The Heart of the City' were largely responsible for the ideology with which the traditional city core was subsequently raped (an ironic, if not cynical, procedure that did not gain its full momentum until a decade later). As De Carlo argued, the Newspeak overtones of this venture were not entirely lost on the critics of Western society, who came to regard the process of urban renewal as a euphemism for the dislocation of the poor.

In the mid-1960s this point still largely escaped most Team X members who, with the exception of Van Eyck, Woods and De Carlo, seemed to prefer to ignore the destruction of our urban heritage in the name of speculation. The postulative capacities of Team X became paralyzed at this juncture, their inventive energies becoming depleted in the face of an impossible situation. Paradoxically, what now endures from their work is not so much their architectural vision as the suggestive power of their cultural criticism

# Chapter 4
# Place, Production and Scenography: international theory and practice since 1962

What the word for space, *Raum, Rum,* designates is said by its ancient meaning. *Raum* means a place cleared or freed for settlement and lodging. A space is something that has been made room for, something that is cleared and free, namely within a boundary, Greek *peras.* A boundary is not that at which something stops but, as the Greeks recognized, the boundary is that from which something *begins its presencing.* That is why the concept is that of *horismos,* that is, the horizon, the boundary. Space is in essence that for which room has been made, that which is let into its bounds. That for which room is made is always granted and hence is joined, that is gathered, by virtue of a location, that is by such a thing as the bridge. *Accordingly spaces receive their being from locations and not from 'space'.*

Martin Heidegger
'Building, Dwelling and Thinking', 1954

No account of recent developments in architecture can fail to mention the ambivalent role that the profession has, played since the mid-1960s – ambivalent not only in the sense that while professing to act in the public interest it has sometimes assisted uncritically in furthering the domain of an optimized technology, but also in the sense that many of its more intelligent members have abandoned traditional practice, either to resort to direct social action or to indulge in the projection of architecture as a form of art. As far as this last aspect is concerned, one cannot help regarding it as the return of a repressed creativity, as the implosion of utopia upon itself. Architects have of course indulged in such unrealizable projections before but, with the classic exception of Piranesi or, more recently, the fantasmagoria of Bruno Taut's Glass Chain, rarely have they projected their images in such inaccessible terms. Both before and after the trauma of the First World War the positive aspirations of the Enlightenment still had the power to carry a certain conviction. Before that, at the threshold of the 19th century, even the most grandiose of Boullée's visions could, one imagines, have been built had sufficient resources been made available, and clearly Ledoux was as much a builder as he was a visionary. What was true of Ledoux was certainly no less true of Le Corbusier, whose vast urban projections could no doubt all have been realized had sufficient power been placed at his disposal. The 412-metre (1,350-foot) World Trade Center, New York, a framed tube structure in the form of twin towers completed to the designs of Minoru Yamasaki in 1972, or the 30-metre (100-foot) higher Sears Tower, Chicago, designed in 1971 by Bruce Graham and Fazlur Khan of Skidmore, Owings and Merrill, have both served to demonstrate that possibly not even Wright's 1,600-metre-high (1 mile) skyscraper of 1956 was necessarily unfeasible. But such mega-buildings are too exceptional to serve as a model for general practice. Meanwhile, as Manfredo Tafuri has suggested, the aim of the latterday avant garde is either to validate itself through the media or, alternatively, to redeem its guilt by executing the rite of creative exorcism in isolation. The extent to which this last may serve as a subversive tactic (Archigram's 'injecting noise into the system') or as an elaborate metaphor with critical implications depends of course on the complexity of ideas involved and on the intent underlying the whole enterprise.

In the case of the English Archigram group, who began to project Neo-Futurist images just before the first issue of their magazine *Archigram* in 1961, it is obvious that their attitude was closely tied to the technocratic ideology of the American designer Buckminster Fuller and to that of his British apologists John McHale and Reyner Banham. By 1960, at McHale's suggestion, Banham had already earmarked Fuller as the redeeming white knight of the future, in the last chapter of his book *Theory and Design in the First Machine Age*. Archigram's subsequent commitment to a 'high-tech', light-weight, infrastructural approach (the kind of indeterminacy implicit in the work of Fuller and even more evident in Yona Friedman's *L'Architecture mobile* of 1958) brought them, rather paradoxically, to indulge in ironic forms of science fiction, rather than to project solutions that were either truly indeterminate or capable of being realized and appropriated by the society. It is this more than anything else that distinguishes them from that other prominent Fuller disciple on the British scene, Cedric Price, whose Fun Palace of 1961 and Potteries Thinkbelt of 1964 were nothing if not realizable and, in theory at least, both indeterminate and capable, respectively, of meeting an evident demand for popular entertainment and a readily accessible system of higher education.

Aside from a certain subversive eroticism (the biologically functionalist parody evident say in Michael Webb's Sin Centre of 1962) Archigram was more interested in the seductive appeal of space-age imagery and, after Fuller, in the Armageddon overtones of survival technology than in the processes of production or the relevance of such sophisticated technique to the tasks of the moment. For all their surface irony, Ron Herron's 'Walking Cities' of 1964 were clearly projected as stalking across a ruined world in the aftermath of a nuclear war. Like Howard Hughes's 'Glomar Explorer' they suggest some sort of nightmarish salvation, rescuing both men and artifacts after a cataclysmic disaster. These leviathans may be regarded as paralleling Fuller's 1962 proposal to erect a giant dome over the whole of midtown Manhattan. This urban iron lung was projected as a geodesic smog shield, a device which could no doubt be made to double as a fallout shelter in the unlikely event of a nuclear near-miss. With comparable nonchalance, Archigram saw no reason to concern themselves with the social and ecological consequences of their various megastructural proposals, of which Peter Cook's 'Plug-In

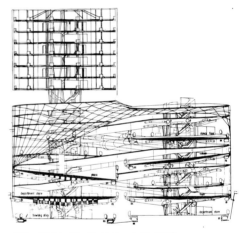

278   Webb, 'Sin Centre' project, 1962.
279   Herron, 'Walking City' project, 1964.

280 Fuller, project for a geodesic dome over midtown Manhattan (river to river, 64th–22nd streets), 1962.

City' of 1964 was a typical example. Similarly, in their obsession with suspended space-age capsules, Dennis Crompton, Michael Webb, Warren Chalk and David Greene felt under no obligation to explain why one might choose to live in such expensive and sophisticated hardware and yet at the same time in brutally cramped conditions. Like Banham acting out the narcissistic gestures of Vishnu in his solipsistic, inflatable bubble, equipped with high fidelity and presumably other conveniences (in homage probably to the philistine ethos of Fuller's ironic lyric 'Roam Home to a Dome': see p. 239), they all proposed space standards that were well below the *Existenzminimum* established by those pre-war functionalists they supposedly despised.

If anything was destined to reduce architecture 'to the level of the activities of certain species of insects and mammals' – to quote Berthold Lubetkin's 1956 attack on the reductivism of Soviet Constructivist architects (his target was Ginzburg's OSA group) – it was surely these residential cells projected by Archigram. Modelled on Fuller's Dymaxion House of 1927 or on his Dymaxion Bathroom of a decade later (see p. 239), these units aspired to being 'autonomous packages', in the sense that they were designed chiefly for individuals or couples. Although this preoccupation with the childless unit may have been an implicit critique of the bourgeois family, the ultimate stance of Archigram was hardly critical, as the following passage from Peter Cook's *Architecture: Action and Plan* of 1967 makes evident:

It will often be part of the architect's brief to investigate the 'possibilities' of a site; in other words to use the ingenuity of the architectural concept to exploit the maximum profit from a piece of land. In the past this would have been considered an immoral use of the talents of an artist. It is now simply part of the sophistication of the whole environmental and building process in which finance can be made into a creative element in design.

The work of Archigram was surprisingly close to that of the Japanese Metabolists, who, reacting to the pressures of Japanese overcrowding, started in the late 1950s to propose constantly growing and adapting 'plug-in' megastructures where the living cells, as in the work of Noriaki Kurokawa, would be reduced to prefabricated pods clipped on to vast helicoidal skyscrapers. Alternatively, as in the projects of Kiyonari Kikutake, they would be attached like limpets to the inner and outer surfaces of large cylinders floating in or on the sea. Kikutake's floating cities are surely among the most poetic visions of the Metabolist movement. Yet, despite the proliferation of off-shore drilling rigs with their working complement dedicated to the extraction of energy, Kikutake's marine cities seem even more remote and inapplicable to everyday life than the megastructures of Archigram. It testifies to the rhetorical avant gardism of the movement that most of the Metabolists went on to establish rather conventional practices. With the exception of Kikutake's Sky House of 1958 and Kurokawa's Nagakin bachelor capsule tower, built in the Ginza, Tokyo, in 1971 (cf. Kurokawa's capsule apartments of 1962), very few Metabolic concepts were realized. Although such frantic futurism is to be distinguished from the intelligent additive urban form proposals advanced by such moderates as Fumihiko Maki and Masato Otaka, Gunther

281    Kikutake, 'Marine City' project, 1958.

282    Kurokawa, Nagakin capsule tower, Tokyo, 1971.

Nitschke had this to say when making an assessment of the Metabolist movement in 1966:

As long as the actual buildings get heavier, harder, more and more monstrous in scale, as long as architecture is taken as a means of expression of power, be it of oneself or of any kind of vulgar institution, which should be serving not ruling society, the talk of greater flexibility and change-loving structures is just fuss. Comparing this structure [Akira Shibuya's Metabolic City project of 1966] with any one of the traditional Japanese structures or modern methods suggested by Wachsmann, Fuller, or Ekuan in Japan, it must be considered a mere anachronism, a thousand years out of date, or to say the least, not an advance of modern architecture in terms of theory and practice.

The decline of the Metabolist vision in Japan came with the evident ideological emptiness of the Osaka Exhibition of 1970. Thereafter the critical lead in Japanese architecture passed from the older Metabolists to the members of the so-called Japanese New Wave, whose work became known largely through the support of two architects of the middle generation, Arata Isozaki and Kazuo Shinohara. While Shinohara's work has remained almost exclusively domestic, Isozaki's stature stems from his double reputation, first as a critical intellectual and second as a public architect whose independent career began with the Oita branch of the Fukuoka Mutual Bank, built in Kyushu in 1966. This successful work led to a whole series of major public structures, including the Gunma Prefectural Museum, Takasaki, dating from 1974.

Isozaki came to the fore internationally in 1968 when he contributed a critical exhibit entitled 'Electric Labyrinth' to the 14th Triennale in Milan. Conceived as a multi-media presentation of the apocalyptic significance of the Hiroshima disaster, this *tour de force* comprising randomly operated pivoting screens and back-projected images established Isozaki's standing with the European avant garde. The Milan Triennale brought him into contact with Archigram and Hans Hollein, and thereafter his work displayed certain aspects of these influences. From Archigram he took the 'high-tech' exuberance of his robot designed for Kenzo Tange's Festival Plaza in the Osaka Exhibition of 1970; from Hollein, his taste for mixing materials with high crafted objects and ironic artistic images, the latter first appearing in the Fukuoka Sogo Bank headquarters in Kitakyushu (1968–71). Apart from his penchant for elaborate interior finishes, Isozaki was inspired,

283

283 Isozaki, Gunma Prefectural Museum of Fine Arts, Takasaki, 1974.

like Kahn, by the *architecture parlante* of Ledoux. Taking Ledoux's emblematic Neoplatonic geometry as his point of departure, Isozaki pursued a gridded high-tech architecture in a series of branch banks designed in the early 1970s, culminating in the *magnum opus* of the Gunma Museum. With this mirage-like, scintillating architecture Isozaki attempted to compensate for the loss of the traditional Japanese 'space of darkness' – the dimly lit, recessive domestic interior which Junichiro Tanizaki had been among the first to lament, in his essay 'In Praise of Shadows' (1933). Sympathetic with Tanizaki's evaluation of the underlit interiors of traditional Japanese buildings but unable to accept the reactionary implications of his cultural nostalgia, Isozaki attempted to evolve a modern equivalent for this traditional illusionistic space. This development reached its peak in the Nagamsami Home Bank (1971), of which he wrote:

This building has almost no form; it is merely a gray expanse. The multi-level grid guides one's lines of sight but does not focus them on anything in particular. At first encounter, the vague gray expanse seems impossible to decipher and utterly odd. The multi-level lattice disperses vision throughout the space, much as various images might be thrown around an area from a central projector. It absorbs all individual spaces that establish strict order. It conceals them, and when that concealment process is over, only the gray expanse remains.

Since the early 1970s Isozaki's work has oscillated constantly between gridded atectonic assemblies (grey expanses) controlled by the superimposition of cubic forms, as in the Gunma Museum and the Shukosha Building in Fukuoka City (1974–75), and a series of barrel-vaulted tectonic structures such as the Fujimi Country Clubhouse near Oita (1972–74) and the Central Library of Kitakyushu City (1972–75). The latest version of this last paradigm is the Museum of Contemporary Art in Los Angeles, under construction in 1984, which is probably his finest recent work.

Unlike the Metabolists, Isozaki and Shinohara and other members of the Japanese New Wave accept the fact that today one can hardly hope to achieve any meaningful relationship between the one-off building and the urban fabric as a whole. This critical attitude has been expressed in a series of extremely formal and introspective houses designed by such architects as Tadao Ando (who will be discussed in the next chapter), Hiromi Fujii, Hiroshi Hara, Itsuko Hasegawa and Toyo Ito, in addition to similarly introverted works by Isozaki and Shinohara.

Ito, who has been influenced to an equal degree by both Isozaki and Shinohara, can be seen as epitomizing the general line of the Japanese New Wave; that is to say, his work is both highly aesthetic and ideologically critical. Like Isozaki and Shinohara he has assumed a fatalistic attitude toward the megalopolis, regarding it as a manifestation of environmental delirium, devoid of sense. He sees the sole possibility for cultural significance to reside in the creation of closed poetic domains, in contrast to the random disorder of the 'Non-Place Urban Realm' (see below). His largest urban work to date, the PMT Building in Nagoya erected in 1978, is a 'paper-thin' structural intervention whose hermetic, largely top-lit form possesses a stoic and acerbic beauty. What we have here is the aristocratic counterform (Isozaki) rather than the mask of a patronizing Populism (Venturi). This much is clear from Ito's essay of 1978, 'Collage and Superficiality in Architecture':

Surface richness in a Japanese city does not consist of a historical accumulation of buildings but rather arises out of a nostalgia for our lost architectural past which is indiscriminately mixed with the superficial icons of the present. Behind an endless desire for nostalgic satisfaction there resides a void without any substance. What I wish to obtain in my architecture is not another nostalgic object, but rather a certain superficiality of expression in order to reveal the nature of the void hidden beneath.

As we have seen, apart from the geodesic dome 'drop-out' culture of the American West Buckminster Fuller's greatest impact has been in Japan and, above all, in Britain, where a continuous 'Dymaxion' development can be traced from the first space-frame and dome projects of Cedric Price and Peter Cook to the more recent work of Foster Associates.

The paradigm of this movement is the Centre Pompidou in Paris, built in 1977 to the designs of the short-lived Anglo-Italian partnership of Richard Rogers and Renzo Piano. The building is obviously a realization of the technological and infrastructural rhetoric of Archigram; and while the full consequences of this approach are becoming evident through everyday use, it is apparent that certain paradoxical achievements may be claimed on its behalf. In the first place, it is an outstanding popular success – as much for its sensational nature as for anything else. In the second, it is a brilliant *tour de force* in advanced technique, looking for all the world like the oil refinery whose technology it attempts to emulate. It seems, however, to have come into being with the minimum regard for the specificity of its brief – for the art and library holdings it was destined to house. It represents the design approach of indeterminacy and optimum flexibility taken to extremes. Not only was it necessary to build another 'building' within its skeletonal volume in order to provide sufficient wall surface and enclosure for the exhibition of art; but also the provision of 50-metre (165-foot) lattice truss spans throughout, in order to ensure optimum flexibility, seems to have proved excessive. In the first instance we have an under-provision of wall surface, in the second an over-provision of flexibility. The additional fact that the scale of the building is quite indifferent to its urban context and that it is incapable of representing its status as an institution is consistent with the ideological position from which it stems, since such concerns

284, 285  Piano and Rogers, Centre Pompidou, Paris, 1972–77.

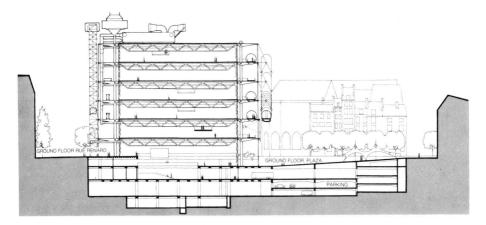

286 Llewelyn-Davies Weeks Forestier-Walker and Bor, strategic plan for Milton Keynes New Town, Bucks., 1972. Schematic road grid laid over the landscape. Residential areas (pale shading) and employment areas (dark) are irregularly intermingled.

were always foreign to the English Dymaxion school of design. One of the unintended ironies of this work seems to derive from the spectacular view of the city which may be gained from the glazed escalator access tubes, hung off the west side of the building. These access ways are now barely adequate to accommodate the average daily attendance of more than 20,000 visitors, a number of whom come not for the cultural facilities offered but for the building and the view.

An equally indeterminate approach was adopted in the 1972 design of the English New Town, Milton Keynes. This city, based on a somewhat irregular street grid, was apparently conceived as an instant Los Angeles to be laid over the agrarian landscape of Buckinghamshire. Its empty irregular network, configurated after the topography, was yet another exercise in indeterminacy pushed to absurdity. Despite the Neo-Classicism of its Miesian shopping centre, its capacity to represent a municipal identity is virtually non-existent. One has no notion of arrival here save for the graphic indication of the legal boundary, and for the casual visitor Milton Keynes seems nothing more than a rather random collection of more or less well-designed housing estates. One thinks by contrast of the orthogonal precision of Wright's Broadacre City, where, despite the relentless dispersal of the urban fabric, places

would have acquired a certain definition by virtue of their orthogonal boundaries. Here, needless to say, what boundaries there are fail to correspond to any perceivable order, and this is hardly surprising given that the structure of the town was influenced by the planning theories of Melvin Webber, whose slogan 'Non-Place Urban Realm' seems to have been adopted as a credo by the official architects of the plan, Llewelyn-Davies Weeks Forestier-Walker and Bor. The fact that this slogan stemmed from Webber's commitment to the Kristaller-Losch central place location theory — then as now, the most dynamic model available for the creation of optimum marketing conditions — could hardly have escaped either the architects or the City Corporation. This selection of an open-ended planning model in accordance with the hypothetical interests of a consumer society was surely a conscious choice.

Within the Hochschule für Gestaltung (HfG) at Ulm in Germany, initially conceived in 1951 by the Swiss architect Max Bill as the institutional successor to the Bauhaus, a rigorous approach to design and technology brought itself in the space of a decade to confront the fundamental contradictions of designing for a consumer society. After Bill's resignation as director in 1956, the HfG embraced a form of 'operational research' by which it intended to evolve a heuristic of design, whereby the forms of objects would be determined in accordance with precise methods for analyzing the nature of their production and use. Unfortunately, this method rapidly degenerated into a form of method-idolatry in which the methodological 'purist' was invariably prepared to forego a solution rather than arrive at a design that had not been ergonomically determined. As far as Herbert Ohl's Department of Industrialized Building was concerned, this led to an emphasis on the design of industrial components to the exclusion of any comprehensive analysis of specific building tasks. Real needs were often overlooked in an effort to produce extremely sophisticated, if relatively simple, prototypical components for the rationalized production of built form. By the mid-1960s the more critical faculty members, Tomás Maldonado, Claude Schnaidt and Gui Bonsiepe, had jointly recognized that this idealization of product design was a dead end, conveniently overlooking in the name of scientific method and functional aesthetics the fundamental contradictions inherent in neo-capitalist society. As far as architecture was concerned this was never more forcibly expressed than by Schnaidt, who in his essay 'Architecture and Political Commitment' (1967) wrote:

In the days when the pioneers of modern architecture were young, they thought like William Morris that architecture should be an 'art of the people for the people'. Instead of pandering to the tastes of the privileged few, they wanted to satisfy the requirements of the community. They wanted to build dwellings, matched to human needs, to erect a Cité Radieuse. But they had reckoned without the commercial instincts of the bourgeoisie who lost no time in arrogating their theories to themselves and pressing them into service for the purposes of money-making. Utility quickly became synonymous with profitability. Anti-academic forms became the new décor of the ruling classes. The rational dwelling was transformed into the minimum dwelling, the Cité Radieuse into the urban conglomeration and austerity of line into poverty of form. The

287  Bill, Hochschule für Gestaltung, Ulm, 1953–55, showing (left to right) workshop block, library, administration building and student housing. In the distance is Ulm Cathedral.

architects of the trade unions, co-operatives, and socialist municipalities were enlisted in the service of the whisky distillers, detergent manufacturers, the bankers, and the Vatican. Modern architecture, which wanted to play its part in the liberation of mankind by creating a new environment to live in, was transformed into a giant enterprise for the degradation of the human habitat.

Later in the same article Schnaidt criticized the achievements of the 'alternative' avant garde of the 1960s:

It is their philosophy that even the most audacious concepts in architecture and city planning are feasible with modern technological aids. This is what lies behind their quest for something resembling space ships, packing crates, filing systems, refineries, or artificial islands. . . .

These futurist architects may well have the merit of taking technology to its logical conclusion but more often than not their attitude ends up in technolatry. The refinery and the space capsule may serve as models of technical and formal perfection but if they become the objects of a cult, the lessons they can teach will

288 Superstudio, 'A Journey from A to B', 1969. 'There will be no further reason for roads or squares'.

penetrable megaliths, faced in mirror-glass, to the depiction of a science-fiction landscape in which nature had been rendered benevolent — in short the quintessential anti-architectural utopia. In 1969 they wrote:

Beyond the convulsions of over-production a state can be born of calm in which a world takes shape without products or refuse, a zone in which mind is energy and raw material and is also the final product, the only intangible object for consumption.

And again in 1972:

The objects we will need will be only flags or talismans, signals for an existence that continues or simple utensils for simple operations. Thus, on the one hand, there will remain utensils . . . on the other, such symbolic objects as monuments or badges . . . objects that can easily be carried about if we should become nomads, or heavy and immovable if we decide to stay in one place forever.

Beyond the rule of the performance principle, which the philosopher Herbert Marcuse had already characterized as defining life in terms of instruments and consumer goods, Superstudio projected a silent, anti-futurist and technologically optimistic utopia where, in the words of Marcuse's *Eros and Civilization* (1962),

The level of living would be measured by other criteria: the universal gratification of the basic human needs, and freedom from guilt and fear — internalized as well as externalized, instinctual as well as 'rational'. . . . In this case the quantum of instinctual energy still to be diverted to necessary labor . . . would be so small that a large area of repressive constraints and modifications no longer sustained by external forces would collapse.

It is significant that Superstudio chose to represent such a non-repressive world in terms of an architecture that was virtually invisible, or, where visible, totally useless and by design auto-destructive (see their self-disintegrating mirror-glass dam for Niagara Falls). For all that they rendered the contradiction of the 'Continuous Monument' as an impenetrable mass

completely miss their mark. This unlimited confidence in the potentialities of technology goes hand in hand with a surprising degree of disingenuousness concerning the future of man. . . . Such visions as these are soothing to many architects: braced by so much technology, by such confidence in the future, they feel reassured and justified in their social and political abdication.

Yet while one might challenge its effectiveness, the architectural avant garde of the 1960s had not entirely abdicated its social responsibility. Many factions existed whose orientation was decidedly political and whose attitude towards advanced technology was by no means uncritical. Of these mention must be made of the Italian Superstudio group, who were, in this respect, among the most poetic. Influenced by the 'unitary town planning' concepts of the International Situationist Constant Nieuwenhuys, who, in his New Babylon of 1960, had postulated a constantly changing urban fabric that would respond to the 'ludic' tendency in man, Superstudio, led by Adolfo Natalini, started in 1966 to produce a body of work which was more or less divided between representing the form of a 'Continuous Monument' as a mute urban sign and producing a series of vignettes illustrating a world from which consumer goods had been eliminated. Their work varied from the projection of vast im-

reminiscent of Boullée, it was nonetheless a metaphysical image, as fleeting and as cryptic as the Suprematist monuments of Malevich or the 'wrapped' buildings of Christo, an artist who, after wrapping the Kunsthalle at Berne in 1968, went on to package and hence to 'silence' most of the institutional monuments of the Western world.

The growing awareness in the early 1960s that in common practice there was a fundamental lack of correspondence between the values of the architect and the needs and mores of the user led to a whole series of reformist moves which sought in a variety of counter-utopian ways to overcome this divorce of the designer from everyday society. These factions not only challenged the inaccessibility of the abstract syntax of contemporary architecture but also tried to devise ways in which architects could serve those poor sectors of the society not normally addressed by the profession. In his book *Supports: An Alternative to Mass Housing* (1972) N.J. Habraken first tackled the problem of building residential stock that could meet the variable needs of its users, and John Turner and William Mangin began in 1963 to write up their experience as consultants to the spontaneous 'squatter' cities then coming into existence around the perimeters of large South American towns. The following situation, as described by Mangin at the time, may be taken as typical of many other cities throughout the Continent:

The tremendous population growth in Peru, together with the centralization of social, political, economic and cultural rewards in Lima, the capital city, has led to recent intensified migration from the provinces to Lima. It is safe to say that at least a million of Lima's two million people were born outside the city. The increase in the numbers of migrants to the city and the subsequent dramatic resettlement of many of them in 'unaided self-help' squatter settlements, 'barriadas', have drawn considerable attention locally and abroad and for the first time made many Peruvians aware of the situation. The city has probably grown in the past in much the same way, but the magnitude and the visibility of the recent influx made it

seem like a new phenomenon. The migrants come from practically all regions and all social classes and ethnic groupings in the country.

Problems of this magnitude, of course, lie beyond the province of architecture as an autonomous discipline and even outside the process of land settlement and building as it is commonly understood. All the same, the scale of the problem, its visibility and the need to confront it in a way that would assist the squatters to build in a more effective manner (the provision in most instances of water and sewer infrastructures), created a general climate in which the forty-year-old Neue Sachlichkeit formula of slum clearance followed by massive rehousing was for the first time subjected to radical reconsideration. Habraken argued that the whole approach needed to be rethought, not only in respect of the Third World but also in the face of growing user discontent in industrialized economies.

The establishment of alternative modes of practice to meet this situation, for both the developed and the underdeveloped world, has proved elusive, and the panacea of 'user participation' (hard to define appropriately and even more difficult to achieve) has only served to make us acutely aware of the in-

289 De Carlo, Mateotti village, Terni, 1974–77.

tractability of the problem and of the fact that probably it can only be effectively tackled on a piecemeal basis, by responding appropriately to specific situations. Nevertheless, advocacy planning remains with us as a radical legacy of the 1960s, although the results of its application have varied widely, from the political manipulation of the underprivileged to the recent achievement of a section of low-rise housing in Terni north of Rome, designed by Giancarlo de Carlo, in accordance with a brief developed as a result of extensive discussions with the local trade union. There is no doubt that this whole undertaking has resulted in housing of remarkable quality and variety, although the manner in which the users' desires were finally interpreted remains a controversial issue.

As far as transforming the practice of the Neue Sachlichkeit was concerned, Habraken and his Foundation for Architectural Research (SAR) in Eindhoven did their technocratic best to take the promise of Yona Friedman's open infra-structural approach, his 'mobile architecture', to its logical conclusion. To this end they proposed a low-rise, multi-storey, *support* structure, whose plan arrangement was undetermined, save for fixed access, kitchen and bathroom zones. Outside these zones the occupant would be free to arrange the plan of his allocated volume in any way he wished. Regrettably, Habraken intended to furnish this spatial matrix with industrialized, modular components fabricated along the lines of the car industry and brought to a level of technical sophistication and structural tolerance which has yet to be attained, even in the wholesale prefabricated building programmes of the Soviet Union. Moreover, like Friedman, he tended to overlook the fact that much of the inherent 'freedom' of the system would automatically disappear once it came under the auspices of monopoly capital. Housing after all has yet to become a truly consumable item. Fortunately, the SAR concept does not stand or fall by its technology alone, and Habraken has opened up a line of research which has yet to be fully explored. A quite remarkable work apparently influenced by Habraken's thought is the distinguished 'expandable' terrace housing built in

Genterstrasse in Munich in 1971 by Otto Steidle and Doris and Ralph Thut.

Populism

The Loosian recognition of the loss of cultural identity that urbanization had brought in its wake returned with a vengeance in the mid 1960s as architects began to realize that the reductive codes of contemporary architecture had led to an impoverishment of the urban environment. The exact manner in which this impoverishment has come about however — the extent to which it is due to abstract tendencies present in Cartesian rationality itself or alternatively to ruthless economic exploitation — is a complex and critical issue which has yet to be judiciously decided. It cannot be denied that the tabula rasa reductivism of the Modern Movement has played a salient role in the wholesale destruction of urban culture; thus the emphasis that the 'Post-Modernist critique has placed on respecting the existing urban context can hardly be discredited. This anti-utopian 'contextualist' critique was already available in the 1960s, first in Colin Rowe's neo-Sittesque approach to urban form (as taught in Cornell University and presented in his book of 1979, *Collage City*), and then in Robert Venturi's *Complexity and Contradiction in Architecture* of 1966 in which he wrote:

The main justification for honky-tonk elements in architectural order is their very existence. They are what we have. Architects can bemoan or try to ignore them or even try to abolish them, but they will not go away. Or they will not go away for a long time, because architects do not have the power to replace them (nor do they know what to replace them with), and because these commonplace elements accommodate existing needs for variety and communication. The old clichés involving both banality and mess will still be the context of our new architecture, and our new architecture significantly will be the context for them. I am taking the limited view, I admit, but the limited view, which architects have tended to belittle, is as important as the visionary view, which they have tended to glorify but have not brought about. The short-term plan, which expediently combines the old and the new, must accompany the long-term plan. Architecture is evolutionary as well as revolutionary. As an art it will acknowledge what is and what ought to be, the immediate and the speculative.

With the publication in 1972 of *Learning from Las Vegas*, written by Venturi, Denise Scott-Brown and Steve Izenour, Venturi's sensitive and sane assessment of the cultural realities confronting everyday practice — the need to set order against disorder and vice versa — shifted from an acceptance of honky-tonk to its glorification; from a modest appraisal of Main Street as being 'almost all right' to a reading of the billboard strip as the transmogrified utopia of the Enlightenment, lying there like a science-fiction transposition in the midst of the desert!

This rhetoric, which would have us see A & P parking lots as the *tapis verts* of Versailles, or Caesar's Palace in Las Vegas as the modern equivalent of Hadrian's Villa, is ideology in its purest form. The ambivalent manner in which Venturi and Scott-Brown exploit this ideology as a way of bringing us to condone the ruthless kitsch of Las Vegas, as an exemplary mask for the concealment of the brutality of our own environment, testifies to the aestheticizing intent of their thesis. And while their critical distance permits them the luxury of describing the typical casino as a ruthless landscape of seduction and control — they emphasize the two-way mirrors and the boundless, dark, disorientating timelessness of its interior — they take care to disassociate themselves from its values. This does not prevent them, however, from positing it as a model for the restructuring of urban form:

Beyond the town the only transition between the Strip and the Mojave desert is a zone of rusting beer cans. Within the town the transition is as ruthlessly sudden. Casinos whose fronts relate so sensitively to the highway turn their ill-kempt backsides towards the local environment, exposing residual forms and spaces of mechanical equipment and service areas.

The irony with which architects from Lutyens to Venturi have sought to transcend through wit the contradictory circumstances under which they are asked to build here seems to degenerate into total acquiescence; and the cult of 'the ugly and the ordinary' becomes indistinguishable from the environmental consequences of the market economy. Between the lines, the authors are brought to concede the superfluity of architectural design in a society that is exclusively motivated by ruthless economic drives; a society which has nothing of greater significance to represent than the giant neon-lit sky sign of the average strip. At the end of their analysis they are almost brought to concede that the loss of the monument is an absence that can hardly be compensated for by the sophistries of the 'decorated shed':

The casino in Las Vegas is a big low space. It is the archetype of all public interior spaces whose heights are diminished for reasons of budget or air conditioning. Today, span is easy to achieve and volume is governed by mechanical and economical limitations in height. But railroad stations, restaurants and shopping arcades only ten feet high reflect as well our changing attitude to monumentality ... we have replaced the monumental space of Pennsylvania Station by a subway above ground and that of Grand Central Terminal remains mainly through its magnificent conversion to an advertising vehicle.

Venturi is determined to present Las Vegas as an authentic outburst of popular fantasy. But, as Maldonado has argued in his book *La Speranza Progettuale* (*Design, Nature and Revolution*) of 1970, the reality would indicate the contrary, that Las Vegas is the pseudo-communicative culmination of 'more than half a century of masked manipulative violence directed towards the formation of an apparently free and playful urban environment in which men are completely devoid of innovative will'.

Be this as it may, the Venturi faction did not take their Populist stand in isolation. On the contrary, they soon acquired a sympathetic following in both academic and professional circles – from the historian/critic Vincent Scully, who initially rallied to their cause with his laudatory introduction to Venturi's *Complexity and Contradiction*, and who went on to confirm his continuing support with his polemic *The Shingle Style Revisited* (1974), and from architects such as Charles Moore and Robert Stern, who, while adopting more varied *ad hoc* attitudes towards the manipulation of form, were nonetheless equally open to exploiting the essentially atectonic nature of the American balloon-frame.

The net effect, at least in Anglo-Saxon circles, has been to stimulate a rather indiscriminate reaction against all forms of modernist expression in architecture, a situation which the critic Charles Jencks was prompt to identify as 'Post-Modern'. In his book *The Language of Post-Modern Architecture* (1977), Jencks effectively characterized Post-Modernism as being a Populist-Pluralist art of immediate communicability. At the end of the first edition of this text, he hailed Gaudí's 'pre-modern' Casa Battló (1906) as an exemplary work, which was readily accessible, inasmuch as the populace could decipher and identify with the iconography of Catalan separatism which it embodied (Jencks is referring here to the lance-like tower and the dragon's back roof representing the ultimate triumph of the Catalan hero St George over the 'dragon' of Madrid). Nationalist mythologies cannot be invented overnight, however, and the sobering fact remains that many so-called Populist works have nothing more to convey than a gratifying cosiness or an ironic comment on the absurdity of suburban kitsch. More often than not Post-Modernist architects use the private house as an occasion for indulging in idiosyncratic obsessions, as is all too evident from the triviality of Stanley Tigerman's Hot Dog and Daisy houses of the mid-1970s.

291  Jahn, Bank of the South West, Houston, 1982 ff.

290  Stern, Ehrman House, Armonk, N.Y., 1975.

Each year American Populism seems to grow increasingly diffuse in its eclectic parodies from the Art Deco conceits of say Venturi's Brant House at Greenwich, Connecticut (1971) and Stern's closely related Ehrman House at Armonk, New York (1975) to the self-styled 'Popular Machinism' (in effect, neo-Art Deco) of Helmut Jahn's typical crystal skyscraper, the high-rise, curtain-walled structure rendered as a giant Wurlitzer organ. These and other Populist divagations indicate that the purging simplicity of 'the dumb

292  Moore, Piazza d'Italia, New Orleans, 1975–79.

and the ordinary' (in Venturi's phrase) has now been left behind, along with the sparsely elegant Trubeck and Wislocki houses which Venturi realized on Cape Cod in 1970.

By scenographically simulating the profiles of classical and vernacular and thereby reducing the architectonics of construction to pure parody, Populism tends to undermine the society's capacity for continuing with a significant culture of built form. The consequence of this for the field as a whole has been a seductive but decisive drift towards a kind of 'tawdry pathos', to use Jencks's felicitous yet ambivalent assessment of the theatrical effects created by Moore and Turnbull in their designs for Kresge College on the University of California's Santa Cruz campus (1974). The cynicism which ultimately motivates such scenographic operations has since been openly conceded by Moore, above all in his account of the design process which led to the Piazza d'Italia in New Orleans (1979). In 1981 he wrote:

I remembered that the architectural orders were Italian, with a little help from the Greeks, and so we thought we could put Tuscan, Doric, Ionic and Corinthian columns over the fountain, but they overshadowed it, obliterating the shape of Italy. So instead we added a 'Delicatessen Order' that we thought could resemble sausages hanging in a shop window, thus illustrating its transalpine location. But now I think there is going to be an Italian restaurant and no sausages. . . . there was a little bit of money left over so we thought we would bang up a temple out front to show that our piazza was behind it. There was enough money too to make a campanile beside the temple to show off our existence and to make more patterns with the verticals of the skyscraper behind. Someday there will be shops around it, like Ghirardelli Square, but for the moment it is just sitting by itself and a little lonesome.

In contrast to the flaccid eclecticism of Moore (who abandoned the constructional purity of his Sea Ranch complex in Sonoma County, California (1964–66) as soon as it was completed), Frank Gehry's domestic work, above all his own deconstructed 'anti-house' (cf. Marcel Duchamp's 'anti-painting') built in Santa Monica in 1979, introduced a genuinely subversive element into the complacent decadence of American Populist architecture. However, this creative resistance has been more than balanced by the uncritical absorption of American Populism into the European mainstream, a cultural transfer effected by Paolo Portoghesi's architectural section of the 1980 Venice Biennale which bore the seductive double title 'The Presence of the Past' and 'The End of Prohibition'. It is significant that the full-size façades of Portoghesi's 'Strada Novissima' in the Arsenal (fig. 309) were realized by scene-builders from the Italian film industry. The only exception was the design by Leon Krier, who, no doubt out of 'moral' deference to his beloved Heinrich Tessenow (see the latter's *Handwerk*

293  Gehry, Gehry House, Santa Monica, Calif., 1979.

*und Kleinstadt* of 1910), insisted on building his façade out of real materials.

## Rationalism

Nothing could be further from the Populist programme, at least at its origin, than the Italian Neo-Rationalist movement, the so-called 'Tendenza', which was clearly an attempt to save both architecture and the city from being overrun by the all-pervasive forces of megalopolitan consumerism.

This return to the 'limits' of architecture was initiated by the publication of two singularly seminal texts, Aldo Rossi's *L'architettura della città* (1966) and Giorgio Grassi's *La costruzione logica dell'architettura* (1967). The first stressed the part to be played by established building types in determining the morphological structure of urban form as it develops in time; the second attempted to formulate the necessary compositional or combinatorial rules for architecture – the intrinsic logic by which Grassi himself had arrived at his own highly restrained expression. While insisting that everyday needs must be met, both men rejected the principle by which form is supposed to follow function – ergonomics – and asserted instead the *relative* autonomy of architectural order. Aware of the tendency of interested rationality to absorb and distort every significant cultural gesture, Rossi structured his work about historical architectonic elements that could recall and yet transcend the rational if arbitrary paradigms of the Enlightenment; the pure form postulated in the second half of the 18th century by Piranesi, Ledoux, Boullée and Lequeu. The most enigmatic, not to say hermetic, aspect of his thought resides in his unstated preoccupation with the Panopticon (cf. Michel Foucault's *Surveiller et punir* of 1975) under the rubric of which he would surely include – after Pugin's *Contrasts* of 1843 – the school, the hospital and the prison. Rossi seems to have obsessively returned to these regulatory, quasi-punitive, institutions which for him, in conjunction with the monument and cemetery, constitute the only programmes capable of embodying the values of architecture *per se*. After the thesis that Loos first set out in his essay *Architektur* of 1910, Rossi has recognized that most mod-

294 Rossi, apartment block for the Gallaratese district of Milan, 1969–73.

295 Rossi, project for Modena Cemetery, 1971. Aerial perspective.

ern programmes are inappropriate vehicles for architecture and for him this has meant having recourse to a so-called analogical architecture whose referents and elements are to be abstracted from the vernacular, in the broadest possible sense. To this end his Gallaratese apartment block, designed as part of Carlo Aymonino's housing complex built on the outskirts of Milan in 1973, was an occasion to evoke the architecture of the traditional Milanese tenement. Similarly his town hall for Trieste, projected in the form of a penitentiary in 1973, was both a homage to the local 19th-century building tradition and a sardonic comment on the ultimate nature of modern bureaucracy. Like Leon Krier who has since taken a similar path, Rossi attempts to evade the twin chimeras of modernity – positivistic logic and a blind faith in progress – by returning to both the building typology and the constructional forms of the second half of the 19th century. Of his contribution to the Gallaratese complex, he wrote:

In my design for the residential block in the Gallaratese district of Milan (1969–73), there is an analogical relationship with certain engineering works that mix freely with both the corridor typology and a related feeling I have always experienced in the architecture of the traditional Milanese tenements, where the corridors signify a life-style bathed in everyday occurrences, domestic intimacy and varied personal relationships. However, another aspect of this design was made clear to me by Fabio Reinhart driving through the San Bernardino Pass, as we often did to reach Zürich from the Ticino Valley. Reinhart noticed the repetitive element in the system of open-sided tunnels, and therefore the inherent pattern. I understood . . . how I must have been conscious of that particular structure . . . without necessarily intending to express it in a work of architecture.

This analogical approach, suspended, as Rossi himself said, between 'inventory and memory', permeates his entire oeuvre, from the bunker-like resistance monument projected for Cuneo in 1962 to the Modena Cemetery of 1971, with its references not only to the traditional ossuary but also, by association, to the factory and to the traditional farm of the Lombardy region.

Other Italians who made important contributions to the Tendenza were Vittorio Gregotti, whose book *Il territorio dell'architettura* (1966) had an extensive influence, and Enzo Bonfanti, who with Massimo Scolari edited the Neo-Rationalist magazine *Contraspazio* in the second half of the 1960s. Finally credit has to be accorded to Manfredo Tafuri, whose writings were a major

296  Reichlin and Reinhart, Tonini House, Torricella, 1974.

influence on the movement, and to Franco Purini and Laura Thermes, whose theoretical projects explored the potential range of the Neo-Rationalist syntax. Paradoxically, the Tendenza has realized very little in Italy, though it has had an impact on Italian city-planning and the historic preservation of urban centres, the classic example being Cervellati and Scannarini's analytical study of Bologna, which influenced the development of that city throughout the 1970s.

The most extensive realization of the Tendenza outside Italy has undoubtedly been in the Swiss region of the Ticino, where a 'rationalist' school of considerable vigour was already flourishing in the early 1960s. While Bruno Reichlin and Fabio Reinhart followed Rossi closely (see their Tonini House in Torricella, 1974), the Ticino School included architects whose work came into being under a much broader Rationalist influence. Typical in this regard is Aurelio Galfetti's Neo-Corbusian Rotalinti House, Bellinzona (1961), which pre-dates the emergence of the Tendenza as an influence by almost a decade. It should also be noted that the Ticinese architects were privileged with links to the pre-war Italian Rationalist movement, in particular Alberto Sartoris and Rino Tami (see below, p. 322).

The 'School of Madrid' was likewise privileged in having a local Rational tradition to which it could refer directly. Despite the interruption caused by Fascism and the subsequent seductions of the 'organic' ideology of Frank Lloyd

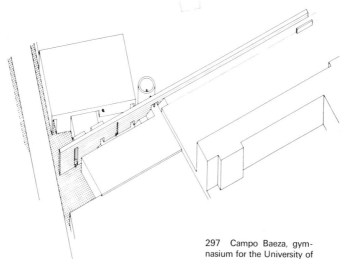

297 Campo Baeza, gymnasium for the University of Madrid, 1983.

298 Ciriani, detail of Noisy 2, Marne-la-Vallée, 1980.

Wright, the continuous cultivation of tectonic reason enabled the Madrid School to sustain a line of thought which brought together three levels of rationality: planning logic, elevational deportment and structural empiricism. This tripartite inter-relation of rational principles is consistently carried over from one generation of Madrid architects to the next, including in the linear development such figures and works as Luis Lacasa (Students' Dormitory, Madrid University, 1935), Alejandro de la Sota (Governor's Building, Tarragona, 1957, and gymnasium of the Colegio Maravillas, 1962), Rafael Moneo and Ramón Bescós (Bankinter, Madrid, 1976), and finally, but from de la Sota's generation, Francisco Javier Sáenz de Oiza (Banco de Bilbao, Madrid, 1980). That the Neo-Rationalism of the younger generation in Spain has been grafted onto this root is borne out by such works as Alberto Campo Baeza's gymnasium projected in 1983 for the University of Madrid. At the same time, more normative connections to the Italian Tendenza are evident in the work of Estudio Dos, Manuel de las Casas, and, – removed from Madrid – in the doctrinaire work of the Basque architects Miguel Garay and José Ignacio Linazasoro, especially their Ikastola School near Irun, completed in 1978.

Since the late 1960s Neo-Rationalism has attained a wide following throughout Continental Europe. In France, its influence is apparent in H.E. Ciriani's Noisy 2 apartment complex in Marne-la-Vallée near Paris (1980). In Germany, Neo-Rationalism has found its principal manifestation in the typological work of Mathias Ungers, Jürgen Sawade and J.P. Kleihues. Recent works of consequence in this regard are Ungers' extension to the Messehalle (1983) and his Architecture Museum (1984), both in Frankfurt. In Berlin a sampling of Rationalist work would surely include Kleihues' Vinetaplatz perimeter housing block in Wedding (1978) and his megastructural hospital in Neukölln (1984).

Particularly significant in the German development was Ungers' adoption of a modified Neo-Rationalist approach to urban form, after his return from the United States in 1975. His thesis of that time, that in the future we shall often find ourselves confronted with the problem of planned metropolitan shrinkage, rather than expansion or renewal, has imparted a certain urgency to his approach. Ungers recommends a fragmentary urban strategy comprising forms of development limited in accordance with the topographical and institutional constraints of a specific task in a particular context. This appears in such projects as his 1976 Hotel Berlin or his 1978 proposal for a multi-use building in the centre of Hildesheim. Where in the Hotel Berlin he opted for a self-contained 'city in miniature', close to the devastated urban landscape of the historic Lutzowplatz, at Hildesheim he attempted to rationalize and reinterpret the received type of the medieval market hall. His only truly contextual realization to date has been his Schillerstrasse perimeter block in Berlin, completed in 1982.

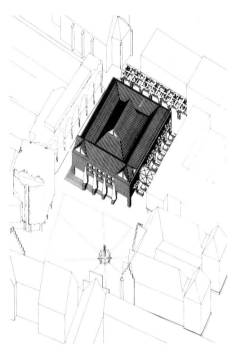

299 Ungers, project for a 'Stadtloggia' in the marketplace at Hildesheim, 1980.

Ungers has been a major Neo-Rationalist theoretician and teacher, first in the Technische Universität in Berlin and then at Cornell University, where for eight years (1967–74) he directed the Department of Architecture. His consistent application of the principle of typological transformation to both teaching and practice gave his pedagogical method great conviction. He made the full range of this

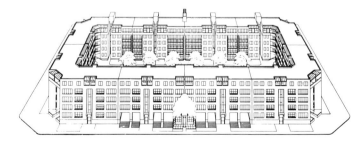

300 Kleihues, perimeter block housing, Berlin-Wedding, 1978. This residential type has the capacity to engender both courtyards and streets.

transformational precept explicit in 1982:

When architecture is seen as a continuous process, in which theses and antitheses are dialectically integrated, or as a process, in which history is as closely involved as the anticipation of history, in which the past has the same weight as looking forward to the future, then the process of transformation is not only the instrument of design, but it is the very object of design. At the same time it becomes possible to make reference to the specific reality of each individual site where the architecture will be built – and therefore to the genius loci – and to discover the poetry of the place and give it expression. In this way the site is used to its best advantage.

The principle of transformation is active in all fields of nature, life and art. It is the principle of formation (Gestaltungsprinzip) capable of organizing divergent elements into a planned totality. Thus the principle of transformation – as it can be grasped for example in the historical transformations of the town plan of Trier – converts a given stabilized organization into chaos and eventually, following the laws of chance, into a new order. A differentiated and planned organisation is submerged over the course of time by chance and spontaneity, which in the end produce an organisation that is genuinely different and

contrasts with the previous one; an organisation, that is, of immediacy and pragmatic necessity.

This grounding of architecture in the dialectic of typological transformation exerted a major influence on the Luxembourg architect Robert Krier, who spent a number of years in Ungers' Cologne studio as his assistant. However where Ungers was to remain open to the free interchange and generation of both type and technique, including industrial technique, Robert Krier and, to an even greater extent, his brother Leon adopted an exclusively craft approach to the generation of tectonic and urban form. Thus we find Leon Krier writing in 1976:

The debate which both Robert Krier and I want to raise with our projects is that of urban morphology as against the zoning of planners. The restoration of precise forms of urban space as against the wasteland which is created by zoning. The design of urban spaces, both traffic and pedestrian, linear and focal is, on the one hand, a method which is general enough to allow flexibility and change and, on the other, precise enough to create both spatial and built continuity within the city . . . we try in our projects to re-establish the dialectic of building and public realm, of solid and void,

301  L. Krier, project for Echternach, Luxembourg, 1970. The continuous pitched roof (centre to bottom right) contains shops, apartments and a school.

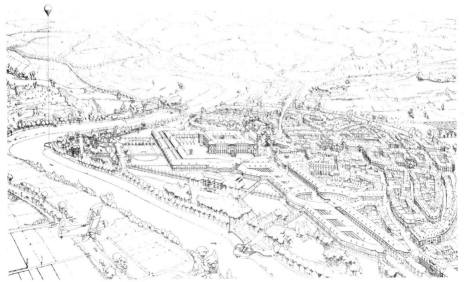

of the built organism and the spaces it necessarily creates around itself . . . the architectural
language we use for fairly large urban parts is
both simple and ambiguous. In Echternach
(1970) we used the same craft which after the
war reconstructed the city, the Abbey, and the
annex buildings.

The weakness of this position is that the building
industry has now been rationalized to such a
degree that it is increasingly difficult to maintain
high-quality craft production as a universal
standard. At the same time there seems no
apparent reason why a project such as Leon Krier's
Royal Mint Square housing for London (1974)
could not have been realized by using a judicious
mixture of craft and rationalized building methods.

302  Meier, High Museum, Atlanta, 1980–83.

In the United States in the 1970s, despite the
following enjoyed by Aldo Rossi, the Tendenza
did not take root in theory and practice. In part this
may be attributed to its lack of relevance to the
American city, which has nowhere the same
typological and morphological complexity as its
traditional European counterpart. The main Tendenza thesis about the 'continuity of the
monument' could have little credibility in a society
where the urban context itself was so unstable. On
the other hand an attempt was made in the second
half of the 1960s to develop a theoretical base as
rigorous and ideological as that achieved by the
pre-war European avant garde. This 'discourse'
arose out of the work of the 'Five Architects', a
loose-knit association of New York-based architects under the leadership of Peter Eisenman.
While two members of the 'New York Five'
grounded their work in extreme avant-gardist
aesthetic practice, namely Eisenman and John
Hejduk, who took the work of Giuseppe Terragni
and Theo van Doesburg as their respective
paradigms, the remaining three, Michael Graves,
Charles Gwathmey and Richard Meier, assumed
the Purist villas of Le Corbusier as their point of
departure. The New York Five's 'modernist'
commitment to the idea of an autonomous
architecture, decidedly removed from what they
saw as the vulgar functionalism of the Neue
Sachlichkeit, was most categorically expressed in
Eisenman's House VI (Frank House) built at West
Cornwall, Connecticut, in 1972, and in certain
polemical projects by Hejduk – his Diamond

House series (1963–67) and above all his Wall
House (1970). While Hejduk has since abandoned neo-avant-gardism to devote his artistic
energies to the creation of urban 'myths' (see his
Berlin Masques, 1981) and Graves has left behind
the Neo-Purism of his early work in favour of a
more decorative Post-Modernist approach (see
below), Gwathmey and Meier have remained
more faithful to their Purist roots, above all Meier,
whose High Museum in Atlanta, Georgia (1980–
83) and Applied Art Museum in Frankfurt
(1979–84) have secured him a reputation as one
of the most significant American *public* architects
of his generation.

The New York Five were not the only architects
of the late 1960s and early 1970s to ground their
work in the aesthetic and ideological premises of
the 20th-century avant garde. The role they played
in New York found its parallel in London in the
work of OMA (Office for Metropolitan Architecture), comprising Rem Koolhaas, Elia and Zoe
Zenghelis and Madelon Vriesendorp. Like Hejduk,
whose early work was 'eclectically' inspired
almost equally by Neoplasticism and the later
Mies, Koolhaas and Zenghelis predicated their
urban projects on the Suprematist architecture of
Ivan Leonidov while at the same time turning to
Surrealist practice for ways of achieving what
Roland Barthes called *'une répétition différente'*.
Aside from giving rise through teaching to a
subsequent generation of Neo-Suprematists,
most notably Laurinda Spear of Arquitectonica,

Florida (Spear House, Miami, 1979) and Zaha Hadid in London (Hong Kong Peak Competition winner, 1983), OMA created major civic design projects in the early 1980s including a villa colony for the Greek island of Antiparos in 1981 and a housing quarter for Berlin in the following year. Where the former was a Neo-Suprematist rendering of an Aegean landscape, the latter was the rendering of a low-rise, high-density scheme in terms of Neoplasticism. However, both of these works must be seen as avant-gardist rather than as rational in the 'classical' sense of that term.

The Krier brothers' credo that 'function follows form', their anti-technocratic attitude and their insistence on the cultural importance of place, all find a parallel in the work and thought of the Dutch architect Herman Hertzberger, who in every other respect could not be further removed from the ethos of the Tendenza. The most crucial influence on the thought and practice of Hertzberger has been Aldo van Eyck, who is responsible for the most consistently sustained and significant critique of modern architecture as an inseparable part of the Enlightenment. In 1962 Van Eyck delivered one of his sharpest attacks on Europocentrism and on the bankruptcy of imperialist culture:

Western civilization habitually identifies itself with civilization as such, on the pontifical assumption that what is not like it, is a deviation, less advanced, primitive, or, at best, exotically interesting at a safe distance.

Five years later, in his magazine *Forum*, Van Eyck anticipated many of the arguments since advanced by the Kriers, including a certain scepticism with regard to the notion of progress:

It seems to me that past, present and future must be active in the mind's interior as a continuum. If they are not, the artifacts we make will be without temporal depth or associative perspective. . . . Man after all has been accommodating himself physically in this world for thousands of years. His natural genius has neither increased nor decreased during that time. It is obvious that the full scope of this enormous environmental experience cannot be combined unless we tele-

scope the past. . . . Architects nowadays are pathologically addicted to change, regarding it as something one either hinders, runs after, or at best keeps up with. This, I suggest, is why they tend to sever the past from the future, with the result that the present is rendered emotionally inaccessible, without temporal dimension. I dislike a sentimental antiquarian attitude toward the past as much as I dislike a sentimental technocratic one toward the future. Both are founded on a static, clockwork, notion of time (what antiquarians and technocrats have in common), so let's start with the past for a change and discover the unchanging condition of man.

The unifying concept with which Dutch Structuralism hoped to overcome the reductive aspect of Functionalism was characterized by Van Eyck as labyrinthine clarity, a concept that has since been fully elaborated by his pupils. Thus Hertzberger wrote of their common notion of 'polyvalent space' in 1963:

What we must look for, in place of prototypes which are collective interpretations of individual living patterns, are prototypes which make individual interpretations of the collective patterns possible; in other words, we must make houses alike in a particular way, such that everyone can bring into being his own interpretation of the collective pattern. . . . Because it is impossible (and it always was) to make the individual setting that exactly suits everyone, we have to create the possibility for personal interpretation, by making things in such a way that they are indeed interpretable.

This precept has been the point of departure from which Hertzberger has evolved the rest of his work, culminating in the erection in 1974 of the Centraal Beheer insurance offices in Apeldoorn, built to his designs in the form of a 'city within a city'. This reinforced-concrete frame and concrete-block structure is ordered about an irregular cluster of working platforms set within a *regular* orthogonal tartan grid comprising floors, columns, light slots and service ducts. Top-lit gallery spaces of varying height separate these 7.5-metre (24-foot) square platforms from each other and allow

303 Hertzberger, Centraal Beheer Building, Apeldoorn, Holland, 1974.

natural light to filter down to the lowest public levels. The suspended platforms provide a network of activity spaces that may be appropriated as either individual or group working stations, through the rearrangement of modular elements comprising desks, seats, light fittings, cabinets, couches and expresso machines, etc. According to Hertzberger this bunker-like labyrinth — reminiscent in its introspection of Wright's Larkin Building of 1904 — has been deliberately left unfinished so as to encourage the 'spontaneous' appropriation and decoration of the space by its immediate users. Hertzberger's antipathy to the mechanistic provision of flexibility, as found in the sophisticated infrastructural propositions of both Habraken and Friedman, seems to have been vindicated here by the apparent spontaneity and ease with which the working spaces have been taken over and modified. And while one can only be circumspect about the rhetorical comparison that Hertzberger draws between the appropriation of space in the Centraal Beheer and the Saussurian linguistic distinction between *langue* and *parole*, there is little doubt that his approach has done something to overcome the chronic inaccessibility of the architectural discourse in a Taylorized age.

The architects of the Tendenza would surely agree with Hertzberger's argument that the functionalist organization of residential units into strictly subdivided areas for living, dining, cooking, washing, and sleeping is in itself a tyranny, and that we should attempt to return to the pre-industrial norm of interconnected rooms, offering an altogether looser fit between volume and activity (cf. Hertzberger's 'Diagoon' experimental houses built in Delft in 1971). On the other hand they would no doubt reject outright his 'casbah' concept, particularly as this appears in the Centraal Beheer, on the grounds that such an introverted type form is incapable of providing representative public space at an urban scale. The Centraal Beheer is, indeed, indifferently related to its urban context. The fact that these Islamic 'bazaar' or 'patio' building types inherently afford no architectural element with which to express the hierarchical status of the entrance is also confirmed at the Centraal Beheer, where the company has found it necessary to put up signs directing visitors to the point of entry.

Productivism
Nothing could be further from the Centraal Beheer than the three-storey glass-walled Willis-Faber and Dumas insurance offices built at Ipswich in 1974 to the designs of Foster Associates. For here all the emphasis has been placed on the elegance of the production itself, on realizing that which Max Bill once defined as the *Produktform*. It is interesting to note that Norman Foster cites just such *Produktformen* as the antecedents for his work, listing for instance Paxton's Crystal Palace, Charles and Ray Eames's own house built of 'off-the-peg' components at Santa Monica, California (1949), SOM's Marine Gunnery School at Great Lakes, Illinois (1954), and Bill's Lausanne Exhibition Pavilion (1963). Following in this line, in opposition to Venturi's populism, Willis-Faber is the undecorated shed par excellence; a form whose only differentiation, aside from its faceted serpentine curtain wall (fig. 245), resides in the swimming pool on the ground floor and the garden terrace restaurant on the roof.

304 Skidmore, Owings and Merrill, Marine Gunnery School, Great Lakes, Ill., 1954.

If Centraal Beheer is a hybrid building — derived in part from the 19th-century arcade (cf. Pomerantsev's New Trading Lines, Moscow, of 1893) and in part from the Middle-Eastern casbah — Willis-Faber with its central escalator access hall lies somewhere between the 20th-century office tower and the 19th-century department store. The case can be made, as G.C. Argan has proposed, that build-

305    Foster Associates, Willis-Faber and Dumas Building, Ipswich, 1974.

ing types embody certain values which were inherent at their inception and which survive any subsequent transposition. It is surely pertinent to the cultural significance of these buildings that in both cases the tertiary industry of informational exchange has come to be housed in spatial types which, in part at least, were once spaces of consumption – the casbah and the department store. It is against this background that Centraal Beheer can be seen as an attempt to overcome the bureaucratic division of labour through the 'anthropological' occupation of its labyrinthine office landscape. As in the traditional casbah, Hertzberger's fragmented *Bürolandschaft* encourages a pattern of behaviour that oscillates constantly between moments of work and moments of relaxation. In Willis-Faber, on the other hand, we are confronted with a *Bürolandschaft* that is a natural successor to Bentham's Panopticon of 1791, an open plan form whose unremitting panorama of order and control is supposedly compensated for by the provision of centralized amenities such as the staff restaurant and the swimming pool. Since these facilities are equally subject to company control the scope of the Panoptic domain appears to be total.

The contrast between these buildings also extends to the ambience established by their detailing. The exposed concrete-block partitions used throughout the Centraal Beheer are supposed to provoke the 'anarchistic' appropriation of the space while Willis-Faber posits the corporate image of a hypothetically egalitarian and affluent society through the absolute impeccability of its pristine skin and interior. Willis-Faber's undulating curtain wall evokes Mies's glass skyscraper proposals of the 1920s, although the actual technique employed, namely frameless glass sheets hung from the roof, like a necklace, connected by weatherproof neoprene joints, invites comparison with the achievements of those American minimalists who, having been trained by Eero Saarinen, came to prominence in the 1970s – Kevin Roche (Ford Foundation Building, New York, 1968, and United Nations Plaza Hotel, New York, 1973), Gunnar Birkerts (Federal Reserve Bank, Minneapolis, 1967), Cesar Pelli (Pacific Design Center, Los Angeles, 1971, and San Bernardino City Hall,

306 Pelli, Pacific Design Center, Los Angeles, 1971.

1972), and the talented but underappreciated Anthony Lumsden, whose most brilliant work remains largely unbuilt (e.g. his project for the Beverly Wilshire Hotel, Los Angeles, 1973).

The Willis-Faber building is Mies van der Rohe's 'almost nothing' stripped of its Classicism and brought through the use of mirror-glass not only to answer the contextual imperative of relating to the scale and texture of the existing urban environment – in this instance, by simply reflecting it – but also to respond to the modernist predicament of the total loss of any commonly accessible, or acceptable, 'received' language. Instead Willis-Faber proffers a range of constantly changing kinaesthetic sensations, opaque and scintillating in overcast light, reflective in the sun, transparent at night. And yet in a paradoxical way it shares with its Dutch counterpart the lack of any naturally inflective syntax, with the result that its entry is almost as invisible as the entrance to the Centraal Beheer.

Productivism in its purest sense is virtually indistinguishable, as a 'modernist' position, from the view which holds that an authentic modern architecture can and should be nothing more than elegant engineering, or certainly a product of industrial design on a giant scale. As I have already indicated, this is a view that has many antecedents in the history of the Modern Movement, not least among them the pioneering work of the French artisan/engineer Jean Prouvé, dating back to his curtain wall detailing of the Roland Garros Aero-club in Paris of 1935 and his modifiable Maison

du Peuple in Clichy, Paris, built in 1939 to designs which were developed in collaboration with the engineer Vladimir Bodiansky and the architects Marcel Lods and Eugène Beaudouin.

In taking Mies literally at his word (i.e. in the cult of 'almost nothing'), one wing of Productivism has concentrated on air-supported, inflatable structures, as exemplified by Yutaka Murata's Fuji Pavilion for Expo '70 at Osaka, or on cable-suspended tent construction, of which the leading exponent is the German architect/engineer Frei Otto. Although Otto's earliest tented structures date from the mid-1950s, he came to prominence with the large tents he designed for the International Horticultural Exhibition staged in Hamburg in 1963 and with the German Pavilion built for the Montreal World Exposition of 1967. Understandably, this whole approach has been largely restricted to temporary constructions, the largest to date being Otto's roof covering the stadium for the Munich Olympics of 1972.

The basic precepts of Productivism may be summarized as follows. In the first place, the building 'task' should be accommodated, as far as is feasible, in an undecorated shed or hangar, this loft structure to be kept as open and as flexible as possible (on the model of the post-Second World War *bürolandschaft* ideal). In the second place, the adaptability of this volume should be maintained by the provision of a homogeneous and integrated network of services – power, light, heat and ventilation (see Cedric Price's concept of well-serviced anonymity). The third precept

307 Otto, German Pavilion at Expo 67, Montreal, 1967.

concerns the necessity of articulating and expressing both the structure and the services, usually achieved by following Kahn's famous separation of *served* and *servant* spaces. This last precept is patently demonstrated in the larger works of Richard Rogers, in his Centre Pompidou and more recently in his headquarters building for Lloyds of London, designed in 1976 and completed some eight years later. The same basic idea is given a more discreet (and ultimately more serviceable) expression in Foster's Sainsbury Centre for the Visual Arts, completed at the University of East Anglia outside Norwich in 1978. Here the servant space is accommodated precisely within the depth of the trussed tubular steel supporting frames and 33-metre spans (cf. Kahn's Salk Institute at La Jolla of 1965: fig. 243). The fourth and all-important precept of Productivism is of course the 'unimpeded' manifestation of production itself, that is the expression of all component parts as *Produktformen* – a hardline rule which is rarely obeyed within the buildings of American minimalists (who show little interest in revealed construction), though both American and British Productivists strive for a smooth all-enveloping 'consumerist' skin. As Andrew Peckham observed of the Sainsbury Centre, '[Foster's] ability to persuade us doesn't hinge on the traditional language of architecture but rather on the language of the modern material world – of industrial production and consumable finishes'.

One of the few basic variables in the Productivist approach is the extent to which the skin or the skeleton is the dominant mode of expression. Until recently, this differentiation permitted one to distinguish between the respective rhetorical attitudes adopted by the Foster and Rogers practices, with the former ultimately favouring the skin and the latter placing the prime expressive burden on the structure. Foster Associates have since modified their approach, however, turning increasingly in their recent work towards the extrinsic expression of structure, most notably in their Renault factory at Swindon, Wiltshire, completed in 1983, and in their headquarters building for the Hongkong and Shanghai Banking Corporation in Hong Kong, designed in 1979. More than any of the more fantastic structures envisaged by Archigram or Buckminster Fuller, this layered skyscraper (comprising three 16.2-metre deep slabs rising to 28, 35 and 41 storeys respectively) invites comparison with the rocket-launching structures of Cape Canaveral – not for its overall size, but for the colossal scale of its articulated components, above all for its double-height deep, giant exposed tubular steel trusses, spanning 38.4 metres, from which the floors are suspended, grouped in sets, seven at the bottom, then six, then five, and finally four floors which top out the structure. Foster's own words are only too eloquent of the strange mixture of reality and techno-romanticism which determined this building's form:

The difficulties of building rapidly and quietly on a tight site have been resolved by a combination of technologies ranging from indigenous craft-based family units to the spin-off from aerospace and other advanced industries. For example the fastest way to place caissons is to hand-dig them – a locally based technique that also happens to be noise-free. Likewise the most elegantly efficient structures to be seen in the Colony are the spider-webs of bamboo scaffolding which mark virtually all construction sites. However given the amount of imported hardware that buildings comprise, as well as an awareness of the very real relationship between weight and performance, the design has been strongly influenced by sources outside the traditional building industry.

308    Foster Associates, Hongkong and Shanghai Banking Corporation headquarters, Hong Kong, 1979–84 (model).

These range from the Concorde design team, to military establishments coping with mobile bridges to take tank loadings to the world of aircraft sub-contractors, particularly in the States.

## Post-Avant-Gardism
The architectural section of the Venice Biennale of 1980, 'The Presence of the Past', announced in various ways the emergence of Post-Modernism

at a global level. While it cannot be defined in terms of a specific set of stylistic and ideological characteristics, the fact that it tends to proclaim its legitimacy in exclusively formal – not to say superficial – terms, rather than in terms of constructional, organizational or socio-cultural considerations (such as were still central to the revisionism of Team X), already separates it, as a *modus operandi*, from the architectural production of the third quarter of the century. Notwithstanding Portoghesi's Biennale thesis, however, the past was already a presence in the major monuments of the period.

Needless to say, the most distinguished American architects of the preceding decades, Mies van der Rohe and Louis Kahn, remained committed to a deconstruction of this historical legacy and to a reassembly of its precepts and components in accordance with the technological capacity of the epoch: the work remained expressive of its time, even if certain tectonic elements and compositional models were patently (and even polemically) determined by historical precedents. Mies van der Rohe's Neue National-galerie in Berlin (commissioned 1961, built 1965–68) and Kahn's Kimbell Art Museum at Fort Worth, Texas (1967–72) illustrate this, the one tied to Schinkel and 19th-century ferro-vitreous engineering, the other to Mediterranean vaulted construction and the tectonics of reinforced concrete. Millennialistic utopianism is of course largely absent from the later work of both men, the focus being instead upon the irreducible nature of tectonic construction and upon its sublime interaction with light, as the two transhistorical conditions of architecture, and, in Kahn's case, upon a form of cosmological, cabbalistic mysticism. Both Mies and Kahn would have seen the advent of Post-Modernism as cultural decadence; and indeed we have Kahn's aphoristic reproach to Venturi, on seeing his proposal for the Philadelphia Bicentennial 'strip', to the effect that 'colour ain't architecture'.

We may claim, in this regard, that no 'master' architects in history were more misunderstood by their immediate pupils and heirs than Mies and Kahn. Mies was patently gratified by his success in formulating the normative American mode of corporate building from 1950 to 1975, the Miesian format becoming standard for a certain

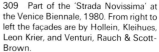

309 Part of the 'Strada Novissima' at the Venice Biennale, 1980. From right to left the façades are by Hollein, Kleihues, Leon Krier, and Venturi, Rauch & Scott-Brown.

sector of development in the postwar world (see Arthur Drexler's 'Buildings for Business and Government', MoMA, 1959), but both he and Kahn tended to find that the latent qualities of their work were better appreciated in Europe. Thus while the Skidmore, Owings and Merrill-dominated Chicago School succeeded in following Mies with verve and audacity, architects like Myron Goldsmith (United Airlines, Des Plaines, Illinois, 1962), Gene Summers (McCormick Place, Chicago, 1971) and Arthur Takeuchi (Wendell Smith Elementary School, Chicago, 1973) all failed to arrive at a fresh point of departure, possibly because they were unable to appreciate sufficiently the Romantic Classical and Suprematist dimensions which lay hidden in Mies's work. In the same way Kahn, despite his disciples of the Philadelphia School (Moore, Venturi, Vreeland and Giurgola), ultimately found a more sensitive following in Italian Neo-Rationalism and Dutch Structuralism.

This eclipse of Late Modernism in America, together with the 'consensus' rejection of what Jürgen Habermas called the 'unfinished modern project', as this had been so fervently integrated into the myth and reality of American development over the past century, is nowhere more

evident than in the current repudiation of Frank Lloyd Wright, particularly when one considers Wright's indisputable status as one of the most fertile architects of this century. It is significant how, apart from the antiquarian art market, Wright continues to be ignored by the American protagonists of Post-Modernism, despite the recent efforts of Charles Jencks to validate Michael Graves by way of Wright in his book *Kings of Infinite Space* (1983). The reason for this amnesia is not hard to find, since Wright has to be counted among those modernists (Aalto would be another) whose work can in no way be dismissed as reductive or inaccessible. One may advance as evidence to the contrary the 200 Usonian houses which Wright built in his own lifetime and think of them as an attempt to render the generic suburb as a cultivated domain.

It is difficult to arrive at the fundamental character of the Post-Modern phenomenon as this has emerged in architecture and almost every other cultural field. From one point of view it has to be acknowledged as an understandable reaction to the pressures of societal modernization and thus as an escape from the tendency of contemporary life to be totally dominated by the values of the scientific-industrial complex. Yet while the utopian emancipatory aims of the Enlightenment may now have to be relinquished in the name of more effective and *reassuring* forms of realism, there is little evidence that modern society either can or, finally, wishes to renounce the fundamental 'benefits' of modernization. Moreover, as Habermas suggested in his Theodor Adorno Prize address of 1980, it is the speed and rapacity of modern development, rather than avant-gardist culture, that is responsible for disruptions and disappointments, together with this apparently popular rejection of the new. In the end, even the staunchest Neo-Conservative will admit there is little chance of resisting, in real terms, the relentless progress of modernization.

If there is a general principle that can be said to characterize Post-Modern architecture, it is the conscious ruination of style and the cannibalization of architectural form, as though no value either traditional or otherwise can withstand for long the tendency of the production/consumption cycle to reduce every civic institution to some kind of consumerism and to undermine every traditional quality. Today the division of labour and the imperatives of 'monopolized' economy are such as to reduce the practice of architecture to large-scale packaging; and at least one Post-Modern architect, Helmut Jahn, has frankly acknowledged that this is how he sees his role. At its most predetermined, Post-Modernism reduces architecture to a condition in which the 'package deal' arranged by the builder/developer determines the carcass and the essential substance of the work, while the architect is reduced to contributing a suitably seductive mask. This is the predominant situation in city centre development in America today, where high-rise towers are either reduced to the 'silence' of their totally glazed, reflective envelopes or alternatively dressed in devalued historical trappings of one kind or another. Indeed Jahn's Popular Machinism must be regarded as an attempt to combine both strategies. Irrespective of whether this dematerialized historicism is made of actual stone and hence of necessity suspended from heavily reinforced steel skeletons, as in the case of Philip Johnson's AT&T headquarters building, New York (1978–84), or whether more moderately it is a decorative curtain wall of glass hung off steel, or even whether, as in the case of Michael Graves's Portland Building in Portland, Oregon (1979–82), it is a painted concrete 'billboard' which enlarges to a gargantuan scale the graphic image of a 'ruined' and hence idealized garden folly, the result is fundamentally the same; that is to say, it is the Populist format of Venturi's 'decorated shed'. In any event, in all three options the impulse is scenographic rather than tectonic, so that not only is there a total schism between the inner substance and the outer form, but the form itself either repudiates its constructional origin or dissipates its palpability. In Post-Modern architecture classical and vernacular 'quotations' tend to interpenetrate each other disconcertingly. Invariably rendered as unfocussed images, they easily disintegrate and mix with other more abstract, usually cubistic forms, for which the architect has no more respect than for his extremely arbitrary historical allusions.

Michael Graves has been a symptomatic figure in this whole development. The method and the substance of his Post-Cubist collages (be they painted or built) changed radically around 1975 as he fell under the influence of Leon Krier's Neo-Classical 'speculations' and as Krier himself proceeded to eliminate all traces of modernist syntax from his own work. (Compare Krier's Royal Mint Square project of 1974 to his Lilliputian St Quentin-en-Yvelines school of 1978, where this expurgation has been brought to its logical conclusion.) Similarly, Graves passed from his still 'modernist' Crooks House project (1976) to the Neo-Classical 'folly' of his Fargo-Moorhead Cultural Center, proposed in 1977 for the twin towns on either side of the state line dividing Minnesota from North Dakota. From this point onwards 'inverted' Ledoux-like motifs prevail in his work, mixed with episodic fragments drawn from Krier, Hoffmann, Gilly, Schinkel, Cubism and even Art Deco.

Graves's largest work to date, the Portland Building, projected him into the centre of the Post-Modern furore with a public building where the most contentious aspect derived from the arbitrary painted configurations of the façade. To start with, the clients vigorously objected to the smallness of the predominantly square, pierced windows, on the grounds that in Oregon the sky is generally overcast, and as a result the windows were slightly enlarged. Then, as built, the building was criticized on architectonic grounds for the

310 Graves, Portland Building, Portland, Ore., 1979–82.

total falseness of its seemingly large windows, much of which consists of heavily tinted plate glass 'drawn' deceptively over solid concrete walls. Finally, and perhaps most seriously, it was challenged for its surprisingly insensitive attitude towards the site. Unlike the Beaux Arts buildings on either side – the City Hall and the County Courthouse – it fails to acknowledge (except for a service entrance) the public amenity of the park to the south, and it also presents, despite its arcaded ground floor, a strangely inhospitable frontage to the surrounding streets.

Graves has since gained commissions which seem to be more suited to his imagistic approach, as one may judge from the diminutive civic scale of the Public Library in San Juan Capistrano, California (1983), with its regionally inflected Spanish Colonial roofs. Even here, however, a feeling begins to obtrude that like Olbrich, to whom his astonishing talent may be compared more revealingly than to Wright, he is more of a designer of *objets d'art* than an architect. With the later Graves, as Peter Eisenman put it, 'a house, for example, is no longer conceived as a house (a social or ideological entity) or as an object (in itself) but rather as a painting of an object'.

As with Graves, so with many figures today who had hitherto occupied Late Modernist positions – not only James Stirling, Philip Johnson and Hans Hollein, but other more recent converts to the Post-Modernist position such as Romaldo Giurgola, Moshe Safdie and Kevin Roche. In each instance, and to different degrees, the discourse of a 'dematerialized' historicism has been selfconsciously embraced and virtually mixed at random with modernist fragments. More often than not the result is an inconclusive and seemingly pointless 'cacophony' in which the architect loses control of his material. This latter-day version of the 'disappearance of the author' is manifest in Stirling's latest work, notably in his Stuttgart Staatsgalerie. While this work is the most distinguished public building of Stirling's late career – emerging, as it has, out of three successive 'neo-classical' designs for German museums in the second half of the 1970s – it is also a strangely mixed and conflictive design. Framed in reinforced concrete, meticulously detailed and finished in finely wrought ashlar, the Staatsgalerie, while far from scenographic, is nonetheless atectonic in its general expression; that is to say, it is closer to Hoffmann and Asplund, above all to Asplund's Woodland Cemetery Crematorium, Stockholm, of 1939, than it is to the avant-gardist, Constructivist precepts which inspired Stirling's early career. The differences between Stirling and Asplund are equally significant, in particular the replacement of Asplund's sense of liberal *civitas* – his feeling for an egalitarian civic identity – by Stirling's 'classical-populism'. I am referring to Stirling's conviction, derived no doubt from modern museum management, that today the museum is not only an edifying institution but also a place of distraction and amusement. This last accounts for the mediation of the overall monumentality of the Staatsgalerie by certain Constructivist-influenced episodes, by a dramatically undulating curtain wall, by outsize tubular handrails, by symbolic aedicules in light tubular steel, in fact a whole plethora of brightly-coloured, toy-like elements designed to appeal to the man in the street.

A similar approach asserts itself in other recent museum work by Stirling, the extension to the Fogg Museum at Harvard and the extension to the Tate Gallery in London. As far as the Tate is

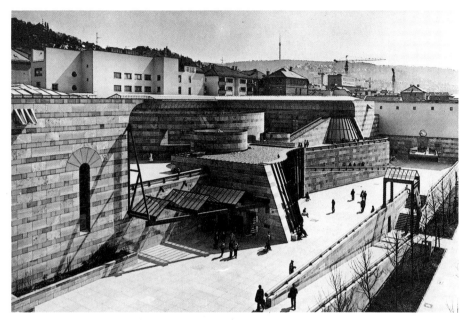

311  Stirling, Staatsgalerie, Stuttgart, 1980–83.

concerned it is as though the tradition of tectonic culture was being consumed before our eyes by the fashionable rediscovery of architectural rendering.

Another form of 'disappearance' is to eliminate the building altogether, to bury it in the earth so that it at once becomes an introverted interior rather than a testament to civic virtue. Hollein's Mönchengladbach museum (1983) and Giurgola's new Australian Parliament Building, now under construction in Canberra, are but two recent examples of this approach.

Hollein seems to be the only figure among the 'Post-Avant-Gardists' who has been able to combine an indulgence in craft aestheticism with a revealing critical distance. This dichotomous brilliance was unequivocally demonstrated in his 'anti-façade' for the Venice Biennale of 1980, wherein he rang the changes from 'reality' to 'illusion' and from 'art' to 'nature' around the theme of the archetypal column (fig. 309). Greater scope for wit and high-quality finish had in fact already presented itself to Hollein some three years earlier, when he realized an elaborate ceramic

exhibition at the Teheran Museum (1977). In many respects that commission served to crystallize his high metaphoric style, which he also demonstrated in his Israeli and Austrian travel bureaus in Vienna realized between 1976 and 1978. It is no accident, as Friedrich Achleitner implied in his essay 'Viennese Positions' (1981), that Hollein is at his best in the design of interiors. Achleitner's brilliant analysis of Hollein's relationship to Viennese culture merits quoting at length:

To do justice to Hollein, one cannot ignore the Viennese reality, where there is a tradition that is too old and a sensibility that is too highly developed with regard to the architectural setting as a counter-reality or a substitute reality. Going right back to Baroque, and maybe even earlier, the ambivalence of the media of music and architecture (arising out of the repression of literature by the Hapsburgs) was favoured above the presentation of evident realities, and came to reflect collective and individual psychic states. The funeral processions and parades of the Hapsburgs had heralded the enactment of the passing away of the aristocratic-upper bourgeois world that preceded the first world war and was reflected on the aesthetic level within the Viennese secession. Vienna possessed a tradition of aesthetic heightening of reality, a long praxis of artificial remoteness. The techniques of montage, collage, alienation, striking allusions and disarming quotation are not cultivated in language alone.

Hans Hollein seems not only to incorporate this tradition, but his works, seen in an extreme perspective, are to the Viennese the unwelcome confirmation of an unchanged situation. The backdrops become visible once more: he possesses the instruments to give them prominence. Or is the travel office perhaps something different from the visual treatment of the satisfaction of needs that are in themselves simple, represented by the task of supplying information and travel tickets? But what many may find disturbing is that the aesthetic handling of the subject does not illustrate the content in a reductive fashion but the subject itself in all its facets. It is not a question, here, of information and travel documents, but of illusions, of desires, of dreams and even of clichés about the aims of travel. The client enters a world of references and illusions, no object is merely itself. The hall itself is not the lobby of a travel bureau but of a railway station, or at least it creates this association. The allusions possess differing

degrees of immediacy; they range from the banal legibility of the airline counter (Adler), of shipping companies (Reling), up to the counter for theatre tickets (moving piece of scenery – the student has to guess the reason for himself) and the most subtle references to Egypt, Greece, India. Illusion and orientation, information and learning are merged together while the money passes through the radiator grill of a Rolls-Royce – a wink at the client.

Nothing could be further from this resistant play with multiple levels of reality than the Taller de Arquitectura's Neo-Social-Realist *mega-classicism*, executed in prefabricated reinforced concrete construction. Confronted with Ricardo Bofill's recent realization of large public housing projects in a number of French new towns – the urban quarter known as Les Arcades du Lac in St Quentin-en-Yvelines (1974–80) and the theatrical Abraxas perimeter block in Marne-la-Vallée (1979–83) – it would be hard to imagine another contemporary Western practitioner who has enjoyed such a close relationship with State power or indeed one who is so simplistically identified with power at this level. Needless to say this identification, together with the worldly success which it inevitably entails, does nothing to legitimize this 'incarceration' of collective dwelling units within a carcass of kitsch classicism. This technically accomplished parallel to Jahn's Popular Machinism understandably entails a total denial of the values placed on the monument by the Tendenza, for while this is by no means the first time that mass housing has been given a monumental form (cf. Karl Ehn's Karl Marx Hof, Vienna, of 1927 and Le Corbusier's Unité d'Habitation, Marseilles, of 1952), not since the time of the Ringstrasse – Loos's *Potemkinstadt* – has the aggregation of dwelling units been so scenographically rendered. It is surely symptomatic of our reactionary period, both from a social and an architectural point of view, that there is little accommodation or representation in Bofill's work of those 'social condensers' – nursery schools, meeting rooms, laundries and swimming pools – that public housing should demand. The absence of such amenities is as reactionary as the brutal nature of the standard apartments which are wilfully encased in these false architraves and

313 Bofill and the Taller de Arquitectura, 'Le Palacio', Les Espaces d'Abraxas, Marne-la-Vallée, 1979–83.

empty columns. Deprived of a terrace, since this does not accord with the assumed syntax, the upwardly mobile resident has to be satisfied with the operatic illusion of living in a palace.

It would be hard to find a more self-effacing contrast to such stupefying rhetoric than Renzo Piano's Menil Museum in Houston, Texas, begun in 1981, where most of the effort has gone into the rationalization and refinement of the construction and above all into the control of natural light. In other words, the emphasis has been appropriately placed on the art rather than the architecture. The exhibits are exposed to the lively (variable) conditions of daylight, and at the same time they are protected from unacceptable levels of ultra-violet light by adjustable reinforced concrete louvers in the ceiling which reduce the illumination from 80,000 to 2,000 lux. The works of art will also be rotated between the top-lit exhibition hall and the fully controlled environment of an

adjacent repository, only forty works from the entire collection being on view at any one time. Worked out in close collaboration with the client, this museum serves to remind us that the thoughtful development of the programme is as important to the final result as any preconception that the architect may have as ·to the aesthetic qualities of the work.

Here we see that despite the apparent 'triumph' of Post-Modernism a reduction in the referential content of form itself may have profound consequences, for the ideal of 'almost nothing' (other than its Miesian manifestations) may still be capable of producing more responsible and responsive environments. One of the most seminal pieces of land settlement built in Europe since the end of the Second World War is undoubtedly Siedlung Halen, realized outside Berne to the designs of Atelier 5 in 1960 (cf. Le Corbusier's Roq et Rob housing of 1949: fig. 215). Today, enveloped in vegetation, this 'carpet housing' still proffers itself as a model for reconciling development with place-creation and with the maintenance of ecological balance. The benefits to be derived from such dense patterns of land settlement – the fact that, say, an enclosed courtyard garden functions as a climatological flywheel, warm in winter, cool in summer – are no longer to be discounted in a world that is threatened with the exhaustion of its non-renewable resources. The current debate as to the

314 Atelier 5, Siedlung Halen, Berne, 1960.

appropriateness or otherwise of modern architectural form seems somewhat irrelevant in the light of such issues.

Building by virtue of its actuality cannot realize itself in terms of the future. For all its relative permanence it has no choice but to exist in its own historical moment. It has as its task the realization of man here and now, so that its object is no longer the idealized projections of the Enlightenment but rather the constitution of the attributes of *place*. In a society mesmerized by Taylor's principle of divided labour and the political economy of consumption and production (extending even to the architect in the economy of his own professional activity), such ontological conditions can perhaps only be achieved through the strategy of creating discontinuous bounded 'enclaves'. A whole set of superficially diverse developments in architecture begin to point to the necessity of this strategy, from the general realization of low-rise high-density housing that followed in the wake of Siedlung Halen (e.g. Neave Brown's housing for Camden in Fleet Road, London, of 1975) to the unrealized concerns of the Tendenza for the reconstitution of the urban monument.

The present loss of the *finite* city as a significant cultural object no doubt partially accounts for the deliquescence of avant-garde architectural thought and for the realization that architecture can no longer pretend to intervene or sustain itself at a global scale. The void left by our seeming incapacity to realize and sustain clearly defined urban domains, together with the civic institutions which they have always traditionally embodied, was until recently ideologically veiled by the apparent benefits of operational planning, a positivistic discipline whose effectiveness in managing the consumer economy is contingent upon its absolute indifference to physical form. Against this, the urban enclave posits itself as an antithesis whose current viability seems to be sustained in part by the present bankruptcy of planning as an effective discipline.

The enclave, however, is only a potential 'what' in a moment when architecture has to re-position itself in order to maintain some sense of continuity and depth in relation to the overall context. In our need to arrive at a viable general method for the practice of architecture in the future, the 'how'

must be accorded a status equal to the 'what'. There is, as Hans Sedlmayr has pointed out, a moment when place and production are fused together to yield that quality of *character* from which we eventually receive our sense of identity. As Christian Norberg-Schultz wrote in his study of the work of Portoghesi and Gigliotti, *Alla ricerca dell'architettura perduta* (1975),

Whereas spatial organization may be described without referring to a particular technical solution, *character* cannot possibly be separated from the process of making. That is the meaning of Mies van der Rohe's well-known statement: 'God is in the details'. The technical revolution of the last hundred years is therefore more than a *technical* revolution. In fact, modern technology does not only serve to solve quantitative and economic problems but, if properly understood, may help us to substitute for the devalued motifs of historicism forms which give our environment character, and thereby make it become a real *place*.

The veil that photo-lithography draws over architecture is not neutral. High-speed photographic and reproductive processes are surely not only the political economy of the sign but also an insidious filter through which our tactile environment tends to lose its concrete responsiveness. When much of modern building is experienced in actuality, its photogenic quality is denied by the poverty and brutality of its detailing. Time and time again an expensive and ostentatious display of either structure or form results in the impoverishment of intimacy; in that which Heidegger has recognized as the loss of 'nearness'. How rarely do we encounter a modern work where the inflection of a chosen tectonic penetrates into the innermost recesses of the structure, not as a totalizing force but as the declension of an articulate sensibility. That modern society still possesses a capacity for such inflection finds confirmation in the finest work of Aalto. Against his inspiring achievement, the present tendency of modern building to be reduced, through the way in which it is built, returns us to the Heideggerian challenge that the conditions of building, dwelling, cultivating and being were once indivisible.

Chapter 5
# Critical Regionalism:
# modern architecture and cultural identity

The phenomenon of universalization, while being an advancement of mankind, at the same time constitutes a sort of subtle destruction, not only of traditional cultures, which might not be an irreparable wrong, but also of what I shall call for the time being the creative nucleus of great civilizations and great culture, that nucleus on the basis of which we interpret life, what I shall call in advance the ethical and mythical nucleus of mankind. The conflict springs up from there. We have the feeling that this single world civilization at the same time exerts a sort of attrition or wearing away at the expense of the cultural resources which have made the great civilizations of the past. This threat is expressed, among other disturbing effects, by the spreading before our eyes of a mediocre civilization which is the absurd counter-part of what I was just calling elementary culture. Everywhere throughout the world, one finds the same bad movie, the same slot machines, the same plastic or aluminum atrocities, the same twisting of language by propaganda, etc. It seems as if mankind, by approaching *en masse* a basic consumer culture, were also stopped *en masse* at a subcultural level. Thus we come to the crucial problem confronting nations just rising from underdevelopment. In order to get on to the road toward modernization, is it necessary to jettison the old cultural past which has been the *raison d'être* of a nation? ... Whence the paradox: on the one hand, it (the nation) has to root itself in the soil of its past, forge a national spirit, and unfurl this spiritual and cultural revendication before the colonialist's personality. But in order to take part in modern civilization, it is necessary at the same time to take part in scientific, technical, and political rationality, something which very often requires the pure and simple abandon of a whole cultural past. It is a fact: every culture cannot sustain and

absorb the shock of modern civilization. There is the paradox: how to become modern and to return to sources; how to revive an old, dormant civilization and take part in universal civilization....

No one can say what will become of our civilization when it has really met different civilizations by means other than the shock of conquest and domination. But we have to admit that this encounter has not yet taken place at the level of an authentic dialogue. That is why we are in a kind of lull or interregnum in which we can no longer practice the dogmatism of a single truth and in which we are not yet capable of conquering the scepticism into which we have stepped. We are in a tunnel, at the twilight of dogmatism and the dawn of real dialogues.

Paul Ricoeur
'Universal Civilization and
National Cultures', 1961

The term 'Critical Regionalism' is not intended to denote the vernacular as this was once spontaneously produced by the combined interaction of climate, culture, myth and craft, but rather to identify those recent regional 'schools' whose primary aim has been to reflect and serve the limited constituencies in which they are grounded. Among other factors contributing to the emergence of a regionalism of this order is not only a certain prosperity but also some kind of anti-centrist consensus – an aspiration at least to some form of cultural, economic and political independence.

The concept of a local or national culture is a paradoxical proposition not only because of the present obvious antithesis between rooted culture and universal civilization but also because all cultures, both ancient and modern, seem to have depended for their intrinsic development on a certain cross-fertilization with other cultures. As Ricoeur seems to imply in the passage quoted above, regional or national cultures must today, more than ever, be ultimately constituted as locally inflected manifestations of 'world culture'. It is surely no accident that this paradoxical proposition arises at a time when global modernization continues to undermine, with ever increasing force, all forms of traditional, agrarian-based, autochthonous culture. From the point of view of critical theory (see the Introduction, p.9) we have to regard regional culture not as something given and relatively immutable but rather as something which has, at least today, to be self-consciously cultivated. Ricoeur suggests that sustaining any kind of authentic culture in the future will depend ultimately on our capacity to generate vital forms of regional culture while appropriating alien influences at the level of both culture and civilization.

Such a process of assimilation and reinterpretation seems to be evident in the work of the Danish master Jørn Utzon, above all in his Bagsvaerd Church, completed in a suburb outside Copenhagen in 1976, wherein pre-cast concrete infill elements of standardized dimensions are combined, in a particularly articulate way, with *in-situ* reinforced concrete shell vaults which span

the principal public volumes. And while this combination of modular assembly and *in-situ* casting may appear at first to be nothing more than an appropriate integration of the full range of concrete techniques which are now at our disposal, the case can be made that the way in which these techniques are combined alludes to a number of dialogically opposed values.

At one level, we may claim that prefabricated modular assembly not only accords with the values of universal civilization but also 'represents' its capacity for normative application, whereas an *in-situ* shell vault is a 'one-off' structural invention built into a unique site. It may be argued, in the light of Ricoeur, that where the one affirms the norms of universal civilization, the other proclaims the values of idiosyncratic culture. Similarly, we may construe these different forms of concrete construction as setting the rationality of normative technique against the arationality of symbolic structure.

Yet another dialogue is evoked as soon as one passes from the economically optimum modular cladding of the exterior (be it the concrete panels or the patent glazing in the roof) to the far from optimum *in-situ* frame and shell vault spanning the nave. Such vaulting, a relatively uneconomic mode of construction when compared say to steel trusswork, has been deliberately selected for its

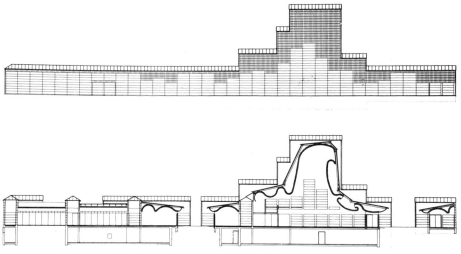

315, 316  Utzon, Bagsvaerd Church, near Copenhagen, 1976: longitudinal elevation and section.

symbolic capacity: the vault signifies the sacred in Western culture. And yet the highly configurated section adopted in this instance can hardly be regarded as Western. Indeed the only precedent for such a section in a sacred context is Eastern – the Chinese pagoda roof, cited by Utzon in his seminal essay of 1962, 'Platforms and Plateaus: Ideas of a Danish Architect'.

The subtle and contrary allusions incorporated into this folded concrete shell roof have far greater consequence than the seeming perversity of reinterpreting an Oriental timber form in Occidental concrete technology; for while the main vault over the nave suggests by its scale and top illumination the presence of a religious space, it does so in such a way as to preclude an exclusively Occidental or Oriental reading of the form by which it is constituted. A similar Occidental/Oriental interpenetration also occurs in the wooden fenestration and slatted partitions which seem to allude both to the Nordic vernacular of the stave church and to the fretted traditional timberwork of China and Japan. The intention behind these procedures of deconstruction and re-synthesis seems to be as follows: first, to revitalize certain *devalued* Occidental forms through an Oriental re-casting of their essential nature; and second to indicate the secularization of the institutions represented by these forms. This is arguably a more appropriate way to render a church in a secular age, where traditional ecclesiastical iconography always risks degenerating into kitsch.

This revitalization of Occidental elements with Oriental profiles and vice-versa by no means exhausts the ways in which the Bagsvaerd Church is inflected with regard to its situation in time and place. Utzon has also given it a barn-like form, using an agricultural metaphor as a way of giving public expression to a sacred institution. But this somewhat cryptic metaphor, associating religion with agrarian culture, may well change somewhat with the passage of time, for when the surrounding saplings have matured the church will for the first time appear within its own proper boundaries. This natural *temenos*, established by a veil of trees, will no doubt encourage a future reading of the building as a temple rather than a barn.

Exemplary of an explicitly anti-centrist regionalism was the Catalan nationalist movement which first emerged with the foundation of Grup R in Barcelona in 1951. This group, led by J.M. Sostres and Oriol Bohigas, found itself caught from the beginning in a complex cultural situation. On the one hand, it was obliged to revive the Rationalist, anti-Fascist values and procedures of GATEPAC (the pre-war Spanish wing of CIAM); on the other, it remained aware of the political responsibility to evoke a realistic regionalism, accessible to the populace at large. This double-headed programme was first publicly announced by Bohigas in his essay, 'Possibilities for a Barcelona Architecture', published in 1951. The various cultural impulses that made up this heterogeneous Regionalism tend to confirm the unavoidably hybrid nature of modern regional culture. In the first place, there was the Catalan brick tradition which dated back to the period of 'Modernismo'; then there was the influence of Neutra and Neo-Plasticism – the latter indubitably stimulated by Bruno Zevi's *La Poetica dell'architettura neoplastica* of 1953. There followed the influential Neo-Realist style of the Italian architect Ignazio Gardella, who employed traditional shutters, narrow windows and wide overhanging eaves in his Casa Borsalino at Alessandria, Italy (1951–53). To this must be added, particularly for the practice of Mackay, Bohigas and Martorell, the influence of British New Brutalism (see their Paseo de la Bonanova apartments in Barcelona of 1973).

The career of the Barcelona architect J.A. Coderch has been typically *regionalist* inasmuch as it has oscillated, until recent date, between a Mediterraneanized, modern brick vernacular first formulated in his eight-storey ISM apartment block built in Barcelona in the Paseo Nacional in 1951 ('traditionally' articulated like the Casa Borsalino with full-height shutters and thin overhanging cornices) and the avant-gardist, Neo-Plastic cum Miesian composition of his Casa Catasus completed at Sitges in 1956.

The more recent deliquescence of Catalan Regionalism is possibly most evident in the work of Ricardo Bofill and the Taller de Arquitectura. For where Bofill's Calle Nicaragua apartments of 1964 displayed an affinity for the reinterpreted brick vernacular of Coderch, the Taller was to adopt an overtly *Gesamtkunstwerk* approach in the late 1960s. With their Xanadu complex built in

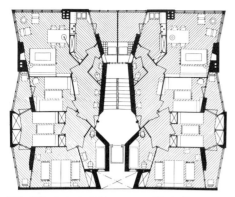

317, 318 Coderch, ISM apartment block, Barcelona, 1951: typical floor plan and view.

Calpe in 1967, they indulged in a form of kitsch romanticism. This obsession with castle images reached its apotheosis in their heroic, but ostentatious, tile-faced Walden 7 complex at Sant Just Desvern, Barcelona (1970–75). With its twelve-storey voids, underlit living rooms, minuscule balconies and its now disintegrating tile cladding, Walden 7 marks that unfortunate boundary where what was initially a critical impulse degenerates into highly photogenic scenography. In the last analysis, despite its

319 Coderch, Casa Catasus, Sitges, 1956: ground plan.

passing homage to Gaudí, Walden 7 displays an affinity for admass seduction. It is an architecture of narcissism *par excellence*, for the formal rhetoric addresses itself to high fashion and to the mystique of Bofill's flamboyant personality. The Mediterranean hedonistic utopia to which Walden 7 pretends collapses on closer inspection, above all at the level of the roofscape where a potentially sensuous environment has not been realized in occupation (cf. Le Corbusier's Unité d'Habitation at Marseilles).

Nothing could be further from Bofill's intentions than the architecture of the Portuguese master Alvaro Siza Vieira, whose career, beginning with his swimming pool at Quinta de Conceição Matosinhos (1958–65), has been anything but photogenic. This much can be discerned not only from the fragmentary evasive nature of the published images but also from a text written in 1979:

Most of my works were never published; some of the things I did were only carried out in part, others were profoundly changed or destroyed. That's only to be expected. An architectonic proposition whose aim is to go deep . . . a proposition that intends to be more than a passive materialization, refuses to reduce that same reality, analysing each of its aspects, one by one; that proposition can't find support in a fixed image, can't follow a linear evolution. . . . Each design must catch, with the utmost rigour, a precise moment of the flittering image, in all its shades, and the better you can recognize that flittering quality of reality, the clearer your design will be. . . . That may be the reason why only marginal works (a quiet dwelling, a holiday house miles away) have been kept as they were originally designed. But something remains. Pieces are kept here and there, inside ourselves, perhaps fathered by someone, leaving marks on space and people, melting into a process of total transformation.

This hypersensitivity to the transformation of a fluid and yet specific reality renders Siza's work more layered and rooted than the eclectic tendencies of the Barcelona School for, by taking Aalto as his point of departure, he has grounded his buildings in the configuration of a specific topography and in the fine-grained texture of the local fabric. To this end his pieces are tight

responses to the urban, land and marinescape of the Porto region. Other important factors are his deference towards local material, craft work, and the subtleties of local light; a deference which is sustained without falling into the sentimentality of excluding rational form and modern technique. Like Aalto's Säynätsalo Town Hall, all of Siza's buildings are delicately laid into the topography of their sites. His approach is patently tactile and tectonic, rather than visual and graphic, from his Beires House built at Povoa do Varzim in 1973–76 to his Bouça Residents' Association Housing in Porto (1973–77). Even his small urban buildings, of which the best is probably the Pinto branch

320–322 Siza Vieira, Beires House, Povoa do Varzim, 1973–76: view, and plans of the upper floor (below) and ground floor (bottom).

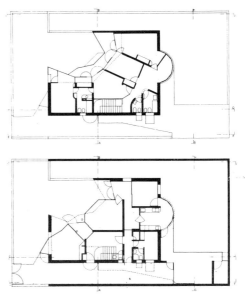

bank built at Oliveira de Azemeis in 1974, are topographically structured.

The projected work of the New York-based Austrian architect Raimund Abraham seems to be informed by similar concerns, inasmuch as this architect has always stressed place creation and the topographic aspects of built form. The House with Three Walls (1972) and the House with Flower Walls (1973) are typical of his pieces of the early 1970s, wherein the project evokes an oneiric image while insisting on the inescapable materiality of building. This concern for tectonic form and for its capacity to transform the surface of the earth has been carried over into Abraham's recent designs made for the International Building Exhibition in Berlin, above all into his recent project for South Friedrichstadt designed in 1981.

An equally tactile attitude obtains in the work of the veteran Mexican architect Luis Barragán, whose finest houses (many of which have been erected in Mexico City, in the suburb of Pedregal) assume a topographic form. As much a landscape designer as an architect, Barragán has always sought a sensual and earthbound architecture; an architecture compounded of enclosures, stelae, fountains and water courses; an architecture laid into volcanic rock and lush vegetation; an architecture that refers indirectly to the Mexican *estancia*. Of Barragán's feeling for mythic and rooted beginnings it is sufficient to cite his memories of the apocryphal *pueblo* of his youth:

My earliest childhood memories are related to a ranch my family owned near the village of Mazamitla. It was a *pueblo* with hills, formed by houses with tile roofs and immense eaves to shield passersby from the heavy rains which fall in that area. Even the earth's color was interesting because it was red earth. In this village, the water distribution system consisted of great gutted logs, in the form of troughs, which ran on a support structure of tree forks, 5 meters high, above the roofs. This aqueduct crossed over the town, reaching the patios, where there were great stone fountains to receive the water. The patios housed the stables, with cows and chickens, all together. Outside, in the street, there were iron rings to tie the horses. The channeled logs, covered with moss, dripped water all over town, of course. It

323 Abraham, project for South Friedrichstadt, Berlin, 1981: detail showing half the site.

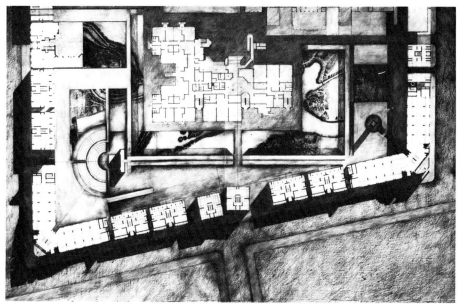

gave this village the ambience of a fairy tale. No, there are no photographs. I have only its memory.

This remembrance was surely influenced by Barragán's life-long involvement with Islamic architecture. Similar feelings and concerns are evident in his opposition to the invasion of privacy in the modern world and in his criticism of the subtle erosion of nature which has accompanied post-war civilization:

Everyday life is becoming much too public. Radio, TV, telephone all invade privacy. Gardens should therefore be enclosed, not open to public gaze. . . . Architects are forgetting the need of human beings for half-light, the sort of light that imposes a tranquility, in their living rooms as well as in their bedrooms. About half the glass that is used in so many buildings – homes as well as offices – would have to be removed in order to obtain the quality of light that enables one to live and work in a more concentrated manner . . .

Before the machine age, even in the middle of cities, Nature was everybody's trusted companion. . . . Nowadays, the situation is reversed. Man does not meet with Nature, even when he leaves the city to commune with her. Enclosed in his shiny automobile, his spirit stamped with the mark of the world whence the automobile emerged, he is, within Nature, a foreign body. A billboard is sufficient to stifle the voice of Nature. Nature becomes a scrap of Nature and man a scrap of man.

By the time of his first house and studio built around an enclosed court in Tacubaya, Mexico D.F., in 1947, Barragán had already moved away from the syntax of the International Style. And yet his work has always remained committed to that abstract form which has characterized the art of our era. Barragán's penchant for large, almost inscrutable abstract planes set into the landscape is perhaps at its most intense in his gardens for the residential districts of Las Arboleadas (1958–61) and Los Clubes (1961–64) and in his freeway monument, Satellite City Towers, designed with Mathias Goeritz in 1957.

Regionalism has, of course, manifested itself in other parts of the Americas; in Brazil in the 1940s in the early work of Oscar Niemeyer and Affonso

324 Barragán and Goeritz, Satellite City Towers, Mexico City, 1957.

Reidy; in Argentina in the work of Amancio Williams, above all in Williams's bridge house in Mar del Plata of 1943–45 and more recently perhaps in Clorindo Testa's Bank of London and South America, Buenos Aires (1959); in Venezuela, in the Ciudad Universitaria built to the designs of Carlos Raúl Villanueva between 1945 and 1960; on the West Coast of the United States, first in Los Angeles from the late 1920s in the work of Neutra, Schindler, Weber and Gill, and then in the Bay Area school founded by William Wurster

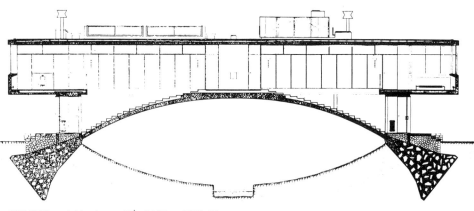

325 Williams, bridge house, Mar del Plata, 1943–45.

and in the Southern California work of Harwell Hamilton Harris. No-one has perhaps expressed the idea of a Critical Regionalism more forcefully than Harris, in 'Regionalism and Nationalism', an address which he first gave to the North West Regional Council of the AIA in Eugene, Oregon, in 1954. This was the occasion when he first advanced his felicitous distinction between restricted and liberated regionalism:

Opposed to the Regionalism of Restriction is another type of regionalism; the Regionalism of Liberation. This is the manifestation of a region that is *especially in tune with the emerging thought of the time*. We call such a manifestation 'regional' *only because it has not yet emerged elsewhere*. It is the genius of this region to be more than ordinarily aware and more than ordinarily free. Its virtue is that its manifestation has *significance for the world outside itself*. To express this regionalism architecturally it is necessary that there be building – preferably a lot of building – at one time. Only so can the expression be sufficiently general, sufficiently varied, sufficiently forceful to capture people's imaginations and provide a friendly climate long enough for a new school of design to develop.

San Francisco was made for Maybeck. Pasadena was made for Greene and Greene. Neither could have accomplished what he did in any other place or time. Each used the materials of the place; but it is not the materials that distinguish the work. . . . A region may develop ideas. A region may accept ideas. Imaginations and intelligence are necessary for both. In California in the late Twenties and Thirties modern European ideas met a still developing regionalism. In New England, on the other hand, European Modernism met a rigid and restrictive regionalism that at first resisted and then surrendered. New England accepted European Modernism whole because its own regionalism had been reduced to a collection of restrictions.

Despite an apparent freedom of expression, such a level of liberative regionalism is difficult to achieve in North America today. Within the current proliferation of highly individualistic forms of expression (work which is often patronizing and self-indulgent rather than critical) only a few firms today display any profound commitment to the unsentimental cultivation of a rooted American culture. An atypical example of current 'regional' work in North America is the sensitively sited houses designed by Andrew Batey and Mark Mack for the Napa Valley area in California; another is the work of the architect Harry Wolf, whose activity has been largely restricted to North Carolina. Wolf's metaphorical approach to place-making was polemically demonstrated in his 1982 competition entry for the Fort Lauderdale Riverfront Plaza. As his description indicates, the intention was to inscribe the city's history into the site through the incidence of light.

The worship of the sun and the measurement of time from its light reach back to the earliest

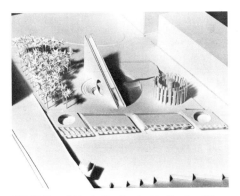

326 Wolf, model for the Fort Lauderdale Riverfront Plaza, 1982.

built at Sutrio in 1954–56.

It is surely understandable that in Europe, where the vestigial city-state was still very much alive, such a regionalist impulse would emerge spontaneously after the Second World War when a number of significant architects were able to contribute to the culture of their native cities. Among those of the post-war generation who remained committed to a regional inflection one may count Ernst Gisel in Zürich, Jørn Utzon in Copenhagen, Vittorio Gregotti in Milan, Sverre Fehn in Oslo, Aris Konstantinidis in Athens, and last but by no means least Carlo Scarpa in Venice.

Switzerland, with its intricate linguistic boundaries and its tradition of cosmopolitanism, has

recorded history of man. It is interesting to note in the case of Fort Lauderdale that if one were to follow a 26° latitudinal line around the globe, one would find Fort Lauderdale in the company of Ancient Thebes – the throne of the Egyptian sun god, Ra. Further to the East, one would find Jaipur, India, where heretofore, the largest equinoctial sundial in the world was built 110 years prior to the founding of Fort Lauderdale.

Mindful of these magnificent historical precedents, we sought a symbol that would speak of the past, present and future of Fort Lauderdale. . . . To capture the sun in symbol a great sundial is incised on the Plaza site and the gnomon of the sundial bisects the site on its north-south axis. The gnomon of the double blade rises from the south at 26° 5′ parallel to Fort Lauderdale's latitude. . . .

Each of the significant dates in Fort Lauderdale's history is recorded in the great blade of the sundial. With careful calculation the sun angles are perfectly aligned with penetrations through the two blades to cast brilliant circles of light, landing on the otherwise shadowy side of the sundial. These shafts of light illuminate an appropriate historical marker serving as annual historical reminders.

In Europe the work of the architect Gino Valle may be considered regional inasmuch as his career has always been centred on the city of Udine. Aside from his concern for the city, Valle made one of the earliest post-war reinterpretations of the rural vernacular of Lombardy in his Casa Quaglia,

327 Valle, Casa Quaglia, Sutrio, 1954–56.

328 Scarpa, Querini Stampalia Gallery, Venice, 1961–63.

321

329 Schnebli, Castioli House, Campione d'Italia, 1960.

always displayed strong regionalist tendencies. The cantonal principle of admission and exclusion has always favoured extremely dense forms of expression, with the canton favouring local culture and the Federation facilitating the penetration and assimilation of foreign ideas. Dolf Schnebli's Neo-Corbusian vaulted villa at Campione d'Italia on the Italo-Swiss frontier (1960) may be seen as initiating the resistance of Ticinese architecture to the influence of commercialized modernism. This resistance found an echo immediately in other parts of Switzerland, in Aurelio Galfetti's equally Corbusian Rotalinti House in Bellinzona (1961) and in Atelier 5's assumption of the Corbusian *béton brut* manner, as this appeared in Siedlung Halen, built outside Berne in 1960 (fig. 314).

Today's Ticinese Regionalism has its ultimate origins in the pre-war protagonists of the Italian Rationalist movement in Switzerland, above all the work of the Italian Alberto Sartoris and the Ticinese Rino Tami. Sartoris's main realizations were in the Valais, most notably a church at Lourtier (1932) and two small concrete-framed houses, built in association with viticulture and under construction between 1934 and 1939, of which the most renowned is the Morand-Pasteur residence at Saillon (1935). Of the compatibility between Rationalism and rural architecture Sartoris wrote: 'Rural architecture, with its essentially regional features, is perfectly at home with today's rationalism. In fact it embodies in practice all those

functional criteria on which modern building methods are essentially based.' Where Sartoris was primarily a polemicist keeping the Rationalist precepts alive throughout the Second World War and its aftermath, Tami was mainly a builder, and the Ticinese architects of the 1960s were able to take his Cantonal Library at Lugano (1936–40) as an exemplary Rationalist work.

Ticinese practice in the mid-1950s, with the exception of Galfetti, was oriented towards the work of Frank Lloyd Wright rather than the pre-war Italian Rationalists. Of this period Tita Carloni wrote: 'We naively set ourselves the objective of an "organic" Ticino, in which the values of modern culture were to be interwoven in a natural way with local tradition.' Of Ticinese Neo-Rationalism in the early 1970s we find him writing:

The old Wrightian schemata were superseded, the chapter of 'big commissions' for the State, with good reformist intentions, was closed. It all had to be begun all over again, from the ground upwards: housing, schools, minor didactic restorations, competition entries as an opportunity to investigate and critically assess the contents and forms of architecture. In the meantime cultural confrontation in Italy, political commitment, and the exacting confrontation with our own native intellectuals, especially Virgilio Gilardoni, meant that history books started to appear on our desks, and above all faced us with the challenge of critically reappraising the whole evolution of modernism, most especially that of the 1920s and 1930s.

As Carloni suggests, the strength of provincial culture resides in its capacity to condense the artistic and critical potential of the region while assimilating and reinterpreting outside influences. The work of Carloni's prime pupil, Mario Botta, is typical in this respect, with its concentration on issues which relate directly to the specific place while adapting methods and approaches drawn from outside. Formally educated under Scarpa, Botta was fortunate enough to work, however briefly, for both Kahn and Le Corbusier during the short period when they projected civic works for Venice. Evidently influenced by these men, Botta went on to appropriate the Italian Neo-Rationalist methodology as his own, while simultaneously

330 Botta, house at Riva San Vitale, 1972–73.

retaining, through Scarpa, an unusual capacity for the craft enrichment of his form. One of the most exotic examples of this occurs in his application of *intonaco lucido* (polished plaster) to the fireplace surrounds of a converted farmhouse at Ligrignano in 1979.

Two other traits in Botta's work may be seen as critical: on the one hand, his constant preoccupation with what he terms 'building the site', and on the other, his conviction that the loss of the historical city can only be compensated for by 'cities in miniature'. Thus Botta's school at Morbio Inferiore is interpreted as a micro-urban realm – as a cultural compensation for the evident loss of civic life in Chiasso, the nearest large city. Primary references to the culture of the Ticino landscape are also evoked by Botta at a typological level, such as the house at Riva San Vitale, which refers obliquely to the traditional tower-like country summer houses or 'rocoli' which were once plentiful in the region.

Aside from these references, Botta's houses serve as markers in the landscape – as indicators of limits or boundaries. The house in Ligornetto, for example, establishes the frontier where the village ends and the agrarian system begins: its main aperture (a large 'cut-out' opening) turns away from the fields and towards the village. Botta's houses are often treated as bunker/belvederes, where the fenestration opens onto choice views in the landscape, concealing the rapacious suburban development that has taken place in the Ticino since 1960. Instead of being terraced into the site, they 'build the site', after the thesis advanced by

Vittorio Gregotti in *Il territorio dell'architettura* (1966). They declare themselves as primary forms, set against the topography and the sky. Their capacity to harmonize with the partially agricultural nature of the region stems directly from their *analogical* form and finish; that is to say, from the fair-faced concrete block of their structure and from the silo or barn-like shells in which they are housed, these last alluding to the traditional agricultural structures from which they are derived.

Despite this feeling for a domestic sensibility which is at once modern and traditional, the most critical aspect of Botta's achievement resides in his public projects; in particular in the two large-scale proposals which he designed in collaboration with Luigi Snozzi. Both of these are 'viaduct' buildings and as such owe something to Kahn's Venice Congress Hall project of 1968 and to Rossi's first sketches for Gallaratese. The 1971 Botta/Snozzi project for the Centro Direzionale, Perugia, is projected as a 'city within a city', and the wider implications of this design clearly stem from its potential applicability to many megalopolitan situations throughout the world. Had it been realized, this centre, conceived as a 'viaduct-megastructure', could have established its presence in the urban region without compromising the historic city or fusing with the chaos of the surrounding suburban development. A comparable clarity and appropriateness obtained in their Zürich Station proposal of 1978, where a multi-level bridge concourse would not only have

331 Botta and Snozzi, project for the alteration of Zürich Station, 1978: the original station building (bottom) and bridge across the tracks.

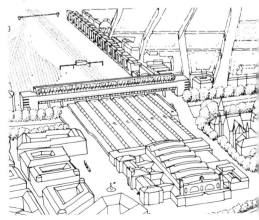

accommodated shops, offices, restaurants and parking but would also have constituted a new head building while some of the original functions were retained in the existing terminus.

It is no accident that Tadao Ando, who is one of the most regionally conscious architects in Japan, should be based at Osaka rather than Tokyo and that his theoretical writings should formulate more clearly than any other architect of his generation a set of precepts which come close to the idea of Critical Regionalism. This is most evident in the tension that he perceives as obtaining between universal modernization and the idiosyncrasy of rooted culture. Thus we find him writing in an essay entitled 'From Self-Enclosed Modern Architecture toward Universality':

Born and bred in Japan, I do my architectural work here. And I suppose it would be possible to say that the method I have selected is to apply the vocabulary and techniques developed by an open, universalist Modernism in an enclosed realm of individual lifestyles and regional differentiation. But it seems difficult to me to attempt to express the sensibilities, customs, aesthetic awareness, distinctive culture, and social traditions of a given race by means of an open, internationalist vocabulary of Modernism . . .

By 'enclosed modern architecture' Ando intends the literal creation of walled enclaves by virtue of which man is able to recover and sustain some vestige of his former intimacy with both nature and culture. Thus he writes:

After World War II, when Japan launched on a course of rapid economic growth, the people's value criteria changed. The old fundamentally feudal family system collapsed. Such social alterations as concentration of information and places of work in cities led to overpopulation of agricultural and fishing villages and towns (as was probably true in other parts of the world as well). Overly dense urban and suburban populations made it impossible to preserve a feature that was formerly most characteristic of Japanese residential architecture; intimate connection with nature and openness to the natural world. What I refer to as an enclosed Modern Architecture is a restoration of the unity between house and nature that Japanese houses have lost in the process of modernization.

In his small courtyard houses, often set within dense urban fabric, Ando employs concrete in such a way as to stress the taut homogeneity of its surface rather than its weight, since for him it is the most suitable material 'for realizing surfaces created by rays of sunlight . . . [where] walls become abstract, are negated, and approach the ultimate limit of space. Their actuality is lost, and only the space they enclose gives a sense of really existing.'

While the cardinal importance of light is stressed in theoretical writings of both Kahn and Le Corbusier, Ando sees the paradox of spatial limpidity emerging out of light as being peculiarly pertinent to the Japanese character and with this he makes explicit the broader meaning which he attributes to the concept of a self-enclosed modernity:

Spaces of this kind are overlooked in utilitarian affairs of everyday and rarely make themselves known. Still they are capable of stimulating recollection of their own innermost forms and stimulating new discoveries. This is the aim of what I call closed modern architecture. Architecture of this kind is likely to alter with the region in which it sends out roots and to grow in various distinctive individual ways. Still, though closed, I feel convinced that as a methodology it is open in the direction of universality.

What Ando has in mind is the development of an architecture where the tactility of the work transcends the initial perception of its geometric order. Precision and density of detail are both crucial to the revelatory quality of his forms under light. Thus he wrote of his Koshino House of 1981:

Light changes expressions with time. I believe that the architectural materials do not end with wood and concrete that have tangible forms but go beyond to include light and wind which appeal to our senses. . . . Detail exists as the most important element in expressing identity. . . . Thus to me, the detail is an element which achieves the physical composition of architecture, but at the same time, it is a generator of an image of architecture.

In their article on the Critical Regionalism of the Greek architects Dimitris and Susana Antonakakis, entitled 'The Grid and the Pathway'

324

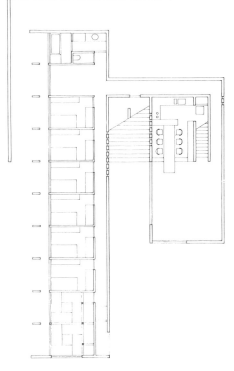

332, 333 Ando, Koshino House, Osaka, 1981: view and ground plan.

(*Architecture in Greece*, 1981), Alex Tzonis and Liane Lefaivre demonstrate the ambiguous role played by the *Schinkelschüler* in the building of Athens and the founding of the Greek state:

In Greece historicist regionalism in its neo-classical version had already met with opposition before the arrival of the Welfare State and of modern architecture. It is due to a very peculiar crisis which explodes around the end of the nineteenth century. Historicist regionalism here had grown not only out of a war of liberation; it had emerged out of interests to develop an urban élite set apart from the peasant world and its rural 'backwardness' and to create a dominance of town over country: hence the special appeal of historicist regionalism, based on the book rather than experience, with its monumentality recalling another distant and forlorn élite. Historical regionalism had united people but it had also divided them.

The various reactions which followed the proliferation of the 19th-century Greek Nationalist Neo-Classical style varied from the vernacular historicism of the 1920s to the committed modernism of the 1930s as this became manifest in the work of such architects as Stamo Papadaki and J.G. Despotopoulos. As Tzonis points out, a consciously regionalist modernism emerged in Greece with the earliest works of Aris Konstantinidis (his Eleusis house of 1938 and his Kifissia garden exhibition of 1940), and this line was developed further by Konstantinidis in the 1950s, in various low-cost housing schemes and in the hotels he designed for the Xenia national tourist organization between 1956 and 1966. In all of Konstantinidis's public work a tension appears between the universal rationality of the trabeated reinforced concrete frame and the autochthonous tactility of the native stone and blockwork which is used as infill. A much less equivocal regionalist spirit permeates the park and promenade that Dimitris Pikionis designed for the Philopappus Hill in 1957, on a site adjacent to the Acropolis in Athens. In this archaic landscape, as Tzonis and Lefaivre point out,

Pikionis proceeds to make a work of architecture free from technological exhibitionism and compositional conceit (so typical of the mainstream of architecture of the 1950s), a stark naked object almost dematerialized, an ordering of 'places made for the occasion', unfolding around the hill for solitary contemplation, for intimate discussion, for a small gathering, for a vast assembly.... To weave

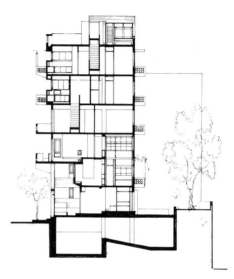

334 Pikionis, park paving on the Philopappus Hill, Athens, 1957.

this extraordinary braid of niches and passages and situations, Pikionis identifies appropriate components from the lived-in spaces of folk architecture, but in this project the link with the regional is not made out of tender emotion. In a completely different attitude, these envelopes of concrete events are studied with a cold empirical method, as if documented by an archaeologist. Neither is their selection and their positioning carried out to stir easy superficial emotion. They are platforms to be used in an everyday sense but to supply that which, in the context of contemporary architecture, everyday life does not. The investigation of the local is the condition for reaching the concrete and the real, and for rehumanizing architecture.

Tzonis sees the work of the Antonakakis partnership as combining the topographic path of Pikionis with the universal grid of Konstantinidis. This dialectical opposition seems to reflect once again that split between culture and civilization remarked on by Ricoeur. Perhaps no work expresses this duality more directly than their Benaki Street apartments built in Athens in 1975, a layered structure wherein a labyrinthine route drawn from the Greek island vernacular is woven into the regular grid of the supporting concrete frame.

As with the largely overlapping categories used in the previous chapter, Critical Regionalism is not so much a style as it is a critical category oriented towards certain common features which may not always be present in the examples cited here

335, 336 Antonakakis, apartment building in Benaki Street, Athens, 1975.

These features, or rather attitudes, may perhaps be best summarized as follows.

*(1)* Critical Regionalism has to be understood as a marginal practice, one which, while it is critical of modernization, nonetheless still refuses to abandon the emancipatory and progressive aspects of the modern architectural legacy. At the same time, Critical Regionalism's fragmentary and marginal nature serves to distance it both from normative optimization and from the naïve utopianism of the early Modern Movement. In contrast to the line that runs from Haussmann to Le Corbusier, it favours the small rather than the big plan.

*(2)* In this regard Critical Regionalism manifests itself as a consciously bounded architecture, one which rather than emphasizing the building as a free-standing object places the stress on the territory to be established by the structure erected on the site. This 'place-form' means that the architect must recognize the physical boundary of his work as a kind of temporal limit – the point at which the present act of building stops.

*(3)* Critical Regionalism favours the realization of architecture as a *tectonic* fact rather than the reduction of the built environment to a series of ill-assorted scenographic episodes.

*(4)* It may be claimed that Critical Regionalism is regional to the degree that it invariably stresses certain site-specific factors, ranging from the topography, considered as a three-dimensional matrix into which the structure is fitted, to the varying play of local light across the structure. Light is invariably understood as the primary agent by which the volume and the tectonic value of the work are revealed. An articulate response to climatic conditions is a necessary corollary to this. Hence Critical Regionalism is opposed to the tendency of universal civilization' to optimize the use of air-conditioning, etc. It tends to treat all openings as delicate transitional zones with a capacity to respond to the specific conditions imposed by the site, the climate and the light.

*(5)* Critical Regionalism emphasizes the tactile as much as the visual. It is aware that the environment can be experienced in terms other than sight alone. It is sensitive to such complementary perceptions as varying levels of illumination, ambient sensations of heat, cold, humidity and air movement, varying aromas and sounds given off by different materials in different volumes, and even the varying sensations induced by floor finishes, which cause the body to experience involuntary changes in posture, gait, etc. It is opposed to the tendency in an age dominated by media to the replacement of experience by information.

*(6)* While opposed to the sentimental simulation of local vernacular, Critical Regionalism will, on occasion, insert reinterpreted vernacular elements as disjunctive episodes within the whole. It will moreover occasionally derive such elements from foreign sources. In other words it will endeavour to cultivate a contemporary place-oriented culture without becoming unduly hermetic, either at the level of formal reference or at the level of technology. In this regard, it tends towards the paradoxical creation of a regionally based 'world culture', almost as though this were a precondition for achieving a relevant form of contemporary practice.

*(7)* Critical Regionalism tends to flourish in those cultural interstices which in one way or another are able to escape the optimizing thrust of universal civilization. Its appearance suggests that the received notion of the dominant cultural centre surrounded by dependent, dominated satellites is ultimately an inadequate model by which to assess the present state of modern architecture.

# Acknowledgments

The individuals who have helped in the preparation of this work are by now too numerous to mention. However, particular credit must be given to those without whom this text would never have come into being; above all the staff at Thames and Hudson. Credit is also due to Julia Bloomfield and Silvia Kolbowski for help on draft versions of the text and to students of mine in both London and New York whose drawings have greatly helped in illustrating the final version; particularly Rene Davids, Jan Glynsteen, Jeremy Hawker, Christian Hubert, William McCleod and David Warner.

I am especially grateful for the criticism and advice I received while writing Part I of this book: to Robin Middleton and Anthony Vidler for Chapter 1, to Anthony Sutcliffe for Chapter 2, and to Pedro Guedes for Chapter 3. I am also indebted to Reyner Banham for his pioneering work in the field of Futurist architecture as it appeared in his *Theory and Design in the First Machine Age* (1960).

Aside from this I owe a debt to those of my colleagues, both architects and architectural historians, with whom I have been associated over the past decade or more; in particular Diana Agrest, Alan Colquhoun, Peter Eisenman, Kurt Forster, Mario Gandelsonas, Leon Krier, Tomás Maldonado, Demetri Porphyrios and John Miller. There remain those who have been influences at a distance: Colin Rowe, Joseph Rykwert, Dalibor Vesely and Manfredo Tafuri.

For illustrations the publishers and I wish to thank Haig Beck and Derek Brampton for help, and to acknowledge the following: Firmenarchiv AEG-Telefunken 90; Albertina, Vienna 71, 72, 73, 75; courtesy Tadao Ando 332, 333; Archigram 279; reproduced by permission of The Architects Collaborative Inc. 93; Copyright *Architectural Design* (1964) 257, 272 (November 1963) 278; Architectural Publishers Artemis 132, 133, 134, 137, 139, 142, 143, 144, 145, 147, 163, 164, 165, 166, 167, 168, 169, 214, 215, 216, 219, 220, 221, 222, 223, 224, 225, 229, 246, 249; *The Architectural Review* 80, 253, 265 (photo de Burgh Galwey) 263; *Arkkitehti*, Helsinki 184; courtesy Atelier 66 335, 336; Bauhaus-Archiv 105, 110, 111, 114, 123; Bibliothèque Nationale, Paris 2, 6, 8; Archives Henry van de Velde, Bibliothèque Royale, Brussels 77; Bildarchiv Foto Marburg 79; Brecht-Einzig Limited 268; Bundesarchiv Koblenz 207; Burkhard-Verlag Ernst Heyer, Essen 120; courtesy G. Candilis 275; Olivier Chaslin 298; Chicago Architectural Photographing Company 34; Chicago Historical Society 43; *Country Life* 30, 200; courtesy Roger Cranshawe 173; John Donat 305; courtesy Fiat 21; FISA Industrias Gráficas 47; courtesy Foster Associates 245, 308 (photo Richard Davies); Henry Fuermann 39; Buckminster Fuller Archives 236, 280; photo Keith Gibson, Hamlyn Group Copyright 57; Glasgow School of Art 58; courtesy Michael Graves (photo Proto Acme Photo) 310; Heins L. Handsur, Vienna 59; Heikki Havas, Helsinki 192; Hedrich Blessing 151, 177, 232, 304; Architectenburo Herman Hertzberger 303; Hessisches Landesmuseum, Darmstadt 61; HfG-Ulm Archives 287; Historic American Buildings Survey (photo Jack E. Boucher, 1965) 35; Studio Hollein

312; IBA, Berlin 323; courtesy Jahn & Murphy 291; S. C. Johnson & Son, Inc. 175; courtesy Philip Johnson 237, 238; Pierre Joly & Véra Cardot 277; Kaiser Wilhelm Museum, Krefeld 88; A. F. Kersting 1, 25; KLM Aerocarto 119; Kunstgewerbemuseum, Zürich 48, 78; Malcolm Lewis 307; E. Mäkinen – The Museum of Finnish Architecture 191; Mas 10; Collection Mattioli, Milan 205; Milton Keynes Development Corporation 286; courtesy Moore Grover Harper (photo Norman McGrath) 292; Museo Civico, Como 68; Museum Bellerive, Zürich 76; Museum of Finnish Architecture 189; Museum of Modern Art, New York, The Mies van der Rohe Archives 146, 149, 226, 227; Museum of the City of New York 14; Bildarchiv der Österreichisches Nationalbank, Vienna 65; courtesy Mrs Dione Neutra 248; Carlos Niño, The Architectural Association 313; Novosti Press Agency 158; Tomio Ohashi 282; courtesy Sir Nikolaus Pevsner 20; redrawn by Stefanos Polyzoides 247; Radio Times Hulton Picture Library 17; Marvin Rand 306; F. Rausser, Bollingen-Berne 314; Retoria, Tokyo (photo W. Fujii) 309, (photo Y. Futagawa) 260, 262, 283, (photo T. Kijajima) 293; Cervin Robinson 211, 239; courtesy Rockefeller Center, Inc. 212; courtesy Richard Rogers (photo Martin Charles) 284; Roger-Viollet 16, 210; Royal Institute of British Architects, London 27, 29; courtesy of Royal Netherlands Embassy 117; Bernard Rudofsky 206; Department of Planning and Design, City of Sheffield 271; Alison and Peter Smithson 264, 270, 273, 274; Staatliche Museen zu Berlin 5; Stadt- und Universitätsbibliothek, Frankfurt 126; Stedelijk Museum, Amsterdam 127; E. Stoecklein 296; Dr Franz Stoedtner 89, 95; Esto/Ezra Stoller 302; Tim Street-Porter 245; Swedish Institute, Stockholm 183; courtesy Salvador Tarragó 46; Plansammlung der Universitätsbibliothek der Technischen Universität Berlin 96, 97; Tennessee Valley Authority 235; United States Information Office 234; Stedelijk van Abbemuseum, Eindhoven 131; Gustav Velin, Turku 186; Photo Welin – The Museum of Finnish Architecture 190

Illustrations have been reproduced from the following publications: Antonin Raymond, *An Autobiography* (Charles E. Tuttle Co., Inc., Tokyo, 1973) 258; Colin Rowe, *The Mathematics of the Ideal Villa* (MIT Press, Cambridge, Mass. 1977) 141; Roger Sherwood, *Modern Housing Prototypes* (Harvard University Press, Cambridge, Mass. and London, 1978) 85, 138; Helmut Weber, *Walter Gropius und Das Faguswerk* (Verlag Georg D. W. Callwey, Munich, 1961) 92.

Acknowledgment is due to The Frank Lloyd Wright Foundation for permission to publish the following illustrations, which are Copyright © The Frank Lloyd Wright Foundation; 36 (copyright 1957), 38 (copyright 1942, 1970), 40 (copyright 1955), 41 (copyright 1963), 172 (copyright 1955), 174 (copyright 1942, 1970), 178 (copyright 1955), 179 (copyright 1958).

The following illustrations of works by Louis I. Kahn are published by Permission of the Trustees of the University of Pennsylvania, by whom all rights are reserved: 240, 241, 243, 244.

# Select Bibliography

*For general works and abbreviations see p. 349*

PART I

Chapter 1

R. Banham, *Theory and Design in the First Machine Age* (London 1960): esp. ch. 1–3.

L. Benevolo, *History of Modern Architecture*, I (Cambridge, Mass. 1971), esp. preface and ch. 1.

T. Buddensieg, *'"To build as one will . . ."* Schinkel's Notions on the Freedom of Building', *Daidalos*, 7, 1983, 93–102.

A. Choisy, *Histoire de l'architecture* (Paris 1899).

L. Dehio, *Friedrich Wilhelm IV von Preussen: Ein Baukünstler der Romantik* (Munich and Berlin 1961).

A. Dickens, 'The Architect and the Workhouse', *AR*, Dec. 1976, 345–52.

A. Drexler, ed., *The Architecture of the Ecole des Beaux-Arts* (New York 1977): with essays by R. Chafee, N. Levine and D. van Zanten.

R. A. Etlin, *The Architecture of Death* (Cambridge, Mass. 1984).

R. Evans, 'Bentham's Panopticon: An Incident in the Social History of Architecture', *AAQ* III, no. 2, Apr./July 1971, 21–37.

— 'Regulation and Production', *Lotus*, 12, Sept. 1976, 6–14.

B. Fortier, 'Logiques de l'équipement', *AMC*, 45, May 1978, 80–85.

K. W. Foster, 'Monument/Memory and the Mortality of Architecture', *Oppositions*, Fall 1982, 2–19.

M. Gallet, *Charles de Wailly 1730–1798* (Paris 1979).

E. Gilmore-Holt, *From the Classicists to the Impressionists* (New York 1966).

M. Girouard, 'Neo-classicism', *AR*, Sept. 1972, 169–80.

J. Guadet, *Eléments et théorie de l'architecture* (Paris 1902).

W. Hermann, *Laugier and Eighteenth-Century French Theory* (London 1962).

— *The Theory of Claude Perrault* (London 1973).

A. Hernandez, 'J.N.L. Durand's Architectural Theory', *Perspecta*, 12, 1969.

Q. Hughes, 'Neo-Classical Ideas and Practice: St George's Hall, Liverpool', *AAQ*, V, no. 2, 1973, 37–44.

E. Kaufmann, *Three Revolutionary Architects, Boullée, Ledoux and Lequeu* (Philadelphia 1953).

— *Architecture in the Age of Reason* (New York 1968).

M. Lammert, *David Gilly. Ein Baumeister der deutschen Klassizismus* (Berlin 1981).

K. Lankheit, *Der Tempel der Vernunft* (Basel and Stuttgart 1968).

N. Lieb and F. Hufnagl, *Leo von Klenze, Gemälde und Zeichnungen* (Munich 1979).

G. Mezzanotte, 'Edilizia e politica. Appunti sull'edilizia dell'ultimo neoclassicismo', *Casa-bella*, 338, July 1968, 42–53.

R. Middleton, 'The Abbé de Cordemoy: The Graeco-Gothic Ideal', *JW&CI*, 1962, 1963.

W. Oechslin, 'Monotonie von Blondel bis Durand', *Werk-Archithese*, Jan. 1977, 29–33.

— *et al.*, *Klassizismus in Bayern, Schwaben und Franken: Architektur Zeichnungen 1775–85* (Munich 1980).

A. Oncken, *Friedrich Gilly 1772–1800* (reprint, Berlin 1981).

A. Pérez-Gómez, *Architecture and the Crisis of Science* (Cambridge, Mass. 1983).

J. M. Pérouse de Montclos, *Etienne-Louis Boullée 1728–1799* (Paris 1969).

N. Pevsner, *Academies of Art, Past and Present* (Cambridge 1940): unique study of the evolution of architectural and design education.

— *Studies in Art, Architecture and Design*, I (London 1968).

J. Posener, 'Schinkel's Eclecticism and the Architectural', *AD*, Nov.–Dec. 1983, special issue on Berlin, 33–39.

P. de la Ruffinière du Prey, *John Soane* (Chicago 1982).

H. G. Pundt, *Schinkel's Berlin* (Cambridge, Mass. 1972).

G. Riemann, ed., *Karl Friedrich Schinkel. Reisen nach Italien* (Berlin 1979).

A. Rietdorf, *Gilly: Wiedergeburt der Architektur* (Berlin 1943).

R. Rosenblum, *Transformations in Late Eighteenth Century Art* (Princeton, N.J. 1967).

A. Rowan, 'Japelli and Cicogarno', *AR*, Mar. 1968, 225–28: on 19th-century Neo-Classical architecture in Padua, etc.

J. Rykwert, 'Classic and Neo-Classic', *Oppositions*, 7, Winter 1976, 39–53.

— *The First Moderns* (Cambridge, Mass. 1983).

P. Saddy, 'Henri Labrouste: architecte-constructeur', *Les Monuments Historiques de la France*, no. 6, 1975, 10–17.

J. Starobinski, *The Invention of Liberty* (Geneva 1964): trans.

D. Stroud, *The Architecture of Sir John Soane* (London 1961).

— *George Dance, Architect 1741–1825* (London 1971).

W. Szambien, *J.N.L. Durand* (Paris 1984).

M. Tafuri, *Architecture and Utopia: Design and Capitalist Development* (Cambridge, Mass. 1976).

J. Taylor, 'Charles Fowler: Master of Markets', *AR*, Mar. 1964, 176–82.

D. Ternois *et al.*, *Soufflot et l'architecture des lumières* (CNRS/Paris 1980): proceedings of a conference on Soufflot held at the University of Lyons in June 1980.

G. Teyssot, *Città e utopia nell'illuminismo inglese: George Dance il giovane* (Rome 1974).

— 'John Soane and the Birth of Style', *Oppositions*, 14, 1978, 61–83.

A. Valdenaire, *Friedrich Weinbrenner* (Karlsruhe 1919).

A. Vidler, 'Architecture of the Lodges: Ritual Form and Associational Life in the Late Enlightenment', *Oppositions*, 5, Summer 1976.
— 'The Idea of Type: The Transformation of the Academic Ideal 1750–1830', *Oppositions*, 8, Spring 1977. (The same issue contains Quatremère de Quincy's extremely important article on type that appeared in the *Encyclopédie Méthodique*, III, pt. 2, Paris 1825.).
— 'The "Art" of History: Monumental Aesthetics from Winckelmann to Quatremère de Quincy', *Oppositions*, 25, 1982, 53–67.
D. Watkin, *Thomas Hope and the Neo-classical Idea* (London 1968).
— 'Karl Friedrich Schinkel: Royal Patronage and the Picturesque', *AD*, XLIX, 8/9, 1979 (special issue on Neoclassicism), 56–71.

## Chapter 2

L. Balmer, S. Erni and U. von Gunten, 'Co-operation between Capital and Labour', *Lotus*, 12, Sept. 1976, 59–71.
H. P. Bartschi, *Industrialisierung Eisenbahnschlacten und Städtebau* (ETH/GTA 25, Stuttgart 1983).
L. Benevolo, *The Origins of Modern Town Planning* (Cambridge, Mass. 1967).
— *History of Modern Architecture*, I (Cambridge, Mass. 1971), ch. 2–5.
— *The History of the City* (Cambridge, Mass. 1980): encyclopaedic treatment of the history of Western urbanism.
C. Boyer, *Dreaming of the Rational City: the Myth of American City Planning* (Cambridge, Mass. 1983).
A. Brauman, *Le Familistère de Guise ou les équivalents de la richesse* (Brussels 1976): English text.
S. Buder, *Pullman: An Experiment in Industrial Order and Community Planning 1880–1930* (New York 1967).
D. Burnham and E. H. Bennett, *Plan of Chicago* (Chicago 1909).
J. Castex, J. C. Depaule and P. Panerai, *Formes urbaines: de l'îlot à la barne* (Paris 1977).
I. Cerdá, 'A Parliamentary Speech', *AAQ*, IX, no. 7, 1977, 23–26.
F. Choay, *L'Urbanisme, utopies et réalités* (Paris 1965).
— *The Modern City: Planning in the 19th Century* (New York 1969): essential introductory text.
G. Collins, 'Linear Planning throughout the World', *JSAH*, XVIII, Oct. 1959, 74–93.
— 'Cities on the Line', *AR*, Nov. 1960, 341–45.
C. C. and G. R. Collins, *Camillo Sitte and the Birth of Modern City Planning* (London 1965).
M. H. Contal, 'Vittel 1854–1936. Création d'une ville thermale', *Vittel 1854–1936* (Paris 1982).
W. L. Creese, *The Legacy of Raymond Unwin* (Cambridge, Mass. 1967).
G. Darley, *Villages of Vision* (London 1976).
J. Fabos, G. T. Milde and V. M. Weinmayr, *Frederick Law Olmsted, Sr.* (University of Massachusetts 1968).
R. M. Fogelson, *The Fragmented Metropolis: Los Angeles 1850–1930* (Cambridge, Mass. 1967).
K. W. Forster, 'Sozialer Wohnbau: Geschichte und Gegenwart', *Archithese*, 8, 1973, 2–8.

A. Fried and P. Sanders, *Socialist Thought* (New York 1964): useful for trans. of French utopian socialist texts, Fourier, Saint-Simon, etc.
J. F. Geist and K. Kurvens, *Das Berliner Miethaus 1740–1862* (Stuttgart 1982).
A. Grumbach, 'The Promenades of Paris', *Oppositions*, 8, Spring 1977.
A. J. Jeffery, 'A Future for New Lanark', *AR*, Jan. 1975, 19–28.
D. Leatherbarrow, 'Friedrichstadt – A Symbol of Toleration', *AD*, Nov.–Dec. 1983, 23–31.
A. Lopez de Aberasturi, *Ildefonso Cerdá: la théorie générale de l'urbanisation* (Paris 1979).
F. Loyer, *Architecture of the Industrial Age* (New York 1982).
— *Paris XIXe. siècle* (Paris 1981).
H. Meyer and R. Wade, *Chicago: Growth of a Metropolis* (Chicago 1969).
B. Miller, Ildefonso Cerda', *AAQ*, IX, no. 7, 1977, 12–22.
G. Peschken, 'The Berlin Miethaus and Renovation', *AD*, Nov.–Dec. 1983, 49–57.
N. Pevsner, 'Early Working Class Housing', reprinted in *Studies in Art, Architecture and Design*, II (London 1968, repr. 1982).
F. Rella, *Il Dispositivo Foucault* (Venice 1977): with essays by M. Cacciari, M. Tafuri and G. Teyssot.
J. P. Reynolds, 'Thomas Coglan Horsfall and the Town Planning Movement in England', *Town Planning Review*, XXIII, Apr. 1952, 52–60.
A. Service, *London 1900* (London and New York 1979).
C. Sitte, *City Planning According to Artistic Principles* (London 1965): trans. of Sitte's text of 1889.
M. de Sola-Morales, 'Towards a Definition: Analysis of Urban Growth in the Nineteenth Century', *Lotus*, 19, June 1978, 28–36.
R. Stern, *New York 1900* (New York 1984).
A. Sutcliffe, *Metropolis 1890–1940* (Chicago 1984).
— *Towards the Planned City: Germany, Britain, the United States and France 1780–1914* (New York 1981).
J. N. Tarn, 'Some Pioneer Suburban Housing Estates', *AR*, May 1968, 367–70.
— *Working-Class Housing in'19th-Century Britain*, AA Paper no. 7 (London 1971).
P. Wolf, 'City Structuring and Social Sense in 19th and 20th Century Urbanism', *Perspecta*, 13/14, 1971, 220–33.
R. Wolters, *Stadtmitte Berlin* (Tübingen 1978).

## Chapter 3

T. C. Bannister, 'The First Iron-Framed Buildings', *AR*, CVII, Apr. 1950.
— 'The Roussillon Vault: The Apotheosis of a Folk Construction', *JSAH*, XXVII, no. 3, Oct. 1968.
P. Beaver, *The Crystal Palace 1851–1936* (London 1970).
W. Benjamin, 'Paris: Capital of the 19th Century', *New Left Review*, no. 48, Mar.–Apr. 1968.
M. Bill, *Robert Maillart: Bridges and Constructions* (New York 1969): English version of a 1949 definitive study of Maillart's work.

D. P. Billington, *Robert Maillart's Bridges* (Princeton, N.J. 1979).

— *The Tower and the Bridge* (New York 1983).

B. Bradford, 'The Brick Palace of 1862', *AR*, July 1962, 15–21: documentation of the British successor to the Crystal Palace.

P. Chemetov, *Architectures, Paris 1848–1914* (Paris 1972): exhibition catalogue and research carried out with M.-C. Gagneux, B. Paurd and E. Girard.

P. Collins, *Concrete: The Vision of a New Architecture* (London 1959).

C. W. Condit, *American Building Art: The Nineteenth Century* (New York 1960).

A. Corboz, 'Un pont de Robert Maillart à Leningrad?', *Archithese*, 2, 1971, 42–44.

E. de Maré, 'Telford and the Gotha Canal', *AR*, Aug. 1956, 93–99.

E. Diestelkamp, *The Iron and Glass Architecture of Richard Turner* (PhD thesis, London University, 1982).

E. Fratelli, *Architektur und Konfort* (Winterthur 1967).

E. Freyssinet, *L'Architecture Vivante*, Spring/Summer 1931: a survey of Freyssinet's work up to that date, ed. J. Badovici.

M. Gayle and E. V. Gillon, *Cast-Iron Architecture in New York* (New York 1974).

J. F. Geist, *Passagen, ein Bautyp des 19. Jahrhunderts* (Munich 1969); trans. *Arcades: The History of a Building Type* (Cambridge, Mass. and London 1983).

S. Giedion, *Space, Time and Architecture* (Cambridge, Mass., 3rd edn 1954): still a classic work despite errors in detail; see 161–331.

J. Gloag and D. Bridgwater, *History of Cast Iron Architecture* (London 1948).

— *Mr Loudon's England* (Newcastle 1970).

A. Grumbach, 'The Promenades of Paris', *Oppositions*, 8, Spring 1977, 51–67.

G. Günschel, *Grosse Konstrukteure 1: Freyssinet, Maillart, Dischinger, Finsterwalder* (Berlin 1966).

R. Günter, 'Der Fabrikbau in Zwei Jahrhunderten', *Archithese*, 3/4, 1971, 34–51.

H.-R. Hitchcock, 'Brunel and Paddington', *AR*, CIX, 1951, 240–46.

J. Hix, 'Richard Turner: Glass Master', *AR*, Nov. 1972, 287–93.

— *The Glass House* (Cambridge, Mass. 1974).

D. Hoffmann, 'Clear Span Rivalry: The World's Fairs of 1889–1893', *JSAH*, XXIX, 1, Mar. 1970, 48.

H. J. Hopkins, *A Span of Bridges* (Newton Abbot 1970): excellent history of bridge construction by a qualified engineer.

V. Hütsch, *Der Münchner Glaspalast 1854–1931* (Munich 1980).

A. L. Huxtable, 'Reinforced Concrete Construction. The Work of Ernest L. Ransome', *Progressive Architecture*, XXXVIII, Sept. 1957, 139–42.

R. A. Jewett, 'Structural Antecedents of the I-beam 1800–1850', *Technology and Culture*, VIII, 1967, 346–62.

G. Kohlmaier, *Eisen Architektur, The Role of Iron in the Historic Architecture in the Second Half of the 19th Century* (ICOMOS, Hanover 1982).

S. Koppelkamm, *Glasshouses and Winter Gardens of the 19th Century* (New York 1981).

J. C. Loudon, *Remarks on Hot Houses* (London 1817).

F. Loyer, *Architecture of the Industrial Age, 1789–1914* (New York 1982).

H. Maier, *Berlin Anhalter Bahnhof* (Berlin 1984).

D. McCullough, *The Great Bridge* (New York 1972): a popular history of the building of Brooklyn Bridge.

C. Meeks, *The Railroad Station* (New Haven, Conn. 1956).

T. F. Peters, *Time is Money: Die Entwicklung des Modernen Bauwesens* (Stuttgart 1981).

J. M. Richards, *The Functional Tradition* (London 1958).

G. Roisecco, *L'architettura del ferro: l'Inghilterra 1688–1914* (Rome 1972).

G. Roisecco, R. Jodice and V. Vannelli, *L'architettura del ferro: la Francia 1715–1914* (Rome 1973).

T. C. Rolt, *Isambard Kingdom Brunel* (London 1957).

— *Thomas Telford* (London 1958).

C. Rowe, 'Chicago Frame. Chicago's Place in the Modern Movement', *AR*, Nov. 1956.

H. Schaefer, *Nineteenth Century Modern* (New York 1970).

A. Scharf, *Art and Industry* (Bletchley, Bucks. 1971).

E. Schild, *Zwischen Glaspalast und Palais des Illusions: Form und Konstruktion im 19. Jahrhunderts* (Berlin 1967).

W. Schivelbusch, *The Railway Journey: Trains and Travel in the 19th Century* (New York 1979).

P. Morton Shand, 'Architecture and Engineering', 'Iron and Steel', 'Concrete', *AR*, Nov. 1932: these pioneering articles were repub. in *AAJ*, no. 827, Jan. 1959, ed. B. Housden.

A. W. Skempton, 'Evolution of the Steel Frame Building', *Guild Engineer*, X, 1959, 37–51.

— 'The Boatstore at Sheerness (1858–60) and its Place in Structural History', *Trans. of the Newcomen Soc.*, XXXII, 1960, 57–78.

A. W. Skempton and H. R. Johnson, 'William Strutt's Cotton Mills 1793–1812', *Trans. of the Newcomen Soc.*, XXX, 1955–57, 179–203.

— 'The First Iron Frames', *AR*, CXXXI, 1962.

T. Turak, 'The Ecole Centrale and Modern Architecture: The Education of William Le Baron Jenney', *JSAH*, XXIX, 1970, 40–47.

K. Wachsmann, *The Turning Point in Building* (New York 1961): gives a contemporary designer's insight into the significance of the work of Paxton, Eiffel, Roebling, Baker, etc.

## PART II

### Chapter 1

C. Amery, M. Lutyens *et al.*, *Lutyens* (London 1981).

C. R. Ashbee, *Where the Great City Stands: A Study in the New Civics* (London 1917): a comprehensive ideological statement by a late Arts and Crafts designer.

E. Aslin, *The Aesthetic Movement* (London and New York 1969).

A. Bøe, *From Gothic Revival To Functional Form* (Oslo 1957).

I. Bradley, *William Morris and his World* (London 1978).

J. Brandon-Jones, 'The Work of Philip Webb and Norman Shaw', *AAJ*, LXXI, 1955, 9–21.

— 'C. F. A. Voysey', *AAJ*, LXXII, 1957, 238–62.

— (and others), *C. F. A. Voysey: Architect and Designer* (London 1978).

K. Clark, *Ruskin Today* (Harmondsworth 1967): certainly the most convenient introduction to Ruskin's writings.

J. Mordaunt Crook, *William Burges and the High Victorian Dream* (London 1981).

D. J. DeWitt, 'Neo-Vernacular/Eine Moderne Tradition', *Archithese*, 9, 1974, 15–20.

D. Gebhard, 'The Vernacular Transformed', *RIBAJ*, Mar. 1971, 98–102.

M. Girouard, *Sweetness and Light: The Queen Anne Movement 1860–1900* (Oxford 1977).

C. Grillet, 'Edward Prior', *AR*, Nov. 1952, 303–08.

N. Halbritter, 'Norman Shaw's London Houses', *AAQ*, VII, no. 1, 1975, 3–19.

E. Howard, *Tomorrow: a Peaceful Path to Real Reform* (London 1898).

C. Hussey, *The Life of Sir Edwin Lutyens* (London 1950).

P. Inskip, *Edwin Lutyens* (London and New York 1980).

A. Johnson, 'C. F. A. Voysey', *AAQ*, IX, no. 4, 1977, 26–35.

W. R. Lethaby, *Architecture, Mysticism and Myth* (London 1892, reprinted 1975).

— *Form and Civilization* (London 1922).

— *Philip Webb and His Work* (London 1935).

— *Architecture, Nature and Magic* (London 1935).

R. Macleod, *Style and Society: Architectural Ideology in Britain 1835–1914* (London 1971): essential for this period.

A. L. Morton, ed., *Political Writings of William Morris* (New York 1973).

H. Muthesius, *The English House* (London 1979): trans. of 1904 German text.

N. Pevsner, *Pioneers of Modern Design* (New York 1949).

— 'William Morris and Architecture', *RIBAJ*, 3rd ser., LXIV, 1957.

— *Some Architectural Writers of the Nineteenth Century* (Oxford 1962): esp. for the reprinting of Morris's 'The Revival of Architecture' (1888).

— *The Sources of Modern Architecture and Design* (London 1968).

— 'Arthur H. Mackmurdo' (*AR* 1938) and 'C. F. A. Voysey 1858–1941' (*AR* 1941), in *Studies in Art, Architecture and Design*, II (London 1968, repr. 1982).

M. Richardson, *The Craft Architects* (London and New York 1983).

A. Saint, *Richard Norman Shaw* (Princeton and London 1978).

A. Service, *Edwardian Architecture and its Origins* (London 1975).

— *Edwardian Architecture* (London 1977).

— *London 1900* (London 1979).

P. Stanton, *Pugin* (London 1971).

F. A. Walker, 'William Lethaby', *AAQ*, IX, no. 4, 1977, 45–53.

R. Watkinson, *William Morris as Designer* (New York and London 1967).

## Chapter 2

A. Bush-Brown, *Louis Sullivan* (New York 1960).

D. Crook, 'Louis Sullivan and the Golden Doorway', *JSAH*, XXVI, Dec. 1967, 250.

H. Dalziel Duncan, *Culture and Democracy* (Totowa, N.J. 1965).

D. D. Egbert and P. E. Sprague, 'In search of John Edelman, Architect and Anarchist', *AIAJ*, Feb. 1966, 35–41.

H.-R. Hitchcock, *The Architecture of H. H. Richardson* (New York 1936, rev. edn. 1961).

D. Hoffmann, 'The Setback Skyscraper of 1891: An Unknown Essay by Louis Sullivan', *JSAH*, XXIX, no. 2, May 1970, 181.

G. C. Manson, 'Sullivan and Wright, an Uneasy Union of Celts', *AR*, Nov. 1955, 297–300.

H. Morrison, *Louis Sullivan, Prophet of Modern Architecture* (New York 1935, reprinted 1952).

J. K. Ochsner, *H. H. Richardson, Complete Architectural Works* (Cambridge, Mass. 1982).

J. F. O'Gorman, *The Architecture of Frank Furness* (Philadelphia 1973).

— *Henry Hobson Richardson and his Office: Selected Drawings* (Cambridge, Mass. and Boston 1974).

L. Sullivan, *A System of Architectural Ornament According with a Philosophy of Man's Powers* (Washington 1924).

— 'Reflections on the Tokyo Disaster', *Architectural Record*, Feb. 1924: a late text praising Wright's Imperial Hotel.

— *The Autobiography of an Idea* (New York 1926 and 1956): originally pub. as a series in the *AIAJ*, 1922–23.

— *Kindergarten Chats and Other Writings* (New York 1947).

D. Tselos, 'The Chicago Fair and the Myth of the Lost Cause', *JSAH*, XXVI, no. 4, Dec. 1967, 259.

F. L. Wright, *Genius and the Mobocracy* (New York 1949): Wright's appreciation of Sullivan's ornamental genius.

## Chapter 3

H. Allen Brooks, *The Prairie School* (Toronto 1972).

— ed., *Writings on Wright* (Cambridge, Mass. 1983).

J. Connors, *The Robie House of Frank Lloyd Wright* (Chicago 1984).

A. M. Fern, 'The Midway Gardens of Frank Lloyd Wright', *AR*, Aug. 1963, 113–16.

H. de Fries, *Frank Lloyd Wright* (Berlin 1926).

J. Griggs, 'The Prairie Spirit in Sculpture', *The Prairie School Review*, II, no. 4, Winter 1965, 5–23.

S. P. Handlin, *The American Home: Architecture and Society 1815–1915* (Boston 1979).

D. A. Hanks, *The Decorative Designs of Frank Lloyd Wright* (New York 1979).

H.-R. Hitchcock, *In the Nature of Materials 1887–1941. The Buildings of Frank Lloyd Wright* (New York 1942): still the finest catalogue *raisonné* of Wright's work 1887–1941.

— 'Frank Lloyd Wright and the Academic Tradition', *JW&CI*, no. 7, 1944, 51.

D. Hoffmann, 'Frank Lloyd Wright and Viollet-le-Duc', *JSAH*, XXVIII, no. 3, Oct. 1969, 173.

A. Izzo and C. Gubitosi, *Frank Lloyd Wright Dessins 1887–1959* (Paris 1977): Franco-Italian exhibition catalogue containing many unpublished drawings.

C. James. *The Imperial Hotel* (Rutland, Vt. and Tokyo 1968): a complete documentation of the hotel prior to its demolition.

E. Kaufmann and B. Raeburn, *Frank Lloyd Wright: Writings and Buildings* (New York 1960): an important collection of Wright's writings, including his seminal *The Art and Craft of the Machine*.

N. Kelly-Smith, *Frank Lloyd Wright: A Study in Architectural Content* (Englewood Cliffs, N.J. 1966).

R. Kosta, 'Frank Lloyd Wright in Japan', *The Prairie School Review*, III, no. 3, Autumn 1966, 5–23.

G. C. Manson, 'Wright in the Nursery: The Influence of Froebel Education on the Work of Frank Lloyd Wright', *AR*, June 1953. 349–51.

— 'Sullivan and Wright, an Uneasy Union of Celts', *AR*, Nov. 1955.

— *Frank Lloyd Wright to 1910: The First Golden Age* (New York 1958): one of the most intelligent interpretations of the early Wright to date.

L. M. Peisch, *The Chicago School of Architecture* (London 1964).

V. Scully, *The Shingle Style* (New Haven, Conn. 1955).

— *Frank Lloyd Wright* (New York 1960).

D. Tselos, 'Frank Lloyd Wright and World Architecture', *JSAH*, XXVIII, no. 1, Mar. 1969, 58ff.

F. L. Wright, *Ausgeführte Bauten und Entwürfe von Frank Lloyd Wright* (Berlin 1910, reissued New York 1965).

— *An Autobiography* (New York 1932, reissued London 1946).

— *On Architecture*, ed. F. Gutheim (New York 1941): a selection of writings 1894–1940.

G. Wright, *Moralism and the Modern Home: 1870–1913* (Chicago 1980).

**Chapter 4**

J. F. Aillagon or G. Viollet-le-Duc, *Le Voyage d'Italie d'Eugène Viollet-le-Duc 1836–1837* (Florence 1980).

T. G. Beddall, 'Gaudí and the Catalan Gothic', *JSAH*, XXXIV, no. 1, Mar. 1975, 48.

O. Bohigas, 'Luis Domenech y Montaner 1850–1923', *AR*, Dec. 1967, 426–36.

F. Borsi and E. Godoli, *Paris 1900* (London 1978).

F. Borsi and P. Portoghesi, *Victor Horta* (Brussels 1977).

F. Borsi and H. Weiser, *Bruxelles Capitale de l'Art Nouveau* (Rome 1971).

Y. Brunhammer and G. Naylor, *Hector Guimard* (London 1978): the best available English monograph on Guimard.

E. Casanelles, *Antonio Gaudí, A Reappraisal* (New York 1967).

J. Castex and P. Panerai, 'L'Ecole d'Amsterdam: architecture urbaine et urbanisme social-démocratie', *AMC*, 40, Sept. 1976, 39–54.

G. Collins, *Antonio Gaudí* (London 1960).

M. Culot and L. Grenier, 'Henry Sauvage, 1873–1932', *AAQ*, X, no. 2, 1972, 16–27.

M. Culot and others, *Henri Sauvage 1893–1932* (Brussels 1976): collected works with essays by L. Grenier, F. Loyer and L. Miotto-Muret.

R. Dalisi, *Gaudí Furniture* (London 1979).

R. Delevoy, *Victor Horta* (Brussels 1958).

— *et al.*, *Henri Sauvage 1873–1932* (Brussels and Paris 1977).

R. Descharnes and C. Prévost, *Gaudí, The Visionary* (New York 1971): contains much remarkable material not available elsewhere.

B. Foucart *et al.*, *Viollet-le-Duc* (Paris 1980).

D. Gifford, *The Literature of Architecture* (New York 1966): contains trans. of Berlage's article, 'Neuere amerikanische Architektur'.

L. F. Graham, *Hector Guimard* (New York 1970).

G. Grassi, 'Un architetto e una città: Berlage ad Amsterdam', *Casabella-Continuità*, 1961, 39–44.

J. Gratama, *Dr H. P. Berlage Bouwmeester* (Rotterdam 1925).

H. Guimard, 'An architect's opinion of l'Art Nouveau', *Architectural Record*, June 1902, 130–33.

M.-A. Leblond, 'Gaudí et l'architecture méditerranéenne', *L'Art et les artistes*, II, 1910.

D. Mackay, 'Berenguer', *AR*, Dec. 1964, 410–16.

S. T. Madsen, 'Horta: Works and Style of Victor Horta Before 1900', *AR*, Dec. 1955, 388–92.

C. Martinell, *Gaudí: His Life, His Themes, His Work* (Barcelona 1975).

F. Mazade, 'An "Art Nouveau" Edifice in Paris', *Architectural Record*, May 1902: a contemporary account of the Humbert de Romans theatre.

N. Pevsner and J. M. Richards, eds., *The Anti-Rationalists* (London 1973).

F. Russell, ed., *Art Nouveau Architecture* (New York 1979).

R. Schmutzler, 'The English Origins of the Art Nouveau', *AR*, Feb. 1955, 109–16.

— 'Blake and the Art Nouveau', *AR*, Aug. 1955, 91–97.

— *Art Nouveau* (New York and London 1962, paperback 1979): still the most comprehensive English study of the whole development.

J. L. Sert and J. J. Sweeny, *Antonio Gaudí* (London 1960).

P. Singelenberg, *H. P. Berlage: Idea and Style* (Utrecht 1972): this definitive work is the only readily available English text on Berlage.

J. Summerson, 'Viollet-le-Duc and the Rational Point of View', in *Heavenly Mansions* (London 1948): still one of the best short introductions to Viollet-le-Duc.

J. Summerson. N. Pevsner, H. Damish and S. Durant, *Viollet-le-Duc*, *AD* Profile, 1980.

F. Vamos, 'Lechner Ödön', *AR*, July 1967, 59–62.

**Chapter 5**

F. Alison, *Le sedie di Charles Rennie Mackintosh* (Milan and London 1973): a catalogue raisonné with drawings of Mackintosh's furniture.

R. Billcliffe, *Architectural Sketches and Flower Drawings by Charles Rennie Mackintosh* (London 1977).

T. Howarth, *Charles Rennie Mackintosh and the Modern Movement* (London 1952, rev. edn. 1977). Still the seminal English text.

E. B. Kalas, 'L'art de Glasgow', in *De la Tamise à la Sprée* (Rheims 1905): an English version was pub. for the Mackintosh Memorial Exhibition, 1933.

R. Macleod, *Charles Rennie Mackintosh* (London 1968).

A. Service, 'James Maclaren and the Godwin legacy', *AR*, Aug. 1973, 111–18.

D. Walker, 'Charles Rennie Mackintosh', *AR*, Nov. 1968, 355–63.

G. White, 'Some Glasgow Designers and their Work', *Studio*, XI, 1897, 86ff.


## Chapter 6

P. Behrens, 'The Work of Josef Hoffmann', *Architecture* (Journal of the Society of Architects, London) II, 1923, 589–99.

F. Cellini, 'La villa Asti di Josef Hoffmann', *Contraspazio*, IX, no. 1, June 1977, 48–51.

J. R. Clark, 'J. M. Olbrich 1867–1908', *AD*, XXXVII, Dec. 1967: still the only comprehensive short account in English of Olbrich's work.

H. Czech, 'Otto Wagner's Vienna Metropolitan Railway', *A&U*, 76.07, July 1976, 11–20.

Darmstadt: *Ein Dokument deutscher Kunst 1901– 1976* (Darmstadt 1976); 5 vol. exhibition catalogue. Vol. V records the 3 main phases of the building of the colony, 1901–14.

H. Geretsegger, M. Peintner and W. Pichler, *Otto Wagner 1841–1918* (New York and London 1970): the only available and comprehensive account in English of Wagner's work.

O. A. Graf, *Die Vergessene Wagnerschule* (Vienna 1969).

G. Gresleri, *Josef Hoffmann* (New York 1984).

I. Latham, *Josef Maria Olbrich* (London 1980).

A. J. Lux, *Otto Wagner* (Munich 1914).

W. Mrazek, *Die Wiener Werkstätte* (Vienna 1967).

C. M. Nebehay, *Ver Sacrum 1898–1903* (New York 1978).

N. Pevsner, 'Secession', *AR*, Jan. 1971, 73–74.

N. Powell, *The Sacred Spring: The Arts in Vienna 1898–1918* (New York 1974).

C. Schorske, 'The Transformation of the Garden: Ideal and Society in Austrian Literature', in *Dargestellte Geschichte in der europäischen Literatur des 19. Jahrhunderts* (Frankfurt-am-Main 1970).

W. J. Schweiger, *Wiener Werkstätte: Kunst und Handwerke 1903–1932* (Vienna 1982); English trans. *Wiener Werkstätte: Design in Vienna 1903–1932* (London 1984).

E. Sekler, 'The Stoclet House by Josef Hoffmann', in *Essays in the History of Architecture Presented to Rudolf Wittkower* (London 1967).

— 'Art Nouveau Bergerhöhe', *AR*, Jan. 1971, 75–76.

— *Josef Hoffmann: Das architektonische Werk* (Vienna 1982).

M. Tafuri, 'Am Steinhof, Centrality and Surface in Otto Wagner's Architecture', *Lotus*, 29, 1981, 73–91.

P. Vergo, *Art in Vienna 1898–1918* (London 1975).

O. Wagner, *Moderne Architektur* (Vienna: I 1896, II & III 1898–1902): for abridged trans. see 'Modern Architecture', in *Brick Builder*, June–Aug. 1901.

— *Die Baukunst unserer Zeit* (Vienna 1914).

R. Waissenberger, *Vienna 1890–1920* (New York 1984).


## Chapter 7

U. Apollonio, *Futurist Manifestos* (London 1973): contains all the basic manifestos.

R. Banham, *Theory and Design in the First Machine Age* (London 1960), esp. ch. 8–10.

G. Brizzi and C. Guenzi, 'Liberty occulto e G. B. Bossi', *Casabella*, 338, July 1968, 22–23.

L. Caramel and A. Longati, *Antonio Sant'Elia* (Como 1962).

R. Clough, *Futurism* (New York 1961).

E. Godoli, *Il Futurismo* (Rome and Bari 1983).

J. Joll, *Three Intellectuals in Politics* (New York 1960): studies of Blum, Rathenau and Marinetti.

G. Kahn, *L'Esthétique de la rue* (Paris 1901).

M. Kirby, *Futurist Performance* (New York 1971).

F. T. Marinetti, *Marinetti: Selected Writings* (New York 1971).

C. Meeks, *Italian Architecture 1750–1914* (New Haven and London 1966): the last chapter is particularly relevant to the Stile Floreale.

J.-A. Moilin, *Paris en l'an 2000* (Paris 1869).

J. P. Schmidt-Thomsen, 'Sant'Elia futurista or the Achilles Heel of the Futurism', *Daidalos*, 2, 1981, 36–44.

J. Taylor, *Futurism* (New York 1961).

P. Thea, *Nuove Tendenze a Milano e l'altro Futurismo* (Milan 1980).

C. Tisdall and A. Bozzolla, *Futurism* (London 1977).


## Chapter 8

F. Amendolagine and M. Cacciari, *Oikos: da Loos a Wittgenstein* (Rome 1975).

V. Behalova, 'Die Villa Karma von Adolf Loos', *Alte und moderne Kunst*, Nov–Dec. 1970.

C. A. and T. J. Benton, *Form and Function*, ed. with Dennis Sharp (London 1975): anthology containing trans. of *Architektur* (1910) and *Potemkinstadt* (1898).

H. Czech and W. Mistelbauer, *Das Looshaus* (Vienna 1976): study of the Goldman & Salatsch building.

— 'The Loos Idea', *A&U*, 78.05, 1977, 47–54.

P. Engelmann, *Letters from Ludwig Wittgenstein* (Oxford 1967), esp. ch. 7.

J. P. Fotrin and M. Pietu, 'Adolf Loos. Maison Pour Tristan Tzara', *AMC*, 38, Mar. 1976, 43–50.

B. Gravagnuolo, *Adolf Loos: Theory and Works* (New York 1982).

J. Gubler, 'Loos, Ehrlich und die Villa Karma', *Archithese*, 1, 1971, 46–49.

J. Gubler and G. Barbey, 'Loos's Villa Karma', *AR*, Mar. 1969, 215–16.

A. Janik and S. Toulmin, *Wittgenstein's Vienna* (New York 1974).

H. Kulka, *Adolf Loos, Das Werk des Architekten* (Vienna 1931).

A. Loos, *Das Andere* (Vienna 1903).

— *Ins Leere gesprochen* (Paris 1921): articles written 1897–1900.
— *Trotzdem* (Innsbruck 1931): articles written 1903–30.
— *Sämtliche Schriften* (Vienna 1962).
E. Altman Loos, *Adolf Loos, der Mensch* (Vienna and Munich 1968).
L. Munz and G. Künstler, *Adolf Loos: Pioneer of Modern Architecture* (London 1966): a study, plus trans. of *The Plumbers, The Story of the Poor Rich Man* and *Ornament and Crime.*
J. Rykwert, 'Adolf Loos: the new vision', *Studio International*, July/Aug. 1973, 17–21.
D. Worbs *et al.*, *Adolf Loos 1870–1933* (Berlin 1984): cat. of an exhibition at the Akademie der Künste, Berlin.

## Chapter 9

M. Culot, *Henry van de Velde Theatres 1904–14* (London and Brussels 1974).
— 'Réflexion sur la "voie sacrée", un texte de Henry van de Velde', *AMC*, 45, May 1978, 20–21.
R. Delevoy and others, *Henry van de Velde 1863–1957* (Brussels 1963): catalogue with essays by Delevoy, Verwilghen, Lebeer, Baudin, Risselin.
D. D. Egbert, *Social Radicalism in the Arts* (New York 1970).
A. M. Hammacher, *Le Monde de Henry van de Velde* (Antwerp 1967).
H. Hesse-Frielinghaus, A. Hoff and W. Erben, *Karl Ernst Osthaus: Leben und Werk* (Reckling-hausen 1971).
K.-H. Hüter, *Henry van de Velde* (Berlin 1967).
P. Morton Shand, 'Van de Velde to Wagner', *AR*, Oct. 1934, 131–34.
— 'Van de Velde, Extracts from Memoirs 1891–1901', *AR*, Sept. 1952, 143–45.
L. Tannenbaum, 'Henry van de Velde: A Re-evaluation', *Art News Annual*, XXXIV (New York 1968): the best overall English account of Van de Velde's contribution.
H. van de Velde, 'Déblaiement d'art', in *La Société nouvelle* (Brussels 1894).
— *Les Formules de la beauté architectonique* (Weimar 1916–17).
— 'Vernunftsgemässer Stil. Vernunft und Schönheit', *Frankfurter Zeitung*, LXXIII, no. 21, Jan. 1929.
— *Geschichte meines Lebens* (Munich 1962): for English extracts see Shand, *op. cit.*
W. Worringer, *Abstraction and Empathy* (New York 1963): trans. of 1908 text.

## Chapter 10

J. Badovici, 'L'Oeuvre de Tony Garnier', *L'Architecture Vivante*, Autumn/Winter 1924.
J. Badovici and A. Morancé, *L'Oeuvre de Tony Garnier* (Paris 1938).
R. de Souza, *L' Avenir de nos villes, études pratiques d'esthétique urbaine, Nice: capitale d'hiver* (Paris 1913).
T. Garnier, *Une Cité industrielle. Etude pour la construction des villes* (Paris 1917; 2nd edn. 1932).
— *Les Grands Travaux de la ville de Lyons* (Paris 1920).

C. Pawlowski, *Tony Garnier et les débuts de l'urbanisme fonctionnel en France* (Paris 1967).
D. Wiebenson, *Tony Garnier: The Cité Industrielle* (New York 1969): best available English text on Garnier.
P. M. Wolf, *Eugène Hénard and the Beginning of Urbanism in Paris 1900–1914* (Paris 1968).

## Chapter 11

J. Badovici, articles in *L'Architecture Vivante*, Autumn/Winter 1923, Spring/Summer 1924, Spring/Summer 1925, and Autumn/Winter 1926.
A. Bloc, *L'Architecture d'Aujourd-hui*, VII, Oct. 1932: special issue dedicated to the work of Perret, with articles by Astruc, Jourdain, Hilberseimer, Le Corbusier, Sarfatti and Vago.
B. Champigneulle, *Auguste Perret* (Paris 1959).
P. Collins, *Concrete: The Vision of a New Architecture* (London 1959).
V. Gregotti, 'Classicisme et rationalisme d'A. Perret', *AMC*, 37, Nov. 1975, 19–20.
B. Jamot, *Auguste Perret et l'architecture du béton armé* (Brussels 1927).
A. Perret, 'Architecture: Science et poésie', *La Construction moderne*, 48, Oct. 1932, 2–3.
— 'L'Architecture', *Revue d'art et d'esthetique*, June 1935.
— *Contribution à une théorie de l'architecture* (Paris 1952).
G. E. Pettengill, *Auguste Perret: A Partial Bibliography* (unpub. MS, AIA Library, Washington 1952).
P. Saddy, 'Perret et les idées reçues', *AMC, op cit.*, 21–30.
P. Vago, 'Auguste Perret', *L'Architecture d'Aujourd'hui*, Oct. 1932.
P. Valéry, *Eupalinos ou l'architecte* (Paris 1923; trans. London 1932): a key to the French classical attitude to architecture after the First World War.

## Chapter 12

S. Anderson, 'Peter Behrens's Changing Concept of Life as Art', *AD*, XXXIX, Feb. 1969, 72–78.
— 'Modern Architecture and Industry: Peter Behrens and the Cultural Policy of Historical Determinism', *Oppositions*, 11, Winter 1977.
— 'Modern Architecture and Industry: Peter Behrens and the AEG Factories', *Oppositions*, 23, 1981, 53–83.
P. Behrens, 'The Turbine Hall of the AEG 1910', *Documents* (The Open University Press, Milton Keynes 1975), 56–57.
T. Benton, S. Muthesius and B. Wilkins, *Europe 1900–14* (The Open University Press, Milton Keynes 1975).
K. Bernhardt, 'The New Turbine Hall for AEG 1910', *Documents* (The Open University Press, Milton Keynes 1975), 54–56.
R. Bletter, 'On Martin Fröhlich's Gottfried Semper', *Oppositions*, 4, Oct. 1974, 146–53.
T. Buddensieg, *Industriekultur. Peter Behrens and the AEG, 1907–1914* (Cambridge, Mass. 1984).
T. Buddensieg and H. Rogge, 'Peter Behrens and the AEG Architecture', *Lotus*, 12, Sept. 1976, 90–127.
L. Burckhardt, ed., *Werkbund: Germania, Austria, Svizzera* (Milan 1977).

J. Campbell, *The German Werkbund – The Politics of Reform in the Applied Arts* (Princeton, N.J. 1978).

C. Chassé, 'Didier Lenz and the Beuron School of Religious Art', *Oppositions*, 21, 1980, 100–103.

U. Conrad, *Programs and Manifestoes on 20th-Century Architecture* (Cambridge, Mass. 1970): an important anthology of manifestos 1903–63, notably *Aims of the Werkbund* (1911) and *Werkbund Theses and Anti-Theses* (1914).

S. Custoza, M. Vogliazzo and J. Posener, *Muthesius* (Milan 1981).

H. Eckstein, ed., *50 Jahre Deutscher Werkbund* (Frankfurt and Berlin 1958).

L. D. Ettlinger, 'On Science, Industry and Art, Some Theories of Gottfried Semper', *AR*, July 1964, 57–60.

W. Gropius, 'Die Entwicklung Moderner Industriebaukunst', *Jahrbuch des Deutschen Werkbundes*, 1913.

— 'Der Stilbildende Wert Industrieller Bauformen', *Jahrbuch des Deutschen Werkbundes*, 1914.

W. Herrmann, *Gottfried Semper und die Mitte der 19. Jahrhunderts* (ETH/GTA 18, Stuttgart 1976): proceedings of an important international Semper symposium.

— *Gottfried Semper in Exile* (ETH/GTA 19, Stuttgart 1978).

— *Gottfried Semper. Theoretischer Nachlass an der ETH Zürich* (ETH/GTA 15, Stuttgart 1981).

F. Hoeber, *Peter Behrens* (Munich 1913).

F. Meinecke, *The German Catastrophe* (Cambridge, Mass. 1950, repub. Boston 1963).

S. Müller, *Kunst und Industrie – Ideologie und Organisation des Funktionalismus in der Architektur* (Munich 1974).

H. Muthesius, 'The Task of the Werkbund in the Future', *Documents* (The Open University Press, Milton Keynes 1978), 7–8; followed by extracts from the Werkbund debate at Cologne, 1914.

— *The English House* (New York 1979): trans. of German original.

H. Muthesius, F. Naumann and others, *Der Werkbund-Gedanke in den germanischen Ländern* (Jena 1914). Proceedings of the Werkbund debate at Cologne, 1914.

F. Naumann, 'Werkbund und Handel', *Jahrbuch des Deutschen Werkbundes*, 1913.

— 'Culture is, however, a General Term, Paris 1900 – a letter', *Daidalos*, 2, 1981, 25, 33.

N. Pevsner, 'Gropius at Twenty-Six', *AR*, July 1961, 49–51.

J. Posener, 'Muthesius as Architect', *Lotus*, 9, Feb. 1975, 104–15 (trans. 221–25).

F. Schumacher, *Der Geist der Baukunst* (Stuttgart 1983): republication of a thesis first issued in 1938.

F. Very, 'J. M. L. Lauweriks: architecte et théosophe', *AMC*, 40, Sept. 1976, 55–58.

G. Wangerin and G. Weiss, *Heinrich Tessenow 1876–1950* (Essen 1976).

H. Weber, *Walter Gropius und das Fagus werk* (Munich 1961).

A. Windsor, *Peter Behrens Architect 1868–1940* (London 1981).

## Chapter 13

J. Badovici, 'Erich Mendelsohn', *L'Architecture Vivante*, Autumn/Winter 1932 (special issue).

R. Banham, 'Mendelsohn', *AR*, 1954, 85–93.

O. Beyer, ed., *Erich Mendelsohn: Letters of an Architect* (London 1967).

R. Bletter, 'Bruno Taut and Paul Scheerbart' (unpub. Ph.D. thesis, Avery Library, Columbia, New York 1973).

U. Conrads and H. G. Sperlich, *Fantastic Architecture* (London 1963).

K. Frampton, 'Genesis of the Philharmonie', *AD*, Mar. 1965, 111–12.

H. Häring, 'Approaches to Form' (1925), *AAQ*, X, no. 7, 1978: trans. of Häring text.

J. Joedicke, 'Häring at Garkau', *AR*, May 1960, 313–18.

— *Hugo Häring, Schriften, Entwürfe, Bauten* (Stuttgart 1965).

— ed., *Das Andere Bauen* (Stuttgart 1982): an anthology of theoretical writings by Häring.

P. Blundell Jones, 'Organic versus Classic', *AAQ*, X, no. 7. 10–23.

— 'Late Works of Scharoun', *AR*, Mar. 1975, 141–54.

— *Hans Scharoun* (London 1978).

K. Junghans, 'Bruno Taut', *Lotus*, 9, Feb. 1975, 94–103 (trans. 219–21).

— *Bruno Taut 1880–1938* (2nd edn, Berlin 1983).

W. Pehnt, *Expressionist Architecture* (London 1973): the most definitive account available.

J. Posener, 'Poelzig', *AR*, June 1963, 401–05.

— ed., *Hans Poelzig: Gesammelte Schriften und Werke* (Berlin 1970).

G. Rumé, 'Rudolf Steiner', *AMC*, 39, June 1976, 23–29.

P. Scheerbart and B. Taut, *Glass Architecture and Alpine Architecture* (New York 1972): trans. of 2 seminal texts.

W. Segal, 'About Taut', *AR*, Jan. 1972, 25–26.

D. Sharp, *Modern Architecture and Expressionism* (London and New York 1966).

— 'Park Meerwijk – an Expressionist Experiment in Holland', *Perspecta*, 13/14, 1971.

M. Staber, 'Hans Scharoun, Ein Beitrag zum organischen Bauen', *Zodiac*, 10, 1952, 52–93: Scharoun's contribution to organic building, with trans.

B. Taut, 'The Nature and the Aims of Architecture', *Studio*, Mar. 1929, 170–74.

M. Taut and O. M. Ungers, *Die Gläserne Kette. Visionäre Architecktur aus dem Kries um Bruno Taut 1919–1920* (Berlin 1963).

A. Tischhauser, 'Creative Forces and Crystalline Architecture: In Remembrance of Wenzel Hablik', *Daidalos*, 2, 1981, 45–52.

A. Whittick, *Erich Mendelsohn* (London 1970).

B. Zevi, *Erich Mendelsohn* (New York 1984).

## Chapter 14

G. Adams, 'Memories of a Bauhaus Student', *AR*, Sept. 1968, 192–94.

H. Bayer, W. Gropius and I. Gropius, *Bauhaus 1919–1928* (Boston 1952).

336

A. Cohen, *Herbert Bayer* (Cambridge, Mass. 1984).

M. Franciscono, *Walter Gropius and the Creation of the Bauhaus in Weimar* (Chicago and London 1971).

S. Giedion, *Walter Gropius: Work and Teamwork* (New York 1954).

P. Green, 'August Endell, *AAQ*, IX, no. 4, 1977, 36–44.

W. Gropius, *The New Architecture and the Bauhaus* (London 1935).

— *The Scope of Total Architecture* (London 1956): important for trans. of seminal texts of the 1920s

R. Kostelanetz, *Moholy-Nagy* (New York 1970): trans. of his basic texts.

L. Lang, *Das Bauhaus 1919–1923. Idee und Wirklichkeit* (Berlin 1965).

S. A. Mansbach, *Visions of Totality: László Moholy-Nagy, Theo van Doesburg and El Lissitzky* (Ann Arbor, Mich. 1980).

L. Moholy-Nagy, *The New Vision* (New York, 4th edn 1947): trans. of *Von Material zu Architektur* (Munich 1928).

— *Vision in Motion* (Chicago 1947).

S. Moholy-Nagy, *Moholy-Nagy. An Experiment in Totality* (New York 1950).

E. Neumann, *Bauhaus and Bauhaus People* (New York 1970).

W. Schedig, *Crafts of the Weimar Bauhaus 1919–1924* (London 1967).

O. Schlemmer, L. Moholy-Nagy and F. Molnar, *The Theater of the Bauhaus* (Middletown, Conn. 1961): trans. of *Bauhausbücher 4*.

J. Willett, *The New Sobriety 1917–1933: Art and Politics in the Weimar Period* (London 1978).

H. Wingler, *The Bauhaus: Weimar, Dessau, Berlin and Chicago* (Cambridge, Mass. 1969): the basic documentary text on the Bauhaus to date.

## Chapter 15

E. Bertonati, *Aspetti della 'Nuova Oggettività'* (Florence 1968): catalogue of exhibition of the New Objective painters, Rome and Munich, 1968.

O. Birkner, J. Herzog and P. de Meuron, 'Die Petersschule in Basel (1926–1929)' *Werk-Archithese*, 13/14 Jan.–Feb. 1978, 6–8.

J. Buckschmitt, *Ernst May: Bauten und Planungen*, vol. 1 (Stuttgart 1963).

M. Casciato, F. Panzini and S. Polano, *Olanda 1870–1940: Città, Casa, Architettura* (Milan 1980).

G. Fanelli, *Architettura moderna in Olanda* (Flornece 1968).

G. Grassi, ed., *Das Neue Frankfurt 1926–1931 e l'architettura della nuova Francoforte* (Bari 1975).

J. Gubler, *Nationalisme et internationalisme dans l'architecture moderne de la Suisse* (Lausanne 1975): very detailed account of the Neue Sachlichkeit in Switzerland, 145–238.

O. Haesler, *Mein Lebenswerk als Architekt* (Berlin 1957).

H. Hirolina, ed., *Neues Bauen Neue Gesellschaft: Das neue Frankfurt die neue Stadt. Eine Zeitschrift Zwischen 1926–1933* (Dresden 1984).

K. Homann and L. Scarpa, 'Martin Wagner, The Trades Union Movement and Housing Construction in Berlin in the First Half of the 1920s', *AD*, Nov.–Dec. 1983, 58–61.

B. Housden, 'Arthur Korn', *AAJ* (special issue), LXXIII, no. 817, Dec. 1957, 114–35.

— 'M. Brinckman, J. A. Brinckman, L. C. van der Vlugt, J. H. van der Broek, J. B. Bakema', *AAJ*, Dec. 1960: a documentation of the evolution of this important firm over 4 generations.

E. J. Jelles and C. A. Alberts, 'Duiker 1890–1935', *Forum voor architectuur en daarmee verbonden kunsten*, nos. 5 & 6, 1972.

S. Lissitzky-Küppers, *El Lissitzky* (London 1968).

D. Mackintosh, *The Modern Courtyard*, AA Paper no. 9 (London 1973).

B. Miller Lane, *Architecture and Politics in Germany 1918–1945* (Cambridge, Mass. 1968).

L. Murad and P. Zylberman, 'Esthétique du taylorisme', in *Paris/Berlin rapports et contrastes/France-Allemagne* (Paris 1978), 384–90.

G. Oorthuys, *Mart Stam: Documentation of his work 1920–1965* (London 1970).

M. B. Rivolta and A. Rossari, *Alexander Klein* (Milan 1975).

F. Schmalenbach, 'The Term Neue Sachlichkeit', *AB*, XXII, Sept. 1940.

H. Schmidt, 'The Swiss Modern Movement 1920–1930', *AAQ*, Spring 1972, 32–41.

C. Schnaidt, *Hannes Meyer, Buildings, Projects and Writings* (London 1965).

G. Uhlig, 'Town Planning in the Weimar Republic', *AAQ*, XI, no. 1, 1979, 24–38.

J. B. van Loghem, *Bouwen, Bauen, Bâtir, Building* (Amsterdam 1932): standard contemporary survey of the achievement of the Nieuwe Zakelijkheid in Holland.

K. P. Zygas. 'The Magazine Veshch/Gegendstand/Object', 1922 (annotated bibliography). *Oppositions*, 5, Summer 1976, 113–28.

## Chapter 16

J. Baljeu, *Theo van Doesburg* (London 1974).

T. M. Brown, *The Work of G. Rietveld, Architect* (Utrecht 1958).

M. Friedman, ed., *De Stijl: 1917–1931. Visions of Utopia* (Minneapolis 1982).

H. L. C. Jaffé, *De Stijl 1917–1931. The Dutch Contribution to Modern Art* (Amsterdam 1956).

— *De Stijl* (London 1970): trans. of seminal texts.

J. Leering, L. J. F. Wijsenbeck and P. F. Althaus, *Theo van Doesburg 1883–1931* (Eindhoven 1969).

P. Mondrian, 'Plastic Art and Pure Plastic Art', *Circle*, ed. J. L. Martin, B. Nicholson and N. Gabo (London 1937).

S. Polano, 'Notes on Oud', *Lotus*, 16, Sept. 1977, 42–49.

M. Seuphor, *Piet Mondrian* (New York 1958).

N. J. Troy, *The De Stijl Environment* (Cambridge, Mass. 1983).

J. H. van der Broek, C. van Eesteren and others, *De Stijl* (Amsterdam 1951): this initiated the post-war interest in the movement, and carries trans. of a number of the manifestos.

T. van Doesburg, 'L'Evolution de l'architecture moderne en Hollande', *L'Architecture Vivante*, Autumn/Winter 1925 (special issue on De Stijl).

C. St John Wilson, 'Gerrit Rietveld 1888–1964', *AR*, Dec. 1964, 399–402.

B. Zevi, *Poetica dell'architettura neoplastica* (Milan 1953).

## Chapter 17

G. Baird, 'A Critical Introduction to Karel Teige's "Mundaneum" and Le Corbusier's "In the Defence of Architecture"', *Oppositions*, 4, Oct. 1974, 80–81.

R. Banham, *Theory and Design in the First Machine Age* (London 1960), esp. section 4.

T. Benton, *Les Villas de Le Corbusier 1920–1930* (Paris 1984).

M. Besset, *Who Was Le Corbusier?* (Cleveland 1968): trans.

P. Boudon, *Pessac de Le Corbusier* (Paris 1969).

P. A. Croset *et al.*, 'I clienti de Le Corbusier', *Rassegna*, 3, July 1980: a special number devoted to the clients of Le Corbusier from the industrialist Bata to the Soviet State.

P. Dermée, ed. (with A. Ozenfant and Le Corbusier), *L'Esprit Nouveau*, 1, 1920–25. (Facsimile reprint New York 1969.)

G. Fabre, ed., *Léger and the Modern Spirit, 1918–1931* (Paris 1982).

K. Frampton, 'The Humanist vs. Utilitarian Ideal', *AD*, XXXVIII, 1968, 134–36.

R. Gabetti and C. Olmo, *Le Corbusier et l'esprit nouveau* (Turin 1977).

P. Goulet and C. Parent, 'Le Corbusier', *Aujourd' hui*, 51 (special issue), Nov. 1965: for early correspondence, documentation, etc.

C. Green, 'Léger and l'esprit nouveau 1912–1928', *Léger and Purist Paris*, catalogue ed. with J. Golding (London 1970), 25–82.

E. Gregh, 'Le Corbusier and the Dom-Ino System', *Oppositions*, 15/16, Jan. 1980.

G. Gresleri, *80 Disegni di Le Corbusier* (Bologna 1977).

— *L'Esprit Nouveau. Le Corbusier: costruzione e ricostruzione di un prototipo dell'architettura moderna* (Milan 1979).

J. Guiton, *The Ideas of Le Corbusier* (New York 1981).

A. Izzo and C. Gubitosi, *Le Corbusier* (Rome 1978): catalogue of hitherto unpublished Le Corbusier drawings.

Le Corbusier (pseud. C. E. Jeanneret), *Etude sur le mouvement d'art décoratif en Allemagne* (La Chaux-de-Fonds 1912).

— *La Peinture moderne* (Paris 1925).

— *L'Art décoratif d'aujourd'hui* (Paris 1925).

— *Une Maison – un palais* (Paris 1928).

— 'In the Defence of Architecture', *Oppositions*, 4, Oct. 1974, 93–108: 1st pub. in Czech in *Stavba*, 7 (Prague 1929) and in French in *L'Architecture d'Aujourd'hui*, 1933.

— *Le Corbusier et Pierre Jeanneret, Oeuvre complète*, I: 1918–1929 (Zürich 1935, repr. London 1966).

— *Towards a New Architecture* (London 1927).

— 'Purism' (1920), in *Modern Artists on Art*, ed. R. C. Herbert (Englewood Cliffs, N.J. 1964), 58–73: timely trans. of the essay 'Purism' which appeared in the 4th issue of *L'Esprit Nouveau*.

— *Le Voyage d'orient* (Paris 1966): record of a journey to Bohemia, Serbia, Bulgaria, Greece and Turkey (1st prepared for pub. 1914).

— *Le Corbusier Sketchbooks*, vol. 7 (Cambridge, Mass. 1982).

Le Corbusier and A. Ozenfant, *Après le Cubisme* (Paris 1918).

J. Lowman, 'Corb as Structural Rationalist: The Formative Influence of the Engineer Max du Bois', *AR*, Oct. 1976, 229–33.

J. Petit, *Le Corbusier lui-même*, (Geneva 1969): important catalogue of Le Corbusier's painting 1918–54.

N. Pevsner, 'Time and Le Corbusier', *AR*, Mar. 1951: an early appraisal of Le Corbusier's work in La Chaux-de-Fonds.

J. Ritter, 'World Parliament – The League of Nations Competition', *AR*, CXXXVI, 1964, 17–23.

C. Rowe, *The Mathematics of the Ideal Villa and Other Essays* (Cambridge, Mass. 1977).

C. Rowe and R. Slutzky, 'Transparency: Literal and Phenomenal', *Perspecta*, 8, 1963, 45–54.

M. P. Sekler, 'The Early Drawings of Charles-Edouard Jeanneret (Le Corbusier) 1902–1908', Ph.D. thesis, Harvard 1973 (New York 1977).

P. Serenyi, 'Le Corbusier, Fourier and the Monastery of Ema', *AB*, XLIX, 1967, 227–86.

— *Le Corbusier in Perspective* (Englewood Cliffs, N.J. 1975): critical commentary by various writers spanning over half a century, starting with Piacentini's essay on mass production houses of 1922.

B. B. Taylor, *Le Corbusier et Pessac*, I & II (Paris and Cambridge, Mass. 1972).

K. Teige, 'Mundaneum', *Oppositions*, 4, Oct. 1974, 83–91: 1st pub. in *Stavba*, 7 (Prague 1929).

P. Turner, 'The Beginnings of Le Corbusier's Education 1902–1907'. *AB*, LIII, June 1971, 214–24.

— *The Education of Le Corbusier* (New York 1977).

R. Walden, ed., *The Open Hand: Essays on Le Corbusier* (Cambridge, Mass. 1977): seminal essays by M. P. Sekler, M. Favre, R. Fishman, S. von Moos and P. Turner.

## Chapter 18

D. von Beulwitz, 'The Perls House by Mies van der Rohe', *AD*, Nov.–Dec. 1983, 63–71.

J. Bier, 'Mies van der Rohe's Reichspavillon in Barcelona', *Die Form*, Aug. 1929, 23–30.

M. Bill, *Mies van der Rohe* (Milan 1955).

J. P. Bonta, *An Anatomy of Architectural Interpretation* (Barcelona 1975): a semiotic review of the criticisms of Mies van der Rohe's Barcelona Pavilion.

H. T. Cadbury-Brown, 'Ludwig Mies der Rohe', *AAJ*, July–Aug. 1959: this interview affords a useful insight into Mies's relation to his clients for both the Tugendhat House and the Weissenhofsiedlung.

L. Glaeser, *Ludwig Mies van der Rohe: Drawings in the*

*Collection of the Museum of Modern Art* (New York 1969).

— *The Furniture of Mies van der Rohe* (New York 1977).

L. Hilberseimer, *Mies van der Rohe* (Chicago 1956).

H.-R. Hitchcock, 'Berlin Architectural Show 1931', *Horn and Hound*, V, no. 1, Oct–Dec. 1931, 94–97.

P. Johnson, 'Architecture in the Third Reich', *Horn and Hound*, 1933 (reprinted in *Oppositions*, 2, 1974, 92–93).

— 'The Berlin Building Exposition of 1931', *T square*, 1932 (reprinted in *Oppositions*, 2, 1974, 87–91).

— *Mies van der Rohe* (New York 1947): still the best monograph on Mies, with comprehensive bibliography and trans. of Mies's basic writings 1922–43.

L. Mies van der Rohe, 'A Tribute to Frank Lloyd Wright', *College Art Journal*, VI, no. 1, Autumn 1946, 41–42.

— 'Two Glass Skyscrapers 1922', in Johnson, *Mies, op. cit.*, 182; 1st pub. as 'Hochhausprojekt fur Bahnhof Friedrichstrasse im Berlin', in *Frühlicht*, 1922.

— 'Working Theses 1923', *Programs and Manifestos on 20th Century Architecture*, ed. U. Conrads (Cambridge, Mass. 1970), 74: pub. in *G*, 1st issue, 1923, in conjunction with his concrete office building.

— 'Industrialized Building 1924', *ibid.*, 81; from *G*, 3rd issue, 1924.

— 'On Form in Architecture 1927', *ibid.*, 102; 1st pub. in *Die Form*, 1927, as 'Zum Neuer Jahrgang'; another trans. appears in Johnson, *Mies, op. cit.*

R. Moneo, 'Un Mies menos conocido', *Arquitecturas Bis* 44, July 1983, 2–5.

N. M. Rubio Tuduri, 'Le Pavillon de l'Allemagne à l'exposition de Barcelone par Mies van der Rohe', *Cahiers d'Art*, 4, 1929, 408–12.

A. and P. Smithson, *Mies van der Rohe, Veröffentlichungen zur Architektur* (Berlin 1968): a short but sensitive appraisal which introduced for the 1st time the suppressed Krefeld factory (text in German and English).

— *Without Rhetoric* (London 1973): important for critical appraisal and photographs of the Krefeld factory.

W. Tegethoff, *Mies van der Rohe. Die Villen und Landhaus Projekte* (Berlin 1981).

P. Westheim, 'Mies van der Rohe: Entwicklung eines Architekten', *Das Kunstblatt*, II, Feb. 1927, 55–62.

— 'Umgestaltung des Alexanderplatzes', *Die Bauwelt*, 1929.

— 'Das Wettbewerb der Reichsbank', *Deutsche Bauzeitung*, 1933.

F. R. S. Yorke, *The Modern House* (London 1934, 4th edn 1943): contains details of the panoramic window in the Tugendhat House.

C. Zervos, 'Mies van der Rohe', *Cahiers d'Art*, 3, 1928, 35–38.

— 'Projet d'un petit musée d'art moderne par Mies van der Rohe', *Cahiers d'Art*, 20/21, 1946, 424–27.


## Chapter 19

C. Abramsky, 'El Lissitzky as Jewish Illustrator and Typographer', *Studio International*, Oct. 1966, 182–85.

P. A. Aleksandrov and S. O. Chan-Magomedov, *Ivan Leonidov* (Milan 1975): Italian trans. of unpub. Russian text.

T. Anderson, *Vladimir Tatlin* (Stockholm 1968).

— *Malevich*, catalogue raisonné of the Berlin Exhibition of 1927 (Amsterdam 1970).

J. Billington, *The Icon and the Axe* (New York 1968).

M. Bliznakov, 'The Rationalist Movement in Soviet Architecture of the 1920s', *20th-Century Studies*, 7/8, Dec. 1972, 147–61.

C. Borngräber, 'Foreign Architects in the USSR', *AAQ*, XI, no. 1, 1979, 50–62.

S. O. Chan-Magomedov, *Moisej Ginzburg* (Milan 1975): Italian trans. of Russian text pub. 1972.

— 'Nikolaj Ladavskij: An Ideology of Rationalism', *Lotus*, 20, Sept. 1978, 104–26.

— see also Kahn-Magomedov.

J. Chernikov, *Arkhitekturnye Fantasii* (Leningrad 1933).

J. L. Cohen, M. de Michelis, and M. Tafuri, *URSS 1917–1978. La ville l'architecture* (Paris 1978).

F. Dal Co, 'La poétique "a-historique" de l'art de l'avant-garde en Union Soviétique', *Archithese*, 7, 1973, 19–24, 48.

V. de Feo, *URSS Architettura 1917–36* (Milan 1962).

E. Dluhosch, 'The Failure of the Soviet Avant Garde', *Oppositions*, 10, Autumn 1977, 30–55.

C. Douglas, *Swans of Other Worlds: Kazimir Malevich and the Origins of Abstraction in Russia* (Ann Arbor, Mich. 1980).

D. Elliott, ed., *Alexander Rodchenko: 1891–1956* (Oxford, Museum of Modern Art, 1979).

— *Mayakovsky: Twenty Years of Work* (Oxford, Museum of Modern Art, 1982).

K. Frampton, 'Notes on Soviet Urbanism 1917–32', *Architects' Year Book*, XII, 1968, 238–52.

— 'The Work and Influence of El Lissitzky', *ibid.*, 253–68.

R. Fülöp-Muller, *The Mind and Face of Bolshevism* (London and New York 1927, repub. New York 1962).

N. Gabo, *Gabo* (Cambridge, Mass. 1957).

M. Ginzburg, *Style and Epoch* (Cambridge, Mass. 1982): trans. of the Russian original of 1924.

C. Gray, *The Great Experiment: Russian Art 1863–1922* (London 1962).

S. Kahn-Magomedov, *Ivan Leonidov* (IAUS Cat. no. 8, New York 1981): a great deal of the material in this cat. was compiled by R. Koolhaas and B. Oorthuys.

— see also Chan-Magomedov.

G. Karginov, *Rodchenko* (London 1979).

E. Kirichenko, *Moscow Architectural Monuments of the 1830s–1910s* (Moscow 1977).

A. Kopp, *Town and Revolution, Soviet Architecture and City Planning 1917–1935* (New York and London 1970).

— *Architecture et mode de vie* (Grenoble 1979).

J. Kroha and J. Hruza, *Sovetská architektonicá avant-garda* (Prague 1973).

El Lissitzky, *Russia: An Architecture for World Revolution* (Cambridge, Mass. 1970): trans. by E. Dluhosch; 1st pub. in German, 1930.

I. G. Liudkovsky, 'On the Choice of the Optimum Types of Suspended Roofs and of their Rearing Contours', *The*

*Russian Engineer*, 26 May 1972: gives brief information on the suspended roofs of V. G. Shukhov, 1894.

C. Lodder, *Russian Constructivism* (New Haven 1983).

B. Lubetkin, 'Soviet Architecture: Notes on Developments from 1917–32', *AAJ*, May 1956.

K. Malevich, 'Recent Developments in Town Planning', in *The Non-Objective World* (Chicago 1959).

— *Essays on Art*, I 1915–28, II 1928–33 (Copenhagen 1968).

V. Markov, *Russian Futurism* (London 1969).

J. Milner, *Tatlin and the Russian Avant-Garde* (New Haven 1983).

N. A. Milyutin, *Sotsgorod. The Problem of Building Socialist Cities* (Cambridge, Mass. 1974): trans. from Russian.

M. F. Parkins, *City Planning in Soviet Russia* (Chicago 1953).

V. Quilici, *L'architettura del costruttivismo* (Bari 1969).

— 'The Residential Commune, from a Model of the Communitary Myth to Productive Module', *Lotus*, 8, Sept. 1974, 64–91, 193–96.

— *Città russa e città sovietica* (Milan 1976).

B. Schwan, *Stadtebau und Wohnungswesen der Welt* (Berlin 1935).

F. Starr, *Konstantin Melnikov. Solo Architect in a Mass Society* (Princeton, N.J. 1978).

M. Tafuri, ed., *Socialismo città architettura URSS 1917–1937* (Rome 1972): collected essays.

— 'Les premières hypothèses de planification urbaine dans la Russie soviétique 1918–1925', *Archithese*, 7, 1973, 34–91.

— 'Towards the "Socialist City": Research and Realization in the Soviet Union between NEP and the First Five-Year Plan', *Lotus*, 9, Feb. 1975, 76–93, 216–19.

J. Wolin, 'Multi-Media Machine Building', *Perspecta*, 13/14, 1971.

K. P. Zygas, 'Tatlin's Tower Reconsidered', *AAQ*, VIII, no. 2, 1976, 15–27.

— *Form Follows Form: Source Imagery of Constructivist Architecture 1917–1925* (Ann Arbor, Mich. 1980).

## Chapter 20

P. M. Bardi, *A Critical Review of Le Corbusier* (São Paolo 1950): an attempt to analyze Le Corbusier's philosophy, including some reference to his urban design.

F. Choay, *Le Corbusier* (New York 1960).

J. L. Cohen, 'Le Corbusier and the Mystique of the USSR', *Oppositions*, 23, 1981, 85–121.

R. de Fusco, *Le Corbusier designer immobili del 1929* (Milan 1976).

M. di Puolo, *Le Corbusier/Charlotte Perriand/Pierre Jeanneret. 'La machine à s'asseoir'* (Rome 1976).

A. Eardley, *Le Corbusier and the Athens Charter* (New York 1973): trans. of *La Charte d'Athènes* (1943).

N. Evenson, *Le Corbusier: The Machine and the Grand Design* (New York 1969).

R. Fishman, *Urban Utopias in the Twentieth Century* (New York 1977).

K. Frampton, 'The City of Dialectic', *AD*, XXXIX,

Oct. 1969, 515–43, 545–46.

E. Girard, 'Projeter', *AMC*, 41, Mar. 1977, 82–87.

G. Gresleri and D. Matteoni, *La Città Mondiale: Anderson, Hebrard, Otlet and Le Corbusier* (Venice 1982).

Le Corbusier (pseud. C. E. Jeanneret), *The City of Tomorrow* (London 1929): 1st English trans. of *Urbanisme* (Paris 1925).

— *When the Cathedrals Were White* (New York 1947): trans. of *Quand Les Cathédrales étaient blanches* (Paris 1937).

— *Des canons, des munitions? Merci! Des logis . . . S.V.P.* (Paris 1938).

— *Les Trois Etablissements humains* (Paris 1944).

— *The Four Routes* (London 1947): trans. of *Sur Les 4 Routes* (Paris 1941).

— (with F. de Pierrefeu) *The Home of Man* (London 1948): trans. of *La Maison des hommes* (Paris 1942).

— *The Radiant City* (London 1967): 1st English trans. of *La Ville radieuse* (Paris 1933).

M. Macleod, 'Le Corbusier's Plans for Algiers 1930–1936', *Oppositions*, 16/17, 1980.

— 'Le Corbusier and Algiers' and 'Plans: Bibliography', *Oppositions*, 19/20, 1980, 54–85 and 184–261.

C. S. Maier, 'Between Taylorism and Technocracy: European Ideologies and the Vision of Industrial Productivity in the 1920s', *Journal of Contemporary History*, 5, 1970, 27–61.

S. von Moos, 'Von den Femmes d'Alger zum Plan Obus', *Archithese*, 1, 1971, 25–37.

— *Le Corbusier – Elements of a Synthesis* (Cambridge, Mass. 1979): trans of *Le Corbusier, Elemente einer Synthese* (1968).

J. Pokorny and E. Hud, 'City Plan for Zlín', *Architectural Record*, CII, Aug. 1947, 70–71.

A. Vidler, 'The Idea of Unity and Le Corbusier's Urban Form', *Architects' Year Book*, XII, 1968, 225–37.

## Chapter 21

B. Brooks-Pfeiffer, ed., *Letters to Apprentices. Frank Lloyd Wright* (Fresno, Cal. 1982).

— *Frank Lloyd Wright. Letters to Architects* (Fresno, Cal. 1984).

B. Brownell and F. L. Wright, *Architecture and Modern Life* (New York 1937): a revealing ideological discussion of the period.

W. Chaitkin, 'Frank Lloyd Wright in Russia', *AAQ*, V, no. 2, 1973, 45–55.

C. W. Condit, *American Building Art: The 20th Century* (New York 1961): for Wright's structural innovations see 172–76, 185–87.

R. Cranshawe, 'Frank Lloyd Wright's Progressive Utopia', *AAQ*, X, no. 1, 1978, 3–9.

A. Drexler, *The Drawings of Frank Lloyd Wright* (New York and London 1962).

F. Gutheim, ed., *In the Cause of Architecture – Wright's Historic Essays for Architectural Record 1908–1952* (New York 1975).

H.-R. Hitchcock, *In the Nature of Materials 1887–1941. The Buildings of Frank Lloyd Wright* (New York 1942).

D. Hoffmann, *Frank Lloyd Wright's Falling Water* (New York 1978).

A. Izzo and C. Gubitosi, *Frank Lloyd Wright Dessins 1887–1959* (Paris 1977).

E. Kaufmann, ed., *An American Architecture: Frank Lloyd Wright* (New York 1955).

E. Kaufmann, 'Twenty-Five Years of the House on the Waterfall', *L'Architettura*, 82, VIII, no. 4, Aug. 1962, 222–58.

M. Schapiro, 'Architects' Utopia', *Partisan Review*, 4, no. 4, Mar. 1938, 42–47.

J. Sergeant, *Frank Lloyd Wright's Usonian Houses* (New York 1976).

N. K. Smith, *Frank Lloyd Wright. A Study in Architectural Contrast* (Englewood Cliffs, N.J. 1966).

S. Stillman, 'Comparing Wright and Le Corbusier', *AIAJ*, IX, Apr.–May 1948, 171–78, 226–33: Wright's Broadacre City compared with Le Corbusier's urban conceptions.

E. Tafel, *Apprenticed to Genius* (New York 1979).

F. L. Wright, *Modern Architecture* (Princeton 1931): the Kahn lectures for 1930.

— *The Disappearing City* (New York 1932).

— *When Democracy Builds* (Chicago 1945).

— *The Future of Architecture* (New York 1953).

— *The Natural House* (New York 1954).

— *The Story of the Tower. The Tree that Escaped the Crowded Forest* (New York 1956).

— *A Testament* (New York 1957).

— *The Living City* (New York 1958).

— *The Solomon R. Guggenheim Museum* (New York 1960).

— *The Industrial Revolution Runs Away* (New York 1969): facsimile of Wright's copy of the original 1932 edn of *The Disappearing City*.

B. Zevi, 'Alois Riegl's Prophecy and Frank Lloyd Wright's Falling Water', *L'Architettura*, 82, VIII, no. 4, Aug. 1962, 220–21.

**Chapter 22**

A. Aalto, *Postwar Reconstruction: Rehousing Research in Finland* (New York 1940).

— *Synopsis* (Stuttgart 1970).

— *Sketches*, ed. G. Schildt and trans. S. Wrede (Cambridge, Mass. 1978).

H. Ahlberg, *Swedish Architecture in the Twentieth Century* (London 1925).

G. Baird, *Alvar Aalto* (London 1970).

R. Banham, 'The One and the Few', *AR*, Apr. 1957, 243–59.

W. R. Bunning, 'Paimio Sanitorium, an Analysis', *Architecture*, XXIX, 1940, 20–25.

A. Chris-Janer, *Eliel Saarinen* (Chicago 1948).

L. K. Eaton, *American Architecture Comes of Age: European Reaction to H. H. Richardson and Louis Sullivan* (Cambridge, Mass. and London 1972).

K. Fleig, *Alvar Aalto 1963–1970* (New York 1971): contains Aalto's article, 'The Architect's Conscience'.

S. Giedion, 'Alvar Aalto', *AR*, CVII, no. 38, Feb. 1950, 77–84.

H. Girsberger, *Alvar Aalto* (London 1963).

R. Glanville, 'Finnish Vernacular Farm Houses', *AAQ*, IX, no. 1, 36–52: a remarkable article recording the form of the Karelian farmhouse and suggesting the structural significance of the building pattern.

F. Gutheim, *Alvar Aalto* (New York 1960).

M. Hausen, 'Gesellius-Lindgren-Saarinen vid sekelskiftet', *Arkkitekti-Arkitekten*, 9, 1967, 6–12, with trans.

Y. Hirn, *The Origins of Art* (London 1962).

H.-R. Hitchcock, 'Aalto versus Aalto: The Other Finland', *Perspecta*, 9/10, 1965, 132–66.

P. Hodgkinson, 'Finlandia Hall, Helsinki', *AR*, June 1972, 341–43.

G. Labò, *Alvar Aalto* (Milan 1948).

K. Mikkola, ed., *Alvar Aalto vs. the Modern Movement* (Jyväskylä 1981).

L. Mosso, *L'Opera di Alvar Aalto* (Milan 1965): important exhibition catalogue.

— *Alvar Aalto* (Helsinki 1967).

— ed., 'Alvar Aalto', *L'Architecture d'Aujourd'hui* (special issue), June 1977: articles from the Centre of Alvar Aalto Studies, Turin.

E. Neuenschwander, *Finnish Buildings* (Zürich 1954).

G. Pagano, 'Due ville de Aalto', *Casabella*, 12, 1940, 26–29.

J. Pallasmaa, H. O. Andersson *et al.*, *Nordic Classicism 1910–1930* (Helsinki 1982).

P. D. Pearson, *Alvar Aalto and the International Style* (New York 1978).

D. Porphyrios, 'Reversible Faces: Danish and Swedish Architecture 1905–1930', *Lotus*, 16, 1977, 35–41.

— *Sources of Modern Eclecticism: Studies on Alvar Aalto* (London 1982).

M. Quantrill, *Alvar Aalto* (New York 1983).

A. Salokörpi, *Modern Architecture in Finland* (London 1970).

G. Schildt, *Alvar Aalto: the Early Years* (Keuruu and New York 1984).

P. Morton Shand, 'Tuberculosis Sanatorium, Paimio, Finland', *AR*, Sept. 1933, 85–90.

— 'Viipuri Library, Finland', *AR*, LXXIX, 1936, 107–14.

J. B. Smith, *The Golden Age of Finnish Art* (Helsinki 1975).

M. Trieb, 'Gallén-Kallela: A Portrait of the Artist as an Architect', *AAQ*, VII, no 3, Sept. 1975, 3–13.

— 'Lars Sonck', *JSAH*, XXX, no. 3, Oct. 1971, 228–37.

O. Warner, *Marshall Mannerheim and the Finns* (London 1967).

J. Wood, ed., 'Alvar Aalto 1957', *Architects' Year Book*, VIII, 1957, 137–88.

S. Wrede, *The Architecture of Erik Gunnar Asplund* (Cambridge, Mass. 1979).

— 'Landscape and Architecture: the Work of Erik Gunnar Asplund', *Perspecta*, 20, 1983, 195–214.

**Chapter 23**

G. Accasto, V. Fraticelli and R. Nicolini, *L'architettura di Roma Capitale 1870–1970* (Rome 1971).

D. Alfieri and L. Freddi, *Mostra della rivoluzione fascista* (Bergamo 1933).

L. Benevolo, *History of Modern Architecture*, II (Cambridge, Mass. 1971), 540–85.

M. Carrà, E. Rathke, C. Tisdall and P. Waldberg, *Metaphysical Art* (London 1971).

G. Cavella and V. Gregotti, *Il Novecento e l'Architettura Edilizia Moderna*, 81 (special issue dedicated to the Novecento), 1962.

S. Danesi, 'Cesare Cattaneo', *Lotus*, 16, 1977, 89–121.

S. Danesi and L. Patetta, *Rationalisme et architecture en Italie 1919–1943* (Venice 1976).

P. Eisenman, 'From Object to Relationship: Giuseppe Terragni/Casa Giuliani Frigerio', *Perspecta*, 13/14, 1971, 36–65.

V. Gregotti, *New Directions in Italian Architecture* (New York 1968).

B. Huet and G. Teyssot, 'Politique industrielle et architecture: le cas Olivetti', *L'Architecture d'Aujourd'hui*, no. 188, Dec. 1976 (special issue): documents the Olivetti patronage and carries articles on the Olivetti family and the history of the company by A. Restucci and G. Ciucci.

S. Kostof, *The Third Rome* (Berkeley, Calif. 1977).

P. Koulermos, 'The work of Terragni, Lingeri and Italian Rationalism', *AD*, Mar. 1963 (special issue).

N. Labò, *Giuseppe Terragni* (Milan 1947).

T. G. Longo, 'The Italian Contribution to the Residential Neighbourhood Design Concept', *Lotus*, 9, 1975, 213–15.

E. Mantero, *Giuseppe Terragni e la città del razionalismo italiano* (Bari 1969).

— 'For the "Archives" of What City?', *Lotus*, 20, Sept. 1978, 36–43.

C. Melograni, *Giuseppe Pagano* (Milan 1955).

L. Moretti, 'The Value of Profiles, etc.', 1951/52, *Oppositions*, 4, Oct. 1974, 109–39.

L. Patetta, 'The Five Milan Houses', *Lotus*, 20, Sept. 1978, 32–35.

E. Persico, *Scritti di architettura 1927–1935*, ed. G. Veronesi (Florence 1968).

— *Tutte le opere 1923–1935*, I & II, ed. G. Veronesi (Milan 1964).

A. Pica, *Nuova architettura italiana* (Milan 1936).

V. Quilici, 'Adalberto Libera', *Lotus*, 16, 1977, 55–88.

B. Rudolfsky, 'The Third Rome', *AR*, July 1951, 31–37.

A. Sartoris, *Gli elementi dell'architettura funzionale* (Milan 1941).

— *Encyclopédie de l'architecture nouvelle – ordre et climat méditerranéens* (Milan 1957).

T. Schumacher, 'From Gruppo 7 to the Danteum: A Critical Introduction to Terragni's Relazione Sul Danteum', *Oppositions*, 9, 1977, 90–93.

G. R. Shapiro, 'Il Gruppo 7', *Oppositions*, 6 and 12, Autumn 1976 and Spring 1978.

M. Tafuri, 'The Subject and the Mask: An Introduction to Terragni', *Lotus*, 20, Sept. 1978, 5–29.

E. G. Tedeschi, *Figini e Pollini* (Milan 1959).

G. Terragni, 'Relazione sul Danteum 1938', *Oppositions*, 9, 1977, 94–105.

L. Thermes, 'La casa di Luigi Figini al Villaggio dei giornalisti', *Contraspazio*, IX, no. 1, June 1977, 35–39.

G. Veronesi, *Difficoltà politiche dell'architettura in Italia 1920–1940* (Milan 1953).

B. Zevi, ed., *Omaggio a Terragni* (Milan 1968): special issue of *L'Architettura*.

**Chapter 24**

R. H. Bletter, 'King-Kong en Arcadie', *Archithese*, 20, 1977, 25–34.

R. H. Bletter and C. Robinson, *Skyscraper Style – Art Deco New York* (New York 1975).

D. Brounlee, 'Wolkenkratzer: Architektur für das amerikanische Maschinenzeitalter', *Archithese*, 20, 1977, 35–41.

E. Clute, 'The Chrysler Building, New York', *Architectural Forum*, 53, Oct. 1930.

C. W. Condit, *American Building Art: The 20th Century* (New York 1961): for the Woolworth Tower and the Empire State Building see ch. 1.

F. Dal Co and S. Polano, 'Interview with Albert Speer', *Oppositions*, 12, Spring 1978.

R. Delevoy and M. Culot, *Antoine Pompe* (Brussels 1974).

Finlands Arkitekförbund, *Architecture in Finland* (Helsinki 1932): this survey by the Finnish Architects' Association affords an extensive record of the New Tradition.

S. Fitzpatrick, *The Commissariat of Enlightenment* (Cambridge, England 1970).

P. T. Frankl, *New Dimensions: The Decorative Arts of Today in Words and Pictures* (New York 1928).

D. Gebhard, *The Richfield Building 1926–1928* (Los Angeles 1970).

— 'The Moderne in the U.S. 1910–1914', *AAQ*, II, no. 3, July 1970, 4–20.

S. Giedion, *Architecture You and Me* (Cambridge, Mass. 1958): esp. 25–61.

R. Grumberger, *The 12-Year Reich* (New York 1971).

H.-R. Hitchcock, 'Some American Interiors in the Modern Style', *Architectural Record*, 64, Sept. 1928, 235.

— *Modern Architecture: Romanticism and Reintegration* (New York 1929).

R. Hood, 'Exterior Architecture of Office Buildings'. *Architectural Forum*, 41, Sept 1924.

— 'The American Radiator Company Building, New York', *American Architect*, 126, Nov. 1924.

C. Hussey and A. S. G. Butler, *Lutyens Memorial Volumes* (London 1951).

W. H. Kilham, *Raymond Hood, Architect* (New York 1973).

R. Koolhaas, *Delirious New York* (New York and London 1978).

A. Kopp, *L'Architecture de la periode Stalinienne* (Grenoble 1978).

S. Kostof, *The Third Rome 1870–1950: Traffic and Glory* (Berkeley 1973).

C. Krinsky, *The International Competition for a New Administration Building for the Chicago Tribune MCMXXII* (Chicago 1923).

— *Rockefeller Center* (London and New York 1978).

B. Miller Lane, *Architecture and Politics in Germany 1918–1945* (Cambridge, Mass. 1968).

L. O. Larsson, *Die Neugestaltung der Reichshauptstadt/Albert Speer's General-bebauungsplan für Berlin* (Stuttgart 1978).

F. F. Lisle, 'Chicago's Century of Progress Exposition: The Moderne or Democratic, Popular Culture', *JSAH*, Oct. 1972.

342

A. Lunacharsky, *On Literature and Art* (Moscow 1973).

W. March, *Bauwerk Reichssportfeld* (Berlin 1936).

W. Oechslin, 'Mythos zwischen Europa und Amerika', *Archithese*, 20, 1977, 4–11.

E. A. Park, *New Background for a New Age* (New York 1927).

A. G. Rabinach, 'The Aesthetics of Production in the Third Reich', *Journal of Contemporary History*, 11, 1976, 43–74.

H. Hope Reed, 'The Need for Monumentality?', *Perspecta*, 1, 1950.

H. Rimpl, *Ein deutsches Flugzeugwerk. Die Heinkel-Werke Oranienburg*, text by H. Mackler (Berlin 1939).

D. Rivera, *Portrait of America* (New York 1963): ills. of Rivera's RCA mural 40–47.

W. Schäche, 'Nazi Architecture and its Approach to Antiquity', *AD*, Nov.–Dec. 1983, 81–88.

P. Schultze-Naumburg, *Kunst und Rasse* (Munich 1928).

A. von Senger, *Krisis der Architektur* (Zürich 1928).

— *Die Brandfackel Moskaus* (Zürich 1931).

— *Mord an Apollo* (Zürich 1935).

A. Speer, *Inside the Third Reich, Memoirs* (New York 1970).

— *Spandau: The Secret Diaries* (London 1976).

—*Architektur 1933–1942* (Berlin 1978). Documentation of Speer's work with essays by K. Arndt, G. F. Koch and L. O. Larsson.

A. Speer and R. Wolters, *Neue deutsche Baukunst* (Berlin 1941).

R. Stern, *Raymond M. Hood* (IAUS Cat. no. 15, New York 1982).

M. Tafuri, 'Neu Babylon', *Archithese*, 20, 1977, 12–24.

— 'La dialectique de l'absurde Europe-USA: les avatars de l'idéologie du gratte-ciel 1918–1974'. *L'Architecture d'Aujourd'hui*, no. 178, Mar./ Apr. 1975, 1–16.

R. R. Taylor, *The Word in Stone. The Role of Architecture in National Socialist Ideology* (Berkeley, Calif., 1974).

A. Teut, ed., *Architektur im Dritten Reich 1933–1945* (Berlin 1967): the largest documentation assembled to date.

G. Troost, *Das Bauen im neuen Reich* (Bayreuth 1943).

J. Tyrwhitt, J. L. Sert and E. N. Rogers, *The Heart of the City* (London 1952).

G. Veronesi, *Style and Design 1909–29* (New York 1968).

A. Voyce, *Russian Architecture* (New York 1948).

G. Wangerin and G. Weiss, *Heinrich Tessenow, Leben, Lehre, Werk 1876–1950* (Essen 1976).

B. Warner, 'Berlin – The Nordic Homeland and Corruption of Urban Spectacle', *AD*, Nov.–Dec. 1983, 73–80.

W. Weisman, 'A New View of Skyscraper History', *The Rise of an American Architecture*, E. Kaufmann Jr., ed. (New York 1970).

B. Wolfe, *The Fabulous Life of Diego Rivera* (New York 1963): details of Rivera's work on the RCA Building 317–34.

## Chapter 25

S. Adshead, 'Camillo Sitte and Le Corbusier', *Town Planning Review*, XIV, Nov. 1930, 35–94.

C. Correa, 'The Assembly, Chandigarh', *AR*, June 1964, 404–12.

M. A. Couturier, Letter to Le Corbusier, 28 July 1953, reproduced in J. Petit, *Un couvent de Le Corbusier* (Paris 1961), 23: trans. in separate booklet obtainable from La Tourette.

A. Eardley and J. Ouberie, *Le Corbusier's Firminy Church* (IAUS Cat. no. 14, New York 1981).

N. Evenson, *Chandigarh* (Berkeley, Calif. 1966).

— *Le Corbusier: The Machine and the Grand Design* (New York 1969).

M. Ghyka, 'Le Corbusier's Modulor and the Conception of the Golden Mean', *AR*, CIII, Feb. 1948, 39–42.

A. Gorlin, 'Analysis of the Governor's Palace at Chandigarh', *Oppositions*, 16/17, 1980.

A. Greenberg, 'Lutyens' Architecture Restudied', *Perspecta*, 12, 1969, 148.

S. K. Gupta, 'Chandigarh. A Study of Sociological Issues and Urban Development in India', Occasional Papers, no. 9, Univ. of Waterloo, Canada, 1973.

F. G. Hutchins, *The Illusion of Permanence. British Imperialism in India* (Princeton, N.J. 1967).

R. Furneaux Jordan, *Le Corbusier* (London 1972), esp. 146–47, 'Building for Christ'.

Le Corbusier (pseud. C. E. Jeanneret), *Des canons, des munitions? Merci! Des logis . . . S.V.P.* (Paris 1938).

— *L'Unité d'habitation de Marseilles* (Souillac 1950); trans. as *The Marseilles Block* (London 1953).

— *Le Corbusier Sketchbooks*, vol. 2 *1950–54*, vol. 3 *1954–57*, vol. 4 *1957–64* (Cambridge, Mass. 1982).

R. Moore, 'Alchemical and Mythical Themes in the Poem of the Right Angle 1947–1965', *Oppositions*, 19/20, 1980, 110–39.

S. Nilsson, *The New Capitals of India, Pakistan and Bangladesh* (Lund 1973).

A. Roth, *La Nouvelle Architecture* (Zürich 1940).

C. Rowe, 'Dominican Monastery of La Tourette, Eveux-sur-Arbresle, Lyons', *AR*, June 1961, 400–10.

J. Stirling, 'From Garches to Jaoul. Le Corbusier as domestic architect in 1927 and in 1953', *AR*, Sept. 1955.

— 'Le Corbusier's Chapel and the Crisis of Rationalism', *AR*, Mar. 1956, 161.

*James Stirling*, RIBA Drawings Collection catalogue (London 1974).

R. Walden, ed., *The Open Hand: Essays on Le Corbusier* (Cambridge, Mass. 1977).

## Chapter 26

R. Banham, Almost Nothing is Too Much', *AR*, Aug. 1962, 125–28.

J. F. F. Blackwell, 'Mies van der Rohe – Bibliography (Univ. of London Librarianship Diploma thesis, 1964, deposited in British Architectural Library, London).

P. Blake, *Mies van der Rohe: Architecture and Structure* (New York 1960).

W. Blaser, *Mies van der Rohe – The Art of Structure* (New York 1965).

P. Carter, *Mies van der Rohe at Work* (London and New York 1974).

A. Drexler, *Ludwig Mies van der Rohe* (New York 1960).

L. W. Elliot, 'Structural News: USA, The Influence of New Techniques on Design', *AR*, Apr. 1953, 251–60.

D. Erdman and P. C. Papademetriou, 'The Museum of Fine Arts, Houston, 1922–1972', *Architecture at Rice*, 28 (Houston 1976).

L. Hilberseimer, *Contemporary Architecture. Its Roots and Trends* (Chicago 1964).

S. Honey, 'Mies at the Bauhaus', *AAQ*, X, no. 1, 1978, 51–59.

D. Lohan, 'Mies van der Rohe: Farnsworth House, Plano, Illinois 1945–50', *Global Architecture Detail*, no. 1, 1976; critical essay and complete working details of the house.

L. Mies van der Rohe, 'Mies Speaks', *AR*, Dec. 1968, 451–52.

— 'Technology and Architecture', *Programs and Manifestoes. . .*, ed. U. Conrads (Cambridge, Mass. 1970), 154: extract from an address given at the IIT, 1950.

R. Miller, ed., *Four Great Makers of Modern Architecture: Gropius, Le Corbusier, Mies van der Rohe, Wright* (New York 1963): mimeographed record of a seminar at Columbia Univ., important for reference to Mies's idea of his debt to the Russian avant garde.

C. Norberg-Schulz, 'Interview with Mies van der Rohe', *L'Architecture d'Aujourd'hui*, Sept. 1958.

M. Pawley, *Mies van der Rohe* (London 1970): includes the rarely published McCormick House and the Social Services Administration Building, Univ. of Chicago.

C. Rowe, 'Neoclassicism and Modern Architecture', *Oppositions*, 1, 1973, 1–26.

J. Winter, 'Dominion Development, *AR*, Jan. 1972, 48–57.

— 'The Measure of Mies', *AR*, Feb. 1972, 95–105.

**Chapter 27**

R. Banham, 'On Trial 2, Louis Kahn, the Buttery Hatch Aesthetic', *AR*, Mar. 1962, 203–06.

C. Bonnefoi, 'Louis Kahn and Minimalism', *Oppositions*, 24, 1981, 3–25.

J. Burton, 'Notes from Volume Zero: Louis Kahn and the Language of God', *Perspecta*, 20, 1983, 69–90.

M. Emery, ed., 'Louis I. Kahn', *L'Architecture d'Aujourd'hui*, no. 142, Feb.–Mar. 1969 (special issue).

R. B. Fuller, 'Dymaxion House', *Architectural Forum*, Mar. 1932, 285–86.

R. Giurgola and J. Mehta, *Louis I. Kahn* (Boulder, Colo. 1975).

H.-R. Hitchcock, 'Current Work of Philip Johnson', *Zodiac*, 8, 1961, 64–81.

W. Huff, 'Louis Kahn: Assorted Recollections and Lapses into Familiarities', *Little Journal* (Buffalo), Sept. 1981.

J. Huxley, *TVA, Adventure in Planning* (London 1943).

J. Jacobus, *Philip Johnson* (New York and London 1962).

P. Johnson, *Machine Art* (New York 1934).

— 'House at New Canaan, Connecticut', *AR*, Sept. 1950, 152–59.

R. Furneaux Jordan, 'US Embassy, Dublin', *AR*, Dec. 1964, 420–25.

W. H. Jordy, 'The Formal Image: USA', *AR*, Mar. 1960, 157–64.

— 'Medical Research Building for Pennsylvania University', *AR*, Feb. 1961, 99–106.

— 'Kimbell Art Museum, Fort Worth, Texas/Library, Philips Exeter Academy, Andover, New Hampshire', *AR*, June 1974, 318–42.

— 'Art Centre, Yale University', *AR*, July 1977, 37–44.

L. Kahn, 'Form and Design', *AD*, no. 4, 1961, 145–54.

A. Komendant, *18 Years with Architect Louis Kahn* (Englewood, N.J. 1975).

R. W. Marks, *The Dymaxion World of Buckminster Fuller* (New York 1960): still the most comprehensive documentation of Fuller's work.

J. McHale, ed., 'Richard Buckminster Fuller', *AD*, July 1967 (special issue).

J. Mellor, ed., *The Buckminster Fuller Reader* (London 1970).

E. Mock, *Built in USA: 1932–1944* (New York 1945).

D. Myhra, 'Rexford Guy Tugwell: Initiator of America's Greenbelt New Towns 1935–1936', *Journal of the American Institute of Planners*, XL, no. 3, May 1974, 176–88.

T. Nakamura, ed., *Louis I. Kahn 'Silence & Light'* (Tokyo 1977): a complete documentation of Kahn's work with articles by Kahn, Scully, Doshi, Maki, etc.

H. Hope Reed, 'The Need for Monumentality?', *Perspecta*, 1, 1950.

H. Ronner, S. Jhaveri and A. Vasella, *Louis I. Kahn, Complete Works 1935–74* (Basel and Stuttgart 1977): awkward format, but the most comprehensive documentation of Kahn's work to date.

P. Santostefano, *Le Mackley Houses di Kastner e Stonorov a Philadelphia* (Rome 1982).

A. Tyng, *Beginnings, Louis I. Kahn's Philosophy of Architecture* (New York 1983).

P. Zucker, ed., *New Architecture and City Planning* (New York 1945), esp. 577–88.

**PART III**

**Chapter 1**

R. Banham, *The New Brutalism* (New York 1966).

M. Bill, 'Report on Brazil', *AR*, Oct. 1954, 238, 239.

W. Boesiger, *Richard Neutra, Buildings and Projects*, I, 1923–50 (Zürich and London 1964).

O. Bohigas, 'Spanish Architecture of the Second Republic', *AAQ*, III, no. 4, Oct.–Dec. 1971, 28–45.

A. H. Brooks, 'PSFS: A Source for its Designs', *JSAH*, XXVII, no. 4, Dec. 1968, 299.

L. Campbell, 'The Good News Days', *AR*, Sept. 1977, 177–83.

F. Chaslin, J. Drew, I. Smith, J. C. Garcias and M. K. Meade, *Berthold Lubetkin* (Brussels 1981).

P. Coe and M. Reading, *Lubetkin and Tecton: Architecture and Social Commitment* (Bristol 1981).

J. L. Cohen, 'Mallet Stevens et l'U.A.M. comment frapper les masses?' *AMC*, 41, Mar. 1977, 19.

A. Cox, 'Highpoint Two, North Hill, Highgate', *Focus*, 11, 1938, 79.

W. Curtis, 'Berthold Lubetkin', *AAQ*, VII, no. 3, 1976, 33–39.

E. M. Czaja, 'Antonin Raymond: Artist and Dreamer', *AAJ*, LXXVIII, no. 864, Aug. 1962 (special issue).

O. Dostál, J. Pechar and V. Procházka, *Modern Architecture in Czechoslovakia* (Prague 1970): best available recent documentation of the Czech Modern Movement.

D. Gebhard, *An Exhibition of the Architecture of R. M. Schindler 1887–1953* (Santa Barbara, Calif. 1967).

— *Schindler* (London 1971).

S. Giedion, *A Decade of New Architecture* (Zürich 1951).

M. Gold, 'Sir Owen Williams KBE', *Zodiac*, 18, 11–29.

G. Herbert, 'Le Corbusier and the South African Movement', *AAQ*, IV, no. 1, Winter 1972, 16–30.

G. Hildebrand, *Designing for Industry: The Architecture of Albert Kahn* (Cambridge, Mass. 1974).

H.-R. Hitchcock and C. K. Bauer, *Modern Architecture in England* (New York 1937).

H.-R. Hitchcock and P. Johnson, *The International Style: Architecture Since 1922* (New York 1932).

— 'England and the Outside World', *AAJ*, LXXII, no. 806, Nov. 1956, 96–97.

B. Housden and A. Korn, 'Arthur Korn. 1891 to the present day', *AAJ*, LXXIII, no. 817, Dec. 1957, 114–35 (special issue; includes details of the MARS plan for London).

C. Hubert and L. Stamm Shapiro, *William Lescaze* (IAUS Cat. no. 16, New York 1982).

R. Ind, 'The Architecture of Pleasure', *AAQ*, VIII, no. 3, 51–59.

A. Jackson, *The Politics of Architecture* (London 1967).

S. Johnson, *Eileen Gray: Designer 1879–1976* (London and New York 1979).

R. Furneaux Jordan, 'Lubetkin', *AR*, July 1955, 36–44.

J. C. Martin, B. Nicholson and N. Gabo, *Circle* (New York 1971).

K. Mayekawa, 'Thoughts on Civilization in Architecture', *AD*, May 1965, 229–30.

E. McCoy, 'Letters between R. M. Schindler and Richard Neutra 1914–1924', *JSAH*, XXXIII, 3, 1974, 219.

— *Second Generation* (Salt Lake City 1984).

A. Morancé, *Encyclopédie de l'architecture de construc-tions moderne*, XI (Paris 1938): includes major pavilions from the Paris Exhibition of 1937, notably those by the Catalan architects Sert and Lacasa and the Czech architect Kreskar.

R. Neutra, *Wie Baut Amerika?* (Stuttgart 1927).

— *Amerika – Neues Bauen in der Welt*, no. 2 (Vienna 1930).

— *Mystery and Realities of the Site* (New York 1951).

— *Survival Through Design* (New York 1954).

— 'Human Setting in an Industrial Civilization', *Zodiac*, 2, 1957, 68–75.

— *Life and Shape* (New York 1962).

D. O' Neil, 'The High and Low Art of Rudolf Schindler', *AR*, Apr. 1973, 241–46.

S. Papadaki, *The Work of Oscar Niemeyer*, I (New York 1950).

— *Oscar Niemeyer: Works in Progress* (New York 1956).

S. Polyzoides and P. Koulermos, 'Schindler: 5 Houses', *A&U*, Nov. 1975.

J. Pritchard, *View from a Long Chair* (London 1984).

A. Raymond, *Antonin Raymond. Architectural Details* (New York 1947).

— *Antonin Raymond. An Autobiography* (Tokyo 1973).

J. M. Richards, 'Criticism/Royal Festival Hall' *AR*, June 1951, 355–58 (special issue).

A. Roth, *La Nouvelle Architecture* (Zürich 1940).

J. L. Sert, *Can Our Cities Survive?* (Cambridge, Mass. 1947).

M. Steinmann, 'Neuer Blick auf die "Charte d'Athènes"', *Archithese*, 1, 1972, 37–46.

— 'Political Standpoints in CIAM 1928–1933', *AAQ*, IV, no. 4, Oct.–Dec. 1972, 49–55.

T. Stevens, 'Connell, Ward and Lucas, 1927–1939', *AAJ*, LXXII, no. 806, Nov. 1956, 112–13 (special number devoted to the firm, including a catalogue raisonné of their entire work).

L. Wodehouse, 'Lescaze and Dartington Hall', *AAQ*, VII, no. 2, 1976, 3–14.

F. R. S. Yorke, *The Modern House* (London 1934).

— *The Modern Flat* (London 1937): general coverage of International Style apartments, including GATEPAC block, Barcelona.

## Chapter 2

L. Alloway, *This is Tomorrow*, exhibition catalogue, Whitechapel Art Gallery, London 1956.

R. Banham, 'The New Brutalism', *AR*, Dec. 1955, 355–62: important for the Neo-Palladian analysis of the Smithsons' Coventry project.

T. Crosby, ed., *Uppercase*, 3 (Tonbridge 1954): important document of the period featuring the Smithsons' presentation at the CIAM Congress in Aix-en-Provence; also contains a short text and collection of photos by N. Henderson.

P. Eisenman, 'Real and English: The Destruction of the Box. 1', *Oppositions*, 4, Oct. 1974, 5–34.

K. Frampton, 'Leicester University Engineering Lab-oratory', *AD*, XXXIV, no. 2, 1964, 61.

— 'The Economist and the Hauptstadt', *AD*, Feb. 1965, 61–62.

— 'Stirling's Building', *Architectural Forum*, Nov. 1968.

— 'Andrew Melville Hall, St Andrews University, Scotland', *AD*, XL, no. 9, 1970, 460–62.

M. Girouard, 'Florey Building, Oxford', *AR*, CLII, no. 909, 1972, 260–77.

W. Howell and J. Killick, 'Obituary: The Work of Edward Reynolds', *AAJ*, LXXIV, no. 289, Feb. 1959, 218–23.

P. Johnson, 'Comment on School at Hunstanton, Norfolk', *AR*, Sept. 1954, 148–62: gives an extensive documentation.

A. and P. Smithson, 'The New Brutalism', *AR*, Apr. 1954, 274–75: 1st pub. of Soho house.

M. Tafuri, 'L'Architecture dans le boudoir', *Oppositions*, 3, May 1974, 37–62.

## Chapter 3

G. Candilis, *Planning and Design for Leisure* (Stuttgart 1972).

K. Frampton, 'Des Vicissitudes de l'idéologie',

*L'Architecture d'Aujourd'hui*, no. 177, Jan.–Feb. 1975, 62–65 (in English and French).

A. Smithson, *Team 10 Primer* (Cambridge, Mass. 1968).

A. and P. Smithson, 'Louis Kahn', *Architects' Year Book*, IX (London 1960), 102–18.

— *Ordinariness and Light: Urban Theories 1952–60* (Cambridge, Mass. 1970).

— *Urban Structuring* (London 1970).

M. Steinmann, 'Political Standpoints in CIAM 1928–1933', *AAQ*, Autumn 1972, 49–55.

— *CIAM Dokumente 1928–1939* (ETH/GTA 15, Basel and Stuttgart 1979).

S. Woods, 'Urban Environment: The Search for a System', in *World Architecture/One* (London 1964), 150–54.

— 'Frankfurt: The Problems of A City in the Twentieth Century', in *World Architecture/One* (London 1964), 156.

## Chapter 4

F. Achleitner, 'Viennese Positions', *Lotus*, 29, 1981, 5–27.

D. Agrest, 'Design versus Non-Design', *Oppositions*, 6, Autumn 1976, 45–68.

Y. Alain-Bois, 'On Manfredo Tafuri's "Theories et histoire de l'architecture"', *Oppositions*, 11, Winter 1977, 118–23.

H. Arendt, *The Human Condition* (Chicago 1958).

G. C. Argan, 'On the Typology of Architecture', *AD*, Dec. 1963, 564, 565.

C. M. Aris and A. Renna, 'Giorgio Grassi: Documentation', in *Construcción de la ciudad*, X, Dec. 1977.

P. Arnell, T. Bickford, K. Wheeler and V. Scully, *Michael Graves, Buildings and Projects 1966–1981* (New York 1983).

P. Arnell, T. Bickford and C. Rowe, *James Stirling, Buildings and Projects* (New York 1984).

C. Aymonino, *Origine e sviluppo della urbanistica moderna* (Venice 1965).

R. Banham, *Theory and Design in the First Machine Age* (London 1960).

R. Banham, N. Foster and L. Butt, *Foster Associates* (London 1979).

J. Baudrillard, *The Mirror of Production* (St Louis 1975): trans. of *Le Miroir de la Production* of 1972.

— *L'Effet Beaubourg: implosion et dissuasion* (Paris 1977).

M. Bill, 'The Bauhaus Idea From Weimar to Ulm', *Architects' Yearbook*, 5 (London 1953).

W. Blaser, *After Mies: Mies van der Rohe – Teaching and Principles* (New York 1977).

I. Bohning, 'Like Fishes in the Sea; Autonomous Architecture/Replications', *Daidalos*, 2, 1981, 13–24.

A. Bonito Oliva, ed., *Transavantgarde* (Milan 1983).

G. Bonsiepe, 'Communication and Power', *Ulm*, 21, Apr. 1968, 16.

G. Broadbent, 'The Taller of Bofill', *AR*, Nov. 1973, 289–97.

N. S. Brown, 'Siedlung Halen and the Eclectic Predicament', in *World Architecture/One* (London 1964), 165–67.

G. Brown-Manrique, *O. M. Ungers: Works in Progress*

*1976–1980* (IAUS Cat. no. 17, New York 1981).

P. L. Cervellati and R. Scannarini, *Bologna: politica e metodologia del restauro nei centri storici* (Bologna 1973).

S. Chermayeff and C. Alexander, *Community and Privacy: Towards a New Architecture of Humanism* (New York 1963).

A. Colquhoun, 'The Modern Movement in Architecture', *The British Journal of Aesthetics*, 1962.

— 'Literal and Symbolic Aspects of Technology', *AD*, Nov. 1962.

— 'Typology and Design Method', in *Meaning in Architecture*, ed. Jencks & Baird (London 1969), 279.

— 'Centraal Beheer', *Architecture Plus*, Sept./Oct. 1974, 49–54.

— *Essays in Architectural Criticism: Modern Architecture and Historical Change* (Cambridge, Mass. 1981).

U. Conrads, 'Wall-buildings – as a Concept of Urban Order. On the Projects of Ralph Erskine', *Daidalos*, 7, 1983, 103–06.

P. Cook, *Architecture: Action and Plan* (London 1967).

G. de Carlo, *An Architecture of Participation* (Melbourne 1972).

— 'Reflections on the Present State of Architecture', *AAQ*, X, no. 2, 1978, 29–40.

R. Delevoy, *Rational Architecture/Rationelle 1978: The Reconstruction of the European City 1978* (Brussels 1978).

G. della Volpe, 'The Crucial Question of Architecture Today', in *Critique of Taste* (London 1978): trans. of *Critica del gusto* (Milan 1960).

M. Dini, *Renzo Piano: Projets et architectures 1964–1983* (Milan and Paris 1983).

P. Drew, *The Third Generation: The Changing Meaning In Architecture* (London 1972).

— *Frei Otto: Form and Structure* (London 1976).

A. Drexler, *Transformations in Modern Architecture* (New York 1979).

R. Evans, 'Regulation and Production', *Lotus*, 12, Sept. 1976, 6–15.

— 'Figures, Doors and Passages', *AD*, Apr. 1978, 267–78.

M. Foucault, *Discipline and Punishment: The Birth of the Prison* (1977): trans. of *Surveiller et punir, naissance de la prison* (Paris 1975).

K. Frampton, 'America 1960–1970. Notes on Urban Images and Theory', *Casabella*, 359–360, XXV, 1971, 24–38.

— 'Criticism', *Five Architects* (New York 1972). Critical analysis of the New York Neo-Rationalist school at the time of its formation, the 'five' being: P. Eisenman, M. Graves, C. Gwathmey, J. Hejduk and R. Meier.

— 'Apropos Ulm: Curriculum and Critical Theory', *Oppositions*, 3, May 1974, 17–36.

— 'John Hejduk and the Cult of Humanism', *A&U*, 75:05, May 1975, 141, 142.

— *Modern Architecture and the Critical Present*, *AD*, 1982 (special issue).

K. Frampton and D. Burke, *Rob Krier: Urban Projects 1968–1982* (IAUS Cat. no. 5, New York 1982).

Y. Friedman, 'Towards a Mobile Architecture', *AD*, Nov. 1963, 509, 510.

M. Gandelsonas, 'Neo-Functionalism', *Oppositions*, 5, Summer 1976.

S. Giedion, 'Jørn Utzon and the Third Generation', *Zodiac*, 14, 1965, 34–47, 68–93.

G. Grassi, *La Costruzione logica dell'architettura* (Padua 1967).

— 'Avantgarde and Continuity', *Oppositions*, 21, 1980.

— 'The Limits of Architecture', in *Classicism is not a Style*, *AD*, 1982 (special issue).

— 'Form Liberated, Never Sought. On the Problem of Architectural Design', *Daidalos*, 7, 1983, 24–36.

— *L'Architecture comme un métier* (Liege 1984).

V. Gregotti and O. Bohigas, 'La passion d'Alvaro Siza', *L'Architecture d'Aujourd'hui*, no. 185, May/June 1976, 42–57.

R. Guess, *The Idea of a Critical Theory: Habermas and the Frankfurt School* (Cambridge, Mass. 1981).

J. Guillerme, 'The Idea of Architectural Language: A Critical Inquiry', *Oppositions*, 10, Autumn 1977, 21–26.

J. Habermas, 'Technology and Science as Ideology', in *Toward a Rational Society* (Boston 1970): trans. of *Technik und Wissenschaft als Ideologie* (Frankfurt 1968).

— 'Modernity – an Incomplete Project', in *The Anti-Aesthetic: Essays on Postmodern Culture*, ed. H. Foster (Washington 1983).

N. J. Habraken, *Supports: An Alternative to Mass Housing* (New York 1972).

M. Heidegger, 'Building, Dwelling and Thinking', in *Poetry, Language and Thought* (New York 1971).

H. Hertzberger, 'Place, Choice and Identity', in *World Architecture/Four* (London 1967), 73–74.

— 'Architecture for People', *A&U*, 77:03, Mar. 1977, 124–46.

T. Herzog, *Pneumatische Konstruktion* (Stuttgart 1976).

B. Huet and M. Gangneux, 'Formalisme, Realisme', *L'Architecture d'Aujourd'Hui*, no. 190, 1970.

T. Ito, 'Collage and Superficiality in Architecture', in *A New Wave of Japanese Architecture*, ed. K. Frampton (IAUS, New York 1978).

M. Jay, *The Dialectical Imagination* (Boston 1973).

C. Jencks, *The Language of Post-Modern Architecture* (London 1977, 4th edn 1984).

N. Kawazoe, 'Dream Vision', *AD*, Oct. 1964.

— *Contemporary Japanese Architecture* (Tokyo 1965).

L. Krier, 'The Reconstruction of the City', *Rational Architecture 1978* (Brussels 1978), 28–44.

R. Krier, *Stadtraum in Theorie und Praxis* (Stuttgart 1975).

— *Urban Space* (London and New York 1979).

N. Kurokawa, *Metabolism in Architecture* (London 1977).

V. Lampugnani, *Josef Paul Kleihues* (Dublin 1983).

T. Llorens, 'Manfredo Tafuri: Neo Avantgarde and History', *AD*, 6/7, 1981.

A. Luchinger, 'Dutch Structuralism', *A&U*, 77:03, Mar. 1977, 47–65.

— *Strukturalismus in Architektur und Städtebau* (Stuttgart 1981).

A. Lumsden and T. Nakamura, 'Nineteen Questions to Anthony Lumsden', *A&U*, no. 51, 75:03, Mar. 1975.

J. F. Lyotard, *The Post-Modern Condition: A Report on Knowledge* (Minneapolis 1984).

A. Mahaddie, 'Why the Grid Roads Wiggle', *AD*, Sept. 1976, 539–42.

F. Maki, *Investigations in Collective Form* (St Louis 1964).

F. Maki and Ohtaka, 'Some Thoughts on Collective Form', in *Structure in Art and Science*, ed. G. Kepes (New York 1965).

T. Maldonado, *Max Bill* (Buenos Aires 1955).

— *Avanguardia e razionalità* (Turin 1974).

T. Maldonado and G. Bonsiepe, 'Science and Design', *Ulm*, 10/11, May 1964, 8–9.

— *Design, Nature and Revolution: Towards a Critical Ecology* (New York 1972): trans. of *La Speranza Progettuale* (Turin 1970).

W. Mangin, 'Urbanisation Case History in Peru', *AD*, Aug. 1963, 366–70.

H. Marcuse, *Eros and Civilization: A Philosophical Enquiry into Freud* (New York 1962).

G. Marinelli, *Il Centro Beaubourg a Parigi: 'Macchina' e segno architettonico* (Bari 1978).

T. Matsunaga, *Kazuo Shinohara* (IAUS Cat. no. 17, New York 1982).

J. Meller, *The Buckminster Fuller Reader* (London 1970).

N. Miller and M. Sorkin, *California Counterpoint: New West Coast Architecture 1982* (IAUS Cat. no. 18, New York 1982).

A. Moles, 'Functionalism in Crisis', *Ulm*, 19/20, Aug. 1967, 24.

— *Information Theory and Aesthetic Perception* (Urbana and London 1966).

R. Moneo, 'Aldo Rossi: The Idea of Architecture and the Modena Cemetery', *Oppositions*, 5, Summer 1976, 1–30.

J. Mukarovsky, 'On the Problem of Functions in Architecture', in *Structure, Sign and Function* (New Haven and London 1978).

T. Nakamura, 'Foster & Associates', *A&U*, 75:09, Sept. 1975 (special issue with essays by R. Banham, C. Jencks, R. Maxwell, etc.)

A. Natalini, *Figures of Stone, Quaderni di Lotus No.3* (Milan 1984).

A. Natalini and Superstudio, 'Description of the Micro-Event and Micro-Environment', in *Italy: The New Domestic Landscape*, ed. Emilio Ambasz (New York 1972), 242–51.

C. Nieuwenhuys, 'New Babylon: An Urbanism of the Future', *AD*, June 1964, 304, 305.

G. Nitschke, 'The Metabolists of Japan', *AD*, Oct. 1964.

— 'MA – The Japanese Sense of Place', *AD*, Mar. 1966.

— 'Akira Shibuya', *AD*, 1966.

C. Norberg-Schulz, 'Place', *AAQ*, VII, no. 4, 1976, 3–9.

H. Ohl, 'Industrialized Building', *AD*, Apr. 1962, 176–85.

A. Peckham, 'This is the Modern World', *AD*, XLIX, no.2, 1979, 2–26: an extended critique of Foster's Sainsbury Centre.

R. Piano, 'Architecture and Technology', *AAQ*, II, no. 3, July 1970, 32–43.

A. Pike, 'Failure of Industrialised Building/Housing Program', *AD*, Nov. 1967, 507.

P. Portoghesi, *The Presence of the Past* (Venice Biennale, 1980).

C. Price, 'Potteries Thinkbelt', *AD*, Oct. 1966, 483.

A. Rossi, *L'architettura della città* (Padua 1966), trans. *The Architecture of the City* (Cambridge, Mass. 1982).

— 'An Analogical Architecture', *A&U*, 76:05, May 1976, 74–76.

— 'Thoughts About My Recent Work', *A&U*, 76:05, May 1976, 83.

— *A Scientific Autobiography* (Cambridge, Mass. 1982).

C. Rowe and F. Koetter, *Collage City* (Cambridge, Mass. 1979).

J. Rykwert, *Richard Meier, Architect* (New York 1984).

M. Safdie, *Beyond Habitat* (Cambridge, Mass. 1970).

V. Savi, *L'architettura di Aldo Rossi Franco Angeli* (Milan 1978).

— 'The Luck of Aldo Rossi', *A&U*, 76:05, May 1976, 105–06.

C. Schnaidt, 'Prefabricated Hope', *Ulm*, 10/11, May 1964, 8–9.

— 'Architecture and Political Commitment', *Ulm*, 19/20, Aug. 1967, 30–32.

H. Skolimowski, 'Technology: The Myth Behind the Reality', *AAQ*, II, no. 3, July 1970, 21–31.

— 'Polis and Politics', *AAQ*, Autumn 1972, 3–5.

A. Smithson, 'Mat-Building', *AD*, Sept. 1974, 573–90.

I. Sola-Morales, 'Critical Discipline', *Oppositions*, 23, 1981.

M. Steinmann, 'Reality as History – Notes for a Discussion of Realism in Architecture', *A&U*, 76:09, Sept. 1976, 31–34.

M. Tafuri, 'Design and Technological Utopia', in *Italy: The New Domestic Landscape*, ed. E. Ambasz (New York 1972), 388–404.

— 'L'architecture dans le boudoir: The Language of Criticism and the Criticism of Language', *Oppositions*, 3, May 1974, 37–62.

— *Architecture and Utopia: Design and Capitalist Development* (Cambridge, Mass. 1976).

— 'Main Lines of the Great Theoretical Debate over Architecture and Urban Planning 1960–1977', *A&U*, 79:01, Jan. 1979, 133–54.

K. Taki, 'Oppositions: The Intrinsic Structure of Kazuo Shinohara's Work', *Perspecta*, 20, 1983, 43–60.

J. Tanizaki, *In Praise of Shadows* (New Haven 1977).

A. Tzonis and L. Lefaivre, 'The Narcissist Phase in Architecture', *Harvard Architectural Review*, IX, Spring 1980, 53–61.

O. M. Ungers, 'Cities within the City', *Lotus*, 19, 1978, 83.

— 'Five Lessons from Schinkel', in *Free-Style Classicism* (*AD*, LII, 1/2, 1982).

A. van Eyck, 'Labyrinthine Clarity', in *World Architecture/Three* (London 1966), 121–22.

— (with P. Parin and F. Morgenthaler), 'Interior Time/A Miracle in Moderation', in *Meaning in Architecture* (London 1969), 171–73.

R. Venturi, *Complexity and Contradiction in Architecture* (New York 1966).

R. Venturi, D. Scott-Brown and S. Izenour, *Learning From Las Vegas* (Cambridge, Mass. 1972).

D. Vesely, 'Surrealism and Architecture', *AD*, no. 2/3, 1978, 87–95.

K. Wachsmann, *The Turning Point of Building* (New York 1961).

M. Webber, 'Order in Diversity: Community Without Propinquity', in *Cities in Space*, ed. Lowden Wingo (Baltimore 1963).

S. Woods, 'Urban Environment: The Search for a System', in *World Architecture/One* (London 1964), 151–56.

— *The Man in the Street: A Polemic on Urbanism* (Baltimore 1975).

## Chapter 5

E. Ambasz, *The Architecture of Luis Barragán* (New York 1976).

E. Antoniadis, *Greek Contemporary Architecture* (Athens 1979).

— 'Pikionis' Work Lies Underfoot on Athens Hill', *Landscape Architecture*, March 1979.

T. Ando, 'From Self-Enclosed Modern Architecture toward Universality', *Japan Architect*, 301, May 1962, 8–12.

— 'A Wedge in Circumstances', *Japan Architect*, June 1977.

— 'New Relations between the Space and the Person', *Japan Architect*, Oct.–Nov. 1977 (special issue on the Japanese New Wave).

— 'The Wall as Territorial Delineation', *Japan Architect*, June 1978.

— 'The Emotionally Made Architectural Spaces of Tadao Ando', *Japan Architect*, April 1980: this issue contains a number of short seminal texts on Ando.

— 'Description of my Works', *Space Design*, June 1981 (special issue on the work of Ando).

K. Axelos, *Alienation, Praxis and Techné in the Thought of Karl Marx* (Austin 1976).

E. S. Badia, *Coderch de Sentmenat* (Barcelona 1979).

C. Banford-Smith, *Builders in the Sun: Five Mexican Architects* (New York 1967).

E. Battisti and K. Frampton, *Mario Botta: Architecture and Projects in the 70s* (Milan 1979).

S. Bettini, 'L'architettura di Carlo Scarpa', *Zodiac*, 6, 1960, 140–87.

B. Bognar, 'Tadao Ando – A Redefinition of Space, Time and Existence', *AD*, May 1981.

O. Bohigas, 'Diseñar para un público o contra un público', in *Contra una arquitectura adjetivida*, ed. Seix Barral (Barcelona 1969).

M. Botero, 'Italy: Carlo Scarpa the Venetian, Angelo Mangiarotti the Milanese', *World Architecture*, 2 (London 1965).

M. Botta, 'Architecture and Environment', *A&U*, June 1979, 52.

E. Bru and J. L. Mateo, *Spanish Contemporary Architecture* (Barcelona 1984).

M. Brusatin, 'Carlo Scarpa, architetto veneziano', *Contraspazio*, 3–4, Mar.–Apr. 1972.

T. Carloni, 'Notizien zu einer Berufschronik. Entwurfs Kollektive 2', in *Tendenzen: Neuere Architektur im Tessin* (Zürich 1975), 16–21.

A. Dimitracopoulou, 'Dimitris Pikionis', *AAQ*, 2/3, 1982, 62.

L. Dimitriu, 'Interview', *Skyline*, March 1980.

— 'Architecture and Morality: An Interview with Mario Botta', *Perspecta*, 20, 1983, 119–38.

S. Fehn and O. Feld, *The Thought of Construction* (New York 1983).

L. Ferrario and D. Pastore, *Alberto Sartoris/La Casa Morand-Pasteur* (Rome 1983).

K. Frampton, 'Prospects for a Critical Regionalism', *Perspecta*, 20, 1983, 147–62.

— 'Towards a Critical Regionalism: Six Points for an Architecture of Resistance', in *The Anti-Aesthetic. Essays on Post-Modern Culture*, ed. H. Foster (Port Townsend, Ore. 1983), 16–30.

— ed. *Tadao Ando: Projects, Buildings, Writings* (New York 1984).

M. Frascari, 'The True and Appearance. The Italian Facadism and Carlo Scarpa', *Daidalos*, 6, Dec. 1982, 37–46.

— 'The Tell-the-Tale Detail', *Via* (Cambridge), 7, 1984.

G. Grassi, 'Avantgarde and Continuity', *Oppositions*, 21, 1980.

— 'The Limits of Architecture', in *Classicism is not a Style* (AD, LII, 5/6, 1982).

V. Gregotti, 'Oswald Mathias Ungers', *Lotus*, 11.

H. H. Harris, 'Regionalism and Nationalism' (Raleigh, N. C., Student Publication, XIV, no.5).

H. Huyssens, 'The Search for Tradition: Avantgarde and Post-modernism in the 1970s', *New German Critique*, 22, 1981, 34.

L. Knobel, 'Interview with Mario Botta', *AR*, July 1981, 23.

A. Konstantinidis, *Elements for Self Knowledge: Towards a True Architecture* (Athens 1975).

— *Aris Konstantinidis: Projects and Buildings* (Athens 1981).

P. Koulermos, 'The Work of Konstantinidis', *AD*, May 1964.

L. Magagnato, *Carlo Scarpa a Castelvecchio* (Milan 1982).

— 'Scarpa's Museum', *Lotus*, 35, 1982, 75–85.

P. Nicholin, *Mario Botta 1961–1982* (New York 1983).

C. Norberg-Schulz, 'Heidegger's Thinking on Architecture', *Perspecta*, 20, 1983, 61–68.

T. Okumura, 'Interview with Tadao Ando', *Ritual, The Princeton Journal, Thematic Studies in Architecture*, I, 1983, 126–34.

D. Pikionis, 'Memoirs', *Zygos*, Jan.–Feb. 1958, 4–7.

D. Porphyrios, 'Modern Architecture in Greece: 1950–1975', *Design in Greece*, X, 1979.

P. Portoghesi, 'Carlo Scarpa', *Global Architecture* (Tokyo), L, 1972.

P. Ricoeur, 'Universal Civilization and National Cultures', in *History and Truth* (Evanston 1965), 271–84.

A. Samona, F. Tentori and J. Gubler, *Progetti e assonometrie di Alberto Sartoris* (Rome 1982).

E. Sanquineti *et al., Mario Botta: La casa rotonda* (Milan 1982).

P. C. Santini, 'Banco Popolare di Verona by Carlo Scarpa', *GA Document* 4 (Tokyo 1981).

C. Scarpa, 'I Wish I Could Frame the Blue of the Sky', *Rassegna*, 7, 1981.

A. Siza, 'To Catch a Precise Moment of the Flittering Image in all its Shades', *A&U*, 123, Dec. 1980.

M. Steinmann, 'Wirklichkeit als Geschichte. Stichworte zu einem Gespräch über Realismus in der Architektur', in *Tendenzen: Neuere Architektur im Tessin* (Zürich 1975), 9–14; trans. as 'Reality as History – Notes for a Discussion of Realism in Architecture', *A&U*, Sept. 1979, 74.

K. Takeyama, 'Tadao Ando: Heir to a Tradition', *Perspecta*, 20, 1983, 163–80.

F. Tentori, 'Progetti di Carlo Scarpa', *Casabella*, 222, 1958, 15–16.

R. Trevisiol, *La casa rotonda* (Milan 1982): documents the development of the house by Botta.

A. Tzonis and L. Lefaivre, 'The Grid and the Pathway: An Introduction to the Work of Dimitris and Susana Antonakakis', *Architecture in Greece*, 15, 1981, 164–78.

J. Utzon, 'Platforms and Plateaus: Ideas of a Danish Architect', *Zodiac*, 10, 1962, 112–14.

F. Vanlaethem, 'Pour une architecture épurée et rigoureuse', *ARQ*, 14, Modernité et Régionalisme, Aug. 1983, 16–19.

D. Vesely, 'Introduction', in *Architecture and Continuity* (AA Themes no. 7, London 1982).

H. Yatsuka, 'Rationalism', *Space Design*, Oct. 1977, 14–15.

— 'Architecture in the Urban Desert: A Critical Introduction to Japanese Architecture after Modernism', *Oppositions*, 23, 1981.

I. Zaknic, 'Split at the Critical Point: Diocletian's Palace, Excavation vs. Conservation', *Journal of Architectural Education*, XXXVI, no.3, Spring 1983, 20–26.

G. Zambonini, 'Process and Theme in the Work of Carlo Scarpa', *Perspecta*, 20, 1983, 21–42.

## GENERAL

L. Benevolo, *Origins of Modern Town Planning* (1967).

— *History of Modern Architecture* (1971).

F. Dal Co and M. Tafuri, *Architettura contemporanea* (1976).

S. Giedion, *Space, Time and Architecture* (1941).

— *Mechanization Takes Command* (1948).

H.-R. Hitchcock, *Architecture: Nineteenth and Twentieth Centuries* (1958/83).

M. Tafuri, *Teorie e storia dell'architettura* (1968).

— *Architecture and Utopia: Design and Capitalist Development* (1976).

## ABBREVIATIONS

| | |
|---|---|
| AA | Architectural Association |
| *AAJ* | *Architectural Association Journal* |
| *AAQ* | *Architectural Association Quarterly* |
| *AB* | *Art Bulletin* |
| *AD* | *Architectural Design* |
| *AIAJ* | *American Institute of Architects Journal* |
| *AMC* | *Architecture Mouvement Continuité* |
| *AR* | *Architectural Review* |
| *A&U* | *Architecture and Urbanism* |
| *RIBAJ* | *RIBA Journal* |
| *JSAH* | *Journal of the Society of Architectural Historians* |
| *JW&CI* | *Journal of the Warburg and Courtauld Institutes* |

# Index

*Figures in italic type refer to illustration numbers*